THE

Practice OF
Social Work IN
North America

Related books of interest

THE

Practice OF
Social Work IN
North America

CULTURE, CONTEXT, AND
COMPETENCY DEVELOPMENT

KIP COGGINS

New Mexico Highlands University

LYCEUM
BOOKS, INC.

5758 South Blackstone Avenue
Chicago, Illinois 60637

© 2016 by Lyceum Books, Inc.

Published by

LYCEUM BOOKS, INC.
5758 S. Blackstone Avenue
Chicago, Illinois 60637
773-643-1903 fax
773-643-1902 phone
lyceum@lyceumbooks.com
www.lyceumbooks.com

6 5 4 3 2   16 17 18 19 20

ISBN 978-1-933478-26-5

Printed in the United States of America.

Library of Congress Cataloging-in-Publication Data

Coggins, Kip, 1956– author.
    The practice of social work in North America: culture, context, and competency development /
Kip Coggins.
        pages cm
    Includes bibliographical references.
    ISBN 978-1-933478-26-5 (alk. paper)
    1. Social workers—North America. 2. Social service—Practice—North America.
    3. Social service—North America. I. Title.
    HV40.8.N7C64   2016
    361.3′2097—dc23
                                                                                                2015026580

The painting on the cover, Cadmium's Coat-tail, was created by noted Chicago artist, Leslie Baum, using watercolor on arches paper.

This book is dedicated to my sister Caprice (Cappi), who has served as the matriarch and grounding force of our ever-increasing extended family since the death of our mother nearly twenty-five years ago. Cappi has been an inspiration to me throughout my career. She has been there for me in times of great joy and deep sorrow, in struggle and celebration. She is without doubt a beautiful and nurturing human being whom our family is so extremely fortunate to have as a member.

I also dedicate this book to Don Robinson, MSW, for all he has taught me about the importance of humility, strength, and the courage to follow one's path in life. Don is one of those special individuals who possess the ability to gracefully blend his knowledge of traditional Indigenous Peoples with his education in social work in a way that serves as an example of highly skilled and professional social work practice. He brings light and love to the lives of all those lucky enough to know him.

Contents

Figures

Preface

North America includes Canada, the United States, and Mexico. Although Mexico is referred to at many points in this book, the two nations of Canada and the United States are the primary focus. This approach to organizing material has been taken because both Canada and the United States have similar and mutually recognized systems of accrediting social work programs designed to prepare developing social work practitioners for work with a wide array of clients and client systems. The histories of both Canada and the United States have long been linked, with social work professionals in both nations tracing their roots to the endeavors of powerful and visionary individuals, primarily women, who sought to better the condition of humankind. Both the United States and Canada have bachelor's, master's, and doctoral programs in social work. The two countries also have a great deal in common in terms of their bachelor of social work (BSW) and foundational master of social work (MSW) curricular structure. While there are some differences, the roles of case manager, clinical practitioner, agency director, community organizer, researcher, and educator in either nation would look familiar to social workers or academics from both sides of the Canada-US border.

So what makes this textbook different from the vast array of offerings already available? To begin with, this book looks at Canadian and American differences and similarities within a changing North American social work practice environment that includes growing Indigenous, ethno-cultural, and racial minority populations, all in a context of increasing social diversity on many levels. This book features several common theories, concepts, and perspectives upon which social work practice is based. However, established social work knowledge is viewed through the multiple and bi-national lenses of cultural diversity, social diversity, social justice/anti-oppressive practice, economic justice, and the importance of the physical environment, both natural and human built. Moreover, different views and different voices are presented as a central feature in terms of furthering social work knowledge and skill development in an era of fundamental social change in which Indigenous Peoples, minority populations, and socially diverse groups are demanding justice for themselves and for the planet.

This textbook represents the realization of a dream that has been many years in the making. *The Practice of Social Work in North America: Culture, Context, and Competency Development* strives to help both students and educators understand the enormous value of developing well-prepared entry-level social work practitioners who will face traditional challenges in working with client systems as well as technological, economic, and even environmental concerns in a rapidly changing and increasingly diverse North American milieu. This textbook includes chapters on ethics, social justice, cultural competence skill development, theory, evidence-informed practice, and material related to working with client systems at the micro, mezzo, and macro levels. In addition, assessment, case management, and clinical practice are presented in a manner that addresses current and developing social work practice environments. This book also includes a final chapter on field practicum placement settings, in which students are introduced to the structure and purpose of professional supervised skill development.

The time has arrived when social work needs to recognize that students, practitioners, and the clients they will serve are becoming increasingly diverse. In addition to social, ethnic, and racial diversity there is also a growing diversity of families headed by single parents, parents who are not married, and parents with a variety of nondominant sexual orientations or gender identities. As a result, the match between social work practitioners and clients will quite often be one in which both are members of different, and perhaps nonmajority, population groups. Therefore, it is crucial that social work educators create a learning environment in which culture and other forms of diversity are included throughout the curriculum and addressed in field practicum settings.

This does not mean that traditional social work knowledge or Euro-Western concepts are obsolete or without value. Instead, the task of contemporary social work education is one of incorporating a developed history of professional knowledge in a way that begins to decenter, but does not summarily discard, Euro-Western theory related to practice. Indeed, many populations have experienced the impact of Euro-Western economic structures, cultural values, social institutions, and social policies. As a result, there are bound to be areas of congruence between majority culture approaches to helping, healing, or treatment and the expectations of clients from a wide variety of distinct ethno-cultural population groups. Nevertheless, recognizing the culture-bound foundations of Euro-Western thought is an essential part of allowing non-Western and nondominant values, perspectives, concepts, and healing traditions the space to flourish, even in a context that is shared with certain Euro-Western theories and techniques. As other systems of thought, practice, and theorizing continue to develop, they will inform social work in a manner that fosters the enrichment of knowledge, skills, and abilities that will be necessary for practice in an emerging age of diversity and change.

The task of this book is therefore immense. It involves honouring the legacy of a profession that has often opposed dominant social structures and economic arrangements that disadvantage those who are in need, vulnerable, marginalized, or excluded. At the same time, another purpose of this text is to advance non-Euro-Western and nondominant forms of theorizing, helping, healing, and treatment in a way that will allow them to become equal partners with existing Euro-Western approaches to working with clients.

Acknowledgment

This book would not be possible without the work of Natalia Medina Coggins. She spent countless hours over the course of four years editing, formatting, and lending creative input to the final version of this textbook. She deserves immeasurable thanks for her attention to detail and her desire to see a quality end product that is both engaging and accessible to students.

Chapter One

Social Work Education in North America

INTRODUCTION

North America has changed in ways that were unimagined since the first professional course in social work was offered at Columbia University in New York, in the summer of 1898. There are now more than eight hundred accredited social work programs across North America, with more entering candidacy each year. It has now been a little more than one hundred years since the 1915 National Conference on Charities and Corrections, during which Abraham Flexner was asked if social work was a true profession. In his answer, he stated that social work was not a true or "fully fledged" profession (Flexner, 1915). This response, likely rooted in the sexist belief that a profession dominated by women could not be truly professional, triggered an obsession for a theoretical and scientific legitimacy similar to that which was and continues to be enjoyed by physicians. While many will argue that this resulted in an overemphasis on evidence-based practice that has undermined the social and economic justice foundation of the profession, it can certainly no longer be said that social work lacks a knowledge base or professional standards in relation to practice. In short, there is no doubt that social work is indeed a profession.

The Changing Face of Canada and the United States

In Canada, data from Statistics Canada indicate a pattern of growing diversity. First Nations (North American Indians), Inuit, and Métis persons, collectively referred to as *Aboriginal*, currently make up 4 percent of the national population, with some provinces, such as Manitoba, fast approaching the 20 percent mark. In Vancouver and Toronto, the next twenty-five years will see a demographic shift resulting in visible minority non-Caucasian populations becoming the majority. At the same time, the rural-to-urban migration of Aboriginal Canadians means that social workers in the urban Canadian context, where more than 80 percent of the population lives, will experience diversity as a central, rather than peripheral, feature of practice. All of this means that social work theory and practice can no longer consider diversity an "add on" component of professional education in the preparation of practitioners.

In the second decade of the twenty-first century, in the United States, there are four states (Hawaii, California, New Mexico, and Texas) in which non-Hispanic whites now actually form the minority. This will increase to eight or perhaps ten states by the early 2020s, if census predictions are realized (Teixeira, 2013). As of 2014, both New Mexico and California had Latino populations that were larger than their non-Hispanic white populations, making Latinos the largest single ethnic group in both states. Already in thirteen states, and within the District of Columbia, minority children form the majority of those under the age of five. In twenty-five other states, minorities now make up more than 40 percent of the under-five age group (U.S. Census, 2011; Yen, 2013). Within the school-aged population of the United States (those from ages five to seventeen) minorities will become the majority by 2020. Moreover, it is projected that 26 percent of all school-aged children at that point will be Latino as well (Frey, 2012).

The Social Work Practice Environment of Canada and the United States

Social work degrees from accredited programs in Canada or the United States are recognized in both countries. Both nations have shared origins in relation to social and economic development with individual case-based models of intervention in social work existing alongside social reform movements such as settlement houses in major eastern and north central urban centres (Edwards, Shera, Nelson Reid, &York, 2006). As social work developed in both Canada and the United States, the curricula of the various programs in all regions of both nations evolved into five basic core areas of social work education.

As can be seen in figure 1.1, social work curricula in Canada and the United States have a generalist foundational requirement that is essentially identical in both nations. All bachelor-level and foundational master-level social work education must provide a solid generalist curriculum that addresses the five core areas of Human Behaviour, Social Policy, Practice, Research, and Field Practicum. In addition, social work students must have a generalist foundation educational experience that exposes them to a wide range of practice settings through a process that fosters knowledge development, skill acquisition, and demonstrated ability to engage in social work intervention at the micro, mezzo, and macro levels.

Micro-level practice is generally understood as work with individuals and families. Mezzo-level practice refers to direct practice with small groups. However, some authors and theorists in social work also see family practice as mezzo-level practice, or as existing somewhere between the micro and mezzo levels of practice. Macro-level social work is generally understood as social work at the organizational level, in which program development, program evaluation, and agency administration occur. Macro-level practice may also take place in the form of community organization in which entire communities are mobilized to bring about positive social, economic, political, or environmental change. Macro practice also involves social policy development at the provincial/state and federal levels. Finally, macro-level practice may also include social research intended to study social problems with the intention of developing social policy or micro-level approaches to practices, with the goal of improving people's lives.

Indeed, in many ways Canada and the United States look quite similar. However, important differences between the two nations exist both in terms of social welfare history and enduring national character. Although the early years of both nations were a time of almost identical approaches to helping those in need, the middle part of the twentieth century was an era of much more robust movement toward institutional social welfare programs in Canada than was the case in the United States. For example, the Family Allowance Act of 1944 was Canada's first universal income support program (Graham, Swift, & Delaney, 2012). By the 1960s, the Canadian health care system moved to a single-payer universal government-funded health insurance program, often referred to as "Medicare." Although Saskatchewan, under New Democratic Party (NPD) leadership, had already instituted a provincial version of universal health care, a national plan did not materialize until 1966 (Nelson, 2006).

Even though the groundwork for institutional (universal) social welfare programs in the United States had been laid by the passage of the 1934 Social Security Act, the social welfare system in the United States has remained almost entirely residual in nature. In the United States, a truly universal approach to health care has yet to develop. Proposals for national health care date back to the 1800s. However, medical associations and private insurance companies have been able to block efforts to cover all citizens and legal permanent residents. Even though the United States does have some forms of nearly universal health care for certain populations, the programs still fail to fully cover all persons within specific intended groups.

Figure 1.1   Five Core Areas of Social Work

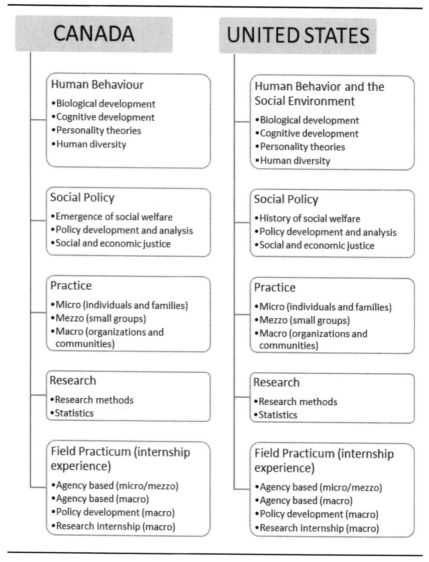

In the United States, Medicare is a program available to American citizens and certain legal permanent residents who have reached age sixty-five. Medicare also covers some individuals with disabilities and persons with renal failure who are younger than sixty-five. The legislation creating Medicare was passed into law in 1965 and now offers public plans (often known as traditional

Medicare) and private managed care options, also called Medicare Advantage Plans and Medicare Part C. Those senior citizens participating in the managed care plans offered under Medicare Part C receive services in much the same manner as other Americans who are covered by private insurance plans through health maintenance organizations (HMOs). This means that Medicare-eligible seniors are restricted to physicians who are part of the network of providers included in their particular plans and that seeking services and practitioners outside of their respective HMOs will require them to pay partially or entirely out-of-pocket to receive care. Although not truly universal because of the cost sharing covered by premiums recipients pay and the limitation to service networks, it is as close to a universal government-funded approach to health care as can be found for the general public in the United States.

The US Department of Veterans Affairs, another government-funded but less truly universal program, provides services to all eligible veterans of the military. While there are veterans who qualify for free health care services as a result of certain service-related conditions, other services may be subject to means testing. So, while veterans do have a certain portion of their health and mental health care covered in some cases, the program is not actually universal, even for the target population it is designed to serve.

Another program, the Indian Health Service (IHS), provides a broad range of health and mental/behavioural health services to enrolled members of federally recognized American Indian tribes in the United States. Although IHS does provide a broad range of health care services, some specialty health care not provided at IHS facilities or tribal clinics must be secured through the use of contract funds that often go to pay private providers. In some cases, a person living far from her or his reservation or tribal service area will need to return home to access contract funds. Even then, contract funds are limited, leaving many to wait for coverage of services. Still, IHS is closer to being a targeted universal program than is the case for veterans' health care. Although IHS provides comprehensive health care coverage for eligible American Indians, it is common knowledge that the health service is underfunded, leading to long waits for treatment, especially, as mentioned, if the condition requires the use of limited contract funds.

There are also state health care programs that attempt to cover all or most of the legal residents within a given state. The most sweeping reform has been in the state of Vermont, where work is under way to create a single-payer government-run health insurance system that will guarantee universal access to health care for all residents of that state (Hsiao, Kappel, & Gruber, 2011). The legislation creating the single-payer system was enacted in spring 2011, with full implementation expected by 2016. The Vermont approach most closely resembles that of Canada. Hawaii has had a nearly universal health insurance program in place since 1974 (Abrams, 2010). The Hawaiian system is an employer-mandated approach to health insurance coverage which also requires copays and some deductibles (costs the individual must pay). In Massachusetts, there are several programs for low-income families and individuals needing health insurance. The state also requires all residents to have health insurance coverage, meaning that those who do not meet low-income thresholds must purchase private health insurance. However, low- and moderate-income families and individuals are eligible for subsidies to help cover the cost of private health insurance.

The most recent attempt by the United States to institute some form of broader health care coverage is the Patient Protection and Affordable Care Act (PPACA), which was signed into law in 2010 by President Barack Obama. Although the act expands access to health care, it by no means covers all uninsured citizens. In addition, unlike the Canadian system, the American approach to health care remains a largely private enterprise that is subject to varying degrees of government regulation. So, whereas the Canadian system is an example of a national commitment to basic health care for all, the American system is more accurately a case of modest insurance reform.

Other components of the American safety net, such as income support, called Temporary Assistance for Needy Families (TANF) includes work requirements along with a sixty-month (five-year) lifetime limit in most cases. Conversely, in Canada income support does not come with a lifetime limit. Moreover, unlike the United States, Canada does not exclude single able-bodied adults or childless couples from eligibility for income support. In the United States, single people living in poverty may have general assistance available in their states, municipalities, or American Indian reservation communities, but the availability of income support for individuals and childless couples is by no means uniform or widespread, with only a few states providing general assistance to those deemed employable. Most US states that eliminated general assistance programs for employable individuals did so in the 1980s and 1990s, and no states in the southeast United States provide any general assistance to individuals whether they are able-bodied or living with a disability. Furthermore, most of the general assistance payments are very low, with the median range of US$215 in 2011 (Schott & Cho, 2011).

This is not to say that Canada is a comparative utopia of universal social welfare programming more like that of Denmark or Sweden. In fact, the expansion of social welfare in the 1960s and early 1970s was followed soon thereafter by a clawing-back or ending of many programs that continued throughout the 1990s (Armitage, 2003). In addition, the Canada Assistance Plan, which began in 1966, was replaced by Canada Health and Social Transfer (CHST) grants to provinces (Canadian Association of Social Workers [CASW], 2012). The CHST grants, which were roughly analogous to the use of block grants in the United States, served to reduce the overall amount of federal support to the provinces, thereby affecting social welfare programming. This was especially so in the wealthier provinces of Alberta, British Columbia, and Ontario, where the largest reductions in federal support occurred (CASW, 2012). The last vestiges of universal income supports from the federal government in Canada ended with the phasing out of family allowances in the 1990s (McGilly, 1998). Although the Universal Child Care Benefit (UCCB) may appear similar to the family allowance, it is counted as taxable income. The lowest-income families, those most likely to be receiving income support, fall below the taxable threshold (Battle, Torjman, & Mendelson, 2006). As a result, the UCCB becomes a de facto program that is more residual than universal in nature. Just as had been the case in the final years of family allowances, increased income means decreased benefits. Although the progressive tax nature of the UCCB is better than a benefit delivered within a regressive tax structure, the program, despite its name, is not truly universal in nature.

Canadian policy makers have moved away from universalism in social welfare and have instead chosen to follow the American model of child tax credits for working parents. In fact, recent changes in the thinking of those who hold political power in Canada would look quite familiar to American social workers. A belief in the forces of the free market to create economic wealth for all, combined with calls for privatization of public services, sound eerily like the disastrous path taken in the United States as that nation has continued to drift to the socially conservative right since the time of Ronald Reagan's presidency in the 1980s.

Social Work Practice Settings

According to the US Bureau of Labor Statistics (2014), for the year 2012, social workers in the United States held 607,300 jobs in a variety of organizations and employment settings, including child welfare, mental health clinics, community mental health agencies, schools (both public and private), hospitals, and of course, group and solo private practice. In addition, social workers can be found on military bases, in college and university counselling centres, in correctional settings, juvenile justice systems, nursing homes, public housing, women's shelters, homeless outreach organizations, addictions treatment facilities and outpatient programs, and scores of other settings, even including government. In line with the more individualistic thinking that prevails in the United States has been a concomitant evolution of social work as a profession for those wishing to provide psychotherapeutic services to clients with mental health diagnoses. Although American social work has had a tradition of espousing the need for broad-based progressive social change that benefits all, especially the poor and vulnerable, the reality is that during the last thirty years many in the United States who want to become social workers generally envision themselves not as social workers serving the poor and marginalized in society, but instead as private practice therapists at some future point (Perry, 2003). By the first decade of the twenty-first century, approximately 40 percent of National Association of Social Workers members identified themselves as being employed in solo or group private practice settings (Green, Baskind, Mustian, Reed, & Taylor, 2007, p. 151).

Social work programs in the United States do emphasize social and economic justice, the need to focus on vulnerable populations through policy advocacy, and the importance of maintaining a collective professional commitment to the poor. However, while professors may admonish students to help the needy, the job market students will enter following graduation, especially at the MSW-level, will provide the most economic rewards for those adopting a more conservative approach to developing their careers. By this, it is meant that those emphasizing individual psychotherapy or casework skill development over community organization and policy advocacy will be more likely to see secure employment and experience career advancement. This has led many to criticize social work for abandoning its original mission to serve the poor and marginalized in society (Bradley, Maschi, O'Brien, Morgen, & Ward, 2012). Even for those who select policy and administration specializations, the commitment to the poor, vulnerable, and marginalized may hold less appeal than the opportunity to rise through the ranks of specific agency management structures and broader state or national social service administration organizations does. As a result, social work students end up being caught between a commitment to the founding principles of the profession and the realities of the postgraduation job market. Lectures and assignments related to poverty, the history of social welfare, progressive social policy, and issues of social justice may be of enormous interest to social work students, but the reality is that employment as a social worker following formal education often leaves little room for advocacy beyond that which is engaged in for specific assigned clients. Efforts to advocate for vulnerable populations or challenge existing oppressive social structures will therefore consist primarily of activities that are subordinate to or entirely outside of agency-defined work-related priorities.

American social workers, like other Americans, are generally socialized within a national milieu of status consciousness connected to both work and wealth. Any conversation with a group of social work professionals in an American context will quickly reveal socially influenced hierarchies within the profession. Direct practice social workers providing case management services are generally regarded as having a lower status than social workers who provide psychotherapeutic services. Likewise, those in "private practice" are often viewed as being more accomplished than social workers in public mental health settings. The exception to this would of course be the person who is the director of the public mental health or social service agency. Administrative positions generally come with higher salaries, and in a profession that is largely female, administration within social work also continues to be an area in which males dominate (Chernesky, 2003; Dewane, 2008; Zunz, 1991), reflecting a larger American social context within which male work continues to be valued more highly than female work.

The vast majority of opportunities for employment in social work are in the area of direct practice with individuals or families. In the United States, case management is most often thought of as the practice realm of BSW graduates and practitioners. This includes discharge planning in hospital settings, case management within many of the public agencies such as child welfare, adult protective services, services to persons with developmental disabilities, and those with long-term mental illness. Master-level social workers, although often employed in many of the same settings, tend to have specialized areas of practice related to mental health, addictions, work with the elderly, corrections, and so forth. In addition, the MSW degree in the United States becomes for many a path to private practice that will allow them to bill Medicaid and/or private insurance, as well as contracting with state or local agencies for the provision of specialized mental or behavioural health services.

In Canada, private practice currently constitutes a small segment of the overall workforce in social work. Nevertheless, it is an area of practice that is growing. Still, however, 93 percent of social workers in Canada are employed by government-run health and social services organizations or are in other government industries (CASW, 2000). In Canada social workers are also employed in the voluntary sector, often called private nonprofit agencies, or simply nonprofit organizations (NPOs). Social workers in Canada, much like the

United States, can be found in various settings including child welfare agencies, schools, general and mental health (psychiatric) hospitals, correctional facilities, adult and youth justice systems, community mental health clinics, and various social welfare-related settings. Moreover, social workers in Canada follow very similar career trajectories with BSW graduates being employed as direct practice case managers who also provide supportive counselling, while MSW graduates become specialists in areas such as mental health, addictions treatment, family therapy, and various types of group treatment, administration, program evaluation, policy planning/development, and of course, research.

CONCLUSION

Although the field of social work and the social work-accrediting bodies of both Canada and the United States have many similarities, notable differences in the conceptualization of the practice context exist between the two nations, especially in relation to the manner in which poverty and social or economic justice are viewed by the broader society. In American society, social justice is most often understood as access to resources and equality of opportunity, whereas Canadian society, while not favouring truly equal redistribution of resources, is more open to reducing the gap between the wealthiest and the poorest segments of society. Social workers in Canada have, in recent times, advocated for equitable distribution of resources as an important avenue to equality of both opportunity and the creation of a just society. This is not surprising given the long-standing differences in national character between Canada and the United States. The United States is a more highly individualistic country in which a much larger proportion of people tend to look negatively at anything that sounds remotely like income-equalization efforts, whereas Canada, although individualistic in its own right, also has a far greater acceptance of government as an entity with the capacity to enhance social well-being through the provision of public tax-funded services and social programs.

In the United States, equality of opportunity is founded on the mythical belief that Americans are rugged individualists who, given the opportunity, will prosper if they are willing to work hard enough. This national sense of *self* fosters both dislike and distrust of those who are unable to become economically self-sufficient. In the United States, government intervention in social welfare is generally seen less as a social good and more as a necessary evil that should be time-limited and relied upon only during periods of extreme and extraordinary need. Many Americans seldom acknowledge or even know the extent to which government programs have profoundly enhanced their lives. A significant number of Americans receiving anything from veterans' benefits, to Medicare for the elderly, to farm subsidies will often vote against their own best interests and in favour of politicians promising tax cuts, less government regulation, and the elimination of the very programs and services upon which they and their family members depend.

The pervasive mistrust of government among Americans has a history that is nearly as old as the nation itself and attempts to create a progressive social welfare apparatus aimed at alleviating poverty and the excesses of capitalism have historically been met with suspicion. Indeed, movement toward even something as basic as universal health care is countered on the political right with warnings of socialist revolution and government control of people's lives. This is combined with religiously based and increasingly vocal social conservatism that in many cases includes racism, homophobia, and xenophobia. The resulting contemporary sociopolitical context has caused American social workers and social work organizations to become focused, out of necessity, on preserving individual civil rights and civil liberties at the expense of more far-reaching goals such as redistribution of wealth and the outright elimination of poverty.

By contrast, Canadians in general have a somewhat more collectivist view of themselves as a nation. Canada, with a more enduring association to France, particularly in the province of Quebec and a longer period of time as part of the United Kingdom, followed by a continued connection as a British Commonwealth nation, has developed an approach to social welfare and social development that appears to Americans more European in nature. Still, it cannot be denied that Canadian society does have a strong socially and fiscally conservative element that at times appears quite like its American neighbour to the south. Under Conservative leadership, recent and recurring calls to explore partial privatization of health care, questions regarding limits on abortion, passage of the Omnibus Crime Bill, austerity measures resulting in the elimination of thousands of federal employees, and constant political promises to lower taxes appear to have been lifted directly out of American conservative political playbooks.

Yet, Canada does still have a collective sense of the importance of fairness, a commitment to maintaining basic health care for all, and a general belief in the value of progressive social change that has yet to adequately develop in the United States. Universal health care, marriage equality, and a host of rights and freedoms Canadians take for granted have still not become reality for many living in the United States. So, while social workers in Canada and the United States share a similar and in some cases common history, some of society's most pressing social welfare and human rights needs, such as health care, constitutionally enshrined gender equality, and marriage equality, have been resolved to a far greater extent in Canada than is the case in the United States.

Living and working within a Canadian context has allowed social workers and their professional organizations to forge ahead with a multitude of more wide-reaching efforts which include putting an end to the centuries-long maltreatment of Indigenous (Aboriginal) populations, as well as calling for a reduction in and eventual elimination of poverty as spelled out in the Report of the Standing Committee on Human Resources, Skills and Social Development and the Status of Persons with Disabilities (Canada, Parliament, House of Commons, 2010). Therefore, while Canadian social workers, like their American counterparts, may be fighting to preserve social programs and services, public will and at least a portion professional energy are still able to be channeled toward improving the lives of the nation's poor, vulnerable, and marginalized.

Social workers in the United States currently practice in a much more hostile environment. In the United States, intensely nationalist sentimentality combined with socially and fiscally conservative policy making has created a regressive approach to human rights and the needs of the poor. As a result, social justice activities engaged in by social workers are directed toward preserving women's rights, the rights of sexual minorities, individual rights, basic human rights, fighting racism and discrimination, and attempting to halt the dismantling of an ever more-tenuous and shrinking social safety net. This, combined with struggling to preserve what remains of opportunities to address poverty at the most basic level, has taken precedence over attempts to influence either politicians or the general electorate that a more equitable distribution of resources should be one of the most important goals of social justice. Furthermore, because this contemporary conservative milieu has existed and intensified since 1980, and has a place in the American psyche that extends back to the founding of the nation, the idea of creating an avenue for equal access to basic services and equality of opportunity is a much better fit with American sensibilities than the idea of redistribution of resources. For Americans, creating opportunity while denying decades or even centuries of socially constructed barriers and mechanisms of disadvantage is far more palatable than facing the truth about the misfit between democratic ideals and a capitalist economic system.

Chapter Two

Canadian and American Codes of Ethics

INTRODUCTION

In the social work profession, there are many codes that serve as guides for ethical practice and against which the ethical behaviour of social workers can be measured when questions of negligence, incompetence, or intentional harm arise in the course of contact with clients. In Canada, each province and territory is responsible for the regulation of social workers through a process of either registration or licensure. In Canada, provincial regulatory bodies, referred to as either associations or colleges, are responsible for regulating the practice of social work, providing opportunities for continuing education, and imposing sanctions on members who violate ethical codes or practice regulations. In the United States, the process of regulation is under the purview of the various state licensing boards. However, the National Association of Social Workers (NASW) Code of Ethics serves as the document that informs many of the licensing violation statutes used to develop sanctions. In the United States, the state chapters of the NASW generally provide training for social workers who need continuing education units (CEUs) to maintain licensure. In addition, the NASW also advocates for social workers and the clients they serve in legislative matters at the state and national level.

Ethics and ethical behaviour have been a major and enduring element of social work programs in the preparation of future practitioners. Whereas the profession of social work in the United States defines ethical practice in accordance with a single code of ethics, social workers in Canada may be guided by different codes depending on the province within which they live and work. Nevertheless, codes such as the British Columbia Association of Social Workers Code of Ethics remain quite similar to the more widely known Canadian Association of Social Workers (CASW) Code of Ethics. In the codes of ethics for social workers in the two nations, similar values and ethical principles address many of the same professional commitments, issues, and concerns, albeit in differing order and at different locations within the two codes.

PROFESSIONAL CODES OF ETHICS CORE VALUES

Figure 2.1   Professional Codes of Ethics Core Values

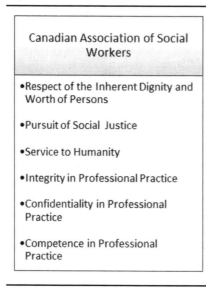

Canadian Association of Social Workers	National Association of Social Workers (USA)
•Respect of the Inherent Dignity and Worth of Persons •Pursuit of Social Justice •Service to Humanity •Integrity in Professional Practice •Confidentiality in Professional Practice •Competence in Professional Practice	•Service •Social Justice •Dignity and Worth of the Person •Importance of Human Relationships •Integrity •Competence

In the social work profession, ethical codes serve to structure both thought and action in a manner that transcends the individual social worker and the specific practice setting. Social work is a profession bound by ethical codes, and as such, practice with individuals, groups, organizations, communities, Indigenous nations, and various levels of society are all measured against the ethical values and organizing principles of the social work profession. As is the case in the United States, the CASW Code of Ethics addresses what Reamer (2005) (in a comparison of US and UK codes), identifies as key purposes served by the American code. These include the establishment of ethical standards, as addressed by core values; professional obligations regarding ethical behaviour; ethical standards intended to ensure professional accountability; a document against which violations of ethical behaviour can be evaluated; and as guidelines for social workers new to the profession. For social work students, especially at the point of entering the field practicum placement setting, thinking about ethical behaviour may very well be something that is of secondary concern, given the overwhelming task of becoming oriented to a new learning environment in which practice skill development is the primary goal. Nevertheless, ethics and professional ethical behaviour will become a foundational component of each practicum student's professional development.

What is perhaps most often heard in discussions of ethics in social work is what to do about ethical dilemmas that arise. A dilemma is defined as "a choice between two evenly balanced alternatives and as a predicament that apparently defies a satisfactory outcome" (*Webster's II Dictionary*, 1984, p. 378). For social workers, dilemmas generally arise when professional values are at odds with agency practices. Students become acutely aware of dilemmas when what they have been learning about ethical behaviour in their classes at university does not match with agency practices in the field practicum setting. When social work practicum placements occur in host settings, meaning environments in which social work services are ancillary, concerns regarding ethical conflicts and dilemmas may arise early on in the placement. For example, in correctional settings, emphasis is always on maintaining the security of the facility (Coggins & Fresquez, 2007). This means that core social work values, such as service to clients, pursuit of social justice, and even confidentiality, may be challenged on a regular basis. In addition, social workers and social work interns in correctional settings will often need to tolerate ambiguity and periods of uncertainty while issues of professional versus host environment value conflicts are being resolved. Dilemmas of this sort are common in nearly all environments that employ social workers as service providers supporting nonsocial work core missions and visions. Hospitals, police departments, schools, juvenile justice facilities, universities, and many others have primary organizational or agency missions that can be at odds with the core mission and values of the social work profession.

Because the world of social work practice is so vast and complex, it is not possible for a field instructor, professor, or anyone else to provide direction to social work interns on what to do in every situation they may encounter in work with clients. Therefore, the focus for classroom and field practicum instructors needs to be placed on guiding knowledge and skill acquisition with an emphasis on nurturing each student's ability to apply what has been learned to new and unfamiliar situations. For social work students, the internship is not a simple apprenticeship. It is not enough for a social work student intern to observe and model the behaviour of her or his field practicum instructor. Social work students are also expected to develop their own practice skills that are informed by knowledge and guided by professional values. The following material includes brief discussions of core social work values that guide practice in Canada and the United States.

Canada—Canadian Association of Social Workers Codes of Ethics

Respect for the Inherent Dignity and Worth of Persons

Under the CASW Code of Ethics, there is an expectation that social workers will uphold human rights of both individuals and groups as they are outlined in the 1982 *Canadian Charter of Rights and Freedoms* and the 1948 *United Nations Universal Declaration of Human Rights*. Concepts such as individual and community self-determination are included in the application of this value as part of social work practice. Respect for the dignity and worth of persons also encompasses the importance of cultural expression in the lives of communities, families, and individuals. In accordance with this particular value, clients' wishes are only to be overridden when laws or imminent harm to self or others are clearly at stake. The Canadian case upon which *duty to warn* has been most clearly defined is that of *Smith vs. Jones* (1999). In this particular case, a patient of a forensic psychiatrist disclosed, in very elaborate detail, his intention to rape and murder prostitutes. The attorney for the psychiatric patient said that the findings of forensic evaluation were protected by attorney-client privilege and could not be disclosed. The Supreme Court of Canada ruled that while client-attorney privilege is the highest privilege accorded by law that it was not absolute, citing compelling public safety concerns as one exception (Felthous & Sass, 2007, pp. 82–83).

Pursuit of Social Justice

In accordance with the CASW Code of Ethics, Canadian social workers are expected to promote fair treatment of all individuals and of larger collectives. The pursuit of social justice also includes a special focus on impoverished, disadvantaged, marginalized, and vulnerable members of society. This includes people with disabilities and those having exceptional needs. Beyond providing resources and services to those in need, the pursuit of social justice calls upon social workers to advocate for social well-being through the equitable distribution of resources, the removal of barriers to accessing services and fair treatment, and the elimination of prejudice and/or discrimination. For social workers, this means looking beyond poverty as a micro-level concern by making the elimination of poverty at the societal level an ethically grounded professional commitment.

As a value, social justice should also foster in social workers the recognition of structural aspects of current social arrangements that have resulted from colonization, capitalism, globalization, and the continued battles against racism, sexism, homophobia, and scores of other forms of intolerance and exclusion that serve to create and maintain populations at risk for marginalization. This will, at times, put social workers at odds with the larger society that categorizes people as those deserving help and fair treatment versus those who are not. Ex-convicts, prostitutes, abusive parents, persons with heroin addictions, and many other populations peripheral to mainstream society, while often marginalized or outright rejected, are still equally deserving of just and fair treatment in accordance with ethical social work practice. Finally, pursuit of social justice should also include efforts by social workers to advocate for clean and healthy living environments, safe housing, safe workplaces, and the advancement of both treaty rights and basic human rights for Indigenous Canadian populations. Advocating for both people and a healthy planet at the local, provincial, national, and global levels are critical to the pursuit of social justice for all.

Service to Humanity

The value of service to others is perhaps the value that most would identify as a motivation for becoming a social worker. The idea of being of service to others and society is as old as the profession of social work itself. The giving of one's ability, time, knowledge, and skill to help those in need has both humanistic and religious foundations in North American social work. The charity and settlement house movements in Canada and the United States led to many important social reforms, as did the social gospel movement which began as a sort of "Christian socialism" in the Canadian Prairie provinces (Heinonen & Spearman, 2010, p. 20). Many social workers and social work students in Canada and the United States speak of their desire to help those in need as a *calling*. This term has religious roots and refers to a feeling or belief that a person has regarding her or his mission in life.

For social workers, the idea of being ethically called or in some way spiritually compelled to serve is also what sustains them when called upon to work long hours, fight for social justice, and advocate for those in need. In their various roles as professionals, social workers put service to clients above their own personal goals. Likewise, professional social workers are expected to use any power or authority they may possess as tools to serve those in need, advance social justice, and, in general, serve humanity.

Integrity in Professional Practice

In the Canadian context, integrity in professional practice is guided by the CASW Code of Ethics, relevant provincial codes and territorial standards for professional practice, and even the International Federation of Social Workers (IFSW) Code of Ethics, an organization with which both Canadian and US social work associations are affiliated. Social workers who behave and practice in an ethical manner do so out of internalized respect for the profession with which they identify. Social workers who practice with integrity will strive to avoid being judgmental or imposing personal moral, religious, or political views, or even preferences on the clients they serve.

Social workers practicing with integrity take the initiative to establish and maintain proper professional boundaries in work with clients, colleagues, and members of the community. In their private lives away from work or volunteer activities, social workers make an effort to act in ways that do not reflect negatively on the profession. When social workers do encounter potential conflicts, they consult the CASW Code of Ethics or their appropriate provincial codes and practice guidelines for direction in matters representing a potential or actual ethical dilemma or conflict. When ethical guidelines are unclear, social workers are expected to seek the advice of supervisors, colleagues, and at times, even their respective provincial regulatory entities.

Confidentiality in Professional Practice

The CASW Code of Ethics highlights the value of confidentiality as being central to professional relationships with client systems. Clients share a great deal of personal information with social workers, and as a result, an expectation of confidentiality is professional obligation that in many situations is also legally mandated. Whenever client information is to be disclosed, social workers need the written consent of the client, the client's legal guardian, or a legal requirement such as a court order. Even the family members of clients cannot receive confidential information without the authorized consent of the client. This of course depends on the age and maturity of the client, if she or he is a minor, or the mental competence of an adult. Moreover, different provincial jurisdictions have varying legal requirements related to confidentiality that impact the disclosure process. Therefore, confidentiality is not absolute. In cases such as imminent harm to self or others, confidentiality will need to be broken. This is also true in cases of child abuse and the victimization of senior citizens.

Clients should always be informed at the beginning of contact with the social worker about the limitations of confidentiality. However, even when information must be shared for compelling reasons such as public safety or a court order, social workers only release the information necessary to achieve the intended purpose.

Competence in Professional Practice

In some Canadian jurisdictions such as Alberta and British Columbia, social workers need to be licensed for certain levels of practice. In locations where licensure is required, continuing education is also needed to maintain licensure. In other jurisdictions, social workers are generally registered. However, all social workers, whether registered or licensed, need to be involved in competence building through continuing education in the form of conference attendance, skill development workshops, and reading of professional journal articles or books. While social workers are ethically bound to practice within their areas of knowledge and expertise, professional development does not end with graduation from a bachelor of social work (BSW) or master of social work (MSW) program. Because the social work value of competence highlights the need of social workers to provide competent services to clients, social workers are both professionally and ethically compelled to develop skills and expand their knowledge base. With new approaches to intervention and emerging technological advances, it is incumbent upon social workers to remain current in the profession.

United States—National Association of Social Workers Code of Ethics

In the United States, and all US territories, social workers are bound by a code that is very similar to the ethical codes in Canada. In fact, the CASW Code of Ethics utilized portions of the 1996 NASW Code of Ethics from the United States in the formation of the 2005 CASW code. The current code being used in the United States has undergone several revisions. In the 1920s, social work pioneer Mary Richmond developed a simple code of ethics for social workers (Pumphrey, 1959). This has been followed by other codes that bring it into the present time.

In the United States, the NASW is the professional organization that represents the social work profession at the national level. The NASW was formed in 1955, and since then, it has developed three codes of ethics: one in 1960, another in 1979, and the current code in 1996 (Reamer, 2006). The 1996 Code of Ethics was also revised in 2008 to include more language about cultural competence and social diversity, antiracist and antidiscriminatory practice, and social/political action directed toward the elimination of structural barriers and oppressive social policies (NASW, 2013). In the United States, the six core values are *Service, Social Justice, Dignity and Worth of the Person, Importance of Human Relationships, Integrity,* and *Competence.* In the following material, the similarity between the Canadian code and the American code will easily become evident.

Service

The value of service goes well beyond helping people in need or connecting clients to service providers. Indeed, service involves much more. The NASW Code of Ethics identifies service as including the professional requirement of putting service to others above self-interest, combined with the primary intention of helping people in need. Along with this, social workers go beyond the individual to address larger social problems that impact marginalized, vulnerable, and disadvantaged populations. To be of service to individual clients and society, social workers need to acquire knowledge, skills, and abilities related to helping people in need, whether they are individuals, families, communities, or entire populations, such as persons with Alzheimer's disease or youth at risk for gang involvement.

The field practicum placement is often the initial context within which Canadian and American social work students receive the opportunity to apply classroom-based learning to work with clients. Practicum students entering their field placements are most often placed in agencies that serve individuals and/or families. In these settings, social work students are often eager to engage and successfully assist their first clients. However, as stated earlier, service is not simply helping individual clients. Some students may become involved in advocacy for victims of gendered violence or the organization of community food and clothing banks for economically disadvantaged families. These activities and many others constitute service. As stated in the discussion of the CASW Code of Ethics, service to humanity also includes involvement in initiatives to create a more just and caring society. So, service for social workers has a much larger and more encompassing meaning that speaks to the foundational belief in humanity and the importance of the social good, which is increasingly being expanded to include the health of the planet upon which we all depend.

Social Justice

Social justice is perhaps the most difficult value for social work students to con-ceptualize and make operational in their field practicum placements; and stu-dents are not alone. Social work practitioners also lose track of this value commitment when the reality of heavy caseloads and seemingly endless paper-work get in the way of thinking about larger social issues. Still, social workers belong to a profession that includes an ethical responsibility to challenge and work toward changing social structures that support racism, discrimination, marginalization, and oppression as well as the economic arrangements that perpetuate poverty. In accordance with the American code of ethics, social workers are expected to pursue social change leading to a more just society, not only for individuals, but for entire populations. This means that a social worker helping an undocumented immigrant from Central America does not stop at finding services for that particular client, but also becomes involved in organizations and activities advocating fair, just, and humane treatment of all people, regardless of immigration status. The value of social justice makes clear the commitment social workers have to support and honour cultural and social diversity in a broad manner that also includes gender, gender expression, sex-ual orientation, religion/spirituality, and disability.

Dignity and Worth of the Person

This NASW core value of the profession carries with it a requirement that social workers treat each person with dignity and respect (Ginsberg, 1998). This respect is inclusive of all the complex variables that define each individual. Although social workers are generally quite accepting of cultural, religious, or sexual orientation differences, accepting clients who are hostile, uncoopera-tive, or engage in self-defeating behaviour is more difficult. Even more chal-lenging are clients with political views that differ from those of the social worker, or attitudes of intolerance regarding racial differences, gender equality, and same-sex sexual orientation. Social workers who have no difficulty expressing genuine respect, care, or concern for abused children or adult victims of sexual violence may find it much more difficult to accord that same respect to the per-petrators of violent acts. Treating each client with dignity and respect, regard-less of their actions or words, is an enormously difficult task. Social workers need to take special care to avoid developing a habit of liking, respecting, and making the effort to serve only the "good" clients (Coggins & Fresquez, 2007).

As social workers, our fair treatment of clients and respect for them as people cannot be affected, as Beister (1957, p. 73) states, "by personal success or failure in things physical, economic, social or anything else."

However, this does not mean that according dignity and respect to all people includes accepting all behaviours without condition. Social workers in correctional and criminal justice systems know this all too well. In many instances, acceptance of the client as a person deserving of dignity and respect must be separated from behaviours that are self-destructive or are harmful to others. Those who work with the most difficult-to-reach populations must be clear with their clients and within themselves that a person, just because she or he is a human being, should be accorded dignity and respect. Nevertheless, behaviour that is antisocial, criminal, destructive, exploitative, and in general harmful to self and/or others cannot be approved of or tolerated. In other words, treating such clients with dignity and respect must necessarily include clear and unambiguous messages about behaviour that is unacceptable as well as that which is acceptable. The establishment of clear behavioural boundaries and expectations, while at the same time according dignity and conveying respect, holds far greater potential for creating a positive working relationship between the client and the social worker.

Importance of Human Relationships

For social workers, a feature of ethical professional practice that clearly stands out is the importance of human relations. In work with both clients and colleagues, social workers recognize that supportive and affirming relationships between people are critical to healthy human development. Social workers recognize that relationships in the form of working alliances between themselves and the clients they serve are critical to the process of problem resolution and change (Coggins & Fresquez, 2007; NASW, 2008). The task of engaging a client in a mutually agreed-upon working relationship with the social worker constitutes the foundational step in problem-solving processes that must be successful before moving on to assessment and intervention phases.

Social workers do not just focus on the relationships between themselves and individual clients. The ethical value highlighting the importance of human relationships is a broad one, including the enhancement of those relationships in many areas. This means that the engagement of families, groups, organizations, and communities are also indispensable aspects of the broader definition of human relationships (NASW, 1996). Human relationships outside of those that involve the client and social worker include not just the most obvious connections one may have with spouses, partners, children, parents, or extended family members, but less immediately obvious ties to friends, religious or spiritual guides, and others with whom we are connected, as human beings, at various levels and degrees of emotional intensity or attachment.

Integrity

The core value of integrity speaks to the importance of trustworthy and ethical behaviour on the part of social work practitioners in their roles as professionals. As professionals practicing with integrity, social workers are expected to promote ethical practice engaged in by colleagues, employing agencies, and within the profession (NASW, 1996). Integrity in the United States, just as is the case in Canada, also involves a monitoring of one's own personal behaviour with the recognition that even when a social worker is not on the job, she or he still has an obligation to avoid conduct that could reflect negatively on the profession as a whole. It is nearly inevitable that social workers will at some point experience a conflict between the values and goals of an employing agency and the ethical values of the social work profession. For some, this may occur as early as his or her field practicum experience, while for others, a conflict may arise in a postgraduation workplace setting. Some conflicts are dealt with easily and quickly, while others may take much longer to adequately resolve. When an ethical conflict or dilemma requires extended time for resolution, the social worker (or student intern) will need to tolerate a period of ambiguity while the opposing tensions of a professional commitment to ethical values are at odds with an employing agency.

Competence

Competence for social workers refers to both current and developing knowledge, skills, and abilities. According to the NASW Code of Ethics, social workers are ethically bound to practice within their areas of competence while also engaging in career-long development of both existing and new areas of expertise. Without a doubt, social workers at the beginning of their careers will have much to learn as they take on workplace challenges, develop new practice interests, and move from one place of employment to another. However, even seasoned social workers should be engaged in competence-building activities that address emerging issues, social challenges, and technological changes. In addition, all social workers need to remain current regarding policy developments affecting client populations and social work practice environments. Because all states have some level of licensure, state social work regulatory boards mandate continuing education in order to comply with licensing requirements. This makes competence more than a social work value. The advent of licensure has created a requirement for career-long learning. In the United States, those who want to continue practicing as social workers must demonstrate attendance at sanctioned trainings that are intended to both maintain and expand social work practitioner competence.

However, competence building cannot be narrowly defined and limited to learning the latest approach related to work with one or another of multiple client populations that fall into any number of diagnostic categories. Competence needs to address all the ethical principles that have been listed above. Social workers need to seek information about changing economic, social, political, and environmental conditions. Trends in employment, immigration, changing population demographics, environmental degradation, and advances in medicine, law, and human rights are all important in relation to competence. Although the tendency or even desire to work toward developing competence in a narrowly defined manner might be attractive, social workers need a broad-based understanding of the world in which we all live. Effectiveness in work with client systems of various sizes requires constant learning in relation to the increasingly complex and globalized environment in which the life is lived.

Ethical Decisions and the NASW/CASW Codes of Ethics

The core values of the NASW Code of Ethics are accompanied by ethical standards that provide a detailed framework for ethical decision making. The ethical standards found in the code are organized around three areas of concern to the social work profession and to practicing social workers. The first centers on decisions that are made by practicing social workers that have potential ethical implications. The second is focused on situations that involve ethical dilemmas in practice. The third area of concern, and the one most often utilized in complaints lodged against social workers, is practitioner misconduct (Reamer, 2005, p. 53). The section of the code that outlines ethical responsibilities of social workers also discusses those responsibilities as they relate to clients, colleagues, practice settings, personal professional conduct, the social work profession, and society. The NASW Code of Ethics covers a great deal of material regarding the responsibilities of social workers in relation to clients. However, there are four areas of specific concern that seem to arise regularly for students entering their field practicum placements: client self-determination, confidentiality, unethical conduct on the part of field instructors or colleagues, and issues of physical contact with clients (Coggins & Hatchett, 2009).

Client Self-Determination

Many social work students become confused about client self-determination in the initial stages of their educational experiences. A renewed concern about proper ethical support of self-determination generally occurs again as students enter their first field practicum placement setting. In accordance with the CASW 2005 Guidelines for Ethical Practice [1.3.1] and the 1996 NASW code [1.02], social workers have an ethical responsibility to promote and support client self-determination. Initially, many students confuse this ethical responsibility with letting clients do whatever they wish. Needless to say, this is not the case. The code also makes it clear that there are times when social workers may be called upon to limit a client's self-determination. For example, social workers do not simply stand aside when clients express or attempt to carry out a desire to cause great bodily harm to themselves or others. Likewise, a client who expresses an intention to sexually molest children or maim and torture animals will need to be made aware of the legal consequences of her or his planned behaviour. However, most cases of client self-determination that may have the potential for negative impact on the client or others are not so clear. For example, a client who decides to return to alcohol use after years of sobriety is not a choice in which a social worker can legally intervene. Likewise, a client with terminal lung cancer who is mentally competent but chooses to refuse treatment is not a decision a social worker can force a client to change.

However, what ethical social workers can and should do is help clients understand the potential consequences of different courses of action. This approach, often referred to as informed self-determination, involves social workers helping clients understand the consequences of their choices or planned actions, and then allowing them to make decisions voluntarily and free of coercion (Reamer, 2006). By helping clients explore and evaluate the positive and negative consequences of choices, social workers encourage, but cannot guarantee, informed and responsible decision making. Client self-determination is perhaps one of the most difficult issues social work students struggle with in courses and field practicum placement settings. Nevertheless, failing to master the skill of fostering client autonomy through self-determination will lead to an approach to practice that is paternalistic or even coersive, even if that paternalism is believed to be in the client's best interest.

Confidentiality

Perhaps the most difficult and anxiety-provoking aspect of professional practice for students is the issue of breaching confidentiality. Facing a situation that calls for breaking confidentiality is difficult not just for social work students in field practicum settings, but for experienced practitioners as well. Although the idea of protecting confidentiality is a deeply held ethical conviction of social workers, there are situations that challenge sound ethical decision making. According to the code, it is always important for social workers to discuss confidentiality and its limits early in the client-worker relationship. This very important practice-related task includes the responsibility of social workers to let clients know about laws in provincial, state, First Nation, and sovereign Native American Nation jurisdictions regarding requirements to report elder abuse, child neglect, physical abuse or sexual exploitation of children, rape, assault, and many other forms of criminal activity. Likewise, social workers need to be clear that a court order or clearly stated intentions to harm oneself or others will result in the disclosure of confidential communication. What become problematic are issues for which ethical codes give little or no guidance.

Of course, the default recommendation for any social worker who is unclear is to seek supervision. This is always the recommendation for social work student interns in practicum settings. In fact, students in practicum settings should never violate client confidentiality without the consent and approval of the field practicum instructor who will of course need to sign off on the action. However, for social work practitioners a supervisor may not always be available or the person seeking guidance may be the top-level supervisor. Ambiguity in this and many other areas of ethical professional behaviour is why social workers seeking continuing education credits should also look for workshops offering ethics training. In fact, many jurisdictions now require licensed social workers to have a certain number of CEUs in the area of ethics.

Not only do the legal obligations of social workers regarding confidential client information change, they differ from state to state and from province to province. For example, personal information in Canada is generally protected under the 2004 revision of the Personal Information Protection and Electronic Documents Act (PIPEDA). However, in Alberta, Quebec, and British Columbia, province-specific legislation protects private businesses, while federal entities are under PIPEDA. In the United States, the privacy of health information, which includes mental health services provided by social workers, is protected by the Health Insurance Portability and Accountability Act (HIPAA) of 1996 and the 2009 Health Information Technology for Economic and Clinical Health Act (HITECH) amendment to HIPAA. In addition to both PIPEDA and HIPAA-HITECH legislation, there are other provincial and state laws protecting privacy. In some jurisdictions, the laws are quite restrictive.

Take for example the 1999 *Smith vs. Jones* Supreme Court decision in Canada or the 1976 court decision, in the case of *Tarasoff vs. Regents of the University of California*. In both cases, rulings by the court have been used to defend doctors, psychiatrists, and social workers who violate confidentiality in order to save the lives of people that their patients or clients intended to harm. However, in 1999 the Texas State Supreme Court rejected the precedent set by the 1976 Tarasoff case when it issued a ruling in *Thapar vs. Zezulka*. In the Texas case, the court ruled that there is no duty to warn a third party of imminent harm. However, the mental health professional who becomes aware of a client's plan to kill another person may (but is not required to) contact law enforcement (Lewis, 2001). Therefore, although a decision to breach client confidentiality is generally understood as protected by duty-to-warn statutes (Dolgoff, Harrington, & Lowenberg, 2012), it is clearly not an absolute protection. Interestingly, the robust defense of confidentiality in the case of *Thapar vs. Zezulka*, which protects information clients share with therapists is contrasted with state laws such as SB-1070 in Arizona, requiring social workers to disclose the immigration status of clients they serve. This places social workers and other human service providers in a difficult ethical situation. In many cases, social workers are faced with the dilemma of obeying the law or violating ethical values (Furman, Ackerman, Loya, Jones, & Negi, 2012, p. 178). Moreover, the act of providing information to law enforcement in an attempt to comply with certain immigration laws actually leads social workers to violate other laws governing confidentiality (Furman et al., 2012, p. 179).

In addition to state and provincial law that may or may not be informed by court decisions supporting a duty to warn, other factors exist that complicate the ability of social workers to assure confidentiality of information shared with them by their clients. Social workers employed by criminal justice or correctional systems may be required by court decree to report specific information about client progress in treatment. Assessments, case notes, and other written materials completed by social workers in juvenile and adult justice environments will often be subject to court orders making them open to review by judges, attorneys, probation or parole officers, and parole boards (Coggins & Hatchett, 2009). What this means for social workers is that discussions of limits to confidentiality may also include informing clients of the reality that what they share has the potential for being quite widely disseminated. As a result, social workers must be particularly careful about what is recorded in client files. Although social workers should always take care to protect the privacy of clients and their family and friendship networks, the multiplicity of persons having access to files in criminal justice environments makes attention to this fact even more acute. The same can be said for other host environments as well. Any setting where multiple individuals have access to client information increases the potential for a violation of privacy. Therefore, social workers employed in these settings and field practicum students placed in these locations need to be even more vigilant regarding the protection of confidential client information.

Unethical Behaviour of Supervisors/ Field Instructors and Colleagues

Confronting unethical behaviour is uncomfortable for social workers and is even more so for students in field practicum placements. Often, students leave the classroom with a large amount of information about ethical practice only to find that their field placement settings are not ideal. Students may see receptionists who ask very personal questions about a client's reasons for visiting a social worker. Office spaces may be divided by no more than temporary cubicle walls. Students may even see conversations about clients taking place in hallways and open boardrooms. These and many other aspects of agency life that appear to be violations of confidentiality can be troubling to students who are attempting to uphold professional standards. Many faculty field liaisons have meetings with students who feel the agency in which they have been placed is violating ethical standards. Indeed, there are incidents of ethical violations that occur in many agencies. However, students should be directed to their field instructors to address what has been observed. In many underfunded agencies, private offices are not feasible for all staff. As a result, there may be one or two private rooms in an agency that are reserved for meetings with clients that are sensitive and confidential in nature. Receptionists may be new to an agency and in need of additional training in relation to compliance with ethical standards and laws related to protecting confidential information. The ability of a student to meet with a field instructor or supervisor to address an ethical issue corresponds with both Canadian learning objectives and American competencies that address the capacity of students to tolerate ambiguity in the resolution of ethical issues or violations and should always be encouraged as a first step in ethical violation resolution processes.

Concerns regarding fellow student interns or even field instructors are even more difficult for students in practicum field placement settings. The NASW Code of Ethics (1996) 2.11 does state that social workers are ethically bound to identify, address, and take steps to correct unethical behaviour engaged in by colleagues. However, students who are new to actual client contact and desirous of good performance evaluations in their field practicum placements may be reluctant to confront what appears to be unethical behaviour (Rothman, 1998). In addition, reluctance may also exist in relation to reporting what appears to be the unethical behaviour of a fellow student for fear of being labeled as someone who monitors and reports the activities of others. With fellow students, the best initial step is to address her or him about what has been observed, discussion of the concern, and allowing that fellow student the opportunity to explain and correct the behaviour. If unethical behaviour continues, the issue should be addressed with the field instructor, after having informed the fellow student of the intention to do so. With field instructors, the problem is fraught with much more fear and anxiety.

Although most field instructors are highly ethical and responsible individuals, there are situations that present challenges far in excess of the typical student concern regarding a perception of ethical conflicts in the placement setting. Take for example the case of a female African American social work student who was concerned about questions she was being asked in supervision. The student went to her faculty advisor, also a person of colour, and said that she was regularly being asked about her sex life during supervision with her Anglo-American male field instructor. When asked to elaborate, the student said that her field instructor was telling her that she needed to be in touch with and comfortable discussing her own sexual activity in order to be effective as a social worker who will ask clients similar questions. However, when the student went on to say that her field instructor said she (the student) knew she was erotic, and in need of an outlet, the student's advisor agreed that the field instructor had clearly violated not only the student's privacy, but had crossed the line into sexual harassment. The student was immediately removed from the placement while the issue was taken to the field liaison, the field director, and to the dean. The resolution included both termination of the affiliation agreement with the agency and involvement of the Equal Employment Opportunity Commission (EEOC) in the form of an investigation. Although this is an extreme case, the fact remains that students do encounter difficult situations in field placement settings and faculty liaisons must be aware that asking a student to first speak with the field instructor is sometimes highly problematic. In many cases, a student needs the support of the faculty liaison when addressing difficult or sensitive issues with a field instructor.

Many social work programs require a field practicum experience as well as a separate field seminar class. This is the typical structure of BSW programs. However, many MSW programs now also include an integrative seminar. Separate field seminar courses are an ideal place to discuss the application of ethical principles to practicum placement settings. Likewise, issues related to ethics that are discussed in the field seminar can also be included in weekly supervision with the agency-based field instructor. The link between the two settings is the weekly journal prepared by the student. By approaching field instruction in this manner, there are several opportunities for students to work through ethical issues, ethical dilemmas, and concerns related to maintaining professional boundaries.

Physical Contact

A final area of concern for social work students in practicum placement settings is the issue of physical contact and professional behaviour in relation to physical contact. Both the NASW and CASW ethical codes are very clear about the issue of sexual contact. The CASW (2005b) Guidelines for Ethical Practice [2.6.1] state that social workers are not to have sexual contact or become otherwise romantically involved with clients under any circumstances. In addition, the CASW Ethical Guidelines [2.5.1] also state that social workers are to avoid physical contact with clients where a potential for harm to the client may exist. This portion of the guidelines on physical contact further states that social workers who make the decision to engage in what they deem to be appropriate physical contact with clients must assume the responsibility for setting clear, appropriate and culturally sensitive boundaries (CASW, 2005a, [2.5.1]). The 1996 NASW Code of Ethics [1.09] states that under no circumstance should a social worker engage in sexual activity with a client. In the same section of the code, social workers are reminded that they should also not engage in other forms of physical contact with clients where a possibility of psychological harm exists. Inappropriate forms of contact, such as cradling or caressing clients, are typical examples (NASW, 1996, [1.09]). Also, identical to the Canadian code, the American code places the responsibility on the social worker when it comes to determining what qualifies as appropriate physical contact.

Although the issue of sexual contact or things such as cradling, caressing, or rocking an adult client may seem very clear and almost a matter of common sense, there still exists a broad range of types of physical contact that are not well defined. What about hugging children? What do you do with a client who wants to embrace you? Are there instances when a kiss on the cheek might be OK? All of these are good questions. However, for social work students in field settings, the answer should be developed in discussions with the field instructor regarding the nature of the setting, the context of the contact, and the appropriate setting of boundaries. A social worker at a Special Olympics event may hug clients at the finish line of a marathon or other event, but not in the group home or at the office. Likewise, a family may encourage a child to hug the social worker at the end point of family therapy, but the social worker would be ill advised to initiate a hug with a child or hug a child without the parents present. In a correctional setting, hugging of any form is nearly always warned against, with a very business-like handshake being the acceptable limit of physical contact with a client (Coggins & Fresquez, 2007). To be ethical, appropriate, and safe, the social work student should consider setting physical contact boundaries early in the relationship with a client. Although comforting a child in crises or embracing a client who has been diagnosed with terminal cancer may seem appropriate, the social work intern should always keep in mind that limited physical contact is the best rule when starting out. There will likely be an entire career to gain skill related to knowing when and what type of physical contact is most appropriate. However, at the point of field practicum and early in one's social work career, a handshake is the best policy. Moreover, the handshake itself should be initiated by the client. Even with an understanding of clear limits and boundaries, the social worker or social work intern should always follow the lead of the client and never force contact with which the client might feel uncomfortable.

Ethical Dilemmas and Case Examples

The following case examples are intended to highlight situations that present ethical dilemmas for social workers involved in work with clients. You, as the reader, are being asked to carefully consider the elements of each case and then develop potential resolutions to the problems presented. Each case also requires a review of the CASW Code of Ethics and Ethical Guidelines or the NASW Code of Ethics and the Ethical Standards to see what guidelines or standards apply and how.

Soheila

Soheila is a fourteen-year-old student who has been referred for social work services after telling the school nurse that she has not had a period for two months and that a home pregnancy test came out positive. During the intake session with the social worker, Soheila says she wants an abortion and asks if the social worker can arrange one. Soheila tells the social worker that she has been secretly dating a twenty-eight-year-old man who had told her he is unable to get anyone pregnant. She begs the social worker not to tell her parents. She says her parents are devout Muslims and she does not know how they will react to the information.

1. What laws might have a bearing on the social worker's actions in this case?
2. Are there CASW or NASW ethical guidelines/standards that provide direction for the social worker in this case?
3. What should the social worker do in this case?

Eduardo

Eduardo is a sixteen-year-old male who is a nondocumented immigrant from central Mexico. He is in an initial session with a social worker at a shelter for homeless youth who have been living on the street. Eduardo has become involved in drug use and admits to sharing a needle with several intravenous drug users. In addition, Eduardo was originally smuggled into the country with the promise of a job, but was instead sold to a man who made him work as a male prostitute. Because he is a nondocumented immigrant, he has no health insurance coverage. Eduardo has recently been ill, experiencing night sweats, bloody stools, and weight loss. Eduardo tells the social worker he must continue to perform sex acts and sell drugs for money in order to feed himself. He has asked the social worker to look up his symptoms on the Internet to see what illness he might have. Eduardo says he is afraid to see a doctor because he fears being deported.

1. What laws might have a bearing on the social worker's actions in this case?
2. Are there CASW or NASW ethical guidelines/standards that provide direction for the social worker in this case?
3. What should the social worker do in this case?

James

A social worker with adult services has received a call from a person concerned about a neighbour who lives alone. The neighbour had contacted adult services regarding a man named James, who has not been seen outside of his home for three days. James is a seventy-three-year-old male of African American descent, living by himself in an inner-city neighbourhood that is economically depressed. When the social worker entered the home, she found James unable to get out of bed. The house was extremely hot inside and the windows were nailed shut. On the table near James's bed, the social worker saw uneaten food that had begun to mould. When questioned about family members, James stated that he has only one child, a forty-four-year-old son, who lives in a suburb about forty-five minutes away. James has been living alone since the death of his second wife, ten months earlier. He was the primary caregiver for his wife who had been diagnosed with Alzheimer's disease five years ago. In the last eight months, James has been in rapidly declining health due in part to complications from diabetes. James states that his son visits him every weekend. According to James, his son says that he is unable to visit more often because of work and the need to take care of his own children who are in their late teens. James says he can care for himself if the social worker will help him get out of bed. James pleads with the social worker not to put him in a nursing home.

1. What laws might have a bearing on the social worker's actions in this case?
2. Are there CASW or NASW ethical guidelines/standards that provide direction for the social worker in this case?
3. What should the social worker do in this case?

Adrian

A female social worker is employed at a counselling centre in a rural northern community serving several Indigenous First Nations. The social worker is the therapist for a twenty-three-year-old man named Adrian. During the fourth session with the social worker, Adrian states that he spent four weeks in the summer with his cousin who lives in the city. He says that while he was there, he attended lots of parties and that during one of those parties he had unprotected sex with two men. The social worker is concerned about the possibility that Adrian may have contracted a sexually transmitted disease, in particular HIV. Adrian says he has a girlfriend, but has not told her about the sex with men that occurred while he was in the city. When Adrian stated the name of his girl-friend and where she was from, the social worker realized that Adrian's girlfriend was one of her relatives. Adrian says he came to the social worker because he knows she will not tell anyone what he has shared in counselling. Adrian is not sure what he wants to do, but says that for now, he would like to continue seeing the social worker to, in his words, "work things out."

1. What laws might have a bearing on the social worker's actions in this case?
2. Are there CASW or NASW ethical guidelines/standards that provide direction for the social worker in this case?
3. What should the social worker do in this case?

Amalia

Amalia is of Latin American descent and lives in an inner-city neighbourhood in a large urban area. Amalia has arrived at a health clinic asking for treatment of several cuts and bruises. After initial wound cleaning and care, the clinic nurse refers Amalia to the social worker. During the session with the social worker, Amalia admits that her husband drinks heavily and abuses her. However, she also admits that she is not a documented legal resident and asks the social worker not to tell anyone about the abuse. Amalia states that in Nicaragua, she no longer has family members she can rely on because all of her close family members have moved away to Belize, Mexico, Canada, or the United States. In addition, she says that she is not welcome in her family because they do not approve of the marriage to her husband. So according to Amalia, she has no family she can turn to, and a return home without family would leave her destitute. Amalia says that she had been deported once before and that if it is found out she is in the country illegally, she will be deported and banned from reentry. She is fearful of both the abuse and of what might happen to her if she is returned to Nicaragua.

1. What laws might have a bearing on the social worker's actions in this case?
2. Are there CASW or NASW ethical guidelines/standards that provide direction for the social worker in this case?
3. What should the social worker do in this case?

CONCLUSION

In addition to the two primary national codes of ethics in Canada and the United States, there are other codes of ethics in different provinces, as well as codes of ethics and mission statements of various racial/cultural groups that are designed to serve as guides for ethical professional practice. For example, the National Association of Black Social Workers (NABSW, n.d.[b]) in the United States, and the Canadian province of Nova Scotia, is an organization that is now approaching a half century of existence. The NABSW has always maintained a commitment to social justice, social change, advocacy, an African American-centric practice orientation, belief in the common destiny of African American people, and the professional obligation to commit oneself as an African American person through volunteerism to causes that will advance the social well-being of African Americans (NABSW, n.d.[b]).

The NABSW has long advocated for African American families. As a professional social work organization, a great deal of effort has been directed toward reducing out-of-home placement of African American children wherever possible. The commitment of the NABSW is guided by the ethical principles that complement and extend the NASW Code of Ethics. The NABSW Code of Ethics (n.d.[a]) includes the following professional commitment statements intended to guide practice and shape the professional identity of African American social workers:

> As Black social workers we commit ourselves, collectively, to the interests of our Black brethren and as individuals subscribe to the following statements:
>
> ■ I regard as my primary obligation the welfare of the Black individual, Black family, and Black community and will engage in action for improving social conditions.
>
> ■ I give precedence to this mission over my personal interest.
>
> ■ I adopt the concept of a Black extended family and embrace all Black people as my brothers and sisters, making no distinction between their destiny and my own.
>
> ■ I hold myself responsible for the quality and extent of service I perform and the quality and extent of service performed by the agency or organization in which I am employed, as it relates to the Black community.

- I accept the responsibility to protect the Black community against unethical and hypocritical practice by any individual or organizations engaged in social welfare activities.

- I stand ready to supplement my paid or professional advocacy with voluntary service in the Black public interest.

- I will consciously use my skills, and my whole being as an instrument for social change, with particular attention directed to the establishment of Black social institutions.

For many Indigenous (Aboriginal) social workers in Canada, the concept of professionalism is further strengthened by both Nation-specific belief systems that guide just and fair treatment of others and by the pan-Indigenous life values known as the *Seven Sacred Teachings*. These teachings have different expressions in the various Indigenous communities across Canada and parts of the United States, but the concepts are universal, providing a framework for living a good, meaningful, thoughtful, and caring existence that is grounded in teachings passed down across the generations through Elders. The Seven Sacred Teachings are humility, honesty, respect, courage, wisdom, truth, and love (Bouchard & Martin, 2009). At the University of Manitoba Inner City Social Work Program, these teachings are also included in the education of social students as a companion to CASW ethical values. In a program serving a student body that is more than 70 percent Indigenous/Aboriginal Canadian, the Seven Sacred Teachings act as a bridge between cultures and as a tool for examining the manner in which certain aspects of social work values from the majority culture echo teachings from Indigenous cultures.

Ethical values and ethical codes cannot answer all questions that arise in contact with clients. In some cases, the CASW, NASW, or other codes and practice guidelines offer clear direction. In cases where this does not occur, laws such as the PIPEDA or the HIPAA-HITECH may give direction. However, there are still times when a law or code does not help social workers resolve ethical dilemmas, or worse, they provide conflicting information regarding how one should proceed. In our current age of political polarization, religious conflict, growing economic disparity, and contact between different societies with different cultural values, ample room exists for the creation of confusion regarding what to do when confronted with an ethical issue or dilemma for which no clear guidance exists. After all, social work values are derived from social values (Dolgoff et al., 2012, p. 27), and when a multiplicity of divergent value orientations exist side by side, so will value-driven behavioural expectations. This may leave many social workers wondering if falling back on personal values is appropriate when professional values do not address the issue or dilemma being faced. For social workers the ability to recognize personal values, social values, and professional values; know where they are congruent and where they are divergent; and then select a path that is most consistent with a professional value orientation is crucial. With social workers, the ability to critically analyze a situation and act in a manner that demonstrates adherence to professional ethical principles and value orientations, even where no clear guidance exists, will prove to be the most appropriate professional course of action.

Chapter Three

Social Justice and Anti-oppressive Practice

INTRODUCTION

The term *anti-oppressive practice* as it relates to social work is seldom heard in the United States. In the United States, the term most commonly encountered is *social justice social work*. However, both include a commitment to the creation of a society that is more fair, just, inclusive, and affirming of many forms of diversity. An anti-oppressive perspective in social work practice recognizes the intersectionality of multiple oppressive forces in society. Critical race theory, colonial and postcolonial cultural hegemony, structural approaches to understanding poverty and oppression, feminist perspectives, client empowerment, and deconstructing disempowering hierarchical relationships are all features of an anti-oppressive perspective in social work practice.

Still, some might posit that good ethical social work is naturally anti-oppressive. However, good social work is subjective. Take, for example, a social worker raised in a Euro-Canadian or Euro-American family and community that values conservative Christian faith, believes hard work inevitably leads to prosperity, and elevates the importance of individualism and individual effort. Add to this a social milieu in which heterosexuality is dominant and viewed as the normal and preferred state for coupling and raising children. Finally, patriotism (especially in the United States) along with the invisibility of privilege within the context of white, economically secure, heteronormative social networks and social institutions completes a picture that makes other lived experiences, such as the realities of multitudes of marginalized populations, somehow strange and hard to understand.

Although there are those in the dominant culture of North America who come from economically advantaged backgrounds who may have a desire to help those in need, that help often comes with deeply held convictions about appropriate behaviour, attitudes, beliefs, and values. Therefore, success in helping the "poor" may unconsciously be gauged by what the social worker understands as the normal, optimal state of functioning for human beings. This, of course, can result in a continuation of oppression as social workers from privilege or those who have internalized the dominant cultural discourse attempt to shape clients' lives in a way that feels familiar or correct. Failures on the part of clients to respond in a manner deemed appropriate by dominant cultural standards are turned back on clients who are blamed for not working hard enough to achieve real and lasting change. Social workers will be destined to replicate oppressive relationships in contact with clients if they lack awareness of differences in social location resulting from the impact of colonization, cultural hegemony, income and health disparities, racism, sexism, heterosexism and homophobia, ableism, ageism, xenophobia, and the compounding effect of these factors as they intersect in people's lives.

UNDERSTANDING OPPRESSIVE FORCES

Oppression within the North American context can occur at different levels, develop over time, target specific populations in certain regions, and create shifting patterns of privilege and marginalization. In some settings, ageism or ableism may predominate, while in others, sexism, homophobia, or fear of cultural differences may result in discrimination. Moreover, discrimination can be subtle or blatant. Although the United States and Canada have legislation banning certain forms of discrimination, this does not mean that these issues have disappeared. In the following sections of this chapter, critical race theory, discrimination faced by sexual minority populations, feminist perspectives, social justice, and economic justice will be highlighted. Nevertheless, it must be remembered that marginalization and exclusion can be made manifest in many ways and for a multitude of reasons. The evolving nature of oppression and the quest of some individuals and groups to secure power, maintain or increase privilege, and marginalize those deemed less worthy of fair treatment remains an ongoing issue. Therefore, the broad categories of thought and theory related to oppressive forces featured in the pages that follow must be understood as a selected versus exhaustive list of oppressive forces impacting and shaping the lives of individuals in North American societies.

Critical Race Theory

Critical race theory in North America was a natural outgrowth of social and economic justice movements of the 1960s. Racism, and the persistent belief in race as a biological reality, has resulted in the racialization of certain groups in North American society. *Racialization* is a social process through which certain populations become identified as different on the basis of physical character-istics that the Euro-American and Euro-Canadian majority identify as belong-ing to a group other than their own (Dalal, 2002). In North America, typical racialized persons are those who have darker natural skin colour and physical features that are viewed as different from populations having origins in north-ern, western, and eastern Europe. Even though the civil rights movements in the middle part of the twentieth century did result in numerous positive changes, racial disparity, racism, and the pervasive negative experiences of racialized populations remain a major social justice concern in social work and in the larger North American context. In Canada and the United States, the con-cept of race has shaped much of the contemporary experience of people who trace their heritage to populations that do not originate in Europe. Even for Europeans having darker skin, marginalization due to perceived racial differ-ences has resulted in groups such as southern Europeans being less fully included in the Euro-American/Euro-Canadian majority that is primarily of northern and western European derivation. In spite of gains made in Canada and the United States, race and racism continue to be pervasive, shaping the context of lived experiences for Euro-Canadians, Euro-Americans, and those with non-European heritage.

Abrams and Moio (2009) identify six key components of critical race theory:

1. Racism is endemic;
2. Race is socially constructed;
3. Racialization is differential, shifting, and shaped by the Caucasian majority holding power in much of North America;
4. Racism gives the Caucasian majority both material power and per-ceived moral authority in social discourse, with change that favours the oppressed happening only when it converges with the interests of those in power;
5. Voices of colour are often excluded from history by the dominant Caucasian majority; and
6. Race can and does intersect with other forms of oppression based on sex, gender or gender expression, economic class, sexual preference, and so forth. (pp. 250–251)

Moreover, critical race theorists argue that an examination and analysis of race and oppression must be careful not to consider all forms of oppression as essentially the same, because in so doing, we run the risk of perpetuating the very marginalization we had sought to avoid (Hutchinson, 2000). For example, a person who is African American, transgender, and homeless will have a level of marginalization that is greater than any single status, condition, or identity alone. In other words, a person who is African American, heterosexual, and middle class in a predominately Caucasian community may experience racism, but her or his degree and type of oppression and marginalization will look quite different from the homeless African American individual who is also transgender. Realizing that many variables of one's life intersect in multiple and often compounding ways is crucial for social workers wanting to develop a more empathic and anti-oppressive approach to understanding those they serve.

Indigenous North Americans, Colonization, and Racism

The history of Indigenous populations in North America has also been one of genocide, segregation, marginalization, forced assimilation, and continued colonial domination. In the European colonies that became the United States and Canada, early contact with Indigenous North Americans began with death. Diseases introduced by Europeans decimated the regions of the Caribbean and the colony of New Spain. European, African, and Central Asian diseases decimated entire villages and regions that had no immunity to new pathogens (Stannard, 1992; Thornton, 1987). Although the initial unintentional spreading of disease was not itself racist in nature, the belief that Indigenous deaths were proof that God had cleared the land for European settlement demonstrates the Eurocentrism of the colonizing European populations.

The English arriving on the eastern seaboard of North America were planning to stay, colonize, and claim the land as their own. Smallpox epidemics that spread among Indigenous populations in what are now the New England states in the United States were taken as convincing evidence that "Indians" were being cleared from the land to make way for English colonization (Fleming, 2003). Growing European colonial populations and a desire for more land led to the policies of genocidal warfare including intentional infection of Indigenous populations with smallpox (Palmater, 2012). For the English, Indigenous Americans were not viewed as fitting participants in fledgling colonial societies. After genocidal warfare (especially in what is now the United States) and removal to reservations (reserves, in Canada), forced assimilation became the policy in both nations.

Although many consider North America to be in a postcolonial period that began for the United States in 1775 and Canada in 1867, the term *postcolonial* is really a misnomer. The most pronounced period of European expansion from the middle of the fifteenth century through the end of the nineteenth century is generally seen as the time of empire building and colonialism (Wolf, 1982). The period after that point until present is often referred to as the postcolonial era. However, colonization as a phenomenon is far from being over worldwide as well as in North America. Histories of colonization, racism, and other forms of oppression have had a profound impact on the social institutions, values, beliefs, attitudes, behaviours, and worldviews of persons in societies that have experienced being colonized (Knopf, 2008). For Indigenous North Americans, colonization began in earnest more than five hundred years ago with the Spanish invasion of the Caribbean and Mexico, followed by colonial empire building on the part of Spain, France, England, and, to a lesser degree, the Netherlands, Sweden, and even Russia in what is now Alaska and coastal British Columbia. It is well documented and widely known that before Canada and the United States existed as nations, Indigenous populations were subjected to enslavement, genocide, forced assimilation, and the theft of their lands by invading Europeans (Koning, 1992). What is not as widely known is the degree of colonization that occurred after independence in the United States and confederation in Canada.

The United States Constitution, Article I, Section 8 established federal control over commerce with foreign nations and "Indian Tribes." In addition, Article I, Section 2 of the same document excludes Indigenous Americans who had not assimilated and become taxpayers from being counted as persons in any state or territory. In fact, as a whole, Indigenous Americans did not become citizens of the United States until 1924. In the United States, Indigenous peoples were subjected to wholesale annihilation as the Euro-American government sought to empty the prairies and the West of Indigenous inhabitants so that the way could be cleared for white European and Euro-American colonization. Those reservation lands that were promised in treaties were reduced many times over as the desire for land was fueled by natural expansion of the Euro-American population combined with European immigration to North America.

The General Allotment Act (Dawes Act) of 1887 was instituted in the United States with the intention of bringing an end to Indigenous forms of land ownership and use. Under the act, reservation lands were divided into one hundred sixty-, eighty-, and forty-acre parcels with the expectation that Indigenous Americans would assimilate to Euro-American culture by becoming farmers. Much of the land that was distributed to Indigenous persons as members of various tribes was not of good quality for either farming or grazing. As a result, the land allotments received were not adequate for Indigenous Americans to become economically self-sufficient. After the allotment process, the remaining lands, called *surplus lands*, were offered for sale to Euro-Americans at extraordinarily low prices or issued as homesteads. Reservation holdings were reduced even further because allotted land could be sold by the property owner after twenty-five years. This resulted in the loss of land to non-Indigenous persons as economically destitute Indigenous landowners sold their property at very low prices. After the initial sale of lands deemed to be surplus, Indigenous lands were also taken through tax default. The surrendered land was subsequently offered for sale to non-Indigenous farmers or ranchers. In the end, two-thirds of the preallotment land base of Indigenous Americans in what is now the United States was lost.

In Canada, the Indian Act of 1876 makes clear that the federal government controls Indigenous Canadians and the lands upon which they live. The Indian Act, which was developed and enacted in accordance with Section 91(24) of the 1867 Constitution Act, gave the federal government full control over Indigenous Canadians and all reserve lands (lands reserved for "Indians"). With this legislation, Indigenous Canadians were made wards of the state, with the federal government having full colonial authority in matters related to Indigenous Canadians. Throughout Canada, the Indian Act and colonial authority has had devastating results. In the Prairie Provinces, the 1872 Dominion Lands Act, much like the Homestead Act in the United States, was designed to reduce Indigenous control of the land and open the prairies for replacement of formerly Indigenous Canadian owners by Euro-Canadians and European immigrants. The Dominion Lands Act was designed to create a permanent change in the racial and cultural character of Western Canada. Under the act, settlers who agreed to accept land were required to live on and cultivate the land. If all requirements of settlement and use were met, the homesteaders secured farmlands at little to no cost.

Residential/Boarding Schools

Another example of colonial domination can be found in the creation of the *residential school system*. In Canada and the United States, generations of Indigenous children were forcibly taken from their parents and placed in residential schools in Canada and boarding schools in the United States. Off-reservation boarding schools for Indigenous American children started with the opening of the Carlisle Indian School at an abandoned military post in Carlisle, Pennsylvania, on October 6, 1879 (Fleming, 2003, p. 194). At the time, Euro-Americans believed that assimilation and off-reservation boarding schools constituted a more benevolent policy than outright extermination. The idea behind boarding schools was quite simple: the US government believed that progress for Indigenous American "Indians" depended on getting them away from their communities, native languages, and cultures (King, 2012). In fact, Indigenous American children at boarding schools often did not go home to their families for months or even years at a time. Instead, they were paired with Euro-American families with whom they would stay during holidays and for whom they would provide free labour as farmhands during the summer (Fleming, 2003). Many boarding schools were established at great distances from reservations. This was done to limit contact between the students and their families. Parents were discouraged from visiting students at the schools to further consolidate the separation of Indigenous youth from their languages, spiritual traditions, and other aspects of culture. Students at the boarding schools wore military uniforms and were forced to march to and from school, meals, church, and daily chores. Disobeying rules resulted in punishment.

In addition to requirements of obedient behaviour, Indigenous children in boarding schools were forbidden to speak their languages. Speaking an Indigenous language could result in punishments ranging from spanking to having one's mouth washed out with soap, to more severe forms of physical brutality. Students were also forced to practice the Christian faith. At the boarding schools, children were housed in dormitories and had virtually no privacy. Moreover, they were encouraged to spy on each other and to report infractions to administrators and teachers. During this time, children in boarding schools were also taught that Indigenous cultures were inferior to the white Euro-American culture.

In Canada, the residential school era began in 1883 under then Prime Minister John A. Macdonald. Residential school student populations surged after 1920 when residential school attendance was made compulsory by the federal government (Frideres & Gadacz, 2012). By the 1930s, residential school attendance was at its peak. The Canadian system was virtually identical to the American system with one exception: US schools were run by the federal government, while the residential schools in Canada, although funded by the government, were operated by Christian churches. This arrangement continued until 1969. The last residential school for Indigenous Canadian children, in the Province of Saskatchewan, closed in 1996.

Asian-Origin Populations

Asian-origin populations with histories in Far-East Asian countries such as China, Korea, and Japan have been subject to negative stereotyping, racialization, legal exclusion, and (in the case of the Japanese) even placement in internment camps in Canada and the United States during World War II. At one point in Canadian and American history, Asian-origin populations were viewed as a threat to North American economies (Abrams & Moio, 2009). Conversely, Asian-origin individuals from China and Japan have also been held up as examples of "model minorities" who are able to achieve academically and commercially without threatening to disrupt the social institutions of the majority culture (Lee & Mock, 2005, p. 272).

In more recent times, southwest Asian populations, and particularly those associated with cultures influenced by Islam, have been less favourably received by Euro-Canadian and Euro-American majorities. This has been especially so since the terrorist attacks on the United States on September 11, 2001, and the more recent rise of the Islamic State (ISIS) in 2014. Southwest Asian populations along with south Asian populations have continued to be viewed as racialized others with little attention to the cultural, linguistic, and religious diversity between and among populations originating in this part of the world (Almeida, 2005). Nevertheless, Canadians have become somewhat more comfortable with a variety of south Asian ethnic groups, while Americans continue to have a greater degree of discomfort with individuals who look and dress differently from those in the majority culture, especially when those differences are either correctly or erroneously connected to Islam.

African American/African Canadian Populations

In the case of African-origin populations in North America, racism continues to defy scientific reality. Although race is clearly a social construct, many in North America continue to see the division of human beings into distinct races as a biological reality that carries with it ideas of character, behaviour, temperament, and so forth. Racism has a long history in Canada and the United States with discrimination and white *nativist* backlash against African-origin populations often looking quite similar in the two countries (Palmer, 1976). This, combined with a history of segregation for African-origin North Americans in the United States and Canada (sometimes legal and at other times social), demonstrates that neither nation has been immune to racist policies and practices directed at people of African heritage. Much like the "black towns" that developed in the

American plains states (most notably Oklahoma) following the end of slavery (Hardaway, 1999), African Americans in Canada were often segregated in communities separate from those of Euro-Canadians in Upper Canada (Winks, 1997). Farther west, in the Prairie Province of Alberta in 1910, Euro-Canadian residents of Edmonton petitioned the government to stem the growth of black settlements in Canada. In response, a one-year moratorium on African American settlement in Canada was passed by the Laurier government, citing the unsuitability of the "Negro race" to the cold climate and requirements of Canada as a reason to prohibit African American immigration from the United States (Payne, 2013).

Latino Populations

In the minds of many Caucasian Euro-Canadians and Euro-Americans, Latino populations have largely been relegated to the position of unskilled farm labour or meat-packing line workers with the added racializing attributes of genetic, linguistic, and cultural difference that departs radically from the Canadian and American majority (Sawchuk & Kempf, 2008). In the United States, Mexican-origin and other Central or South American populations have been viewed by many on the socially conservative political right as an invading social and cultural force that threatens to change American society. The fear is that the core national culture of the United States will move from one based on values, culture, and language derived from Northern and Western Europe to a society that has western Mediterranean and Indigenous foundations. Coupled with this fear of a profound culture shift are the enduring stereotypical assumptions of a biological predisposition to involvement in criminal behaviour, gangs, and the illegal drug trade. In addition, Latinos in the United States are regularly suspected of having questionable legal status related to residency.

In the United States, people who have origins in the diverse cultures south of the border between the United States and Mexico are also often seen as being a drain on the social welfare system, with many non-Latinos having the erroneous assumption that Mexicans and other Latino populations come to the United States simply to receive welfare. The fact that most recent immigrants, and all nondocumented immigrants, are wholly ineligible for income support and other forms of social assistance has not had a demonstrable impact on dispelling the myth. Finally, the stereotype of laziness among Mexican-origin and other Latino populations exists in spite of engagement by many low-income Mexican Americans, Mexican nationals, and immigrants from Central

America or South America in physically demanding labour, for long hours, at low pay.

Endemic Racism

In Canada, Indigenous (Aboriginal) Canadians often experience the same sort of negative stereotyping that is largely directed toward other racialized population in the United States. In Canada, Indigenous persons are widely viewed as a drain on the social welfare system that Euro-Canadians believe they as taxpayers are forced to fund. In urban areas, Aboriginal Canadians are characterized as likely to be involved in the illegal drug trade, suspected of being members of gangs, assumed to be addicted to alcohol or drugs, and viewed as dangerous to Euro-Canadians (Palmater, 2012). These stereotypes persist into the present and create uneasy relations between Indigenous Canadians and other populations within Canada. However, while non-Indigenous Canadians have the option of avoiding Indigenous individuals and communities to a large extent, Indigenous Canadians cannot avoid experiencing life as negatively racialized persons with the larger national context. The endemic nature of racism should come as no surprise to anyone in social work. An examination of Indigenous North American issues in Canada and the United States, the historic and contemporary experience of African Americans in the United States and African-origin populations in Canada, or the treatment of Latino and southwest Asian-origin populations in both nations will quickly expose the power of dominant-culture discourse in relation to shaping the experience of groups that are characterized as being outside of the cultural, social, linguistic, and phenotypic "norm" of the majority North American society.

Sexual Minority Populations

In all of North America, including Mexico, some progress has been made regarding the fight for civil rights and social inclusion of sexual minority persons. However, this inclusion and acceptance has been uneven. Persons who identify as lesbian, gay, bisexual, transgender, queer, questioning, or intersex (LGBTQQI) still face many barriers in relation to securing basic civil rights. The degree of rights and freedoms afforded to sexual minority populations varies by nation and region of residence. For example, since 2005 same-sex marriage has been legal throughout all of Canada in a manner that includes all the rights and freedoms afforded to opposite-sex couples. While at the same time, in the United

States marriage equality had only been achieved in some states, while it was explicitly banned in others (Robinson, 2013). However, with the recent (June 2015) US Supreme Court decision, same-sex marriage was determined to be a right guaranteed by the US Constitution and marriage equality became legal nationwide. Finally, Mexico has been evolving rapidly since 2009 when same-sex marriage was legal in only two jurisdictions.

Canada

The struggle for fair and equal treatment of sexual minority populations in Canada has developed over decades with the majority of positive changes occurring since the 1960s. In 1969, same-sex sexual activity was decriminalized following the passage of the Criminal Law Amendment Act, 1968–69 (S.C. 1968–69, c. 38), an omnibus crime bill that introduced numerous changes to the federal criminal code. However, the event that created the legal framework for actual equality of sexual minority populations did not take place until patriation of the constitution in 1982, which included the Canadian Charter of Rights and Freedoms. Charter Section 15, which addresses equality rights, has since been interpreted as guaranteeing the rights of same-sex couples, culminating in the passage of marriage equality in 2005. Still, legislation has not eliminated discrimination and the acceptance of difference continues to be problematic. For example, gay, lesbian, and transgender youth still experience bullying in school (Burtch & Haskell, 2010). Moreover, while gay male couples and lesbian couples are now free to legally marry, work still remains in relation to furthering civil rights for those individuals who identify as transgender, intersex, or as in some way outside of the male-female binary conceptualization of sex and gender.

United States

The United States has been less successful in developing uniform protections for sexual minority populations. Although same-sex sexual activity has been decriminalized, this did not occur nationwide until 2003 with the US Supreme Court decision in *Lawrence v. Texas* (Tribe, 2004). Moreover, the United States lagged behind Canada and even Mexico in relation to recognizing same-sex marriages or civil unions in all states. In the United States, legally wedded same-sex couples, unlike opposite-sex couples, did not enjoy uniform legal recognition of their unions throughout the nation until the Supreme Court decision on June 26, 2015. Prior to that time a move from one state to another often resulted in the loss of legal recognition as a married couple (Robinson, 2013).

The United States also has additional serious challenges in relation to living up to the promise of equality and freedom for all. In many parts of the United States, the discrimination faced by sexual minority populations continues unabated. In more than half of the states, individuals can have their employment terminated simply for being identified as a lesbian, gay, or transgender person (Burns & Krehely, 2011). While it is often pointed out that progress toward social inclusion continues in the United States, it cannot be denied that marginalization and exclusion resulting from homophobia and heterosexism continues, and in some areas has even intensified.

Mexico

Within Mexico, same-sex marriage was initially only granted in the state of Coahuila and the federal district (Distrito Federal) which includes Mexico City. Rights were expanded when the Mexican Supreme Court ruled that all legal marriages performed in Distrito Federal must be recognized by all thirty-one states, thereby extending full matrimonial rights nationwide (Agren, 2010). Therefore, a same-sex couple married legally in Distrito Federal must have the legality of their marriage upheld, even if they move to another Mexican state that does not have marriage equality (Robinson, 2013). Since the ruling, Mexico has continued to move forward with a series of court rulings that allow marriage for all same-sex couples in Coahuila, Quintana Roo, and Distrito Federal as well as limited marriage or civil union rights in many others. As a result of these rapid changes, it is believed that Mexico will have full same-sex marriage access nationwide in the near future (Feder, 2015).

FEMINIST PERSPECTIVES

Generally speaking, feminist social work practice strives to engage and work with clients in a manner that is not oppressive and does not serve to keep in place the gender-based inequalities that exist in society (Baines, 1997). When a feminist perspective, or more generally feminism, is referred to by most social workers, the common understanding is that some sort of social movement addressing the oppression of women began in the 1940s in Quebec and in the 1960s in the United States (Backhouse & Flaherty, 1992). The general assumption is that feminism was an outgrowth of many other civil rights movements that were on the rise in North America. However, feminism has roots that run much deeper in Canada and the United States. From the earliest days of European invasion, Indigenous North American women were involved in resisting colonization and the reduction in status that resulted from assimilation to European concepts of the role of women in society (Frideres & Gadacz, 2012; Jaimes & Halsey, 1992). During slavery in the American South, African American women were crucial in organizing resistance to oppression and facilitating the escape of slaves to freedom. Many American schoolchildren have read about African American activist Harriet Tubman who is famous for fighting to end slavery and for helping slaves escape to northern states and later to Canada. During the Mexican Revolution, Indigenous and Mestiza women fought alongside men to secure freedom from colonial Spain (Linhard, 2005; Macias, 1980). Latina/Chicana women also figured prominently in the farm labour movements of the United States, and Indigenous American women were crucial to the formation and growth of the American Indian Movement (Gonzales, 2009; Jaimes & Halsey, 1992).

While much of North American feminist history includes the stories of courageous women, what is often missing are the contributions, accomplishments, and voices of Indigenous women, African American/African Canadian women, sexual minority women, women of Asian origin, and Latina/Chicana women. As Beverly Guy-Sheftall (1995, p. xiii) states, "the history of American feminism has been primarily a narrative about the heroic deeds of white women." Indeed, Canada and the United States, from the fight for the right to vote to the battle for constitutionally enshrined equality for women, it has been white middle-class women who have been in the limelight, with low-income women, minority women, and those from outside of the mainstream being marginalized or worse, never recognized for their contributions to the feminist movements in North America (Prendergast, 2011).

Feminist Perspectives of Marie Weil

The oppression, freedom, or equality of women in any society is influenced by multiple intersecting factors. Regional, provincial, state, and national policies related to women can serve as limiting or affirming forces in the lives of those living in various societies. In addition, religious institutions, ethnic group membership, socioeconomic status, education, and many other factors can be either supportive and affirming, or serve as oppressive and limiting influences in the lives of women when considered in conjunction with the multiple layers of additional oppression created by race, disability, immigrant status, or sexual minority identity. As a result, the worldviews and organizing efforts of women can be quite different. In her work on women and organizing, Marie Weil identifies four different feminist perspectives that demonstrate distinctly different worldviews in relation to women in society. Weil's (1995) perspectives are described as liberal, socialist, radical, and women of colour.

According to Weil, the *liberal feminist perspective* emphasizes the importance of equal rights. The liberal perspective focuses on gender equality and the dispelling of gender-based stereotypes. Liberal feminists advocate for reform. However, that reform is conceived of as taking place within the current political and economic structure of North American society. For liberals, the goal is creating a society in which women have equality of opportunity.

Those who identify with the *socialist feminist perspective* focus on the elimination of gender-based oppression and discrimination as well as fighting for social and economic justice. Socialist feminists firmly believe that economic arrangement within capitalist societies serve to support and perpetuate the oppression and marginalization of women, people of colour, sexual minorities, persons with disabilities, and those living in poverty. Socialist feminists advocate for drastic, revolutionary political change and social restructuring that would decenter white, male, capitalist supremacy by creating a society that eliminates all forms of discrimination, distributes resources more equitably, and ends the oppression of women, minorities, and vulnerable populations.

The *radical feminist perspective* places a clear emphasis on the elimination of patriarchal social structures through the creation of a society that is based on feminist values. The radical perspective is one that sees male power and privilege as oppressive forces responsible for much of the oppression that exists in the world. Radicals advocate revolutionary change, but unlike socialist feminists, radicals are more exclusively focused on the ascendency of women and the creation of a society that places feminist values at the centre.

The *women of colour perspective* differs from the other three in that race is seen as often being equal to (and sometimes more important than) gender in relation to oppression. Those more closely identified with the women of colour perspective do see gender-based oppression as a critical issue, but within a framework of advocacy that strives to eliminate all forms of oppression. This particular approach connects the oppression of women with racism directed toward people of colour and those living in poverty. Rather than advocating for revolution, as is the case with radical and socialist feminists, those who identify with the women of colour perspective are more likely to fight for political change that creates opportunities for women, minorities, those living in poverty, and other oppressed populations.

Feminist Approaches of Margaret Matlin

In a similar manner, Margaret Matlin (2004) outlines three different feminist approaches: liberal, cultural, and radical feminism. Much like Weil's description of liberal feminism, Matlin's review of feminist literature identifies *liberal feminists* as those who emphasize gender equality in a manner that affords women the same rights and opportunities as men, but within existing economic and political structures. Therefore, liberal feminism is centered on reforms that emphasize equality of opportunity.

Radical feminists, as described by Matlin, focus on oppression that forms the foundation of laws, policies, and cultural practices that permeate North American society. As is the case with radical feminism described in Weil's model, creating healthier and more affirming social and cultural contexts for women will require a dramatic shift in social and political structures that are currently viewed as perpetuating sex and gender inequality, a devaluing of women, and multiple forms of violence against women.

Matlin identifies *cultural feminists* as a third group of feminist activists and scholars who have a distinct orientation that differs from liberal and radical feminists. Cultural feminists emphasize the importance of valuing women and elevating the status of female values such as nurturing, caregiving, and cooperation, rather than aggression which is viewed as having resulted from societies dominated by men (Matlin, 2004, p. 6). Unlike liberal feminists, cultural feminists believe that society needs dramatic restructuring in a manner that values and affirms women rather than focusing on gender similarity and reform directed at achieving male and female equality within the existing North American political context.

NEOLIBERALISM AND NEOCONSERVATISM

Neoliberalism, as it relates to social welfare, is best understood as a retreat from the post–World War II expansion of social welfare that had occurred in Canada, the United States, and indeed much of the world that was characterized as industrialized in that time. Social welfare programming, education, health care, unionization, and the expansion of civil rights all shaped and were shaped by

Figure 3.1   Neoliberalism versus Neoconservatism

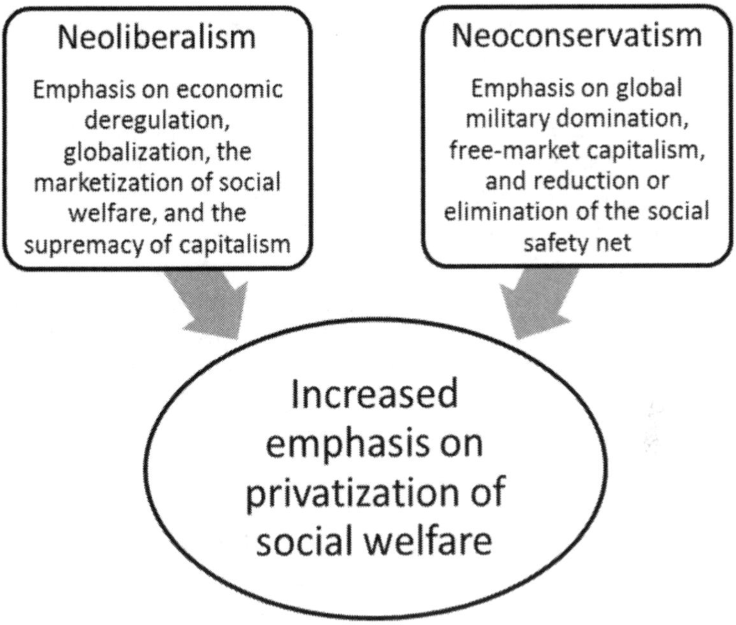

Neoliberalism

Emphasis on economic deregulation, globalization, the marketization of social welfare, and the supremacy of capitalism

Neoconservatism

Emphasis on global military domination, free-market capitalism, and reduction or elimination of the social safety net

Increased emphasis on privatization of social welfare

a time in which North America was undergoing massive social, political, economic, and technological change. A large part of that change began with civil rights movements that expanded rapidly from the 1950s onward and quickly grew to include a focus on the plight of the poor (Harvey, 2005).

By the 1960s, a robust welfare state was developing in the United States and Canada with both nations moving in the direction of Western Europe where post–World War II governments had worked to create a social safety net, decrease the disparity between the wealthiest and poorest segments of society, and to improve incomes and living standards for all. This was particularly true for Scandinavian countries (Harvey, 2005). The European approach to improving overall standards of living and the general quality of life for citizens and legal residents was done through the creation or expansion of institutional (universal) and residual (means-tested) social welfare programs such as health care, education, assistance to low-income individuals and families, unemployment benefits, public pensions, disability insurance, and so forth. Although Canada attained many social welfare developmental objectives to a far greater degree than the United States, both countries were on a similar trajectory that would lead to social citizenship that would include entitlement to certain protections, supports, and freedoms resulting from being a citizen or legal resident of an economically advanced nation and society (Graham, Swift, & Delaney, 2012).

Although Canada and the United States have seen retrenchment in relation to social welfare, with Quebec retaining the most European-like social welfare system, Canada has retained more of a belief in social citizenship that benefits all than can be said for the United States. Even in the best and most socially progressive of times, the United States has always been a reluctant welfare state. The flush of civil rights, social justice, and the movement toward an expansion of social welfare that flourished in the 1960s struggled in the 1970s under President Richard Nixon, and finally ended with the election of Ronald Reagan in 1980. It was at this time that neoliberal and the rapidly developing neoconservative ideology began to take root in North America and the United Kingdom.

In his book *The Inconvenient Indian*, Thomas King (2012) discusses the dichotomy of savage versus civilized that has characterized the history of contact between Indigenous North Americans and Euro-Canadians/Euro-Americans. King states that beliefs about civilization and capitalism have been fused in a manner that acts as a powerful toxin contaminating all of our major institutions. King (2012) states:

> Under its influence democracy becomes not simply a form of representative government, but an organized principle that bundles individual freedoms, Christianity, and capitalism into a marketable product carrying with it the unexamined promise of wealth and prosperity. (p. 79)

The concept of neoliberalism is explained quite effectively by this quote, and nowhere is King's quote more true than in the United States where large numbers of wealthy and working-class citizens support neoliberal policies aimed at dismantling antipoverty programs and establishing regressive tax structures, while at the same time supporting neoconservative military expenditure (Naylor, 2010).

As an ideology, neoconservatism has its roots in the backlash to liberal social welfare policies of the United States, Canada, and the United Kingdom in the 1960s and 1970s. In the 1980s, US President Ronald Reagan, Canadian Prime Minister Brian Mulroney, and British Prime Minister Margaret Thatcher all set out to dismantle existing and developing public social welfare based on collectivist principles. As neoconservatives, they espoused the hollow rhetoric of individual liberty, hard work, and the idea that inability to thrive economically was a result of personal failure (Moses, 2004). Neoconservative ideology rejects the idea that anything should be done about economic or social barriers that exist for women, minorities, or other marginalized groups, believing instead in the Social Darwinian concept that society is composed of those who will succeed and those who will fail. Moreover, some neoconservatives believe that failure of some is necessary to strengthen society overall. This Social Darwinian approach harkens back to the work of nineteenth-century sociologist Herbert Spencer who first coined the term *"survival of the fittest"* in his development of the social evolutionist concepts that would become Social Darwinism (Werth, 2011, p. 118). Much like the industrialists of the late nineteenth and early twentieth century, the neoconservatives in the twenty-first century have adopted an approach to social welfare that views assistance to those in need as fostering dependence, which will weaken society in the long run.

Beyond withdrawing from commitments to social welfare, neoconservatives, especially in the United States, embarked on a path of military imperial world domination. During the 1980s, American neoconservatives in the Republican Party, led by Republican President Ronald Reagan, diverted revenues and resources to a massive military buildup and an interventionist policy directed at shaping the world to their liking. Militarism, coupled with nationalism and conservative fundamentalist Christian hegemony, has resulted in a modern-day colonial mission under the guise of spreading democracy, which has become a worldwide effort directed toward nation building, or more accurately, nation shaping. In 2012, the United States had a military budget of $682 billion—more than China, Russia, the United Kingdom, and Japan combined (SIPRI, 2012). In the United States, the result has been reduced spending for social welfare and the actual infrastructure needed for economic development at home. Moreover, a myriad of social welfare programs originally designed as a buffer against the excesses of capitalism have either been cut or eliminated.

Social and Economic Justice

In 2011, the most progressive major political party in North America, the New Democratic Party of Canada, changed the preamble of their constitution to eliminate references to socialism, opting instead for a move toward the political right in an attempt to position themselves for a run at securing a majority in the Canadian Parliament. Likewise, the Democratic Party in the United States has, over several decades, moved from a progressive social welfare platform to a more centrist and even right-of-center position. This is evidenced by the fact that in 1996 then President Bill Clinton signed into law the Personal Responsibility and Work Opportunity Reconciliation Act, which replaced Aid to Families with Dependent Children (AFDC) with Temporary Assistance to Needy Families (TANF). TANF included lifetime limits, work requirements, and the denial of social assistance benefits for those convicted of certain drug offences. In addition, the legislation barred new immigrants from receiving assistance. Even under US President Barack Obama, who has been touted as a socially progressive leader, there has not been a return to calls for more progressive social welfare policies and programs. In 2009 and 2010, the Democrats were neither able nor completely willing to bring forward a proposal for a single-payer health insurance system that would have provided universal coverage to all citizens. Instead, the Patient Protection and Affordable Care Act, the legislation that did pass, keeps private insurance corporations in place, which fits with neoliberal ideology that values private market arrangements over public solutions.

Throughout North American society, much of the impetus to eliminate economic disadvantage and disparity has been replaced by a desire to help the poor through the creation of what many on the political left and right have called *ladders out of poverty* (Reed, 2012). What this sort of thinking does is create the belief that poverty will never be eliminated. Therefore, the next best choice is to save those who are bright, capable, and willing to work hard to pull themselves out of the abyss. This approach to poverty and the poor is rife with assumptions about intelligence, initiative, or even social desirability and exposes a sociocentrism based on economic class, power, and privilege. Such thinking about poverty is not new by any means and has long been the preference of many politicians who more often than not come from wealth and do not want to upset the status quo.

CONCLUSION

In Canada and the United States, various codes of ethics that guide social work practice contain language related to social justice. Social work stands alone as a profession with a foundational and enduring commitment to social justice (Lundy, 2011). Yet, even within the profession, much needs to be done to work toward the goals set by mission statements and ethical codes. Canadian and US social work ethical codes speak of social justice, while economic justice is handled much more carefully, directing social workers to be committed to equality of opportunity, access to services, and so forth. Although the Canadian Association of Social Workers (CASW-ACTS, 2005a) directs social workers to advocate for the equitable distribution of resources, nowhere is wealth redistribution specifically identified. In the United States, the ethical code of the National Association of Social Workers (1996, 2008) stops short of including economic justice and instead has increased the emphasis placed on cultural competence and social diversity.

Clearly, emphasizing the importance of equality in relation to race, ethnicity, culture, gender or gender expression, sexual preference, and many other forms of social diversity is crucial. This, combined with efforts to eliminate racism and discrimination and to advance social inclusion, is critical to ethical anti-oppressive social work practice and furthers the cause of social justice. However, economic justice is also critical. In the 1960s and early 1970s, the idea of broad-based social change and social activism in the form of advocacy for civil rights and antipoverty programming dominated the social work landscape (Specht & Courtney 1994). At that time, *Rules for Radicals* by Saul Alinsky (1971) was required reading for nearly all social workers. Now this once-famous community organizer is scarcely known by many graduates of social work programs that emphasize the preparation of specialized micro-level practitioners and agency or program managers who will fit nicely within the neoliberal and evermore privatized world of services to those in need. Alinsky (1971, p. 18) once said that America is comprised of *The Haves, The Have Nots,* and *The Have a Little but Want Mores.* In Alinsky's description of the class struggle in American capitalist society, *The Haves* (the wealthy) and *The Have a Little but Want Mores* (the middle class) are allies in the cause that favours existing economic and political structures, because the middle classes want not only to maintain their accumulated wealth, but also to move into the wealthy or upper class. Therefore, they often support the creation of opportunities for economic class mobility, but tend to look negatively upon attempts to redistribute wealth downward to those among *The Have Nots* who are in economic need.

What Alinsky did not foresee was the manner in which racism, nationalism, social conservatism, religion, and even fear of terrorism would be used by the political right to rally large numbers of Euro-Americans who might otherwise benefit from a progressive tax structure and antipoverty programming to support neoconservative causes. For example, in the United States the shift in public support for economic assistance, especially to poor nonwhites, has decreased significantly since 1984 (Niemi, Weisburg, & Kimball, 2010). Moreover, Euro-American voters who are lower income and working class have come to identify with the antiwelfare, antigovernment, neoconservative ideology of the Republican Party in ever-increasing numbers. In the 1970s, 60 percent of lower-income Euro-American voters identified as Democrats, but by the 1990s, that number had dropped to 40 percent; and although some movement toward the Democratic Party occurred in 2008, by 2010 that brief reversal had vanished (Hacker & Pierson, 2013, p. 143). Much like conservatives in the United States, conservatives in Canada have demonized big government with the promise that capitalism, economic growth, and lower taxes would benefit all citizens. The language used emphasizes the importance of willingness to work hard at succeeding in a society based on free-market principles. What this sort of rhetoric does is foster the belief that those who are poor are quite often unmotivated as well.

All across North America a retreat from democratic socialist values has been evident since the high point of activism in the late 1960s. For most Canadians, Americans, and the social workers in both nations, the idea of radical wealth redistribution has been largely abandoned since the rise of neoliberal/neoconservative ideology in the 1980s. Since then, social work has been moving away from its collective professional commitment to the poor and into the arena of individual psychotherapy and private practice—a shift that began in earnest in the United States in the 1990s (Specht & Courtney, 1994). With the movement toward privatization and an increased emphasis on individual psychological distress, social work has returned in many ways to the zeitgeist of the 1920s in which people's problems were understood in terms of individual inability to cope with intrapsychic issues exacerbated by the stresses of daily living. Problems from trauma, to anxiety, to depression, to post-traumatic stress are now regarded as internal battles people must wage (with the help of therapy) in order to feel whole and well adjusted. Indeed, mental illness is a real concern and one that social work as a profession should continue to address. However, the socioeconomic and sociopolitical context within which life is lived in North America is not a neutral factor. Although there are voices out there attempting to focus attention on larger economic, social, political, and environmental concerns, the fact remains that social work has become first and foremost a profession that provides individual solutions for what are largely understood as individual problems.

Still, social work and social workers are not entirely to blame for the shift toward a market-driven and increasingly privatized neoliberal/neoconservative society. In many cases, social workers are simply responding to societal realities that shape the working environments where they are employed. After all, social workers have limited power to effect policy change at the provincial/state and national levels. Yes, it is true that some social workers enter politics and become elected officials. However, reaching the numbers needed to form decisive voting blocs, create powerful lobbies, and influence politicians remains elusive with the exception of all-too-infrequent examples in which social work efforts have resulted in legislative victories.

What this means for most direct-practice social workers is that they, as agency employees, must find ways in which social and economic justice can be realized in their daily interactions with clients. Without a doubt, every instance of social or economic injustice cannot be met with a broad-based effort to redistribute wealth. However, when opportunities arise or can be created, social workers are, as a matter of ethical and moral obligation, bound to take action. Still, some degree of economic justice can be realized on a smaller scale in the form of economic advocacy for individuals, families, or entire groups in need. Even when limited efforts result in some form of income support or the distribution of tangible material goods, economic justice has in some small way been made very real.

This does not mean that social workers abandon the fight to create a more just, fair, and equitable society and refocus instead on micro-level solutions that avoid addressing larger systemic problems within neoliberal/neoconservative capitalist economies. On the contrary, as Carniol (2005) makes clear, social workers who apply anti-oppressive principles in their practice must attend to micro-level efforts directed toward assisting disempowered and marginalized individuals while also seeking opportunities to advocate for economically disadvantaged, vulnerable, and marginalized members of society at the macro level.

When it comes to students, and especially to recent graduates of social work programs, academics and more privileged members of professional organizations need to realize that expecting all social workers to be tireless advocates for social change can become itself an oppressive stance. Instead, social work students should be helped to see the importance of balancing the realities of the contemporary workplace environment with professional ethical values and principles that shape our interaction with those we serve at the individual, family, group, organizational, community, and societal level. Social workers who can see the current realities of clients' lives through the lens of an ongoing struggle to ensure social and economic justice will be better prepared to be truly anti-oppressive practitioners.

Chapter Four

Multiculturalism and Cultural Competence in Social Work

INTRODUCTION

This chapter explores knowledge acquisition in relation to culture and multi-culturalism as key elements of social work education and practice. Canada and the United States have large and growing populations of people with origins in societies that differ in ways large and small from North American majority cultures based in Caucasian Euro-Western assumptions about normative behaviours, language, beliefs, attitudes, and so forth. The federal governments of Canada and the United States have developed categories for identifying minority populations. Furthermore, these categories are socially and politically constructed, including a mix of racial, cultural, and ethnic group identities.

Figure 4.1   Most Common Differences in Terminology

CANADA	UNITED STATES

•Indigenous (Aboriginal) Canadian
   •First Nation
   •Inuit
   •Métis
	•Native American / Native Indian
	   •Native American / Native Indian
	   •Alaska Native
	     •American Indian
	     •Yupik
	     •Inupiat
	   •Native Hawaiian

•African Canadian	•African American
•Latin American	•Latino or Hispanic
•Visible Minority	•People of Color

A discussion of common terms in social work practice that are related to racial, social, and cultural diversity has been included in this chapter. This has been done to clarify some of the confusion that exists regarding the use and meaning of language related to work with clients who may be culturally and socially different from the social worker with whom they come into contact. This chapter will also include a detailed discussion of important considerations regarding multiculturalism and practice in social work. Finally, although social workers in Canada and the United States recognize growing multiculturalism and emerging forms of diversity, most social work education still approaches culture from the perspective of Anglo-Canadian/French-Canadian and Anglo-American social workers intervening with clients from culturally distinct populations who at some future point are expected to assimilate into, or at least accommodate, the majority culture of either nation. What is most often missing is the reality of social and cultural change that is reshaping North American society and impacting social work practice contexts. Therefore, culture, multi-culturalism, and critical practice considerations will be discussed with the intention of initiating the paradigm shift that must occur as social work arrives at the middle of the second decade in the twenty-first century.

CULTURE

One of the most enduring classic definitions of culture is that which was developed by Edward Tylor, a British anthropologist (1832–1917). Tylor's definition is still well known to students of cultural anthropology. According to Tylor (1958),

> Culture, or Civilization taken in its widest ethnographic sense, is that complex whole which includes knowledge, belief, art, morals, law, or any other capabilities and habits acquired by man as a member of society. (p. 1)

Although Tylor believed in the unity of humankind as a single species, he borrowed from Darwinian thinking the idea that human cultures evolved from primitive to complex, with European societies representing the pinnacle of cultural development. Europeans in the era of exploration and colonization had often viewed and characterized non-European (especially nonwhite) societies as simple, homogeneous, and less complex than those of Europe. When advanced cultures were encountered in the Americas, Africa, and Asia, ethnocentric Europeans found them to be lacking in religious, moral, literary, or artistic development equal (meaning identical) to that of Europe. As a result, European societies continued to be viewed as superior. The original proclivity of early European anthropologists was to present non-Europeans in overly simplistic terms, emphasizing uniformity of clearly bounded cultural systems (Wolf, 1982). Although the degree of predictability of cultural expression in non-Western societies sought by the Europeans was a naïve endeavor, the task of defining culture for the purpose of predicting values, behaviours, beliefs, and attitudes has become even more implausible within the increasingly global nature of contemporary human existence. Our collective exposure to and participation in the global community has added new levels of diverse cultural and social expression that further highlight the importance of understanding variability within societies or populations identified as specific cultural groups.

In the 1960s and 1970s, many in the field of anthropology were beginning to seriously rethink the scientific approach to understanding cultural differences. Most of the early ethnographers (those who studied particular non-Western populations) seemed to describe cultures that developed among non-European populations as static, uniform, and able to be catalogued in much the same manner as one would describe the collective habits of nonhuman species. A good example of this shift away from earlier anthropological inquiry can be found in the 1973 book *Interpretation of Cultures*, by anthropologist Clifford Geertz who challenged the earlier more positivist approaches to defining culture by questioning the very motivation for studying the cultures of those we identify as "the other." In his book, Geertz discusses the earlier work of sociologist Max Weber who spoke more of social construction of meaning within societies. Geertz (1973) writes,

> Man is an animal suspended in webs of significance that he himself has spun. I take culture to be those webs, and the analysis of it to be therefore not an experimental science in search of law but an interpretive one in search of meaning. (p. 5)

For Geertz and others in the era of increasing contact between culturally different populations, the idea of discovering and recording fixed and immutable behaviours, attitudes, and beliefs within a given society became increasingly untenable. As a result, many anthropologists began to examine culture from the standpoint of its impact on socialization. Take for example the definition of culture developed by anthropologist Conrad Kottak. For Kottak (1991, p. 2) culture is defined as the process of transmitting, through "learning, traditions and customs that govern the behaviours of people exposed to them" with the effect of producing some degree of consistency in behaviour and thought within a given society.

For Kottak, culture is also understood as existing at different levels. For example, a small French Canadian town, a Native American reservation, a Spanish New Mexican community, an African American neighbourhood, a Mennonite farming community, or an urban ethnic enclave will all likely have certain aspects of social life that many will be able to identify as a local culture or way of life. These distinct local communities are embedded within larger regional contexts, which in turn are part of nations. Finally, all nations exist within an ever-more globalized environment having elements of a common or shared international culture (Kottak, 1991).

For Kottak (1991) and many other anthropologists, different forms of small-scale social organization occurring within larger, more complex levels of a

Figure 4.2   Levels of Culture

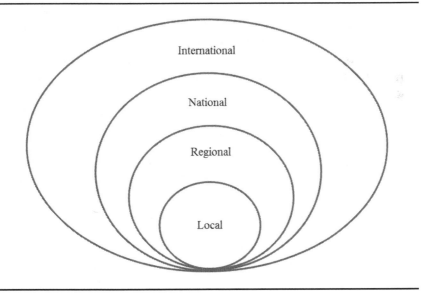

International

National

Regional

Local

region and nation are identified as subcultures. However, others make a distinction between societies such as those of Indigenous Canadian First Nations or Indigenous Hawaiian Homeland communities, and intentional communities based on political belief or concepts of cooperative living. Indigenous Canadian First Nations societies and Indigenous Hawaiian Homeland communities are small-scale or minority societies having distinct cultural histories dating back in time to well before the formation of the state-level Euro-Western governments with which they must now contend. Intentional communities are quite different, and more accurately understood as subcultures within the larger majority North American cultural context (Coggins, 1996). The key difference between intentional subcultures and small-scale or minority cultures can be best understood when one considers how each has come into existence. What makes contemporary Indigenous First Nations and other ethnic cultures distinct and different from the majority culture of any state-level society is that they were not initially formed as the result of a collective dissatisfaction with (or other reactions to) life as majority culture individuals within a state-level society.

Conversely, persons who are part of regional and national cultures who create intentional communities as a reaction to aspects of the majority culture they find objectionable, or simply inconsistent with their beliefs, are not the same as societies that existed before state-level national values, beliefs, and policies developed into majority cultures. Even in the case of the distinct populations and cultural forms that result from the blending of different social and cultural entities, syncretic (culturally blended) systems arising in the wake of contact between culturally distinct populations are still quite different from intentional communities or groups of people who identify with a particular organized religion or political ideology.

The Métis in the Canadian Prairie provinces and the Genízaro of New Mexico developed syncretic cultural forms resulting through the process of ethnogenesis. *Ethnogenesis* refers to the blending of distinct populations resulting in new hybrid syncretic cultural systems that include characteristics different from those found in the two or more populations from which the new societies emerged (Hanson & Kurtz, 2007, pp. 3–4; Jones & Perry, 2012, p. 304). The Genízaro and the Métis came into existence through the blending of Indigenous and European forms of cultural expression and economic activity (Hanson & Kurtz, 2007). In the case of the Métis, the process of ethnogenesis even included the development of a distinct language known as Michif (Bakkar, 1997).

Figure 4.3   Distinct Cultures versus Subcultures

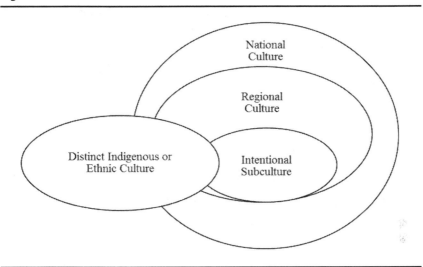

Added to the difference between distinct cultures and subcultures are the issues of colonization and oppression that impact cultural expression and the development of tension in relation to larger regional and national cultures. For those in subcultures such as the intentional communities of the 1960s in Canada and the United States, often referred to as communes, the vast majority of the youth who joined did not come from families, communities, or societies that had been subjected to colonization, physical and cultural genocide, or geographic, legal, or social segregation. However, Indigenous North Americans, Canadian visible minority populations, African Americans, Asian Americans, Latino populations, and many distinct European ethnic groups, especially those from eastern and southern Europe, have experienced pressures to abandon their distinct forms of social organization and cultural expression, and instead adopt majority Canadian or American cultures (McGoldrick, Giordano, & Garcia-Preto, 2005). Therefore, social workers need to be careful not to assume that all differences in human expression are distinct cultural forms or that all cultural forms have similar histories in terms of development or continuation in relation to social and political pressures exerted by the much larger North American state-level societies in Canada and the United States.

A social worker cannot assume that she or he has either a complete or accurate understanding of any client's individual sense of self in terms of identification with a particular ethnic population, an Indigenous Nation, a lin-guistic community, or a collective sense of cultural history that is shared with others. This is precisely why it is important to explore the cultural identity of those served by social workers in a manner that allows each client to deter-mine who she or he is in relation to self within and between various socio-cultural contexts.

Understanding Common Terms

For social workers and their professional organizations, culture has become a key area of focus for ethical and effective practice. However, many practitioners and even educators have a difficult time grasping the concept of culture, let alone communicating cultural knowledge in conference workshops or class-room settings. Attempts to develop a more nuanced understanding of culture has left the social work profession struggling to understand culture and multi-culturalism in a way that will honour the individuality of clients, while at the same time providing some broader direction to social workers regarding pop-ulation-based differences in culture that will be of value in cross-cultural inter-actions (Coggins & Hatchett, 2009).

To begin this process, social work students and practicing social workers need to develop a clear understanding of the difference between certain terms. Quite often, social work students are taught in a manner that leads them to believe that terms such as *culture*, *multiculturalism*, *race*, *ethnicity*, and *diversity* are interchangeable. This leads to a great deal of confusion. It also speaks to the fact that many educators are themselves confused about the meaning of these terms.

Race

Race in North America can be understood in two different ways. The first is a general folk understanding of race in which people are believed to be made up of broad groups such as Negroid, Caucasoid, Mongoloid, and Australoid populations, with various subgroupings. The second and more contemporary conceptualization of human difference that is now widely ascribed to by anthro-pologists and other social scientists is that race is socially constructed (McLeod, 2010). Nevertheless, many people still think of race in terms of the outdated categories of major groupings with attendant and often negative stereotypical characteristics.

Culture

Culture has to do with human behaviour that is shaped through socialization within a given society (Winkelman, 1999). People are not born with a culture that is determined genetically, as is the case for skin colour, hair texture, eye colour, and so forth. Those who conflate race and culture make two basic mistakes: first, assuming that racial categories exist as discrete biological entities, and second, that behaviours, beliefs, and attitudes are biologically determined in the same manner as one's physical appearance.

Ethnicity

Ethnicity is something that refers to people who identify as being part of a population with a common culture, history, and often a place of origin (Ariel de Vidas, 2008). Ethnicity is not the same as race. However, ethnicity as a replacement for race has its problems as well. As Efird (2010, p. 806) states, "ethnicity draws its power from the very same bogus assumptions about immutable, heritable 'ethnic' characteristics and behaviour." This leads many to believe that persons such as those of Italian, Polish, Irish, West African Yoruba, Mexican, or any other ethnically identified descent will consistently think and act in particular culturally determined ways. Social workers who succumb to the belief in predictable ethnically determined consistency in client behaviour may become confused or even dismayed by unique and highly varied forms of expression within specific identified ethnic populations, precisely because their clients do not conform to what they as social workers may have been taught about cultural expression.

Multiculturalism

Multiculturalism at its most basic level refers to the existence of a culturally pluralistic society (Gould, 1995, p. 199). The problem with multiculturalism in North American social work is that the term *multicultural* is generally understood as referring to those who are not of white European heritage. In truth, multiculturalism encompasses people of all cultures, including Euro-Western populations that form the majority cultures of Canada and the United States. However, social workers and social work educators who say they serve multicultural individuals and families are most often intending to convey that they strive for cultural sensitivity in work with persons from non-Caucasian populations. In other words, the term and indeed the concept of multicultural is often improperly used and not well defined. When social workers discuss multiculturalism, the term needs to be understood as inclusive of all without separating and excluding from the discussion those Euro-Western populations that have traditionally held social and economic power within North American society. By speaking of multiculturalism as existing only among non-Euro-Western populations, privilege and dominance are accorded to those in the majority culture who escape having their cultures analyzed to identify difference, while at the same time making the voice of the majority that which is legitimate and even normative. As Gould (1995, p. 204) states, "a collectivist perspective in a multicultural worldview does not exclude White people, it just gives them an equivalent rather than a dominant voice." In other words, we all have culturally influenced values, beliefs, attitudes, and behaviours. Moreover, the North American majority culture, while dominant in terms of those who are socialized within it, is neither better nor worse. It is instead just a social and cultural context that exists alongside, and at times blended with, many different and equally valid forms of cultural expression.

Diversity

Diversity is a common term in social work that includes cultural differences, physical difference, individual expression, gender, gender expression, sexual orientation, different degrees and types of ability/disability, and many other forms of human variation or aspects of the human condition (Krentzman & Townsend, 2008). Put simply, diversity is the "opposite of homogeneity" (Barker, 2003, p. 126). Diversity is also a term often used by educators and practitioners as a replacement for race or even ethnicity. Because of the inclusiveness and affirming connotation of the term, diversity fits comfortably with empowering approaches to social work practice. However, diversity as a preferred term, even though its use is envisioned in a positive and uplifting manner, may serve to mask the tension that exists in relation to the discussion or recognition of socially constructed categories of race, class, or even heteronormativity, and the impact of those social constructs on individuals and entire populations.

Cultural Competence

The term *cultural competence* in social work has been in regular use since the 1990s with the National Association of Social Workers (NASW) developing practice standards related to cultural competence in 2001 (Colvin-Burque, Zugazaga, & Davis-Maye, 2007). However, cultural competence as a concept is not fully embraced within social work. Many involved in social work practice and education question the very idea of leading students and practitioners to believe that they can develop demonstrable mastery of information and techniques for application to practice with people from a wide variety of non-majority North American populations. Moreover, there are those who argue cultural competence is not a well-defined concept and can perhaps never be achieved (Johnson & Munch, 2009). This may in fact be true if we consider all the variability found within pluralistic and culturally distinct populations worldwide. However, the goal of cultural competence should not be a task of learning a laundry list of traits in the same manner as one would learn diagnoses from the fifth edition of the *Diagnostic and Statistical Manual of Mental Disorders* (DSM-5). Cultural competence should instead involve the development of a way of thinking, reflecting, and acting that recognizes the existence of a broad range of diversity in relation to culturally based values, beliefs, attitudes, and behaviours.

MULTICULTURALISM FOR SOCIAL WORK

In 1998, the Council on Social Work Education (CSWE) sponsored a gathering of Indigenous North American, Latino/a, African American, Asian American, sexual minority, religious minority, and majority culture social work academics and doctoral students to discuss cultural competence and multiculturalism in social work education. The meeting was held at the University of Michigan, which resulted in a series of intense and vigorous discussions regarding cultural competence in social work education and the concept of multiculturalism within social work. At the end of the three-day period, the task force agreed on a definition of the term *multiculturalism* that was designed to clarify what is meant by multiculturalism within a complex and pluralistic society. This definition was an attempt to eliminate confusion regarding multiculturalism and to create something that could guide educators, students, and practitioners in the process of developing cultural competence. The definition agreed upon is as follows:

> Culture is a contestable set of traditions and customs, differentially transmitted and received through learning, which forms the beliefs and shapes the behaviors of people exposed to them, and can or may provide a shared sense of peoplehood.

> Thus, multiculturalism for social work is defined as multiple cultures between and within nations, institutions, organizations, communities, groups, and individuals.
>
> Multiculturalism therefore must examine the important influence of multiple cultures of nation; ethnicity; ancestry and family; association and community; identity; interpretation of meaning; personal experience; the struggle with oppression; and the result of privilege.
>
> Finally, multiculturalism in social work must also include an emphasis on structural power and acknowledge social construction over time, with the recognition that many voices may be missing at this historical point in time. (Coggins & Hatchett, 2002, p. 134)

This particular definition of multiculturalism addresses intersectionality which is crucial to understanding identity and identity development. What is also highlighted by this definition is the danger inherent in emphasizing memorization of behavioural traits that are linked to socially constructed, politically designated, and often artificially bounded social systems. For example, Mexico has hundreds of Indigenous groups (Meyer & Beezley, 2000), other populations with bloodlines that can be traced to Africa, Asia, and Europe, and a large Mestizo (mixed Indigenous and non-Indigenous) population that forms the majority of Mexican society (Castellanos, Nájera, & Aldama, 2012). Yet, when people from Mexico cross the US border or arrive in Canada as immigrants or guest workers, an assumption is made that all are native Spanish speakers who derive their identities from a uniform pan-Mexican majority culture. This definition of ethnic belonging imposed from outside obscures and marginalizes many Indigenous and non-Indigenous ethnic identities through a process of homogenization that occurs within the minds of Anglo-Canadians and Anglo-Americans north of Mexico. Even social workers and social work educators participate in this process by teaching about Mexican culture as if the entire country of Mexico constitutes one large uniform national ethnic identity, when in reality many immigrants who move north from Mexico are Indigenous Mexicans from populations that have retained Indigenous languages and cultural practices (Gutiérrez Nájera, 2012).

Sadly, the same can often be said about social work education and cultural competence in relation to other nonmajority ethnic populations. As stated earlier, the shift in social work education that must occur is one in which attention is given to understanding each client on her or his own terms. This does not, however, mean that understanding cultural difference should be abandoned in favour of emphasizing individuality and uniqueness devoid of any attempt to address culture. Social workers who take such an approach ignore the importance of cultural influences in the lives of their clients (Brisbane, 2000). Culture is important, and social workers need to develop skill in understanding cultural differences. However, the practice of discounting culture and the opposite, attributing every word, thought, and action to a cultural template for behaviour, robs clients of their basic humanity. Instead, social workers need to become skilled at recognizing the impact of culture not just in the lives of their clients, but in their own lives as well.

Critical Practice Considerations

In preparation for social work practice with culturally different populations, the existing assumption is often that of working with an Anglo-Canadian or Anglo-American middle-class social work student who is encountering a client who identifies as being part of a population outside of the Caucasian North American majority. However, North America is becoming increasingly diverse, meaning that any combination of worker and client can occur. For example, the US-Mexico border city of El Paso, Texas, is and has been a minority-majority community and region since the time of the Treaty of Guadalupe Hidalgo in 1848. Minority-majority simply means that those populations designated as minorities in a national sense constitute the majority in certain states, territories, regions, or municipalities.

According to the US Census (2010), in El Paso the white non-Hispanic/Latino population is slightly above 13 percent. In a city with more than 825,000 residents, this means that the Anglo-American population is statistically and numerically small. The city also has a bachelor of social work (BSW) and master of social work (MSW) program that graduates predominately Mexican American social workers, most of whom remain in the area. As a result, the likelihood of encountering an Anglo-American social worker is low. Therefore, preparing social workers in this, and other minority-majority regions, with approaches to cultural competence skill development based on antiquated concepts of Anglo-Canadian/Anglo-American cultural dominance and numerical majorities does not match the realities of multitudes of contemporary pluralist and minority-majority practice environments.

The idea of educating social workers in relation to culturally sensitive practice with "others" ignores existing and emerging demographic shifts occurring across the United States and Canada. Currently the United States has four states that are minority-majority states and a minority-majority federal district. The US Census (2010) reports Hawaii at 77.1 percent minority population, followed by the District of Columbia at 64.7 percent, California at 60.3 percent, New Mexico at 59.8 percent, and Texas at 55.2 percent of residents counted as part of federally designated minorities. In addition, there are many more municipalities having minority-majority populations.

Statistics Canada (2013) projects that fully one third of the nation's population will be constituted of visible minority persons by 2031. In addition, the Aboriginal population in Canada (First Nations, Métis, and Inuit) is projected to be between 4 and 5 percent of the total national population by 2031, with some provinces such as Manitoba already at 16.7 percent of residents identifying as Aboriginal (Statistics Canada, 2013). With minority and Indigenous students continuing to enter social work as a profession, the North American cultural landscape, as it relates to practice, will be one in which people of varied cultural backgrounds will encounter nonmajority individuals as clients and social work service providers. Therefore, preparing for social work practice will require increased attention to cultural differences and diverse experiences that shape the worldviews of clients and practitioners. This means that social workers preparing for practice in a changing sociocultural milieu will need to take into consideration several critical practice concerns.

First—Interest in Cultural Differences Is Crucial

Without a doubt, reading information about the cultures of various societies, ethnic groups, and populations is a good place to start. Attending workshops that focus on skill building in relation to work with those who are culturally different is another important first step. In addition, spending time in communities that are culturally different from one's own can foster increased awareness of the importance of culture in shaping what people value, as well as what they believe and how they engage in interaction with others. Becoming familiar with culturally shaped expectations of appropriate behaviour, forms of social and family organization, and spiritual traditions, along with the views people may hold about themselves and the cultures of the societies with which they identify, can be of assistance when it comes to engaging clients in a collaborative helping process that is culturally appropriate and affirming. Although learning about the cultures of populations a social worker encounters on a regular basis is of critical importance, situations will inevitably arise in which a social worker encounters individuals from societies with cultures that she or he has little to no knowledge of. In addition, even in cases where a reasonable degree of knowledge about certain populations does exist, there is no guarantee that a particular individual client will fit what the social worker may have learned about the culture of the community, ethnic group, or population with which the client identifies.

Second—Culture Is Dynamic and Variable

The degree of each individual's identification with the culture of a particular group considered with the changing nature of cultures creates a dilemma for social workers. Social workers cannot expect to learn about culture by memorizing traits as one would medical diagnoses or mathematical formulas. Neither should a social worker abandon learning about culture by adopting an approach that treats each client as a cultureless entity. No social worker has the time to study each and every culture associated with the multitudes of populations found in North America, let alone understanding the manner in which each culturally distinct society is changing and/or developing as a result of internal and external forces. Therefore, it is necessary to develop knowledge, skills, and abilities in relation to social work intervention that honour cultural and individual differences in the lives of clients encountered in a variety of situations. This, as stated earlier, means taking an interest in learning about cultural differences between and among different populations, societies, and nations. It also means understanding that culture, cultural knowledge, and culturally based behaviours will be understood and expressed differently at the community, family, and individual level.

Coggins and Hatchett (2009) present the *Reciprocal Exploration Model*, which utilizes an approach to cross-cultural knowledge generation and assessment that honours the experiences of people within different cultural contexts versus using clients as cultural experts who must either enlighten social workers about the culture(s) with which they identify, challenge the social worker's knowledge, or validate the social worker's cross-cultural expertise. Instead, reciprocal exploration involves a discussion of culturally based traditions, beliefs, and behaviours, done in a manner that is intended to establish mutual awareness of cultural differences that do or may exist between the client and social worker. Reciprocal exploration may involve a discussion of cultural differences in any number of areas. Things such as anger, grief, depression, expressions of happiness, and demonstrations of respect can differ markedly from one society to another. As culture is explored, understood, and discussed, the client and social worker build a bond that comes from a deeper understanding of each other. In addition, a thoughtful examination of culture may also help the client see where she or he has strong, affirming, conflicted, tense, or tenuous connections to perceived traditional beliefs and practices of an identified cultural community (Coggins & Hatchett, 2009).

The reciprocal exploration model may involve discussions of any number of behaviours, beliefs, attitudes, values, expectations, and so forth, with the intention of creating understanding on the part of the social worker in a manner that validates the lived experiences of clients. A good example of reciprocal exploration would be that of an Indigenous social worker from the southwest United States who was working with a client in a reservation community in the northern Great Plains. During the course of several sessions, the client discussed a recurring dream in which Elders offered her roasted meat. The social worker stated, "You have talked about this dream before. For my people, dreams are important, and you have said that dreams are important in your

Figure 4.4 Reciprocal Exploration Model

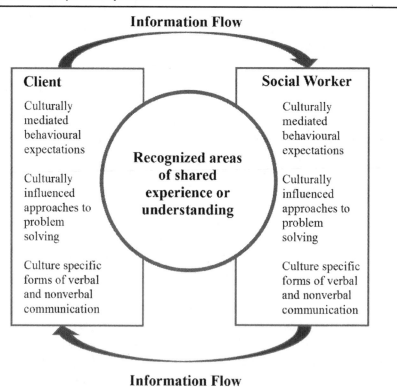

culture as well. But I don't know what the significance of meat is in your dream, in terms of your traditions. Do you have any idea?" When the client spoke, she said, "I was taught that being offered meat in a dream means that I will die if I accept the food." This was followed with a revelation by the client that she had been thinking of taking her own life.

Whether the client's understanding was wholly accurate on a broader scale within her culturally distinct society is not as important as the fact that she had been taught a particular interpretation of the dream. The key issue in this interaction between client and social worker is that the social worker validated the client's lived experience and accumulated knowledge in a manner that honours her understanding of herself within the context of her culture. This example also shows that a reciprocal exploration approach to intervention is not an exhaustive discussion of cultural similarity and difference. It is instead a closer examination of cultural difference in key areas, as the need arises. In addition, those familiar with the basic elements of social work practice will recognize that reciprocal exploration utilizes the communication technique of clarification with an emphasis on understanding cultural differences for the purposes of increasing empathic understanding in cross-cultural contact between social workers and clients.

Third—Intersectionality Matters

In pluralistic social contexts such as those found in much of North America, the worldviews of social workers and the clients they serve are influenced by the intersection of multiple culturally based social values, attitudes, beliefs, and behaviours that are characterized by varying and shifting degrees of tension and congruence. For example, a client who is an urban-dwelling, but reservation-born and -raised Diné (Navajo) person may utilize technologically based Euro-Western approaches to identifying and treating health concerns. However, this same person may also not feel complete in terms of addressing illness until returning to her or his home community for a traditional Diné healing ceremony. In addition, the decision to engage in both approaches to diagnosis and healing may represent tension between beliefs about the efficacy of Euro-Western forms of treatment and Indigenous healing traditions, or conversely, comfort with a culturally blended approach to health care. Because people served by social workers may have varying degrees of identification with Indigenous, ethnic, local, regional, and national cultures, it is important to understand how these varying degrees of conflict and congruence between culturally based worldviews can influence a client's conception of what constitutes a problem, as well as what might be the most appropriate steps to take in problem resolution.

Fourth—Lives Are Lived in a Multiplicity of Sociocultural Contexts

Social workers need to develop skill in working collaboratively with clients to develop culturally appropriate helping or healing plans that resonate with clients' worldviews. Life choices clients make, such as delaying marriage, remaining single, choosing not to have children, or seeking a university degree, are decisions that take place within a broader familial, social, and cultural context in which there may be support, acceptance, tension, or even conflict. If social workers do not strive to understand the manner in which individual, collective, and macro-societal imperatives intersect within the lives of those they serve, a major and very important component of effective intervention with clients from culturally different populations will be missing.

Fifth—Sexual Minority Populations Face Unique Challenges

Sexual minority populations live within social and cultural contexts on many levels from local, to regional, to national, and even international. Social work with individuals who are part of sexual minority and racial or ethnic minority populations must include recognition of the manner in which a client's minority cultural identity may come into conflict with her or his sexual orientation or gender identity (Akerlund & Cheung, 2000). This requires an awareness of the types and degrees of discrimination, oppression, affirmation, or acceptance, which may be encountered by racial or ethnic minority persons who identify as lesbian, gay, bisexual, transgender, queer, questioning, intersex (LGBTQQI), or any other sexual or gender identity that is outside of the more common heterosexual majority. Being an identified member of a sexual minority group can result in increased vulnerability to physical harm, denial of civil rights, and even rejection by one's own cultural community of identity, thus magnifying marginalization and oppression that is often experienced at the intersection of minority cultural communities, sexual minority identity, and the larger dominant society.

Beyond issues that are part of the LGBTQQI experience found at the intersection between sexual or gender identity and identified race or ethnicity are issues of religion and exclusion or marginalization that may foster hostility toward sexual minority individuals. For example, in African American and African immigrant populations religious institutions have long provided for the material and spiritual needs of their members. Nevertheless, there can be resistance by churches or other religious organizations to helping or including LGBTQQI persons because of beliefs about those who are seen as having broken the laws of God and gone against the teachings of the Bible, Koran, or Torah. This rejection by religious organizations and leaders often results in a sense of alienation among LGBTQQI individuals who may have traditionally looked to religion and fellow worshipers as sources of material or emotional support (Hatchett, Duran, & Timmons, 2000). Because cultural identity and religious identity are so closely linked for certain minority communities and individuals, being excluded or marginalized by religious institutions can be particularly traumatic.

Sixth—Immigration Experiences Shape Worldviews

Immigrants to Canada and the United States arrive in North America with very diverse backgrounds, knowledge about the nations to which they are immigrating, levels of education, experiences in the nations from which they are emigrating, and expectations or even fears regarding life in a new country. If we compare someone who is immigrating to Canada as a refugee from a war-torn region of Africa with a person of African American descent from New York City who has accepted a faculty position at a university in Ontario, we will find vast differences in the experiences of both. Although both may share African heritage, the experiences of a refugee from Africa will be vastly different from that of an African American academic. Consequently, there will be differences in each person's worldview with many of those differences being quite pronounced.

In this example, the African American academic will quite likely have been born, raised, and educated within a social context marked by varying degrees of racism toward persons of African heritage. In addition, African American intra-group attitudes regarding hair texture, skin colour, levels of education, and status linked to personal wealth or poverty may seem quite foreign to the African refugee for whom tribe or ethnic group, language spoken, and religious affiliation will be the more likely basis for the forms of oppression she or he may have experienced. The physical environment, the social context, access to health care, levels of education, and differences in the types and degrees of oppression can result in people of similar or common ancestry developing very different views of themselves and the world around them. In the case of the two immigrants in this example, knowledge about immigrant experiences or being a member of a visible minority would need to be considered in the context of very different life experiences as members of a collective and as individuals.

Seventh—Culture Impacts Problem-Solving Processes

Clients and social workers can and often do have different views about what constitutes a "problem." Take for example a situation from the 1980s in which a man and woman, in their twenties, working at a summer resort in New York, became emotionally close and physically intimate followed by a decision to move in together and live as a couple. In this example, the woman was Irish American and the man was African American. The woman asked her closest friend, a social worker, to be with her when she told her mother about the decision. The young woman's mother became very upset and said she did not approve. When the issue of racism was addressed, the young woman's mother said, "I'm not worried about him being black; heavens no. I just don't approve of a man and a woman living together before they are married. What would people think? Let them get married first." Clearly, the problem in this case was viewed by an older woman as violating a more traditional morality, whereas her daughter and the social worker assumed race would be the issue.

Another example has to do with a female university student from Micronesia, a group of islands in the Southwest Pacific, and involves visits with a social worker at the counselling centre on campus. The Micronesian woman has been speaking with the social worker about her boyfriend who is from a neighbouring island. She states that her mother is very angry about the relationship. After several missed sessions with the social worker, the woman returns and announces she is pregnant. The social worker asks about the increased stress this news has placed on her relationship with her mother. The woman from Micronesia tells the social worker that her mother was very happy about the new grandchild. Confused, the social worker asked, "Why the change?" The client explained that on her island, parents become upset about relationships, especially when the intention of sending children away is to have them concentrate on their studies. However, once a pregnancy occurs, no one wants to think badly of the developing child for fear that bad thoughts will harm the developing fetus.

The lesson from both examples is that we cannot assume as social workers that we know or can anticipate (from any particular cultural perspective) what people from another culture will view as a problem. Likewise, we cannot make assumptions about expectations or experiences in relation to culturally influenced problem solving. A social worker raised and educated within a North American majority cultural milieu may approach problem solving from a perspective that values individual choice over collective consensus or the need to consult family elders. Conversely, a social worker attempting to be culturally sensitive might assume that clients from traditionally collectivist societies will be disinclined to adopt an individualistic approach to addressing a problem when indeed that might be exactly what is sought.

The lesson here is one in which social workers need to acknowledge the influence of culture(s) in everyone's life, including their own. This means understanding that all of us, as human beings, have culturally based behavioural expectations that are not just influenced by a myriad of social and cultural factors, but are also dynamic, shifting and changing with time, life course transitions, personal experiences, and so forth. Flexibility in the development of intervention plans that resonate with a wide range of worldviews will have far better results than memorizing laundry lists of cultural traits followed by rigid scripted interventions that often do not match client realities or capture the complexity of clients' lives.

CONCLUSION

Social work has long approached the task of teaching about cultural difference with an assumption that cross-cultural communication involves mostly Caucasian majority culture social workers engaging and helping non-Caucasian clients. However, as client and social work practitioner populations continue to diversify, Euro-Western majority culture assumptions about foundational knowledge, appropriate professional practice, and the utility of evidence-based approaches to work with clients will continue to be challenged. This does not mean that scientific inquiry regarding work with clients is to be abandoned. Indeed, research regarding the development of *best practices* should undoubtedly continue. Yet, it must also be acknowledged that the development of effective approaches to intervention with clients will need to incorporate different and emerging cultural forms that profoundly impact worldview development. As this chapter has demonstrated, cultural competence cannot be thought of as something that one masters and then applies. Instead, the goal of developing competence is better understood as something we all strive toward with a clear recognition that achieving cultural competence will never be truly realized due to the dynamic, shifting, and changing nature of culture.

Beyond cultural competence, the idea of intersecting variables presented by racism, classism, ableism, sexism, ageism, homophobia, and the marginalization of those who represent emerging social or cultural forms demonstrate the complexity of social, political, and cultural contexts within which social work practice takes place. To further complicate the practice environment, corporate colonization, growing income inequality, and environmental degradation all have an impact on the various client populations served by social workers. Therefore, the idea of practice that strives to understand difference from a position of preference for middle-class Euro-Western cultural attitudes, beliefs, and behaviours is not only outdated, but quite narrow in focus. In the twenty-first century, the old social work adage of *meeting the client where the client is* must now include a recognition of how that client is embedded in multiple systems that are impacted by environmental, social, cultural, economic, and political forces at many levels, ranging from local, to regional, to national, and even international. Helping those in need of social work services requires a broad base of knowledge in relation to many forces that shape each person's current lived reality. This, combined with an ability to help clients achieve positive personal outcomes that resonate with their culturally and socially shaped worldviews, while at the same time respecting the life rights of others, will be the task of social work in an ever-more multicultural and socially diverse practice context.

Chapter Five

The Individualized Worldview

INTRODUCTION

The *individualized worldview* (IWV) is designed to facilitate teaching, assessment, self-reflection, and even research. As a *tool for teaching*, the model allows for the representation of the multiple factors that must be considered in a discussion of worldview development. As an *assessment tool*, the IWV can be applied by the social work practitioner to organize an examination of the multiple contexts within which the lives of clients are lived and comprehended. When utilized as a *tool for self-reflection*, the IWV assists students and practitioners in exploring the multiple factors that have impacted their own unique assessments of what motivates behaviour, shapes belief, and influences human agency.

As a *tool for research*, the IWV model emphasizes a phenomenological orientation. The IWV simultaneously explores multiple influences on the worldview development of individuals by examining the manner in which larger cultural, social, environmental, techno-environmental, and political conditions interact with innate abilities, personality characteristics, and biological factors in fashioning the contexts through which lives are experienced and understood. This is of particular importance when considering the development of research projects in which cultural relevance, anti-oppressive approaches to gathering data, and guarding against culture-bound researcher bias come into question. Although the model is designed to focus on worldview development in individuals, the factors examined act as a reminder to researchers of the multiple lenses through which they and their research project participants view the world.

To understand the meaning of an *individualized worldview*, one must first understand the meaning of worldview. For example, the *concept of worldview* can be understood as existing in an organized established system among those within a distinct cultural group, a group of religious believers, or at a more personal level involving views on life and humanity (Van der Kooij, De Ruyter, & Miedema, 2013). A person's worldview holds profound potential for influencing her or his beliefs, behaviours, expectations of behaviours in others, basic assumptions about life, and so forth. Therefore, understanding the worldview of an individual is an important initial step in work with clients (Leigh, 1998). For

81

social work practitioners and students who strive to approach clients with sensitivity to culture and other life-shaping factors, the concept of worldview development is of extreme importance.

Developing skills related to understanding how clients conceptualize their closeness to or distance from various cultural groups, combined with culturally mediated expectations related to attitudes, behaviours, beliefs, and the internalization of group-held values, are crucial factors in social work education related to worldview development. In addition to cultural identity, social workers need to pay close attention to the impact of a multitude of factors that shape the worldviews of clients. Culture and identification with a particular cultural group is only one facet of an individual's overall sense of self within the world. Furthermore, the interaction between a client's cultural identification and other life influences or factors holds the potential for creating various degrees of either tension or congruence.

THE INDIVIDUALIZED WORLDVIEW

The IWV emphasizes twenty-five areas that can be addressed in determining important influences or factors that shape people's lives. Indeed, there are other factors that influence people's lives; therefore, the IWV model needs to be understood as inclusive but still not exhaustive in relation to understanding the multifaceted lives of individuals embedded in multiple systems. Utilizing an approach to understanding clients in context helps the social work practitioner or other service provider avoid the temptation to make assumptions about behaviour based on what has been learned regarding various populations designated as being outside of the cultural majority. This dismantles the all-too-common recommendation of designating the client as cultural informant or the professional practitioner as cultural expert by instead allowing space for the exploration and understanding of each client's unique worldview (Ortega & Faller Coulburn, 2011).

Within each of the areas presented in the IWV model, there are key considerations intended to remind us all that while something, such as disability or ability, needs to be thought of in terms of shaping worldview, many other factors will also play a role in creating the contexts within which lives are lived. Therefore, this chapter will include key considerations for each of the twenty-five areas featured in the IWV model followed by a brief discussion intended to encourage thinking about worldview development.

Figure 5.1   The Individualized Worldview

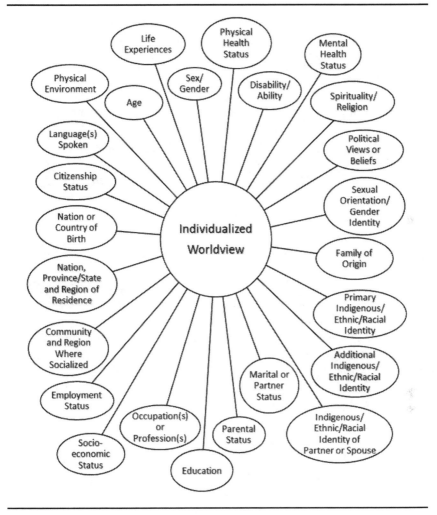

Age

Age and one's age cohort have a profound influence on worldview. For example, events, such as the 2001 terrorist attacks on the Twin Towers in New York City, remain firmly and clearly etched in the memories of adults in North America, and indeed the world. For most people who were in their preteen years or

Figure 5.2   Age

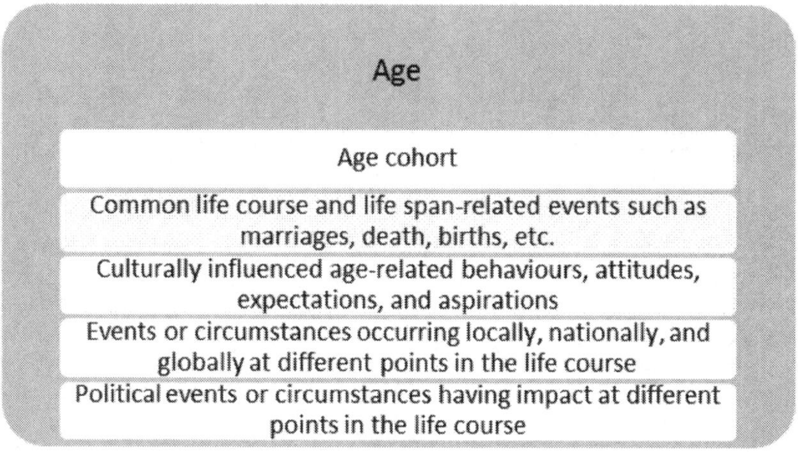

older on the day the attacks occurred, it remains relatively easy to recall where we were and what we were doing. However, for those who were very young at the time, or those born after that date, September 11, 2001 is a historical event that they themselves either don't remember or did not live through. The same is true for countless world, national, and local events. In the province of Manitoba, the record flood of 1950 resulted in the construction of a floodway designed to divert future floodwaters around Winnipeg. The floodway was completed in 1968 and is estimated to have saved the capital city of that province billions of dollars in damage that would have otherwise occurred (Manitoba Historical Society, 2013). Again, for those old enough to remember life before the floodway, the 1950 flood will always be experienced as a collective, and, in many cases, a very personal, tragic event. However, for those who were too young to remember or not yet born, the floodway is a fixture of the landscape that is almost taken for granted by those living behind its protective dikes.

Time periods and the events that occur within them are not experienced in the same manner by all people. It is true that each of us as human beings will have very personal life events and experiences that may or may not have been shared with others in our age cohort. Moreover, broader socially constructed categories such as race, ethnicity, gender, and countless other "identifiers" locate individuals at different places in hierarchies of privilege. As a result of individual and collective social location, people will experience events common to an age cohort in very different ways. This can be seen in the following example of childhood and adolescent memories shared by two women from the same rural community in the Great Lakes region.

The stories of these women who went through adolescence in the late 1970s and early1980s demonstrate just how such differences occur. One woman, of English heritage, recalls summers in a town beside the lake. She speaks fondly of the shop owners and feels quite nostalgic about her carefree adolescence as the child of a local sawmill owner. She says that she never once felt unsafe because she was surrounded by a caring family within a close-knit community. The other woman, of Indigenous (Aboriginal) heritage, remembers several times when she and her mother were followed while shopping in town and on more than one occasion accused of stealing. Although she had some very close non-Indigenous friends and remembers fun-filled days at the beach, she also recalls being referred to as "savage." In addition, she has a particularly painful memory of being spit at when Indigenous fishing and hunting rights were being asserted. The Indigenous woman lived through the same period as the woman of English heritage, but being of Indigenous ancestry located her in a socially marginalized population. Therefore, the Indigenous woman did not recall summers by the lake as completely carefree times.

Age also influences worldview in terms of the timing and occurrence of life course events. For some, there exist strong familial, cultural, and even religious influences on the timing of marriage, giving birth, and the assumption of certain roles within family and community life. Age, timing of life events, social roles, socially based behavioural expectations, and obligations to community and family serve to inform and direct choices people make throughout life. Added to this is ageism within the larger North American context. Starting new businesses, careers, educational programs, or even having children are generally associated with young adulthood, meaning that persons who are outside of expected norms in relation to the completion of life tasks or the achievement of certain career or personal goals are in countless ways, large and small, out of sync with society, as so illustratively stated by the sixty-year-old father of a five-year-old girl who said, "I can't tell you how many times I have been told how precious my granddaughter is."

In addition to the timing of life events, there are career and even behavioural expectations linked to one's age group. For example, a weekend of alcohol consumption, dancing at nightclubs, and falling asleep on a friend's couch may be universally perceived as inappropriate, but it is much more likely to be overlooked or excused if engaged in by a twenty-two-year-old than would be the case for a person who is fifty-four years old. Likewise, young adults who join Voluntary Service Overseas (VSO) in Canada or the Peace Corps in the United States, will often be received quite favourably. However, if the same decision is made by a forty-year-old high-paid professional, her or his choice to do so will most likely be viewed as what many call a bad career move.

Age also influences other areas of life. As people in North America reach middle age, roughly between the ages of forty to fifty-nine years, they often begin to worry about their health, preparing for retirement, and caring for their aging parents, among other concerns (Fiore, 2011). However, aging can and does look quite different within different populations. Among older African Americans, Asian Americans, Indigenous North Americans, and Latinos, being "old" comes with an expectation of meaningful inclusion in family networks that have expanded with the arrival of grandchildren and perhaps even great-grandchildren. Although this is the cultural expectation, changing patterns of residence related to work and career have meant that families are now more geographically dispersed. Still, people from ethnic or social groups that are more collectivist in nature will tend toward more meaningful inclusion of elderly family members.

In some culturally distinct populations, such as certain Asian-origin communities or Indigenous North American societies, the elderly, and especially those viewed as Elders, are quite highly regarded and sought out for their wisdom and knowledge. As was once said by an older woman from Ohkay Owingeh Pueblo in New Mexico, "Today is a feast day here at the pueblo and it is my sixty-fifth birthday, too. I am so happy today, because that means I have reached the time of my peak intelligence, at least in my culture." As the woman went on to speak, she clearly demonstrated that she understood aging was not seen in the same way by all cultures. She continued by revealing how her Anglo male employer at an addictions treatment centre wanted her to consider retiring due to age, citing potential problems with a mentally and emotionally demanding job. Clearly, when a person is socialized and lives within a society that places high value on elderly members, the thought of aging will be seen through a cultural lens that differs markedly from the North American majority culture. Therefore, age and aging within different cultural and social contexts will have an impact on the development of one's view of the world.

Life Experiences

Figure 5.3   Life Experiences

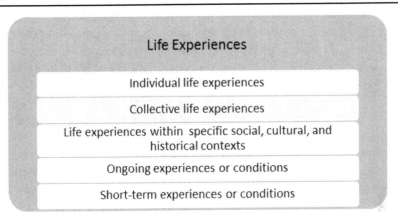

> ## Life Experiences
>
> Individual life experiences
>
> Collective life experiences
>
> Life experiences within specific social, cultural, and historical contexts
>
> Ongoing experiences or conditions
>
> Short-term experiences or conditions

Within the lives of clients, there exist nearly infinite numbers of unique individual experiences that can shape worldview development. There are, for example, those whose parents have or had military careers, resulting in multiple geographic relocations which did not foster the development of a connection to a single location one would call "home." Some individuals have been raised around people who look and speak very much like themselves, while others were born into the only minority families in their respective communities or neighbourhoods.

As one woman from a rural Canadian community stated, "We were the only Aboriginal kids in town. The teachers at school just called us the kids with black hair." Conversely, an Anglo-American male university student, raised on a Native American reservation in New Mexico, regularly stated that he did not feel like he fully fit in anywhere. He often remarked, "I know I am not Native American, but I grew up on the reservation, so I spoke the local Native language from an early age." He further stated, "When I am there visiting, it feels like home, but I look different. When I am in the white world, I look like I fit in, but I feel different." Anyone working with either of these individuals as clients could not make assumptions about culture based on physical appearance. Knowing someone means not presuming, but instead exploring what has shaped the way she or he views the world and her or his sense of fit within that world.

Some life experiences are very personal and unique, while others are shared. For example, a woman from Dearborn, Michigan, who felt very fearful of anti-Muslim sentiments after September 11, 2001, experienced her sense of fear along with thousands of others in the largest Muslim community found in North America. In the same year, a woman from an all-Anglo-American community near Dallas was feeling culture shock when her spouse accepted a military assignment in El Paso, Texas. The woman explained to her social worker that she was feeling very isolated because everyone else in her neighbourhood was Mexican American. Eventually she did fit in, but the fit occurred surprisingly when she enrolled in Spanish classes where she met three African American women from her part of Texas.

Considering individual experiences includes recognizing that some experiences might be discrete and short term, while others are shared and extend over longer periods. Moreover, experiences can take place, as noted in the above examples, in settings that are culturally familiar or noticeably culturally different. Examples of collective and individual life experiences could be virtually endless. However, the lesson for those working with clients in any setting is that the client's story should shape the understanding of worldview development versus being predetermined by attempts to decide which racial, ethnic, or Indigenous population template defines a person.

Sex and Gender

Figure 5.4   Sex and Gender

Sex and Gender
Culturally influenced statuses
Culturally influenced behavioural expectations
Federal, provincial/state, and local rights, freedoms, or limitations experienced
Social location and associated existence or lack of privilege
Workplace experiences

According to a United Nations report by Goldberg (2010), the Netherlands, Denmark, and Sweden are ranked as being the top three most equal countries on earth in relation to the status of women and men, whereas the Democratic Republic of Congo, Niger, and Yemen are at the bottom of the 169 nations which were ranked (Goldberg, 2010). In the same report, Canada ranked sixteenth, while the United States was in thirty-seventh place (Goldberg, 2010). Although the United States may have high levels of female participation in higher education and the labour force, the teenage pregnancy rates and the high number of women who die in childbirth brought the United States down to a rank just above Bulgaria (Goldberg, 2010). In the United States, the Constitution does not include language regarding the equality of women. Although the Equal Rights Amendment and the push for equality of women and men dates back to the 1920s in the United States, equality for women remains an unfulfilled promise of a nation whose pledge of allegiance promises liberty and justice for all. Still, even in nations such as Canada, where the federal Charter of Rights and Freedoms constitutionally guarantees equality and protection from discrimination based on race, national or ethnic origin, colour, religion, sex, age, or mental or physical disability, women do not enjoy social inclusion and status equal to that of men. For example, Canadian women in the labour force, especially in the private sector, still earn less than their male counterparts (Drolet & Mumford, 2012).

Gender is a particularly important lens through which people view the world. Gender is most often understood as a person's sex, either male or female; however, the two are not the same thing, and they are not necessarily even connected. Whereas sex (male, female, or intersex) constitutes the biological attributes with which a person is born, gender is a social construction. Oral histories and written historical records of contact between Europeans and Indigenous populations of North and South America indicate that prior to colonization, many Indigenous societies recognized nonbinary (male or female) forms of gender and sexuality (Morgensen, 2012). In other words, the expectations that different societies have for persons of different sexes develop within cultural contexts. Therefore, while a person may be born female, she might at some point live as a man, woman, or select another gender based on available options existing in her culture and social context.

Physical Health Status

Physical health status can have a profound impact on worldview at any one point in time. In addition, the influence of physical health on worldview also

Figure 5.5   Physical Health Status

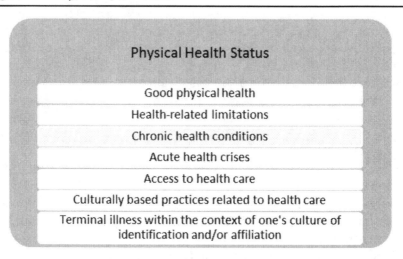

Physical Health Status

Good physical health

Health-related limitations

Chronic health conditions

Acute health crises

Access to health care

Culturally based practices related to health care

Terminal illness within the context of one's culture of identification and/or affiliation

changes and shifts with time. Often, theorists do not consider the importance of physical health when discussing worldview development. However, when looking through the lens of physical health, physical illness, or one's experiences in relation to a wide range of health conditions, physical health does indeed impact how one views the world around her- or himself.

In the current era, human populations are beset with various chronic and often interrelated health conditions such as heart disease, asthma, diabetes, and a seemingly endless list of other illnesses that require ongoing monitoring and management (CDC, 2009). Anyone who has a chronic condition is fully aware of the limitations represented by the need to constantly evaluate external conditions for possible impact on one's health. For example, a man with adult-onset asthma may have recently become aware that his condition is exacerbated by high levels of humidity as well as certain pollens of highly allergenic plants. The man lives in a semiarid region and now when he makes travel or vacation plans, he must check weather forecasts, typical climate, and levels of allergenic pollens. In his specific case, weather or outdoor conditions require more vigilance with any planned activities. In addition, travel to particularly humid locations also requires that any necessary medications are readily available. The same man may recall a time, before the onset of his asthma, when he traveled to many places, some quite remote, never once thinking of a potentially life-threatening asthma event. His current health condition now causes him to view some places as dangerous, and life now seems less carefree than it did in the past.

Culture is another important consideration in terms of physical health status. Culture and the impact of culture on health practices is something widely known and often discussed in terms of contact between health care professionals and patients. In addressing the importance of culture and understanding general widely encountered cultural practices, Galanti (2000) states:

> Cultural generalizations will not fit every patient whom physicians see, but knowledge of broad patterns of behavior and belief can give physicians and other health professionals a starting point from which to provide the most appropriate care possible. (p. 336)

While this is good general advice about being culturally sensitive, it does not address the much larger issue of how health status impacts each and every one of us in terms of how we think about our activities on a daily basis. While cultural practices do shape perception of illness and worldview, we do not often think of the manner in which health in general impacts a very fluid and evolving worldview, especially in those for whom chronic and terminal illnesses require a degree of attention to personal care that may not even be consciously considered among those with overall good health.

Access to health care is another aspect of worldview. For many people in metropolitan areas of Canada, health care is generally available with few barriers to accessing services. However, rural populations and those living in remote reserve-based First Nations communities often have barriers in relation to accessing the health care services that are widely available to Canadians living in more densely populated areas. In addition, concerns related to the provision of culturally relevant and appropriate services for Indigenous Canadians remain a difficult issue in a nation that has prided itself on providing health care for all since the 1960s.

In the United States, the issue of health care access is even more problematic. The Patient Protection and Affordable Care Act (PPACA) of 2010 is designed to achieve health care coverage for all, by requiring US residents to purchase private health insurance. For low-income residents, subsidies and an expansion of Medicaid would guarantee that nearly all Americans are insured. However, since the passage of the PPACA, the US Supreme Court has ruled that states could opt out of Medicaid expansion. As a result, economically disadvantaged people in more than twenty mostly southern and staunchly conservative states are not covered by Medicaid because their states have refused to expand this vital health care program for the poor. Many individuals not receiving health care coverage in those states are economically disadvantaged Euro-Americans, African Americans, and Latino Americans. In addition, a large number of single mothers are not covered by Medicaid who otherwise would have been covered if the states they live in had chosen to accept the federal offer of subsidies for coverage of the poor (Kenney, Dubuy, Zuckerman, & Huntress, 2012). Therefore, ease of access to health care, something many take for granted, is not always a reality for the poor and for remote populations, even in places like Canada. What this means is that many people have a worldview that includes fear of what might happen in the case of serious illness, combined with anxiety related to what might happen if, as is the case in the United States, the hospital emergency room is your only option and one that will prove enormously costly if exercised.

Disability/Ability

Figure 5.6   Disability/Ability

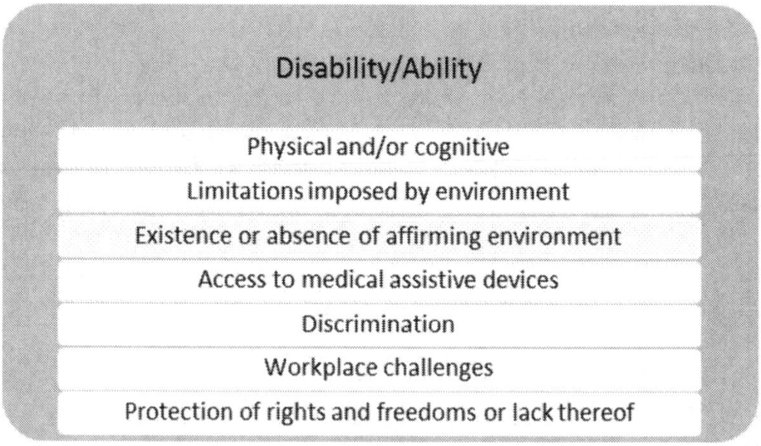

Disability/Ability

Physical and/or cognitive

Limitations imposed by environment

Existence or absence of affirming environment

Access to medical assistive devices

Discrimination

Workplace challenges

Protection of rights and freedoms or lack thereof

Physical disability, cognitive disability, and serious mental illness impact the way in which individuals experience the world around them. For persons with physical disabilities, the physical environment presents multiple challenges that may go unnoticed by those who are at this point in time able-bodied. Getting from one place to another is fraught with obstacles for those in wheelchairs. People using walkers, canes, or those who are blind, also face challenges that can be made increasingly difficult when weather extremes of heat or cold are considered. In the United States, the Americans with Disabilities Act (ADA) was passed in 1990. The ADA (1990) covers physical and mental disabilities and was designed to remove barriers to mobility as well as access to participation in the workforce. In Canada, legislation regarding persons with disabilities has been handled on a province-by-province basis with no federal legislation currently in place. Although many locations have legislation that mandates accommodations and the removal of barriers that will facilitate inclusion, advocates in Canada are still working toward federal protection for persons with disabilities.

Physical and cognitive disability influence worldview at the individual level as each person adjusts to her or his disability. Moreover, this process shifts, changes, and evolves over time. However, the social and political context within which persons with disabilities live has a profound impact as well. Affirming environments help persons with disabilities to live with dignity on many levels. This includes the creation of home settings that facilitate maximum participation in private and public spheres by eliminating the barriers that isolate persons with disabilities from the rest of society (Gibson et al., 2012). Nations, states, provinces, and communities that are affirming of persons with disabilities will foster environments in which developmental or adjustment processes are likely to have more positive outcomes than is the case in places where discrimination and exclusion are more pronounced. However, in the process of advocating for social inclusion, care must be taken to avoid paternalism (Schur, Kruse, & Blanck, 2013). Persons with disabilities should be understood as having highly valuable views of the world that make them uniquely qualified to lead efforts related to redesigning public and private spaces in ways that help all members of society in the transformation from thinking in binary categories of ability and disability to an understanding of people as differently abled.

Mental Health Status

Many parts of this book are about mental health in context. It is important to remember that mental health, mental illness, and our assumptions as human beings about what we can and should expect out of life in terms of happiness,

Figure 5.7   Mental Health Status

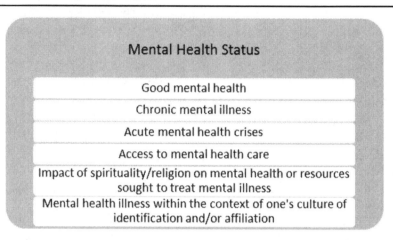

Mental Health Status

Good mental health
Chronic mental illness
Acute mental health crises
Access to mental health care
Impact of spirituality/religion on mental health or resources sought to treat mental illness
Mental health illness within the context of one's culture of identification and/or affiliation

contentment, and freedom from stress or sadness, shape and are shaped by the status of our mental health. In addition, the interaction between mental and physical health is critical to the manner in which the world around us is perceived and experienced nearly every day of our lives.

Good overall mental health is something that few people think about until an acute mental health crisis occurs or a chronic mental illness develops and then worsens to the point that life is negatively impacted. Globally, serious mental illness accounts for 30 percent of health-related impairments (Sarinen, Matzanke, & Smeall, 2011; Towers Watson, 2012). Major mental illness includes conditions such as schizophrenia, major depression, bipolar disorder, obsessive-compulsive disorder, attention deficit hyperactivity disorder, anxiety disorder, post-traumatic stress disorder, panic disorder, intermittent explosive disorder, social phobia, specific phobias, and various addictive disorders (Schachar & Ickowicz, 2014, p. 84).

Chronic mental illness shapes daily life in a multitude of ways, big and small. A person with schizophrenia may need to cope with unrelenting auditory hallucinations. An individual with anxiety may constantly dread a panic attack. Someone with depression could spend days on end isolated from others and living with a bleak outlook on life. Post-traumatic stress changes personalities making someone almost unrecognizable at times in terms of behaviour. In old age, debilitating conditions such as Alzheimer's disease gradually robs individuals of their own sense of self. Although some progress has been made in terms of understanding mental illness, persons with serious mental health conditions still experience a substantial degree of stigma and in many cases discrimination as well.

Another concern related to mental illness is culture. While mental illness does indeed exist in all populations, conditions and treatment in North America are still largely defined in Euro-Western terms. Many persons and populations attribute health conditions and mental illness to a number of causes ranging from scientific-biological to social factors or even spiritual contamination resulting from the actions or ill wishes of others (Purnell, 2014). Even though many cultures have trusted approaches to treating many health and mental health concerns, minority culture approaches to treatment are often only utilized if they support Euro-Western assessment, diagnosis, and intervention strategies. This means that even the experience of mental illness is subject to colonizing by dominant social structures that often shape the definition of mental illness and the context within which mental illness is treated.

While Euro-Western diagnoses and clinically tested treatments for mental illness cannot be summarily dismissed in favour of culture-specific approaches, neither should traditional approaches to treatment automatically be discounted or be considered less effective. Among non-Euro-Western minority populations a wide range of clients and client preferences exist in relation to mental health concerns and ideas about what constitutes preferred treatment. There are those who feel more comfortable with culture-specific identification of problems combined with traditional non-Euro-Western approaches to treatment or healing. Others may prefer an entirely Euro-Western process. Some clients may prefer to sequence or even blend non-Western and Euro-Western approaches to treatment. This can be seen in more traditional East or South Asian-origin population groups in which Euro-Western diagnoses may be accepted as valid or appropriate, but traditional treatment is preferred. Likewise, persons from Indigenous North American populations may in some cases also feel comfortable with Euro-Western diagnoses but prefer instead to use traditional approaches to treatment and healing. The point is that knowing about the potential impact of mental illness on the lives of clients should be combined with an understanding that cultural differences exist, and that clients may have highly variable views in terms of preferred approaches to addressing their needs.

Spirituality/Religion

Figure 5.8   Spirituality/Religion

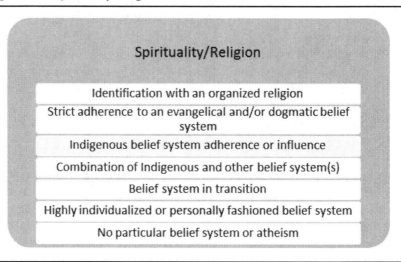

Spirituality/Religion

Identification with an organized religion

Strict adherence to an evangelical and/or dogmatic belief system

Indigenous belief system adherence or influence

Combination of Indigenous and other belief system(s)

Belief system in transition

Highly individualized or personally fashioned belief system

No particular belief system or atheism

In much of the published material regarding the preparation of social work or other helping professionals for practice, spirituality and religion are discussed as something that should be addressed in an assessment of a client. In that respect, this text is no different. Since the 1990s, the importance of spirituality and religion in the lives of clients has appeared in an increasing number of textbooks directed at practitioners of social work, counselling, and related professions. It is now widely understood that belonging to a religious community can provide a sense of direction, connection, and purpose for many (Payne, 2014).

Although many publications in the spiritual/religious category of professional practice mention spirituality, in North America, Christian belief systems predominate. This is not surprising because many North Americans identify as belonging to one of the Christian-based faiths. However, there are multitudes of other belief systems. Some are organized and scripture-based such as Islam, Judaism, or Hinduism, while others are not (Toropov & Buckles, 2004). There are also many North Americans who are spiritual but not religious, some who are atheist or agnostic, and others who practice Indigenous religious or spiritual traditions that predate European colonization. Among certain client populations, being part of larger community of believers has served a sustaining and even protective function in people's lives. It is widely known that African American populations in the United States have a long history of connection to religious organizations, most of which have also played a role in providing for church members in times of need, such as funerals, health crises, and so forth. Among Latino populations, the Catholic Church in particular has exerted a great amount of influence on the structure of culture and daily life. Like Catholicism, other denominations of Christianity, the various branches of Judaism, and the major types of Islam have all had an influence well beyond the internal spiritual life of believers. Indeed, all major world religions have served the purpose of influencing and shaping the attitudes, beliefs, and behaviours of large segments of society. So clearly, religion does have an impact on the lives of clients encountered by professional practitioners such as social workers, and it is important that social workers understand the role of religion or spirituality in clients' lives.

While it is crucial to recognize that religion or spirituality may be very important in the lives of clients, one must not forget that aspects of religion and spirituality can shift and change over the course of a person's life. Some clients may have come from devout religious backgrounds and have since moved away from religiosity or perhaps even become atheist. Others may be in the process of returning to the religious traditions of their youth, while some may have developed a belief system that combines elements of two or several religious/spiritual traditions.

With Indigenous populations in Canada and the United States, a history of religious persecution and forced conversion has been replaced by an environment in which Indigenous spiritual practices are being revived, with many now returning to non-Christian traditions (Johnston, 2012). For Indigenous North Americans, the period of criminalization of their ceremonies combined with forced conversion to Christianity has left many communities divided. Years of residential/boarding school indoctrination created generations of people who were taught to despise and reject their own cultural and spiritual beliefs. In most cases, Indigenous peoples were told that their pre-Christian lifeways and belief systems were evil and corrupt (King, 2012). Years of what amounted to cultural genocide and reprogramming left some confused or even negative about their own worth and value, a feeling that included Indigenous precolonial religious/spiritual belief systems.

To understand the influence of religion or spirituality on the lives of people requires nonjudgemental openness to a wide variety of belief systems and traditions. The spiritual/religious lives of individuals can range from devout practice of an organized faith, to a blending of traditions, to atheism. For some people, the spiritual path in life may also be in transition from one belief system to another, as has been the case for many Indigenous North Americans who within recent decades have begun to return to ceremonies and spiritual beliefs that are grounded in non-Christian Indigenous cultures tracing their roots back to precontact and precolonial societies. The key to understanding worldview, in relation to religion, spirituality, or even atheism, is to engage people in a process of exploration regarding the importance of belief or nonbelief in their lives.

Political Views or Beliefs

Figure 5.9   Political Views or Beliefs

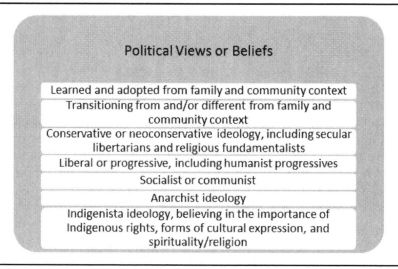

Political Views or Beliefs

Learned and adopted from family and community context

Transitioning from and/or different from family and community context

Conservative or neoconservative ideology, including secular libertarians and religious fundamentalists

Liberal or progressive, including humanist progressives

Socialist or communist

Anarchist ideology

Indigenista ideology, believing in the importance of Indigenous rights, forms of cultural expression, and spirituality/religion

Social work, like many other professions, has traditionally avoided the topic of politics in work with clients. While it is true that social workers have an ethical obligation to engage in work with clients, regardless of political beliefs held by those needing services, it must be understood that clients can and often do hold political beliefs that not only influence their worldviews in profound ways, but also quite often differ from beliefs held by their social workers. As noted in the key considerations above, people can hold widely divergent beliefs in terms of political views. However, hearing someone state that she or he is conservative, liberal, progressive, socialist, or even anarchist needs to be understood in terms of how political belief or ideology has shaped worldview. Moreover, understanding how a person has arrived at a political point of view at this particular point in time may provide insight regarding social, economic, and religious/spiritual forces that have shaped current thinking.

For example, a person might identify as being Indigenist (derived from the term *Indigenista*), indicating a belief in the importance of Indigenous rights, forms of cultural expression, and religion/spirituality (Engle, 2010). A person who states a firm belief in humanist progressive thinking may be very much in favour of social programming, but wary of involvement by religious organizations in the provision of social services. On the other end of the progressive-conservative spectrum, there are secular libertarians and religious fundamentalists who may distrust government, but who also have very divergent beliefs regarding issues such as marriage equality and the separation of church and state. Political beliefs are often learned in family and community contexts and can even impact who people go to in times of need, or who they feel comfortable working with if and when social workers or other professionals become involved in their lives.

Sexual Orientation and Gender Identity

Figure 5.10   Sexual Orientation and Gender Identity

Sexual Orientation and Gender Identity

Same sex, opposite sex, or bisexual identity

Gender transitioned, transitioning, or undecided

Social and cultural attitudes toward sexual orientation

Affirming or oppressive experiences related to the sexual identity development process

Federal, provincial/state, and/or local freedoms or limitations oppressive experiences

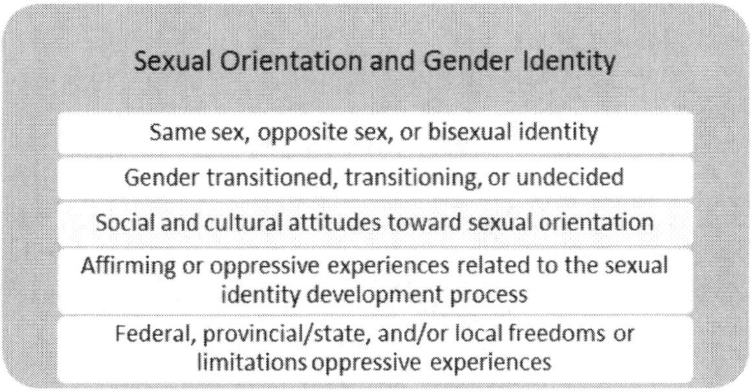

The wide variety of differences in sexual orientation and gender identity are aspects of life that should be a valued and celebrated as part of being human. Instead, sexual minority populations are all-too-often marginalized, excluded, and discriminated against. In North America, marriage equality in terms of same-sex partners being able to legally wed has changed dramatically since the period of intense civil rights activity in the 1960s and 1970s. In Canada, same-sex marriage has been legal nationwide since 2005. In the United States, with the Supreme Court decision in June 2015 legalizing same-sex marriage, all states must now recognize marriages between same-sex couples. As mentioned in chapter 3, Mexico is moving in the same general and more inclusive direction. Still, sexual orientation and gender identity that fall outside of the heterosexual dominant mode continue to be a reason for discrimination. There are indeed many cases, subtle and pronounced, of exclusion and marginalization due to sexual orientation or gender identity. In extreme circumstances, assault, injury, and even murder can occur at the hands of those who for religious, political, or cultural reasons are unwilling to embrace the full inclusion of people from sexual minority populations in society.

When one thinks of worldview development and sexual orientation or gender identity, it cannot be forgotten that people come from a wide range of family, cultural, social, and political environments in which being a sexual minority person is experienced in radically different ways. Added to the vast array of either affirming or marginalizing experiences are the differences one encounters as someone who identifies as female and lesbian or male and gay versus individuals with transgender or fluid and changing gender identities. In Canada and the United States, same-sex marriage has become much more accepted. However, transgender individuals and persons with other identities continue to be much more marginalized (Knegt, 2011).

Family of Origin

Figure 5.11   Family of Origin

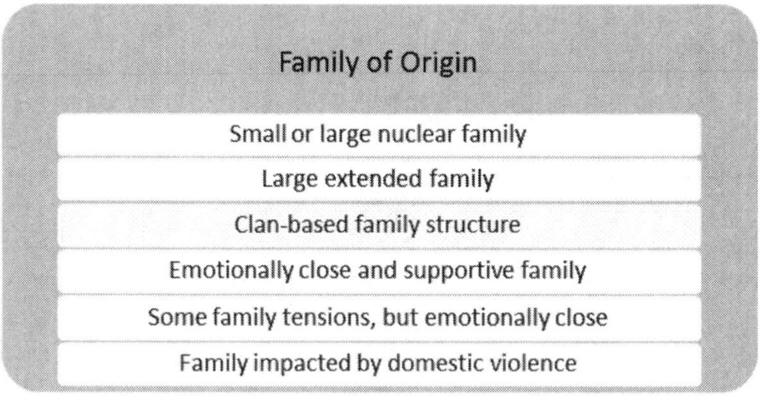

Family of Origin

Small or large nuclear family

Large extended family

Clan-based family structure

Emotionally close and supportive family

Some family tensions, but emotionally close

Family impacted by domestic violence

The cliché *families come in all shapes and sizes* is literally quite true. Families are shaped by culture, social forces, and even political decisions made by governments in relation to what constitutes a family. Families can be large or small. There are families with same-sex parents, opposite-sex parents, and single parents. There are blended families that occur when children resulting from previous adult relationships are brought together into a single household. Some families have children who are adopted, while other families are comprised of children in substitute (foster) care. In some families, the extended family network is what shapes the developmental experience of individuals raised within them, while other families are organized around a nuclear structure that is conceptually and physically distinct, and separate from others in the extended family network. Euro-Canadian and Euro-American majority cultural concepts of family have a tendency to focus on the primacy of the nuclear unit with grandparents and other extended family members considered important but secondary. This is different from many Latino, African American, or Asian-origin families in which grandparents may be central figures in the lives of children. In certain Indigenous societies, family membership may be clan-based, with individuals being viewed as members of larger collectives versus being defined solely in terms of distinct nuclear structures. Moreover, for those who have been raised in cultural contexts that differ from the North American majority, family may be understood as one thing at home among family members, and another in the external environment that is shaped by the social and legal definitions of the larger majority culture.

Aside from culturally, socially, and legally influenced family structures, there are issues of difference in relation to nurturing or potentially harmful aspects of the family environment. Some individuals recall family life during childhood as emotionally close, loving, and caring, while others might remember childhood experiences as times of violence and fear. Still others may have memories of good times and bad; and depending on the developmental stage of the individual, family discord and violence may have a lasting impact that can take years of work in adulthood to effectively resolve. Therefore, when a person is asked about family, it is important not to assume a common or shared understanding of what that means. Exploring the meaning of family and the emotions attached to those meanings are critical to understanding each person's sense of self in the present.

Primary Indigenous/Ethnic/Racial Identity

Figure 5.12   Primary Indigenous/Ethnic/Racial Identity

Primary Indigenous/Ethnic/Racial Identity

Close and positive connection

Marginal to distant connection

Identity in transition

Involvement with a larger community of culture

Identity development within a context of affirmation occurring at various levels

Identity development within a context of racism and/or prejudice occurring at various levels

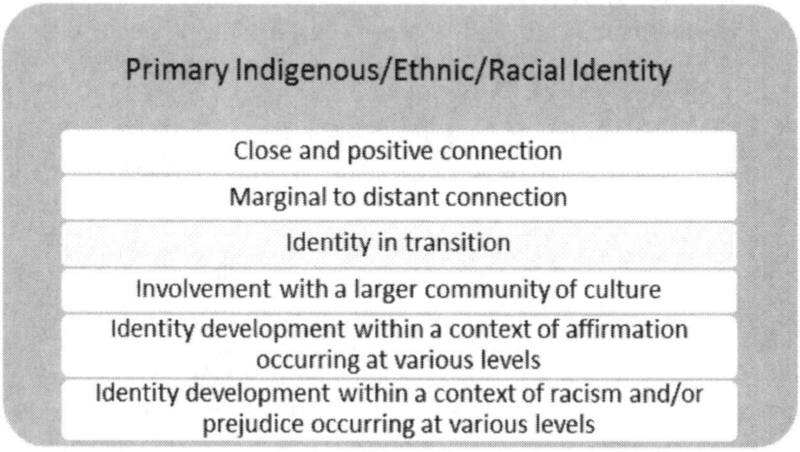

Worldwide, race and ethnicity combine with racism, economic advantage based on identity, and power that privileges some identities while disempowering or marginalizing others. Moreover, socially constructed concepts of race, combined with shifting social, political, and economic forces, can result in constantly evolving racial or ethnic forms. A good example of this sociopolitical phenomenon is found in the difference between Indigenous identity in Guatemala and southern Mexico versus the United States or Canada. In Mexico and much of Central America, Indigenous identities are shaped by several factors such as language, connection to known Indigenous communities, and biological connection to an Indigenous population as defined by appearance that includes physical features and manner of dress. If someone in Mexico or Central America has biological Indigenous heritage but lives away from ancestral villages, maintains no connection, and speaks and dresses like the Mestizo majority, he or she will be considered Mestizo, not Indigenous. This differs from Canada and the United States, where legal definitions outweigh cultural and social definitions. A person in the United States who meets the blood quantum threshold for legal definition as a member of a federally recognized tribe will be defined as Indigenous; this, in spite of limited or no linguistic, cultural, or social connection, as has occurred in some cases (Clark, 2004). Conversely, people in the United States or Canada may be culturally and linguistically connected to an Indigenous community, but legally defined as non-Indigenous by the federal government.

In North America, any visible African heritage identifies a person as African American or African Canadian, while in countries such as Brazil, racial categories abound, with a recognition that multiple forms of African, Indigenous, and European mixed identities can exist (Harris & Kottak, 1963). Persons having African heritage in North America were historically defined as the racial "other" to facilitate exploitation in the form of free or cheap labour, whereas Indigenous (Native Americans) were defined out of existence through the use of blood quantum standards in order to facilitate expropriation of land (Clark, 2004). What has happened as a result of many generations of identity being defined from outside by colonial authorities, regulations, and the resulting social constructs is that in many cases African American/African Canadian and Indigenous North American populations have now come to define themselves in the same manner, thus perpetuating the practices of colonial powers.

Aside from social and legal definitions of racial, ethnic, or Indigenous identity are the very personal experiences of identity development taking place within sociopolitical and sociocultural contexts that may include covert and overt experiences of racism. A person's sense of self that develops in societies characterized by racism, prejudice, and exclusion will likely be impacted negatively. Conversely, those societies that welcome diversity and are affirming of racial and cultural differences have the potential to impact identity development positively. Therefore, knowing a person's racial, ethnic, or Indigenous identity without exploring the social and cultural milieu within which that identity developed will provide only limited insight regarding worldview.

Additional Indigenous/Ethnic/Racial Identities

Figure 5.13   Additional Indigenous/Ethnic/Racial Identities

Additional Indigenous/Ethnic/Racial Identities

Additional identities to which there is a strong connection

Additional identities that are embraced and valued

Additional identities to which there is some connection

Additional identities that are seldom acknowledged or denied

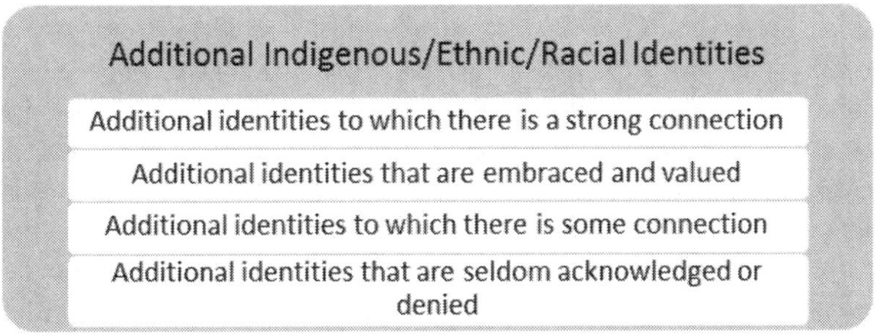

The population of North America is becoming increasingly diverse. Therefore, many individuals who identify with a particular ethnicity, racial group, or Indigenous population may also have additional heritage with which they identify to greater or lesser degrees. For example, many Indigenous North Americans in the United States and Canada also have Euro-Canadian or Euro-American ancestry in their backgrounds. For some, that ancestry may simply be known, whereas for others, it might represent a significant component of personal identity. The same is true for many African Americans who have not only African and European heritage, but often Indigenous North American heritage as well. For some African Americans, there may be a close and well-established connection to other identities, whereas for others European or Indigenous ancestors represent little more than a footnote in their family histories.

For many generations in North America, the social expectation of assimilation combined with the privileged position of Euro-Americans and Euro-Canadians led many to deny other racial heritage if they could "pass for white." As a result, connections for many were severed in a way that represented permanent loss for future generations. For example, a man from the southern United States who was engaged in an assessment process with a social worker spoke of his home town in Mississippi where the courthouse opened up family records in the 1960s, allowing people to take possession of their family's original birth certificates and other documents. He went on to say, his family was "part black" on his mother's side, but they were told to never admit or talk about it. He remembered his mother burning boxes of documents, so no one would ever know or try to prove this part of the family ancestry. While it seemed extreme to him at the time, he now understands that antimiscegenation laws banning interracial marriages would have made his grandparents or parents criminals prior to the civil rights era. Undoubtedly events similar to this one have taken place many times over as people have tried to erase the past.

For each of us as human beings, identity can be multilayered. For some, knowing all the pieces of the past may be easily accessible and welcomed aspects of shared family histories. For others, certain elements of heritage may be denied and linked to family secrets that even include feelings of shame. Now that many people are trying to explore their ancestry, they may have little more than vague family stories of some untraceable past. While there are those who have turned to genetic testing to determine their ancestry, experts in the field of genetics have warned that ethnic ancestry via DNA testing is not as accurate as people would like to believe, and the results will not identify a particular ancestor, just broad population groups (American Society of Human Genetics,

2008). Clearly, ancestral identity remains important for many individuals. The growing desire for people to know the populations and places their ancestors have come from demonstrates the importance of connection to the past in order to shape a sense of belonging and self-understanding in the present. When considering the worldview of any human being, it is crucial to remember that ancestry can be a discussion that is linked to a host of feelings, beliefs, and contested family histories, especially when the issue of additional identities becomes the area of focus.

Indigenous/Ethnic/Racial Identity of Partner or Spouse

Figure 5.14   Indigenous/Ethnic/Racial Identity of Partner or Spouse

Indigenous/Ethnic/Racial Identity of Partner or Spouse

Congruence or similarity of traditions and/or lifeways

Affirming of differences which includes celebrations of traditions and/or lifeways

Mutual respect for differences with little blending of traditions and/or lifeways

Adjustments that move between periods of tolerance and tension

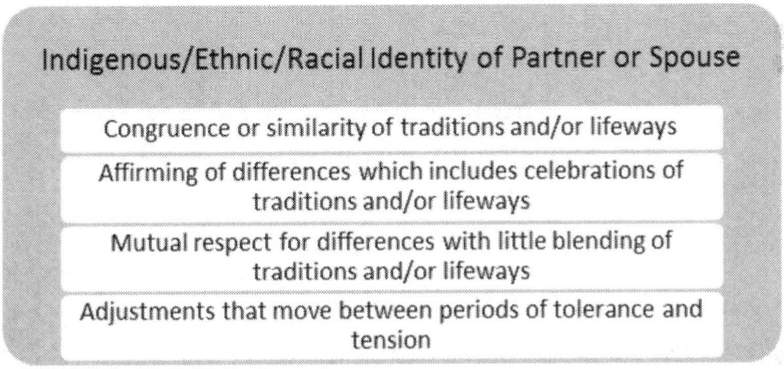

Whenever two people join as a couple in a committed intimate relationship, there are always differences that need to be negotiated. Even if both are from the same ethnic or cultural background, their understanding of themselves and each other in terms of identity can include shared values, beliefs, attitudes, and behavioural expectations as well as minor and even major differences. When each person in a couple comes from what their respective societies define as different racial or cultural backgrounds, all of the typical issues of adjustment and compromise exist as well as additional issues related to differences in perceived race and/or culture. For some, there is a willingness to celebrate cultural and/or racial differences. For others, these differences can cause tension for the pair or tension within and between their families of origin.

Where differences are minor, any adjustments may be smooth due to a higher likelihood of multiple shared cultural and social understandings. When differences are great or historic ethnic/racial discord is a factor, there can be strain within the relationship as well as varying degrees of acceptance or disapproval from family and community members on both sides. When differences present challenges, more time needs to be spent developing awareness and negotiating culturally based approaches to everything from childrearing to interacting with the other spouse or partner's family of origin. For some couples, these issues may not be easily resolved or even negotiable and can result in separation or divorce. For others, shifting periods of tolerance and tension may exist as new aspects of cultural differences arise, are worked through, and resolved in a way that allows each person in the relationship to feel validated and valued. Still, ethnic and racial differences may result in less favourable adjustments that privilege the race, culture, or ethnicity of one partner over another. In such cases, simmering tension diminishes the potential for creating affirming environments for individual development, healthy bonding as a couple, or providing a nurturing milieu for raising children.

Marital or Partner Status and Parental Status

Figure 5.15   Marital or Partner Status and Parental Status

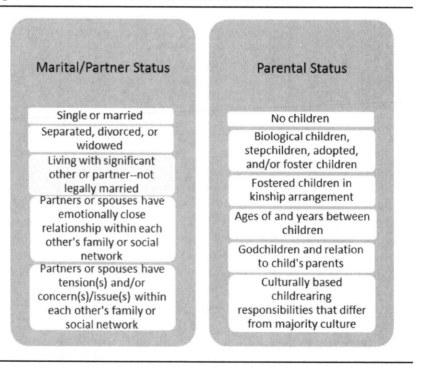

Marital/Partner Status	Parental Status
Single or married	No children
Separated, divorced, or widowed	Biological children, stepchildren, adopted, and/or foster children
Living with significant other or partner--not legally married	Fostered children in kinship arrangement
Partners or spouses have emotionally close relationship within each other's family or social network	Ages of and years between children
	Godchildren and relation to child's parents
Partners or spouses have tension(s) and/or concern(s)/issue(s) within each other's family or social network	Culturally based childrearing responsibilities that differ from majority culture

Partner or marital choices influence worldviews in multiple ways. Life with a partner can take many forms. A person might be in a legally recognized marriage, a socially recognized union, divorced, widowed, separated, or living in a close intimate relationship that has not been formalized in any particular way. The choice of a partner can be accepted and even celebrated by families of origin, or it can be a source of tension that may eventually lead to rejection. When considering the question of partner or marital status, there is also the option being single, remaining single, or choosing life as a single person following divorce, separation, or death of a partner or spouse.

When it comes to parenting, whether someone is in a relationship with another person or not, being a parent has a profound impact on the way one looks at the world, and it is a crucial component of understanding a person's worldview. Although there is a tendency to think of parenting in terms of someone raising their biological children, the role of parent is filled by different caregivers in many ways. There are those who have adopted children or who serve as parents for children in substitute (foster) care. In some situations, the foster parent might also be a relative who is now occupying a parental caregiving role due to something such as illness or incarceration of a child's parent or parents.

In Asian-origin, African American, and Indigenous North American families, grandparents play a very important caregiving role. This differs from the majority culture concept of grandparents as occasional caregivers, who are expected not to interfere in the nuclear families of their adult children. Another caregiving role that is common in many families is the role of godparents. In African American and Latino populations, the role of godparent may be particularly important for some families. Serving as the caregiver for children of extended family members or friends is taken very seriously in certain cultures. For Latino individuals and families for whom *compadrazgo* (coparenting/ godparenting) is highly valued, godparents play an important coparenting role in extended family networks (Gill-Hopple & Brage-Hudson, 2012). Although many people think of godparents as having traditionally stepped in when biological parents have died, godparents in Latino cultures often play an active part in the extended family network within which children are raised and socialized. The extended family as the socializing and caregiving unit is also important in many Indigenous North American communities found in rural reserve/ reservation settings and urban environments. Collective coparenting styles can take many forms. However, in societies in which collectivist cultures predominate, there is a tendency toward greater involvement by a wide range of relatives in the socialization of children.

Education and Occupation(s) or Profession(s)

Figure 5.16   Education and Occupation(s) or Profession(s)

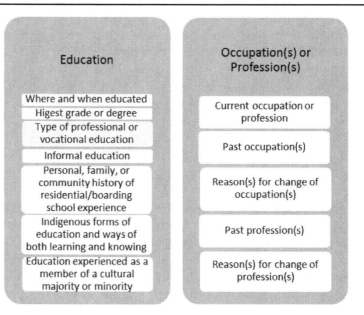

Education exerts a profound influence on worldview. Public school systems, private schools, religious schools, colleges, and universities shape the way individuals look at the world and themselves as part of that world. Within institutions of higher learning, fields of study or professional educational experiences shape the way students view the world. For example, business, medicine, and social work will produce graduates who are likely to see economic issues, poverty, and moral dilemmas from very different perspectives. Students from the Euro-American or Euro-Canadian majority may very well have more of a sense of connection to dominant culture educational systems than is the case for African American/African Canadian, Indigenous, South Asian, or Latino students, who often experience a feeling of disconnect with institutions that privilege Euro-Western cultural knowledge and approaches to knowledge acquisition.

Another important component of education is the recognition of knowledge that is acquired through culturally different systems, such as those found among Indigenous populations or non-Western immigrant populations that bring with them ways of knowing that are outside of dominant Euro-Western approaches found in North American educational institutions. Finally, uneasiness with Euro-Western systems may also be connected to a past that includes forced assimilation, which has been the case for Indigenous North Americans in Canada and the United States. A history of residential/boarding school atrocities still lingers in many communities, making it difficult for some to feel entirely comfortable with and trusting of non-Indigenous educational systems.

Professions and occupations also influence worldview. Work as a teacher, social worker, correctional officer, auto mechanic, or computer programmer will influence how one sees the world. Likewise, those employed in lucrative and growing occupations might have very different concerns from people employed in dying or threatened occupations. As is the case with employment histories, one's occupation or chosen profession may change moderately or even drastically over the course of a lifetime, potentially creating profound changes in worldview.

Socioeconomic Status and Employment Status

Figure 5.17   Socioeconomic Status and Employment Status

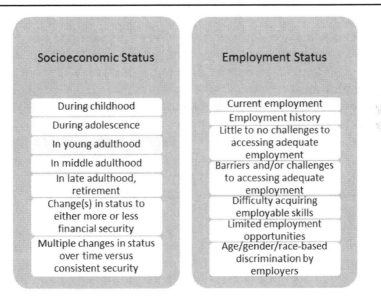

Socioeconomic Status	Employment Status
During childhood	Current employment
During adolescence	Employment history
In young adulthood	Little to no challenges to accessing adequate employment
In middle adulthood	Barriers and/or challenges to accessing adequate employment
In late adulthood, retirement	Difficulty acquiring employable skills
Change(s) in status to either more or less financial security	Limited employment opportunities
Multiple changes in status over time versus consistent security	Age/gender/race-based discrimination by employers

Many of the issues in relation to socioeconomic factors have been discussed in earlier chapters of this text. However, it is important to mention the profound impact social and economic forces can have on the lives of individuals, families, and even entire communities. In capitalist countries such as Canada and the United States, employment and income exert an important influence on worldview. Many people derive their identities from the work they do and from being able to work. Those who are injured and cannot work, or those who have retired often experience a profound sense of loss because so much of their identity has been shaped by the work they have done.

Socioeconomic factors and experiences that have occurred during the course of people's lives can have a definite impact on their worldviews. There are still those alive today who survived the Great Depression of the 1930s. Many of those individuals remember that time as being marked by such deprivation that to this day, they do not feel comfortable unless they have well-stocked food pantries and readily available cash. For their children, grandchildren, and great-grandchildren, such behaviour might seem odd. However, when one views any economic comfort as potentially temporary, the motivation to plan for difficult times makes sense. Immigrants to Canada and the United States often exhibit some of the same behaviours, warning their children that they need to be frugal, save their money, and be prepared in the event of an economic catastrophe.

Economic deprivation is often discussed and thought of in terms of individual choices having individual solutions. In the United States, it is common to see unemployed people blaming themselves for not working hard enough or not being sufficiently skilled. Rarely is the capitalist system questioned. However, it is no secret that obstacles to upward mobility and economic security exist in North America. Racism, gender discrimination, and barriers to education or skill acquisition also factor into economic issues. For example, if one is aware of broader structural forces that create or perpetuate poverty, the reaction to an economic downturn, such as that of 2008–2010, will be perceived quite differently than is the case for those who see economic difficulty as evidence of personal failure. While job loss and a reduction in earning capacity may still be enormously difficult, an awareness of larger forces causing suffering for many may make those experiencing hardship less likely to see unemployment or underemployment as evidence of inadequacy or personal failure.

Employment status includes full-time employment, part-time employment, underemployment, and employment in a job that does not meet basic needs, as is the case in the United States where many of the working poor wage a battle against impossible odds. As reported by Berman (2013), a study conducted by Wider Opportunities for Women (WOW), a nonprofit organization based in Washington, DC, found that the federal minimum wage in the United States would not constitute a living wage, even in Hanson County, South Dakota, which has the lowest cost of living in the nation.

For many people, employment history can—and often does—include times when they have struggled financially. For some, this has meant moving from one job to another just in an attempt to develop some sort of financial security. For example, rural Newfoundland and Labrador have struggled since the 1990s to maintain economic and even social viability in the face of ongoing out migration (Higgins, 2008). This is a pattern that repeats itself across the continent as rural regions, reserves, reservations, and even old industrial cities lose population to areas experiencing economic growth or at least presenting better opportunities to become and remain employed.

For many, this has meant the development of employment histories that involve substantial upheaval and change. As the environment of economic globalization continues, employment histories that feature life in one location with the same employer are likely to become increasingly rare. For the sake of being employed, many people are faced with the hard choice of leaving home, culture, community, and land to which an attachment may span generations. Some do not leave, opting instead for a life that includes struggling to stay in a single place—a choice that may ultimately prove futile in terms of being gainfully employed.

Community and Region Where Socialized and Region of Residence

Figure 5.18   Community and Region Where Socialized and Region of Residence

Community and Region Where Socialized	Nation/Country, Province/State, and Region of Residence
Urban advantaged or urban disadvantaged	Urban or rural residence
Rural advantaged or rural disadvantaged	Lifetime residence in the same location
Culturally distinct or multicultural community	Region of residence far from or close to region of origin
Mutliple and varied communities	Region of residence in a nation/country other than place of origin
Individualistic or collectivist cultural context	Living in a community that is either ethnically, culturally, and/or economically similar or different from region of origin
Regular or part-time First Nation/Métis/Inuit or Indigena community residence	

Where a person is raised and socialized has the potential for creating a lasting impact on worldview. Understanding people in current context requires knowing where they have come from in individual and collective historical terms. For example, a person may be an urban dweller now, but an investigation of where she or he was socialized might reveal something quite different, such as a family and ethnic group history in a rural location that is generations deep. In addition, knowing if a person was raised with a relative degree of economic comfort or deprivation is important as well. Simply knowing a person came from a small town does not reveal a history of poverty or privilege, marginalization or exclusion, and many other experiences that form someone's sense of self in relation to where she or he was raised and socialized.

Socialization in childhood can take place in collectivist cultural contexts or in settings where individualism and competition are important social values. Some people have grown up in very diverse communities, while others only encountered people who were racially, culturally, and socioeconomically quite similar to themselves. There are those who were raised, socialized, and have remained in the same community, while others have lived in a wide variety of geographic and cultural environments. Finally, there are those who have connections to Indigenous communities which will endure throughout adulthood. For example, it is not uncommon for people raised in traditional Indigenous reservation-based societies to return home upon retirement. This pattern is quite common in the US Southwest, where Diné and Pueblo populations move home even after many years of life in distant cities and other states.

People live in a variety of social and cultural contexts. Some live in rural areas and others in large sprawling metropolitan regions. There are those who now live in places that are far from their original homes. On the other end of the spectrum are those who have been lifetime residents of a single location. Some people live in communities where most of the residents who surround them are ethnically and culturally quite similar to themselves, while others may find most of the people they associate with on a daily basis to be culturally different. Within Canada and the United States, there are even distinct Indigenous populations found on reserves or reservations that are surrounded by the territories of larger state-level societies formed by colonizing powers. Clearly, people inhabit many different environments—some by choice and others as a result of political forces, economic forces, social factors, or even environmental degradation. The important lesson in all of this is that simply knowing where a person has been raised, socialized, and/or currently resides does not provide a reliable understanding of her or his worldview. The only way to truly develop an understanding of worldview is through an exploration of the very subjective personal experience and interpretation of meaning that each person possesses in relation to where she or he lives and has lived.

Nation or Country of Birth and Citizenship Status

Figure 5.19   Nation or Country of Birth and Citizenship Status

Canada, the United States, and Mexico have populations that consist of persons descended from Indigenous societies, those who trace their roots to various waves of European colonization or immigration, later more diverse immigrant streams, and others who have very recently arrived in North America. A person's nation or country of birth can impact worldview in multiple ways. The point at which someone leaves a nation of birth may mean that she or he has a more difficult time adjusting to a new host nation. This may be of particular concern for elderly immigrants, whereas children are widely known to adjust more quickly and integrate more successfully with the societies found in their new nations of residence.

When it comes to citizenship or citizenship status, there are many people born and raised in the major nations of North America (the United States and Canada in particular) who may seldom think of citizenship issues. Although Indigenous North Americans have a history of physical and cultural genocide at the hands of colonizers, and continue to have ongoing conflicts with the state-level colonizing powers that formed Canada and the United States, they, along with non-Indigenous Canadians and Americans, are much more likely than some recent immigrants to have lived their lives without fear of widespread armed religious or ethnic war on a broader national or regional scale. As a result, a decision to live or work for a period of time in a nation outside of Canada or the United States does not come with the same sense of loss that might be experienced by a refugee who may never be able to return home. Moreover, returning home for most native-born Canadians and Americans involves little more than having the proper documentation, money for travel, and the ability to drive or fly to their respective nations of origin. Therefore, a sense of feeling forever cut off from where one was born does not exist. This alone creates a profoundly different subjective understanding of living in a host nation.

Immigrant populations in North America also include persons who are undocumented. In Canada and the United States, undocumented immigrants live in fear of deportation. Status as an undocumented immigrant leaves that person vulnerable to abuses by employers and very limited access to health or mental health care. For women in particular, being an undocumented immigrant increases vulnerability in relation to victimization by intimate partners who may use their undocumented status to intimidate and control them (Aleman, 2014). Because of language barriers and fear of deportation, some will avoid all contact with law enforcement. Being undocumented also means having little access to needed social services. For social workers serving undocumented clients, simply trying to find services for which their clients are eligible is a challenge.

Difficulties such as oppressive poverty, war, or widespread drug and gang violence occurring outside of Canada and the United States have created immigrants who are often cut off from their homelands and families. The disruptions and life-altering changes resulting from forced immigration can leave many with a profound sense of loss. Some immigrants arriving in the United States or Canada with high hopes of acceptance and success are often faced with limited employment opportunities, anti-immigrant sentiment, or even outright racism, which can tarnish their hopes and dreams of a new life in a new land. Conversely, others speak of their adopted homes as being welcoming on many levels, a comment often heard particularly by immigrants to Canada, which has had a national commitment to multiculturalism since 1971 (Esses & Gardner, 1996). Undoubtedly, immigrants face a multitude of positive and negative experiences that impact worldview development. Moreover, reasons for immigration combined with the political, social, and economic milieu of their North American destinations intersect in ways that make for highly subjective and unique outcomes in terms of worldview development.

Language(s) Spoken

Figure 5.20   Language(s) Spoken

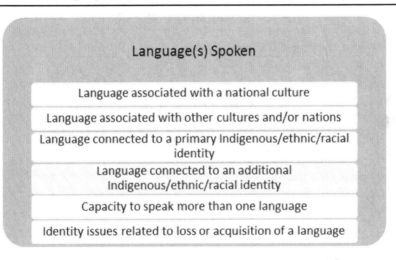

Language is very important, as it connects people to others and forms a critical component of shared peoplehood. Language is associated with a connection to national, regional, ethnic, and Indigenous cultures. Regional accents, speech patterns, and dialectic differences demonstrate connections to cultural communities. Language and the ability to speak a nondominant language, being bilingual, or multilingual can connect people to others beyond themselves.

The importance of a nondominant language is often not fully appreciated until it is gone. The Sea Island Gullah in South Carolina and Georgia have seen cultural and societal remnants of their African language fade in the face of coastal development and out migration. As a group, young Hispano (Spanish) Americans in New Mexico and Colorado are far less proficient in Spanish than their parents or grandparents. Among young Indigenous North Americans in Canada and the United States, Indigenous language proficiency is fading fast in many areas. Loss of one's language that is a connection to a specific cultural group can lead to a profound sense of identity loss (McCarty, Romero-Little, Warhol, & Zepeda, 2014). Indigenous Elders often lament the loss of language noting that a disconnection from Indigenous language also means a loss of ability to engage in ceremonies based in their respective Indigenous languages. Signs of language loss include fluency being found only among older speakers and the loss of language used in public domains, such as in school, at cultural observances, and at home (Crawford, 1996, p. 45).

Physical Environment

Figure 5.21   Physical Environment

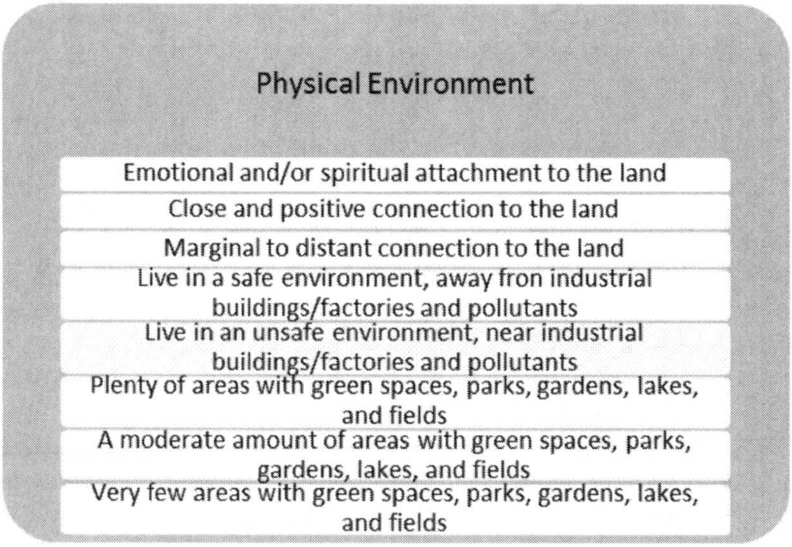

Physical Environment

Emotional and/or spiritual attachment to the land
Close and positive connection to the land
Marginal to distant connection to the land
Live in a safe environment, away fron industrial buildings/factories and pollutants
Live in an unsafe environment, near industrial buildings/factories and pollutants
Plenty of areas with green spaces, parks, gardens, lakes, and fields
A moderate amount of areas with green spaces, parks, gardens, lakes, and fields
Very few areas with green spaces, parks, gardens, lakes, and fields

Petroglyphs of coiled snakes are signs that a natural spring or pool of rainwater is nearby. The head of the snake glyph points in the direction of the water. The Spaniards thought the snake glyphs pointed to buried treasures the Indians had hidden. The Spaniards did not understand: fresh water is the treasure. (Silko, 1993, p. 29)

The words of Indigenous North American author Leslie Marmon Silko speak to the sacredness with which Indigenous North Americans have traditionally viewed the total natural environment. The natural physical environment is what sustains us all. It does not matter where we live. The earth is the only home we humans have. Unfortunately, the physical environment is often narrowly understood as the immediate surroundings such as a house, an apartment, or a neighbourhood. When thinking of the physical environment, especially the natural environment, the importance of a deep connection or a profound disconnection is revealing in terms of worldview. The physical environment has an impact on worldview that includes concerns related to sense of safety or levels of toxins and carcinogens in one's food, water, and surrounding soil. However, the physical environment represents much more. Research indicates a link between healthy natural environments and psychological well-being (Bowler, Buyung-Ali, Knight, & Pullin, 2010). Most people would prefer parks, gardens, lakes, oceans, forests, deserts, mountains, and fields to concrete cityscapes, even when those human-built structures are well maintained. For some, especially those from rural and remote regions, the environment defines how they have become who they are. As King (2012) states, many Indigenous people speak of a spiritual connection to the earth, and "that relationship is equally available to non-Natives, should they choose to embrace it" (p. 266).

When assessing a client or reflecting on yourself, think of the common questions and concerns about safety and possible environmental contamination, but ask other questions as well. Is there a strong cultural, spiritual, or emotional connection to a particular place? Is there a positive or negative sense about your current residence? How do you connect to your physical environment? Do you see the earth you walk on as a living thing or as an inanimate medium of plants, rocks, minerals, and water? Your answers reveal the manner in which physical environmental variables shape your worldview, your motivations in this existence, and indeed your life on this planet, just as the answers from others will reveal the thinking that shapes who they are and how they see themselves. Opening yourself up to hearing how others see the human-made and natural worlds within which they live can build understanding and even empathy. Looking within to reflect on your own views about your environment creates valuable insight.

CONCLUSION

One of the most problematic issues with cultural competence skill development has to do with the desire of professional practitioners in social work and other fields wanting to find that "one simple way" to quantify culture. However, as this chapter has demonstrated, understanding culture and the expression of culture at the level of the individual is exceedingly complex. Countless practitioners have long wanted a set of guidelines regarding the cultures of various populations that could serve as a template for designing culturally sensitive interventions. Unfortunately, much of the history of social work education in North America has fostered the belief that culture (meaning non-Euro-Caucasian culture) can be clearly identified and categorized in a manner that creates a list of cultural traits and beliefs for vast numbers of different populations. The same could be said for nursing, psychology, and psychiatry as well. In many faculties and schools of social work, attempts to include faculty members from various politically identified minority populations has been followed with an expectation that they will enlighten students and colleagues regarding broad value and belief systems as well as the intricacies of their respective presumed cultures. This has placed undue pressure on minority faculty members to be the all-knowing experts on culture. In addition, these same minority faculty members are called upon time and time again to teach "culture" to social work students—a practice that relieves majority culture faculty from the need to increase their own understanding of cultural diversity in its many and complex manifestations.

Those social work educators and practitioners who are less comfortable with the rigidity of a trait list approach may have opted for what appears to be a more scientific approach. Many practitioners have long wanted to utilize a central tendency or modal personality approach, much as Anthony Wallace (1952b) did in the study of the Tuscarora People of upstate New York, and then apply those findings to work with each individual identified as being a part of a particular population. Nevertheless, creating a truly effective cultural identity or trait assessment tool akin to the Minnesota Multiphasic Personality Inventory (MMPI) has eluded social workers and other helping professionals for decades.

Within the Euro-Western medical field, culture has generally been viewed as a barrier to treatment. Admittedly, there are a few exceptions such as the work by Arviso-Alvord and Cohen-Van Pelt (1999), which attempts to bridge the worlds of Euro-American medicine and Indigenous (in this case Diné) concepts of health and wellness. However, the vast majority of written material intended for use by medical professionals begins with the unquestioned belief that a Euro-Canadian/Euro-American approach to the treatment of health and mental health conditions is superior to all other belief systems. Therefore, when culture is encountered, it is viewed at best as something to be respected, and at worst, a nuisance. In either case, culture is still seen as a barrier to providing truly professional care.

In spite of the shortcomings mentioned above, social work has been somewhat more successful at opening the door to work with populations that differ from the Anglo-Canadian and Anglo-American majority cultures that predominate in North America. But still, the belief that nonmajority societies and their respective cultures are somehow static, predictable, and reducible to a list of recommended practitioner behaviours misses the point of individual, family, and community complexity. It is important for social workers to understand that culturally based beliefs and behavioural traits do exist, and that cultures do indeed differ. However, it is also important to realize that while certain attitudes, beliefs, and behaviours may predominate within culturally distinct populations, the degree to which individuals resemble a cultural archetype or ideal is bound to vary widely. Each of us, as human beings, will have a way of looking at the world (and ourselves within it) that has been influenced by many factors. Therefore, the exploration of multiple individual, familial, ethnocultural, community, macrosocietal, and environmental factors that influence the manner in which each person develops her or his unique and evolving worldview is critical in meeting the client where she or he currently is at this point in time.

Chapter Six

Getting Started with Clients

INTRODUCTION

Getting started with clients is perhaps one of the most stress-producing and even feared tasks for those who are at the beginning of their preparation for careers as social workers, counsellors, or other types of professional helpers who engage clients in helping or healing processes. In recognition of that concern, this chapter opens with a review of core skills related to engaging clients and developing a working alliance. This initial period of contact between professional helpers and clients is crucial for the development of an alliance in which both become partners in working toward treatment, helping, or healing objectives. However, before an initial assessment can proceed to the point of collaborating on the development of a treatment, helping, or healing plan, the professional must first engage the client in opening up about the problem(s) for which she or he may need help. The use of various techniques related to building empathy, gathering information, checking for accuracy, and developing a collaborative working relationship with clients will form the foundation of trust that is necessary for the helping or healing process to begin.

In human service fields such as social work, counselling, family practice, and clinical psychology, humanistic theory has played an important role in organizing thinking about the engagement process. Carl Rogers's person-centered approach is an example of work with clients that is based in humanistic theory. A person-centered approach provides a foundation for the process of engaging clients, developing a collaborative relationship, and initiating work on issues that are of concern to clients who have sought or been referred for services. While humanistic theory is seldom used as a basis for counselling or therapy, Rogers's person-centered approach, along with Maslow's beliefs in human potential and the ability of people to make important positive improvements in their own lives, continue to give shape to basic assumptions of social workers and other like-minded helpers regarding the innate goodness and worth of human beings.

The discussion of problem solving included in this chapter lays the conceptual groundwork for the presentation of social work case management appearing later in chapter 15 of this book. The material on problem solving includes historical and contemporary elements of the problem-solving process as a professional activity, as well as a discussion of what constitutes effective and ineffective problem solving. Finally, cultural and social aspects of problem solving are presented for consideration as elements of an overall anti-oppressive approach to practice with culturally different, marginalized, or vulnerable populations.

The material on crisis management, followed by suicide prevention and intervention, has been included as a reminder of important critical issues faced by social workers and other helping professionals in work with clients experiencing profoundly destabilizing and potentially life-threatening situations at various points in time. Although this material could have been included in several of the other chapters in this book, it has been placed in this particular chapter because the management of a crisis or what to do about a suicidal client are concerns often shared by many students who enter helping professions. Although crisis management and suicide-prevention approaches have been written about extensively, the material provided in this chapter is intended to give the reader a starting point for the further development of skills related to work with those for whom a crisis and/or suicidality may be major concerns.

ENGAGEMENT AND THE DEVELOPMENT OF A WORKING ALLIANCE

The working alliance, also called the therapeutic alliance or the therapeutic working alliance, is that collaborative relationship and working agreement that is established between the social worker and the client. A nonthreatening environment in which a client feels safe to address issues and concerns is believed by many to be critical in relation to problem solving that will lead to emotional well-being or desired behaviour change (Bachelor, 2013). The idea of engaging clients is perhaps one of the tasks that causes the greatest degree of anxiety among social work students and new social work practitioners. The concern many have is that clients will not feel comfortable around them and will therefore not be willing to open up and talk to them about problems or concerns.

Direct and Closed-Ended Questioning

Although nearly all noncrisis interactions with clients start with some version of the open-ended question *"What brings you here today?"* many of the initial questions social workers and other types of helping or counselling professionals ask clients are direct or closed-ended. *Direct* and *closed-ended* questioning at the beginning of a session is designed to get specific information efficiently. Much of the demographic information social workers use in assessments such as name, date of birth, primary ethnic/racial or indigenous identity, preferred gender identity, and language or languages spoken will be gathered using a direct questioning approach. Likewise, asking clients about the number and age of children and of course place of residence will be done with a direct questioning approach. However, asking the client a series of questions in rapid succession can create discomfort. Moving at a moderate pace and allowing for conversation will make the collection of demographic information less intimidating. For example, a social worker might start by saying, "I have to gather a bit of basic information about you before we get started. If you feel uncomfortable at any point or wonder why I am asking a particular question, please ask me to stop and I will explain why I am requesting specific information." In addition, social workers can make the initial session more personable by breaking up direct questioning with brief comments or periods of conversation.

As the initial session proceeds, the social worker will continue to use direct closed-ended questions, but this will be done more infrequently and only for reasons such as making sure information is being clearly understood, to gather specific relevant details accurately, or to more clearly focus attention on specific issues. Closed-ended questions have a limited place in work with clients and need to be limited to getting specific answers to questions versus encouraging clients to explore thoughts, feelings, and issues (Good & Beitman, 2006, p. 72).

Open-Ended Questioning

The use of open-ended questions is intended to encourage clients to more freely engage in the discussion of thoughts, feelings, and the situations that resulted in contact with a social worker, counsellor, or other helping professional (Evans, Hearn, Uhlemann, & Ivey, 2008, p. 41). Open-ended questions are used throughout the session with the client and are from time to time punctuated with closed-ended questions that serve to complete information. For example, a woman may tell her social worker that she avoids arguing with her spouse's father out of respect. The social worker might perhaps use a closed-ended question such as asking how often the father-in-law visits, followed by an open-ended question regarding what she (the client) finds so aggravating about her father-in-law.

Active Listening and Attending Behaviour

Listening to a client while at the same time letting her or him know that you are paying close attention to what is being said is a skill that needs to be developed and practiced. Active listening is more than just nodding your head and occasionally saying "OK." Active listening involves culturally appropriate eye contact, allowing for comfortable personal space, and demonstration, through the use of body language, that you as a social worker, counsellor, and so forth, are available to and interested in your client. In figure 6.1, using a new

Figure 6.1   E-N-G-A-G-E-S

| E | Eye Contact |

•Maintaining a moderate level of eye contact is important. Looking away too often may be interpreted as disinterest whereas maintaining an overly intense gaze can be disturbing. Make sure you understand age and cultural differences regarding appropriate eye contact.

| N | Nodding |

•Use of head nodding to convey attention to a client is important, but should not be excessive or continuous.

| G | Grammatical Style |

•Matching the client's grammatical style does not mean mimicking an accent or using certain slang terms. It means matching the level of language that is comfortable for the client. In general, avoid professional jargon or highly technical language. Also, consider that some clients may have limited proficiency in the language you use within the context of professional work.

| A | Avoiding Distracting Behaviour |

•Avoiding distracting behaviours means when you are with the client, you should not concentrate on excessive note-taking, eating, answering phone calls, etc. Also, an overly positive and upbeat tone of voice, fiddling with pens or other objects, twirling of the hair, etc., can be distracting or even annoying.

| G | Gauging |

•Gauging the difference between what a client says and what is communicated by facial expression or body language is important. Remember that body language may be more expressive in some cultures and less expressive in others.

| E | Express Understanding |

•Expressing your attention to a client and your understanding of what s/he is saying can be done by the use of utterances or single words, such as "Yes" or "OK." Let the client know you are listening and understanding what is being said. In some instances, culturally specific approaches may be either more or less active in regard to utterances, single words, or brief statements.

| S | Space |

•Personal space is important and is also influenced by culture. It is important to understand that you as a social worker, counsellor, therapist, etc., should be aware of cultural differences and strive to establish a comfortable space for meeting with clients that will also accommodate differing personal space preferences.

(Adapted from Good and Beitman, 2006)

mnemonic device, *E-N-G-A-G-E-S*, explains the components of active listening to which social workers and other helping professionals must attend in their work with clients.

Clarification

The use of clarification in sessions with clients might involve open-ended or closed-ended questioning. A client may use an unfamiliar term for which a social worker or counsellor would request explanation. For example, a social worker or counsellor might say, "I am not familiar with that word. Could you tell me what it means?" If the social worker or counsellor thinks she or he understands a term or phrase but wants to be certain the client assigns the same meaning, a closed-ended question might suffice. For example, a young client might use a common term such as *qué onda*, which is Spanish slang. The social worker or counsellor could say, "I have heard *qué onda* before. I understand it to mean *What is going on?*, *What's happening?*, or *How is it going?* Is that how you use the term?" Clarification may also be used to confirm the accuracy of a client's statements or intended meaning following a summary or a reflection. In any case, checking in with the client to make sure that what has been communicated reflects what the client intended to say is facilitated by the use of clarification.

Reflection

Reflections can be either simple or complex. Simple reflections recap what a client has stated in a manner that stays close to what the client has actually said. Simple reflections are often used at the beginning of a session. For example, a client may say, "I am so pissed off with the way the teacher spoke to me about my son." The social worker using a simple reflection might respond with, "I can hear that you are very upset by this." In the use of simple reflection, avoid just repeating the client's words. Doing so does not truly communicate understanding and can perhaps leave the client feeling frustrated or even angry. After more information has been communicated and understood, a more complex form of reflection can occur. This type of reflection, often referred to as the reflection of feelings, is one of the most important skills for social workers and other helping professionals (Sevel, Cummins, & Madrigal, 1999, p. 20).

Reflection of feelings may include what the client has said and what has been conveyed in tone of voice as well as through nonverbal communication. A social worker or counsellor might, for example, hear a client's statement of anger and respond with a reflection of feelings by saying, "I think I hear more in what you say than just anger. I also hear that you felt discounted, almost as if what you said didn't matter." By reflecting feelings, the social worker in this very brief example acknowledged the client's anger, but went on to address thoughts and emotions that were perhaps communicated in other ways, or based in part on statements made by the client earlier in the session.

Another example of reflection of feelings can be found in the interaction between a social worker in an urban setting and a client from a remote First Nation reserve. In this example, the client states that she feels very alone in the city. She makes this comment many times and then adds that she also has very little help from her family. The social worker, using reflection of feelings might respond to the client's comments by stating, "From what you are telling me, I hear that you feel lonely and that you wish you had more support from your family. I also get the sense that life here has been a big adjustment and you feel like you have to do everything on your own." Again, reflection of feelings involves more than just what the client has said. The use of this type of reflection addresses emotions connected to what has been communicated. In addition, this approach to reflecting also creates the opportunity for further exploration of issues presented by the client.

Paraphrasing

"Paraphrasing feeds back to the client the essence of what has just been said. The listener shortens and clarifies the client's comments" (Ivey & Ivey, 2007, p. 154). Paraphrasing differs from reflection because the purpose of paraphrasing, on the part of the social worker or counsellor, is to facilitate a clear understanding of what the client is saying, while also attempting to develop a better understanding of the client's subjective experience of a feeling, an experience, an event, or situation. A brief example would be the case of a client in a session with a social worker following a negative interaction with a foreman at work. The client might say something like, "That foreman at work is whacked. Every time I ask him a question, he goes off on me like I just challenged him to a fight." The social worker's paraphrased recounting of the client's comment might be something like, "The foreman at work gets extremely agitated, to the point of raising his voice and sounding quite angry whenever you ask him a question. Is that correct?" Verifying accuracy of the paraphrase is important. Any paraphrasing that is done needs to be checked out with the client by inviting modification or revision of the paraphrase to make sure it is accurate.

Summarizing

Summaries are "essentially reflective" (De Jong & Berg, 2008, p. 28). Summaries involve listening to what clients have said and then restating key elements that capture the essence of what has been communicated. Summaries can occur at several points during the session. When used in this way, they generally cover the span of a few minutes or even a few statements. Summarizing what clients have said can also be a good way to get a session moving again when a client seems to have become stuck. Summarizing at the end of a session, or using a summary of a previous session at the beginning of a new session, can also be useful as it serves to focus the conversation. A social worker using summarization before a session might start by saying something like, "Last week we spent a lot of time discussing your growing desire to return home to Georgia. Maybe this week we could talk more about your interest in going back to the place you call home."

Beyond reflecting what has occurred in a single session, summaries can also be used to recap what has been done during several sessions. This is a common approach in motivational interviewing (chapter 12), and can reinforce gains made during the treatment/healing/helping process. For example, a social worker in a session with a client may comment on gains the client has made and encourage a process of summarization by stating, "Perhaps it would help if today we reviewed the positive changes you have made so far."

Providing Information

Clients come into contact with social workers and other professional service providers for a number of reasons; some are simple, such as needing information about income maintenance, education, or employment services, while others involve issues of child safety, mental illness, addictions, sexual victimization, domestic violence, or any number of problems, events, or situations that are far too many in number to list here. Because the North American context represents a patchwork of service providers, it is important that social workers, counsellors, and other helping professionals be aware of programs and eligibility criteria for services in the community and region.

However, information giving is not limited to information about programs and services. Social workers, counsellors, and other providers of human services may also be in the position of supplying clients with information about different forms of mental illness, drug abuse and chemical dependency, the dangers of unprotected sexual activity, the warning signs of child abuse, and a whole host of health and mental health concerns or risks. The important thing to remember is that information giving is not advice giving. Information giving is providing clients with the knowledge that can inform their choices, whereas advice usually involves telling clients what you as a professional think they ought to do. The codes of ethics and ethical practice guidelines for social workers in Canada and the United States make it very clear that client self-determination is a critical component of professional practice, making information giving, not advice giving, the more respectful and appropriate approach to helping clients.

HUMANISTIC THEORY

The humanistic theoretical perspective in social work represents another reaction to the dominance of psychoanalytic theory in social work and psychology. Although humanism never developed the centrality and acceptance in practice that occurred for cognitive-behavioural therapy and even certain postmodern therapies (Payne, 2014), it has still played an important role in social work. Practitioners who use humanism as a foundation for work with clients have certain basic assumptions regarding human behaviour and personality development. Humanist concepts such as the belief in human potential and the capacity for people to improve themselves are still central tenets of social work practice, which sets humanism and social work apart from the more deterministic and technical approaches to treatment (Payne, 2014, p. 273).

Humanistic approaches to human behaviour, personality development, and work with clients are grounded in the belief that human nature is innately positive (Alloy, Acocella, & Bootzin, 1996). This differs markedly from the Judeo-Christian concept of original sin and the reductionist psychoanalytic view of humans as animals in search of ways to satisfy instinctual sexual and aggressive drives within the confining rules of civil society (Alloy et al., 1996). In addition, unlike behaviourists who conceive of human action as being shaped in response to stimuli in their environments, humanists see people as being motivated by a desire to create meaning and purpose in life.

Humanistic theory is relevant to social work because of the importance placed on the subjective experience of individuals. For humanists, individual experiences and the manner in which those experiences are both processed and understood is viewed as being critical in terms of their influence on human behaviour (Nye, 1981). In this respect, humanism and cognitive-behavioural theorists share some common ground. Humanists, in much the same way as cognitive behaviourists (see chapter 11), believe that a person's subjective understanding of any given situation is more important in terms of emotional response and concomitant behaviour than the actual event or situation itself. As a result, intervention with clients, from a humanistic perspective, is focused on developing as closely as possible an understanding of the client's subjective sense of her or his lived experience, followed by helping the client free her or himself from problematic emotions linked to negative events in life.

Person-Centered Approach

Carl Rogers's person-centered therapy comes out of humanistic theory. It is likely the most well known and widely used of the humanistic approaches to work with clients (Payne, 2014). Although social workers, counsellors, or other practitioners generally do not use Rogerian approaches to the exclusion of others, the basic elements of Carl Rogers's humanistic person-centered approach remains with us today. In social work education, the Rogerian belief in the value of internal resources, unconditional positive regard, empathy, empowerment, and the realization of one's full potential still shapes the manner in which students are taught to view clients. Those who incorporate Rogerian person-centered perspectives in work with clients believe in the importance of a positive and affirming therapeutic relationship. Rogerian principles foster an acceptance of clients by social workers, counsellors, or other helpers, with the belief that as they (clients) feel accepted, they will become more accepting of themselves. Moreover, this increased self-acceptance will allow clients to more fully experience their own humanity, thereby removing what has blocked them from realizing their full potentials. Rogers believed that creating the proper facilitative therapeutic climate is crucial to empowering positive change in clients. According to Rogers, clients have within them what is needed to alter negative self-concepts and damaging self-directed behaviours, and that it is the task of therapists or counsellors to help their clients access those internal resources (Rogers, 1986). In general terms, Rogers believed that people who were helped to become self-aware could move forward to self-acceptance, self-expression, abandonment of defensiveness, and finally arrive at a point where they could be open and honest with themselves and others, leading them to even greater self-awareness in a cycle of growth and personal development.

Figure 6.2   Cycle of Growth and Development

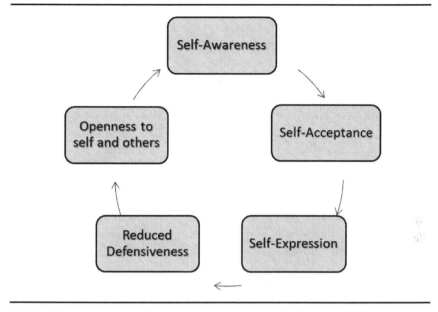

For Rogers, the key elements of helping clients realize their potential are found in the therapeutic techniques of developing empathy, being congruent and genuine with clients, and unconditional positive regard.

Empathy

Most people have some understanding of the concept of empathy. Empathy is not the same as sympathy. Sympathy is feeling sorry for another person. However, empathy involves trying to think of how you might feel if you were placed in another person's circumstances. A very old saying in English is "Don't judge another person until you have walked a mile in her/his shoes." In other words, try to understand the experience of another person from her or his perspective. *Empathy* for social workers, counsellors, or other professional helpers is best described as attempting to come as close as possible to understanding the client's subjective experience. The basic engagement skills of using open-ended questions, reflection of feelings, paraphrasing, asking for clarification, and always checking with the client for accuracy are examples of techniques used to develop empathy. According to Rogers, developing empathy is one of the most important tasks of a therapist engaged in work with a client (Rogers, 1957). Rogers's description of empathy involves trying "to sense the client's private world as if it were your own" (Rogers, 1957, p. 99). However, for Rogers, just as is the case in the education of social workers and other helping professionals today, empathy also requires that the professional practitioner not become lost in the client's subjective experience to the point that she or he becomes consumed and immobilized by the client's emotions (De Jong & Berg, 2008).

Genuineness

Genuineness describes a way of being emotionally present, warm, natural, and congruent with the emotional state of the client (Sharma, 2012). Unlike therapists in the psychoanalytic tradition, who are more emotionally reserved, those professionals who use person-centered approaches in work with clients make a point of being emotionally present and even sharing their reactions to the feelings clients express. Whereas a more reserved and distant therapist might ask a client "How does that make you feel?," a practitioner using a person-centered approach would be more inclined to say something like, "That sounds very difficult. I can sense how alone and afraid you must have felt."

Another aspect of genuineness is self-disclosure. Self-disclosure in service of the client occurs when the social worker, counsellor, or other professional shares something that may be of value in helping that person feel that she or he is being heard and understood. For example, a social worker might say something like, "I also lost my mother to cancer. I understand the helplessness you describe when you feel like there is nothing more you can do." By sharing her own feelings, the therapist in this example is also modeling disclosure in a way that can make the client feel more comfortable to do the same. Essentially, those using the person-centered technique of genuineness see it as involving a willingness on the part of the social worker, therapist, and so forth, to take down the traditional barrier between her- or himself and the client, allowing for true collaborative work.

Unconditional Positive Regard

Work with clients from a Rogerian perspective begins with the foundational concept of unconditional positive regard, which bears a great deal of similarity to the social work value of dignity and worth of the person. Applying the concept of unconditional positive regard in work with clients means that the social worker, counsellor, or other professional helper must truly value clients as human beings (Coggins & Hatchett, 2009). This does not mean that all behaviour is approved of, but instead that clients are viewed as having worth simply as a function of their humanity, and should therefore be treated with dignity and respect (Sue, Sue, & Sue, 1994).

Critique of Person-Centered Therapy

Person-centered approaches to therapy have been criticized for vagueness in terms of principles, opposition to diagnosis in mental health, and the strong emphasis placed on client self-evaluation as the primary measurement of outcomes in therapy (Sharma, 2012, p. 37). Humanistic approaches such as person-centered therapy have also been criticized for being most effective with clients who are generally more educated, articulate, and willing to engage in discussions about difficulties experienced at the point of life transitions or in relation to adjusting to new or changing life circumstances. With those who have a serious mental illness or have difficulty even engaging in discussions about feelings due to distorted perceptions of reality, person-centered therapy may be of diminished effectiveness (Sharma, 2012, p. 37; Sue et al., 1994). Still, there have been several studies that lend support to the effectiveness of unconditional positive regard, developing empathic understanding, and the use of genuineness as tools for engaging clients.

Criticism aside, it is important to remember humanistic perspectives in social work and other similar helping professions have, much like the concept of problem solving, become so commonplace that they now constitute basic unquestioned assumptions about respectful and even ethical work with clients. For marginalized persons from racial, ethnic, or sexual minority populations, humanistic approaches have represented an important step in the direction of hearing the voices of those to whom the larger majority culture had long been dismissive or even hostile.

Abraham Maslow and Self-Actualization

For nearly anyone in social work, psychology, or counselling, the name *Maslow* is associated with the term *self-actualization*. While Maslow did popularize this term, it was first used by Kurt Goldstein, a psychiatrist (Frick, 1995, p. 227).

Abraham Maslow thought of human aspiration to seek self-actualization as a goal of personal development that occurred in steps. For Maslow, the fulfillment of basic, midlevel, and higher level needs recognized the importance of attending to basic human needs before moving on to the highest level of development, which is self-actualization (Maslow, 1970). For students in social work and other helping professions, the idea of attending to basic needs may seem to be common sense. However, in the 1950s and 1960s, Maslow's ideas about human behaviour and potential for growth toward self-actualization ran counter to the mainstream emphasis on pathology (Hutchinson & Charlesworth, 2013). Maslow's concept of a hierarchy of needs, developed in 1954, emphasized the importance of meeting lower level needs as a way of helping clients develop in the direction of improved self-esteem and eventually self-actualization. Although Maslow saw all levels of need as being part of human instinct, he also made it clear that lower level needs had to be at least partially fulfilled in order to address higher level needs (Hutchinson & Charlesworth, 2013; Maslow, 1970).

Figure 6.3   Maslow's Hierarchy of Needs

In Maslow's hierarchy, the most basic level of *physiological needs* relates to human survival and includes fulfilling the need for water, food, clothing, shelter, and so forth. Basic physiological needs are followed by *safety needs*, which involve feeling reasonably free from potential harm along with having some degree of stability and predictability in life. After basic needs for survival and safety are met, the next level is that of *psychological needs*. Psychological needs are focused on fulfillment in relation to being accepted and loved by others as well as having a sense of belonging. The psychological needs are often divided into lower level love and social belonging needs, followed by self-esteem that is derived from a sense of confidence and achievement combined with a respect for self and others (Maslow, 1954). The final stage in Maslow's humanistic conceptualization of human growth and development is *self-actualization*. Experiencing self-actualization requires that lower level needs must be met. Once lower level needs are met and tasks related to them have been mastered, the person is free to live up to her or his fullest potential. In 1969, Maslow added self-transcendence as a step beyond self-actualization to explain motivation for things such as self-sacrifice related to altruism and the struggle for social progress (Koltko-Rivera, 2006).

Although Maslow has been criticized for developing theoretical constructs that do not hold up well to empirical validation, the beliefs of psychological freedom and the ability to be all we are capable of being had its beginnings in the humanistic psychological movement of which Maslow was an important part (Bell, 2011, p. 122). Moreover, the concept of meeting basic human needs identified in Maslow's hierarchy represents a useful tool for beginning social workers, counsellors, psychologists, and other helping professionals because it provides a simple and accessible approach to understanding relatively concrete steps needed to help clients improve physical, psychological, and emotional well-being.

Indeed, it is true that much of the human potential movement largely ignored structural poverty, oppression, and the fact that people from culturally distinct non-Western societies do not value individualism to the same degree as Euro-Western societies. In addition, the hierarchical model also privileges middle- and upper-middle-class Euro-Canadians and Euro-Americans over persons from minority populations who must attend to the ever-present requirements of meeting lower level needs. This is due to a combination of factors that include historic and ongoing racism, marginalization, maltreatment, and proportionately higher rates of poverty, effectively barring them from ever fully reaching self-actualization and beyond. Nevertheless, those new to the helping professions and the application of theory to practice benefit from using a model that encourages them to match client needs with services in a manner that recognizes the importance of meeting basic needs first.

PROBLEM SOLVING

In 1957, Helen Harris Perlman's textbook on casework had a formula that went something like, a *person* with a *problem* goes to a *place* and is engaged in a *process* (Perlman, 1957). Nearly all social workers educated in the late 1950s through the 1980s, which includes many social work educators still teaching today, will recall the elements of the problem-solving approach first devised, practiced, and recorded by Perlman. The idea of problem solving was actually quite radical at the time. Psychoanalytic theory and Freudian psychotherapy had permeated the social work profession. In addition, the medical model approach, which emphasized diagnosis and treatment, regarded the client as a rather passive character in the process. As a result, clients were expected to regard the therapist as holding the knowledge and answers to their problems. This left clients awaiting the illuminating interpretation of the therapist to set them free from unconscious thoughts, fears, and memories buried in early development that stood in the way of mental health. Perlman set social work on a different course, one that enlisted clients as collaborators in identifying and working toward solutions to problems in their lives. The concept of including clients as partners in the problem-solving process is now central and quite mainstream in social work practice. However, it was nonetheless radical in a profession that had become very comfortable with a medicalized and pathologizing approach to work with clients. Chapter 15, which is devoted to case management, demonstrates the degree to which problem-solving approaches in practice have influenced the social work profession.

Across North America, there are multitudes of case managers devoted to engaging clients in various updated forms or variants of problem-solving processes every day. As is the case with any approach in social work and other helping professions, questions about the effectiveness of problem solving have existed for quite some time. There are those who claim a problem-solving approach is culture bound, having been derived from white Euro-Western culture, and that it may not be appropriate or even effective for persons from certain non-Western populations (Galan, 2001; Sue, 1981). Conversely, there are those who point to many decades' worth of research that demonstrate problem solving and its variants have been quite effective with a wide variety of clients from diverse cultural and social backgrounds (Dobson, Backs-Dermott, & Dozois, 2000; Reid, 1988; Reid & Fortune, 2002). In either case, it cannot be disputed that problem solving as an approach to work with clients has had an enormous impact on social work and other professions that serve clients in need.

However, even Perlman's approach to addressing problems and the many problem-solving models that followed her original formulation do not fully capture the degree to which problem solving is an unavoidable part of being human and alive. It is not as if we are only called upon to solve problems on rare and extraordinary occasions. We all solve problems countless times every day of our lives. However, because we are able to master solving many of the problems we encounter each day, the mastered tasks that require some degree of problem-solving ability are no longer perceived as problems. In fact, they become so commonplace that we often perform many of them with little thought regarding all the steps involved.

For example, making coffee, preparing toast, warming tortillas, cutting up fruit, heating beans, chopping chiles, making pancakes, or getting a bowl of cereal with milk all seem like mundane tasks related to making a breakfast. However, when breakfast needs to be prepared, each element of the meal represents a component of problem solving. The same can be said for driving an automobile. Those who have learned to drive a car can remember how difficult it was in the beginning to coordinate all the tasks and functions involved. Yet, as one becomes familiar with driving, the complexity of those tasks are mastered to such a degree that many of them are done without the driver being consciously aware. This does not diminish the fact that driving a car represents a series of decisions and actions that constitute problem solving as it relates to getting from one place to another. Likewise, those who use public transportation may initially feel anxious about getting on the correct bus or train, and becoming familiar with schedules, regular stops, and so forth. However, once mastered, using a bus or train system becomes comfortable, presenting few challenges, creating minimal stress, and evoking very little anxiety. Again, the point here is that every day we as humans engage in problem solving as a means of making it through life.

Anyone who has experienced a loss of ability to easily perform the tasks commonly called *activities of daily living* can tell you that learning or relearning how to make it through each day is filled with problem solving in relation to tasks that need to be mastered. Problem solving only becomes a "problem" when demands exceed the capacity of an individual to address a particular situation or effectively complete a task. When this occurs, the problem encountered is perceived as a threatening and stress-producing event (Cormier, Nurius, & Osborn, 2009). By recognizing that mastering the tasks of life is an ongoing process, clients can be helped to see that they already possess different problem-solving skills. Therefore, asking for or needing help with a problem is less a case of failure than it is of exceeding existing capacities required to deal with a particular challenge encountered in life.

Effective versus Ineffective Problem Solving

In social work, counselling, and other related helping professions, problem-solving is a common term used to describe the process a client is engaged with a professional. However, it is worthwhile to note that problem solving is often done without seeking professional help at all. For all of us, client and professional service provider alike, problem-solving occurs along a continuum from very ineffective and even potentially harmful (life damaging) to very effective in a manner that promotes physical or mental well-being, facilitating future skill development (life enhancing). Helping clients distinguish between healthy/effective and unhealthy/potentially harmful problem-solving strategies is an important component of professional practice for social workers and other helpers. For example, a client who is experiencing depression that exceeds coping capacity may choose to seek the help of professional social workers, psychiatrists, counsellors, and/or specific healers or helpers who have been trained in and sanctioned by recognized communities of culture. Conversely, this same client may also choose to deal with depression by consuming alcohol or using addictive pain medication. Although both approaches constitute problem-solving strategies and actions, the latter may have dire health, social, and even legal consequences. Moreover, the consequences of life-damaging problem-solving strategies and actions is that others within the client's social network will likely experience fallout from choices that are not life enhancing. The task of social workers and others who engage clients in problem-solving processes is to present and discuss potential outcomes for actions taken in the course of trying to resolve problems encountered in life. This means discussing positive and negative individual and family/social network effects that could result from each course of action.

Figure 6.4   Effective versus Ineffective Problem Solving

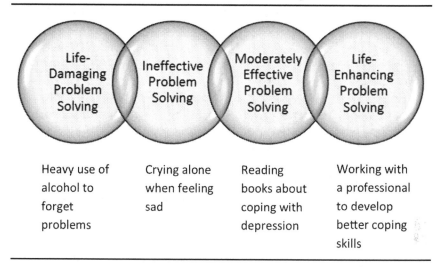

Life-Damaging Problem Solving	Ineffective Problem Solving	Moderately Effective Problem Solving	Life-Enhancing Problem Solving
Heavy use of alcohol to forget problems	Crying alone when feeling sad	Reading books about coping with depression	Working with a professional to develop better coping skills

Problem Solving through an Anti-oppressive Lens

In the previous chapter, the *individualized worldview* was presented as a way to understand the manner in which multiple individual, familial, cultural, social, macrosocietal, and environmental factors shape the way in which people view themselves and the world around them. Therefore, while it is important to understand innate abilities clients may or may not have regarding their capacity to cope with challenges in life, it is also important to be aware of the larger environmental context within which problem solving occurs.

Different people have different strengths and challenges in relation to coping with problems encountered in life. The size and adequacy of formal and informal support networks will vary by context and over time, in some cases quite dramatically. Some clients possess problem-solving skills that have been developed in very different societies, geographic locations, or cultures. Therefore, approaches to problem solving that may have worked well in particular environmental, social, or cultural contexts are perhaps not as well suited to the new or emerging social and physical environmental realities within which clients now live. In North America, this is especially true for migrants coming to large urban centres from remote rural locations, persons who are from culturally distinct nonmajority populations who now find themselves within majority culture contexts, and immigrants who arrive in Canada or the United States from a wide variety of countries around the world. The problem of fit between capacities and contexts can go the other way as well. Although less common, migrants from urban to rural settings or from mid-latitudes to remote northern regions will need to develop problem-solving skills to fit their new environments.

Finally, for all people facing challenges in life, the buffer that is afforded by access to money and other private informal or formal types of support can mean the difference between inconvenience, problem, or even crisis. So, when helping professionals assess the problem-solving skills possessed by clients, it cannot be forgotten that income, available social supports, the physical environment, racism, oppression, innate abilities, and even opportunities afforded by more privileged social location will all impact where people start in the process of trying to cope with stressors presented in life.

CRISIS INTERVENTION AND COUNSELLING

What Is a Crisis?

In *The Social Work Dictionary*, a *crisis* is defined as either an "internal experience of emotional change and distress" or as a social phenomenon "in which a disastrous event disrupts some essential functions of existing social institutions" (Barker, 2003, p. 103). James and Gilliland (2013) describe a *crisis* as "something that arises from a traumatic event that is unpredictable and uncontrollable" (p. 7). Kanel (2012) presents *crises* as being those events, conditions, times, or situations in life that

1. involve subjective distress related to a traumatic or hazardous event;
2. are common and occur at transitional points in development across the life course;
3. are situational involving deaths, accidents, assaults, and unexpected traumatic events; and
4. result from a failure of typical coping mechanisms. (pp. 9–12)

All crises have precipitating events. In other words, something occurs that brings the mismatch between available resources and coping capacities to the forefront. The example of the two family crises presented later demonstrates the degree to which social supports and existing coping skills within individuals and family systems can ameliorate or exacerbate a potential crisis situation. Clearly the Mexican American extended family was more capable of rallying resources because they had more resources available within the extended family network. Moreover, their familiarity with their community, local culture, and health care system reduced the amount of stress that could have occurred had that knowledge been lacking. As a result, the hospitalization of a family member was distressing, but not beyond the capacity of the problem-solving skills possessed by the family system. Conversely, the woman from Pakistan was linguistically, culturally, and socially isolated, which created an immediate crisis requiring more social work involvement in the development of a culturally appropriate and relevant way to help the family system increase its capacity to resolve the current crises and more effectively manage potential crises in the future.

The event that triggers a crisis can be of a medical, psychological, emotional, environmental, interpersonal, or even spiritual nature. Although some may see any contact between clients and social workers or other helping professionals as the result of a crisis, practitioners who have regular daily contact with clients tend to think of crises as being situations or events that require immediate attention to avoid or mitigate potential harm. Crises can come in many forms and have varying levels of intensity. There are crises involving subjective distress that do not pose an imminent threat to life but are nonetheless very unsettling for those who experience them. Other crises, such as medical emergencies, car accidents, physical abuse, sexual victimization, and natural or human-created disasters, can range from life disrupting to life threatening. Symptoms of major mental illness that occur with clients who have diagnosed conditions such as schizophrenia or bipolar disorder also represent crisis situations, especially when they lead to psychiatric emergencies as is the case with rapid and acute onset (Knox & Roberts, 2008). In addition, crises can begin with one person or in one location, and then develop into events that impact other individuals, families, and even communities. James and Gilliland (2013, p. 9) refer to this as the process of "metastasizing" in that much like a cancer, a crisis has the potential to impact and in essence infect other persons and systems. In Canada and the United States, we have all seen cases of crises such as suicide in rural communities that appear to spread and claim new victims, becoming community-wide crises versus isolated events. In addition, the well-publicized cases of victimization that spread to cyberbullying, which eventually culminated in suicide on the part of victims, demonstrates the growing link between technology and the metastasizing effect of crises events. Clearly, crises, the impact of crises, and the varying responses to them have the potential of spreading far beyond the person(s) and precipitating events initially involved.

Intervention

During the evaluation of potential danger in crisis assessment, the social worker or helping professional will often be brought into contact with others such as police officers, firefighters, psychiatrists, child welfare workers, and in many cases, the members of a client's family who may themselves be in crisis. Threats to safety in a client's environment may be present in the form of natural or human-created disasters as well as from other persons. Child abuse, elder abuse, domestic violence perpetrated by intimate partners, and many sorts of harmful or even lethal threats presented by others are common examples of imminent danger. Likewise, impending flood, approaching storms, chemical explosions or spills, and the aftermath of these events represent danger and themselves can trigger other crises in those who are already medically or psychologically vulnerable. For example, a child who has already experienced evacuation due to flooding may have post-traumatic stress related to the event that is triggered by warnings of another impending flood. In the case of this young individual, the physical environment presents a threat that could become a crisis, while her/his response to that threat has/may have already resulted in a state of subjective distress or even panic.

Actions on the part of clients regarding suicide pose additional dangers. Assessment of lethality regarding potential suicide requires quick action but cannot ignore the importance of environmental supports and stress factors, medical conditions and medications to which the individual has access, drug and alcohol use, and of course, demonstrated coping ability on the part of the client (Eaton & Ertl, 2000). Actual suicide attempts involving drugs, firearms, knives, or other lethal means are current crises that warrant immediate action, and if the person attempting suicide lives, the fact that an attempt has been made places that person at greater risk for future attempts (Borges et al., 2010).

Because a crisis situation requires rapid assessment, it is important for the social worker, crisis counsellor, or other professional helper to be certain that she or he is attending to those functions that will increase the likelihood of achieving more favourable outcomes. Roberts (1991, 2000, 2005) conceptualizes the process of crisis intervention as consisting of seven stages that begin when encountering a client who is experiencing a crisis. According to Roberts, these stages have a specific sequence, sometimes overlap with one another, and are essential to the process of effective crisis intervention. The social worker or other professional intervening in the crisis works quickly toward stabilization of the situation. This is followed by crisis resolution, and finally, skill acquisition through which clients develop mastery. As Roberts (1991) shows, these stages are as follows:

1. Plan and conduct a thorough biopsychosocial and lethality/imminent danger assessment.
2. Make psychological contact and rapidly establish the collaborative relationship.
3. Identify the major problems, including crisis precipitants.
4. Encourage an exploration of feelings and emotions.
5. Generate and explore alternatives and new coping strategies.
6. Restore functioning through implementation of an action plan.
7. Plan a follow-up and booster sessions. (adapted, pp. 3–17)

Examples of Crisis Events within Two Different Families

The first family in this example is that of a geographically and emotionally close Mexican American extended family in the US Southwest. On an early afternoon day in October, the mother of three children (ages six, eight, and ten) was rushed to the hospital with acute appendicitis. When the father of the three children was contacted at his workplace, he called his sister who went to the school to meet the children. When the children were brought to the principal's office their *tía* (aunt) was there to let them know that their mother was fine, she had an emergency operation, and they were told that they could speak with her by phone shortly. They were also told they could see her at the hospital after dinner. The children were taken to the aunt's house to eat and then went with their father, aunt, uncle, and one grandmother to the hospital early that evening.

The capacity of the extended family system to manage the crisis was clear. The children, although initially upset, were surrounded by familiar and trusted family members. The hospital social worker was able to meet with several extended family members to make sure that the mother who had been hospitalized would have necessary assistance at home during her recovery. Therefore, a life event that could have been extremely traumatic, especially for young children, instead demonstrated the capacity of a family system to marshal resources, protect vulnerable members, and effectively take action. In an assessment and discharge plan for the hospitalized woman, the social worker noted the well-developed problem-solving skills of all family members and the reduction in stress experienced by the client and her children as a result of an extended, well-functioning, and supportive social support network. Of course, not all situations so easily present such richness of support, cooperation, or ability to take quick action. This is why it is so important for social workers to thoroughly assess social support networks to locate strengths, challenges, and entry points for the provision of concrete tangible assistance (cash and in-kind services) and emotional supports (family and friendship networks as well as access to supportive counselling) that can be called upon in times of need.

In another example of crisis, a small family from Pakistan, consisting of a married couple (male and female) and their two-year-old son, were living in an apartment in the US Midwest, while the father of the family completed a university engineering degree. The three of them were housed in a family complex on campus. In the first semester at the university, the father of the family was becoming increasingly angry about American racism toward Muslims and made a personal vow to keep his wife and son isolated from the influences of the host culture as much as possible. As a result, the family seldom left their apartment except to go grocery shopping and on rare occasion to attend a mosque about ten miles (seventeen kilometres) away. Contact with family in Pakistan was done by phone. However, little information regarding difficulties experienced in adjusting to North American culture was shared with them.

In March of the second semester of his educational program, the father of this small family was hospitalized with what had been described as a mild heart attack. When his wife was contacted at home, she became panic stricken. She spoke Urdu and very little English, she could not drive a car, she did not know how to navigate the local bus system, and she did not know her way to the hospital where her husband had been taken. After she had frantically knocked on several doors in her complex, she found a woman from Bangladesh at home. The woman spoke English and a form of Urdu found in parts of Bangladesh. Once the Pakistani woman was calmed enough to speak, she was able to say what she thought had happened. She was in an extremely emotional and fearful state because she believed that her husband would soon be dead. The woman from Bangladesh contacted the hospital where the Pakistani woman's husband had been taken. She was referred to the social work unit and was finally able to get basic information about the woman's husband. With the social worker's help, the wife of the man who had been hospitalized was able to speak briefly with him via mobile telephone, which helped to reduce her level of anxiety.

Once the husband of the woman from Bangladesh arrived home, she went to the hospital with the woman from Pakistan. Acting as an interpreter, she assisted the social worker in the completion of an initial assessment that demonstrated a great deal of isolation. Because this small family had very few contacts in the community, the mild heart attack became a major stress-inducing crisis. The social worker involved in the case needed to deal with the immediate health crisis and aftercare needs of the client. However, the need to work with both the husband and wife, regarding the development of a network of supports, had to be done in a manner that fit with the culture of the family and addressed racism and concomitant feelings of anger on the part of the husband. In this case, the social worker made an effort to involve the family with others in the mosque they had been attending. This, combined with the willingness of the nearby Bangladeshi couple to act as cultural guides in the new land, served to reduce tension and give the father of this small family some sense of relief. After the initial visit with the social worker at the hospital, a connection with a social worker was made through the mosque. Slowly, the family began to build a network of friends that helped them reduce feelings of isolation, anger, and stress.

Suicide as a Public Health Concern

Although the history of suicide as a public health concern in North America dates back to the late 1950s and early 1960s, it was not until the latter half of the twentieth century that suicide became a more central public health concern. In 1987, the National Task Force on Suicide in Canada produced a comprehensive report on the problem of suicide. The report included nine recommendations regarding what needed to be done in terms of advancing a suicide research agenda. However, by 1995, only some of the recommendations had resulted in action (Tanney, 1995). More recent suicide prevention research and efforts in Canada include recognition of social and economic factors in suicide that contribute to higher rates of suicide completion among certain populations.

In the mid-1990s, the US Surgeon General formed the Call to Action to Prevent Suicide group of public and private agencies. This group included departments within the US Department of Health and Human Services (U.S. DHHS) and grassroots organizations made up of those who had survived the loss of a loved one to suicide, attempters of suicide, community activists, and health and mental health clinicians (U.S. DHHS, 1999). During 1998, through suicide mobilization, the group became energized in their attempts to impact public policy. Utilizing 1996 guidelines developed by the United Nations, this group created a set of recommendations that could form the basis of a national strategy on suicide prevention. In October 1998, The Surgeon General's Call to Action to Prevent Suicide, held a national conference in Reno, Nevada, to engage in an analysis about what was known and the potential response to suicide (U.S. DHHS, 1999). Key points developed at this conference were as follows:

1. Suicide prevention must recognize and affirm the value, dignity, and importance of each person.
2. Suicide is not solely the result of illness or inner conditions. The feelings of hopelessness that contribute to suicide can stem from societal conditions and attitudes. Therefore, everyone concerned with suicide prevention shares a responsibility to help change attitudes and eliminate the conditions of oppression, racism, homophobia, discrimination, and prejudice.
3. Some groups are disproportionately affected by these societal conditions, and some are at greater risk for suicide.
4. Individuals, communities, organizations, and leaders at all levels should collaborate to promote suicide prevention.
5. The success of this strategy ultimately rests with individuals and communities across the United States.

The results of their efforts were broad recommendations regarding suicide intervention and prevention that went well beyond the individual to identify the role society plays in suicide. In July 28, 1999, key recommendations of this group were presented in the comprehensive National Strategy for Suicide Prevention, October 1999 Report (U.S. DHHS, 1999).

Suicide represents a particular type of problem solving, but as is the case with problem solving in general, clients who may be or become suicidal will have different levels of problem-solving capacity, resources, protective factors, and risks in relation to coping with those events that contribute to or exacerbate situations in which suicide is contemplated, attempted, or completed. For social workers and others involved in assessing and intervening in potentially lethal situations regarding suicide, it is important to know the warning signs of suicide and the risk or resiliency factors in the lives of those who are at risk for attempting or completing a suicide. Adapted from Rudd, Joiner, and Rajab (2001), Dahlberg and Krug (2002), and the Mayo Clinic (2012), figure 6.5 addresses the risk factors in assessment for suicide and any questions or concerns.

Figure 6.5   Risk Factors in Assessment for Suicide

RISK FACTORS IN ASSESSMENT FOR SUICIDE

•QUESTIONS AND/OR CONCERNS

Suicidal History

- Is there a history of suicide attempts?
- What was attempted?
- When did it occur?
- Was psychotherapeutic treatment sought?

Stressors or Precipitating Events

- Are there financial issues?
- Has there been a job loss?
- Has the client experienced a marked change in economic stability?
- Do serious relationship problems exist?
- Have there been losses through death?
- Has the client become estranged from family members and/or friends?
- Has there been a life threatening or life changing medical diagnosis?

Symptoms

- Does the client report feeling depressed in combination with low self-esteem?
- Is drug or alcohol use or abuse a factor?

Hopelessness

- Look for evidence of hopelessness found in comments such as, there is nothing to live for; I would be better off dead; no one would miss me; or I don't see things ever getting better.

Suicidal Thinking and Behaviour

- Is the client currently thinking about suicide?
- Is there a history of thinking about suicide?
- Has the client developed a plan to carry out her or his suicide?
- How long has the client been thinking about suicide?
- Does the client have access to guns, knives, etc., that are part of her or his plan?
- Has the client actually rehearsed a plan either by thinking it through or by gathering the necessary means to carry through with a suicide?
- Has the client committed self-injurious acts that have the potential for being lethal?

Warning Signs

- Active suicidal ideation; profound sense of hopelessness; reckless behaviour, such as driving dangerously, overdosing on drugs, consuming dangerous amounts of alcohol; expressing feelings of being trapped with no alternatives but ending life; anger, anxiety, or agitation; giving away valued or prized possessions; contacting people to say goodbye.

Individual and Familial Protective Factors

- Having a family, children, others who are emotionally close and supportive; being able to recognize reasons to live (a sense of hope); supportive relationships with social workers, physicians, psychiatrists; strong spiritual or religious commitment; moral objection to killing oneself.

Community and Social Protective/Risk Factors

- Is there access to quality psychiatric and outpatient psychosocial support?
- Is the community welcoming and supportive of those with mental health issues that might lead to suicide?
- Is there a local, regional, and national recognition of the importance of suicide prevention?
- Are potential social, cultural, economic, and environmental factors being addressed at multiple levels within the clients' community, province, state, First Nation, or by the federal government?

It is important to remember that the very nature of social work means practitioners will come into contact with clients who have a potential for suicide. The same is true for other helping professionals who work with individuals experiencing problems related to mental illness, substance abuse, income insufficiency, domestic violence, racism and oppression, homophobia, multiple forms of marginalization, and scores of other issues that bring people in need into contact with professional helpers. The person-centered skills necessary for engaging clients are critical in cases of potential suicide. Developing rapport with clients is facilitated by helping professionals who work to communicate genuineness, respect, and acceptance (Roberts, 2005). Social workers, psychologists, counsellors, and psychiatrists should all be aware that suicide is a potential concern in many settings such as schools, child welfare agencies, mental health clinics, psychiatric treatment centres, and even correctional facilities, to name but a few. Nevertheless, the body of existing research on suicide is missing a key insight that unfortunately can only be provided by those who are no longer with us due to having completed suicide. Therefore, the information about warning signs, intervention, and prevention needs to be considered in light of the fact that there is much we do not know and much that needs to be learned.

CONCLUSION

Within the helping and healing traditions of many cultures worldwide, the importance of a positive link between helpers and clients has long been recognized. *Curanderas/os*, North American Indigenous healers and helpers, and even spiritual practitioners are aware that client trust in the healer and the process will lead to more favourable outcomes. In the contemporary North American context of professional working relationships between mental health practitioners and clients, the concept of the therapeutic alliance can be traced to the early psychodynamic theorists (Horvath, 2015). Since that time, there have been numerous studies designed to measure the importance of this relational element in the healing process for persons with a variety of issues related to mental health and overall well-being. While there are some studies that indicate the importance of a therapeutic alliance may be limited, many others demonstrate a clear link between the quality of the client-professional helper relationship and positive treatment outcomes (Krupnick et al., 2014). Therefore, training for those in social work, clinical psychology, counselling, marriage and family therapy, and related disciplines needs to include an emphasis on the acquisition of those skills that facilitate the development of a therapeutic or working alliance with clients (Ellis, 2015). Many social work programs offer at least one specific course in the engagement process. However, the critical nature of that bond between professional practitioner and client means that the concept of developing a therapeutic/working alliance should be a component of all practice-focused courses due to the influence of this critical aspect of the client-worker relationship on treatment outcomes.

Along with the development of critical skills for engaging clients, those in social work and other helping professions must keep in mind the importance of understanding client problems, issues, and concerns within the context of an assessment that examines strengths and challenges in relation to problem-solving capacities. Humanistic theory provides a framework for professional helping relationships that focus on client capacities for change versus an emphasis on deficits. While Rogers and Maslow, who are featured in this chapter, have been criticized by many postmodern theorists for not attending to structural aspects of the problems clients face, both of these mid-twentieth-century theorists emphasized the importance of client strengths and positive human potential. Rogers in particular spoke of the need for professional helpers to be engaged in the client-worker relationship with a genuine care for those seeking help—a concept that is directly linked to the importance of the therapeutic alliance.

Problem solving and crisis intervention as presented in this chapter have highlighted the link between cultural, social, economic, and other macro-societal variables in relation to difficulties faced by individuals and families. The use of an anti-oppressive/social justice lens in understanding individual problem-solving capacities reminds all of us that people have varying degrees of economic, social, cultural, and internal resources when it comes to facing challenges presented during the life course. Finally, although this chapter has included some information on suicide assessment and prevention, it is an ethical obligation within social work, as it is in other helping professions, that we as professionals continue to build competence in relation to knowledge and skill. Therefore, the information on suicide provided in this chapter should serve as an inspiration to seek additional knowledge and foster skill development in relation to work with those in our many culturally diverse societies of North America who are at risk for suicide.

Chapter Seven

Research and Evidence-Informed Practice in Social Work

INTRODUCTION

Although some social work students may go on to be researchers, the vast majority of those who seek a social work degree in North America plan to work directly with clients. While direct practice settings seldom require those who work with clients to engage in research, it is still important that social workers are sufficiently knowledgeable about research to be informed consumers of research findings. This chapter utilizes plain language to explain the importance of research and research findings. The intention is to guide readers through a discussion of research in a manner that demonstrates how they, as developing practitioners, can and will use evidence from research to guide their work with clients in their practicum placement settings and in their future careers as social workers.

In our roles as students, practitioners, researchers, and as those who utilize or critique research, we need to be aware that randomized controlled trials (RCTs) give us only a limited view of the world. As Albert Einstein once said, "We know nothing at all. All our knowledge is but the knowledge of school-children. The real nature of things we shall never know." With this in mind, it should be remembered that RCTs can quantify the "known" world and make some of what is unknown "knowable." However, RCTs cannot be the only tool for seeking knowledge of how the world works. Dismissal of qualitative methods, practice wisdom, and good old-fashioned trial and error, results in narrowing the pool of acceptable tools for examining and understanding the world around us. The challenge for those in social work, psychology, and the social sciences is not to think only in terms of studies that fit the pure RCT experimental model. Rather, we should be increasing our efforts to design new measures that capture the effectiveness of many forms of seeing, knowing, being, and helping. After all, no one would ask a builder to construct an entire house using only one tool. We need to expand our toolboxes to properly construct and measure the ways in which we help others. By listening to the voices of Indigenous Peoples, those from non-Euro-Western traditions, feminists, or practitioners with long careers of successful engagements with clients, we in social work can begin to break out of our endless obsession to fit a pure scientific experimental model as proof that we are worthy. This does not mean that we entirely abandon the use of RCTs and other positivist forms of inquiry. It only means that we need to be aware of the limitations of quantitative research as it currently exists. Included with this is a recognition that when it comes to engaging with clients, many approaches employed by social workers, psychologists, psychiatrists, counsellors, and other helpers have yet to be studied in terms of effectiveness, regardless of the method employed.

A Word about Evidence-Based Practice in Social Work

Although over time there has been some attention given by those in the helping professions to the study of larger systems such as communities, the vast majority of research related to work with client systems has been focused on evidence-based practice with individuals. In North America academic research related to mental health concerns and social problems continues to be concentrated at the micro level. The current biomedical model of research activities in North America has a strong bias toward interventions aimed at changing individuals, not addressing larger social structures that create environments within which social or behavioural concerns are embedded (McGibbon & Hallstrom, 2012). Social research examining the impact of racism, environmental degradation, unrelenting poverty, or any of a number of macro-societal or macro-environmental variables impacting individual well-being, although valued, does not have the same status or receive the same attention from researchers as projects focused on the pathology of individuals. Even in social work, the profession known for reaching out to families and communities more than any of the helping professions, attention on intrapsychically oriented work with individuals occupies a higher status. This bias exists in conference workshops, continuing education opportunities, and even the definition of evidence-based practice that is found in *The Social Work Dictionary*, which states the following:

> The use of the best available scientific knowledge derived from randomized controlled outcome studies, and meta-analyses of existing outcome studies, as one basis for guiding professional interventions and effective therapies, combined with professional ethical standards, clinical judgments, and practice wisdom. (Barker, 2003, p. 149)

Indeed, most social workers think of research related to evidence-based practice in micro-level (individual) terms with an emphasis on effective therapies, ignoring other important elements of practice, such as case management and client advocacy, let alone intervention with larger systems or advocacy on behalf of entire populations. This does not make such activities less important; it instead highlights the continued bias toward approaches to intervention that are more amenable to randomized controlled studies versus more complex aspects of practice that include multiple and confounding variables in the real world. This push toward evidence-based practice also forces social work into a more medicalized service delivery paradigm that gives little consideration to the artful and creative aspects of practice that are very important, but difficult, to measure.

So while evidence-based practice in social work is indeed important, it must be remembered that those more easily manualized and heavily researched approaches to practice constitute only one aspect of a very broad field among the helping professions. Therefore, while it is crucial that social workers develop knowledge and skill related to research-based clinical practice, it is also equally important to examine the contribution to knowledge made by practice approaches that have yet to be subjected to extensive empirical validation. In fact, as a profession, we as social workers should be demanding that more work be done to find the appropriate tools for evaluating social work effectiveness with systems of various sizes instead of relying on the narrow and often less applicable findings of efficacy studies. Through building competence in relation to all levels of social work, micro to macro, and by seeking to understand the value of multicultural and Indigenous ways of knowing and healing, we as social workers will enrich and expand our knowledge and skill as practitioners.

TERMINOLOGY RELATED TO RESEARCH METHODOLOGY IN SOCIAL WORK

Before proceeding with a discussion of evidence-based practice and research in social work, it is important to clarify some key terms social work students and practicing social workers encounter in textbooks, articles, lectures, and even workshops. Terms used in social work can often be misused by those who do not have a clear understanding of differences in meaning.

Perspective

A *perspective* is neither a theory nor an evidence-based approach to practice, but instead an outlook that serves to shape the way in in which certain problems, conditions, issues, or populations are viewed (Hutchinson & Charlesworth, 2013). Examples of perspectives that are common in social work are the *strengths perspective* and the *people-first perspective*. The adoption of a *strengths perspective* in social work involves identifying the strengths found in individuals, families, groups, and communities; however, it also includes an acknowledgment of the ability of client systems to endure and overcome difficult events or circumstances, even in situations where problem solving may have resulted in only partial success. Social workers who adopt a strengths perspective will approach assessment with attention to tangible and intangible resources for positive problem solving that can be found in client systems (Saleebey, 2002, pp. 14–16). For example, a social worker assessing strengths in a very low-income US-Mexico border community might emphasize the fact that community members have developed many informal and semiformal networks of mutual support that people can depend on in personal or community-wide problematic or crisis situations. Another example would be that of a recently unemployed client in need of assistance who, with the help of social worker, is able to recognize the importance of all the long hours she has worked for years, just to ensure that her children are given time to study and do well in school.

People-first language is a manifestation of the *people-first perspective* which focuses on the person and makes any condition secondary. Person-first language is now quite common in social work and is used when referring to clients with mental illness, physical disability, medical conditions, and so forth. For example, a social worker using the person-first perspective in referring to clients would say something like "She is a person with schizophrenia" versus the more antiquated approach in which someone might say "She is schizophrenic."

Model

The Social Work Dictionary describes a *model* as a "representation of reality" (Barker, 2003, p. 276). Models are not theories, but can represent concepts based in theories. For example, the *individualized worldview model* used in this book is based on sociological, social structural, ecological systems, cultural ecological, critical race, political, feminist, and other theories commonly taught in social work and other helping professions. Therefore, the individualized worldview becomes a theory-based visual representation of many factors that are important to consider in understanding the unique life circumstances of clients.

Theory

Theory should not be confused with fact or truth. In a discussion of epistemology and knowledge, theories can perhaps be best understood as originating in the realm of belief for which verification is sought through many forms of observation and testing. There are many theories that exist in relation to psychosocial development, human behaviour, personality development, mental health problems, and the effectiveness of various forms of psychotherapeutic treatment. With theory, it is important to remember that theoretical orientations will shape the manner in which social work practitioners understand client systems and client issues. For example, if a social worker believes that the problems of individuals are generally intrapsychic in nature, she or he will approach intervention quite differently from another social worker who views human behaviour as a response to external environmental conditions. In either case, theory based in beliefs about human behaviour will impact what the social worker understands as appropriate intervention and desirable treatment outcomes. In chapters 8 through 13, the role of theory in shaping practice will be discussed at greater length.

Hypothesis

A *hypothesis* starts as a desire to see if an expectation or assumption about an outcome is valid. A hypothesis is more specific and limited than a theory, and usually involves something such as testing the effectiveness of a medication, a psychotherapeutic intervention, a physical activity, and so forth. "Hypotheses (predictions) are the testable assumptions about the research group (population) that you expect will be confirmed by your research" (Verhoeven, 2011, p. 91). When many hypotheses having a specific theoretical foundation are appropriately tested, the outcome of each research project related to a particular theory may then be said to either support or not support the theory in question.

Figure 7.1   Theory and Hypothesis

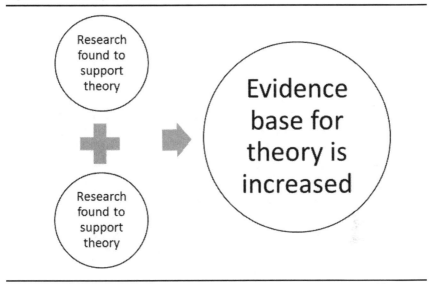

For example, someone may want to study the impact of eating oranges on weight control. If a researcher suspects that a specific manner and amount of orange consumption will result in weight loss, that suspicion can form the basis of a hypothesis. If that is then followed with random controlled testing of individuals who eat oranges being compared with those who do not, the outcome will either demonstrate no connection between orange consumption and weight loss, or that oranges consumed in particular forms and amounts do appear to contribute to weight loss. Research into weight loss, or anything else for that matter, is much more complex than this simple example suggests. However, the point is that to properly test any hypothesis, the research question and the methodology must be repeatable—meaning that other researchers could replicate the process—and falsifiable—meaning that the findings, if not actually accurate, can be found to be false.

Ontology

Ontology is "the study of being, existence, or reality" (Baines, 2011, p. 14). Ontology has to do with our assumptions about the world. Ontology involves ideas, beliefs, and theories about the nature of things in the world and the way our thinking about the world is organized. First developed by Swedish botanist Carl Linnaeus in the 1700s, the grouping of living things found in the well-known biological taxonomy is a good example of ontology from the perspective of the natural sciences (Paterlini, 2007). Linnaeus organized living things into major *Kingdoms*, such as the plant kingdom or the animal kingdom, and from that point, through a series of branching divisions ending in species. For example, humans are part of the *Animal Kingdom*; the *Phylum* of Chordata (having backbones); the *Class* of mammals; the *Order* of primates; the *Family* of Hominidae (which includes all great apes); the *Genus* of Homo, which includes modern humans and closely related ancestors; followed by the *Species* of Sapiens, from which the scientific name homo sapiens is derived.

The work of Linnaeus has impacted science to the present day. His approach to developing a taxonomy that organizes life forms remains relevant as a tool for naming new species of plants and animals. As a result of widespread adoption of Linnaeus's biological taxonomy, most people accept his original idea as truth—a truth that has, in turn, influenced what many understand as knowledge versus belief.

Another example of ontological thinking can be found in Bloom's taxonomy of learning domains. In 1956, Benjamin Bloom was instrumental in the

Figure 7.2   Biological Taxonomy

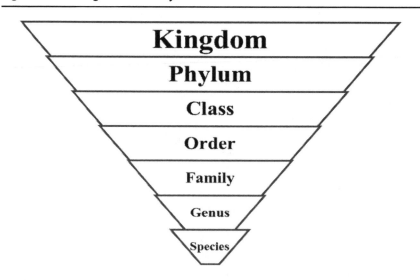

development of a taxonomy related to learning that was intended to promote critical and advanced thinking in education (Anderson et al., 2000). In accordance with Bloom's taxonomy, thinking is divided into the following levels, each requiring a higher degree of complexity in the thinking process. An example of *knowledge* acquisition in relation to Bloom's taxonomy would be reflected by a person's ability to identify behaviourism as a theory. A person who can distinguish between behavioural and psychodynamic theories is demonstrating *comprehension*. Someone who is able to show how behavioural concepts are applied in work with clients is engaging in *application* of theoretical concepts. If a person can then accurately break down behavioural theoretical concepts into component parts, she or he is demonstrating skill in *analysis*. If after all of this, a person working with behavioural concepts is then able to construct a behaviourally based approach to intervention by organizing behavioural theoretical concepts into a workable model, she or he is demonstrating capacity for the *synthesis* of what has been learned. Finally, if the person who has created a model for behaviourally based intervention is now able to devise an approach to testing the effectiveness of various techniques, she or he is demonstrating the ability to engage in the *evaluation* of her or his work.

Figure 7.3   Bloom's Taxonomy of Learning Domains

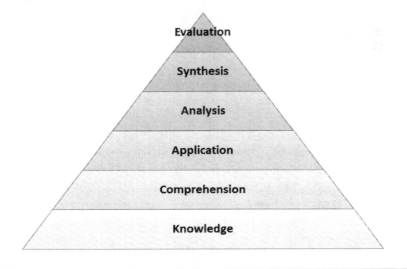

Taxonomies are used in all cultures as a way of organizing, classifying, and naming things. Those taxonomies derived from Euro-Western thought in areas such as economics, biology, physics, business, and psychology have come to dominate our collective understanding of what is knowledge based on truth. However, among Indigenous populations worldwide, folk taxonomies have been devised that include rich and complex categorizations of many components of the environment within which they have developed. For example, the Indigenous Peoples of central Mexico, for whom agriculture was very important, had as many as fifty different soil classifications before the arrival of Europeans in North America (Krasilnikov & Tabor, 2003). The point here is not to pit Euro-Western ontologies against Indigenous ontologies, but instead to remind us all that truth and the world as we understand it can be different for different peoples. Truth and the knowledge that flows from it can be shifting, contextual, have areas of overlap with the truth and knowledge of others, and in many ways is socially constructed.

Epistemology

The Social Work Dictionary defines *epistemology* in two ways. First, epistemology is defined as "the study of the nature, methods, and limits of knowledge" and second, quite simply as "how we know what we know" (Barker, 2003, p. 145). Epistemology, as a branch of philosophy, is primarily concerned with distinguishing between knowledge that represents truth and knowledge that is belief, which may or may not be true. Therefore, belief and truth overlap, with true knowledge found somewhere in the middle. When we say we seek the truth, it may turn out to be more elusive and variable than we had initially thought. To illustrate this point, consider this: something such as a heart attack is an irrefutable and potentially fatal event, but beliefs about underlying causes shift with cultural contexts and change over time. Some societies may attribute the heart attack to diet, others may blame stress. Some may see an imbalance between the physical body, the mind, and the spirit as the root cause of heart failure. So, finding what is believed to be the cause and what may need to be done to facilitate a cure will be based on differential understanding of the knowledge that occurs where truth and belief intersect. Our conceptualizations of existence, human nature, networks, hierarchies, law, morality, and many more aspects of life are influenced by our views of how the world is organized, and the knowledge we derive from those understandings.

Figure 7.4   Epistemology and Knowledge

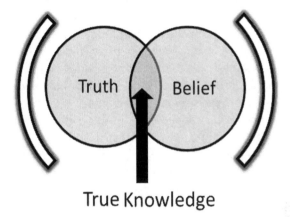

True Knowledge

Clearly, deciding on what is true can be problematic. At one point in history, ancient Europeans and others believed the earth was flat and held that assumption to be absolutely true. As a result, knowledge about ocean travel included a fear that one could actually reach the end of the earth. We now know that such "knowledge" was actually a belief that was found to be wrong many centuries ago (Bartlett, 1996). The important thing to remember is that knowledge is always subject to change. As various types of scientific and other forms of inquiry expose flaws in our beliefs about what is true, we must incorporate that new knowledge with the understanding that future inquiry may again cause a shift in beliefs about what we trust as fact-based knowledge.

Take for example the unquestioned beliefs about homosexuality held by social workers just a few decades ago. Before 1973, the *Diagnostic and Statistical Manual of Mental Disorders* (DSM) listed homosexuality as a mental illness. The vast majority of social workers believed this to be true. It was a case of belief and truth coming together to generate knowledge. Yet, during 1973 to 1986, all DSM references to homosexuality as a mental illness were removed (Herek, 2012). Same-sex relationships are now widely understood as very normal in regard to physical attraction, sexual behaviour, and human bonding. What is it that created this change? First, it must be understood that widespread homophobia in North American society influenced belief, which in turn biased research about same-sex relationships. This impacted what came to be understood as truth. Because accepted truth and widespread belief overlapped to a great extent, knowledge that was generated by flawed research became undisputed fact. However, those individuals with same-sex sexual attractions did not accept the socially constructed "truth" regarding sexual orientation and pathology. Years of fighting for social justice have resulted in the current state of affairs in which same-sex relationships and same-sex sexual attraction are being increasingly accepted as well within the "normal" range of sexual and affectional behaviour in societies across the globe.

Another formerly unquestioned issue, erectile dysfunction (ED) in men, was for generations believed by many clinical social workers to be the result of unconscious issues that needed to be uncovered, interpreted, and resolved. Years later, it was found that decreased blood flow and arterial damage are the major causes of ED, and although psychological symptoms almost always accompany the problem, psychological therapies alone have not been proven to be effective (Buvat, 2012). Moreover, while performance anxiety may be a cause for episodes of sexual dysfunction in healthy younger men, it is now well known that diabetes, obesity, alcohol consumption, damage to erectile tissue, and medications with sexual side effects tend much more often to be the problem. Research into the issue made what was once knowledge just a faulty belief.

One final example is that of anorexia nervosa, a dangerous and potentially fatal condition in which a person refuses or constricts food intake resulting in extreme weight loss, concomitant health complications, and even death. In North America, in the 1980s and early 1990s, many therapists were involved in helping young adults and adolescents in the process of recalling repressed memories of childhood sexual abuse. At one point, some therapists and even researchers were espousing a belief that nearly all people had been sexually abused at some point in their childhood. It was at this time that anorexia nervosa became linked with sexual abuse to such a degree that many therapists believed the primary cause of the condition was childhood sexual abuse. This belief led to accusations of abuse which created an enormous amount of unnecessary grief for those already devastated by the potential loss of a loved one due to anorexia nervosa.

The *Diagnostic and Statistical Manual of Mental Disorders, Fourth Edition, Text Revision* (DSM-IV-TR) describes anorexia nervosa as a condition in which the actual cause is not known (First & Tasman, 2004, p. 1105). Anorexia nervosa is now understood as having many potential biological, psychological, social, and even hereditary risk factors. Although childhood sexual abuse may be one risk factor for the development of this condition, it is by no means the only factor and cannot be considered the only potential cause. A belief that gained widespread clinical consensus, in some circles, became truth for many and subsequently was passed off as knowledge. As inquiry into anorexia nervosa continued, the complex nature of the condition has fostered changes in belief, a new conceptualization of truth, and therefore, a shift in knowledge. So how we know what we know is clearly subject to change as inquiry into the human condition continues in combination with the shifting social construction of lived realities.

CONDUCTING RESEARCH

Social work students need to develop the skills that will make them good consumers of research findings, as students in field practicum placement settings and as practitioners upon graduation. The fact is that most graduates of social work programs across North America will be involved in direct practice with clients. Very few will be researchers, and those for whom research is a major interest and focus often go on to receive doctoral degrees. Therefore, the intention here will be to provide a synopsis of common terms and concepts that are of particular importance to social work students and practitioners.

Methodology

Methodology involves the tools and techniques different societies develop to discover facts or truths, and build knowledge. When we examine knowledge, how we learn and determine what we know, what we are able to know, and how we will go about discovering that knowledge, we utilize different approaches to arrive at the answer. The approaches we use constitute our methodologies. The most well-known and widely used methodologies are identified as part of the Euro-Western tradition in scientific inquiry. However, as has already been stated, Europeans were not alone in their desire to understand the world around them. Indigenous and non-Western societies also had, and in some cases continue to have, long traditions of inquiry about the world around them. Following European colonial expansion and the growth of Euro-Western industrialization, science, as conceived of by Euro-Western societies, became the dominant foundation for inquiry. This in turn has shaped what students learn about research and scientific methodology. Although Euro-Western thinking dominates the discourse in relation to research, students and researchers must remember that it is not the only way of thinking about or studying the many types of phenomena in the world around us.

Research is generally divided into the broad methodological categories of qualitative research and quantitative inquiry. *Qualitative research* is an approach in which the researcher immerses her- or himself in the information (the data) that results from engagement in observation, participant observation, semi-structured or structured interviews conducted with key informants, and the identification of salient features that emerge in the process. Qualitative data and data collection processes are often useful in the examination of large complex systems such as groups, communities, organizations, or institutions. However, the difficulty of qualitative research findings is that they are specific to the systems studied and are often not able to be generalized to society at large (Kreuger & Neuman, 2006). *Quantitative research* is deductive in nature and is a process in which the researcher strives to carry out studies in which rigor, precision, and objectivity are emphasized. Properly conducted quantitative research is intended to produce findings that are generalizable to a larger population (Whittlesey-Jerome, 2009, p. 204).

Researchers utilizing qualitative methods are most often concerned with developing a more complex understanding of social phenomena or cultural systems. Qualitative research is capable of producing findings that are rich in con-

Figure 7.5   Qualitative versus Quantitative Research

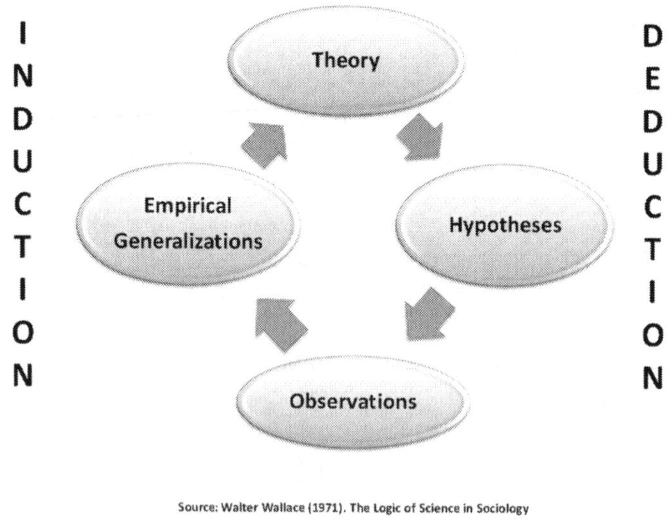

Source: Walter Wallace (1971). The Logic of Science in Sociology

textualized meaning. Methods used in qualitative research are common in cultural anthropology and are also used by other social scientists, including social workers. Cultural anthropologists are regularly confronted with situations where researchers may enter communities not knowing what information will be uncovered about beliefs, attitudes, social structures, social institutions, family constellation patterns, and so forth. The inductive approach used by anthropologists to understanding culturally different populations employs the aforementioned activities of *observation, participant observation, semistructured interviews*, and *structured interviews*. These four approaches are key components of ethnographic methodology. *Surveys* are often included as an additional and quantitative component of ethnographic methodological approaches in research.

Figure 7.6   Ethnographic Methodology

Ethnographic Methodology	Activities Engaged in by the Researcher
Observation	Observation involves looking at and recording all facets of the phenomenon, community, or activity without judgment. Observation requires a meticulous examination and documentation of everything that is seen, heard, felt, or otherwise experienced.
Participant Observation	Participant observation requires that the researcher become involved in community life (or the activities of a population being studied) as a participant, while also observing and recording what occurs.
Semi-Structured Interviews	Semi-structured interviews address broad areas of concern or interest. For example, a researcher might ask community elders to talk about the major concerns they have related to the status of seniors in their society.
Structured Interviews	Structured interviews are focused on specific research questions. In structured interviews the researcher might ask questions about specific topics such as crime, child discipline, preservation of language, and so forth.
Surveys	Surveys are generally quantitative in nature and include questions that require participants in the study to select from specific pre-set categories. Surveys are often used as a follow-up to other ethnographic methods. For example, community elders who say crime is a concern might be asked a series of questions about crime to quantify the actual level of concern within a particular area or within a specific population.

In social work, the more common ethnographic methodological approaches utilized are observation, semistructured interviews, structured interviews, and survey questionnaires. Although one could argue that social workers in certain settings are participant observers as well, very few social workers actually enter, live in, and study communities in the same manner as anthropologists. Nevertheless, there are occasions when social workers are professionals in and members of certain communities or populations impacted by social, economic, environmental, or other conditions that need to be studied in order to determine the most appropriate approaches to intervention. In such situations, the social worker-as-researcher will need to take particular care to ameliorate bias that can result from being intimately connected to an issue, problem, concern, or cause.

Quantitative research utilizes descriptive statistics and inferential statistics to analyze data, examine patterns, and uncover relationships between variables in a study (Krysik & Finn, 2007). Quite simply, *descriptive statistics* describe things in a numerical fashion. Descriptive statistics are often found in the analysis of survey responses to any number of topics, concerns, or issues. Asking registered voters whom they intend to vote for in an election, tallying those responses, and grouping the responses into categories that form a report would be a good example of descriptive statistical analysis.

Inferential statistical analysis is more complex and involves the use of data collected from a sample of a population with the intention of drawing conclusions about the entire population. *Generalizability,* or *external validity,* is the process of making inference about the applicability of the findings to larger populations. High external validity increases the generalizability to other groups and situations, while low external validity limits the generalizability to a very specific situation. Social workers involved in either conducting research or planning to apply research findings need to remember that results from a single study cannot automatically be generalized to an entire population. It is only after several studies have been completed that researchers are able to refer to a body of evidence indicating the effectiveness of a particular intervention (Coggins & Hatchett, 2009).

Efficacy Trials/Studies

Efficacy trials/studies that are of interest in social work are those that contrast some type of therapy or treatment to a comparison group under well-controlled conditions, which makes this a popular method of research. In 1995, researcher

Martin Seligman developed an outline regarding a proper critique of any research findings that are designed to measure the efficacy of treatments used in psychotherapy. Seligman's (1995, p. 965) outline includes eight criteria that are necessary for any study to be considered *ideal*:

1. Random assignments of research study participants to treatment and control groups.

2. Rigor in the development of control groups, which include participants who receive no treatment, as well as those assigned to a placebo group that receives interventions containing credible therapeutic elements or ingredients.

3. Structured, manualized, and highly detailed protocols for the delivery of specific therapy or treatment to ensure fidelity to the specific psychotherapeutic interventions under study.

4. Research study participants are involved in psychotherapy for a fixed number of sessions.

5. Target outcomes are clearly determined and include both observation and participant self-reporting of, reduction in or increase of, specific symptoms, behaviours, etc.

6. A blind study approach in which both participants and diagnosticians, also referred to as raters, are unaware of the group to which participants are assigned. For the most part, efficacy studies of psychotherapy are single-blind, since the treatment is known to both the therapist and the patient.

7. The inclusion of research study participants with a single diagnosed disorder, meaning that dual diagnosed individuals are typically excluded.

8. Research study participants are engaged in thorough follow-up assessments for a fixed period of time after the end of the study. (p. 965)

Creating and completing "ideal" research projects designed to evaluate the efficacy of specific treatment techniques in psychotherapy often does not mirror the real world within which social workers, counsellors, psychologists, and other helpers practice. The disconnect between the controlled nature of efficacy studies and the reality of mental health practice environments makes the findings from efficacy studies something that is not easily generalized to work with clients (Ablon & Jones, 2002). Social work practitioners in mental health settings should keep in mind that findings from efficacy studies need to be viewed with caution. Techniques or treatment protocols determined to be effective in the controlled environment of clinical trials often do not produce the same results when used in a typical practice setting where multiple intervening variables can impact outcomes. Nevertheless, research related to psychotherapy continues to focus on studies conducted in highly controlled settings (Roseborough, 2006).

Effectiveness Trials/Studies

Effectiveness trials/studies are different from efficacy trials in that they are designed to evaluate the usefulness of different approaches to intervention in real-world settings that more closely approximate the environments within which social workers and other practitioners encounter clients (Flay, 1986, p. 451; Nathan & Gorman, 2007, p. ix). Effectiveness studies in psychotherapy research will, like efficacy studies, be conducted with a specific population such as individuals diagnosed with depression, obsessive compulsive disorder, or anxiety. However, effectiveness trials are intended to examine the impact of particular forms of psychotherapy as they occur in "real-world" settings (Glasgow, Lichtenstein, & Marcus, 2003, p. 1263). This means that a more natural and less rigidly manualized approach to treatment is utilized with the intention of evaluating the effectiveness and usefulness of various approaches when they are applied to client cases in which intervening variables (family, employment, community, dual diagnoses, etc.) are present.

Although effectiveness trials may sound appealing to social workers and other mental health practitioners, it must be recognized that they also have drawbacks. When an effectiveness trial approach is used, it becomes much more difficult to determine what may be responsible for improvement in client well-being, because multiple variables can influence outcomes (Ablon & Jones, 2002). For this reason, there are researchers in psychotherapy who recommend constructing research projects in which efficacy and effectiveness are employed, with efficacy used to evaluate specific approaches to treatment, followed by effectiveness trials in real-world environments. It has been argued that combining both approaches will lead to more solidly grounded evidence-based practice in psychotherapy (Glasgow et al., 2003).

Ethics Review

Formal research ethics board review and approval is required when human subjects are involved, and the findings of a study are to be more widely disseminated (U.S. DHSS, 2009). Ethics boards are often referred to as an Institutional Review Board (IRB) in academic settings in the United States. In Canada, the same process involves submitting the research proposal to a Research Ethics Board (REB) for review (often simply referred to as ethics review), a process that is required in all research projects involving human subjects. A class project in which students meet with service providers and write a report or even complete a more formal assessment of an agency would not necessarily be subject to ethics review. However, if in the process clients of an agency or members of a community were asked to participate in a survey questionnaire as part of a study or evaluation of a program where the findings would be shared outside of the agency and for purposes beyond evaluation and program development, an ethics review would be necessary.

A good example of the boundary between the need for agency approval and the additional need for ethics review can be found in the case of a master's level social work student completing her field practicum experience in a hospice agency. As part of her field practicum placement, the student was given the task of surveying the family members of hospice clients following the death of a member in hospice care. Because the survey was initially used as a tool to inform current agency practice and perhaps improve service, the review process was not necessary. However, when agency administration wanted to publish their findings and present at national conferences, the issue of ethics review became important. Because the social work student had conducted the survey as a component of assigned tasks in her field practicum placement setting and not as a research project, the issues of not having an ethics review approval prevented the student from presenting the findings at a national conference. Why would this be the case if clients had voluntarily agreed to the survey? It would be a violation of ethics because no one ever informed the participants of the intention to share the information they provided more broadly or in any public forum. Had that intention been made clear early on, the student could have worked with her graduate advisor and faculty field instructor to draft and submit a proposal to the university ethics review board. Moreover, this would need to have been done before any data collection had begun.

EVALUATING MICRO-LEVEL PRACTICE

For most social work students graduating from BSW and MSW programs, the evaluation of their own practice generally involves the use of *single-subject research designs*, also referred to as single-case experimental designs, which can be applied when the sample size is one or when a small number of individuals are considered as one, as occurs with a family or treatment group. The single-subject design is most often used to measure changes in emotional states or behaviours. The intention of a single-subject approach to tracking changes that result during treatment is to see if change occurs during that time, and to determine, if possible, whether or not emotional and behavioural changes might be attributed to the treatment process. In a single-subject design approach, the assessment provides baseline data against which changes reported by the client and/or those observed by the social worker serve as a measure of treatment effectiveness. Basically, the assessment with the client constitutes the nontreatment phase, which is followed by intervention or treatment. Changes are regularly recorded, providing a measurement of changes that occur or do not occur during each phase of treatment (Gay & Airasian, 2003, p. 383).

McMillan (2004, pp. 227–228) summarized the five characteristics of single-subject research designs: *reliable measurement, repeated measurement, description of conditions, baseline and treatment conditions,* and the *single-variable rule.*

1. Reliable measurement: These designs involve multiple measures of behaviour, therefore it is important for the instrumentation to be reliable. Conditions for the data collection should be standardized and observers need to be trained, as consistency in measurement is especially crucial in the transition before and after the treatment.

2. Repeated measurement: The same behaviour is measured over and over again. This step differs from most experiments, in which the dependent variable is measured only once. Repeated measures are necessary to obtain a clear pattern or consistency in the observed or targeted behaviour over time and to control for the normal variation of behaviour that is expected within short time intervals.

3. Description of conditions: A clear, detailed description of the conditions of measurement and the nature of the treatment are needed in order to strengthen internal and external validity.

4. Baseline and treatment conditions: Each single-subject study involves at least one baseline condition and one treatment condition. The *baseline condition* refers to a period of time in which the target behaviour (dependent variable) is observed and recorded as it occurs without a special or new intervention. The baseline behaviour provides the frame of reference against which future behaviour is compared. The *treatment condition* is the period of time during which the experimental intervention or treatment is introduced and the target behaviour continues to be observed and recorded. Both the baseline and treatment phases of the study need to be long enough to achieve stability in the target behaviour.

5. Single-variable rule: During single-subject research, only one variable should be monitored for change.

During the first phase in a single-subject research design, students and/or clinicians focus on establishing a baseline. Behaviours are tracked through observation and scored on clinical measures. During phase two, the intervention phase, students/clinicians offer treatment. What is produced is the most basic type of single-subject design, the *A-B Design*, with A being the baseline condition or control period and B being the treatment condition period.

A-B Design Case Example

In this case example, the A-B design would show how a clinical social worker would track changes in "feelings of anxiety" in a client over an eight-week period. The baseline week(s) is represented in part A; with part B represented in the eight-week treatment phase or intervention period. Relying on the client to self-report symptoms, the baseline data for the client include the first four weeks prior to engaging in the initial assessment session and treatment with a clinical social worker. This is followed by asking the client to self-report changes during the first eight weeks of treatment. In this case, the social worker utilized a scale (1–10) to measure the "feelings of anxiety" the client experienced throughout each day of each week:

[ ] one (1)—"no symptoms of anxiety"

[ ] two (2)—"somewhat mild symptoms of anxiety"

[ ] three (3)—"mild symptoms of anxiety"

[ ] four (4)—"somewhat moderate feeling of anxiety"

[ ] five (5)—"moderate feelings of anxiety"

[ ] six (6)—"somewhat elevated feelings of anxiety"

[ ] seven (7)—"elevated feelings of anxiety"

[ ] eight (8)—"somewhat severe feelings of anxiety"

[ ] nine (9)—"severe feelings of anxiety"

[ ] ten (10)—"very severe feelings of anxiety"

Figure 7.7   A-B Design Case Example

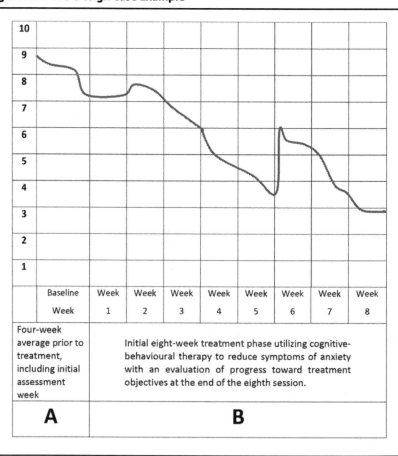

Although the single-subject A-B design is a common approach to tracking client progress, it must be understood that intervening variables that are not attributable to the intervention may impact treatment. In the example given above, the increase in anxiety in week six occurred at the same time the client had a minor car accident. For reasons such as this, it is important that clinical social work students and practitioners be aware that those events occurring in clients' lives outside of clinical sessions make it difficult to state with certainty that change in the emotional states or behaviours of clients can be directly attributed to specific interventions during treatment. With a single-subject approach to the assessment of progress, the best a clinical practitioner can do is indicate that the period of treatment is associated with a reduction in symptoms or an improvement in behaviour.

CONCLUSION—UTILIZING RESEARCH FINDINGS IN PRACTICE

For social workers and other helping professionals, there are two important ways in which research findings inform practice. First, practitioners serving client systems of various sizes need to be informed consumers of research. This means understanding what constitutes a good study. Nathan and Gorman (2007) outline the dominant Euro-Western approach to evaluating the validity of research articles by ranking studies on a scale from one through six. The three most common types of studies encountered by social workers are referred to by Nathan and Gorman (2007, pp. vii–viii) as type 1 studies, type 2 studies, and type 3 studies. *Type 1 studies* are considered to be the most rigorous and follow strict scientific research protocols, such as those mentioned above in the description of efficacy trials, also called RCTs or random controlled studies. Type 1 studies ensure the use of random selection of participants as well as treatment and control groups. In addition, type 1 studies regularly involve a double-blind approach, meaning that participants and those administering and recording the intervention do not know if they are in a treatment or control group. *Type 2 studies* are those that have some clinical significance, but may be missing certain aspects of type 1 studies, such as randomization of participants. While type 2 studies do not meet the standard of type 1 studies, they often make an important contribution and, therefore, their findings should not be discounted. *Type 3 studies* are of much more limited use, and they often lack a number of elements necessary to be considered methodologically sound.

Therefore, such studies provide little useful data about the applicability of a particular intervention or treatment method. However, type 3 studies may be valuable in relation to suggesting areas of interest that could be followed up in more rigorously designed studies. Type 3 studies may appear as articles in professional journals as those that use nonprobabilistic (meaning nonrandom) approaches to selecting participants. Often, such studies will state that a convenience or haphazard approach was used to select participants. Such an approach is most common in qualitative, mixed qualitative and quantitative, and exploratory research. The findings of such research projects may guide researchers' efforts in the formulation of more rigorous studies, but as stated, offer little in the way of data that are generalizable to those who were not involved in the research.

The second important issue in the preparation of social workers for practice has to do with the current limitations of the existing body of research. Many potentially valid approaches to treatment, healing, and intervention or service have not yet been studied or are derived from cultures in which Euro-Western research methodologies may not offer appropriate tools for evaluating effectiveness. In addition, a great deal of valuable practice wisdom exists among professionals but has never been researched or evaluated. Because so much remains to be discovered and uncovered, social workers and other helping professionals need to rely on knowledge that is combined with critical and creative thinking. Practice must therefore be research informed, but not strictly research defined.

Chapter Eight

Indigenous North American Theory and Practice

INTRODUCTION

To begin the process of understanding theories of personality and approaches to problem resolution or healing, this chapter starts with a brief review of Indigenous North American and early syncretic (culturally blended) healing systems that existed before the advent of the European theories with which most social workers and other professional helpers are familiar. Although Indigenous-based approaches are not a common feature of social work or counselling education in North America, Indigenous healing and helping in a multitude of culturally distinct Indigenous societies has a history that predates Euro-Western psychology and psychotherapy by many centuries. Throughout Canada and in many regions of the western and southwestern United States, the north central Great Plains of the United States, and the upper Great Lakes states of Michigan, Minnesota, and Wisconsin, the growth of Indigenous North American populations has sparked an interest in developing approaches to helping and healing that validate and resonate with the cultures of Indigenous Peoples. As a result, this chapter includes historical and theoretical foundations of Indigenous healing or helping traditions, as well as techniques relating to Indigenous North American theories of mental illness, mental wellness, and the role of healers and clients in the process of identifying and addressing client concerns. This means that beyond mental health alone, Indigenous approaches to helping and healing include the journey toward a more holistic sense of balance that involves physical, psychological, spiritual, and emotional aspects of life.

INDIGENOUS NORTH AMERICAN DEVELOPMENTAL THEORY

As is true with Indigenous theories for application to counselling or therapy, there is no *one* Indigenous theory of psychosocial development. Different societies in the precontact period had culturally specific conceptualizations of human growth and developmental stages as well as specific tasks and roles that accompanied various periods in life. Indigenous North American Tewa anthropologist, Alfonso Ortiz, from northern New Mexico, describes the life stages of Tewa children as consisting of being welcomed into the community as an infant, followed by a period of innocence until the child is between six and ten years of age. After the initial period of innocence children go through a rite of initiation that introduces them to gender-specific tasks in community life (Ortiz, 1969, pp. 37–38). Another rite after age ten, referred to as *finishing*, brings the child into the ritual organization of the community based on her or his designation as a member of the summer or winter people of the village which is divided into two halves called moieties (Ortiz, 1969, p. 43). Beyond puberty and into adulthood, Tewa individuals, much as individuals in other pueblo societies, were traditionally viewed as transitioning through life stages that solidified their place in the community at both the level of obligation to extended family network, and in regard to participation in the community-wide ritual cycle (Underhill, 1991). Included with this were milestones such as marriage, parenting, and grandparenting, as well as fulfilling roles based on gender, age, and status—all of which were, and in many communities still are, expected to occur at certain points in the life cycle.

Cree/Métis Canadian researcher and author Kim Anderson writes specifically about the life stages of Indigenous women with a description of life for children, life changes that come with puberty and adolescence, early adulthood, middle adulthood, and old age. Furthermore, each life stage described by Anderson includes challenges, tasks, roles, and expectations that occur in the life trajectory of Indigenous women (Anderson, 2011). As is the case with Pueblo peoples of the southwest United States, Indigenous women in Canada are viewed as living richly contextualized lives with many linkages to others, creating a complex web of spiritual, social, familial, and individual transitions that constitute the stages and phases of the life course. These changes may be discussed by using metaphors such as a medicine wheel or grand medicine lodge, but all Indigenous North American societies, just as many other Indigenous societies worldwide, have had traditions of viewing life as something that is composed of physical, psychological/cognitive, social, and spiritual changes that occur in the lives of individuals in the context of larger social collectives.

Without a doubt developmental theories, and indeed all theories, occur within the context of socially constructed ideas of what it means to be both human and a productive or contributing member of society. If, for example, a society values individualism and individual effort, theories about personality development, such as *object relations theory*, will emphasize the importance of separating from the mother or primary caregiver and becoming increasingly

Figure 8.1   Indigenous North American Developmental Theory

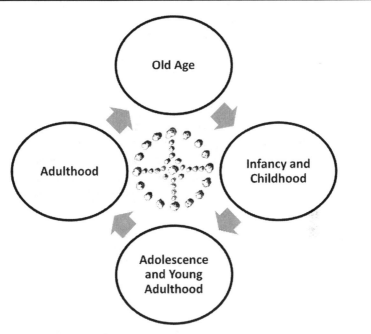

independent. However, in collectivist societies, as was (and in many places still is) the case for Indigenous North American populations, proper development involved progress toward finding one's place within the collective. Therefore, it becomes quite clear that an assessment of mastery in relation to expected "normal" developmental tasks depends on the cultural values of the society within which one is raised and socialized.

Within Indigenous societies past and present, it is understood that not all people proceed through life stages or achieve life milestones in the same way or at the same time. When expected psychosocial developmental changes and life course events occur within the parameters of what is considered appropriate or *on time*, there is little question about the progression of one's life within the context of family and community. However, the completion of developmental tasks, and fulfilling expected roles within familial and community contexts, do not always occur in predicted ways and at commonly or traditionally expected points in the life course of all individuals. In some non-Indigenous societies, rigid beliefs about developmental milestones in life can marginalize those who fall outside of normative expectations. However, Indigenous North American societies have generally included space within a larger family or community context for those who do not fit typical expectations in terms of the life course. One good example would be that of a Diné woman who became a parental figure for her much-younger siblings following the death of their biological mother. Over time, she came to be viewed as their mother and was even referred to as such. Another example of role flexibility in an Indigenous context would be that of an Anishinabe man who had no biological children of his own, but he fulfilled the role of a nurturing and guiding parent to the children of his siblings. There are countless examples of exceptions to culturally specific expectations regarding what is considered normal life course development within Indigenous societies. However, the overarching belief in the need to find a welcoming space for all who wish to be contributing members of family and community has a long history in sociocentric (also known as collectivist) Indigenous populations of North America.

INDIGENOUS THEORY, PRACTICE, AND EUROPEAN CONTACT

Long before the arrival of Europeans in modern-day Canada, the United States, or Mexico, Indigenous populations of North America had culture-specific approaches to helping/healing and systems for categorizing persons with various forms of both physical and mental illness. Hundreds of years before the Spanish arrived in what is now Mexico, the Nahuatl peoples of the Aztec Empire had highly developed forms of what would be recognized today as psychiatry and psychotherapy, including the use of "talk therapy" and herbal preparations designed to treat recognized forms of mental illness (Morales, Sheafor, & Scott, 2012, p. 406). In the pre-Hispanic Aztec Empire, there were even hospitals and Indigenous research projects that tested the effectiveness of different plant-based medicines (Torres, 2006). When the Spanish arrived in Mexico, their beliefs about illness, and, in particular, mental illness, were not nearly as advanced as those of the Aztecs. The Spanish still believed mental illness and physical illness were punishments from God or caused by devils possessing the body (Morales et al., 2012, p. 407). Following Spanish invasion, much of the written knowledge of the Aztecs was burned or otherwise destroyed. With disease, war, and colonization, the Spanish system replaced that of the previous Indigenous societies. However, pre-Hispanic folk practices did remain vital to the treatment of a variety of illnesses.

After many centuries of Spanish and Indigenous contact in Mexico and the US Southwest, a form of healing that is used for various physical, mental, and spiritual illnesses developed (Cotto, 2008). This form of healing, known as *curanderismo*, is still in use among Spanish New Mexican, Mexican, and Mexican American populations. *Curanderismo* has elements of Indigenous North American approaches to healing combined with Spanish Catholicism and some aspects of ancient Moorish culture (Torres, 2006). The term *curanderismo* comes from the Spanish word *curar*, meaning to cure or heal. Although *curanderismo* is found throughout Latin America and the southwestern United States, methods of healing used by practitioners vary by region. For example, in some parts of Mexico and in Texas, the influence of Catholicism may be more pronounced, whereas *curanderas* and *curanderos* (healers) of northern New Mexico will often have a noticeable Indigenous American influence in their approaches to treatment of those seeking services.

The *curanderismo* system of healers has many specializations. There are spiritual-medical practitioners; herbalists, known as *yerberas/os*; *parteras* who specialize in childbirth; and massage/chiropractic specialists, known as *sobadores*, who also remove negative energy from the body. *Hueseras/os*, (bone setters) were more common in earlier times when people lived a more rural existence. However, *hueseras/os* are still present in remote areas of Mexico and parts of New Mexico. *Curanderismo* as a system of healing even includes counsellors known as *consejeras* or *consejeros*. *Curanderismo* as a healing system demonstrates its Indigenous roots in the emphasis placed on returning the client to a state of balance and wholeness. In addition, healing to *curanderas/os* will often be viewed as having physical, emotional, psychological, and spiritual components, all of which may need to be emphasized to lesser or greater degrees depending on the problem for which the client has sought services. This idea of treating the total person and attending to multiple aspects of life makes *curanderismo* a more holistic method of treatment that does not compartmentalize ailments into mental or physical categories as is the case in westernized approaches. However, advances in research related to physical and mental health demonstrate that the once-clear boundaries between the two are becoming increasingly blurred. For example, it is now accepted fact that depression can be accompanied by physical pain, and has even been identified as a risk factor in coronary heart disease (Chavez, Ski, & Thompson, 2012). In other words, it appears that *curanderas/os* have long been correct in recognizing the need to treat the whole person in order to achieve the best results.

The healing and helping systems of Indigenous North Americans were not confined to Mexico and the US Southwest. Precontact societies across North America had well-developed and multifaceted helping/healing systems in place long before the arrival of Europeans (McCormick, 2009). Canadian social worker Pah Teen O-Wug Migisi Innini (English name: Ronnie Beaver), of the Eabametoong Ojibway First Nation in northwestern Ontario speaks of healing and the concept of *"mino pimadiziwin"* or the "good life" as something all people should work toward. However, unlike the Euro-Western concept of the good life which is conceived of as material wealth, power, and privilege, *pimadiziwin* for Anishinabe people has to do with caring for the earth and other living creatures, listening to the teachings of the elders, having good relations with other people, and living life in a balanced, respectful way (Beaver, 2013). Beaver also refers to the various healing and helping roles found in traditional Anishinabe communities. These roles include medical and spiritual healers, herbalists, traditional elders, and counselling healers, all of whom played important roles in precontact Indigenous societies, and in many places continue to do so to this day (Beaver, 2013).

Cree social worker Don Robinson, MSW, from Manitoba, utilizes the Cree concept of *ma-min-no-ta-mowin*, meaning to think deeply and be conscious of one's thoughts (personal communication, April 3, 2013). In his years of practice and teaching, Robinson has emphasized the importance of working with clients to foster deep thought, reflection, and understanding of the personal will needed to make these changes. Such an approach requires an assessment of each client's presenting problem(s) and current life circumstances, combined with an accounting of her or his life journey up to this particular point in time. Similar to the narrative therapy concept of understanding the *problem story* that has influenced the *dominant story*, an accounting of one's life journey examines those circumstances that have shaped or contributed to life as it is currently experienced and understood by the client.

This approach also involves looking at the stages of one's life up until the present, with a discussion of when problems arose and how they were dealt with (or not dealt with) in childhood, adolescence, adulthood, or old age. By examining where the life path became confused and life unbalanced, *ma-min-no-ta-mowin* is an important component of the healing/helping process that represents important work on the part of the client. This, combined with appropriate ceremonies, helps the client regain balance and return to a path of health and positive growth of mind, body, and spirit. This holistic orientation to health discussed by Robinson can also be seen in concepts found among Indigenous

Peoples of the US Southwest. The whole human path of Coggins (1990), follows the teachings of Tom Lujan Jr., of Taos Pueblo, who shares the Tewa concept of life beginning with the idea of innocence and "good direction" at birth, followed by the potential for misdirection in the life journey as a result of difficulties, maltreatment, misfortune, and personal choices. For Lujan, as is the case for Robinson, helping clients begins with understanding where they are now, combined with an examination of the life journey that has led them to this current point in time.

Indigenous approaches to healing are not passive like those of the early European psychoanalysts. For psychoanalytical purists, therapy was a long-term engagement intended to help the client uncover deeply buried emotions of which she or he may not even have been consciously aware. The belief was that by interpreting the meaning of thoughts and dreams, the therapist would clear the way for the client to resolve internal conflicts and thereby achieve improved mental health (Borden, 2009). In Indigenous approaches, helping does not end at bringing thoughts forward into the realm of consciousness. For Indigenous-centered practitioners, problem identification and an exploration of the life journey is always followed by an action phase that requires participation of the client as a partner in her or his own healing. The client must act with conscious intention to address, face, or acknowledge what must be done to bring about healing. This is why the will of the person in treatment is important. Without the personal will to move forward with the healing process, healing in its fullest sense cannot occur.

INDIGENOUS-CENTERED HEALING OR HELPING AND EVIDENCE-BASED PRACTICE

In speaking of what we, as humans, are able to quantify or even understand, Carlos Castañeda (1984, p. 55) discusses the teachings of Don Juan Matus by saying the world in which humans exist is made up of the known, the unknown that is knowable, and a vast incalculable amount of existence that is beyond human reach in the realm of the unknowable. It should be clearly understood by all people in the helping professions that there are many things we do not yet know, or even know how to measure. In addition, as Don Juan told Carlos, there is an infinite amount of existence that will forever be beyond our reach. For example, will we ever be able to truly measure pain, happiness, anger, contentment, or many other human sensations or emotions? At this point in time, we can only observe bodily reactions or rely on people to self-report what they experience. Yes, we can measure brain function, but will that truly tell us how happiness or romantic love feels in a way that can be quantified in the same manner as measuring the heat from a flame? Indeed, there is a great deal of the human experience that cannot yet be adequately or properly measured.

As mentioned in chapter 7, the current state of affairs, especially in relation to social work and mental health, is one in which evidence-based practice approaches are seen as the most effective means of treating diagnosed mental illness. Without a doubt, the move toward the use of techniques that have been researched and found effective does hold promise for improving services provided by social workers and other mental health practitioners. However, Indigenous-based approaches to practice cannot simply be dismissed and should not be viewed as failing to have an evidence base. The mistake that is often made with Indigenous North American approaches to helping and healing is assuming that Euro-Western practices are based in science (making them inherently better) and that Indigenous approaches to helping and healing are not. Indigenous-based approaches to healing and helping need to be viewed within the context of millennia of trial and error regarding what works and what does not. The limitations inherent in a study of Indigenous healing practices stem in part from the challenges of adapting Western research methodologies within Indigenous communities (Schiff & Moore, 2006, p. 63). An insistence on validating Indigenous methods using Euro-Western standards demonstrates a violation of an important question used by all ethical researchers, which is whether or not the instruments being used actually measure what is being studied. Many would argue that for Indigenous-informed practices to be accurately measured, different tools will need to be developed and accepted as being equal in validity to Euro-Western random controlled outcome studies. As Duran and Duran (1995, p. 6) state, "A post-colonial paradigm would accept knowledge from differing cosmologies as valid in their own right, without having to adhere to a separate cultural body for legitimacy."

It is interesting to think that findings from studies of Euro-Western innovations such as eye movement desensitization and reprocessing (EMDR) combined with attention to physical sensation are hailed as groundbreaking in relation to the treatment of posttraumatic stress disorder (PTSD) (Bergmann, 2012), while the practice of using *barridas* (brushing the body with rue or other herbs) and recounting trauma, as is the case in *curanderismo*, is dismissed as untested folk medicine. Both use a similar approach to treating symptoms that appear following trauma, but the treatment used by *curanderas/os* in an Indigenous-based folk system of healing does not have the status of outcomes that result from Euro-Western–style funded research. Indeed, beyond the question of proper measurement for Indigenous-based practice approaches, the question of inadequate tools for many methods of "talk therapy" needs to be asked. If we only use approaches that are easily manualized and subjected to random controlled trials, then we will end up rejecting a multitude of valid and valuable practice methods.

COMPONENTS OF SOCIAL WORK TREATMENT/ HEALING/HELPING FROM AN INDIGENOUS-INFORMED OR -CENTERED PERSPECTIVE

Indigenous North American conceptualizations of illness and healing have traditionally emphasized the need for balance in all areas of life. Unlike the mind/body dualism that developed in Euro-Western societies, Indigenous North American approaches to healing, in relation to health and mental health, often emphasize the need to treat the total person, meaning psychological, emotional, spiritual, and physical aspects of existence (Belanger, 2014).

Figure 8.2   Indigenous-Based Techniques

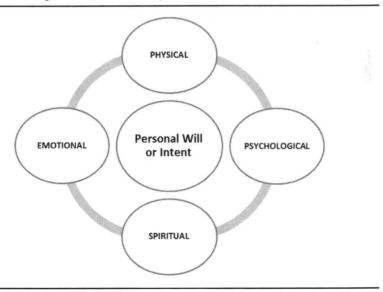

Indigenous approaches to healing emphasize a need to constantly work toward balance in these four areas of life as a means of attaining optimal integrated health (Coggins, 1990). Therefore, an Indigenous-informed or -centered approach to assessment and work with clients emphasizes an examination of where and how life might be out of balance, followed by the development of a plan to engage the client in a process of rebalancing. Counselling or therapy from an Indigenous perspective may also include or be followed by case management activities such as referral to other helpers/healers, either in the form of Euro-Western service providers, or traditional Indigenous practitioners. All of these actions are undertaken in an attempt to help the client toward a more balanced state of being.

Another concern, particularly in the area of mental health, is the belief that any and all Indigenous North American methods of treatment have nothing in common with Euro-Western practices. Conceptualizing differences in such a manner demonstrates an inability, or an unwillingness, to see where approaches to treatment have recognizable similarity. This practice of looking for common ground, versus continually emphasizing difference, has a long tradition in Indigenous North American cultures (Coggins & Hatchett, 2009). For example, Motivational Interviewing (MI) would be considered by many to be a more Euro-Western approach to treatment of addictions and mental health or behavioural issues. Yet, MI emphasizes a nonconfrontational and client-affirming approach that fits quite well with Indigenous cultural values and communication patterns. Another example would be the importance of dreams and the emphasis placed on developing insight as part of Indigenous-centered healing. This is an aspect of treatment that Indigenous-informed or -centered practice shares with certain Euro-Western insight-oriented approaches to clinical work with clients. In particular, Adlerian psychotherapy, with its emphasis on dream analysis that respects cultural differences in the process of interpretation, has a great deal in common with Indigenous-centered practice that by nature must be capable of accommodating a wide variety of distinct Indigenous cultures and blended cultural forms. As stated earlier, Indigenous-informed or -centered healing also emphasizes an active and collaborative role for clients (Belanger, 2014). In this respect, actions by clients that are part of the "homework" engaged in outside of treatment sessions have some similarity to the evidence-based techniques of cognitive-behavioural therapy commonly used by practitioners trained in the Euro-Western tradition of treating mental illness.

In deciding on what approaches to use with Indigenous clients, it must be remembered that Indigenous Peoples often face a combination of collective and individual stress on a daily basis. The loss of land, racism, genocide, cultural genocide, erosion of rights, and years of colonization all combine to create economic, political, environmental, and social conditions in which mental illness, behavioural problems, substance abuse, and suicide have become serious public health concerns. As a result, an approach to treating conditions such as depression and anxiety that conceptualize mental illness in strictly biomedical terms is insufficient. Therefore, Euro-Western treatment approaches that have not been expanded to include a wider focus on social, economic, and environmental justice will have limited impact (Cohen, 2006). Although Indigenous North American approaches to healing/helping, or those approaches that are Indigenous-informed or -centered, can vary widely by Indigenous society or community, nearly all Indigenous-based practices will emphasize the following:

1. An assessment that is holistic, exploring physical, emotional, psychological, and spiritual aspects of life that will result in an understanding of the present state of being.

2. An engagement of the client in an examination of where and how life has become unbalanced, beginning with the present state of being, and followed by a thoughtful exploration of the past that includes a deeper understanding of the client's life journey.

3. Collaborative development of a plan to address changes or actions that are needed to reestablish proper balance. Included with this is an assessment of the person's will to think deeply and commit to change.

4. The inclusion of other healers both traditional and nontraditional, when and where appropriate, to facilitate movement toward optimal physical, psychological, spiritual, and emotional health.

Holistic Evaluation Models

Holistic evaluation models may be of greater use in work with Indigenous North Americans and other culturally different populations or persons for whom harmony and balance are important life goals. The following evaluative tool is heavily influenced by Indigenous North American theory and philosophy in that it emphasizes personal development in psychological, spiritual, emotional,

Figure 8.3   Holistic Model

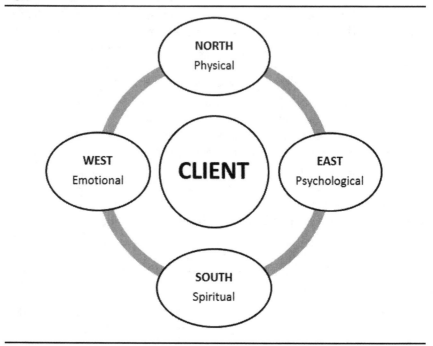

and physical spheres of life. The model features four directions and four realms of existence within which treatment/healing/helping objectives are featured. This model is intended to help practitioners evaluate their work with clients in a manner that is more consistent with holistic treatment/healing/helping approaches and outcome objectives.

East: Psychological Evaluation

This realm of client evaluation corresponds with the acquisition of new knowledge as well as the capacity to communicate what has been learned in the process of work toward the achievement of agreed-upon objectives related to healing or helping. Evaluation in the psychological realm includes a measurement of both what is observed by the social worker/helper/healer as well as what is reflected upon and subjectively experienced by the client in relation to

1. evaluation of success in work toward collaboratively agreed upon objectives linked to effective problem-solving strategies;

2. evaluation of success in work toward collaboratively agreed-upon objectives linked to desired changes in behaviour;

3. evaluation of progress related to the achievement of insight regarding the internal and external forces that impact mental health and influence behaviour; and

4. recognition of the importance of balance between psychological, spiritual, emotional, and physical realms of life.

South: Spiritual Evaluation

The spiritual realm of a client evaluation is not related to a one-dimensional understanding of specific religious traditions that supplement treatment/healing/helping. Neither is it the purpose of a holistic Indigenous-centered evaluation to measure engagement in an organized religious or spiritual community. Rather, the spiritual evaluation is intended to assess the degree to which clients have developed an understanding of themselves in relation to many aspects of existence ranging from self to family, community, the natural environment, and the total universe. Some people may be very involved in an organized religion while others may identify as agnostic or even atheist. For this reason, the term *spiritual* as it is used here is very broadly defined. Spirituality can occur along a continuum from participation in organized religion to a sense of connection with the earth and one's inner self that may be achieved through prayer, meditation, or time spent in the natural environment. Nevertheless, social workers and other healers or helpers using this holistic evaluation tool should also consider the needs of those who may be uncomfortable, even with the very broadly defined term spiritual, and be willing to replace that term with something like *sense of purpose, one's existence,* or a term that is comfortable for a client who may prefer more secular humanist language regarding the evaluation of progress toward objectives. Evaluation in the spiritual realm includes a measurement of both what is observed by the social worker/helper/healer as well as what is reflected upon, subjectively experienced, and clearly communicated by the client in relation to

1. development of self-understanding regarding a personal meaning of spirituality (or *purpose in life*);

2. incorporation of culturally based and/or personally meaningful healing practices, ceremonies, or activities critical to spiritual (or *internal positive nurturing*) development;

3. demonstration of ability to reflect upon the ways in which spirituality (or *deep self-understanding*) can serve as a positive guiding force, and an internal support; and

4. recognition of the importance of spiritual (or *personal internal*) development as part of a balanced and healthy way of living.

West: Emotional (Introspective) Evaluation

In this realm of holistic evaluation clients are helped in the development of an ability to look within themselves and reflect on the many levels and manifestations of their beliefs, attitudes, assumptions, feelings, and emotions. Evaluation in the emotional (introspective) realm includes a measurement of what is observed by the social worker/helper/healer as well as what is reflected upon, subjectively experienced, and clearly communicated by the client in relation to

1. accurately identifying emotions and emotional states;

2. demonstrating ability to understand the manner in which persons, places, situations, or larger social and environmental variables influence emotional states;

3. developing strategies related to addressing undesirable emotional states; and

4. demonstration of ability to implement change strategies.

North: Physical (Biological and Environmental) Evaluation

As human beings, we are influenced by the physical environment within which we live. This realm involves an evaluation of client capacity to go beyond a basic health and wellness approach to physical existence. Evaluation in this area includes the importance of understanding the impact of the physical environment on biological, psychological, spiritual, and emotional aspects of existence. Evaluation in this realm includes an assessment of client progress in relation to

1. understanding of the manner in which physical aspects of life (including place attachment) impact emotions and behaviours;

2. ability to identify one's own specific physiological and affective responses to the physical environment;

3. demonstration of ability to achieve collaboratively agreed-upon objectives linked to desired changes in behaviour; and

4. capacity to develop approaches to life that address emotional, spiritual, and psychological components of physical health and well-being.

CONCLUSION

Identifying Indigenous North American theories and theorists in relation to behavioural or mental health practice is a difficult task indeed. Naming theories, methods, and approaches to practice after people such as Freud, Adler, Jung, Horney, Erickson, Beck, and scores of others is something most social workers, psychologists, and helping practitioners do not even question. In the Euro-Western tradition of theory generation and treatment technique development, specific people are associated with specific ideas or methods. In social work, theories of personality development and concomitant treatment techniques tend to be attributed to or even named after individuals or groups of like-minded practitioners. However, Indigenous North American healers/helpers did not strive to name theories or techniques after themselves. Neither did traditional healers put forward their ideas in an attempt to establish supremacy of one specific healing approach over another. Instead, Indigenous healing practices developed in multitudes of collective healing communities that traced their knowledge back to learning that was handed down across generations with a strong spiritual connection to the earth and the natural cycles of existence. Therefore, it is difficult to name specific theorists within Indigenous traditions. The act of claiming healing methods that you firmly believe are a gift from previous generations as your own ideas would simply not fit with Indigenous knowledge transmission.

Chapter Nine

Early Euro-Western Theories and Techniques

INTRODUCTION

Since its inception, psychoanalytic theory of the late nineteenth and early twentieth centuries has served as a backdrop for theories and theorists engaged in either refuting or advancing psychoanalytic concepts. Among those influenced by Sigmund Freud are some names that are quite familiar to social workers and others in the fields of psychiatry, psychology, and counselling. Although Freudian psychoanalytic theory has fallen out of favour among many contemporary social work practitioners, the concepts developed during the life of Freud, and those psychoanalytic theorists who have based their work on his original concepts, remain with us today. In this chapter, and those that follow, we will see that social work language and indeed the broader society outside of the profession have been impacted by the many stages and ages of Euro-Western theory development. Psychoanalysts, behaviourists, humanists, feminists, cognitivists, and many others have left their mark on the social work profession. However, before discussing the more contemporary theories and theorists that have built on, modified, or rejected the work of Freud and the early psychoanalysts, it is important to begin with a brief journey through the work of some of the prominent early Euro-Western psychoanalytic theorists and researchers. This will help us understand the development of personality theories and the practice approaches that have resulted from them. Moreover, a review of early Euro-Western psychoanalytic theory will give us a better sense of the history of psychiatry, social work, psychology, and counselling that has shaped the beliefs many of us still have regarding the psychological and social worlds of individuals.

PSYCHOANALYTIC THEORY

Perhaps the most well-known or at least the most popularized approaches to conceptualizing and addressing problems of a psychiatric nature are derived from psychoanalytic theory. The psychoanalytic movement, which is most closely identified with Sigmund Freud, began in the late 1800s in Vienna. Soon after its inception, psychoanalytic theory and psychoanalysis became a world-wide phenomenon (Wolitzky, 1995). The key concepts that are central to Freudian psychoanalytic theory have even influenced language in the United States, Canada, and elsewhere. The terms *id*, *ego*, and *superego* are part of every-day speech, with concepts such as conscious and unconscious thoughts being accepted as factual elements of intrapsychic processes versus theoretical con-structs (Borden, 2009). Likewise, nearly everyone is familiar with the term *denial*, using it in mental health settings and even casual conversations. It is also true that most of us in North America, whether we are helping professionals or not, believe as the early psychoanalysts did, that early childhood constitutes the most important time of an individual's life, in terms of personality development.

For Freud, the intrapsychic world of his patients was viewed as the most critical area of focus in relation to addressing emotional problems such as anx-iety, depression, and other mental disturbances. For Freud, the foundation of human behaviour was believed to be the result of what he called primitive drives. These drives were seen as basic, biological, and instinctual in nature. Of all the basic human drives, Freud focused most intensely on sexual and aggres-sive drives. Furthermore, Freud believed that societies developed rules in order to prevent people from exploiting one another to satisfy basic sexual and aggressive desires or urges (Nye, 1981). For Freud, emotional disturbances were believed to be rooted in the frustration experienced when one's sexual or aggressive desires have been suppressed in order to comply with the rules of civil society. As a result, the mismatch between efforts to achieve satisfaction of basic drives and meeting social expectations of proper behaviour led to intrapsychic conflicts that were unconscious in nature.

To understand Freud, it is important to have an understanding of his tri-partite conceptualization of the mind and his stages of personality develop-ment. Freud's conception of thinking and emotion in individuals is based on his topographical model. Freud's model divides the mind into three areas of awareness in relation to thoughts. For Freud, thoughts existed at the uncon-scious, preconscious, and conscious levels. In addition to the levels of awareness in relation to one's thoughts, Freud also viewed the personality as being lodged within the mind, and having three components, which he called the *id*, the *ego*, and the *superego* (Jordan & Franklin, 2011). Freud's Tripartite Model of the Mind is analogous to an iceberg, where much of what constitutes the actual floating mass of ice remains below the surface—or as is the case with the human mind, in the preconscious or unconscious realms.

Figure 9.1   Freud's Tripartite Model of the Mind

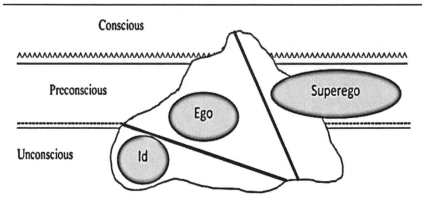

The id is most properly understood as the basic instinctual drives found in all human beings. In Freud's conceptualization of the mind and the human personality, the id was the driving force of human behaviour and was thought to reside completely within the unconscious (Pear, 2010, p. 149). The ego, found at all levels (unconscious, preconscious, and conscious) is that portion of the psyche that is rational and practical (Kail & Cavanaugh, 1996, p. 12). The ego interacts with the world by developing ways of gratifying those basic instinctual drives found in everyone. However, because the real world has rules and regulations imposed by culture, law, and the environment, the satisfaction of these drives must be controlled and channeled into acceptable behaviour. For example, if the id says, "I'm hungry," the ego searches for food. If the hungry person is in a store and sees potato chips on a shelf, the most logical path to satisfying hunger would be to grab the bag, open it, and eat the chips. However, society says that the chips must be paid for first. If not, society will impose sanctions forcing the hungry person to comply with the law and be punished for violations of expected behaviour. This is where the superego comes into play. Because the ego is all about satisfying id-based drives, the superego must serve the function of controlling the ego. The superego is the component of the personality that recognizes socially constructed limitations related to satisfying basic drives, causing the person to develop appropriate ways of redirecting instinctual urges.

The superego is that part of the personality that most people would understand as the conscience (Coggins & Hatchett, 2009). According to Freud, the superego becomes internalized by age five, meaning that rules of proper behaviour and the importance of following social rules and the direction of significant adult figures occurs as a natural response. For example, a nine-year-old child who is away visiting grandparents engages in bedtime rituals, such as brushing her teeth, because she has internalized certain behavioural expectations and no longer needs prompting. The superego becomes the "moral agent" of the personality (Borden, 2009) and serves to guide individual behaviours and actions. While the ego serves the function of navigating the real world to meet the urges of basic drives, the superego can be understood as the component of the personality that will ensure socially acceptable satisfaction of instinctual needs. Freudian psychoanalytic theory also includes an emphasis on the stages of psychosexual development. Psychosexual development, in Freudian theory, begins at birth and reaches mature completion in early adulthood. The five major stages of Freudian psychosexual development are divided into *oral, anal, phallic, latency,* and *genital* components, each having an age at which they normally occur, and each being accompanied by expected behaviours (Sadock, Kaplan, & Sadock, 2007).

The oral stage is the initial stage of psychosexual development, lasting from birth until about eighteen months of age. It is during this stage that infants are believed to find gratification of instinctual urges (food for survival) orally, through sucking and swallowing in the beginning, and then through biting and chewing as the child begins to grow and develop (Waters & Cheek, 1999). The oral stage is followed by what Freud had called the anal stage. Freud and Freudian theorists identify this stage as one that can begin as early as the start of the first year, and last until approximately age three. It was asserted by Freud

Figure 9.2   Freud's Psychosexual Developmental Stages

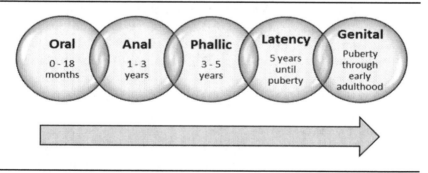

that the anal stage marked a shift in the developing child's attention from the mouth to the anal region. The ability to control the retention and expulsion of fecal matter is considered an important part of this stage of development (Sadock, Kaplan, & Sadock, 2007). Not surprisingly, this is also the stage during which toilet training in Euro-Western cultures became, and remains, an important developmental task.

The third major stage of development in the Freudian scheme, following the anal stage, is the phallic stage. The phallic stage was believed by Freudians to last from year three through the fifth year of life. During the phallic stage, the child is believed to become more focused on the genital area. Because Freud and his followers developed their theories in a male-dominated and patriarchal society, the male sexual organs were believed to be of the greatest interest to males and females. This overemphasis of the importance of male genitalia resulted in the development of the concept of "penis envy" in which females, lacking a penis, repress wishes to have male genitals (Reber, 1995, p. 548). However, Freud's beliefs about penis envy were not shared by all of his contemporaries. For example, Melanie Klein, Karen Horney, and Alfred Adler all believed that women were not envious of male genitalia, but were instead desirous of the degree of privilege and power males had in European and Euro-Western societies in the late 1800s and the early 1900s.

The phallic stage of development is also well known as the time during which the *Oedipus complex* must be resolved. Freud was of the belief that during this stage, male children in particular had desires to possess (as love objects) their mothers. Freud called this the Oedipus complex, a phenomenon also referred to as the Oedipal conflict (Steele, 2010). The name for this developmental event comes from the mythological character in the Greek tragedy *Oedipus Rex*. In the story, Oedipus kills a man and marries his wife, only to find later that the woman is his mother. In the end Oedipus blinds himself.

According to Freud, resolution of the Oedipal conflict is completed successfully when the male child replaces desires to possess his mother through an identification with his father (Arlow, 1995). Freud did not believe that females were as capable as males in terms of resolving the Oedipal conflict. Freud did, however, believe that females and males were in need of resolving incestuous desires for their opposite-sex parents by developing a strong identification with the parent of the same sex (Nye, 1981).

In the Freudian developmental scheme, the latency stage or period follows the phallic stage. Psychoanalytic theorists see latency as starting at the successful resolution of the Oedipal conflict and continuing until puberty begins

(Laplanche & Pontalis, 2006, p. 234). Freud believed that during this stage, sexual and aggressive urges are redirected into other activities, such as play and many forms of learning. Freud also believed that this was the developmental stage marked by increased identification with one's gender through play with same-sex peers (Nye, 1981).

Following latency is the genital stage of development, which is also the final stage of development according to Freud. The genital stage begins with puberty and ends in early adulthood. In this final stage, the young adult is expected to develop mature sexual attraction to an opposite-sex partner who then becomes the love object that replaces parents. Freud also saw this as the time in life when individuals take on the full complement of adult responsibilities, including attention to her or his primary love object, family responsibilities, and the world of work (Waters & Cheek, 1999).

Freudian theorists were of the belief that individuals needed to successfully complete each psychosexual stage of development in order to effectively and fully progress to the next. For Freudians, emotional disturbances were the result of difficulties experienced in the completion of each developmental stage. Although psychoanalysts of the late 1800s and early 1900s primarily treated women, Freud and his contemporaries were most concerned about male development. For example, the purists in Freudian theory believed that humans were inherently bisexual, with heterosexual or homosexual orientations developing as a result of parenting. According to Freud, experiences with parents such as having a weak father and a domineering mother would create an environment in which a male child would not adequately identify with the same-sex parent. As a result, he could develop a sexual attraction to other males (Freud, 1905).

Although Freud himself believed in bisexuality as the original state of human sexual attraction, contemporaries of Freud argued that heterosexuality was the normal state, and that same-sex sexual attraction represented a perversion. This belief became so pervasive throughout the fields of social work, psychology, and psychiatry that it was not until 1973 that homosexuality as a diagnosed mental illness was slated for removal from the *Diagnostic and Statistical Manual of Mental Disorders* (Spitzer, 1981). Indeed, the teachings of Freud and other psychoanalytic theorists during the late nineteenth and early twentieth centuries represented advances over earlier time periods in European and Euro-Western North American societies. However, the fact that mental health and medical professionals (including social workers) took these theories as absolute truth served in many cases to further the oppression of women, persons with same-sex sexual attractions, and those from cultural backgrounds that did not fit Central European and Euro-Western North American norms.

Defense Mechanisms

The concept of *defense mechanisms* in psychoanalytic theory is of extreme importance in understanding psychoanalysis and psychoanalytically oriented therapy. In fact, defense mechanisms as a theoretical construct remain in regular use to this day, particularly in the field of addictions treatment. Defense mechanisms are believed to be employed by the ego as a way of managing feelings of anxiety created by unacceptable urges, impulses, or overwhelming demands presented by daily life (Herma & Arlow, 2000). The following examples represent common ego defenses that are often associated with psychoanalytic theory.

Repression—During the time of Freud and his contemporaries, repression was a commonly identified defense mechanism employed by clients (referred to as patients). In simple terms, repression occurs when the mind does not allow unacceptable thoughts or impulses to reach the level of consciousness. For example, a woman who is the caregiver for her terminally ill spouse may feel trapped at home and overwhelmed with his care. Placing him in a skilled nursing facility would make her life less stressful. However, because she views herself as a caring and devoted spouse, the thought of removing him from the home is an unacceptable desire which never reaches the level of conscious thought.

Suppression—As with repression, unacceptable thoughts and impulses are involved. However, in the case of suppression, the thoughts, memories, or impulses have already reached the level of consciousness. An example of someone engaging in suppression would be a person who may read a book, take a walk, or listen to music as a way of focusing attention on something other than disturbing thoughts. A person may also use drugs or alcohol to suppress painful memories.

Regression—Regression is best understood as returning to a former stage of psychosexual development when facing unacceptable impulses, thoughts, or memories becomes overwhelming. Regression was often spoken of during the early days of psychoanalytic theory development. In fact, many psychoanalysts still discuss regression in clients who may appear to have had a setback in progress toward treatment goals. An example of regression would be a client who uses smoking, eating, or drinking to soothe her- or himself following sessions where the subject of abandonment during early childhood is discussed. In Freudian terms, the client would be seen as returning to an oral stage of development.

Projection—This defense mechanism involves the attribution of one's own negative thoughts such as anger or hatred to others. This is believed to occur because she or he cannot accept being a person who would have those feelings. A typical example of projection would be the case of someone who states that particular individuals are judgmental and negative when in fact she or he is the person experiencing the identified emotions or having a desire to engage in behaviours that are being attributed to others. By projecting unacceptable feelings and behaviours onto others, the person who engages in projection avoids confronting her or his own unacceptable thoughts or emotions.

Denial—Different from repression, denial is a refusal to recognize that a condition exists or that an unpleasant event has occurred. The most common example of denial is the refusal of some people to wear seat belts while driving, even though they know that car accidents can result in death. Another example of denial would be a man who refuses to accept that his aging father has terminal cancer, stating instead that "he always pulls through these things and ends up just fine." With denial, unlike repression or suppression, an individual avoids confronting unacceptable thoughts or emotions by creating a subjective reality in which an undesirable condition or state of events does not exist. In the field of addictions, denial of problems related to alcohol or drug use is often the focus of early intervention leading to treatment.

Rationalization—Persons engaging in rationalization will attempt to give what they think are believable explanations for contradictory information, unacceptable behaviour, or what they may see as unacceptable feelings. For example, a person with an arrest record related to intoxication may state that she or he does not have a problem with alcohol, and that the police just wait outside bars to catch those who have one or two drinks at the end of a stressful day at work. The person engaging in a rationalization of this type will use the act of convincing others as a means of avoiding unacceptable thoughts or behaviours in her- or himself.

Intellectualization—Intellectualization is the process of expressing a well-developed cognitive understanding of an issue or problem while at the same time divorcing oneself from the experiential or emotional components involved. In the field of addictions, a person using intellectualization could be someone who is capable of describing all the negative aspects of alcohol use, but refuses to examine her or his own problematic drinking behaviour.

Reaction Formation—Consciously thinking or behaving in direct opposition to unacceptable thoughts or impulses is at the core of reaction formation. By changing unacceptable urges into their opposites, reaction formation often serves to reinforce new, acceptable, and more positive behaviours. One of the best examples of reaction formation is that of the former cigarette smoker. A former smoker who engages in reaction formation to actively oppose unacceptable urges to smoke may become a staunch antismoking advocate. In doing so, the desire to smoke is replaced by a wish to improve the health of self and others through efforts to end tobacco use.

Displacement—Displacement is a defense mechanism that involves displacing feelings that may cause anxiety, such as aggression toward a feared object, by directing those feelings toward a substitute. The classic example of displacement is the person who is angry at her or his boss, but is fearful of being terminated if the anger is expressed openly. Instead, she or he may demonstrate verbal aggression toward a coworker, or direct angry comments at a spouse, because of the diminished likelihood of severe consequences.

Sublimation—Sublimation is redirection of unacceptable impulses into socially acceptable behaviours or activities. The classic example of sublimation used by many generations of psychology professors (although somewhat implausible) is the college student who redirects sexual urges and impulses into activities such as studying.

Transference and Countertransference

An additional and very important concept in psychoanalytic theory is *transference* and its reverse *countertransference*. Transference is believed to occur when a client transfers feelings from past relationships or experiences onto her or his therapist (Fall, Holden, & Marquis, 2004). An example of transference would be a client who becomes angry at suggestions made by a therapist and states,

"You are just like my mother, always telling me what to do!"Transference is generally considered to be an expected and natural stage of the therapeutic process. In general, psychoanalysts believe that identifying and working through transference is crucial for clients engaged in therapy (Nye, 1981).

Countertransference occurs when the therapist transfers feelings from past relationships and events to her or his interaction with the client. Psychoanalytic theory carries with it an expectation that the therapist will remain objective in work with a client. Therefore, unlike transference, countertransference is generally viewed negatively, as problematic, and even counterproductive in relation to helping clients work through their problems (Wolitzky, 1995).

Psychoanalytic Techniques

For early psychoanalysts, there were certain key elements seen as essential to treating clients in psychotherapy. Even now, two components of treatment remain crucial to those practitioners who base their work on psychoanalytic theory. These are free association and interpretation (Fall, Holden, & Marquis, 2004).

Free association—Perhaps the most important of psychoanalytic techniques involves asking the client to say whatever comes to mind. It is believed that allowing thoughts to be expressed without attempting to filter or direct what is being said will serve as an opening to what is going on within the mind of the client. Although not exactly a window into the unconscious, free association is believed to bring forth thoughts the client may be having, but of which she or he is not entirely aware.

Interpretation—Interpretation requires that the psychoanalyst listens for clues or patterns in what the client says, either during free association or in recounting thoughts or dreams. By identifying how the client's words and thoughts are linked to unconscious and unresolved feelings, unmet needs, and anxiety-provoking urges or impulses, it is believed that the therapist helps the client to recognize psychic blockages, and in doing so, frees her or him to resolve issues that get in the way of achieving mental health.

Dreams

The interpretation of dreams is of particular importance in psychoanalysis (Luborsky, O'Reilly-Landry, & Arlow, 2011). For Freud and others, dreams were regarded as windows into the unconscious. Some of the early psychoanalysts saw dreams as having very specific and established symbolic meaning that could only be interpreted through a psychoanalytic lens. Others, such as Adlerian psychoanalysts, believed that dreams needed to be understood within the context of the lives of their clients (Mosak & Maniacci, 2011). Dreams and their interpretation still play an important role in the process of psycho-analytically oriented psychotherapy. However, contemporary psychotherapists are much more likely to take an Adlerian approach to dream interpretation, recognizing that what appears in dreams must be understood as relating to specific and unique experiences in the lives of their clients.

Without a doubt, the discussion of dreams can be important for clients involved in therapy, whether the therapist or counsellor is psychoanalytically oriented or not. In fact, dreams hold special meaning in many cultures. It is common knowledge for Latina/o social workers and counsellors that dreams, and understanding the messages conveyed through dreams, play an important role in the lives of many Mexican, Central American, and Caribbean Latina/o clients. In traditional Hawaiian culture, dreaming was of particular importance not just to individuals, but also to entire groups. Dreams could guide people in the resolution of a problem or serve as a "creative force in life" (McDermott, Tseng, & Maretzki, 1980, p. 17). In many Indigenous North American cultures, dreams are often viewed as a mechanism used by the deceased to convey information or give guidance to the living. In fact, it would be difficult to find traditional Indigenous cultures anywhere in the world where dreams do not have particular importance as a factor in the psychological, emotional, and even spiritual lives of human beings. Therefore, dreams need to be viewed as having importance in work with clients. Dreams may indeed be conceived of as a window into the thoughts of clients, but as Adler warned, they must be understood within the context of the client's life circumstances. Moreover, dreams must also be interpreted in a culturally appropriate, congruent, and meaningful way.

ADLERIAN PSYCHOLOGY (INDIVIDUAL PSYCHOLOGY)

Different from Freudian psychoanalysts and behaviourists, Alfred Adler had a view of human nature that was more positive. Few social workers know much about Adler, but many are quite familiar with his ideas. Adler introduced the ideas of birth order and personality development, the concept of inferiority feelings that lead to low self-esteem, and even the concept of achieving optimal functioning and personal fulfillment that Maslow would later identify as self-actualization.

Adler broke with Freud on many issues, and was among those who argued against overemphasizing concepts such as the Oedipal conflict and the idea of *penis envy* in women, positing instead that what women wanted was not male genitalia, but male power and social freedom (Mosak & Maniacci, 2011). According to Adler, the only path to positive relations between men and women was to be found in a society that valued gender equality, making Adler an early feminist among those in the field of psychiatry (Fall, Holden, & Marquis, 2004).

Although many social workers and other counselling professionals may not readily recall Adler, most find themselves drawn to the tenets of human personality development and practice techniques found in his work. Adler saw human beings as creative self-determined individuals, able to practice free will. This differs from psychoanalytically and behaviourally oriented theorists who understood human actions as something based in instinctual drives or as a set of responses to environmental stimuli. Adler emphasized what he called holism. This is an important component of his theory that later developed into what is known as *Individual Psychology*. The Adlerian concept of holism as it pertains to the human personality is best understood as interconnected patterns of thinking, behaving, and feeling (Fall, Holden, & Marquis, 2004, p. 114). In addition, Adler rejected the mind-body dualism commonly found among psychiatrists and psychoanalytic theorists of his day, opting instead for an approach to understanding human personality development that emphasized biological and psychological aspects of being, embedded in a physical and social context.

According to Mosak and Maniacci (2011), in practice, therapy from an Adlerian perspective has four major components:

1. The establishment of a good working relationship between the therapist and client.
2. Exploration of multiple life dynamics that impact the client's view of self as well as how the client lives her or his life.
3. Interpretation of client thoughts, dreams, and behaviours with the intention of creating insight.
4. Helping the client to redirect or reorient her or his life to achieve greater happiness and to optimize healthy functioning. (p. 84)

Adler saw the therapist and client as equals—a stance that was quite unlike psychoanalysts of his day who assumed a position of superiority, expecting that clients would passively receive their wisdom. Adler's idea of relationship building is easily recognizable to social workers and other helping professionals in that it has a great deal of similarity to the phase of intervention known as engagement, during which a working or therapeutic alliance is developed.

It could be argued by those who have studied Adler in depth that many of the theories and methods used in contemporary clinical social work, counselling, and clinical psychology originated with Alfred Adler. Humanistic psychologies, ego psychology, rational emotive behavioural therapy, and even cognitive therapy owe a great deal to the work of Alfred Adler. Adler's holistic phenomenological approach to understanding and assessing human beings differed radically from Freud. In fact, Adler would likely have been more comfortable with beliefs about human existence found in Indigenous North American approaches that emphasize understanding the connection between the mind, spirit, body, and the natural environment as the key to holistic health.

In Adler's work, one can find concepts that later became incorporated in a wide array of sometimes seemingly divergent perspectives ranging from cognitive-behavioural therapy to postmodern therapies. For example, the *miracle question* used in postmodern solution-focused brief therapy (SFBT) can be traced back to the Adlerian technique of asking *the question* (Ansbacher & Ansbacher, 1956) in which clients were encouraged to talk about how their lives would be different if the problem for which they were being treated did not exist. Adler's work related to the *person and environment connection* would seem quite familiar to those who utilize an ecological systems approach in assessment and intervention (Borden, 2009). Even the most lauded of evidence-based therapies, cognitive-behavioural therapy, owes the foundational idea of cognitive distortions to Adler's belief that neurosis is the result of distorted perceptions that Adler called "basic mistakes" (Mosak & Maniacci, 2011, p. 71).

Adler emphasized the importance of understanding clients in terms of their "social embeddedness" (Fall, Holden, & Marquis, 2004, p. 115), making his work something that would be very familiar to contemporary social work students and practitioners who universally emphasize the crucial importance of assessing the social networks of clients. The recognition of family, society, and structural impediments such as poverty and gender inequality put Adler in a category that was quite different from Freudian and many Neo-Freudian therapists who adopted a much more socially conservative approach, focusing instead on intrapsychic conflict as the major obstacle to optimal mental health and even economic success.

CARL JUNG

Jung was initially a follower of Freud, but he broke with Freud in the early 1900s and went on to develop a distinctly different approach to psychotherapy that was in many ways much more spiritual and philosophical. Although Jung is not well known by most social workers and counsellors in the twenty-first century, many are familiar with and even utilize Jung's concepts of introversion and extroversion when describing personality types. In fact, many clinicians who use the Myers-Briggs Type Indicator (MBTI) instrument to assess personality types in clients may be wholly unaware that much of the MBTI is based on Jung's personality types (Pittenger, 2005). Another important contribution of Jung was the fact that he was one of the first psychoanalysts to focus on the importance of the early mother-child bond (Douglas, 2011, p. 124).

Those who have read the work of Jung will likely recall his concept of the *collective unconscious* which is understood as a sort of universal knowledge that all human beings share (Jung, 1964). This collective unconscious includes archetypes. Jung's four main forms of archetypes included the shadow, the anima, the animus, and the self (Papadopoulos, 2006). The *shadow* constitutes that part of our internal psychological selves (our psyche) of which we are often largely unaware. The shadow is often the part of ourselves that we dislike, and as a result we dislike those characteristics when we see them in others. For example, if a person did not like judgmental individuals, and later found that many of her or his family members and friends perceived her or him to be judgmental, it would be a difficult thing to admit. The judgmental part of who that person is would be defined by Jungian psychotherapists as the shadow.

Anima (female) and *animus* (male) aspects of the individual were thought by Jung to exist in all of us. Although Jung believed that every person has female and male components to their personalities, it is still the case that he based his concepts on the gender stereotypes that existed during his time (Papadopoulos, 2006), leaving his theoretical constructs of male and female components of personality open to criticism by feminist theorists.

The shadow, anima, and animus, when considered with the Jungian concept of the self, constitute the four main archetypes that Jung believed are found within all of us as human beings. The *self* is the entire range of psychic

phenomena in human beings and therefore was believed by Jung to constitute the personality as a whole (Adler & Hull, 1971).

Two additional concepts of Jung that should be mentioned are the persona and synchronicity. The *persona* is what a person projects to the outside
world. Jung likened it to the masks worn in ancient Greek theatre (Jung, 1964).
The persona involves behaving in socially acceptable ways in order to create
harmonious social relations. *Synchronicity* is a Jungian term that is used to
describe the seemingly inexplicable events that occur in one's life. For example, when a person finds that real-life experiences match the content of a
dream, the two are said to be synchronous. For Jung, synchronicities were
thought to occur at key points in people's lives, such as times of crisis, critical
turning points, or when one is engaged in intense creative activity (Peat, 1987).
A good example of synchronicity would be that of a woman living many miles
from relatives (but who also has an intense and growing desire to reconnect
with her extended family) finding the perfect job opportunity in her community of origin while on vacation visiting family members.

Jung had a more holistic view of the person than was true of the reductionist approach employed by strict Freudian psychotherapists. However, Jung
did believe in several key elements of Freudian psychoanalytic theory, such as
the importance of analyzing transference reactions in his patients, the importance of understanding the function of defense mechanisms, and the analysis
of dreams (Douglas, 2011). Nevertheless, Jung did not simply adopt Freud's
concepts in an unchanged and unchallenged form. He instead adapted them
to fit with his idea of human nature that emphasized wholeness, balance, and
an integration of physical, spiritual, and psychological elements of existence
that often appear more Eastern than Euro-Western in orientation.

NEO-FREUDIAN THEORISTS

Anna Freud and Ego Psychology

It is interesting that many social workers, counsellors, and others who claim to
reject Freudian concepts still believe, as do ego psychologists, in the tripartite
structure of the mind that emphasizes the importance of the id, ego, and superego in governing human behaviour and emotion (Sadock & Sadock, 2007). Ego
psychology as a theoretical foundation for practice is most often associated
with the work of Anna Freud (daughter of Sigmund Freud) and Erik Erikson,

who will be discussed in chapter 10. Erikson focused on psychosexual development whereas Anna Freud stressed the importance of defense mechanisms (Corey, 2009b). Ego psychology emphasizes client capacities to engage in problem solving when faced with demands from the external environment. Social workers and other helpers trained in the practice application of ego psychology are generally engaged in "ego-supporting" or "ego-modifying" interventions in relation to work with clients (Payne, 2005, p. 89). Ego-supporting interventions are directed at problems being experienced in the present that may have overwhelmed the client's capacity to cope. A good example of an ego-supportive intervention would be helping a client through a crisis such as the death of a family member.

Ego-modifying interventions involve working with clients to address long-established behavioural patterns or emotional responses that prevent the client from achieving her or his optimal level of functioning. A good example of an ego-modifying intervention would be working with a client who complains about wanting to leave the stresses of her job at the office, but still engages in work-related activities at home, even on her days off. In this case, the social worker or counsellor would need to spend more time helping the client identify problematic behaviour patterns, unconscious fears or thoughts, and the regular use of defense mechanisms as a means of maintaining her current approach to life. Generally speaking, ego-supporting interventions tend to be more short-term in nature, while ego-modifying interventions quite often require longer periods of time to effectively address and resolve problems (Coggins & Hatchett, 2009).

Karen Horney

The Neo-Freudian movement in psychoanalytic theorizing included women such as Karen Horney (pronounced "horn-eye") who, like Adler, rejected a great deal of Freudian beliefs about women. In much the same manner as Adler, Horney also argued that what Freud called penis envy in women was actually a desire to have male power and privilege, not male genitalia (Pear, 2010). A female perspective on development can be seen in Horney's work. She developed a much broader and more advanced relationship-based theory of development that went well beyond Freud's narrow sex and aggression drive theory to include a desire to be loved, a wish to be safe, and the importance of cultural and familial factors as influences on child development. Her theory of personality development is known as *holistic psychology* with an emphasis on viewing each person as a unitary whole, influenced by the environment within which she or he is cared for and socialized (Sadock, Kaplan, & Sadock, 2007).

Object Relations Theory

Object relations refers to a Neo-Freudian theoretical orientation. Object relations are those *internal structures* (images, understandings, beliefs, emotional responses to others) that human beings internalize in early childhood development. Internal structures serve as a blueprint for establishing and maintaining future relationships (Greenburg & Mitchell, 1983, p. 20). Object relations theory is most commonly associated with Melanie Klein, Margaret Mahler, Edith Jacobson, Ronald Fairbairn, and Harry S. Sullivan. Object relations theory, often referred to as a psychodynamic theory, places a greater emphasis on relationships. In addition, object relations theory, although emphasizing the importance of early child development, also considers adult human relationship development as something that is important and occurring continually across the life span. In accordance with contemporary object relations theory, those objects (parents, grandparents, siblings, caregivers, and others) with whom attachments are formed serve as the foundation for the child's developing sense of self (Greenburg & Mitchell, 1983). Therefore, an object relations-oriented understanding of attachment would view a rejecting caregiver, an unsafe and chaotic environment, or experiences of abuse and deprivation as holding the potential for creating feelings of mistrust, low self-esteem, and behavioural problems that may persist into adulthood. Conversely, healthy and stable early attachments and caregiving environments are believed to result in the capacity for healthy relationship development throughout life. Object relations theorists emphasized relationship seeking over the Freudian idea of pleasure seeking as the driving force in human behaviour. As a result, clinicians who base their work on object relations theory will focus on the importance of relationships in the course of therapy.

For object relations-oriented clinicians, psychopathology is believed to be rooted in traumatic self-object internalizations occurring in childhood that get acted out in adult relationships. The main focus of therapy is therefore one of identifying and resolving self-destructive relational patterns. The belief is that through an insight-oriented exploration of unconscious and deeply internalized maladaptive approaches in relating to others, the client will become enlightened and then work toward internalizing new and healthier ways of building relationships. As is the case with other Neo-Freudian approaches, object relationists maintain the tripartite structure of the mind (id, ego, and superego) and defense mechanisms as important constructs. In addition, those practitioners who approach therapy from an object relations theoretical orientation emphasize the importance of Freudian concepts such as transference, countertransference, and the analysis of dreams, albeit in a more Adlerian manner. Still, object relations theory is, like many of the Neo-Freudian approaches to therapy, very individually oriented, giving far more attention to the internal psychological and emotional lives of clients than is the case for interventions that recognize the tremendous impact of external environmental factors on well-being.

CONCLUSION

It cannot be forgotten that the ideas of Freud, his contemporaries, and those who followed developed a way of conceptualizing and treating mental illness that was rooted in the Central European culture of the late 1800s and the early 1900s. When their ideas reached North America, the dominant society on this continent was profoundly racist and organized around the belief in the superiority of Euro-Western culture. In addition, women during that time were believed to be inferior to men, and poverty was viewed as a personal rather than social structural failure. Psychoanalytic theory fit very well with the cultural assumptions of the new nations of Canada and the United States. For decades, beliefs about human behaviour and personality development shaped by psychoanalytic theory served to oppress women, minorities, and the poor. This led many in the middle of the twentieth century to abandon psychoanalysis as an approach to work with those experiencing depression, anxiety, or other problems. Nevertheless, there are still those who ground their clinical work in psychoanalytic theory. However, contemporary psychoanalytic practitioners tend to more often use terms such as *psychodynamic* or *insight-oriented therapy*. Although there are some who maintain a more purely Freudian approach, most utilize modified and updated versions of psychoanalytic psychotherapy. While these approaches to treatment may be based in original psychoanalytic thinking, they have in some cases been modified, and in others, transformed.

Still, it cannot be argued that the early theorists of the psychoanalytic movement are no longer relevant. Psychoanalytic theory as a foundation for practice has had a profound and lasting effect on the fields of psychiatry, psychology, and even social work. The very idea of thoughts being buried deep within one's unconscious mind still has wide appeal for clinical mental health practitioners. Even now, many of the terms that are used to discuss symptoms of mental illness or to identify diagnostic categories are rooted in psychoanalytic theory. As the practice environment of North America becomes increasingly diverse, psychoanalytically oriented work with clients could simply fade in importance and be replaced by new and developing approaches. However, what is more likely is that psychoanalytically based psychotherapy will continue to modify, transform, and evolve. Psychoanalytic theory may not have the broad appeal it once enjoyed. Yet it is undeniable that the legacy of those early psychoanalytic theorists will remain important as a force that inspires defensive support and spirited dissent resulting in the continuing evolution of contemporary clinical practice.

Chapter Ten

Theories of Individual Development

INTRODUCTION

Developmental theories that are used by social work students and practitioners as a way of understanding human behaviour can be considered as belonging to one of several broad categories. First there are theories of development that are best understood as holistic and non-Euro-Western. These would include Indigenous North American concepts (discussed in detail in chapter 8) and other holistic non-Euro-Western formulations found worldwide. Another group of theories would be those that are more familiar to people who have been educated in the dominant Euro-Western tradition. For social work, psychology, counselling, and other helping professions, the work of European and Euro-Western (largely male) theorists such as Freud (detailed in chapter 9), Erikson, Bowlby, Ainsworth, Gilligan, Vygotsky, Piaget, and Bandura are among those that populate this area of the psychosocial developmental theory landscape, along with moral and spiritual developmental theorists such as Kohlberg and Fowler.

In the 1970s, developmental thinking was strongly influenced by the field of sociology with the introduction of life-course theories that considered the contexts within which lives were lived as well as the importance of life events. From about the 1980s into the present era, the importance of a dimensional approach that examines cognitive, social, and physical changes has coincided with growing interest in aging populations. Along with this, there has been a concomitant shift in research interests from the more traditional focus on early child development to changes that occur toward the end of the life course. Finally, from about the 1990s forward, culture has resurfaced as playing a very important role in human development.

ERIK ERIKSON

For many in social work and psychology, Erikson's stages of psychosocial development are likely what comes to mind when discussing developmental theory. Erikson devised a theory of development that included social and environmental influences—something that had not been a focus of Freud who instead emphasized instinctual drives. According to Erikson, there are eight stages in life, with six occurring during the period of physical growth and development in youth (infancy through early adulthood), while the other two stages focus on adulthood and old age. Erikson is known to have studied many cultural groups, including the Indigenous North American societies of the Yoruk in present-day California and the Lakota in the upper Great Plains region of what is now the United States (Fiore, 2011, p. 32). This is perhaps why Erikson, unlike Freud, believed that there was no irreversible intrapsychic problem in development.

In accordance with Freudian theory, the human personality was seen as fixed early in development. This means that neurosis, psychosis, and mental illness experienced in adulthood can be traced to intrapsychic personality structures formed in the early stages of psychosexual development. Although psychotherapy in adulthood can help clients make adjustments to life, the personality is still understood as being formed in a manner that is resistant to change. Erikson viewed development and change differently. Much like Indigenous North American beliefs about healing, in Erikson's developmental theory there always existed room for renewal and continued psychosocial growth (Fiore, 2011, p. 32). As a result, Erikson's departure from the idea of a formed and unchanging underlying personality structure led him to deviate from traditional psychoanalytic theoretical concepts related to personality development. In Erikson's model, there is hope for positive and healing change. For Erikson, the central concept is that an unresolved or ineffectively resolved psychosocial crisis at any one stage will have an impact on the stages that follow. This can perhaps be best understood by the use of the slang term *baggage*. The slang term *baggage* in North American English refers to unresolved relationship issues or traumatic experiences in life that people carry with them (like heavy luggage) into new relationships or situations. This baggage that people carry from one relationship or situation to another becomes problematic when feelings connected to negative emotional responses emerge in the context of new relationships or situations—even when the circumstances of those relationships or experiences are in some cases quite different. For Erikson each stage presents a particular psychosocial crisis with two potential outcomes, one positive and the other negative. In addition, successful resolution of each psychosocial crisis corresponds with positive age- and stage-related outcomes.

Difficulties experienced in relationships, or typical life stressors that elicit reactions based in feelings of mistrust, shame, a sense of inferiority, and so forth, stem from the incomplete or ineffective resolution of stage-related psychosocial crises that need to be worked through so that healthier relationships and

Figure 10.1   Erikson's Psychosocial Developmental Stages

Psychosocial Crisis
• Positive Outcome
Basic Trust versus Mistrust (0 – 2 years of age)
•Capacity to trust and form healthy attachments to others.
Autonomy versus Shame & Doubt (2 – 3 years of age)
•Developing an increasing sense of mastery in relation to control of various bodily functions, language, and mobility.
Initiative versus Guilt (3 – 5 years of age)
•Increased autonomous exploration of the physical and social world combined with a realization of the capacity to initiate interaction with others.
Industry versus Inferiority (5 – 12 years of age)
•Understanding of cultural, social, and familial rules as well as ability to interact with others found in an ever expanding social network.
Identity versus Role Confusion (12 – 18 years of age)
•Mastering the creation of an integrated sense of self that combines various elements of developed and developing identity.
Intimacy versus Isolation (18 – 25 years of age)
•Developing the ability to be both emotionally and physically intimate with others through participation in reciprocal, healthy, and enduring relationships.
Generativity versus Stagnation (25 – 65 years of age)
•Developing a purpose in life that combines commitment to society, family, and self, leading to a sense of personal fulfillment.
Integrity versus Despair (65 – end of life)
•A capacity to view relationships, work, experiences, achievements, and activities in life as having been worthwhile, creating an overall sense of an integrated purposive existence.

responses to stressors can develop. For example, forming intimate relationships involving openness and vulnerability may be difficult for a person who never resolved basic trust issues from early in childhood. Likewise, an elderly person who is unable to see value and worth in her or his life may become annoyed, bitter, or depressed when hearing or thinking about the lives of other elderly individuals who seem much more complete, rewarding, and full by compari-son. However, as mentioned earlier, unlike Freud and his staunchly psycho-analytic contemporaries, Erikson believed that crises at any stage in life could, with help, be worked through and resolved, leading to healing and emotional growth.

JEAN PIAGET

In many ways, the work of Swiss developmental psychologist Jean Piaget forms the foundation of cognitive developmental theory used in social work, psy-chology, and education. Piaget was born in 1896 and lived well into the twen-tieth century, dying in 1980 at the age of eighty-four. During his lifetime, Piaget studied the cognitive development of children and adolescents. Piaget and other cognitive theorists, such as Lev Vygotsky, represented a departure from psychoanalytic developmental theorists in that the work of cognitivists focused on conscious thought, along with the development of capacity to organize, store, and process information. Piaget theorized that during the process of mat-uration humans develop ever-more complex cognitive structures that allow for the organization of information in the form of mental structures referred to as *schema*, which is a single category, or *schemata*, representing the plural form.

A simple example of the process involved in developing schemata would be to think of a filing cabinet where folders with information are categorized and stored, or the screen on a computer that has folders for information belong-ing to the same category. In either case information is stored in a way that makes sense to the person who created the file folders. When new information is encountered, it will either be stored in an existing category, a process known as *assimilation*, or it will require the creation of a new category, a process known as *accommodation* (Atherton, 2013). As children develop, they will constantly need to create new schemata to process information that does not fit an exist-ing category. Piaget created a developmental stage approach to describe the process of increasing complexity in cognitive capacity and ability in human beings from birth into early adulthood. Even those who do not recall Piaget's name are often familiar with his stages of cognitive development.

Piaget's most enduring contributions have been his particular insights related to physical and cognitive maturation, and the connection of that devel-opment to the increasing capacity of children to understand the world around them. The work of Piaget has inspired much research. More current research

Figure 10.2   Piaget's Stages of Cognitive Development

Sensorimotor   Ages 0 - 2 years

- During this first stage of development, children go through stages such as developing an awareness that they exist separately from people and things in their environments and that they can cause things to happen such as pushing a toy to make it move.
- Near the end of this stage they develop *object constancy* meaning that they know objects or people still exist even when they are not currently visible.

Preoperational   Ages 2 - 7 years

- In this stage, children acquire language and are able to understand and use things such as words and pictures to symbolize objects.
- They are also able to count and classify objects into similar groupings. At this stage, the understanding of past, present, and future develops. Concrete thinking continues to dominate.

Concrete Operational   Ages 7 - 11 years

- During this stage, thinking remains largely concrete.
- Children develop the capacity for basic empathy.
- Logical thought is demonstrated by increased ability to organize objects, identify patterns, understand reversibility in mathematics, and recognize, for example, that two different shaped glasses can hold the same amount of water; a concept also known as "conservation."

Formal Operational   Ages 11 years and older

- During this stage, children develop the capacity for abstract thought and become capable of engagement in logical scientific reasoning such as that which is required for hypothesis testing.
- As adulthood approaches, abstract reasoning deepens as well as the ability to understand things, such as competing ideologies.
- However, not all people reach the stage of formal operations. Many remain in the concrete operational stage.

(Adapted from Atherton, 2013)

---

has caused many to question or even reject Piaget's original categorization of developmental stages (Fiore, 2011). Still, the initial vision he provided remains an inspiration to developmental psychologists, educators, social workers, and others.

LEV VYGOTSKY

Although both Piaget and Vygotsky understood action on the part of the child as an important building block in relation to cognitive development, Piaget saw that development as natural and occurring in the physical environment while Vygotsky saw human action in children as developing within the context of history, society, and culture (Tryphon & Vonèche, 1996). In other words, Piaget believed that cognitive and motor skill development in children was biologically based, while Vygotsky emphasized the role of adults and others in the life of the child who facilitated learning in cultural contexts and in accordance with cultural norms and expectations. Vygotsky was of the belief that the cognitive development of children was greatly affected by language. For Vygotsky, the fact that language could facilitate knowledge and skill acquisition is seen as very important. Likewise, the presence of an adult or older child who had mastered a skill could help a developing child increase her or his intellectual development. For example, if a child was unable to figure out how to open a door that required turning a lock while also turning a handle, another person might have the child turn the lock while she or he turned the doorknob and opened the door. This would then be followed by asking the child to perform the task alone, only offering verbal instructions or actual assistance if needed, and then only until the child was able to perform the task without assistance.

The process of moving from assisted task completion to unassisted completion demonstrates one of Vygotsky's central ideas regarding child development, which is the division of learning capacity into three zones. The *first zone* is that of a child's current knowledge. A *second zone* represents potential knowledge that the child is capable of acquiring, but may need the assistance of others in order to do so. The *third zone* is that which is beyond the child's current developmental stage. This concept of dividing development into three zones is known as the Zone of Proximal Development (ZPD) Model. In Vygotskian thinking, it was important to understand that the gap existing between a child's current level of independent problem solving, and what he or she is capable of learning with guidance, is where cognitive development occurs (Vygotsky, 1978).

Scaffolding is an important component of Vygotsky's theory. However, Vygotsky did not actually use the term *scaffolding* himself. Wood, Bruner, and Ross (1976), introduced the use of the term to describe the supportive structure provided by guidance in learning, much like scaffolding on the exterior of a building under construction supports the structure until it can stand on its own.

Figure 10.3   Vygotsky's Zone of Proximal Development Model

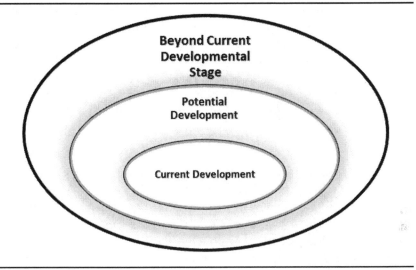

Scaffolding represents the assistance that aids new learners in acquiring previously unknown or not-yet-mastered skills and knowledge. The term *scaffolding* is still used in education and it refers to the concept of building on previous knowledge or skill that a student has developed.

LAWRENCE KOHLBERG AND MORAL DEVELOPMENT

Kohlberg's stages of moral development were clearly an attempt to think of morality as developing in stages. Kohlberg's foundational research involved interviews with seventy-two boys in Chicago, Illinois. The boys were ten to sixteen years of age, and in the study they were presented with a series of moral dilemmas they were asked to resolve (Crain, 1985). The following is an example of the type of dilemma Kohlberg (1963, p. 19) presented in his research:

Heinz Steals the Drug

In Europe, a woman was near death from a special kind of cancer. There was one drug that the doctors thought might save her. It was a form of radium that a druggist in the same town had recently discovered. The drug was expensive to make, but the druggist was charging ten times what the drug cost him to make. He paid $200 for the radium and charged $2,000 for a small dose of the drug. The sick woman's husband, Heinz, went to everyone he knew to borrow the money, but he could only get together about $1,000, which is half of what it costs. He told the druggist that his wife was dying and asked him to sell it cheaper or let him pay later. But the druggist replied, "No, I discovered the drug, and I'm going to make money from it." So Heinz got desperate and broke into the man's store to steal the drug—for his wife.

Should the husband have done that?

The answers of the participants in the study were analyzed for the reasoning behind selecting either a *yes* or *no* response to the question. From the analysis of responses to this and other dilemmas, Kohlberg developed six stages of moral development that were organized in a manner similar to that of Piaget.

A brief summary of Kohlberg's findings begins with children in the first stage of development who are most concerned about knowing and doing what is right or wrong as a way of either avoiding punishment or being rewarded for good behaviour. At the second level or stage of development, children begin to

Figure 10.4   Kohlberg's Stages of Moral Development

1) Avoid punishment *2) Gain reward*	• Pre-Conventional Birth to 9 years of age
3) Gain approval and avoid disapproval *4) Duty and guilt*	• Conventional 9 to 20 years of age
5) Agreed upon rights *6) Personal moral standards*	• Post-Conventional Beyond 20 years of age, but not attained by all

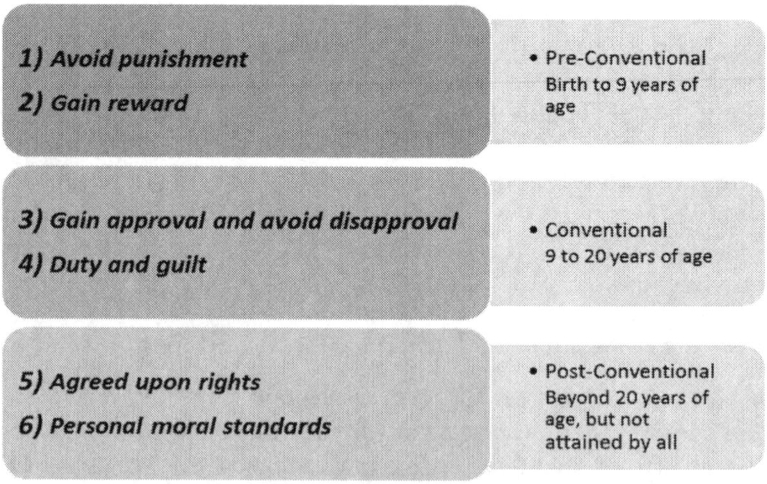

see that there are different views on an issue and that there is not just one right or wrong action. As a result, the idea of pursuing one's own interest emerges as an option, especially if the opportunity exists to exchange favours or make deals with others (Crain, 1985, p. 127). At stages three and four, which represent late childhood, adolescence, and early adulthood, a shift from legal concerns to one that recognizes exceptions based on motives, such as life preservation, may outweigh following rules. This thinking was viewed by Kohlberg as being linked to preserving society (Crain, 1985). Finally stages five and six involve the development of principles and values that lead to the creation of a just society.

AINSWORTH, BOWLBY, AND ATTACHMENT THEORY

Mary Ainsworth and John Bowlby were both critical in relation to the study of attachment in human beings. For both Ainsworth and Bowlby, attachment in humans was viewed as something that connected people to one another at a deep and enduring emotional level (Ainsworth, 1973; Bowlby, 1969). Ainsworth was born in the United States, but received the bulk of her education in Canada, completing her bachelor's, master's, and doctoral degrees in psychology from the University of Toronto. Unlike many of the Euro-Western male theorists and researchers of her time, Ainsworth had field tested her initial ideas about the importance of attachment while conducting research in the 1950s in the African nation of Uganda (Grossmann & Grossmann, 1999). Later, Ainsworth returned to the United States and continued her work, observing mother-child interactions to identify salient patterns regarding attachment (Miserandino, 2012).

John Bowlby was born in England. He began his work as a physician and child psychiatrist, and he was initially a follower of Freudian psychoanalytic theory. However, Bowlby moved from an emphasis on psychoanalytic theory to that of ethology. Bowlby was interested in *ethology*, which is the study of survival and adaptation in animals, with attention to the evolutionary value of certain behaviours (Hinde, 1989). Many who have studied psychology will recognize the name Konrad Lorenz, whose work has been instrumental in modern ethological studies (Dewsbury, 1992). Bowlby was intrigued by the work of Lorenz and other ethological theorists and embarked on a study of the importance of attachment in humans.

Bowlby developed a theory of attachment that was a variant of *object relations theory* (Bowlby, 1988), which itself was a form of psychoanalytic/psychodynamic theory. In his theory, Bowlby emphasizes the importance of a healthy and nurturing bond between caregiver and child. However, his work later included an examination of attachment beyond infancy into adulthood and the transmission of attachment across generations (Stalker & Hazelton, 2008). When one considers the development of children raised in out-of-home placements or in institutional settings, the issue of attachment becomes critical. It is now known that children who do not receive nurturing in a manner that allows for secure attachment often have difficulty with attachment as adults (Miserandino, 2012). Moreover, those who do not receive proper or adequate nurturing may be less capable of nurturing their own offspring, thus giving rise to a transgenerational challenge as they relate to providing a secure nurturing environment.

From the theorizing of Bowlby combined with the theories and experimentation of Ainsworth, ideas about human development and the importance of attachment evolved. In the 1960s and 1970s, Ainsworth's team of researchers conducted studies on attachment that resulted in the identification of three attachment styles in children: secure, avoidant, and ambivalent (Miserandino, 2012). *Secure attachment* was observed in children with a sensitive and responsive mother who provided affection and bodily contact. The second group included those whose mothers were less affectionate and tended to avoid close bodily contact. This type of attachment was referred to as *avoidant attachment*. The final group consisted of children whose mothers either ignored or were otherwise inattentive to their babies but did not avoid close bodily contact. Ainsworth and her team identified this group as being *ambivalent* and having both anxiety and ambivalence demonstrated in terms of the attachments they formed with their mothers (Ainsworth, Blehar, Waters, & Wall, 1978). Main and Solomon (1990) added a fourth type of attachment, which they called *disorganized/disoriented attachment*. Children in this category had mothers who may themselves have experienced trauma in childhood and were therefore fearful in terms of developing attachments to them in the period of infancy and childhood. As was noted in the discussion of Bowlby, difficulties with attachment may develop a transgenerational quality, making the provision of a secure base more difficult for those who never received that in their own development (Miserandino, 2012).

Attachment theory has long been of interest to those who provide psychotherapeutic services. The idea that early attachment issues continue into adulthood is of particular interest to psychoanalytically oriented therapists who strive to understand clients' internalized models of themselves and of attach-

Figure 10.5   Attachment Theory

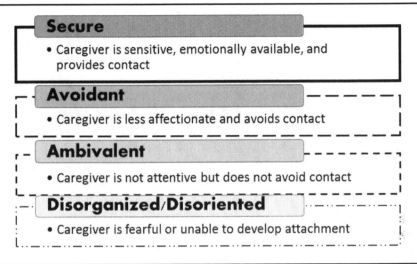

ment figures. It is believed that therapists can be of help to their clients by providing a secure base for the process of exploring and modifying internalized models of self and others (Bretherton, 1992, p. 768–769). Even some postmodern approaches to therapeutic work with clients acknowledge the importance of nurturing and the impact of early experiences on the development of self-image. One very good example would be narrative therapy.

Attachment theory remains important in social work, psychology, counselling, child development, education, and many other professions or disciplines. Moreover, the belief that attachment in infancy and early childhood impacts adolescent and adult capacity to develop attachments with others has been the subject of a great deal of research. Although Ainsworth's studies regarding attachment have been criticized, the criticism has been focused on her methods rather than the validity of attachment theory. Ainsworth is also criticized for not giving adequate attention to the role of fathers as caregivers. Finally, there has also been criticism regarding the role of culture in attachment that some feel has not been sufficiently recognized or explored. Nevertheless, Ainsworth's basic concept of the important role healthy and secure attachments play in development continues to be viewed as valid.

FEMINIST CRITIQUES OF MALE-DOMINATED EURO-WESTERN APPROACHES

Carol Gilligan is perhaps the most notable of early feminists who provided a critique of male-centric Euro-Western approaches to studying development in humans. Gilligan was among those early feminist researchers who brought attention to the fact that most developmental theorists valued separation and individuation over attachments and relationship network building (Congress, 2008). In 1970, Gilligan was a research assistant for Lawrence Kohlberg. As Gilligan continued with her own research, she became very interested in the development of girls and women. As a result, she grew increasingly critical of Kohlberg's work because his research subjects were primarily young white males. Gilligan felt that models based on males and the male view of individual rights ignored women and the importance of relationships in the lives of women. Therefore, she developed her own stage theory that emphasized a balanced understanding of self in the context of relationships with others versus the Euro-Western highly individualized and autonomous male ideal of a highly developed person (Gilligan, 1982). Other feminist theorists, such as Surrey (1991) and Miller (1991), have also been critical of Euro-Western male-oriented theories of attachment that place an inordinate amount of attention on separation and individuation as being more important than the development of attachments and maintenance of relationships.

ALBERT BANDURA AND THE SOCIAL LEARNING THEORY

Ideas about human development based in behaviour theory now include many adaptations, modifications, and resultant hybrid forms of behaviourism used as both theoretical constructs and as applied theory for practice. Albert Bandura's ideas about learning differed from behaviourists and cognitivists in that he focused on the importance of both observation and modeling as elements of behaviour shaping in human beings (Hutchinson & Charlesworth, 2013).

Many students make the mistake of viewing social learning theory as little more than copying the behaviour of others. However, according to Bandura, simply observing the behaviours of others will not automatically lead to replication of those behaviours in an individual. Other factors are involved in the development of an imitative response. Relationship components, such as admiring, identifying with, or wanting to emulate the behaviours of another person are necessary elements of an imitative response. In other words, there needs to be some type of positive connection between a role model and a person who might imitate her or his behaviours (Kaplan & Sadock, 1998). In addition to role modeling in regard to imitative behaviour social learning theory also emphasizes the importance of the environment within which the person is learning, imitating, and internalizing the behaviour.

For example, a child who has a beloved caregiver that sings may also begin singing in an attempt to replicate behaviours modeled by the caregiver. If the social environment supports the behaviour, the child will continue to sing. As singing improves, the model and the environment are impacted and in turn encourage more of the favourable behaviour. This example of the bidirectional influence of personal internal characteristics, behaviour, and a favourable environment represented by the child's model, and others who appreciate singing, illustrates what Bandura (1989) referred to as *triadic reciprocal determinism.*

Social learning theory conceives of behaviour as being far more than simple imitation. While the basic behavioural concepts of operant conditioning are involved in social learning, environmental factors, such as motivation to replicate behaviours modeled by a person with whom a connection exists, are considered important as well (Bandura, 1977). If personal characteristics

Figure 10.6   Bandura's Triadic Reciprocal Determinism

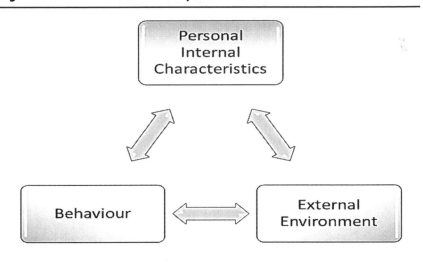

render someone unable to replicate a particular behaviour, or if other conditions, such as a supportive environment or model, do not exist, acquisition of the behaviour will likely not occur (Bandura, 1977). In 1986, Bandura published his ideas again with a change in name from social learning theory to social cognitive theory (Bandura, 1986). According to Bandura, the new name for the theory was more appropriate because it demonstrated recognition of the important role played by cognitive influences in relation to human motivation (Bandura, 2006).

GLEN ELDER AND THE LIFE COURSE THEORY

The life course perspective of Glen Elder focuses on the development of human beings in a manner that differed from earlier theorists. Elder grounded his work in a systems and ecological theory as opposed to earlier psychosexual, psychosocial, or cognitive formulations. The life course approach of Elder does not place an inordinate amount of emphasis on early childhood. Rather, it considers the entirety of life from birth to old age and death (Fiore, 2011). Human development occurs within social and cultural contexts and is impacted by events that take place during life. Therefore, development is not seen as purely biological or as happening only within cultural contexts or social networks. Instead, life course developmental theory emphasizes the importance of physical and cognitive development within the context of sociocultural networks that exist at particular points in time. Therefore, a person's age will mean that social, political, cultural, economic, and even technological factors will play a role in development.

Malcolm Gladwell's book *Outliers* is a fascinating study of the manner in which opportunity is shaped by one's age cohort, historical point in time, and the confluence of privilege, opportunity, and innate ability. In the book, Gladwell points out that both Bill Gates and rival Steve Jobs, while clearly talented when it comes to computers and computer programming, were also extraordinarily lucky in terms of opportunity (Gladwell, 2008, pp. 55, 66). Both were born at the right time to take advantage of the boom in computer science. In addition, they lived in places where they had access to computer labs within which their talents could flourish. Had they been born a decade earlier or later, they may not have had lives that developed in the same way. In addition, had either man been born in a remote community or in an inner-city environment, without access to computers, computer labs, or all the connections to the computer technology industry that was on the verge of phenomenal expansion, their lives might have been quite different. The point here is that unlike other theories that are silent on variables beyond biological development and the social environment, life course theory recognizes that many variables intersect in ways that impact individual development. For Elder, studies of development that did not take into account these multiple variables were missing key questions regarding the life course and the relationship between environmental and personal change (Elder & Rockwell, 1979).

Elder's Four Primary Principles of Life Course Theory

As outlined by Harrigan, Baldwin, and Hutchinson (2013), Elder developed four primary principles of the life course theory:

- Principle One—Historic times and places: Life is seen as being embedded in historical time which shapes the context within which life is lived at different chronological ages and at different points in history.
- Principle Two—Timing: The impact of life events on development is contingent upon when the event occurs.
- Principle Three—Linked lives: The relationships that exist within one's social network can and do influence development.
- Principle Four—Constructionism: Individuals play a role in constructing their own life courses through personal choices and actions, but within the constraints and opportunities presented by social and economic circumstances at a particular point in time. (pp. 384–386)

LEVINSON AND THE SEASONS OF ADULTHOOD

In addition to Elder's conceptualization of the life course and his four principles of life course theory, there is also Daniel Levinson, another important early life course theorist. Levinson developed a theory in relation to the different stages (what he called *seasons*) of adulthood. The fact that Levinson focused on adulthood and not childhood makes his work particularly interesting. Prior to the 1970s, nearly all theory generation regarding development was focused on the period from birth through early adulthood, with an inordinate amount of attention being focused on the early years of childhood (Fiore, 2011). The central concept in Levinson's work was one of understanding adulthood and the way in which people's lives are structured at any given point in time. For Levinson, those elements that structure lives are centered on relationships ranging from close, intimate, and familial, to collegial and social. Therefore, a person who is a spouse or partner of someone, a parent, a coworker, or a close friend will have her or his life structured within and around those relationships.

For Levinson, the seasons of adulthood consist of alternating periods of stability and transition. In stable periods, life has a predictable pattern and relationships are relatively constant. Conversely, transition periods are marked by changes, often major, in which familiar and formerly stable life structures must be altered to accommodate a new reality or changing conditions. According to Levinson (1978, p. 64), the lives of adults are not identical, but his theory did propose a sequence of universal times represented by transitions and common factors that impact all people. In addition, Levinson's sequences of life structures are realistic in that he did not assume that all people would reach old age having resolved problems encountered during transitional periods. For Levinson, the belief was that life may be full of changes, but not all changes lead to continued positive growth and development. The key concepts in Levinson's theory include life trajectories, life transitions, turning points, and the importance of linked lives (Elder, 1996).

Life trajectory is the long view of life. The changes that occur over the course of a person's life represent her or his trajectory. For example, a person who volunteered for local projects in her First Nations community, later became a youth mentor in high school, graduated and then attended university to become a social worker, would appear to be on a path toward professional employment helping others. If that same person then graduated with a university degree and accepted a position as a school social worker, she would have an identifiable life trajectory that resulted in her career choice.

Life transitions are the life events that occur at particular points in time. If we continue with the example of the social worker and her life trajectory, becoming a volunteer, graduating from university, and securing full-time employment all represent specific transitions in life. Other common transitions people experience include things such as getting married, having children, starting a career, retiring, etc.

Turning points are transitions that lead to significant changes in one's life and have the potential to change a person's life trajectory. For example, a young man at university in Canada might decide to participate in a "study abroad" program which results in a ten-week stay in Guatemala. While there, he has the opportunity to join an international organization devoted to developing ecologically sustainable economies in developing nations. He joins the organization and ends up spending much of his career in Central and South America. Clearly the decision to study abroad, which coincided with a life-changing opportunity, represents a turning point in this man's life.

The importance of linked lives holds that each individual is embedded in networks of relationships that evolve, shift, expand, and contract over time. Lives are lived in the context of multiple interconnected relationships. As human beings, our lives are generally linked to those of others. From childhood through adulthood and into old age, we live in the midst of networks that give shape, meaning, and sometimes purpose to who we are, both as individuals, and as a part of collectives. The manner in which our lives are linked to others has the potential to impact us in many ways as we collectively experience happiness, sadness, change, and loss—all of which give rise to new patterns and the development or loss of linkages with others.

Levinson's theory of the seasons of adulthood has been criticized for its focus on male developmental stages. He later included women, even writing a book titled *Seasons of a Woman's Life* (Levinson & Levinson, 1996). However, like many male theorists of his time, women were often an afterthought. Nevertheless, the ideas presented by Levinson, much like Elder, shifted the focus in developmental theory away from early childhood and to a more balanced approach that examined the entire life course. Still, neither theorist included the importance of the physical environment in terms of life course development. Place attachment and spiritual connection to the land is something that most Euro-Western theorists fail to address. In addition, the importance of the land will become even more crucial to understanding development in the face of global climate change. The shifting of climate zones and the looming concern over climate refugees will add another element to life course theories in coming decades. As climate creates economic and social disruptions, millions of people are likely to experience life transitions that will impact their life trajectories in ways we do not yet fully understand (U.S. Global Change Research Program, 2014).

LIFE SPAN APPROACH TO DEVELOPMENT

All social workers and other helping professionals who provide services to individuals and families should become familiar with life span development as it relates to the physical, cognitive, and emotional changes that occur during life. Life span development includes both continuities and changes in an individual that occur throughout the life from conception and birth to death (Shaffer, Wood, & Willoughby, 2002). In fact, while many textbooks on human behaviour in the past twenty years have included psychodynamic, cognitive, and life course theories, the overall structure of most has tended toward organization of material in a typical life span approach beginning with an intense focus on conception, birth and childhood, followed by varying degrees of emphasis on adulthood, old age, and death.

Life span approaches to understanding development are derived from psychological theories and theorists. Therefore, an emphasis is placed on understanding the normative processes of development and aging. This differs from life course theories which emphasize the importance of the social and cultural contexts within which life is lived. For social workers and other helping professionals, the life span perspective is of value because it teaches us to think in terms of age-related developmental changes in the lives of clients. A life span perspective, when applied to work with clients, especially in families with young children, most often involves assessment that is organized by age and stage, with an emphasis on tracking progress toward developmental milestones such as crawling, walking, talking, and so forth. However, a life span developmental approach is also regularly applied to the assessment of physical, cognitive, and emotional development in adolescence, adulthood, and old age.

At various points along the way from conception and birth to old age and death, there are transitions, changes, and risks that have the potential to develop into crises for individuals and those in their family or social networks. At every stage in life, health risks are present. These risks might be the result of environmental pathogens, such as viruses and bacteria, or produced by the social network within which people live. Abuse and neglect of children would be one example of a social network risk to children early in life, whereas peer pressure to become involved in drug use would be a risk more likely found in the social networks of adolescents. At the other end of the life span, the elderly are also vulnerable to abuse and neglect from caregivers within their social net-

Figure 10.7   Life Span Development Approach

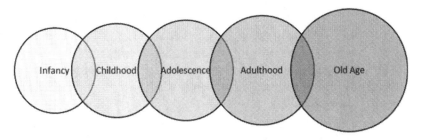

Lifespan Risks Associated With Specific Stages				
Developmental delays	Developmental delays	Identity issues: cultural/ethnic sexual/gender	Barriers to advanced education or training	Retirement
Abuse and neglect	Learning disabilities	Negative peer group influences	Income, employment, and career stresses	Income insufficiency
Income insecurity	Income insecurity	Income insecurity	career stresses	Chronic illness, dementia
Sexual victimization	Abuse and neglect	Abuse and neglect	Income insecurity	Limited access to health care, dental care
	Exploitation and sexual victimization	High risk behaviours	Parenting issues and multigenerational caregiving responsibilities	End-of-life issues Loss and bereavement
		Exploitation and sexual victimization		

works, many of whom are spouses and adult children (Cohen-Mansfield & Werner, 1998).

The use of a life span approach serves as a reminder that certain problems, issues, or concerns can become more prominent at certain points in time. For example, transition points in life such as those that occur between childhood and adolescence, late adolescence and early adulthood, early adulthood and full adulthood (around age thirty), and during the transition from middle age to old age, are times during which people can be particularly vulnerable (Fiore, 2011). Therefore, it is important for those who work with clients to be aware of age- and stage-related risks that may be present at different periods in the life-long developmental and aging process. Within each of the stages, there are common risk factors that extend across the life span. These include risks such as exposure to environmental toxins, limited access to health care, limited access to mental health care, and income insufficiency and/or income insecurity. Likewise, people of any age can become victims of abuse or sexual exploitation. However, life stages also represent times during which certain risks may be more prominent or prevalent.

CONCLUSION

Professional social workers, therapists, counsellors, or other helping professionals do need to have knowledge of human development. Understanding what constitutes normal expected development and what represents a potential concern is of immense importance to those who provide services to individuals and families as well as those who are involved in creating policies that impact program development and funding for social services. It is important for social workers and other professionals to stay up to date on information about early developmental milestones, as well as age-related physical and cognitive changes. Although much has been written about human development, there are many factors with the potential to influence development that have not been researched or published to the same extent as others. Gender differences, sexual orientation, gender identity, cultural differences, socioeconomic conditions, sociopolitical contexts, the physical environment, enduring racism and marginalization, ability/disability, and countless other aspects of life can impact the physical, cognitive, emotional, and spiritual development of individuals. For example, among many Indigenous North American populations, the continuing impact of both historic and contemporary colonial domination, the devastation of cultures, the unravelling of social systems, and the disruption of patterns of subsistence have had an enormous individual and collective impact on Indigenous developmental trajectories. Likewise, the pervasive racism that persists in relation to African Americans, and in particular African American males, cannot be ignored when considering development across the life span. Therefore, care needs to be taken when thinking of "normal" or "expected" life course development, with the recognition that many influences on the life course of individuals from racial, ethnic, cultural, sexual, and other minority populations can have a profound influence.

Since the turn of the twenty-first century, social work in particular has moved toward the adoption of a multidimensional approach in relation to human development and behaviour. A prime example would be the human behaviour textbooks of Elizabeth Hutchinson and contributors (2011) and Lisa Fiore (2011) which address biological, psychological, social, cultural, spiritual, physical environmental, and even global contexts within which human beings develop. The recently emerged or perhaps reemerged multidimensional approach is critical to contemporary professional practice. Development does not occur in a biologically, socially, culturally, politically, or economically neutral milieu. The interplay between person and the total (not just social) environment must be considered in our attempts to fully understand human development and human behaviour in context.

Chapter Eleven

Cognitive-Behavioural Theory and Practice

INTRODUCTION

Cognitive-behavioural therapy has become a widely used approach for the treatment of mental health conditions in practice with individuals, especially those experiencing problems with depression and anxiety. However, cognitive-behavioural therapy, often referred to simply as CBT, is also a commonly used approach in the treatment of posttraumatic stress disorders, phobias, addictions, and eating disorders. In fact, CBT has become a popular therapy for a wide range of mental and behavioural health conditions that range from depression to schizophrenia. The primary goal of CBT is consistent with the medical model approach common in psychiatry, which is focused on symptom reduction and improvement of functioning (Hofmann, Asnaani, Vonk, Sawyer, & Fang, 2012, p. 428).

BEHAVIOURAL FOUNDATIONS

For many in social work and counselling fields, behaviourism is often seen as something that is better suited to laboratory environments in the field of experiential psychology. Nevertheless, those working in mental health and other human service settings utilize behavioural approaches to intervention on a regular basis. Many social workers and others employed in child welfare settings have an entire repertoire of behaviourist recommendations for parents that range from time-out strategies to extinguish bad behaviour, to a multitude of reward strategies for anything from brushing teeth to completing homework. In family therapy and addictions treatment, many social workers—and other counselling professionals who do not consider themselves to be at all behaviourally oriented—regularly use techniques such as behaviour rehearsal and role-playing in work with their clients. Those social workers who are employed in residential treatment settings for youth, adults, and even those in correctional facilities, develop and work within programs that rely heavily on behaviour theory through the creation of reward systems designed to increase positive behaviours and reduce negative behaviours. Social workers in practice with individuals may, for example, also use techniques such as systematic desensitization as a way of helping their clients manage symptoms of obsessive-compulsive disorders or to overcome phobias (Spiegler & Guevremont, 1998).

At the time that Freudian psychoanalytic theory was gaining popularity in North America, behaviourism as a theoretical orientation was also developing. Behaviourism represented a radical departure from psychoanalytic theory. Whereas psychoanalysts were concerned with uncovering behavioural motivations buried deep in the unconscious of their patients, behaviourists focused instead on the manner in which the combination of environmental conditions and human responses to those conditions created and maintained certain behaviours in individuals.

Greater awareness of radical behaviourist theory began with the work of John B. Watson, author of *Psychology from the Standpoint of a Behaviourist* published in 1919 (Wozniak, 1994). Another very important behavioural theorist, familiar to many students in introductory-level psychology, is B. F. (Burrhus Frederick) Skinner. Skinner identified his type of behavioural theory as Radical Behaviourism. Skinner's most well-known works began with *The Behaviour of Organisms: An Experimental Analysis,* published in 1938, followed by many books and articles, reaching a high point in theoretical consistency in 1971 with the publication of *Beyond Freedom and Dignity* (Leigland, 2007). For radical behaviourists, human behaviour was seen as being controlled by stimuli in the environment. As a result, behaviour was viewed as a response to a stimulus (or stimuli) being presented. Unlike psychoanalytically oriented therapists, who preferred to focus treatment on an exploration of early life events and problems in attachment to love objects such as parents or caregivers, behaviourists maintained a focus on the present and worked toward the goal of changing the response of clients to their environments, as well as managing environmental stimuli that served to maintain problematic behaviours. For example, whereas psychoanalysts saw alcohol addiction as stemming from unresolved issues in the oral stage of development (Miller, 2010, p. 24), behaviourists asserted that the pleasurable feelings, peer support, or altered states associated with alcohol consumption reinforced drinking behaviour. This underlying assumption about what influenced human behaviour resulted in very important differences between psychoanalytic and behaviourist approaches in the treatment of many mental and behavioural health conditions.

Radical behaviourism views personality development as a process of learning and behaviour shaping that occurs as a response to stimuli in the environment of the individual (Hayes, Follette, & Follette, 1995). Radical behavioural theory posits that the shaping of a person's response to specific environmental stimuli results in a form of conditioning which in turn influences behaviour. Skinner identified two basic forms of conditioning. The first was *respondent* or *classical conditioning*, and it involved responses to stimuli that developed over time (Nye, 1981). A good example of respondent conditioning would be a person whose mouth begins to water as a result of smelling a favourite food. Because eating that particular food brings pleasure, the odour emitted by the food becomes the stimulus that activates salivary glands in anticipation of eating. Respondent conditioning is therefore a simple stimulus and response sequence. *Operant conditioning* is the other form of conditioning, and according to Skinner, it differs from respondent conditioning because it goes beyond the simple stimulus-and-response understanding of behaviour with a focus on creating behaviour change.

Types of Reinforcements

Figure 11.1   Stimulus and Response

Stimulus / Response	Addition of (appetitive or aversive) stimulus	Removal of (appetitive or aversive) stimulus
Increase of behaviour or response	*Positive Reinforcement*	*Negative Reinforcement*
Decrease of behaviour or response	*Positive Punishment*	*Negative Punishment*

Perhaps the most easily recognized and understood form of operant conditioning is that of *positive reinforcement*. This form of reinforcement generally involves the introduction of an appetitive stimulus, such as a pleasurable or desired event, object, or sensation, which if satisfied, will serve to reinforce and increase a given behaviour. A very good example of positive reinforcement would be a child receiving praise for helping with chores around the house. Because the child seeks approval from parents (appetitive stimulus), which is satisfied by praise, the child will be more likely to engage in the behaviour again, strengthening the connection between stimulus and response.

Another important and commonly misunderstood form of influencing behaviour is *negative reinforcement*. Negative reinforcement is done by removing an aversive stimulus in order to increase a particular behaviour. If, for example, a parent of a ten-year-old child says the child's allowance will be reduced by twenty-five cents for every hour of delay in completing homework, the child will want to preserve the weekly allowance and will be more likely to complete unfinished homework. Moreover, if the negative reinforcement is understood by the child as preserving something highly valued and important (the allowance), and the regimen is repeated regularly, the child may become more diligent about homework completion in order to avoid allowance reduction. Another more direct example might be the act of fastening one's seat belt in a car with an audible and annoying bell that continues to ring until the seat belt is properly connected. Eventually, the driver of the car may resort to fastening the seat belt prior to turning the car on, because doing so means the bell never goes off. If the desire to avoid the annoying bell results in lasting behaviour change, negative reinforcement would be seen as successful.

Punishment is intended to decrease or eliminate a behaviour and can be either positive or negative. *Positive punishment* (or most commonly referred to simply as punishment) is the introduction of an aversive stimulus to decrease a particular behaviour. For example, if a child were to be sent to a room to sit alone each time she or he hit the family dog, the child would soon learn not to hit the dog if she or he did not want to be isolated from others. This action, while clearly grounded in behaviourist principles, is generally understood by a parent or caregiver as simply getting a child to comply with family or household rules.

Negative punishment, also called extinction or omission training, involves the removal of an appetitive stimulus, such as a pleasurable object, sensation, or activity in order to decrease or extinguish a particular behaviour. An example of extinction that is familiar to many parents and caregivers would be that of the child who threatens to hold her or his breath until demands for food, toys, or engagement in pleasurable activities are met. If it is made clear that holding one's breath will not achieve the desired outcome, and the behaviour of the child is consistently ignored, she or he will soon abandon the breath-holding approach to satisfying an appetitive stimulus.

Another very interesting example of extinction can be found in the experience of an inmate at a US penitentiary, who tried repeatedly to get fellow substance abuse treatment group members to join him in a campaign of resistance to requests for compliance with rules imposed by the prison authorities. Each week as the treatment group ended, he attempted to recruit people for his plan. As the weeks passed and no group members were willing to join him, he eventually stopped trying and even asked for a transfer to another facility. Because attempts to address his appetitive stimulus for resisting authority consistently remained unsatisfied, he finally stopped attempting to form a group of inmates willing to engage in disruptive behaviour.

For behaviourists, the environment is seen as playing a major role in shaping and controlling behaviour. Therefore, behaviourally oriented social workers, psychiatrists, psychologists, and counselling practitioners place a primary emphasis on working in the present to create behavioural change in the client. Behavioural assessment includes an examination of environmental stimuli and client actions that serve to maintain maladaptive behaviours or responses to environmental stressors (Spiegler & Guevremont, 1998). It then follows that behaviourally oriented treatment will focus on manipulating environmental conditions and modifying client responses to the external physical and social milieu. This is also known as behaviour shaping, which involves the use of reinforcements and/or punishments, in a successive approximation, in order to reach the target behaviour goal. A client's past is only seen as valuable in regard to identifying when maladaptive behaviours started, and what environmental conditions and client responses to those conditions help to maintain the behaviours now deemed problematic.

Behaviour Therapy

As is the case with all forms of social work intervention or helping, treatment from a behaviourally based theoretical orientation begins with assessment. As with any assessment, behavioural assessments include a process of problem identification, a discussion of the problem history, and an exploration of how and when the problem began, as well as client attempts to resolve the problem for which help is now being sought. However, as mentioned earlier, behaviourally based interventions will differ radically from psychoanalytic approaches because the social worker, psychiatrist, psychologist, or counsellor, will emphasize environmental factors that contribute to the maintenance of problematic or maladaptive behaviours (Hayes et al., 1995). This means that little time will be spent exploring the client's past in terms of childhood, relationships, subconscious or unconscious feelings, or difficulties related to healthy psychosexual development which may take many sessions to uncover and resolve. Behaviour therapy is instead a structured and time-limited approach to treatment in which treatment goals and objectives are established early on, with an emphasis on the elimination or reduction of maladaptive behaviours versus developing insight. Behaviourally oriented practitioners work closely with the client in a collaborative process of problem identification. Together, the client and practitioner identify environmental conditions that are involved in the maintenance of problematic or maladaptive behaviours which then become the focus of treatment (Hayes et al., 1995).

As stated earlier, treatment outcomes in behaviour therapy emphasize the elimination of undesirable behaviours as well as increasing desired behaviours. An example of a behaviourally grounded approach to changing behaviour can be seen in work with a person who smokes cigarettes made from tobacco. It is now well known that smoking the highly processed and chemical-laden tobacco commonly found in most cigarettes leads to addiction coupled with serious health risks. In fact, nicotine is now known to be a very highly addictive substance making smoking cessation difficult in terms of treatment (D'Souza & Markou, 2011). Although a client may want to stop smoking, the concern about health hazards is seldom a motivation unless that individual has been

Figure 11.2 Behaviour Shaping with Successive Approximations

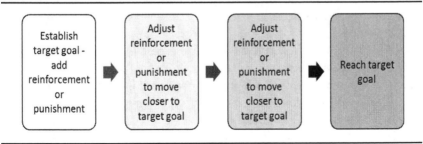

diagnosed with a specific life-threatening illness linked to tobacco use. Even then, smoking cessation is not an easy task. In behavioural terms, the pleasure or anxiety reduction associated with smoking is initially a more powerful motivator to continue tobacco use than a health condition that may or may not develop. In other words, the rewards of smoking outweigh potential risks, even when those risks are known and understood. In addition, people can also associate other pleasurable activities with smoking, such as interacting with friends, reading, watching television, or having a morning cup of coffee.

A social worker attempting to help a person with smoking cessation might begin with more typical suggestions such as replacing smoking with other pleasurable activities that do not involve tobacco. Cooking a healthy meal, walking, swimming, and even meditating are all examples of an approach to treatment in which a problematic or undesirable behaviour is replaced with another more positive, or in this case, health-promoting behaviour. Another potential approach is to attempt the creation of a negative association to smoking beginning with targeting the desire to smoke. A technique that targets the urge to smoke may involve the introduction of unpleasant stimuli such as the smell of wet cigarette butts soaking in water, an audio recording of a person coughing, viewing pictures of cancerous lungs, and so forth. From a behavioural perspective, this technique, known as *aversive conditioning*, can be understood as creating a negative association to tobacco use that would cause the smoker to link the desire to smoke with unpleasant images, sounds, smells, or thoughts, hopefully resulting in smoking cessation.

Although there are many well-developed smoking cessation programs involving nicotine replacement and behavioural or cognitive-behavioural therapies, the intention of this brief example has been to highlight behaviourally based concepts in relation to work with clients. Behavioural theory and behaviourist approaches to work with clients abound in the helping professions. Indeed, there are multitudes of other examples that have been published in books and research articles. In juvenile justice facilities and adult correctional settings, entire treatment programs for drugs, alcohol, and aggressive behaviour have been fashioned using behaviourist principles. In public school systems across North America, behaviourism figures prominently in programs designed to create or maintain safe and functioning learning environments. Although many social workers, counsellors, or psychologists might not want to think of themselves as being behaviourally oriented, the work they engage in regularly does, without a doubt, draw upon behaviourist concepts and techniques.

COGNITIVE FOUNDATIONS

The cognitive foundations of cognitive-behavioural therapy can be traced back to the work of developmental theorist Jean Piaget. Those aspects of Piaget's developmental theory that figure prominently in cognitive-behavioural therapy have to do with the manner in which information is understood and stored. Of particular importance is the concept of the *schema* (singular), or *schemata* (plural), which constitutes cognitive structures involved in the organization of perceptions, thoughts, and memories that become internal representations of the external world, and include the development of patterned approaches to thinking and acting in relation to problem solving (Walsh, 2013, p. 113). According to Piaget, knowledge that is collected and stored by children during various stages of development is necessary for them to make sense of the world around them.

The process of organizing information into the various schemata is referred to as *adaptation*, which results from a process of either *assimilation* or *accommodation* (Walsh, 2013, p. 113). The process of assimilation is one in which new knowledge is stored in the brain in a way that fits with an existing category or *schema* that forms part of an individual's understanding of the world. However, not all new information fits into existing categories. When this occurs, the individual must make modifications to mental structures that allow for the inclusion and understanding of new experiences and realities. The process by which new information is understood and stored is called accommodation (Kail & Cavanaugh, 1996). An example of this would be a child who has a pet dog and calls all other nonhuman animals a dog. This may mean other household pets, such as cats, are also referred to as dogs. When the child is corrected and taught that cats are different from dogs, the child switches from the process of assimilation to one of accommodation in which a new category, "cats," becomes another schema in which information is stored. Throughout life, humans engage in the processes of assimilation and accommodation as new information is either understood as fitting within existing structures or requiring cognitive reorganization through the creation of new schemata.

In terms of cognitive theoretical foundations of cognitive-behavioural therapy, the belief is that mental structures or schemata that become part of a person's understanding of how the world functions can also include inaccurate assumptions of the meaning of life events as well as overly negative self-assessments. When this occurs, those individuals who develop distorted views of the world (and most especially of themselves) believe that their views are accurate representations of reality. In accordance with the cognitive theoretical elements of cognitive-behavioural therapy, it is these inaccurate perceptions of life—often combined with highly critical self-assessments—that can lead to mental health conditions such as major depression or anxiety as well as negative and harmful behaviours such as substance abuse.

Cognitive-Behavioural Therapy

CBT involves elements of teaching, coaching, and reinforcing positive behaviours in clients (Somers, 2007, p. 7). However, behaviour change alone is only one part of cognitive-behavioural therapeutic work with clients. How clients think about their lives, the problems they are coping with, or the difficult situations they face, constitute important areas of attention in cognitive-behavioural approaches to treatment, healing, or helping. Contemporary CBT owes a great debt to cognitive therapy. Cognitive therapy emphasizes the importance of cognitive processing as being critical to understanding the manner in which all of us as human beings respond to a wide variety of conditions and events in our lives (Beck & Weishaar, 1989). In particular, cognitive therapy as an approach to treatment posits that what a person thinks about any particular event in her or his life is of greater importance than the actual event itself (Sue, Sue, & Sue, 1994).

Cognitive and behavioural concepts that form the theoretical foundation for CBT represent a blending of behaviourism with the cognitive therapy for depression originally developed by Aaron Beck (Leahy, 2004, p. 29). Beck credits the rational emotive behavioural therapeutic approaches of Albert Ellis for inspiration. However, as stated in chapter 9, *cognitive distortions*, which form one of the defining elements of CBT, can be traced all the way back to the work of Alfred Adler, who first discussed neurosis in his patients as resulting from distorted perceptions of reality in the form of "basic mistakes" (Mosak & Maniacci, 2011, p. 71). Much like Bandura's original social learning theory, cognitive therapy also conceives of the internal world of clients as being shaped by the environment and innate (meaning natural and already-existing) aspects of personality (Beck, Freeman, & Associates, 1990). Beck utilized the *cognitive triad* as a model to identify those aspects of cognition that influenced the manner in which clients would think about themselves and the world around them. For Beck, the cognitive triad was initially used to depict the three realms of cognition that could become distorted in depressed clients. However, the cognitive triad as a way of thinking about how thoughts and beliefs form perceptions

Figure 11.3   Cognitive Triad

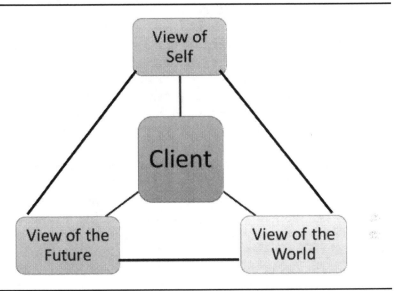

that influence behaviour has utility in terms of describing how clients view themselves in a variety of situations.

As a model, the cognitive triad focuses attention on what shapes thoughts and beliefs a person has about self, the world, and the future (Freeman & Reineke, 1995). For example, people who see the world as dangerous, hostile, and uncaring will likely have more negative beliefs about the future than those who believe in the innate goodness of human beings and the potential for collective positive change. Likewise, someone who sees her- or himself as being a victim of fate versus possessing the capacity to effectively problem solve will undoubtedly view the world in a different and potentially less-positive manner.

Cognitive therapy is based on the belief that our survival as humans beings relies on our ability to process information within our physical and social environmental contexts (Beck & Weishaar, 1989). For cognitive therapists, mental illness such as depression can be the result of faulty information processing that leads to negative and distorted thinking (Howatt, 2000, p. 137). Identifying and understanding distorted and negative thinking that leads to depression is clear in Beck's work. Beck discussed depressed clients as having developed a *systematic bias* in relation to information processing that resulted in negative self-perceptions, often in conjunction with negative views of the world and the future (Beck & Weishaar, 1989).

However, cognitive therapy goes beyond knowledge acquisition alone. Cognitive therapy also considers what Beck had identified as "affective valences," meaning that emotions are connected to specific events in the lives of individuals and that the information stored in the form of various schemata includes feelings related to that information (Freeman & Reineke, 1995, p. 189).

The majority of schemata were believed by Beck to develop during infancy and childhood. It is during this period that humans acquire a sense of self that is shaped by caregivers and others around them. Initial feelings of being loved, valued, and having worth develop during these early stages of life (Freeman & Reineke, 1995). It is also during this time that beliefs about safety, danger, and predictability of the external environment are thought to develop. In much the same manner as psychodynamic theorists, cognitive therapists place emphasis on the importance of infancy and early childhood as being a crucial developmental period in relation to emotional and behavioural health. In addition, the theoretical foundation for cognitive therapy includes a belief that the problems encountered in early developmental periods of life will have an influence in terms of responses to persons, relationships, and events during adolescence and adulthood (Ingram, 1984).

Cognitive Distortions

The theoretical concept that is central to cognitive therapy involves distorted perceptions that individuals develop in relation to themselves, the world, and their futures, as a result of the often-negative messages received from caregivers and other important figures in the social environment, especially, as mentioned above, during infancy and early childhood. Cognitive distortions are thus understood as misperceptions occurring in the thinking process that cause individuals to see themselves and events in their environments in a manner that is not an accurate reflection of reality. Although countless individuals are likely to have distorted thinking that may not accurately reflect their realities to some degree, it is the more serious types of cognitive distortions resulting in mental illness or problem behaviours that bring people into contact with social workers and other helping professionals.

Cognitive distortions may at times appear to be similar to defense mechanisms found in the work of psychoanalytic theorists. However, unlike defense mechanisms, cognitive distortions are not seen as protecting the ego from anxiety-provoking thoughts. Instead, cognitive distortions are more often associated with negative self-perceptions and assessments of the environment that often increase anxiety or depression, and therefore foster an inaccurate view of self and one's environment. The following descriptions of several cognitive distortions that are commonly encountered in the literature on cognitive therapy and CBT are accompanied by examples to help clarify their meaning.

Catastrophizing is a very common form of distorted thinking. Those who catastrophize anticipate negative outcomes in nearly all situations. In other words, they expect the worst. Moreover, this catastrophizing occurs in spite of evidence to the contrary. For example, a teacher with numerous positive evaluations may still view herself as a failure in her work and life. As a result, she becomes very nervous every time a regular evaluation is scheduled. Although her teaching skill has always received a high ranking, she engages in catastrophic thinking, predicting that this time she will be rated negatively.

Magnification is a process of viewing a situation or event as having far more significance than is actually the case. The phrase "blowing things out of proportion" captures the essence of magnification. A good example of magnification would be that of a social work student who becomes anxious and consumed by feelings of inadequacy about his ability to complete a difficult program of graduate study simply because unfamiliar terms and concepts are encountered on the first day of classes. Clearly, no one can realistically be expected to master an entire course worth of new material on day one. However, those who engage in magnification, as was done by the student in this example, will tend to see events and situations as being much more important or significant predictors of overall competence than they actually are. In addition, the self-assessment of personal competence arrived at by those who magnify situations is generally quite negative and self-critical.

Minimization is the opposite of magnification. The psychodynamic concept of denial, as a defense mechanism, is similar to minimization. Individuals who minimize events do not accord the degree of importance to them that they should. A good example of minimization would be that of a man who says he has no problem with alcohol use or abuse, even though he has been incarcerated for nearly killing a person due to driving while intoxicated. The man instead states that he was just in the wrong place at the wrong time and that everything will be fine once he appeals his case and demonstrates to the judge that the whole thing was a big misunderstanding. Another example would be a woman who dismisses the seriousness of a stage four cancer diagnosis in her mother, stating instead that lots of people get these diagnoses all the time and end up being just fine.

Dichotomous thinking is also commonly referred to as polarized thinking or "black-and-white" thinking. A person who engages in dichotomous thinking may be described as someone who assesses things as being either extremely positive or extremely negative, with very little room for other more complex possibilities. In other words, she or he does not think of events, people, or situations as potentially having positive and negative qualities. Dove, Byrne, and Bruce (2009) found that overweight women who engaged in dichotomous thinking tended to remain depressed whether or not they had success in weight loss, whereas women who did not engage in a high degree of dichotomous thinking were more likely to experience depression that is linked to weight gain or larger body mass. In other words, those who think dichotomously will see any degree of obesity as evidence of imperfection or failure and will continue to assess themselves negatively even when success in weight loss has been demonstrated. As is the case with dichotomous thinking, little room exists to see self or others as having good and bad qualities or moving in the direction of personal improvement. Failure to be perfect is viewed as failure in general. As a result, those who engage in dichotomous thinking will experience difficulty with more nuanced assessments of self, others, life, and perhaps even future prospects.

Overgeneralization is a type of cognitive distortion that involves taking one experience or event, usually negative, and generalizing feelings about that event to other often-unrelated events or life circumstances. This type of cognitive distortion can be seen in the example of a high school student who has difficulty with classmates in one class and then states "My whole day at school is horrible" even though all other classes are actually uneventful. With this particular student, the emotions connected with the problematic class have been generalized to the entire educational experience. Another example might be a person who applies for a job, becomes one of the finalists for the position, and is not selected. Instead of seeing her- or himself as having been among a select few, she or he instead sees not being the final choice as evidence of overall failure as a person.

Personalization occurs when someone interprets difficult or negative events in life as somehow being specifically directed at her- or himself, or being caused by her or his actions. The commonly heard remark "You take things so personally" captures the essence of personalization. Those who exhibit behaviours or make comments that are characteristic of personalization generally see the actions or remarks of others as critical, judgemental, negative, and directed at them. For example, a man sees a friend across a busy street. He shouts hello and waves to the friend, but gets no response. Instead of thinking "He didn't see me," the man begins to ask himself what he did to make his friend not want to acknowledge him in public.

Selective abstraction involves taking something out of context and believing it to be accurate while ignoring all other evidence to the contrary. For example, a university student who believes that anything less than perfect is a sign of failure might become depressed and very self-critical after receiving a grade of ninety-eight out of one hundred on a paper. The same student may remark that the missed points are evidence of stupidity and limited potential while ignoring the fact that the paper was nearly flawless.

Negative filters constitute another form of cognitive distortion that involves the maintenance of a negative self-image by filtering out evidence of worth or competence. Those for whom a view of the world is influenced by this form of distortion will quite often filter out compliments, expressions of praise, or evidence of positive attributes. This, combined with the tendency to dwell on the negative details of many situations, serves to maintain a negative view of oneself, one's world, and a pessimistic view of what will likely occur in the future.

Figure 11.4   Negative Filters

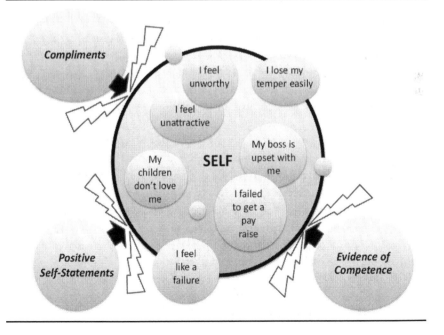

Four Basic Cognitive-Behavioural Techniques

Howatt (2000) identifies basic CBT techniques as belonging to one of the following four broad categories:

1. Reducing anxiety in the initial session
2. Drawing out basic assumptions and beliefs held by the client
3. Testing those basic assumptions and beliefs against existing evidence
4. Modifying problematic assumptions and beliefs that cannot be supported by existing evidence

However, maximum effectiveness of CBT requires a genuine collaboration between the therapist and client, with the client being willing to truly and actively participate in the process of challenging cognitive distortions, engaging in the testing of basic assumptions, and working to modify maladaptive behavioural patterns (Hofmann et al., 2012, p. 428). Therefore, the categories of techniques referred to above should not be understood as something the therapist does alone. Because CBT requires a great deal of investment and work on the part of the client, mutually agreed-upon and understood objectives are crucial to positive treatment outcomes.

Mental health practitioners engaged in therapeutic interventions based on CBT will generally begin the treatment process by acting to *reduce client anxiety*. Most people have never been engaged in therapy designed to treat mental health conditions. Therefore, the clinical social worker, psychologist, or mental health professional often needs to begin by utilizing basic elements of client engagement such as communicating openness, warmth, and genuine concern for the client. These elements, along with other components of establishing a working alliance (as discussed in chapter 6), are critical to reducing anxiety related to engaging in therapy. For some clients, the initial session may also include very basic information, such as clarifying the difference between friends, advisers, counsellors, and those who provide psychotherapeutic services. During this process, the clinical social worker, psychologist, or mental health professional will likely need to explain basic elements of client and mental health practitioner relationships such as confidentiality, the limits of confidentiality, and the process of professional treatment.

The initial session(s) will also include some form of assessment designed to identify problems and concerns that will be the focus of treatment, which with cognitive-behaviourally oriented therapy also includes early development of treatment objectives. Although many approaches to assessment exist through-out the literature, CBT requires focused attention on key aspects of clients' lives that contribute to the maintenance and/or exacerbation of emotional or behav-ioural problems. Williams and Garland (2002) have identified five core areas for cognitive-behavioural assessment that examine

1. life circumstances or situations, which includes relationship issues and other identified problems;
2. altered thinking (cognitive distortions);
3. altered emotions, which are problematic changes in mood or feelings;
4. altered physical feelings or symptoms; and
5. altered behaviours or activity levels. (p. 176)

Cognitive-behaviourally oriented clinical practitioners assert that finding the reason for a problem in mood or behaviour, although important, is less crit-ical in terms of treatment outcomes than understanding the altered thinking that influences the emotional health and physical well-being of the client. What-ever the original cause of emotional disturbance or problematic change in behaviour, altered emotions and behaviours can be maintained or even made more intense by unhealthy and unhelpful thinking, thereby making the response to an original problem itself a problem that must now be addressed (Williams & Garland, 2002, p. 178). The emphasis in therapy on emotional and behavioural responses to problems experienced in life is crucial to under-standing cognitive-behavioural therapeutic techniques. Therefore, techniques involved in broad categories of drawing out basic assumptions, testing basic assumptions, and modifying basic assumptions are all directed at changing the client's response (emotionally and behaviourally) to problems encountered in her or his life.

Drawing out basic assumptions is the step that follows reduction of anxiety. This involves engaging clients in a process of identifying and articulating basic assumptions about themselves and about their lives. Through this process, clients are helped to understand the manner in which they think and feel about themselves, the world around them, and their place within that world. For this reason, cognitive-behaviourally oriented practitioners do not maintain singu-lar focus on problem behaviours as is the case for strict behaviourists. Instead, they also explore more deeply what clients think and feel. As mentioned earlier, *affective valences* are the emotional components of clients' lives that are linked to stored information. It is believed by cognitive-behaviourally oriented therapists that faulty or problematic emotion-information linkages can result in distortions that do not reflect reality and are not supported by objective evidence in the environment of the client.

Testing basic assumptions occurs through a process of encouraging clients to justify beliefs about themselves, the world, and what the future may hold. However, cognitive-behavioural therapists engaging clients in this process also ask them to produce evidence to support their beliefs. A common approach to testing the validity of thoughts and beliefs involves *identifying discrepancies* in evidence presented by clients. As clients present conflicting information or ideas about "cause and effect" that do not seem to fit together in a consistent or logical manner, the therapist will ask the client to defend or explain the connection. If a client engaged in a process of testing basic assumptions cannot produce a plausible reason or reasons why a particular view of the world, of others, or of her- or himself should be accepted, that belief is open to being identified as a distorted perception of reality that can be challenged and targeted for modification.

An example of identifying discrepancies and engaging a client in a basic assumption testing process can be found in the case of a woman who was experiencing mild depression, low self-esteem, and some anxiety related to the conclusion that she is a "bad mother." The example begins with the client in her third session with a clinical social worker. At the beginning of the session, the client states that she is not a good mother to her three-year-old daughter and five-year-old son. This is the same statement she has made at the beginning of the two previous visits, which were followed by forty minutes of attempting to convince the social worker that she tries very hard to be a good mother. In the third session, the social worker remarks, "Each of the last two weeks you have said you are a bad parent and then you spend much of the session talking about everything you do to be a good parent. You have no involvement with child welfare, your children are healthy, appropriately dressed, well fed, and when I have seen them here at the office, they appear happy and loving." The social worker then asked the client what proof she has of her poor parenting skills. When she could not produce any evidence beyond saying that her mother thinks placing young children in day care is bad and that women should stay at home instead of working, the social worker asked the client if she has proof of this connection between day care and bad parenting. In addition, the social worker was able to produce articles regarding day care and positive adjustment in children. The articles were discussed with the client and then given to her to read again at home. This was followed by questions regarding the client's obser-vation of other children in day care. When the client stated that the other chil-dren were just fine, the social worker then remarked, "So what you are telling me is that it's just your children who are harmed by day care, not anyone else's chil-dren." The client responded by saying, "When you put it that way, it does sound kind of silly. I guess I shouldn't let my mother get to me so much."

In this particular case, the idea of being a "bad parent" because of placing children in day care was a distorted sense of self that was challenged through the identification of discrepancies between what the client thought and what the social worker had observed. This was then subjected to a process of testing basic assumptions that did not support the assertion of bad parenting based solely on the placement of children in day care. As sessions with this client con-tinued, the relationship she had with her mother became the focus of her treat-ment, which included several weeks of identifying cognitive distortions and challenging basic assumptions, which, in turn, was followed by a process of modification leading to a view of self that was more appropriately grounded in testable reality.

Modifying assumptions that cannot be supported by existing evidence con-stitutes the fourth broad category of techniques used by cognitive-behavioural therapists. The process of modifying cognitive distortions involves work dur-ing sessions as well as the assignment of tasks or "homework" that occurs between sessions. Sessions tasks, such as testing basic assumptions, may be followed by modeling and cognitive rehearsal that the client will be asked to reflect upon and practice between sessions. Homework may also include the use of audio recordings from sessions. These recordings can be listened to by clients between sessions to remind them of issues addressed in work with their therapists.

Additional Techniques

Modeling is a very important technique used by cognitive-behavioural thera-pists. It involves role-playing activities that are designed to help clients improve their ability to respond differently and more effectively to difficult or problem-atic situations in life. The client sees the behaviour of the therapist as a model to overcome her or his own behavioural problems. In CBT sessions, therapists may ask clients to take on the role of a critical parent, coworker, partner, and so forth. The therapist will then engage in a role-playing exercise with the client in a way that demonstrates responses consistent with behavioural changes being worked toward in treatment. Of course, the role-play technique can take on many forms with the client and therapist assuming different roles for different purposes. However, the intention of modifying behavioural responses to persons, places, or situations remains central.

Another important technique is *cognitive rehearsal*, which involves asking the client to imagine a problematic situation and then envision a preferred or more favourable outcome. The therapist asks the client to rehearse positive self-statements, positive thoughts, and to construct a mental image of a desired outcome or changed reaction to certain elements of one's environment. This CBT technique is often used in addiction treatment with clients who are coached in the development of strategies they will need when confronted by people and situations that could trigger a desire to return to addictive behaviours. For example, a client in treatment for heroin addiction states that he knows of three people who sell drugs in the neighbourhood near his home. In treatment, the client is asked to imagine ways to and from work that will reduce the likelihood of encountering those individuals. In addition, the client is also asked to rehearse in his mind and in sessions with a therapist or treatment group members what he will say if approached by a drug dealer. This process might begin with modeling through role-playing in individual and group therapy sessions and be continued outside of treatment in the form of cognitive rehearsal. For example, the client might even be asked to use a mirror and rehearse modeled and practiced statements of drug refusal while looking directly at his own reflection. The intention of this sort of cognitive rehearsal is to help the client build a repertoire of healthier responses to emotionally stressful situations that in the past might have led to problematic behaviours followed by feelings of failure and concomitant negative self-assessments.

Another technique of CBT involves asking clients to maintain *journals* that include a daily record of feelings, thoughts, actions, and emotional or behavioural responses to people, places, and situations. The journal entries help clients recall emotions, physical responses or sensations, and even basic assumptions about themselves, others, or life in general that have changed to varying degrees during the course of treatment. The client and therapist can then review journal entries as a part of regularly scheduled sessions. The review of journals in treatment helps the client and therapist identify improvement and areas of concern in need of ongoing or increased attention.

CBT may also involve the use of more strictly behavioural approaches in treatment. For example, *systematic desensitization, aversive conditioning* (mentioned earlier in the behaviour therapy section of this chapter), and *stress inoc-*

ulation are also techniques used by cognitive-behavioural therapists. Systematic desensitization is commonly used in the treatment of phobias. Systematic desensitization may begin with engaging a client in imagining an anxiety-provoking situation and culminate over the course of treatment with a real-life experience in which the client is supported through the process of facing her or his fears, with positive and encouraging statements from the therapist.

A good example of systematic desensitization can be found in the case of a client in the northeastern United States who had a morbid fear of hypodermic needles. Her fear was so debilitating that she refused to receive injections of any kind. Because the client had a trip to a tropical country planned as part of her employment, she would need to be vaccinated against certain diseases. Failure to do so would mean not making the trip and then suffering the consequences of difficulty at work. The stress of the situation resulted in a self-referral to a clinical social worker known to specialize in cognitive-behavioural techniques to help clients overcome phobias and face other fears.

Following an assessment and identification of the behavioural issues the client wanted to achieve in treatment, the client and social worker began their collaborative effort to address the hypodermic needle phobia. The clinical social worker in this case started by having the client talk about her fears. As the client began to feel anxiety, she was engaged in deep-breathing exercises and was reassured by her therapist, in a soft voice, that needles will not harm her and that the medicine they deliver will help her stay healthy. Once the client could talk about needles without anxious feelings, the therapist introduced pictures of hypodermic needles and continued the treatment process with additional steps from visiting a physician's office, to observing patients remaining calm while receiving injections, to actually holding a needle. Near the end of the treatment process, the client was accompanied by the social worker to the physician's office for her first series of vaccinations. The client was able to receive her second set of vaccinations on her own without experiencing the usual debilitating anxiety.

Stress inoculation, like systematic desensitization, is intended to reduce anxiety in clients. However, stress inoculation targets potential stressful reactions to experiences that have not yet occurred. Meichenbaum and Deffenbacher (1985) divide stress inoculation into the three phases: *education, rehearsal,* and *implementation.* During the education phase, clients are provided with information regarding what to expect in specific situations. In the rehearsal phase, the person has an opportunity to practice her or his reaction to a potentially threatening situation by role-playing an activity or event in safe and familiar surroundings. In the implementation phase, the person actually engages in the activity or experiences the event. Stress inoculation is commonly used for people who are scheduled to undergo surgery (Meichenbaum & Deffenbacher, 1996). For example, in the case of a child who needs surgery, the process of stress inoculation may begin with reading the child stories about surgery. This initial educative step may then be followed by engaging the child in play that features topics such as hospitalization and medical procedures. As a final step in stress inoculation, a series of visits to the pediatric ward of the hospital may be scheduled to familiarize the child with the pre- and postoperative environment, which may even include meeting other children recovering from surgery. The intention is to reduce anxiety about surgery by making the entire process less mysterious and more familiar.

CONCLUSION

Cognitive-behavioural therapy, with its behavioural and cognitive foundations, fits well with the highly individualistic orientation of the North American majority culture. While many practitioners in the field of mental health treatment point to the evidence base for CBT, it, like other popular but less researched forms of individual therapy, share certain common features. For example, psychodynamic psychotherapy and CBT, while viewed by many as being the polar opposites of each another, focus almost exclusively on internal causes for emotional problems clients experience in their lives. Mental health practitioners who utilize the theoretically diverse approaches to individual treatment found in CBT, psychodynamic psychotherapy, solution-focused therapy, and even person-centered therapy generally do not address larger social, political, economic, and structural elements of the problems people may face in their daily lives. Environmental destruction, place attachment, endemic racism, and a host of other variables that impact individual and collective health and wellness are generally not the focus of CBT or other individualistic approaches to mental health treatment that often appear to conceive of clients' home and community environments as neutral or of secondary importance in relation to developing and working toward treatment objectives.

Nevertheless, cognitive-behavioural therapy is an increasingly popular approach to treatment for a wide variety of mental and behavioural health problems. Meta-analytic studies of CBT indicate strong support for its use in the treatment of depression, anxiety disorders, somatoform disorders, bulimia, anger control problems, and general stress (Hofmann et al., 2012, p. 438).

Indeed, the list of mental and behavioural health problems for which CBT is shown to be effective seems to grow with each passing year. However, feminist theorists and other critical theorists argue that the highly specific focus on symptoms, which is the hallmark of CBT, ignores the impact of social oppression in the lives of clients (Payne, 2014, p. 153). While effective with certain mental health conditions, CBT is of limited use in many of the complex social, economic, political, and environmental contexts where much of social work practice takes place. Finally, CBT as a preferred approach to treatment for economically disadvantaged clients is less clear, due to the limited amount of research in this area. The same can also be said for ethnic minority persons whose cultures may differ markedly from Euro-Western populations (Hofmann et al., 2012, p. 438).

Chapter Twelve

Ecological Systems and Postmodern Practice Theories

INTRODUCTION

Ecological systems theory in social work reflects an understanding of human systems that draws on concepts from ecology and systems theory. One of the most cherished perspectives in social work, the *person-in-environment* perspective, is an ecological systems concept featuring a balanced approach to assessment and intervention that places an emphasis on the client and her or his environmental context (Allen-Mears & Lane, 1987). Indeed, those who advocate the use of an ecological systems approach in work with clients firmly believe that a balanced emphasis on person and environment is critical to effective social work practice (Compton & Galaway, 1999, p. 35). Ecological systems approaches to assessment and practice in social work make social work unique among the helping professions. This chapter provides a basic understanding of ecological systems as a theoretical orientation whereas upcoming chapters build and expand on the ecological systems perspective that has so profoundly influenced contemporary social work practice.

Also included in this chapter is information related to the theoretical foundations and techniques of three major postmodern practice theories: narrative therapy, solution-focused brief therapy, and motivational interviewing. These three theory-based approaches to work with clients are perhaps among the most familiar and widely used postmodern approaches to work with individuals and families. While all three of these theories are identified as postmodern, they have been selected for inclusion in this chapter because of the broad range of difference they represent in relation to problem orientation, techniques used by practitioners, and the approach taken to formulation of treatment/healing/helping goals and objectives.

ECOLOGICAL SYSTEMS THEORY AND PRACTICE

Payne (2014) identifies four concepts found in ecological systems theory that are common elements of social work practice in North America. He states that those who are engaged in practice that has been grounded in ecological systems theory will in general first begin by examining the connection between various systems in the lives of clients. The second step is followed by working with clients to identify life stressors. During the identification of stressors, the social worker's third step is to also look for evidence of client capacity for adaptation within environmental contexts, which is followed in the fourth and final phase of intervention by work toward fostering resilience in clients (Payne, 2014, p. 185). Ecological systems-based approaches to treatment/healing/ helping generally involve change efforts that begin with understanding social and other environmental factors impacting clients, while at the same time evaluating client responses to environmental stressors. The identification of life stressors includes examining the connection and/or interaction between the client and family members, friendship networks, work groups, and systems such as schools, places of employment, religious/spiritual communities, human service agencies, and so forth. Once the source(s) of stress within and between systems have been identified, the social worker collaborates with the client to fashion an intervention plan that will reduce the difficulty or stress experienced at that interface.

Major theoretical foundations for the ecological systems approach to assessment in social work practice can be traced to key theorists, such as Bronfenbrenner, Germain and Gitterman, and Pincus and Minahan. Germain and Gitterman's *life model* emphasizes an understanding of ecological principles that shape social work practice. Many social workers educated in North American social work programs are familiar with basic assumptions about professional practice that have their origin in the work of Germain and Gitterman's life model approach. For example, the life model approach to practice addresses poverty and oppression within the context of harsh and unresponsive sociocultural environmental conditions, difficulties in interpersonal relationships, and the response of clients to life events or problems experienced at various points in the life course (Gitterman & Germain, 2008). Preparation for ecological systems-based practice that is consistent with the life model approach has long required knowledge of human behaviour beyond that of life span-related physical and cognitive change. Social workers who strive to be competent ecological systems-oriented practitioners also need to be aware of the manner in which social, cultural, and economic factors influence the lives of clients within the broader environmental contexts of family, community, and even nation.

In the early 1970s, Pincus and Minahan developed another well-known ecological systems-based approach to work with clients. Pincus and Minahan's

Figure 12.1   Characteristics of Practice—Based on the Life Model

1	Professional practice in relation to individuals, families, groups, communities, and in the arena of political advocacy
2	Professional practice based in social work values and ethical practice guidelines
3	Professional practice that emphasizes the importance of skill development for work with diverse populations
4	Social justice practice that focuses on empowering clients and client populations
5	The integration and professional application of various modalities, methods, and skills necessary to intervene effectively with and on behalf of clients and client populations
6	Approaching work with clients in a manner that emphasizes partnership and collaboration
7	Collaborating with clients to assess multiple systems and environmental variables that impact their lives
8	Conducting client assessments in a manner that honours life stories
9	Recognizing the pervasive importance of social and physical environments in the lives of clients
10	The significance of culture in the lives of clients
11	Evaluation of professional practice
12	The importance of contributing to knowledge building in social work

(Adapted from Germain & Gitterman, 1980)

work emphasizes a systems and ecological orientation to assessment and intervention that identifies problems within and between systems, and then directs change efforts accordingly. Moreover, the manner in which Pincus and Minahan (1973) conceptualize ecological systems and social work practice moves away from an intense and often-singular focus on client adaptation, and instead directs social work intervention efforts, when warranted, toward intervening in other systems that are having a negative impact on client well-being or client capacity to achieve optimal functioning. In the systems and ecological approach of Pincus and Minahan, Payne (2005) identifies four basic systems of importance in assessing and working with clients. Those systems

Figure 12.2   Systems and Ecological Approach—Pincus and Minahan

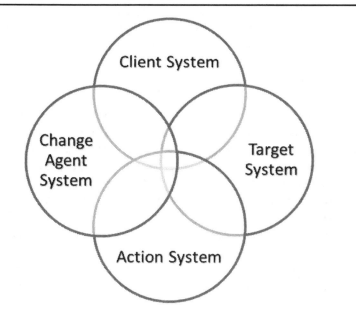

are the change agent system, the client system, the target system, and the action system.

Generally, the social worker or other mental health practitioner, and the agency that sponsors that person, constitute the *change agent system*. However, because intervention from a truly ecological perspective includes the client as well, the change agent system also involves actions and efforts on the part of the client. The *client system* is represented by the person or people with whom the change effort has been designed. The goal of systems and ecological interventions based on Pincus and Minahan's model is to work toward a positive outcome for the client system. Although this chapter is focused more specifically on work with individuals, the client system may range in size from an individual, to a family, or even an entire community.

In accordance with the Pincus and Minahan model, the *target system* is the person, policy, or practice that will need to be changed in order to derive the desired benefit for the client system (Netting, Kettner, & McMurtry, 2004, p. 319). Because an ecological systems approach to assessing and intervening with clients focuses on multiple aspects of clients' lives and lived experiences, the target for change may range from a behaviour engaged in by the client to poli-cies of agencies or even governmental entities. Last, the *action system* is com-prised of those persons with whom the change agent system must engage in an effort to achieve desired positive outcomes for particular client systems (Netting et al., 2004, p. 321).

Germain and Gitterman's life model, Pincus and Minahan's ecological sys-tems perspective model, and other ecological systems theoretically oriented approaches to practice do not offer a great deal of direction regarding what to do in relation to individual, couples, family, or group therapy. There have been attempts by some, such as Willi (1999), who have presented concepts related to providing supportive therapy and assisting clients in shaping personal *niches* that facilitate regulation of emotions and thought. However, ecological psy-chotherapy does not provide guidance in relation to techniques in the same manner as psychodynamic, cognitive-behavioural, narrative, solution-focused, or other forms of therapy. This is perhaps because ecological psychotherapy focuses less on diagnosing or working with diagnosed mental illness and more on the difficulty clients experience at that interface between themselves and other systems within the external environment. It is therefore the reciprocal and reinforcing nature of the relationship between the client system and sys-tems external to the client that become the focus of attention in ecological psy-chotherapy. So while ecological systems theory may not be particularly useful as a foundational theory for individual, couples, family, or group therapy, it is extremely valuable in relation to teaching social workers and other helping pro-fessionals to think in broader environmental terms when developing compre-hensive biopsychosocial cultural assessments that will form the foundation of treatment or service plans that may or may not include referral for clinical psy-chotherapeutic services.

THREE POSTMODERN PRACTICE THEORIES

Narrative Therapy

Narrative therapy is an approach to work with clients that focuses on examin-ing people's lives through their life stories. Narrative therapy has been used with a wide variety of clients ranging from those with moderate depression to persons having serious mental health conditions such as anorexia and bulimia. Narrative therapy has been applied to work with individuals, families, and groups. It has been widely used in school settings, and has been used in treatment for persons in recovery from drug and alcohol addiction. Narrative therapy has even been used in work with older adults as a strategy to assist them in altering negative and problem-focused life stories (Kropf & Tandy, 1998).

Treatment for clients working with narrative therapists does not have the clearly defined beginning, middle, and end phases that are more commonly encountered in cognitive-behavioural therapies. Likewise, termination is not prominently featured early on in the client-therapist relationship. Instead, termination occurs when both parties agree that treatment objectives have been met and that the transformational process is well under way. Unlike brief time-limited approaches that are increasingly popular, narrative therapy has a decidedly slower pace. In its ideal form, narrative therapy is a way of working with clients that does not emphasize quick identification of treatment objectives and rapid movement toward termination. Rather, it is the process of personal or familial transformation that is the focus of the interaction between therapists and clients. Much like Indigenous North American approaches, narrative therapy is complete when clients arrive at a point of deep self-understanding and commitment to positive growth and change.

In a manner that appears similar to Adlerian psychotherapy, the rational-emotive behavioural therapy of Ellis, and the cognitive therapy of Beck, narrative therapy examines the negative thinking that has shaped clients' views of themselves and the world around them. However, narrative therapy is not a cognitive-behavioural or psychodynamic approach to treatment/healing/helping. This is because there are key differences between the problem-focused approaches of the aforementioned forms of psychotherapy and the positive strengths-oriented approach of narrative therapy. The goal of therapy grounded in narrative concepts is to create a strong therapeutic bond that will open up dialogue intended to foster positive transformational change in the lives of clients (Wong, 2008). For example, whereas psychodynamic and even cognitive therapy may examine early childhood experiences to locate the genesis of problems experienced by clients, narrative therapy searches the past to locate evidence of strength and positivity. In other words, narrative therapy is a nonpathologizing approach to clinical work with clients that sees them as the experts in their own lives, much in the same manner as Carl Rogers's humanistic person-centered therapy.

Narrative therapy, unlike most of the forms of therapy used in Canada and the United States, did not originate in either Europe or North America, but instead grew out of the work of Australian Michael White and Canadian-born New Zealander David Epston. Although narrative therapists do help clients with identified problems, the examination of life stories is interpretive in nature, much as one would find in the anthropological work of Clifford Geertz. Perhaps not surprisingly, Geertz completed a great deal of his anthropological field work in nearby Indonesia. In his book *The Interpretation of Cultures*, Geertz (1973) develops his framework for symbolic anthropology which focuses attention on the role symbols play in constructing public meaning. Geertz (1973) writes:

> Man is an animal suspended in webs of significance that he himself has spun. I take culture to be those webs, and the analysis of it to be therefore not an experimental science in search of law but an interpretive one in search of meaning. (p. 5)

It is this interpretive approach to understanding behaviour and meaning in human beings that became so critical to the development of narrative therapy. Ethnographic research in anthropology, when properly and ethically conducted, seeks to understand the meaning of thought, belief, and behaviour within a given society. Ethnographers strive to avoid judging and instead work toward developing as much as possible a subjective understanding of life as it is interpreted by those who live within the community of culture under study. The combination of symbolic anthropological explanations of culture with the strengths-based approach of humanistic theory had a profound and lasting impact on White and Epston, leading to the eventual development of what is now known as narrative therapy.

The basic premise of narrative therapy is to approach work with clients in a manner that is respectful and nonblaming (Morgan, 2000). In this respect, narrative therapy and Indigenous North American approaches to therapy share the concept of *commitment to kindness* that respects and honours clients as whole persons when it comes to understanding the totality of their lived experiences. For narrative therapists, problems are seen as being separate from clients who are viewed not as people with deficits, but as individuals possessing skills that they can access through guidance and use to address the problems they experience in their lives (Morgan, 2000).

In summary, narrative therapy includes the typical person-centered approaches to engaging clients, followed by the assessment process in which the client is asked about the presenting problem that has brought her or him into contact with the clinical social worker, counsellor, or therapist. Once engaged in the treatment/healing/helping process, narrative therapy relies heavily on techniques that include the following:

1. Externalization
2. Mapping the dominant (problem) story
3. Deconstructing the dominant (problem) story
4. Reauthoring a new counterstory
5. Creating an audience (hypothetical and/or actual) to support the new counterstory

Externalization

The technique of externalizing, or creating a separation between a person and her or his problem-saturated story, is a key component of psychotherapy from a narrative perspective (Ramey, Tarulli, Frijters, & Fisher, 2009, p. 262). It is believed that once externalized, the problem does not hold the same power as is the case with something that is seen as inside of oneself. In addition, externalizing a problem is seen as decreasing the subjective sense of guilt and shame that is experienced by someone who sees her- or himself as being the embodiment of a problem, and therefore, flawed. When the problem experienced by a client is objectified or personified, it can then be open for examination by the therapist and the client. Externalization, as a therapeutic technique, involves

1. giving the problem or problems attended to in treatment a persona;
2. using the client's own words to create names for problems and central characters in problem stories;
3. listing the problems that have been externalized; and
4. describing the manner in which personified problems influence or dictate emotions and behaviours in the life of the client.

This process of placing the problem outside of the client allows the client and therapist to begin constructing the "dominant story," which is a way of seeing oneself in the world that the client, and indeed others, have come to understand as a true and accurate representation of reality (Monk, 1997). Typical themes for dominant stories may begin with the way people describe themselves, such as "I am a loser" or "I am weak because I am unable to manage my emotions." Labels or descriptions, such as "I am always an angry person," "I am a bad child," or "I am a discarded elder," can lead to negative stories people create about themselves. The self-blame and shame that people carry disempowers them, leading to feelings such as marginalization, depression, diminished self-worth, and perhaps manifesting in self-destructive behaviours.

The first step in constructing the dominant story that people create about themselves and their lives begins by giving a name to the problem and the central character in the dominant story. The externalization process allows the problematic nature of the dominant story to be converted into an external dialogue that the therapist and client can examine and comment on. When problematic emotions and behaviours have been externalized, the client and therapist can work as allies to address the problem(s). For example, the therapist might ask the client about a problem of "worrying" that has been identified by the client. The therapist might then encourage externalization by suggesting that the client assign a name to the person who worries all the time—something like "worried (client's name)" or "anxious (client's name)." The problem(s) identified by the client can also be given a name that does not have any connection to the client's name, or simply called "It." A very basic example would be that of a boy who spoke of the way he felt inside when he engaged in bad behaviour by calling the central character in his problem story "cousin, Jimmy it."

Early on in the history of narrative therapy, there were those who criticized the rather open approach to externalizing. This is something that was addressed by White (2006) with the development of a much more precise approach to externalization that utilized the Vygotskian concept of scaffolding (White, 2007). A map of the process, created by White, has five levels and involves movement from basic naming in the externalizing process to higher level thinking that involves plans for action. A therapist using White's mapping process might work with a client to create a map of the problem similar to one in the following example in which the client begins by naming, and thereby externalizing her or his concern with anger, followed by understanding how anger controls her or his life, and ending with actions she or he will take to address anger. Figure 12.3 is adapted from White (2006) and shows how the process would progress from one level to the next.

Understanding the Dominant Story

The dominant story that people have about themselves and their lives is influenced by family, community, and society (Monk, 1997). Dominant stories for clients who are seen by narrative therapists generally revolve around emotional and behavioural concerns that have been identified by the client or others with whom the client interacts. Questions that the therapist and client address together will help create an understanding of the meaning, power, and impact

Figure 12.3   Externalizing and Mapping a Client's Problem

		What is possible to know
5.	Articulate plans for action that are not confined or defined by the problem	"I am going to start walking and meditating to help me with my anger"
4.	Articulate abstract concepts related to life separate from the problem	"Being free from anger is important to me"
3.	Reflect on the negative consequences that are associated with the problem	"I don't want to end up bitter and alone"
2.	Explore negative consequences associated with the problem	"I am always feeling angry and it keeps people from getting close to me"
1.	Name and characterize the problem	"Mean Chris" or perhaps just "Anger"
What is known and familiar		

TIME ➤➤➤

of the dominant story on the life of the client. A discussion of the dominant story serves to expose what supports the continuation of the dominant story and how that story is subjectively experienced by the client. The process begins with the development of an externalizing dialogue that is used to discuss the problematic nature of the dominant story. As the problematic dominant story is made external, the client participates in this process and is encouraged to explore how the dominant story came to be what defines her or his life.

As stated earlier, dominant stories are shaped by interactions of the client with those in her or his family, community, and even the larger society. As the dominant story takes shape and becomes consistent and continuous, it is believed to be internalized by the client as a defining component of identity. For example, a woman who married an abusive man was told by her mother, her church, and her husband that she had created the situation in which she was living. Her dominant story became one of poor choices, failure to please others, and needing to be resigned to her fate. An important part of exploring the history of problematic dominant stories is to look for and acknowledge the effects of power relations. In the case of this particular woman, her personal story of powerlessness and failure was supported by many of the people and social institutions around her.

For disempowered people, the internalization of negative self-perceptions combined with a belief in limited ability to change, can also develop in response to oppressive social contexts (Payne, 2006, pp. 21–22). In Canada, many of the survivors of the Indian residential school era still carry with them enormous amounts of shame, anger, and feelings of being "less than" other Canadians simply because they are Indigenous. The development of this pervasive sense of not being valued or valuable has influenced the dominant story of Indigenous Canadians, reflecting the power of colonization in the lives of those exposed to racism and injustice. Therefore, recognizing power relations and naming the injustice is of immense value in the process of reauthoring one's story.

Mapping the Dominant Story

While working with clients to externalize the problems uncovered in the telling of the dominant story, the therapist adopts an investigative journalist approach in which she or he first asks detailed questions about the genesis and development of the dominant story while also listening for information that can be included in the creation of a new story, also referred to as a counternarrative, or simply a counterstory. Listening to a detailed account of how the dominant story developed will often reveal information that does not fit with the problem-laden dominant story, and can be used to create a new more-positive and life-affirming counternarrative (Gonçalves, Matos, & Santos, 2009).

For example, a man who characterized himself as "worthless" and a "drunk" was recalling a time when he went to the river to consume alcohol. He recounts that after only a few sips of whiskey, a car went off the bridge and into the water. He describes how he rushed out to the car, kicked out the window, and saved a woman and her small child. He also says that he had attended a public ceremony where he received a plaque and a letter commending him for his deeds. The therapist in this case planted the seed of a new story when she said to her client, "So, you call yourself worthless, but that woman and child would not be alive had it not been for you." In addition, the story was remembered and later used in the creation of a new story. This process of listening for information about the dominant problem story and what could be used to create a preferred or counterstory is referred to by narrative therapists as the technique of *double listening*. The technique of double listening is simply listening closely for information that can be included in the reauthoring process that will result in the creation of a new and more-positive counterstory.

Deconstructing the Dominant Story

Narrative therapy was not designed to be a fast-paced approach to treatment. The idea of constructing and deconstructing dominant stories takes time, dialogue, reflection, thought, and the development of a plan to create a new counterstory. The deconstruction process follows the mapping of the dominant problem story, in which assumptions the client has about life and self are explored. When the dominant problem story is constructed and understood, the therapist can engage the client in the deconstruction process. This may begin with simple questions such as asking the client if she or he prefers living life according to the dominant story, followed by a discussion of the hypothetical—in other words, asking the client what life would be like if things were different.

It is also during this phase that unique outcomes in life situations are examined to see how they counter the dominant problem story in the lives of clients. Recall the man who saved the woman and child from a car submerged in the river. This event did not fit with his dominant story of being "worthless." A therapist who has been engaged in double listening will recall events, situations, and outcomes that do not fit the client's self-image that has resulted from identifying with the dominant problem story. Asking the client how she or he would think or behave in a "different life" can also be combined with questions about what he or she would need to do in order to be like the person in a life that differs from the one currently being lived according to the dominant story.

Deconstructing the dominant story also involves acknowledging that the client can make choices and take actions that do not fit the dominant problem story. Seeing when and where the client has acted in ways that do not fit with the dominant story can be combined with inviting the client to critique the externalized dominant problem story. This technique is consistent with the strengths-based narrative therapeutic emphasis on recognizing and supporting the development in clients of a sense of efficacy, which means having the power and ability to make positive changes in one's life.

Reauthoring a New Counterstory

The reauthoring process builds on and flows from the deconstruction of the negative dominant problem story. When engaging clients in the reauthoring process, the therapist uses examples of exceptions provided by the client to initiate the creation of a new story, the *counterstory*. Reauthoring returns power to the client who now becomes the driving force behind developing a new self-image. She or he has been a participant in the deconstruction of the dominant problem story and is now engaged in the formation of a new more-positive and life-affirming existence through the process of authoring a counterstory that will become the new dominant story in her or his life. The reauthoring process builds on strengths and allows clients to create and inhabit preferred lives and relationships (Madigan, 2013, p. 456). Using once again the example of the man who saved the woman and child from a car that had plunged into the river, we can see actions and events that do not fit the dominant problem story of his life. The narrative therapist in this case asked the client to describe what was different about his actions on that day, followed by saying, "What do you think that woman, her child, and others at the ceremony who saw you get the plaque would say to describe you if I were to ask them about you as a person?" The client in this case was then asked how it felt to be seen as different from his usual self-perception—as living a story that is different from the dominant story that describes his life.

Creating an Audience to Support the Counterstory

The technique of using exceptions to initiate the reauthoring process is followed by creating an audience for the counterstory. In the case of the hero in the water rescue, the client was asked to imagine what others would say about him if asked. Clients also often have examples of what friends, coworkers, and family members have said that run counter to their negative dominant problem stories. Therefore, hypothetical and actual comments or reactions of others can be drawn into the creation of audiences for the development of a new, healthier, and more-positive counterstory. It is at this point in treatment that discussion transitions away from the problem story to an identity grounded in the new counterstory.

Critique

To date, most of the criticisms of narrative therapy have been directed at what researchers and scholars have identified as inconsistencies in relation to theory and method. Narrative therapy has been criticized for operating within the context of a social constructionist view of the world which is seen as compromising the objectivity needed to test therapeutic interventions. Narrative therapy is also criticized for not having been sufficiently subjected to the rigorous empirical studies needed to support claims of effectiveness. Etchison and Kleist

(2000) state that a focus on qualitative outcomes commonly found in narrative therapy is not in line with the current emphasis researchers in mental health place on quantitative research methods and results. Yet more recent research, such as the work of Vromans and Schweitzer (2010), which utilized a time-limited manualized approach to narrative therapy, lends support to the use of this particular type of psychotherapy in work with adults who have been diagnosed with major depression. Perhaps the debate over narrative therapy speaks to a deeper divide in psychotherapy that is captured by what Clifford Geertz (1973) said of anthropology regarding whether anthropology is an experimental science in search of law or an interpretive science in search of meaning. This debate still rages in psychotherapy regarding the various approaches to mental health work with clients. In addition, narrative therapy may quite simply be one of those approaches to treatment for which accurate measurements of effectiveness have not yet been adequately developed.

Solution-Focused Brief Therapy

The *solution-focused brief therapy* (SFBT) approach to work with clients is most often linked to Steve de Shazer and Insoo Kim Berg, who, in the mid-1980s, were part of a larger treatment team at the Milwaukee Brief Family Therapy Center in Milwaukee, Wisconsin. As is the case with narrative therapy, SFBT is rooted in postmodern theory and views clients as capable of creating new more-positive images of themselves beyond those that are narrowly focused on current problems (Cooper & Granucci Lesser, 2008, p. 196). SFBT as an approach to work with clients emphasizes the importance of identifying preferred solutions rather than focusing on past events or problems.

Therapists using SFBT emphasize the importance of envisioning a future in which the problems experienced by the client in the here and now have been resolved (De Jong and Kim Berg, 2008). With SFBT, the mental health practitioner and client work in close collaboration to find solutions. Much like person-centered and strengths-based approaches to work with clients, SFBT assumes that people are resilient, having the strength within them to make positive changes in their lives (De Shazer et al., 2006). SFBT also shares the resiliency orientation of motivational interviewing that strives to recognize and foster competence in clients (Miller & Rollnick, 2002; Miller, Zweben, DiClemente, & Rychtarik, 1994). However, what makes SFBT so different from even the most closely related postmodern therapies is that the focus in treatment/healing/helping is always on solutions. In fact, therapists using SFBT do not ask clients to provide many details about the duration and severity of problems, nor do they focus on finding possible causes for problems (De Jong & Kim Berg, 2008, p. 17). Instead, the identification of problems is shifted quickly to an emphasis on possible solutions. In addition, the number of sessions for clients engaged in SFBT will typically be fewer than six (Corey, 2009a).

Basic Assumptions of Solution-Focused Brief Therapy

The basic assumptions of solution-focused brief therapy are designed to maintain a focus on solutions to problems versus the problem-centered or even deficit orientation commonly encountered in other approaches to treatment/ healing/helping typically used by social workers, psychiatrists, psychologists, and counsellors (Corey, 2005). Those who collaborate and work with clients in accordance with the basic assumptions of SFBT engage in assessment and problem identification only to the degree necessary to find what the client is seeking help for, to identify negative ways of thinking that block movement

Figure 12.4   SFBT Orientation

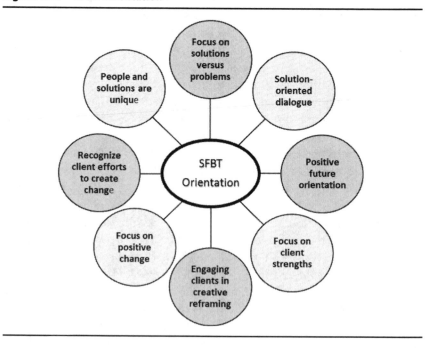

toward positive change, and to give direction to the type of solutions that will be sought in the process of treatment, helping, or healing (Corey, 2005). SFBT is decidedly future oriented and emphasizes the importance of using future-oriented dialogue.

Client strengths are identified early in the process and are built upon to fashion solutions that have been identified by clients. By engaging clients in positive reframing that encourages the adoption of a new perspective, clients are able to examine their life situations and the solutions they may desire in a way that had not been possible before due to being blocked by negative problem-focused thinking. Finally an SFBT approach to work with clients in the process of treatment/healing/helping means firmly believing that all people are unique and so too are the solutions to problems they present. In this way, SFBT is very person centered and very postmodern, rejecting standardized approaches to treatment and what constitutes an effective outcome in work with clients.

Key Concepts and Tools of Solution-Based Brief Therapy

According to De Shazer et al. (2006), key concepts and tools related to treatment/healing/helping in SFBT include the following:

1. A respectful, hopeful, and collaborative approach to work with clients
2. Looking for previous solutions
3. Looking for exceptions
4. Present- and future-focused questions versus past-oriented focus
5. Compliments
6. Inviting the clients to do more of what is working (SFBT goals)
7. Miracle question
8. Scaling questions
9. Constructing solutions and exceptions
10. Abandoning a problem focus in which the therapist is concerned about missing signs of what has caused or is maintaining a problem, and adopting a solution focus in which the therapist is concerned instead with missing signs of progress and solutions
11. Coping questions
12. Experiments and homework assignments

A Respectful, Hopeful, and Collaborative Approach—One of the most important elements of SFBT is the manner in which the therapist approaches work with the client. Because SFBT is future- and solution-focused, the client is viewed as the source of strength for change. The role of the therapist is to maintain a positive and hopeful demeanor, demonstrating a belief in the capacity of clients to be resilient and capable of developing and actualizing solutions.

Looking for Previous Solutions—SFBT therapists maintain that most people have problems in the past that they have effectively solved. Although problem solution may have been in a different context, the fact that attempts to solve problems have been successful is seen as a strength that can be drawn upon in devising new solutions. Even if problems have recurred, previous brief successes are viewed as evidence of potential to generate more successful attempts at creating lasting solutions.

Looking for Exceptions—Although clients may not have previous problem-solving efforts that were entirely successful or able to be repeated, certain behaviours or events may represent exceptions to problem-saturated ways of looking at life. For example, a middle school student who characterized his days at school as being full of difficulty was engaged by a therapist in the process of looking for exceptions to this very general and negative statement. Once it was discovered that there are certain classes and specific locations in the school that represent positive parts of each day, the student was encouraged to explore the reasons for that difference. This was then followed by a discussion of the manner in which the components of positive experiences and places could be used to generate solutions to problems in other parts of his day.

Present- and Future-Focused Questions—The use of questions in SFBT differs from that of other approaches to therapy in that questions become the primary approach to treatment/healing/helping. SFBT is not a confrontational therapy in which the therapist regularly challenges clients. SFBT therapists will redirect clients from a process of recounting the past, and problems related to past events, to one of working on the present while generating solutions that are future oriented. However, the process of doing so is more of an invitation to move toward solution generation versus confronting the client in regard to dwelling on the past. For example, a therapist might say, "I hear you talking again about the past and what you see as failures. However, your recent success at work was very interesting. Could we talk a bit more about that?" In this case, the therapist redirected the client away from a problem-focused past orientation to what is happening in the present. This was done through the identification of recent success in problem solving that could then be built upon to generate additional and more far-reaching future-oriented solutions. This brief example highlights the basic assumption of SFBT, which is that problems are most effectively solved by maintaining a focus on what is currently working as well as what clients would like to see in their lives in the way of solutions.

Compliments—Compliments are another very important element of SFBT. Providing validation for what clients are already doing well in their lives, while simultaneously acknowledging the problems they have faced, is intended to reassure clients that their concerns have been heard and to commend them for being able to function in spite of difficulty (Berg & Dolan, 2001). During the course of therapy, the uncovering of previous solutions to the presenting problem or other problems in the life of the client can highlight how the client has responded effectively to difficult life events, situations, or transitions. A therapist using compliments might say something like, "You were able to defuse the fight between your sister and her husband without anyone getting hurt. I know that must have been hard to remain calm, but you did and that is a very good skill to have when it comes to managing tense situations like the one you are facing now." Once the SFBT therapist has helped the client to recognize skills and abilities that can be applied to solution generation, the client can then be invited to continue doing more of what has been found to be effective as a means of facilitating movement toward solutions to identified problems.

Solution-Focused Goals—SFBT therapists and their clients work together to identify solutions in the form of clear and specific objectives that are directed toward the attainment of broader end-state goals. This is often done by helping the client identify smaller, more quickly achievable objectives versus starting with large end-state goals. In addition, framing favourable treatment outcomes in terms of arriving at a solution is preferable to identifying success in terms of eliminating a problem. For example, a client who wants to eliminate feelings of stress and anxiety might be helped to reframe a treatment goal in terms of developing a feeling of calmness. In addition, the small successes related to a goal can then be broken down into objectives and action steps. Finally, goals that are structured in terms of solutions can be more easily scaled.

Figure 12.5   SFBT Goals

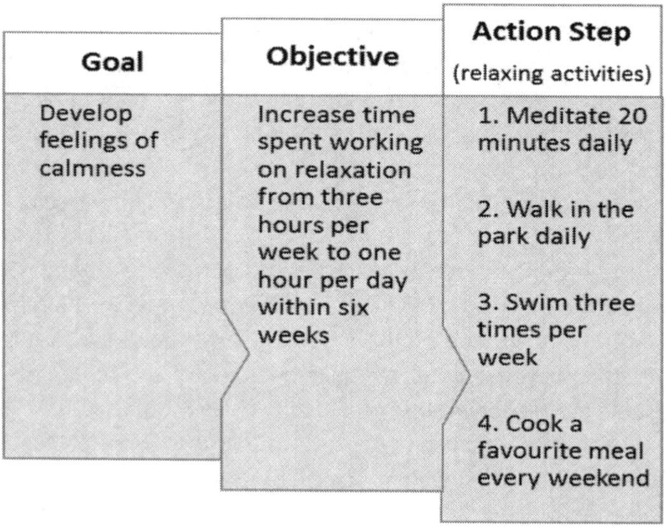

Goal	Objective	Action Step (relaxing activities)
Develop feelings of calmness	Increase time spent working on relaxation from three hours per week to one hour per day within six weeks	1. Meditate 20 minutes daily 2. Walk in the park daily 3. Swim three times per week 4. Cook a favourite meal every weekend

Miracle Question—It is quite common for clients in the midst of one or several problems to have difficulty setting goals or devising solutions. Using the *miracle question* to generate the solutions emphasized in SFBT requires engaging clients in a future-oriented process in which they are asked to envision themselves living in a world where the problem(s) that have been so central in their lives do not exist. Although most often identified with SFBT, it was actually Alfred Adler who first used the miracle question approach in work with clients. Adler would ask clients to think of how their lives might be different if their most difficult problems disappeared overnight. He also often followed this with asking clients to act "as if" this had occurred (Mosak & Maniacci, 2011, p. 91). This *acting as if* concept constitutes a behavioural component of SFBT that is linked to the miracle question because it involves rehearsal of new solution-focused behaviours, self-perceptions, and desired situations.

For example, a woman in a session with a social worker says that her current job is very stressful. She goes on to say that her workplace is a toxic environment and that the woman who is the director makes a point of targeting and humiliating employees for minor errors related to a complex system of documentation for which no training and very little direction has been provided.

The social worker in this case finds that the client is struggling with solution-focused thinking. At this point, the miracle question technique is used. The social worker asked the client to envision the perfect solution to her situation. When the client struggles with the concept, the social worker states, "If you woke up tomorrow and this entire problem were solved, what would have happened and what would your world be like?" The client responds by saying that her boss would have been replaced, and she could wake up feeling happy about going in to work. The social worker then asked how likely it is that the boss will be replaced. When the client says "not very likely," the next question is, "So what needs to happen to help you to feel happy at work?" This last question by the social worker leads to the concept of scaling.

Scaling Questions—Scaling is a way of helping clients measure their own progress toward goals and objectives. Whether clients have developed goals and objectives on their own or through being engaged in the process via the miracle question technique, scaling encourages clients to reflect and self-evaluate. Scaling most often starts with the answer to the miracle question. The client is asked to create a scale from zero through ten, and then reflect on feelings and the severity of the problem prior to the initial appointment

Figure 12.6   Constructing Solutions and Exceptions

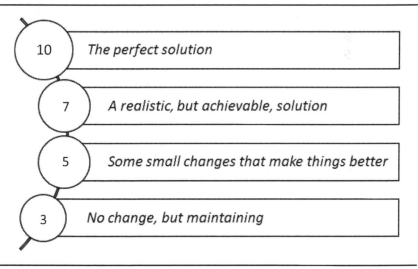

versus the day after the miracle had occurred. Generally, the perfect solution to a problem is not entirely realistic. Therefore, clients are encouraged to use the perfect solution as an inspiration to develop good but more-realistic goals and objectives.

In the process of developing a scale, clients start with where they are now and include what they have done to keep the problem from getting worse. This is followed by envisioning perfect and realistic solutions. As work with the clients proceeds, the social worker, counsellor, or other helping professional will ask clients where they place themselves now and what it might take to get to the next level. It is important to remember that SFBT emphasizes smaller achievable objectives with more concrete measurable steps versus starting with abstract end-state goals.

The social worker in the case of the client presented above followed the use of the miracle question discussion with scaling. For the client, scaling allowed her to regain a sense of competence by identifying strengths related to being able to still get her work done in her current hostile environment. Over a five-week period, the client in the toxic work environment went from using ineffective attempts to please her boss to actually seeking and securing new employment. Although she had started the SFBT process feeling paralyzed and demoralized, the solution-focused approach helped her achieve a realistic objective, which she discussed in her final session by saying, "I guess the miracle came true. I got rid of my boss!"

Coping Questions—Problems may often seem intractable. When progress toward solutions seems slow or absent, the practitioner using SFBT may ask what are called *coping questions*. Coping questions focus not on problems, but on what the client has been doing to keep problems from getting worse. In this way, clients are helped to reframe what might be seen as a failure in a manner that supports continued work toward solutions. For example, a client may have set a goal of being more active, losing weight, and eating healthier foods as a way of improving his self-image and self-esteem. After three weeks of very slow weight reduction, he may feel demoralized. A practitioner using SFBT might ask the client what he has been doing to stay focused on his goal in spite of difficulty versus simply giving up as so many people do. Coping questions are important, because many clients become overwhelmed by focusing on problems to the point of not being able to identify their own strengths and capacities.

Experiments and Homework Assignments—It is common for social workers, counsellors, and other healers/helpers to assign homework to clients for the period between sessions. However, unlike homework one might expect from a cognitive-behaviourally oriented practitioner, those who approach work with clients from a solution-focused perspective will generally ask them to engage in behaviours or activities based on something they are already doing that supports their work toward desired goals. For example, a social worker working with a client who has established a goal of stress reduction listens while the client states that last week she did something different. She says that while she normally goes from home to work and back home, a friend who walks every day asked her to take a forty-minute walk after work. While the client said she has declined the offer in the past, this time she went walking. The client added that she felt much more relaxed after she finished. Hearing about the client's exception to her regular routine, the social worker suggests an assignment that could be an experiment to be discussed in the next weekly session. The social worker asks the client if she could take a daily walk with her friend and report on her stress level in one week. The assignment in this example was based on something the client has done that is different (an exception) and that also had a positive outcome.

Applications of Solution-Focused Brief Therapy

SFBT has shown considerable promise as an effective approach to treatment/healing/helping for clients with a wide range of presenting problems (De Shazer, 1988; Miller et al., 1994). Recent research by Gingerich and Peterson (2013) lends support to SFBT as an effective approach to work with clients having many types of psychological and behavioural problems, with the strongest evidence linked to SFBT for adults with depression. Recent meta-analytic studies indicate that SFBT is similar in effectiveness to cognitive-behavioural therapy and that results are often achieved in fewer sessions (Gingerich, Kim, Stams, & MacDonald, 2012). This may make SFBT a good initial approach in a number of psychological and behavioural problems, especially with clients who cannot or will not remain in therapy that requires multiple sessions over a more extended period of time.

Motivational Interviewing

Motivational interviewing (MI) is a postmodern, nonconfrontational form of therapy that has its foundation in Rogerian person-centered approaches to work with clients (Miller & Rollnick, 2002). It is designed to help clients develop an understanding of their ambivalent feelings regarding behaviour change, with the intention of motivating them to move toward making positive changes in their lives (Treasure, 2004). MI also draws upon the transtheoretical stages of change model developed by Prochaska, DiClemete, and Norcross (1992). The MI approach, as is true for the stages of change model, makes the assumption that change will not occur until clients are motivated by a desire to achieve or maintain something of value in life (Miller & Rollnick, 2002). For example, a person may have said many times that she or he does not want to stop using alcohol. However, when a diagnosis of type 2 diabetes is given by a medical doctor and that diagnosis includes problems linked to heavy alcohol consumption, the fear of chronic illness leading to death may motivate a client to initiate changes in behaviour. Another example might be that of a person who has smoked tobacco cigarettes for many years, but is only motivated to quit after receiving a diagnosis of lung cancer. Whatever the reason, motivation on the part of the client (or potential client) is essential for treatment to be effective. The central premise of MI is one of creating desire for change through the use of person-centered concepts, such as warmth and respect versus coercion and threat of consequences for noncompliance (Treasure, 2004). The *stages of change model*, as adapted from Teater (2013), includes understanding the five components: precontemplation, contemplation, preparation and/or planning, action, and maintenance.

1. *Precontemplation* is when the individual does not recognize the existence of a problem and has no intention of changing.
2. *Contemplation* is when there is recognition of a problem, but the individual is not yet ready to commit to change.
3. *Preparation and/or planning* involve the steps taken to address the problem and engage in actions required to bring about change.
4. *Action* is when the individual engages in the actions necessary to create change in her or his behaviour. In other words, the necessary changes are actually being made.
5. *Maintenance* is when the individual engages in activities necessary to maintain change once it has occurred. This is the post-six months, up to a five-year period.

The "stages of change model" does not indicate a specific amount of time for each stage. However, anyone engaged in a change process will, in accordance with the model, need to move through all stages in the same order to accomplish the stage-specific tasks required for change to occur (Prochaska & Prochaska, 2009). Although the original model did not include a relapse phase, it is now known that change, and in particular change related to addictive behaviour, often includes periods of relapse. Therefore, helping clients understand that relapse can occur at any point in the change process is important. Moreover, this is true whether the practitioner is using MI or other approaches to treatment, helping, or healing.

MI was initially designed for use with persons who have alcohol problems (Teater, 2013). As a result (with the exception of health promotion), the application of MI to other populations has not been as extensive as is the case for SFBT and narrative therapy. Still, MI is used in work with clients outside of the addictions field. MI shares certain common features with narrative and solution-focused approaches. Most notable is that all three are positive, noncoercive, and nonconfrontational. In addition, all three approaches utilize a strengths perspective in work with clients. Finally, MI, SFBT, and narrative therapy all view clients as having the necessary internal resources and potential

Figure 12.7   Motivational Interviewing—Basic Principles

Express Empathy
- Demonstrate to the client a genuine desire to understand her or his subjective experience.

Develop Discrepancy
- Help the client identify where and how personal goals do not fit with current behaviours.

Avoid Resistance and Argumentation
- Do not force an issue. If the client is not ready to discuss an issue, come back to it later. Do not argue or engage the client in a debate about the need for change. Doing this will cause resistance.

Support Self-Efficacy
- Believe in the client's ability to change and acknowledge successes related to making positive change.

resilience required to make changes in their lives. The four basic principles of MI identified by Venner, Feldstein, and Tafoya (2006) and Teater (2013) include expressing empathy, developing discrepancy, avoiding resistance and argumentation, and supporting self-efficacy.

Express Empathy

The intention of MI therapists is that their clients will become motivated to work toward change. This is done through the use of focused and strategic reflective listening combined with helping clients develop discrepancies between current behaviour and important personal values or life goals. The process of engaging clients begins with expressing empathy in much the same manner as Carl Rogers's person-centered therapeutic approach. In other words, the professional who is working with the client begins by attempting to understand that person's subjective reality. This is achieved through the use of open-ended questions, reflective listening, paraphrasing, clarification, and summarizing—all common elements of engagement used to develop a working alliance with a client.

Develop Discrepancy

Developing discrepancy as a motivational interviewing technique is critical to creating motivation for change. In MI, developing discrepancy means that clients are helped to come to an understanding of what they value in life, what they would like to achieve, and the negative impact current behaviours are having on reaching important personal goals (Venner et al., 2006). Although other approaches to therapy, such as cognitive-behavioural therapy, emphasize identifying discrepancy between behaviours, thoughts, and personal life goals, MI is very clear that the client, and not the professional practitioner, must be the one to see and verbalize the discrepancy.

For example, a client in a session with a social worker who uses MI might be asked if she or he sees anything that stands in the way of reaching a desired goal of completing a university degree. The use of an open-ended question approach may lead to an admission that drinking heavily is getting in the way of studying for university exams. At this point, the social worker might use reflection to intensify and bring into focus what the client has said. The social worker might say, "So I hear you telling me that drinking is getting in the way of your studies and you worry that you might not graduate." If the reflection is accepted and perhaps refined by the client, the idea of mismatch between behaviour and the goal of graduation is further explored. The client in this case would likely be encouraged to discuss in greater detail how the two do not fit together. As this is done, the client becomes the one to develop and elaborate upon the discrepancy between personal values, life goals, and behaviours that do not facilitate living the way she or he might want to. Although this approach may take more time than other more confrontational therapies, those who use MI firmly believe that it results in fuller acceptance of the discrepancy by the client who might otherwise resist the observation had it come from the social worker or counsellor.

Avoid Resistance and Argumentation

Arguing or debating with clients regarding change will not make change happen more quickly. According to MI practitioners, the more a social worker, psychologist, counsellor, or other helper fights for change, the more she or he is likely to encounter resistance from the client (Venner et al., 2006). With MI, the realization that change is necessary results from the more careful and measured approach to directing the client toward change through the use of techniques such as reflection of statements and feelings, developing discrepancy, and supporting self-efficacy. If resistance is encountered, the practitioner working with the client needs to try another approach or perhaps return to the topic when the client is ready.

Support Self-Efficacy

Social workers, psychologists, counsellors, and other professional helpers using MI for the purposes of engaging and working with clients must also adopt the core Rogerian principle of genuineness. As stated in chapter 6, genuineness involves a willingness and commitment on the part of the professional helper to develop a true collaborative working relation with clients which includes removing the typical professional barriers that exist in professional relationships. This does not mean crossing professional boundaries and becoming the client's close friend. Rather, genuineness means being real, emotionally available for the client, and having a willingness to be a partner in the treatment process.

Those who approach treatment/healing/helping from the MI perspective emphasize the importance of being a partner in work with clients. This partnership includes truly believing in clients and their ability to bring about change in their lives. In this respect, MI also appears to share the *commitment to kindness* with Indigenous approaches to practice (chapter 8). Having a commitment to kindness, much as one would in relation to unconditional positive regard, demonstrates to clients that the professionals they work with care for and about them. At times, it may be difficult to support self-efficacy in clients. This is especially true when clients are angry, negative, or when progress seems slow or nonexistent. In accordance with MI principles, when a social worker, psychologist, counsellor, or other professional helper is a kind, caring, and positive partner in the treatment/healing/helping process, her or his support, combined with a willingness to believe in the client, is seen as an important motivator for change. However, as with all aspects of MI, the motivation to change and the actions engaged in to make change happen must come from the client.

Motivational Interviewing and Client Populations

MI is a nonconfrontational person-centered approach to work with clients. It may not be well suited for clients who prefer or need a more direct approach from the service provider (Teater, 2013). However, MI does have a solid base of evidence regarding effectiveness with persons who have substance use disorders (Madson et al., 2013). In addition, MI has been found to be effective with a variety of populations beyond just those with substance use disorders for whom behaviour change is the goal of treatment (Dunn, Deroo, & Rivara, 2001). For example, a 2003 meta-analysis of controlled clinical trials using adaptations of MI found that persons with problems involving diet and exercise also respond well to treatment based on MI principles (Burke, Arkowitz, & Menchola, 2003).

CONCLUSION

While ecological systems theory does indeed represent a shift away from the intensely intrapsychic or symptom-based orientation of assessment from a psychodynamic or cognitive-behavioural perspective, there are those who believe it still does not go far enough in examining environmental influences in the lives of clients. As Zapf (2009) would argue, the actual physical environmental part of the partnership between ecology and systems theory is lost in most discussions of the contemporary ecological systems theoretical foundation of social work in North America. Instead, emphasis is placed predominately on the social environment, with attention to physical environmental influences on the daily lives of clients being a less central, and therefore less important, additional consideration. Only in cases of natural disasters such as droughts or hurricanes, environmental destruction brought about by human actions, or the displacement of rural populations does the natural environment get mentioned. Seldom does the physiological, psychological, spiritual, or cultural importance of natural or even human-made environments receive the attention they should in a comprehensive ecological assessment and service plan development process.

When it comes to the popular postmodern therapies featured in this chapter, they, much like ecological systems theory, represent a move away from deficit-based models for client assessment and treatment. Nevertheless, each of these three approaches to practice has strengths and limitations in relation to client populations for whom they might be of use. Narrative therapy has been characterized by some as being of limited use for work with clients who are unwilling or unable to participate in the treatment process. Because narrative therapy requires a great deal of collaboration between the client and the mental health practitioner, a narrative approach to treatment/healing/helping indeed may not be the best choice in all cases. Nevertheless, narrative therapy is a widely used and respected approach to psychotherapeutic work with many different types of clients from very different circumstances and backgrounds. Narrative therapy also has many enthusiastic followers around the world who strongly believe in the effectiveness of the approach in not just helping but also healing clients.

Because MI, like narrative therapy, is not a brief therapy approach, social workers and professional helpers working with nonvoluntary clients in time-limited situations may find MI to be less useful than SFBT or other brief forms of intervention. Although there are conflicting reports on the overall effectiveness of MI, beyond substance abuse and health behaviour change, there does appear to be evidence for MI as an effective approach for use with clients who are ambivalent about change. Moreover, research also seems to support the effectiveness of MI with persons from ethnic minority populations who were involved in treatment that was not delivered in a manualized fashion (Hettema, Steele, & Miller, 2005).

As is the case with narrative therapy and motivational interviewing, SFBT is a collaborative and nonconfrontational, but fast-moving approach to work with clients. Because the emphasis on working toward solutions is addressed immediately, work can begin in the first session. Still, some client populations, such as those preferring a more Indigenous-centered treatment/healing/ helping approach may not be good candidates for SFBT alone. Likewise, very elderly persons, or those with end-stage terminal illness, might prefer approaches such as life review or reminiscence therapy. Nevertheless, a very interesting and important aspect of SFBT is the ease with which it can be combined with other therapies. Whereas some approaches to practice emphasize methodological purity, SFBT emphasizes "doing what works." Therefore, adjunct therapies and even pharmacotherapy could be encouraged by SFBT practitioners without violating the principles of SFBT, as long as they are working (Trepper et al., 2012, p. 33).

Chapter Thirteen

Family Practice Theories and Intervention

INTRODUCTION

Social work with families can be traced to the settlement house movement of the late 1800s. Jane Addams, who had been a central figure in the establishment of Hull House in Chicago, focused much of her attention on families. Since that time, helping families has remained a major area of practice for social work as well as other helping professions such as marriage and family therapy. Nevertheless, many professional practitioners are uncomfortable with the thought of working with families due to fear of being overwhelmed by the perceived immensity of managing interactions with so many clients at one time. Ironically, while many may want to shy away from working with families as clients, helping families improve their ability to provide a nurturing environment for the socialization of children is crucial to the goal of creating a healthier society overall.

Those who either work or plan to work with families need to be aware that families are seldom entirely cut off from the world around them. Instead, they are embedded in socioeconomic and sociocultural contexts that differ by neighbourhood, community, region, state, and even nation. Moreover, the natural and human-made physical environments within which families live add additional variables that need to be considered when assessing and planning for work with family systems. In this chapter, family practice theory, assessment, and intervention are explored from an ecological systems perspective that includes attention to cultural differences, and social justice/anti-oppressive practice concerns. In addition to assessment, this chapter also includes a description of how to use tools such eco-maps and genograms as part of assessment and treatment/healing/helping for families with a variety of needs. This chapter closes with a detailed family example that demonstrates various aspects of service planning combined with an assessment of family members in relation to risk factors, protective factors, needs, and potential professional social work or family worker interventions.

WORKING WITH FAMILIES

As had been stated in chapter 10, attachment experiences in childhood have an impact on people as they mature. If early nurturing experiences are negative or lacking, difficulty with attachment to others can even influence the development of healthy relationships in adulthood (Cohen Konrad, 2013, pp. 59–60). The relationship that forms between children and their caregivers can have an effect on many aspects of people's lives. Hardy and Bellamy (2013, p. 2) state: "early attachment relationships are linked to health outcomes through the impact of emotion regulation on physical health." Attachment relationships are critical because they not only shape how infants relate to caregivers, but they also help to shape the foundation of how people relate to others in adulthood. More importantly, early experiences with either nurturing or troubled attachments will influence how adults relate to their own children (Bretherton & Munholland, 2008).

Attachment occurs in all cultures, but it can take different forms depending on how the culture of a particular society or population is organized. In addition, each caregiver has a way of understanding childrearing that is shaped by many social and cultural experiences within and outside of the family. For example, in Canada and the United States, Indigenous North American family systems have been impacted by colonization and policies of forced assimilation. The residential school system in Canada and the boarding school system in the United States were government-funded and orchestrated attempts to remove Indigenous children from their families and communities with the intention of breaking the cycle of Indigenous cultural transmission from one generation to the next. The result of colonizing governmental policies aimed at eradicating Indigenous cultures, religions, and languages also had a very damaging impact on attachment, leaving many young people with limited knowledge about parenting because of the austere, regimented, and often abusive lives they lived in residential/boarding schools. The result of the residential/boarding school era is that in some families, the children and grandchildren of residential/boarding school survivors may have been raised by adults who themselves face obstacles to forming nurturing attachments. This difficulty with attachment stems from those needing a nurturing environment being raised by caregivers for whom a healthy capacity to foster attachment had been broken long ago.

The Psychocultural Model

The relationship between culture and personality has long been an interest of anthropologists. For anthropologists in the field of psychological anthropology or *culture and personality*, it is believed that collective and individual factors shape personality. Winkelman's Psychocultural Model examines four particular realms within which the culturally influenced adult personality is shaped. These four realms are the *innate skills and potential* (what is possessed by the individual), the child's *learning environment, cultural history,* and the *maintenance or cultural system* (Winkelman, 1999).

Innate skills and potential refers to the talents (called gifts in some cultures) that people are born with. However, innate skills and potential are much more. Innate skills have to do with personality qualities that emerge early in development and remain with people throughout life. Innate skill and potential is seen in some individuals who are very artistic, mathematically inclined, able to

Figure 13.1   Winkelman's Psychocultural Model

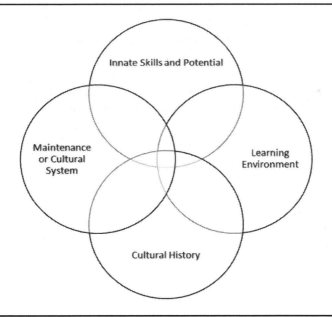

learn languages easily, have a seemingly natural capacity to form relationships with others, and so forth.

The child's *learning environment* includes the social network and physical environment within which she or he is initially socialized in terms of learning how to walk, speak, and interact with others. The learning environment is also where attachment experiences first take place. Within the learning environment, children develop their behavioural styles and learn about relationships between themselves and their caregivers, and between themselves and others in their immediate social network. The learning environments of children also include role expectations associated with age, sex, and status (meaning caregiver, child, sibling, etc.) within the family system.

The *cultural history* of a population group has an impact on personality development as well. Cultural history includes creation stories; stories of migration (voluntary and forced); relationships to the land; religion; changes that have occurred over time; when, where, and how population group identity has been shaped by persecution or privilege; and how particular population groups view themselves in the current social and political context in a regional, national, and global sense.

The *maintenance or cultural system* includes language, religion or spirituality, as well as family organization, kinship patterns, and how communities are structured (Winkelman, 1999, p. 70). Cultural systems also include the multiple manners in which people organize societies in terms of economic activity, governance, various roles occupied by members of the society that can be based on gender, age, earned or inherited status, and the degree and nature of social stratification that exists. For Indigenous North American First Nations, Métis populations, African Americans/African Canadians, Latino Americans/Latino Canadians, Asian Americans/Asian Canadians, and many other minority groups, cultural systems are also heavily influenced by contact with Euro-Western majority cultures in Canada and the United States. Therefore, development from childhood into adulthood needs to be understood in the context of bicultural and often multicultural settings which may include tension at the interface between sometimes very different cultural systems.

What Is a Family?

Images of family in popular Canadian and American national cultures generally perpetuate the stereotype of two young adult middle-class majority culture heterosexual parents in a first marriage with their own biological children.

However, this is not the only type of family, and in some settings, not even the most common type of family encountered by social workers, counsellors, marriage and family therapists, or other professionals who work with families. Blended families, single-parent families, families in which parents are same-sex couples, and families in which parents have never been married have continued to increase (Statistics Canada, 2012; U.S. Census Bureau, 2012). Therefore, a definition of family that is broad and inclusive is needed. In the late 1990s, social work educators and researchers Garvin and Tropman developed a definition of family that seems to become increasingly relevant with each passing year. They define family as "a set of individuals who have economic and other commitments to each other, who are likely to meet each other's needs for intimacy, and who usually maintain a joint household" (Garvin & Tropman, 1998, p. 127). Their definition is broad enough to capture many family types and could even be understood as encompassing the idea of families who may not share a household, but are otherwise connected to one another. It is important for social workers and others who work with families to assess family systems from a strengths-based orientation identifying the important, supportive, and nurturing qualities of a diverse range of family types, while also assessing the challenges presented by families in relation to meeting the needs of all persons who are members.

Culture

The influence of culture on family structure is far more critical in terms of knowledge than many professional practitioners realize. Furthermore, it must be kept in mind that assumptions about culture in relation to family structure, family roles, and the connection to extended family members often does not translate fully or well from one sociocultural context to another. Culture does indeed have a strong influence on the way families are organized and the manner in which they function. For Euro-Canadian and Euro-American majority culture families the nuclear family structure and the general emphasis on separation and individuation may be normative and highly valued. Conversely, certain European ethnic, Asian-origin, Latino, and Indigenous North American populations tend toward maintaining connections with larger extended family networks which include multiple members at each generational level from siblings through grandparents (Martin & Yurkovich, 2014; Morales & Sheafor, 1998). Likewise, African American families often include large multigenerational kinship networks (Hegar & Scannapieco, 1999).

Another aspect of kinship in Indigenous North American families is the inclusion of those who have no actual blood relation, but have become members of a family as a result of long-standing affiliation (Winkelman, 1999). The same holds true for African American families in which there is a long tradition of fictive kinship (Chatters, Taylor, & Jayakody, 1994). For Indigenous North American families, kinship may also include clan members or others within the community to whom a familial connection is known and recognized (Winkelman, 1999). In addition, a number of Indigenous North American societies are matrilineal, meaning that family descent and the identification of clan membership will be through the mother. Those working among more culturally distinct matrilineal populations, such as reservation dwelling Diné (Navajo) peoples of the US Southwest, need to be aware that families may be constituted very differently. In Diné families adhering to a traditional family constellation pattern, women and those descended from their mother's clan represent the most appropriate entry point for engaging a family in a treatment/helping/ healing process. This is because children are viewed as being most closely affiliated with the clan and extended family of their mother (Nydegger, 2014).

Social workers, counsellors, and family therapists engaging Mexican American and other Latino families should be aware that a hierarchical male-dominated family structure is a more typical pattern in Latino societies (Sue, 2006, p. 286). This means that those practitioners who initiate contact with Latino families in which a mother and father are present, should acknowledge the importance of male heads of household as a show of respect. This small act at the point of contact with the family can increase the likelihood of approval for engagement of family members in a treatment/helping/healing process. While the cultural ideal of Latino families is one in which males are heads of households, the current reality is that many are headed by a single parent who is often female. In addition, same-sex couples are becoming more common in various Latino communities, meaning that family structure, hierarchies, and patterns of communication will be highly variable and unique to the family unit in households that do not fit the more traditional pattern.

Sexual Minority Families

Social workers and others who work with families also need to be aware of the fact that a growing number of children are being raised in families where the parents of children in the household may be same-sex couples or persons with nondominant sexual preferences or gender identities. While such families face many of the same issues and concerns of all families in relation to the safety and well-being of their children, there are still barriers to acceptance and inclusion. Families in which parents do not fit the majority culture heterosexual model face additional stresses related to living and working in a society that continues to harbour prejudice toward sexual minority persons who do not fit within accepted sexual preference or gender identity categories (Knegt, 2011).

Social workers or other helping professionals who have fundamentalist religious beliefs may experience personal conflict in work with sexual minority parents and their children if those religiously based beliefs teach intolerance in regard to same-sex sexual orientation or gender identities that do not conform to Euro-Western male-female binaries. In order to be effective with sexual minority clients and approach them with a true sense of unconditional positive regard, tolerance is not enough. Social workers, marriage and family therapists, counsellors, and others who work with families need to develop the capacity to be affirming of the qualities, unique strengths, and potential for love and nurturing that exist in families that do not fit the heterocentrist standard of North American majority culture and society. Professionals working with families need to openly embrace existing and emerging forms of diversity and ideas of what constitutes a healthy, loving, nurturing, and supportive family.

Families with Special Needs

For nearly four decades now, children with special needs related to developmental disabilities have been served in the homes of their families and in various independent or assisted independent living settings in their communities. Still, many children with developmental disabilities tend to remain in the parental or caregiver home (Stancliffe et al., 2012). For much of the twentieth century and before, children, such as those with Down syndrome, did not often live beyond early adulthood, with many dying in early adolescence (Esbensen, 2010). However, those with Down syndrome are now living much longer and experiencing more age-related health complications. As a result, other health conditions, such as diabetes, heart problems, and the development of Alzheimer's disease, have become a concern related to caregiving (Stancliffe et al., 2012). For those who work with families that include special needs children, assessment and intervention now needs to include service planning in the present as well as helping families prepare for the care of dependent adult children with special needs once parents or caregivers are no longer able to do so.

THE FAMILY LIFE CYCLE

Beginning in the 1990s, Betty Carter and Monica McGoldrick began to write about the life stages of families with attention to the challenges family systems face during the life course. The family life cycle approach does provide some very good direction in terms of thinking about the stages a family will go through during the life course of the family as a system, and of the individuals who are members. The original concept of the family life cycle has been continually updated and revised since its inception with the inclusion of work by Joe Giordano and Nydia Garcia-Preto, who along with McGoldrick, served as coeditors on the well-known textbook *Ethnicity and Family Therapy*, first published in 2005. The importance of culture highlights the need to understand that families will see developmental stages, life transitions, and expected behaviours quite differently, depending on values, beliefs, and behavioural expectations that are shaped by culture. Still, the idea of work with families has continued to focus on the North American concept of the nuclear family unit.

Figure 13.2   North American Majority Culture Family Life Cycle

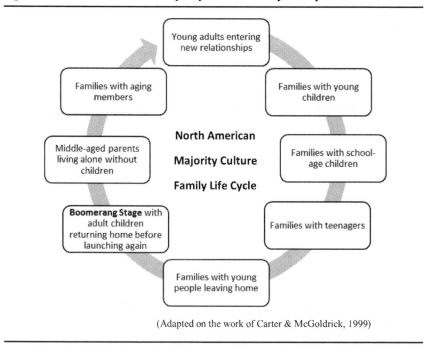

(Adapted on the work of Carter & McGoldrick, 1999)

However, the middle-class nuclear family focus of many Euro-Western models of the family life cycle does not capture the multigenerational nature of households and family systems among culturally different populations, particularly those who are collectivist in orientation. For example, the idea of children individuating and moving out to form their own nuclear families does not reflect the realities of many Indigenous, Latino, African American, or other non-majority population groups in which family members do not individuate in the same way, meaning severing most connections to the parental household and often moving great distances to start their own nuclear families. An alternative way to think about family life cycle development would be considering each individual in a context of relationships organized around her or his role and age cohort within the collective.

While this is more common among collectivist minority populations, it should not be assumed that people identified as being from the Euro-Western North American majority culture do not maintain a strong connection with the parental household, siblings, or extended family members. Some indeed do, especially in rural areas. In addition, as family systems are influenced by the

Figure 13.3   Collectivist Conceptualization of the Family Life Cycle

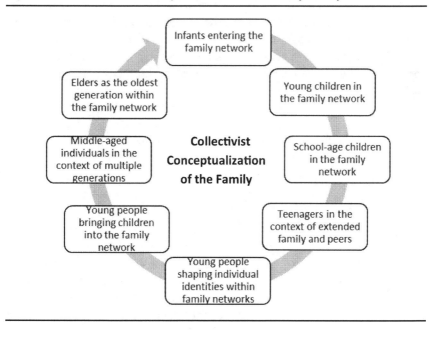

majority culture, some individuals from collectivist cultural backgrounds organize their family lives along the lines of middle-class majority culture expectations regarding the formation of nuclear family-focused systems that have separated from a collectivist style of extended family involvement.

Contact with Families

What brings families into contact with social workers, marriage and family therapists, counsellors, and other professional practitioners? Most often, families will first come into contact with professional family workers through child welfare systems, public school systems, youth justice/juvenile justice systems, and other institutions or organizations encountering families that are often in crisis or have exceeded their capacity to effectively problem solve without some sort of outside support. Clinical social workers specializing in family therapy, clinical psychologists, and marriage and family therapists also come into contact with families through these systems. However, that contact is generally the result of a referral initiated by a social worker. Although some families seeking family therapy services may be self-referrals, they are far less common.

Issues that result in the referral of families for a variety of services are many. The physical, sexual, and emotional abuse of young children represent common initial points of social work or other professional contact with families. Another common reason for contact with social workers, counsellors, or other service providers involves behavioural problems experienced at school or in the home. For younger children in the school setting, signs of potential child abuse often alert teachers who then refer children to Child Protective Services. In other cases, such as aggression in the classroom, children may be referred directly to counsellors or social workers within the school itself. Depending on the age of the child, such referrals may be limited to individual treatment or helping. However, many referrals will also require some degree of work with parents/caregivers, or even the entire family.

While early childhood is often a time when parents or caregivers, and those who work with families are most concerned with childhood health, safety, and development, preadolescence and adolescence present a different set of concerns. Although cognitive, physical, and emotional development are still very important, the transition from childhood to a preadult life stage can be a time of risk for emotional isolation, depression, identity crises, and suicide. In fact, as mentioned in chapter 6, adolescence and old age are the two most critical stages of life in terms of risk for suicidal behaviour (Fiore, 2011). During teenage years, physical changes, social changes, and mounting pressures to find one's place within a network of peers can be profoundly unsettling. While some navigate the emotional highs and lows of this developmental period, few do so successfully without having a social network that includes parents, caregivers, extended family members, friends, or others, such as teachers and social workers, to whom they can turn for support and guidance.

The Adolescent Transition

For young people between late childhood and early adulthood, there are a number of factors that are associated with increased risk for suicide. Although popular social fiction about youth in North America characterizes teenage years as a time of happiness, optimism, and freedom from stress, adolescence is actually filled with challenges and potential hazards, all of which can contribute to placing young people at higher risk for depression, anxiety, chemical dependency/addiction, and suicide. As Davidson and Linnoila (2011) state, the more prominent risk factors for suicide are

1. substance abuse (both chronic and acute);
2. mood disorders, schizophrenia, and borderline personality disorders;
3. loss of a parent and other major family disruptions;
4. same sex sexual preference;
5. having a family member who has committed suicide;
6. experiencing rapid social change or disruption;
7. emphasis on suicide in the media (coverage of suicide related stories); and
8. access to lethal means, such as guns. (p. xi)

Sexual preference and gender identity development are critical concerns during adolescence. Having understanding caregivers or parents as well as supportive social networks embedded in affirming communities can serve as protective factors for youth who identify as having sexual orientations or gender identities that do not fit with dominant heterosexual expectations (Hatzenbuehler & Keyes, 2013). Yet many lesbian, gay, bisexual, and transgender (LGBT) youth lack necessary supports and protective factors, placing them at increased risk for suicidal ideation and behaviour (Hatzenbuehler,

2011). While creating an affirming society may be a daunting task better suited to long-term planning and continued advocacy, addressing certain elements of the social environment on behalf of clients is possible. For example, social workers and school counsellors involved in helping LGBT youth may also include interventions such as working to implement antibullying policies that also address sexual orientation and gender identity differences in school environments. Hatzenbuehler and Keyes (2013) have found that schools with antibullying initiatives that include language related to LGBT individuals serve as a protective factor for youth with nonheterosexual sexual orientations and gender identities.

For preteens and teenagers, behavioural issues are also reasons for family contact with social workers and other professional practitioners. In addition to behavioural problems surfacing at school, preteen and teenage youths are at a point in life where problematic behaviour outside of home and school environments is more likely to result in contact with law enforcement. Substance use and abuse, criminal activity, violation of community curfews, and gang involvement are among the more common reasons young people become involved with youth justice/criminal justice systems, meaning that families may then have to contend with mandated case management and family therapy services.

Referrals throughout the Life Course

Contact with social workers and other professionals who work with families in crisis may occur through a variety of channels with schools, law enforcement, youth justice/juvenile justice systems, health care systems, and hospitals being some examples of common referral sources. Family members at all age levels from childhood through adolescence, adulthood, and even old age can experience mental illness, problems stemming from their own substance abuse or that of another family member, suicidal thoughts that can escalate to suicidal behaviours, acute medical emergencies, the development of chronic physical illness, sexual victimization and/or physical abuse, and of course death.

In early adulthood, a multitude of problem life circumstances, health conditions, and ongoing identity development concerns may result in persons seeking services from social workers or other mental health providers. While some aspects of treatment/helping/healing may be highly individualized, the inclusion of family members in the process also occurs in many cases. During late adolescence and early adulthood, the onset of serious mental illness such as schizophrenia is a risk (Gogtay, Vyas, Testa, Wood, & Pantelis, 2011). In addition, problems related to other forms of major mental illness and difficulties stemming from substance use and abuse often result in family therapy or intervention that includes a client's family members to varying degrees.

In the middle adult years, career-related stress, acting as caregiver for aging relatives and adolescents still in the home, and developing chronic health conditions are reasons individuals and families come into contact with social workers and a variety of other service providers. Women in particular experience the stress identified with the *sandwich generation* (those caring for aging parents and children) because caregiving responsibilities are still primarily attended to by women (Halpern, 2013). During this time, substance use disorders or other addictions may develop as clients seek outlets from life stresses. Life span and life course developmentalists, such as Levinson, see the midlife transition as one in which people begin to evaluate their achievements, often realizing that dreams they once had are now out of reach or need to be changed. Some people are quite capable of creating new and different dreams as they reach their middle years, while others have a great deal of difficulty coping with the loss of their youth, often precipitating what is commonly referred to as a *midlife crisis*. Middle age is also a time of loss of parents, older relatives, or even spouses, partners, siblings, or other middle-aged and extended family members.

FAMILY THEORY AND INTERVENTION

While engagement skills that are useful with individuals are also important in work with families, clearly families are not just a collection of individuals. Family members exist within relationship networks. Those professional helpers who work with families need to think of the total family system as the client, which requires a shift in focus away from the individual (Franklin & Jordan, 1999). As mentioned, families have a variety of constellations. There are nuclear families, extended families and blended families, as well as families with adoptive and other nonbiologically related members. Families, and the way they are defined from within and outside of the unit, will be influenced by culture. In turn, that culture may be derived from the larger Euro-Canadian/Euro-American society, the Franco-Canadian society, or one of any number of Latino, African/African American/African Canadian, Indigenous North American, Asian-origin, or other populations. Families may also have members with mental illness, chronic health conditions, or disabilities—all of which impact family life in ways that differ from the majority culture ideal or "norm" that for many decades has been the standard by which progress toward treatment goals has been gauged.

For much of the past thirty to forty years, treatment/helping/healing with families has been dominated by a general systems and communication theoretical orientation which has strongly influenced the vast majority of family therapy models (Franklin & Jordan, 1999). General systems-based approaches to work with families are likely to be familiar to many professionals who work with families because they themselves were undoubtedly educated in programs that based family intervention in systems theory. While change has taken place in terms of family work, systems theoretical approaches continue to be a presence in the field of family therapy.

Structural Family Therapy

In the 1960s, Salvador Minuchin worked with colleagues at the Philadelphia Child Guidance Clinic to develop an approach to family therapy that focused on family structure (Walsh & McGraw, 2002). Minuchin and colleagues were frustrated by the apparent ineffectiveness of Freudian psychoanalytically oriented family therapy. They instead chose to take a problem-oriented approach to work with families that was directive, present- and future-oriented, and also pragmatic. Although rejecting Freud, Minuchin's structural family therapy shows evidence of Adlerian concepts, in particular, a goal-oriented focus and the emphasis on the positive qualities of human nature, including the capacity to change (Walsh & McGraw, 2002, p. 48). The structural approach spends far less time delving into family history. The bulk of assessment and work are therefore directed toward addressing current problems and concerns as well as restructuring the family in a manner that will provide a better path forward.

Structural family therapy views families as being composed of subsystems. In ideal situations, families are understood as needing to be arranged hierarchically, with parents representing one subsystem and children another (Kaslow & Celano, 1995).

Figure 13.4   Structural Family Therapy Subsystems

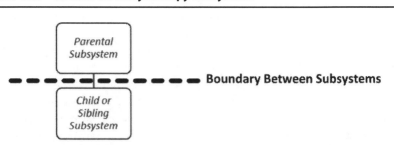

Those who ground their work in structural family systems theory for practice believe that reestablishing the parent subsystem above that of the children or sibling subsystem in a family hierarchy leads to better outcomes (Walsh & McGraw, 2002). Structural family therapists maintain that when subsystem boundaries are diffuse, the family can become *enmeshed*, meaning that all members are overly involved in each other's lives, thus not allowing for sufficient autonomy. At the other end of the spectrum are *disengaged* families. These families are characterized by very little emotionally warm and supportive communication. In disengaged families, communication between subsystems has often broken down, with family members withdrawing from one another and from the family unit. Some of the more common terms that have origins in the language of structural family therapy are alignments, alliances, boundaries, coalitions, and triangulation (Kaslow & Celano, 1995).

There are three phases in structural family therapy. The first phase is *joining,* the second phase is the *assessment,* and the final phase is *restructuring.* During the first phase of joining with the family, the therapist strives to understand the presenting problem from the family's perspective. This is followed by the

Figure 13.5   Common Terms in Structural Family Therapy

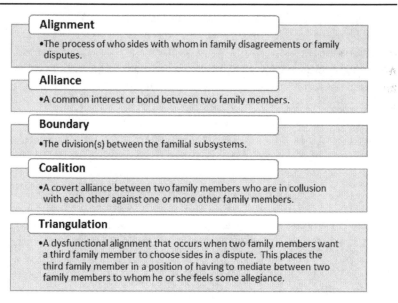

Alignment
•The process of who sides with whom in family disagreements or family disputes.

Alliance
•A common interest or bond between two family members.

Boundary
•The division(s) between the familial subsystems.

Coalition
•A covert alliance between two family members who are in collusion with each other against one or more other family members.

Triangulation
•A dysfunctional alignment that occurs when two family members want a third family member to choose sides in a dispute. This places the third family member in a position of having to mediate between two family members to whom he or she feels some allegiance.

(Adapted from Coggins & Hatchett, 2009)

assessment phase in which the family therapist must uncover communication patterns within the family in order to determine the structure of family sub-systems (Minuchin, 1974). Once family structure and communication patterns between subsystems have been assessed, the therapist moves on to the final phase of treatment, which is *restructuring*. In the final phase, the therapist works with the family to develop relational and communication patterns that are more effective. In addition, the final phase also includes the restoration of the family hierarchy with the parental subsystem above that of the sibling subsystem (Howatt, 2000).

Bowenian or Family of Origin Therapy

Murry Bowen, also a family structuralist, developed an approach to work with families that was in many ways similar to the structural family therapy of Minuchin. Bowen considered families to be made up of subsystems in much the same manner as Minuchin. However, for Bowen, the important task in ther-apy was to help the family become a healthy, supportive, connected, and uni-fied emotional unit. In Bowen's approach to work with families, the term *collusion* appears. Collusion takes place when two family members (usually a parent and child) have developed an alliance against another family member, which is often the other parent (McWhirter, McWhirter, McWhirter, & McWhirter, 1998). Bowenian family therapy focuses on emotional and behavioural issues, with the reduction of symptoms and relief of anxiety being central to the Bowenian approach (Howatt, 2000). A well-known assessment and treatment tool originating in the work of Bowen is the *genogram*. In a Bowenian approach, the genogram (discussed in the ecological systems theory section of this chap-ter) is used to visually depict family subsystems and map the points of stress and tension that exist within and between those subsystems (Walsh & McGraw, 2002).

Strategic Family Therapy

The third traditional family systems theory-based approach to work with fam-ilies is strategic family therapy. For strategic family therapists, the emphasis is on communication. Strategic family therapy is most often identified with Jay Haley, who used a brief form of intervention that took a targeted approach to solving specific problems presented by families in treatment (Walsh & McGraw,

2002, p. 64). Haley was influenced by Gregory Bateson, Minuchin, Montalvo, and others at the Philadelphia Child Guidance Clinic. As a result, Haley's strategic theory shows attention to communication theory and family systems theory. While Haley is generally identified as the founder of strategic family therapy, Virginia Satir was likely its most famous practitioner. Similar to other strategic therapists, Satir firmly believed that true understanding of family dysfunction lies in identifying problems in communication patterns between family members at verbal and nonverbal levels. Satir's technique of *family sculpting* was used to encourage family members to express their perceptions and feelings regarding family communication by physically displaying the way in which they saw family members relating to one another at the level of emotions and interaction.

In an example of the sculpting technique, a clinical social worker encountered a client in her late teens who had trouble putting her feelings into words while in front of her parents. The social worker suggested that the young woman instead create a family scene, without using words, which could describe her feelings. Her parents agreed, and the woman went to work placing her parents in chairs back to back, while she stepped out of the office and then looked in through a very slightly open door. When the client, supported by the clinical social worker, shared the meaning of her sculpture, it was revealed that both parents are physically close but they do not really talk about feelings. She then said that she herself feels excluded, much like an outsider looking in. The session was very emotionally powerful and opened up a dialogue in this small family of three that led to a weekly outing and family meeting in which everyone got to share feelings, whatever they might be. For Satir, as is the case for strategic family therapists in general, her approach to family intervention was focused on change and the development of healthy communication that is clear and congruent with the emotional reality of family members (Howatt, 2000).

Solution-Focused Family Therapy

Solution-focused family therapy (SFFT) and narrative family therapy represent alternatives to therapies based on family systems theory. Both of these postmodern family therapies utilize a strengths perspective that focuses on identifying exceptions to ineffective problem solving or negative self-perceptions. These exceptions are then used as examples of capacity for change. They form the basis of perceptual transformations and solutions that will result in positive growth and more effective problem solving. SFFT follows the same premise as solution-focused brief therapy for individuals. Emphasis is placed on assessing current attempts at problem solving to see what has or has not worked. The SFFT approach avoids pathologizing family members. Very little time is spent exploring the past or seeking the root cause of problems. Instead, assessment focuses on identifying problem-solving patterns that have not led to eliminating or mitigating the problem. This is combined with identifying exceptions to the problem situation. This means identifying when the problem has not been a problem and why. The identification of barriers and exceptions related to problem resolution is followed by working toward developing solutions, which in accordance with SFFT, is "the real work of therapy" (Walsh & McGraw, 2002, p. 9).

Narrative Family Therapy

Narrative family therapy is grounded in narrative therapy that originated in Australia as a new way to approach work with families (Rambo, West, Schooley, & Boyd, 2012). Narrative family therapy, like other postmodern therapies, does not engage in pathologizing the family. The narrative approach to family therapy is family-centered and strives to define the family in a broad sense, which means taking direction from the family about their own membership. As a result, the narrative approach may be multigenerational, constructed along culturally determined lines, and may involve fictive kin. Narrative family therapy includes engagement, assessment, and treatment/helping/healing that allows the story of the family and the family's identity to emerge. During the treatment/helping/healing process, narrative family therapy utilizes a number of techniques, which have already been discussed more fully in chapter 12. The primary techniques used in narrative family therapy are

1. externalization of the problem or problems;
2. mapping the development of the dominant (problem) story;
3. detailed discussion and deconstructing of the dominant (problem) story;
4. engagement of the family in reauthoring a new (counter)story of who they are; and
5. creating an extended family, friendship network, and even community audience to support the new counterstory.

Ecological Systems-Based Work with Families

Since shortly before the turn of the twenty-first century, those providing family therapy services have increasingly embraced more of an ecological systems theoretical perspective. This shift has also included a move to more socially and culturally relevant perspectives that go beyond nuclear family-focused interventions to include extended family networks and even other systems that may impact the family as a unit (Franklin & Jordan, 1999). Gender, sexual preference, ethnicity, culture, race, First Nation/tribal society, and many other factors impact the ways in which family members understand themselves in terms of connection to one another and their place in community and/or society. The evolving roles of women and men, combined with society-changing technological developments, are factors that must be considered when thinking of families in context. Although social workers in particular have long worked with minority, economically disadvantaged, and often marginalized families, the family systems theory-based approaches that were used for many years did not pay adequate attention to external environmental variables that impacted families referred for treatment.

Although many family therapists in the last half of the twentieth-century worked with families living in poverty, the focus of treatment approaches based in family systems theory tended to give only minimal attention to the larger environmental context. Intervention with families during this period most often emphasized attention to behavioural, emotional, and communication issues that would be more typical of work with stable one-earner middle-class North American families living in middle-class suburban environments. As a result, majority culture middle-class Euro-Western values and conceptualizations of family structures dominated family systems theoretical formulations. What was often ignored during this period is the way in which national, regional, and community environments had been profoundly altered by neoliberal and neoconservative social policies in conjunction with the forces of economic globalization.

The economic downturn of 2008 was an event that greatly exacerbated an erosion of the middle class—a phenomenon that had been occurring since 1980, especially in the United States. In 2014, the *New York Times* featured an article in which Canada was identified as having a middle class that was wealthier than their American counterparts (Babad, 2014). However, in a *National Post* article, Marr (2014) pointed out that Canada being identified as having the wealthiest middle class in the world only means that Canada is, for the time being, leading what is still a shrinking middle-class worldwide. Given the widening gap between rich and poor, combined with a rapidly shrinking middle-class, issues faced by many families at this point in time cannot be captured or addressed by emphasizing a family systems theoretical approach to the exclusion of larger environmental concerns.

Therefore, an ecological systems approach that focuses on understanding family systems within larger contexts has become necessary. An assessment of family problems or challenges must also examine the impact of rapidly changing economic, social, and physical environments in order to provide a more balanced approach to identifying and targeting change efforts. This may also require a double-pronged effort in which social workers and other practitioners engage in social and environmental policy advocacy while simultaneously helping families develop skills needed to cope with rapidly changing environments that often include employment concerns, availability of health care, mental health care, social services, employment or training opportunities, and even the degradation of the physical environment.

Multisystemic Family Therapy or Multisystemic Therapy

Multisystemic Therapy (MST) is a good example of a broad-based ecological systems approach to work with adolescents that engages multiple systems, such as schools, peers, and the family, in the treatment process (Walsh & McGraw, 2002). Originally developed by Scott Henggeler, multisystemic family therapy, also called multisystemic therapy, was designed for adolescents who have serious behavioural problems, are also often engaged in substance abuse, and in many cases are involved with youth justice/juvenile justice systems. The emphasis placed on empowering adult caregivers to resume their roles of authority over youth bears some resemblance to structural therapy in which the parental subsystem is empowered to take control at the top of the family hierarchy. With MST, social workers, family therapists, and others involved with the service delivery team provide services structured around a home-based model. However, in order to be successful, caseloads need to be low so that social workers and others can devote the time necessary to families that have multiple needs. As outlined by Henggeler, Schoenwald, Borduin, Rowland, and Cunningham (2009), there are nine MST principles.

The first principle is *finding the fit*, which requires an assessment of the total environment of the youth. In the process, the social worker or other professional in the role of MST therapist collaborates with the family to examine conflict and complementarity in relation to other persons and systems.

Focusing on positives and strengths, the second principle, is a critical component of MST. Social workers and others involved in work with the family utilize a strengths approach as a tool for engaging the youth and her or his family.

In the third principle, *increasing responsibility*, the social worker and others involved in working with young people and their family members help to identify and promote responsible behaviour. The goal is to increase a commitment to appropriate prosocial behaviour and a willingness to work toward reduction and elimination of problematic behaviour.

Present-focused, action-oriented, and well-defined interventions, utilized in the fourth principle, help to maintain an emphasis on the here and now. Problems are clearly defined and targeted for change that can be made immediately. MST is not insight oriented in the same manner as psychodynamic therapies. Instead, attention remains focused on present-oriented solutions.

By *targeting sequences*, the fifth principle, MST therapists examine the connection between various elements in the life of a youth that serve to maintain or exacerbate problem behaviours and target those links for intervention to create positive change. These links can be found within and between various elements of the environment, including family members, friendship and peer groups, schools, the community, and so forth.

Within the sixth principle, *developmentally appropriate* interventions are designed to be age appropriate and to match the developmental needs of clients. A developmental emphasis stresses getting a youth back on track in terms of age-related social, academic, and/or vocational skill development that will be necessary for successful transition into adulthood, especially for youth approaching later stages of adolescence.

Continuous effort, the seventh principle, refers to interventions that involve the deliberate practice of new skills. This affords the youth and her or his family the opportunities to internalize behaviours that will sustain positive change. In addition, continuous effort includes a commitment to recognizing and resolving problems as they arise versus letting them become larger and more difficult to manage. Finally, continuous change includes a commitment to recognizing and admitting that sustaining positive change requires regular adjustments.

The eighth principle of *evaluation and accountability* refers to the effectiveness of interventions by the MST therapist and other professionals involved in work with the family. MST therapists avoid assigning blame for interventions that do not seem to work. Instead, approaches to work with families that do not produce desired results are evaluated and modified or changed. All people involved, including MST therapists, case managers, and other MST team members, are responsible for the effectiveness of interventions with families receiving services.

The last and ninth principle of *generalization* refers to the skills developed by families as a result of MST interventions that can then be used to address problems that arise once service has been ended. The MST intervention process builds on family strengths and depends on the commitment of family members to maintain changes once the MST team is no longer involved.

MST in Combination with Other Approaches

MST is easily combined with individual therapy, such as cognitive-behavioural therapy, solution-focused therapy, narrative therapy, and group or individual treatment for substance abuse. MST also includes interventions with other systems to effect change for youths with serious behavioural problems. For example, a young person may be failing in school and arguing with teachers. The reason for failure may be related to emotional problems or even admitted reading and comprehension difficulties that are uncovered in therapy. The social worker using MST as an overarching approach to work with a family might then refer the youth for educational or even neuropsychological testing, followed by meeting with school staff to determine needed supports.

MST was particularly popular in the 1990s when the family preservation/family enhancement movement was flourishing. The MST approach to work with multiproblem families does have empirical support regarding effectiveness (Henggeler, 2011). However, because of the intensive nature of this particular approach to work with adolescents who have serious behavioural and substance use problems, often in conjunction with criminal offences, many agencies have backed away from programs that have low social worker-to-client caseloads, opting instead for increased caseloads and a return to residential treatment or incarceration for youthful offenders, in spite of the fact that studies have shown the effectiveness of MST and other approaches to family preservation in terms of saving money in the long run through reductions in the incarceration rates of youth and the improvement of family functioning that decreases the need for ongoing services.

Families with Aging Members

In recent decades, life expectancy has increased in Mexico, the United States, and Canada, with Canadians having the most favourable rates in North America. According to *The World Factbook*, produced by the US Central Intelligence Agency (U.S. CIA, 2013a), life expectancy for a child born in Canada in 2014 was 81.67 years. While in the United States, a child born in 2014 was considered likely to live, on average, to an age of 79.56 years (U.S. CIA, 2013b). Of course, females tend to live longer than males, and poverty greatly increases the likelihood of dying at a younger age. The same report identifies Mexico as having the shortest overall life span of all three major North American nations, with an average life expectancy of 75.43 years. Still, the fact remains that people are living longer and the population of elderly continues to increase in all three countries.

The landscape of service delivery to families in Canada and the United States is changing as the population of persons age sixty-five and older continues to grow. According to the Statistics Canada (2012) *Census in Brief* report, individuals age sixty-five and older accounted for 14.8 percent of the total Canadian population—an increase from the 13.7 percent in 2006. The United States Census (2010) reported the population of persons age sixty-five or older accounted for 13.0 percent of the total population; and, like Canada, those sixty-five and older are expected reach 20 percent of the total population by 2030. Along with aging comes an increased need for social workers and other professionals who will specialize in the provision of mental health, case management, and other services designed to meet the needs of an aging population. Moreover, the aging population will be more diverse. In the United States, elderly persons from nonwhite and nonmajority racial and ethnic groups have been projected to experience a 217 percent increase from 1999 through 2030 (Greene, 2008). This means that knowledge of aging will need to include an understanding of differences in the social and cultural context of clients as well.

For social work, as a profession, this means more students receiving a bachelor of social work (BSW) or master of social work (MSW) might want to consider work with the elderly through concentrations, specializations, or certifications in service to aging populations. This shift in focus from an emphasis on young families to one that includes many generations, often in the same household, will be critical for the provision of care to aging clients in the context of family (Greene, 2008). In addition, this process of specialization will need to include more training in relation to the management of chronic health conditions, including diabetes, different forms of dementia, cardiovascular conditions, pulmonary diseases, and various cancers, just to name a few. As people age, they often respond differently to medications. Elderly clients may have problems with sufficient absorption of nutrients, and of course, experience depression in connection to the accumulation of losses that include family members and friends. Finally, the loss of independence is another concern in aging as elderly individuals become increasingly dependent on others for their care. All of these variables combined make work with the elderly and their families a challenging field for social work practice now and well into the future.

Assessment

For aging clients, as is the case with all family members, a multidimensional comprehensive assessment is an important first step (see chapter 14). The assessment will aid in identifying risks and protective factors that are present in the client's environment. However, in preparing assessments with aging clients, social workers need to pay special attention to concerns that include not only health conditions and medications, but also the capacity for clients to engage in the two types of *activities of daily living* (ADLs). The first, *basic activities of daily living* (BADLs) involves typical or routine self-care tasks. One of the key aspects of BADLs for aging individuals is that of proper toileting. Tasks such as the completion of the acts of urinating or defecating, and the capacity to clean oneself properly afterward, are crucial BADLs for all persons and represent an important aspect of comprehensive assessment with aging clients. Other BADLs in the area of personal care would be those related to oral hygiene, such as brushing teeth or caring for dentures, or personal grooming which includes brushing, combing, or styling hair. Likewise, the ability to bathe or shower without assistance, to dress oneself, eating without being helped by others, and attending to other routine tasks, which may require functional mobility must also be explored in an assessment with an elderly client. The second group of ADLs are collectively referred to as *instrumental activities of daily living* (IADLs). IADLs are those more complex tasks that involve physical coordination or a higher level of cognitive reasoning, planning, decision making, and organization: for example, the ability to shop for groceries and clothing; the completion of housework, including cleaning floors, vacuuming, washing dishes, and doing laundry; balancing a checkbook and going to the bank; preparing food and meals; the successful management of medication regimens; the use of technology, such as a computer; using the telephone to make appointments with health care providers; and driving a car or using public transportation.

Another important component of assessment with aging clients involves looking for signs of potential abuse. While it is true that many families try to do as much as they can for their elderly family members, social workers and others who work with elderly clients need to be vigilant for signs of elder abuse. In Canada and the United States, abuse of the elderly is generally understood as taking five basic forms: physical, emotional, sexual, financial, and neglect. While most communities have protective services workers to whom family social workers or other professionals can refer clients, it is still important to recognize major warning signs of abuse in aged clients. Those at greatest risk for abuse are isolated older persons who also have mental health problems. Although many people think of elder abuse as being perpetrated by strangers, the majority of older persons who are victims of abuse report having been abused by their partners, spouses, or adult children (Acierno et al., 2010; Statistics Canada, 2007). Spouses or partners providing care may be coping with their own age-related health problems or even dementia, which adds to the stressors in the home. For adult children, the stress of work, other family concerns, and finances can all result in emotional overload causing them to lash out at parents who have multiple health care and mental health care needs.

Treatment/Helping/Healing with Aging Clients

At this time, life in the biological human form is finite. In other words, all of us will die at some point. The goal of social workers and other professionals who work with the elderly is to increase the quality of life for aging clients by helping them limit the period of debilitating illness (known as morbidity) in aging to a short span at the end of life (Hubert, Bloch, Oehlert, & Fries, 2002). However, for many clients and their families, the knowledge required to manage or avoid chronic health and mental health conditions may be quite limited. Therefore, social workers and other professionals working with aging clients need to be prepared to offer a wide range of supports that include therapy or counselling, psychoeducation, and a broad range of case management services designed to meet the needs and accommodate the wishes of aging clients and their families.

Aging is a time during which physical decline and isolation can lead to depression. It is now well known and documented that health conditions and various medications used to manage those conditions can also contribute to depression in elderly clients. According to the Centers for Disease Control and Prevention fact sheet (2012), among the groups at greatest risk for suicide in the United States are elderly males, with elderly white males being in the highest risk group of all. In addition, those elderly white males committing suicide are most likely to do so with a firearm (Kaplan, Huguet, McFarland, & Mandle, 2012). In Canada, elderly males are also at greater risk for suicide (Fässberg et al., 2012). However, whether male or female, depression in the elderly is associated with increased suicide and completed suicides. In addition, elderly suicide often occurs without warning and tends to be more lethal (Fässberg et al., 2012). Therefore, monitoring depression closely is particularly important with aging clients.

According to the National Alliance on Mental Illness (NAMI), depression in the elderly may be overlooked because it is considered to be a normal part of aging and is often thought of as expected sadness in relation to accumulated losses (NAMI, 2009). In addition, family members may mistakenly think that symptoms of depression are just part of aging-related various illnesses.

There are, of course, other mental health conditions experienced by older persons, such as anxiety, bipolar disorder, psychosis, dementia, schizophrenia

Figure 13.6   Symptoms of Depression in Older Persons

Symptoms of Depression in Older Persons

- Problems with memory
- Increased confusion
- Withdrawal from people and activities
- Changes in appetite, especially not wanting to eat
- Weight loss
- Complaints of pain that are not specific
- Difficulty sleeping
- Irritability
- Increased requests to be helped with activities of daily living (ADLs)
- Decreased physical activity and slower gait
- Demanding behavior

(Based on information from NAMI, 2009)

(which will likely have started much earlier in life), and problems with substance use and abuse. Many of the treatments for mental health conditions discussed in this text have also been found to be effective with elderly clients, and are often combined with pharmacological interventions. However, some older adults may be less well suited to the fast-paced and time-limited therapies that are increasingly popular. While research does demonstrate the effectiveness of cognitive-behavioural therapy with older adults, elderly clients have also been found to respond particularly well to reminiscence therapy, reminiscence group therapy, and grief group support (Wilson & Rice, 2010, pp. 126–128).

Integrative reminiscence therapy is an approach to treatment or healing in which the social worker or other helping professional engages the client in a process of working through emotions that are connected to negative events in the past. During the process, the family of the client may be involved to help the older person resolve past conflicts. This might even include family members from the same age cohort as the older person for whom the treatment or helping intervention has been initiated. During reminiscence therapy, clients are helped by a clinical social worker/therapist as they examine the course of their lives to find exceptions to the negative view they currently hold of the manner in which their lives have unfolded. By looking for exceptions, clients are able to construct new and more-balanced views of themselves in terms of how they have lived their lives. Negative events are not simply dismissed. They are instead understood, processed, and put in perspective. The goal of integrative reminiscence therapy is to help the client find meaning and worth in life (Watt & Cappeliez, 2000). Integrative reminiscence therapy is also used in nursing homes and group home settings in which people from the same age cohort can help one another in the process of examining positive and negative experiences in life, helping them see that others struggle with the same issues of trying to develop a balanced image of oneself that accepts the negative, but also acknowledges the positive (Wu, 2011). Through this process, clients begin to create a well-rounded self-image that balances negative self-assessments by also incorporating positive aspects of self (Watt & Cappeliez, 2000).

Instrumental reminiscence therapy still utilizes an approach to treatment that asks clients to review their lives. However, instead of focusing on emotions linked to negative events in the past, clients are involved in assessing their ability to cope with and overcome difficulties. Instrumental reminiscence therapy focuses on remembering past problem-solving strategies that can be used to cope with current difficulties. For example, a client might reveal that she was always pro-active when it came to facing problems. Such a revelation can be incorporated into the treatment/healing process to help the client design a plan to face problems in the present. The problem-solving skills clients reveal can also be of use in helping others, such as group treatment participants, in the resolution of (or adjustment to) problems they currently face (Watt & Cappeliez, 2000).

As stated earlier, aging is an important and growing area of practice for social workers, nurses, health professionals, counsellors, and many others who work with families, spouses, partners, and close friendship networks involved in caring for older persons. Helping families with aging members goes well beyond dealing with issues of loss, depression, and fear or anxiety related to declining health. Those who work with elderly clients and their families must also be prepared to guide them through the maze of the often-confusing eligibility criteria related to health care and mental health care services. In addition, aging clients and those who care for them will often be in need of guidance regarding decisions and choices that involve end-of-life decisions such as the updating of wills, understanding the legal obligations and limitations of those who might become power of attorney for elderly family members, and what to do in regard to hospice care or the use of extraordinary measures to extend life. Support for caregivers during elder care crises and protracted periods of caregiving will be critical for entire family or friendship caregiving systems. Therefore, it is crucial that social work and other professions continue to develop practitioners capable of meeting the growing area of service needs related to elderly clients and those on whom they depend for care.

FAMILY SYSTEMS ASSESSMENT AND INTERVENTION

Ecological assessments take a broad view of situations families are facing. Like family systems theoretical approaches, ecological assessment of families avoids identifying a person or persons as causing problems faced by the family. Instead, ecological assessment seeks to identify family relational stresses or challenges within the context of an environment that presents risk and protective factors. Ecologically based approaches to assessment and ecological systems theory for work with families actually represent a comprehensive approach to treatment, helping, or healing. The identification of risk and protective factors may result in work with a family that includes a combination of case management, family therapy, and even individual intervention for problems specific to certain family members.

Multicontextual Ecological Family Assessment

Figure 13.7   Ecological Systems Assessment

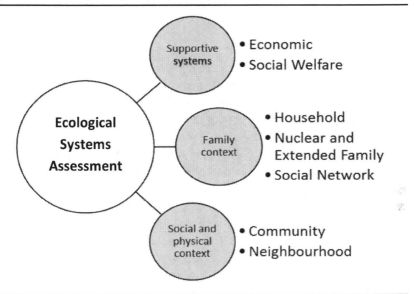

Supportive systems includes an assessment of economic resources, or in simple terms, having enough income or other resources to meet the basic needs of family members. For social workers and others who are engaged in helping families, this may include immediate and longer term intervention strategies. In the short term, families may need referrals to food and/or clothing banks as well as emergency cash or vouchers to purchase needed items such as food or medicine. Intermediate assistance in relation to securing income support would involve helping families acquire social assistance. A longer term intervention might involve aiding certain family members in the location of employment, or perhaps referring them to education and skill development programs that will increase their employability. Assessing for and intervening in relation to overall social welfare involves helping families gain access to needed health care services, mental health care services, addiction/chemical dependency treatment services, housing assistance, and multiple additional services intended to address or avert crises by stabilizing family living situations.

Family context represents the quality of relationships between family members combined with behaviours exhibited by individuals throughout the social network in which the family is embedded. This includes those living in the same household as well as family members who may reside elsewhere, but are still an important part of family life. Planning for family intervention directed toward appropriate and culturally relevant treatment, helping, or healing starts with assessing for risk and protective factors in the home or household as well as throughout family and friendship networks. This even includes those who are not family members but may represent either risk or protective factors.

Risk factors can be represented by substance use or abuse, major mental illness, family violence, difficulty in relation to effective problem solving, ineffective or nonexistent communication between family members, and any other aspect of family life that presents an obstacle to healthy optimal functioning. Protective factors may exist in the form of effective problem solving in specific areas or between certain family members. Individuals, such as grandmothers, uncles, cousins, or close family friends may be emotionally healthy, mature, and stable individuals who are able to exert a calming effect in tension-filled family conflicts. Moreover, these individuals may be recruited by helping professionals as allies in the treatment/helping/healing process.

The *social and physical context* of families is represented by the communities and neighbourhoods within which they live. Communities can have many risk or protective factors that include things such as the availability or lack of recreational or social services for youth and families, living wage employment opportunities for those needing to work, and access to education or technical training. Communities may also be settings in which families from racial, ethnic, religious, or sexual minority populations experience varying degrees of acceptance, fair and just treatment, respect for their human rights, and a sense of inclusion or marginalization.

Within neighbourhood settings, an ecological systems-oriented assessment is focused on identifying risk and protective factors presented by the immediate physical environment. For families, this includes adequacy and safety of housing arrangements, safety of the environment in terms of air quality, possible risks presented by soil contamination, access to safe drinking water, and any other potential hazard that may negatively impact the health, development, and safety of individual family members. Protective factors in neighbourhoods would include things such as adequate and safe parks or open land, safe schools, absence of crime or gang activity, the availability of nutritious food, and a well-maintained infrastructure or healthy and intact natural environment.

The Use of Assessment and Intervention Tools

Genograms and Eco-Maps

Two particularly popular and useful tools that help guide ecological systems-based assessment and intervention are genograms and eco-maps. A *genogram* is a visual approach to depicting family members, generational subsystems, and the relationships that exist between individual family members. In general, genograms feature multiple generations along with other information about family members (McGoldrick, Gerson, & Petry, 2008). Genograms should not be a singular endeavour completed by the social worker or family therapist. The value of completing a genogram in conjunction with family members is to include them in thinking about their own families and the relationships that exist between family members across generations. Genograms visually depict the quality and type of relationships in families, but they also include information regarding family members who are victims of domestic violence or who have problems with substance abuse, addiction, mental illness, physical illness, and so forth. In addition, genograms include information about deaths, births, pregnancies, miscarriages, divorces, adoptions, and other important events impacting family systems.

Although written materials and online sites devoted to genogram construction have very specific information regarding symbols that are used to create genograms, many practitioners, including the author of this text, have found it quite useful to include clients in the development of symbols with personal meaning. In other words, personalizing the process to fit the family is more important than making the family fit the process. For example, a social worker engaged in treatment with an Indigenous North American household of four, provided them with basic symbols for male, female, and death of a family member. Beyond that, all four members of the household, which included a female head of household, a grandmother, and two teenage children, developed a genogram with specific symbols of importance to them. The grandmother wanted to make sure that extended family members appeared on the genogram. The female head of household chose to include her ex-husband and his parents. The two teenage children, ages thirteen and fifteen, proposed giving each family member an animal. The grandmother very much liked this idea and the genogram process moved ahead with all family members becoming enthusiastically involved. Although there were contentious and sad moments in treatment, family members were able to openly and collectively discuss the quality and strength of relationships, whether tense, negative, close, distant, or nonexistent.

Eco-maps are another ecological systems tool that can be used to visually depict the environment of an individual client or a family system (Goldenberg & Goldenberg, 2013). Eco-maps are used to help clients and the professional practitioners working with them in the process of identifying risks, stresses, protective factors, and supports that exist within their environments (Compton & Galaway, 1999). Eco-maps are also of value in regard to targeting problem solving and planned change efforts. While genograms provide a visual representation of family communication and relational patterns, the eco-map is used to identify and examine systems and persons external to the family or household which have an impact on the family system.

Case Example, Including Genogram and Eco-Map

The following case example is of a fictitious family, which is being presented for the purposes of displaying a genogram and an eco-map, along with a treatment/helping/healing plan. The Musa family, a multiethnic and multicultural family system, includes blood relatives and fictive kin. The Musa family resides in the western Canadian province of British Columbia. This family has undergone immense and disruptive changes in the past year. This case presents multiple variables, issues, and concerns that need to be considered in the development of a plan for services related to treatment, helping, and healing. First, an assessment of the family will be presented, in detail.

The Musa Family

I. Identifying Information

Name: the Musa family
Ages and gender of family members:

> Father: Rashid, deceased, born in Pakistan
> Mother: Martha, age forty-three, born in Canada
> Son: Anthony "Tony," age fifteen, born in Canada
> Daughter: Marie, age thirteen, born in Canada
> Family Friend: Federico Quintana, age sixty-seven, born in the United States

Current Family Situation: The Musa family resides in a single-family home in White Rock, a town near Vancouver. Rashid Musa died one year ago in a tragic car accident on the Vancouver Blaine Highway during a heavy fog. Prior to his death, Rashid had been employed as a grounds keeper with the Vancouver public school district. Two months ago, Martha Musa received an eighteen-month prison sentence for trafficking drugs. However, her current projected release date may be as early as one year from now. She was transported to Fraser Valley Women's Facility four weeks ago. Fraser Valley is a federal facility. Martha has been sent there because her drug offence was a federal crime.

While Martha Musa is incarcerated, Tony and Marie Musa are residing in their home with a family friend and godparent Federico Quintana. The house the family lives in is completely paid for. The utilities are covered by the survivor's benefits the family receives through the Canada Pension Plan.

II. Reason for Referral and Referral Source

The Musa family was referred to Family Preservation and Reunification Services through the Ministry of Children and Family Development (MCFD). According to the protective services caseworker, Marie and Tony were living in the home, unsupervised, following the incarceration of their mother. The situation was brought to the attention of MCFD workers when Marie and Tony began to have multiple absences from school combined with failing grades. When the school social worker asked Marie about her home life, Marie began to cry and stated that her mother was in prison. Since that time, a family friend and godparent of both children, Federico Quintana, has been living in the home with Tony and Marie. Martha filed the guardianship paperwork designating Federico as guardian before she (Martha) was incarcerated. Guardianship will be in force until Martha returns home.

III. Client's View of the Family Situation

Marie and Tony express anger toward their mother for her incarceration. Their mother, Martha, claims that she had planned to transport drugs only one time to help "make ends meet." She states that the death of her husband left her with several outstanding financial commitments and that she was slipping further into debt. Tony and Marie claim that they would have worked to help their mother, who had never been employed outside of the home. Since her arrival at the prison, Martha has been placed on antidepressant medication. Martha claims that she feels a great deal of shame in relation to her actions. While in prison, she has been involved in computer classes and hopes to gain employment as a secretary upon release. Martha states that she believed Federico was in the home all along. When she found out otherwise, she became very upset and angry, especially with her son, Tony. Tony states that he believes that he and his sister could have managed until their mother was released. He has admitted being angry at his sister for telling the school social worker about their problems.

IV. Information about the Family from Other Sources

The school social worker states that neither of the Musa children had ever been in trouble at school and that both were "good students." The caseworker from MCFD claims that a background check of the family friend, Mr. Quintana, did not uncover any criminal record or information that would otherwise disqual-ify him to continue as temporary guardian. According to the caseworker, Federico Quintana is a widower, whose children have moved out of the area. Mr. Quintana lives alone in his own apartment. According to the caseworker, Mr. Quintana stated that Tony wanted to manage things on his own and that he (Federico) was willing to let him try.

V. Major Issues Related to Family Functioning

Clearly, the death of Rashid Musa has resulted in a major disruption in the func-tioning of this family. All family members speak fondly of Rashid and both chil-dren state that they loved their father very much.

Martha's incarceration has also placed an enormous strain on this family's sense of integrity. During the initial family meeting with the MCFD caseworker, Marie cried and stated that she is afraid her family is falling apart after her father's death.

VI. Additional Information

The Musa family is under a tremendous amount of strain. Multiple factors have created a sense of crisis in relation to keeping the family together. The sudden death of Rashid Musa and the subsequent incarceration of Martha Musa have resulted in multiple losses, changes in family routines, and many unresolved issues related to grief, shame, anger, and resentment. The distance of the prison from the family home (about fifty kilometres/thirty-one miles) will make regu-lar visits a potentially costly aspect of treatment. Federico Quintana has volun-teered to drive the children to the prison weekly. However, funding for the trips could become an issue.

An examination of the family history has revealed no past problems in rela-tion to chemical dependency or mental illness in either parent. In fact, accounts of the family's history by both children, by Martha, and by Federico Quintana give all indications that this family was functioning in a manner that they themselves characterized as "normal" with only minor and short-term problems related to setting rules and boundaries that are typical of most families with teenage and preteen children.

The Musas have relatives in Pakistan on the father's side. Family members in Pakistan are aware of the death of Rashid Musa and eight family members attended his funeral. Martha has relatives in Hamilton, Ontario. Her family is also aware of the death of Rashid Musa. Martha's family is aware of her incarceration. However, the family in Pakistan is not. Although Rashid Musa was Muslim, he did not practice his religion. Martha is Italian Canadian and she states she is Roman Catholic. Both children have attended the local Catholic Church on high religious holidays, such as Christmas and Easter, but neither Martha nor her children profess to be "religious" people.

Mother: Martha Musa, age forty-three, was born in Ontario and moved to British Columbia with her husband, Rashid, shortly after she and Rashid were married. Martha met Rashid while they were in high school. Rashid had moved from Pakistan to Hamilton and was living with an uncle while he, Rashid, attended his senior year of high school. Rashid's parents wanted their son to go to school in Canada in hopes of building a more economically secure future for himself. Although Martha and Rashid were married in the Catholic Church, Martha also traveled to Pakistan with Rashid, where they were married in a Muslim ceremony. The fact that Martha would travel to their country and agree to be married in their faith as well made Rashid's parents very happy. Rashid worked for a short period of time as a grounds keeper for the public schools in Hamilton, Ontario, when a chance to move to British Columbia arose. Martha and Rashid agreed the move represented a good opportunity.

During the early part of their marriage, Rashid and Martha tried several times to have children. However, Martha had difficulty becoming pregnant. Finally, at age twenty-eight, Tony was born. Two years later, Marie was born. Martha states that the birth of both children made her husband very happy. She still recalls seeing him in the hospital room holding his newborn children and remarking about how precious and beautiful they were.

Rashid died last year on his way to work. He was involved in a tragic accident in heavy fog. His vehicle was hit by a large semitruck. Rashid's death was sudden and devastating. Martha states that her husband was a loving and caring man who always made sure she was taken care of. Martha states that Rashid did not want her to have to work outside of the home, and Martha states that she enjoyed caring for her children and family. However, she now feels that if she had worked outside of the home, the death of her husband might not have been such a financial and personal shock to her or to her family. While in prison, Martha has been involved in computer classes and hopes to gain employment as some type of clerical worker upon release.

Martha has two sisters and one brother. Both of Martha's parents are still living. Her mother, Carmen, is sixty-two years old, and her father, Anthony, is sixty-four years old. All of the members of Martha's family of origin still live near Hamilton, Ontario. Martha's sisters are Gloria, age forty-one, and Alice, age thirty-nine. Martha's brother, Tony, is age thirty-eight. All three are married. However, Gloria and Tony (Anthony Jr.) have no children. Martha's parents were devastated by the news of the incarceration. This was due in part to the fact that Martha's sister Alice had been married to a man (Brent) who is currently incarcerated for drug use and trafficking. Martha's sister is divorced from this man but has three children from him. Since the incarceration and divorce had been financially devastating for Martha's sister, Martha's mother, Carmen, now cares for Alice's children while her daughter is at work. Martha's father had planned to retire from his job as a janitor for a large bank. However, Alice's situation made him decide to work for a few more years to help her out. As a result of this arrangement, Martha's mother was unable to come to British Columbia to help Martha with the children.

Martha's brother Anthony Jr. "Tony" is a writer for *Canadian Geographic Magazine*. He has traveled around the country and many parts of the world. He is married to a woman from Japan, named Miako. Martha's brother was very fond of Rashid and is emotionally close to Martha. While Martha has been in prison, her brother has been her biggest emotional support.

Son: Anthony Musa (called Tony), age fifteen, was born in White Rock, British Columbia. Tony was particularly close to his father. Until recently, Tony had been an excellent student in school. Tony was on the soccer team up until his father's death. Tony and Rashid would often go fishing together, and Tony recalls a family trip to San Diego, at age twelve, when he went deep sea fishing with his father. Tony recalls talking with his father about wanting to go to Pakistan. Rashid had planned to take his family to Pakistan after his son graduated from high school. Tony feels that his father took good care of the family, and now Tony wants to prove he can do the same.

At the present time, Tony is angry with his mother for several things. He is extremely embarrassed that his mother is in prison. Some of Tony's classmates have found out that Tony's mother is in prison, and Tony was in one fistfight with a young man who asked Tony if his mother was a "crack whore" or just a "whore." When he last spoke with his mother, Tony began to cry and stated,

"How could you do this to us? How could you do this to Dad?"Tony is also angry with his sister for letting the school social worker know what was going on in the home. Tony told Marie, "It is our business and nobody else's." Although Tony likes Mr. Quintana a great deal, he (Tony) resents the fact that his mother and MCFD have arranged for Mr. Quintana to reside in the home to supervise Tony and Marie until their mother's return.

Daughter: Marie Musa, age thirteen, was born in White Rock, British Columbia. Marie has been devastated by the loss of her father and the arrest of her mother. Marie is also upset by the anger directed toward her from her brother. Marie has a great deal of fear about her present and future life situations. Marie fears that her mother will be assaulted in prison. Marie is also worried that her brother will get in trouble at school. She knows he has been in one fight already, and worries that he will be suspended or expelled, bringing even more shame to the family. Marie was also very close to her father. Marie and her father used to ride their bikes together in the neighbourhood. Marie is particularly interested in plants. Her father would often take her to the schools in the area to show her how to care for different trees, shrubs, and flowers. Marie states that her father used to say that in Pakistan women usually stay home with the children, but that she (Marie) might want to go to college and study about plants. She says he even told her that there are people at places like the San Diego Zoo whose only job is to care for the plants.

Like Tony, Marie is angry with her mother. However, Marie's anger is in relation to her own sense of abandonment and fear that what her mother has done will destroy the family. Marie is afraid she will end up in foster care and that she, her mother, and her brother will never see each other again. Marie is also angry at her father for dying. However, she does not let others know about those feelings.

Family Friend: Federico Quintana, age sixty-seven, was born in the United States. Federico is an elderly Mexican American male. He moved to British Columbia in his early twenties to be near his wife's family. Federico is a dual citizen of the United States and Canada. He had worked at the school alongside Rashid, until he (Federico) retired two years ago at age sixty-five. Mr. Quintana was very much a father figure for Rashid, and taught Rashid a great deal about plants and grounds maintenance. Federico had been married for more than forty years, until his wife's death four years ago. He says he would have never made it through the grief of losing his wife, Emily, if it had not been for the Musa family. Federico was also devastated by Rashid's death. He cried at the funeral and told Rashid's family that Rashid had been like the son he never had. Federico Quintana is referred to as *abuelo* ("grandpa" in Spanish) by Tony and Marie.

Mr. Quintana has two daughters, Blanca and Selena. Blanca lives in Santa Fe, New Mexico, and Selena lives in Kelowna, British Columbia. Federico's daughters visit for Christmas each year. Both of Federico Quintana's daughters are married. As a result, Federico has two sons-in-law and five grandchildren (two boys and three girls). Federico's daughters want him to retire in either New Mexico or the Okanagan Valley in British Columbia. However, he says that White Rock is his home.

When thinking about why he let Tony Musa try to take care of the household alone, Mr. Quintana feels some sense of guilt that the social worker from MCFD became involved. He had wanted to let Tony be "the man of the house" and take care of the family after Rashid's death. Although he is now living in the home, Mr. Quintana still wants to let Tony make some of the major decisions about family matters. He has in a way tried to provide *consejo* (Spanish for "guidance") for Tony in much the same manner as he had done for Rashid.

Father: Rashid Musa, age forty-four at time of death, was born in Pakistan. Rashid had been the sole income for his nuclear family of four. Rashid was born and raised in Pakistan near the border with India in a small town with a population of about fifteen thousand. Rashid had an uncle in Ontario with whom he was sent to live while completing high school. While in Canada, Rashid met and eventually married his wife, Martha. Rashid became a Canadian citizen following high school and moved with Martha to British Columbia where he had been a grounds keeper for the public school district until his death. Rashid had been employed by the local public school district for more than twenty years. When he arrived in British Columbia, he soon became friends with Federico Quintana. Mr. Quintana had been an important support for Rashid. Rashid had often turned to Mr. Quintana for advice. Rashid often had Mr. Quintana and his wife, Emily, over to his house, and (according to Martha) considered Mr. and Mrs. Quintana to be part of the family.

Rashid has three sisters and four brothers who still live in Pakistan. His sisters are Endira, age forty-one, Asfia, age forty-seven, and Yalda, age fifty. His brothers are Malik, age thirty-nine, Mohammed, age forty-three, Raheem, age forty-nine, and Mahmood, age fifty-two. Rashid was closest to his brother Mohammed, who was closest to him in age. Rashid's father, Aban, a small business owner, had been run over and killed by a bus in Lahore three years after Rashid had married Martha. At that time, Rashid and Martha traveled to

Pakistan to be with the family. Rashid's mother, Malika, now lives with her eldest son in Pakistan.

Great-grandparents: Great-grandparents (grandparents to Martha and Rashid) on both sides had passed away before either Tony or Marie had been born. Rashid's grandparents had all lived as farmers in a very small village in Pakistan. Martha's grandparents on her mother's side, Domenico and Lydia, lived in Ontario but were born in Italy. Martha's grandparents on her father's side, Antonio and Costantina (Tina), had moved to Hamilton, Ontario, from

Figure 13.8   Genogram Musa Family

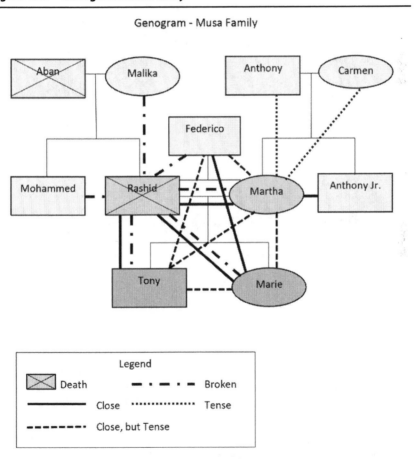

Figure 13.9　Eco-Map Musa Family

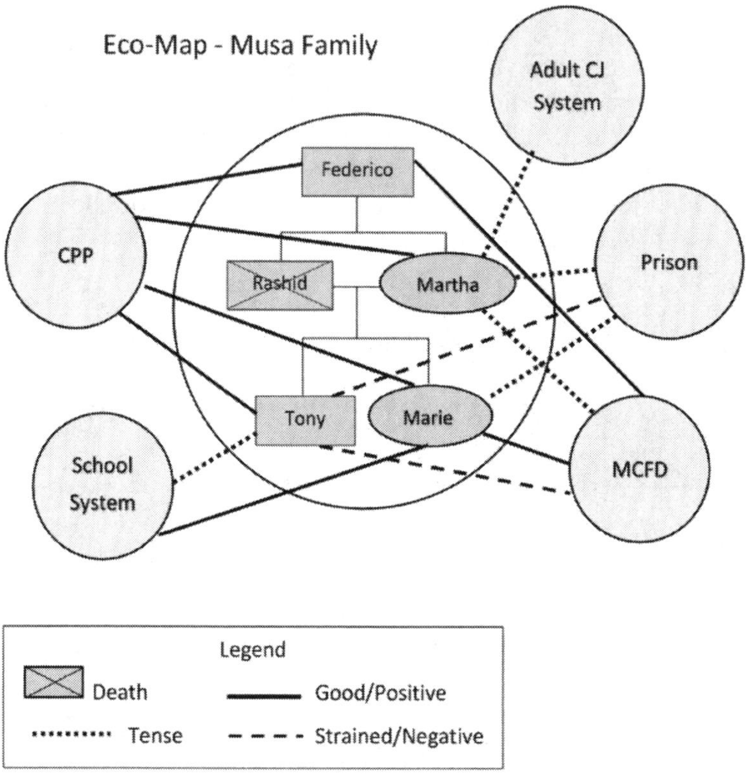

Eco-Map - Musa Family

Legend
☒ Death　　—— Good/Positive
•••••••••• Tense　　— — — Strained/Negative

Montreal, Quebec. Martha was very close to her paternal grandfather. She still misses his comfort and advice. Both of Martha's grandfathers had died of coronary heart disease. Martha's grandmother died of unknown causes, listed only as "natural causes."

The following is a *Risk and Protective Factors Assessment* for the Musa family, which also includes identified needs and possible interventions related to the development of a comprehensive treatment/helping/healing plan.

By engaging the Musa family in the creation of a genogram and eco-map, combined with identifying risks, protective factors, needs, and possible interventions, the social worker can develop more-targeted approaches to treatment, helping, and healing. In the case of the Musa family, grief work is clearly a central issue. However, if a clinical social worker, family therapist, or other professional helper were to initiate grief work without assessing for all the

Figure 13.10a   Treatment-Helping-Healing Plan—Rashid and Marie

Risk Factors	Protective Factors	Needs	Possible Interventions
Death of Rashid	His family home is paid for and CPP survivor's benefits are meeting basic family needs	None	The social worker needs to make sure that all potential benefits and supports have been accessed to help the family
Incarceration of Martha	Involved in prison programming	To complete sentence without incident	Social work case management services
Martha: Grief	Brother Anthony Jr.	Opportunity to process grief	Grief counseling services, support group involvement, and family therapy
Martha: Depression	Taking anti-depressants and enrolled in training opportunities	To process loss, shame, and anger with herself and others, and to regain a sense of self-worth	Psychiatric monitoring, clinical social work services, and referral for post-release employment assistance

Figure 13.10b   Treatment-Helping-Healing Plan—Tony

Risk Factors	Protective Factors	Needs	Possible Interventions
Tony: Grief	A desire to keep his family together	Opportunity to process grief	Grief counseling services, attend support group, and family therapy
Tony: Academic problems	None identified	Support at school	School social work services
Tony: Behavioural problems	None identified	Opportunity to process anger	Clinical social work services
Tony: Tension in relationship with his sister	A desire to play a protective role	Opportunity to process anger and shame	Family therapy
Tony: Tension in relationship with Federico	History of emotionally positive connection with Federico	Opportunity to process anger and shame	Clinical social work services

Figure 13.10c   Treatment-Helping-Healing Plan—Marie

Risk Factors	Protective Factors	Needs	Possible Interventions
Marie: Grief	Federico and the family preservation social worker	Opportunity to process grief	Grief counseling services, attend support group, and family therapy
Marie: Academic problems	None identified	Support at school	School social work services
Marie: Anxiety	Federico and the family preservation social worker	To feel reassured that her family is being helped	Clinical social work services
Marie: Tension in relationship with her brother	Emotionally positive connection with Federico	To regain a close bond with her brother	Clinical social work services

Figure 13.10d   Treatment-Helping-Healing Plan—Federico

Risk Factors	Protective Factors	Needs	Possible Interventions
Federico: Grief	Daughters call regularly	Opportunity to process grief	Grief counseling services, attend support group, and occasional inclusion in family therapy
Federico: Limited income	None identified	Support in caregiving role	Income support for childcare and transportation for family visits
Federico: Risk of burnout	None identified	Support in caregiving role	Respite services

other problems facing the family, the work related to grief might soon be overshadowed by economic needs, caregiver burnout, and other complications that could derail effective service delivery. Clearly, a wraparound approach in which multiple services are not just accessed, but also coordinated in a manner that does not overwhelm the family or duplicate efforts while leaving some needs unmet, would be useful in the case of the Musa family.

CONCLUSION

The intention in the chapter has been to introduce the reader to information about the diversity of work with families while still maintaining a focus on common approaches to intervention. The emphasis placed on ecological systems theory has been intentional, as has the degree of space devoted to sexual minority and non-Euro-Western cultures and societies. Nevertheless, there are aspects of work with families that are noticeably missing. For example, therapy with children has not been addressed. In addition, the importance of substance use and abuse which is discussed in chapter 17 was only mentioned here. Also, couples therapy was not addressed in this chapter. End-of-life issues, such as the preparation of wills, advance directives, or power of attorney procedures, were also not presented in a detailed form. Still, the information provided in this chapter should make the idea of engaging in work with families less intimidating for students and novice practitioners, while also providing an important review of theory for those who have been in the field of direct practice with families for many years.

Chapter Fourteen

Micro-Level Biopsychosocial-Cultural Assessment

INTRODUCTION

Of all the skills a social worker might have or acquire, few are more crucial than the capacity to engage client systems of various sizes in a process of comprehensive assessment. All change efforts in social work, from crisis intervention to policy development, must begin with an assessment. In social work, assessment should be comprehensive. Social workers need to work collaboratively with clients in the exploration, analysis, and evaluation of the often-complex character of presenting problems. The holistic nature of competent social work practice is what makes social work different from other professions. In medicine, the human organism, and quite often very specific organ systems, becomes the focus of intervention. In psychometrics (psychological testing), the assessment of personality and measurement of behavioural and cognitive deviation from societal norms becomes central. In psychiatry, the management of symptoms of major mental illness assumes primacy in treatment. In the field of finances, everything having to with the protection of and acquisition or accumulation of wealth, coupled with the reduction of personal debt, takes precedence over all other concerns. In criminal justice, emotions, physical well-being, spirituality, and financial security are all secondary to the importance of legal matters.

In this chapter, emphasis will be placed on assessment related to work at the direct-practice level with individual clients. Although intervention with larger systems is covered in other chapters of this text, assessment at the individual level has been selected as a stand-alone chapter because bachelor of social work (BSW) or master of social work (MSW) graduates most often begin entry-level employment working with individual clients in a variety of settings. The professional practice of social work at the level of assessment with the individual is much more holistic in nature than assessment in many other helping professions. The primary dimensions of life that include the biological, psychological, social, and cultural aspects of existence represent a complex of linked and intersecting facets of the contexts within which clients live out their lives from day to day. Assessment of individuals with attention to these dimensions

320

forms the very foundation of professional service provision and helps to define the direction of work with any particular client. The biological, psychological, social, and cultural dimensions of people's lives intersect in ways that profoundly influence everything from beliefs about problem definition to what constitutes a general sense of well-being. Therefore, holistic assessment in social work not only serves to identify what has contributed to and maintained a problem(s) experienced by a client, but also holds clues related to client strengths that can be incorporated in the collaborative process of culturally appropriate treatment, helping, or healing plan development.

MICRO-LEVEL BIOPSYCHOSOCIAL-CULTURAL ASSESSMENT

In social work, the competent holistically oriented practitioner takes an approach to assessment and intervention that emphasizes collaborating with the client to investigate and evaluate multiple biological, psychological, social, and cultural variables that constitute or impact the environment within which the client lives and functions. This is followed by targeting interventions in a manner that may address one or multiple concerns. Such an approach will likely include the mixing, phasing, and sequencing of a number of different

Figure 14.1   Intersecting Assessment Domains

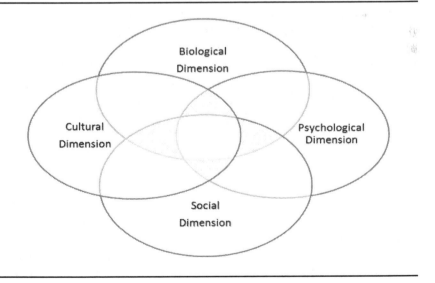

intervention methods or techniques designed to address different goals during a period of work with a client.

For example, a client who is referred for social work services for help with feelings of depression may also be experiencing employment or financial difficulties that are made more acute by a sense of isolation that is perhaps exacerbated by a limited social support network. During the initial assessment phase, potential health, safety, and service need concerns may be uncovered, requiring from the social worker the capacity to engage in case management and counselling activities simultaneously. Once the most critical unmet service needs are attended to, the social worker will address other concerns such as working to help the client identify, develop, strengthen, or expand social supports. While social supports are assessed, the social worker will also engage the client in an exploration of feelings of depression that include when, where, and in what manner her or his depression began and progressed. During the assessment process, the social worker will also examine other influences on client well-being that involve racism, classism, homophobia, ableism, ageism, gender discrimination, or other forms of socially constructed and maintained oppression.

Social workers need to approach assessment with the ability to filter information through various lenses that serve to clarify and direct the intervention process in a manner that assists in the development of short- and long-term goals and objectives. As clients with a variety of life circumstances and problems or concerns are encountered, a social worker may assume different roles depending on the needs of the client. Moreover, a social worker in any number of client-worker relationships may need to assume several roles at any one time. Indeed, the holistic nature of social work requires a broad range of knowledge and skills in identifying many elements of presenting problems, and an ability to determine what sort of intervention may be most appropriate at any given point in work with clients. This is why initial assessment within a broadly defined ecological framework makes sense.

Some may argue that an ecological approach to understanding clients and the problems they face in life assumes a neutral and depoliticized stance. It is true that various ecological systems-based approaches, such as the life model of Germain and Gitterman (1980) emphasize the development of adaptive abilities in the client while saying little about confronting oppressive forces. Still, the value of thinking in ecological terms should not simply be dismissed. Because most ecological systems approaches are concerned with difficulty experienced at the interface between the client and external systems, the importance of identifying the subjective experiences of clients within complex environmental contexts helps to establish the beginning point. In other words, the old social work mantra of *"starting where the client is"* means understanding how clients are experiencing the worlds within which they live. The challenge for social work is to go beyond simply helping clients adapt by also fighting to create a more environmentally, socially, and economically just society.

This is where anti-oppressive principles come into play. A client may have a multitude of familial, social, cultural, political, economic, and environmental systemic factors impacting her or his life. Furthermore, these factors can be conceptualized using an ecological approach. In addition, assisting clients in developing adaptive capabilities for short-term amelioration of problems or problematic conditions can result in a marked immediate reduction of distress. However, good social work does not stop at simply identifying individual distress and alleviating suffering. Social work as a profession has an obligation to improving the social conditions that cause or contribute to human suffering.

What is required, then, is an assessment of the ecological reality of clients' lives with an added emphasis on social and economic justice that for many people, such as Indigenous Peoples, now includes attention to the protection of the natural environment as well. Macrosocietal forms of oppression can be found in the areas of economics, race relations, social class, gender, religion, the marginalization of sexual minorities, and even environmental racism directed at disempowered communities of colour. Attention to these macrosocietal influences on the lives of people has been labeled in various ways. In the United States, the terms *social justice* and *social and economic justice* are commonly understood as referring to multiple oppressive forces that must be addressed by social work as a profession. In fact, the National Association of Social Workers (NASW) Code of Ethics makes special mention of the obligation of social workers to work toward the elimination of multiple forms of discrimination. In addition, the same code calls upon social workers to engage in social and political action intended to "prevent and eliminate domination of, exploitation of, and discrimination against any person, group, or class on the basis of race, ethnicity, national origin, colour, sex, sexual orientation, gender identity or expression, age, marital status, political belief, religion, immigration status, or mental or physical disability" (NASW, 2008, [4.02 and 6.04]).

Likewise, in Canada the ethical guidelines found in the Canadian Association of Social Workers (CASW) Code of Ethics (section 8.0) call on social workers to participate in social action that is directed toward the "prevention and elimination of domination or exploitation of, and discrimination against, any person, group, or class on the basis of age, abilities, ethnic background, gender, language, marital status, national ancestry, political affiliation, race, religion, sexual orientation or socio-economic status" (CASW, 2005a, [8.2.1]). Furthermore the Canadian and American codes include language related to respect for cultural difference, and the importance of access to needed resources, services, and opportunities. However, in Canada macrosocietal foci directed toward social and economic justice, and the approaches to client services that result from the actualization of these professional commitments and principles will most often be referred to as anti-oppressive practice. Canadian anti-oppressive practice has the same roots as American social justice practice, drawing on a large body of knowledge, including feminist, Marxist, postmodern, critical, anti-colonial, antiracist, and Indigenous perspectives (Baines, 2011).

Looking at the ecological context of client problems through the lens of anti-oppressive practice principles requires the social worker to examine the manner in which political, economic, and social structures create barriers and oppressive conditions for persons from populations such as racial, cultural, social, and sexual minorities, as well as immigrants, women, persons with disabilities, and many others. Furthermore, capitalist economic arrangements, globalization, corporate colonization, and environmental racism all combine in myriad and intersecting ways to further marginalize vulnerable populations and individuals. This is why social work assessment at the micro level must also address those macrosocietal factors that influence the daily lives of the clients they serve.

Figure 14.2   Ecological Systems and Anti-oppressive Lens

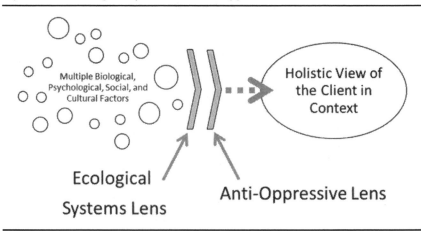

Biological Dimension

The biological portion of most assessments often ends at making sure the client has had a medical examination, and by accounting for any medically based needs. However, the biological aspects of a client's life include the human body, the physical environment, and the impact of that environment on the human organism. The biological aspect of a biopsychosocial-cultural assessment must be a true and multifaceted *person-in-environment* approach to understanding a client within a given physical context. Therefore, intervention, especially at the micro level, must not negate the importance of the larger physical environmental context.

Social workers are generally well trained in relation to assessing social networks, access to income and other supports, affordable housing, and so forth. However, social workers seldom assess for additional aspects of the physical environment. The physical environment is that milieu of earth, air, water, weather, climate, shelter, food, bacteria, viruses, chemicals, and all other aspects of physical existence within which every individual lives out her or his life. The common approach to social work assessment from early in the development of the profession has been one of placing many important biological elements of life in a peripheral realm outside of the more familiar psychological, social, and economic aspects of inquiry which then become the focus of intervention. This means that social workers often opt for emphasizing a limited sphere of concerns. As a result, the physical environmental context may be briefly addressed or entirely ignored. Therefore, a good assessment must include not only the more traditional exploration of social networks and emotional distress or well-being, but also the reaction of the human organism to a broad range of physical environmental conditions and the interplay between social and physical environmental factors impacting the lives of clients.

In our rapidly changing world, human beings are experiencing the effects of degradation in the natural environment on many fronts. In North America, oil and natural gas exploration have in some cases resulted in groundwater contamination, increased releases of volatile organic compounds, heavy metal concentrations in surface soils, and a myriad of other problems (Schmidt, 2011). The full extent to which this sort of activity will impact the health of people and other living organisms is not well known. However, the documented impact to date points in the direction of increased birth defects, respiratory illness, increasing cancer rates, and other diseases (Schmidt, 2011).

In 2013, the Conservative government of Canada, long known for its close relationship with mineral extraction industries, ordered the closing of the internationally known and respected Experimental Lakes Area in Ontario, while at the same time weakening the environmental protections for Canadian waters and land. These moves silence important environmental research and threaten the health of entire communities and regions. Particularly hard hit are Indigenous (First Nations) populations in areas where mining and fossil fuel exploration foul the land and waterways, contaminating not only precious water resources, but also the very animals and plants Indigenous Canadians have depended on for millennia (Davidson-Hunt, Deutsch, & Miller, 2012; Muir & Booth, 2012).

Environmental degradation and health may also be compounded by other factors in the lives of clients. Health conditions can and do impact mental health, resulting in diminished capacity to function either physically or cognitively (Bodnar & Wisner, 2005). However, the experience of racism, sexism, ageism, ableism, homophobia, or any of a multitude of forms of oppression can also compromise a person's mental and physical well-being (McGibbon & Hallstrom, 2012). Studies of race and health outcomes in the United States show that a growing number of researchers are now hypothesizing that racism has a negative impact on health (LaVeist & Isaac, 2013, p. 67). Therefore, any assessment of a client's health in relation to the physical environment should not ignore the added potential impact of any of a number of forms of discrimination and oppression on health and mental health. Although race is generally understood as a social construct, it is mentioned here because evidence points to the increasing awareness that lived experiences impacted by racism and other forms of oppression or discrimination can and do negatively influence overall well-being.

In addition to racism and discrimination, there is the need for awareness on the part of social workers regarding the variable reaction of human beings to weather phenomena and general weather conditions. People are often influenced by specific weather-related events, and regularly occurring weather conditions. Some individuals who live in northern regions with long periods of reduced sunlight or even daylight during winter are known to experience a form of depression known as *seasonal affective disorder* (SAD). SAD is a condition in which depression increases as intensity of sunlight and hours of daylight decrease.

Clients with respiratory problems such as asthma may have sensitivity to conditions of high humidity and poor air quality, which can result in an exacerbation of symptoms leading to fatigue and depression associated with chronic shortness of breath, wakening at night, and more frequent morning symptoms of the illness (Goldney, Ruffin, Fisher, & Wilson, 2008). For these clients, attention to physical health and coping with chronic breathing difficulties will be the central focus or concern. Intervention and the counselling or resource needs-identification activities engaged in by the social worker will need to be part of a service team effort that supports the primary concern of the client that is related to physical health.

Emotional states resulting from acute physical illness will require that restoration or improvement of physical health be the primary focus of intervention with supportive counselling as a secondary component. In cases such as chronic illness that require long-term management, or terminal illness where palliative care is the only remaining option, social workers need to assume various roles, often simultaneously. In some cases, social workers will need to play the role of case manager, ensuring that clients have continuous health care coverage, needed medical devices, and access to appropriate health care professionals. At other times, the focus of intervention may shift to providing supportive counselling, or with some clients, longer term therapy. Social workers may even be called upon to facilitate the connection of clients with religious/spiritual healers or practitioners. Whether helping clients cope emotionally or securing needed services, physical illness represents a requirement of flexibility based on what the client needs at any given point in the process.

Another important consideration in assessment is the interplay between psychological aspects of being and the emotional responses of clients to the natural or human-made environments within which they live, work, and interact. Clients may, for example, have a strong emotional and/or spiritual connection to a particular location. Understanding the emotional and spiritual attachment of clients to a particular place can be of immense value in the completion of an assessment upon which an intervention or planned change process will be based. The importance of attachment to the land has been noted in work with Indigenous North American clients (Zapf, 2010). For many Indigenous people, feelings of connection to land often have deep spiritual and emotion-laden elements that span across many generations. For Indigenous Peoples of the US Southwest, the importance of connection to the land is quite common, with those ties extending to individuals who have lived major portions of their lives in distant places. It is widely believed that Indigenous persons born in the mountains, high deserts, and river valleys of the region must return to the village, pueblo, or reservations of their youth for the circle of life to be complete. Among Native Hawaiian Peoples, there are many accounts of the importance of home as a place of physical and spiritual connection from which health and wellness flow (Kana'iaupuni & Malone, 2006). The same is true for others such as the people of Walatowa (Jemez Pueblo), New Mexico, who regard the earth as the original mother of all human beings, as sacred, and as the "source of their existence" (Sando, 2008, p. 17).

In the boreal forest region of Canada that straddles the border between Manitoba and Ontario, the Pimachiowin Aki Corporation, a coalition of several Ojibwe (Anishinaabe) First Nations have come together to work toward protection of the land. The work they have been engaged in demonstrates the importance of attachment to place. Those involved in the project have been working to have the area declared as a United Nations Educational, Scientific, and Cultural Organization (UNESCO) World Heritage site (Davidson-Hunt, Deutsch, & Miller, 2012). Their work as Indigenous Peoples demonstrates the strong emotional, physical, and spiritual connection to the land that has sustained them since long before the Europeans arrived in their part of the world. Any social work intervention with Indigenous persons from this region would need to address the issue of attachment to place. Ignoring this key aspect of identity could result in missing important elements of a client's sense of self.

However, one should not make the mistake of believing that a place attachment is found only among Indigenous Peoples. Many immigrants to Canada or the United States have throughout history reported feelings of grief and loss in relation to leaving their homelands. Irish immigrants of the 1800s and early 1900s produced multiple poems and songs about their home and the deep emotional connection to the land left behind. Immigrants in more recent times have expressed similar feelings about leaving home. Baffoe (2009) states that many immigrants that are part of the African diaspora still see their ancestral homes in Africa as their true homes—a connection that even includes a distinct desire to have their bodies returned home for burial upon death (Odhiambo Atieno, 1992). The importance of the *person-place bond* is an undeniably critical component of worldview development for many people. It is a multifaceted and complex aspect of individual and group identity (Churchman & Mitrani, 1997). Attachment to place includes a complex blend of historical, social, and emotional elements that involves memory, time, experience, familiarity, and a deep feeling of belonging. In many cases, this sense of belonging has cultural and spiritual components that define who we are as human beings. Therefore, attachment to place is an important consideration in any assessment, and may be particularly critical in work with those individuals and groups who place a high degree of importance on an enduring connection to the land they see as their place of origin.

In contrast to deeply positive emotional connections to specific physical places, some environmental contexts hold memories of past interactions or experiences with or within one's physical setting that can be coupled with emotionally charged reactions to concrete and visible elements of specific locations. Take the case of a woman who has memories of abuse she endured as a student in a residential school for Indigenous Canadian children who were forced by the Canadian government to attend these facilities. Her belief that she will not fully heal until the now-empty and crumbling building is completely destroyed, and the grounds spiritually cleansed, is an example of the powerful influence human-made physical environments can have on a person's sense of emotional well-being. For this particular client, an exploration of residential school experiences may lead to cultural reconnection through participation in healing ceremonies, developing mechanisms for coping with visible reminders of her abuse, or personal empowerment through connecting with others in a community-wide campaign to raze the structure that symbolizes the pain of entire generations.

A somewhat different example of the manner in which environmental concerns are crucial in the assessment process engaged in with individuals can be found in a community-based project related to opportunities for physical activity in an inner-city neighbourhood of El Paso, Texas. In this particular example, social work students were paired with kinesiology students at the University of Texas–El Paso to work with junior high school students in developing strategies for increasing physical activity. The goal was one of prevention regarding the future development of obesity and type II diabetes in those students participating in the project. Social work students involved in the assessment project found that the neighbourhood targeted presented two particularly problematic barriers to increased physical activity. First, most students lived in small houses or crowded apartments in which space for indoor exercise was severely limited or simply nonexistent. Second, although the climate in the region would easily allow for outdoor physical activity from the end of September through the end of April, the location of the target neighbourhood was prone to numerous wintertime smog alert days during which outdoor activity was not recommended. Without a doubt, typical comprehensive assessments completed by social workers do not generally take into account the impact of air quality, space for physical activity, and the interplay between the two, but they should. Social workers need to be trained to give far greater consideration to what may seem peripheral to the assessment of mental health, physical health, or service-related concerns.

Clearly, a strong positive connection or a negative reaction to the physical environment may have a profound impact on a client's mental health. Therefore, the physical world of the client is a very important aspect of the assessment process. Nevertheless, as stated earlier, consideration of the physical world, either natural or built, all too often remains a minor component of most assessments when it may in fact represent the central focus of the most needed and productive work with a client. Social workers should also think of the biological portion of an assessment as looking well beyond the more obvious or typical issues of medical evaluation, crime, and feelings of personal security within a given neighbourhood. An inclusive assessment of the physical environment also requires an exploration of the impact of environmental factors such as air quality, access to safe drinking water, comprehensive quality health care, affordable and nutritious food, and opportunities for physical activity necessary to maintain good health which in turn contributes to emotional well-being.

For social workers adopting a more holistic approach to work with clients, a solid understanding of the biological component of a comprehensive assessment may mean that intervention will focus not just on helping clients cope with difficult conditions, but more importantly, becoming involved in changing those problematic conditions that impact clients on a daily basis. This may mean devoting time to fighting for clean drinking water and against environmental classist/racist practices that locate landfills, heavy industry, and other health hazards in or near disempowered communities of colour and limited income. Therefore, physical health and the physical environment within which the client lives must be viewed as a key element of a truly holistic assessment.

Psychological Dimension

The psychological dimension of a comprehensive assessment involves examining the interaction between the mind of each individual housed in a physical body and continuous contact of that person with the external environment. The psychological lives of clients include cognitive capabilities, emotional states, and overall mental health. It must be remembered that the constant interplay between physical and mental health exists in all of us. When social workers engage with clients in an assessment of psychological aspects of their lives, internal emotional states are most often explored initially through the mechanism of client self-report. Self-report forms the foundational understanding of a client's subjective experience in relation to states of emotional distress or well-being. Indeed, client self-report is an extremely valuable source of information, but it is not the only information used to assess a client's psychological and emotional health.

Some social work practitioners like to utilize different psychological tests to confirm the presence of mood disorders or to identify personality disorders. It should, however, be understood that psychological tests designed to identify underlying "psychological problems" may give a less-than-accurate picture of a client's emotional state. This may be because persons taking any particular test might give false or misleading answers, or simply may not understand the test being administered. In addition, some psychological tests may be insufficiently validated as appropriate tools for measuring anxiety, depression, or other conditions, rendering the results of little use. Furthermore, psychological tests often have some degree of cultural bias, making the interpretation of the results problematic when working with clients from outside of majority Canadian or American cultures.

Therefore, client reports of symptoms and even the results of certain tests cannot on their own constitute a thorough assessment of mental states or conditions. Social workers need to consider that information received from clients and collateral sources will need to be supplemented by other approaches such as paying close attention to behaviours and responses to questions exhibited by clients during the assessment process. This includes observing clients to watch for cues such as nonverbal communication in the form of silence, differences in culturally influenced body language, or physiological responses that may be consistent with or differ greatly from what clients may say. For example, a client who is crying but states "I am fine" should lead any social worker to question the discrepancy between what is said and what is observed. Other behaviours such as minimizing traumatic events may indicate difficulty on the part of clients in addressing painful memories or experiencing feelings of vulnerability.

It is also important to understand, as mentioned earlier, the very real connection between physical and mental health. In recent years, the evidence of the link between mood disorders and health conditions has been growing, with an understanding that physical illness can affect mood, and mood disorders such as depression can impact physical health (Evans et al., 2005). In some research projects the mind-body bidirectional influence of health and mental health can be seen in findings that reveal more medical problems in persons with depression, and more depression in persons with medical conditions (Rieckmann et al., 2012; Whooley, 2012). In addition, many medications, including some psychiatric medications, can have unintended side effects that influence organ systems within the body, which in turn can impact mental health (Goldberg & Ernst, 2012). There exists an almost-infinite list of health concerns or conditions that impact the lives of clients. Dementia, intellectual disabilities, traumatic brain injury, autism, fetal alcohol spectrum disorder, limitations on cognitive capacity, developmental disabilities, and a myriad of other, biological, environmental, or medical factors that influence brain function, calling into question the degree of capacity for autonomous thought or action in clients who are affected. In cases of severely compromised clients, social workers may need to gather important information from collateral sources, usually the primary caregivers of the client. Nevertheless, even clients who may seem incapable of participating in the assessment process should be included to the greatest degree possible—a task that often calls for creativity on the part of the social worker. Take for example the social worker in a hospital working with a sixty-nine-year-old male patient who had suffered a stroke. The patient could not speak, so the assessment was completed with information provided by the patient's daughter. However, the social worker made a point of including the client in the process. Each time information was given by the daughter, the social worker asked the client to squeeze her (the social worker's) finger if he agreed. This was also done for verification of other information. Six weeks later, when the man regained the capacity for limited speech, he asked his daughter to call the social worker and thank her for making him feel like an important part of the process.

Social Dimension

The social portion of a comprehensive assessment involves a history of clients' lives that feature major life events and a vast array of relationships. A social history should include a description of family and friendship networks as well as changes or disruptions in those networks. Divorces, deaths of loved ones, moves from one community or region to another, and other life events are important to examine in terms of how and why social support networks expand and contract in response to life changes. As a time line of life events is recorded with a client, an understanding of the depth and continuity of supportive and problematic social relations will evolve. For example, a client who marries and then later divorces may also mourn the loss of once-important and close relationships with the siblings, parents, and extended family members of her or his former partner. In addition, marital or partner status changes can become complicated by disagreements, arguments, and even court battles over child custody or child support. Furthermore, children, whether young, adolescent, or adult, can feel torn between loyalty to and love for parents and other extended family members on both sides of a difficult divorce.

When clients recount the death of grandparents, parents, siblings, children, or extended family members, the disruption to the life of the client can range from minor to profound and can have a permanent impact, as is most often the case in something such as the death of a child. Coping with death in the midst of a large and supportive social network is quite different from death in which emotional and economic resources are limited or largely unavailable. A well-developed social history that assesses for supportive individuals, families, and even communities, along with available resources, is crucial to the formulation of an intervention plan designed to assist clients in coping with acute crises or mitigating the impact of chronic challenges. Although recording social histories and social networks can help the client and social worker identify challenges or problems, the process also holds potential for exploring successes in problem solving and the capacity for resilience. Individual clients and even entire family systems may have previous positive problem-resolution experiences and built-in protective factors that can lessen the negative impact of acute family crises or difficult transitional periods. The task of the social worker is to work with the client to identify personal and systemic strengths.

Without a doubt, a larger network of social supports is of enormous value. However, some clients have limitations on social support network development or maintenance that has been impacted by geographic relocation, physical or mental illness, assuming the role of a primary caregiver, or even death of one's close friends or family members. In addition, life changes can include loss of socially defined status, something that is a common occurrence in the lives of immigrants to Canada and the United States. Those immigrants who were part of large and integrated networks in their home countries may find themselves marginalized as a result of racism, discrimination, or simply culture shock due to unfamiliar social norms or language barriers.

Electronic Networks

Approaches to preparing professional direct-practice service providers in the completion of assessments are often founded on beliefs, theories, and research about human behaviour that existed prior to the current technoenvironmental context of personal computers, the Internet, and social network sites. As a result, a more traditional assessment of a client's social network might miss the importance of an individual's Internet-based social support system. Age and comfort with social network sites does hold the potential for generationally influenced misunderstanding between the helping professional and the client. Older social workers, counsellors, and so on, may be less comfortable with social networking sites as a place for maintaining or developing social support networks. Chou, Hunt, Beckjord, Moser, and Hesse (2009) note that younger age is associated with more frequent use of social networking sites, and that using these sites to discuss health and mental health issues was more common in the eighteen to twenty-four age group. Additional studies have found that utilization of social network sites can actually reduce loneliness by helping people feel more connected to others, maintain relationships during geographic separation, and develop new networks of friends (Burke, Marlow, & Lento, 2010).

For clients who have limited opportunities for face-to-face interactions with others as a result of illness, disability, or caregiving responsibilities, the Internet does present a great deal of potential for participation in support groups, connection with friends and family, and even entertainment. However, Internet use must be examined in an assessment to evaluate the usefulness of online activities in regard to social support networks for client systems. In much of the literature related to social networking, social capital is featured prominently. Social capital, simply stated, includes "features of social life, networks, norms, and trust, that enable participants to act together to pursue shared objectives" (Putman, 1995, p. 67). The primary shared objectives for members of a social support network that are of concern to social workers would be related to the important functions of providing emotional or informational supports that supplement concrete (food, clothing, shelter, or monetary) resources to those within a mutually supportive constellation of family and/or friends. Social capital for individual clients and family systems in the current era include face-to-face and online components of relationships. Furthermore, clients can develop "bridging capital," which features weak relationships between many individuals, or "bonding capital," characterized by strong ties with smaller groups of individuals (Hopkins, Thomas, Meredyth, and Ewing, 2004, p. 370).

When assessing electronic social network-based support systems, it is important to evaluate the type and strength of the relationship. Asking questions about the nature of support, provided by those with whom one communicates electronically, can help social workers collaborate with clients to determine the level of bonding capital versus bridging capital within the social media-based realm of relationships. This can in turn provide valuable information about strengths and challenges presented by existing social and emotional support networks that can be counted upon to provide various types of resources for clients in times of need.

The Human-Animal Bond

Much information can be found in the literature about the importance of the bond that exists between humans and their pets. In North America, this bond most often takes the form of a connection between people and their dogs or cats. Animals can be very important sources of support during periods of depression, loss of human family members through death, or when other stresses of life or work become difficult to handle (Risley-Curtiss, 2010). The connection between humans and their pets involves true feelings of affection (Toray, 2004). Caring for pets can become an activity that brings normalcy, continuity, and predictability to those who feel that other parts of their lives are in turmoil. Because many view their pets as part of the family (Risley-Curtiss, 2010), they should also be addressed in the completion of a comprehensive assessment of a client's social network.

To understand the emotional ties between pets and their owners, one need only recall natural disasters such as Hurricane Katrina in the United States in the summer of 2005. During and after the hurricane, many shelters and those operations put in place to evacuate people to shelters would not accept pets. As a result, owners became separated from their beloved companions or simply refused to evacuate without them. The collective anger, grief, and sense of profound loss experienced during and after Hurricane Katrina led to the passage of an amendment to the Stafford Disaster Relief and Emergency Assistance Act in the form of Public Law 109-308, or the Pets Evacuation and Transportation Standards (PETS) Act of 2006. In accordance with the PETS Act, all emergency preparedness operations must put in place plans that take into account the needs of pets and service dogs following major disasters or emergencies.

Clearly, pets are an immensely important part of people's lives. However, many social workers and other helping professionals receive little to no training about the need to include pets in the evaluation of individual support networks. Some clients, especially isolated and elderly clients, may become very emotionally attached to pets, viewing them as friends or even surrogate children (Toray, 2004). As a result, the emotional support and increased life satisfaction derived from the bond individuals have with their animal companions needs to be recognized and included in an assessment. Likewise, when the loss of a pet occurs, the grief experienced is real and profound (Weisman, 1991). Therefore, clients who have had deep and enduring relationships with pets will need to be understood, validated, and supported during their loss. This is especially important if the client has a limited support network outside of the relationship with her or his pet (Toray, 2004).

Cultural Dimension

For each of us, culture influences every facet of our lives. Culture shapes our understanding of what is socially acceptable, socially preferred, and socially unacceptable. Our beliefs about gender and gender-specific roles and behaviours are shaped by the cultures within which we have been socialized. Our understanding of appropriate roles, social statuses, and the behaviours linked to them are learned through the process of enculturation. Culture influences our understanding of age-related behavioural expectations and what we see as the proper timing of life course-related events. Our conceptualization of and adherence to specific religious or spiritual traditions are shaped by the cultures of the societies within which we live. The very milieu within which identity development (and beliefs about those defined as "other") occurs is within the context of multilayered cultures of ethnicity, community, region, and nation (Coggins & Hatchett, 2009). As has been discussed in earlier chapters of this text, culture as a factor shaping one's sense of self, others, the world, and reality is multilayered, complex, and sometimes creates internal conflict as opposing values and beliefs are encountered and internalized by those exposed to them. For others, a sense of cultural loss can be a profound and broadly experienced condition, as has been and continues to be the case for many Indigenous North Americans. Cultural loss and disconnection may create feelings of emptiness, longing, and an intense wish to reconnect with the language, spirituality, and knowledge that are part of one's very personal experience of a larger collective history and identity.

Although many social work texts emphasize the importance of knowledge related to minority populations in terms of values, beliefs, attitudes, and behaviours, it is not advisable or wise for social workers to approach clients from cultures other than their own with a laundry list of population group characteristics that clients are expected to fit. In fact, even assuming that clients from one's own ethnic/racial group have the same experiences, level of cultural knowledge, or desire for cultural connection would be a mistake. Culture, as we have seen in previous chapters, is complex. As a collective, certain populations may exhibit a higher incidence of a particular behaviour, such as not speaking loudly or avoiding confrontation, but that does not mean every client from a culturally distinct or different population group will do so. For example, it is widely known that males over fifty years of age may be at higher risk for heart disease and diabetes. However, no social worker would immediately assume that all male clients over fifty have heart trouble. The same is true for assumptions about cultural knowledge. Latino clients over the age of sixty may, for example, be more likely to speak Spanish. However, we cannot assume this is always the case. A large part of being sensitive to culture includes understanding that the expression of cultural traits will vary widely at the level of the individual. This does not mean that social workers should be blind to cultural difference—quite the opposite. Social workers should be prepared to utilize tools such as the *Individualized Worldview* model to formulate an understanding of the lives of clients within various cultural, social, environmental, and economic contexts.

Biopsychosocial-Cultural Assessment Format

The *Biopsychosocial-Cultural Assessment* is a process of exploration, investigation, examination, and evaluation in which client and social worker collaborate in collecting and organizing information for the purpose of deciding on a plan of action that may variously be referred to as a treatment plan, a healing plan, a planned change process, an intervention plan, a change plan, a helping plan, or even a work plan. Regardless of the term(s) used for the interaction between social worker and client, it is critical that the assessment not be viewed as a cataloguing of past problems and previous treatments. Client strengths and successes need to be featured in an assessment as well. Moreover, the recording of client strengths is not simply an exercise in respect or an attempt to bolster client self-esteem. Emphasizing client strengths and successes will help give shape and direction to a plan of action designed to address whatever presenting problem has been identified in the initial phases of the assessment process.

It is also important that a social worker completing an assessment keep in mind certain commonsense considerations. For example, assessments of children will involve a great deal of information about the families within which children live. Clearly, when assessing a five-year old, a discussion of work history will be in relation to the parent(s) of the child. The same will be true for many other components of the assessment. Likewise, with young children, developmental and health histories will be of particular importance, with much of the information being provided by parents or primary caregivers.

Work histories, life-course time lines, health histories, and much of the information gathered in terms of legal, education, and social histories will look quite different for adolescent clients than would be the case for others. People in their sixties, seventies, or eighties are at a very different point in the life course, and will therefore have assessments that differ vastly from children, youth, young adults in their twenties or thirties, or even other adults who are in their forties or fifties. In addition, work histories need to address clients' levels of education, skilled worker training, and economic conditions in the communities where they reside. For example, a work history for a healthy, skilled, well-educated young person, who has large gaps in employment, while residing in an urban area with low unemployment, will indicate something quite different from a similar individual residing in a community or region with high unemployment and few job opportunities. The key for any social worker in the completion of an assessment is to be a creative, investigative, critical thinker who is capable of not only asking questions, but also recognizing the importance of responses within the context of the client's physical, social, economic, political, and cultural milieu.

I. Demographic Data

The collection of demographic data is generally related to documentation required in various agency settings. Clearly, recording a person's identified ethnicity will tell a social worker very little about that individual's particular sense of cultural identity or connection. Likewise, identification of sex/gender or gender identity will not immediately tell someone reading the file about life experiences related to that identity. However, demographic information can give a quick overview of key variables such as age, language preference, parental status, marital status, and of course, the person's name.

a) Client's Name:
b) Date of Birth:
c) Sex/Gender or Gender Identity:
d) Marital or Partner Status:
e) Parental Status (including ages of children):
f) Primary Ethnic and/or Racial Identity (including additional identities, if applicable):
g) Language(s) Spoken by Client:
h) Primary (preferred language):

II. Presenting Problem, including Client's Views of the Problem

Describe the current problem or problems for which the client has been referred or is seeking assistance. Include referral sources if necessary. Also include the client's view of the problem or problems. Include direct quotes of client statements. Remember to include information related to what the client has done in an attempt to resolve the problem or problems before coming to you. Ask the client how long the problem has gone on and what life was like prior to the problem for which she or he now seeks help. In addition, do not forget to identify strengths the client brings to the problem identification and problem resolution process.

III. Developmental and Health History

Find out if the client was the product of a normal birth and pregnancy. Were there any difficulties experienced during the course of childhood development? Does the health history include accidents, prolonged illnesses, specific childhood diseases, and so on? What is the client's current health status? Has the client been evaluated by a physician? Is the client taking any medication? Does the client use herbal remedies? Does the client exercise or does she or he engage in physical activity as a part of work? Find out if the client seeks culture-specific religious or spiritual healers or other alternative practitioners to address health problems. Also ask about successes or positive outcomes the client has had regarding the maintenance or improvement of her or his health.

IV. Physical Environmental Context

Gather information regarding the client's current living conditions. Some questions related to adequate food, clothing, shelter, and transportation may have been addressed as part of the presenting problem. If not, an assessment of the environmental context should include attention to more than the basics of adequate living space, access to food, and questions of personal safety. When discussing the environmental context with a client, explore concerns related to sufficient heating and cooling, presence of environmental dangers such as mould, exposed electrical wiring, asbestos or lead in the home, safe drinking water, presence of functioning bathing and toileting facilities, and so forth.

Social workers assessing the environmental context in urban areas should also engage clients in discussions of neighbourhood safety, outdoor air quality, access to grocery stores that sell affordable and nutritious food, proximity to outdoor spaces such as yards or parks, and the safety of these spaces, especially for use by children. In rural areas, social workers need to determine many of the interior environmental safety factors that are important for urban residents. However, rural inhabitants may supplement food supplies through gardening, hunting, and fishing. Determining the degree to which these activities contribute to food security is important. Also, if rural inhabitants do not hunt, fish, or garden, an assessment of access to adequate, affordable, and nutritious food becomes even more critical. Travel to distant shopping centres, and the high cost of food in these locations will mean that rural individuals may be under particular stress in attempts to feed their families and themselves.

Finally, an assessment of the environmental context should include a discussion of the client's emotional response to the home, neighbourhood, community, and region within which she or he resides. Exploring the attachment a person has to the place where she or he lives can provide some insight regarding the client's sense of well-being. Some clients may have an enduring emotional and spiritual attachment to their respective communities and regions of residence, while others, for any number of reasons, may wish to be elsewhere. Whatever the case may be, social workers who overlook a client's emotional and/or spiritual attachment to or feeling of disconnection from a specific environment may be missing crucial information that will be of profound importance in a truly collaborative intervention, treatment, or planned change process.

V. Mental Health, Chemical Dependency, and Addictive Behaviour Treatment History

This portion of the assessment includes information related to client perceptions of overall mental health, any mental illness diagnoses, hospitalizations for mental illness, and the use of medications prescribed to treat specific mental health problems. When recording a history of mental health and mental illness, it is also important to explore the occurrence of mental illness in other members of the client's family of origin. Also ask if the client has ever used alcohol or other chemicals to manage periods of depression, anxiety, and so forth, which will naturally lead to questions about chemical dependency in the client.

A chemical dependency history will include information about chemical use, abuse, and dependency in the client. A chemical dependency history will also include inpatient and outpatient treatment for chemical dependency and the level of chemical abuse and/or dependency in the client's family of origin. A client's family of origin may include biological members, adoptive parents and/or siblings, extended family members, and even fictive kin. Questions related to gambling addictions, Internet use addictions, and other addictive behaviours that may have had a negative impact on the lives of clients should also be included in this portion of a comprehensive assessment.

As is the case with other elements of a comprehensive assessment, it is important to ask about successes clients have had in their attempts to overcome substance abuse or addiction problems, as well as determining what has been effective in relation to positive resolution of possible mental health concerns connected to substance use and abuse. When assessing for treatment of mental health or chemical dependency problems, an examination of treatment history should not be limited to Euro-Western approaches alone. Some clients may have sought the services of culture-specific religious/spiritual healers or alternative practitioners in an attempt to treat mental illness or chemical dependency, as well as other addiction problems. The social worker should therefore ask about the effectiveness of these approaches to treatment and the desire or potential for a non-Euro-Western or blended approach to addressing any current concerns the client may have.

VI. Employment and Income History

The employment and income history section of the assessment should include information related to current and past employment. It is important to ask what the client's employment experiences have been. In this section, information about socioeconomic status, current and past, should be included. If the client has experienced periods of unemployment, care should be taken to avoid pathologizing a sporadic employment history, opting instead to explore barriers that may have been encountered by clients who have not had consistent employment.

When attempting to determine sources of income, questions about a wide range of supports that include money, housing, and goods such as food or clothing will help to create a more comprehensive understanding of the client's situation in relation to self or family maintenance. It should not be automatically assumed that clients who are unemployed are receiving public assistance. Some may be receiving assistance from private sources such as family members or friends. Others may receive financial support from a variety of sources, including religious organizations. In some cases, if public assistance could be of use, knowing the type and amount of existing support may be helpful in making a referral for various forms of assistance from public, religion-based, or private nonprofit (voluntary) organizations.

An examination of employment and income history should also include what the client sees as high points or achievements. Clients may recount work histories that span many decades and include long periods of stability. Understanding the full range of client work experiences, combined with changes in socioeconomic status over time, will allow for the identification of strengths- and difficulties-related challenges involved in securing work and needed income.

VII. Education History

An education history should include information related to the client's current level of education. However, an education history should also involve gathering information about a client's perception of successes or difficulties experienced in relation to formal education. It is important for social workers to ask clients about favourite subjects in school, struggles related to learning, and whether or not they have ever been placed in special education classes or programs. If clients have been enrolled in special education courses or received other supportive services in educational settings, questions about the duration of and reason(s) for those services will facilitate a deeper understanding of the education experience.

In completing an education history, it is important not to ignore the value of learning that has taken place outside of majority culture educational institutions. People who have been taught skills such as farming, fishing, hunting, collecting and utilizing herbal medicines, and any number of learning experiences that are not captured in discussions focused on Euro-Western majority culture formal educational systems deserve to have that knowledge validated in an assessment. For example, many Indigenous North American societies have systems of traditional knowledge acquisition that require rigorous study and years of training. The same can be said for other non-Euro-Western populations. Therefore, conceiving of education history in broader terms will allow for a fuller understanding of the experiences of individual clients, and increase the potential of identifying client strengths related to learning.

VIII. Legal History

Gathering information for the completion of a legal history involves an exploration of the contact a client may or may not have had with the criminal justice system at either the adult or juvenile level. If the client is currently in a correctional facility or involved in some form of community corrections such as parole or probation, much of the information about offences and sentencing may be in an existing client file. However, if the client's offences have occurred in the past, information about experiences with criminal justice systems that are not already in an existing file will need to be provided by the client.

Questions about experiences with criminal justice systems should not be limited to types of crimes, duration of incarceration, release dates, and so forth. Social workers assessing clients in relation to legal histories should also ask about the impact of incarceration, parole, probation, and so forth, on the client and the client's family. Questions about the manner in which involvement with criminal justice systems has impacted a client's ability to secure work and remain employed are very important in the development of an intervention or service plan. Likewise, asking if the client has ever been involved in programs designed to help ex-offenders and the success of that involvement is important in the identification of strengths and challenges.

IX. Social History

The completion of a social history begins with aiding clients in the construction of their life stories. Comprehensive social histories form an account of numerous events and experiences that result in a description of the client's life journey from early childhood up until the present. Information related to the lives of clients should feature the important social roles clients fill or have filled as children, parents, partners, spouses, friends, and so on. In a social history, it is also important to have the client discuss any friction that may now exist or has existed in the past between competing demands of the various roles identified.

The creation of comprehensive social histories feature experiences at the level of the individual within the context of multiple systems that include families, friends, coworkers, colleagues, and communities, all of which are in turn embedded within a complex structure of limitations or opportunities imposed or created by various physical, social, political, and economic environments. The process of identifying and recording social network changes over time will give the social worker and the client a document that can be reviewed and discussed in a way that may help shape the direction of any treatment, healing, or helping plan that is created. Life events, individual choices, the choices made by others, and the impact they have on limiting, expanding, or changing one's social network are crucial to understanding the way clients experience and perceive their places within the world. The end result should be an increased awareness of each client's view of life that is shaped by the blending history, current circumstances, and their view of the world around them in a way that influences each individual's sense of capacity to effect change, as well as what sort of change may be necessary, appropriate, or desired.

X. Additional Information

The final section of the comprehensive biopsychosocial-cultural assessment should include any additional information related to the client that has not been covered in another part of the assessment. For example, the client may disclose the use of non-Euro-Western complementary alternative medicines (CAM) or other forms of treatment for health and mental health conditions. These can range from the use of acupuncture and herbal medicines or remedies, to culturally specific healing and ceremonial practices that have long histories of use within certain culturally distinct populations. In many cases, clients may have sought the services of culturally specific healers/helpers such as traditional counsellors, herbalists, or even spiritual/medical practitioners from within the client's cultural group. Others may have attempted the use of meditation and contemplative therapies that may be from outside of their own cultural traditions.

Discussion of the effectiveness of healing practices that are outside of and different from more dominant Euro-Western treatment modalities should be explored in a nonjudgemental fashion. Many practices found within non-Euro-Western cultures can be very effective, and may have resulted in the resolution of specific problems for clients who have sought practitioners who are trained in various culturally based forms of healing or helping. Clients who engage in the process of recounting their life journeys should be respected, supported, and genuinely praised for past and current attempts to solve problems. In addition, the adoption of an anti-oppressive approach to assessment and intervention involves the recognition of client strengths, which in some cases will include nonmajority approaches to treating physical conditions and mental illness, addressing culturally defined and embedded problems, or coping with difficulties in life.

CONCLUSION

Most agencies that host social work students as field practicum interns have approaches to assessment that are designed to fit their specific needs and populations. In some locations, such as hospitals, brief assessment may be emphasized. In public and private clinical practice settings, the assessment process may be viewed as an initial step in service planning and an ongoing element of treatment or healing. There are practice settings that provide social workers with detailed templates for assessment, while others have more broad or general guidelines. Nevertheless, comprehensive assessment as presented in this chapter draws attention to various dimensions of human existence that need to be taken into consideration, regardless of the particular assessment tool utilized by any one agency.

This chapter has been designed to emphasize the multifaceted nature of a comprehensive approach to assessment that examines problems, needs, and challenges, while at the same time highlighting the importance of a strengths and empowerment perspective in work with clients. The use of an ecological systems theoretical foundation and an anti-oppressive orientation to assessing problems faced by clients is intended to encourage social workers to think beyond narrow conceptualizations of the assessment process. By attending to physical, psychological, social, and cultural dimensions of the human experience, it is hoped that the approach to comprehensive biopsychosocial-cultural assessment that has been the focus of this chapter will help social work students and practicing social workers in the development of a more holistic understanding of the clients they serve.

Chapter Fifteen

Case Management in Social Work

INTRODUCTION

Social work is a broad and diverse profession. However, some skills are common across work settings. For example, social workers should be well versed in the completion of comprehensive biopsychosocial-cultural assessments for micro-level practice as well as having the skills that are needed to assess larger systems such as organizations and communities. Case management represents another core set of important skills social workers need, even if their professional goals are focused on clinical practice or policy development. For clinical practitioners, the need to engage in case management will inevitably arise in work with clients who face multiple economic, social, health, or other barriers that can complicate the treatment or healing process. For social workers involved in agency administration, knowledge of the core components of case management can be of enormous benefit in regard to staff supervision or resource allocation. A solid understanding of case management can also inform decisions for social workers at the level of program or policy development. Case management is foundational to social work. Therefore, no social worker can be truly prepared for professional practice without understanding the historical and contemporary importance of case management to social work.

While case management is often seen as a bachelor of social work (BSW)-level function that many aspire to move beyond, the reality is that assessing, planning, linking, monitoring, and evaluating client progress in relation to planned change requires skill that is often overlooked and undervalued. In this chapter, the history, purpose, and importance of case management will be combined with an overview of essential skills. In addition, other important aspects of case management such as supportive counselling and the critical functions of problem identification, problem prioritization, and problem partialization will be featured along with other components of case management such as supportive counselling, termination/case closure, and evaluation.

CASE MANAGEMENT AND SERVICE PLANNING

Case management in social work has a long history that dates back to the beginning of the profession, and it has remained an important component of social work practice (Popple, 2008; Stuart, 2008). The primary goal of case management is one of linking those in need with service providers that will be able to meet those needs. In the early days of the profession, case management was but one of many functions that were carried out by those who identified themselves as social workers. However, case management as a full-time activity in social work experienced enormous expansion in the 1960s when Canada and the United States embarked on a course of massive deinstitutionalization that emptied institutions designed to care for persons with mental illness and disabilities (Heinonen & Spearman, 2010; Popple & Leighninger, 2011).

The original idea behind deinstitutionalization was actually quite humane and even progressive. Persons with mental illness and various disabilities had often languished in large institutions for years or even lifetimes, living routinized existences away from their home communities and families. With deinstitutionalization the plan was to have community centres staffed by social workers who would serve as case managers, easing the transition into the community of those released from institutions. Unfortunately, the initially noble plan of supported reintegration into society was not followed by sufficient funding. As a result, the deinstitutionalization movement increased the number of chronically mentally ill homeless, a problem made even more acute as a result of decreased funding (especially in the United States) from the 1980s through the present (Popple & Leighninger, 2011). This has meant that social workers employed as case managers have needed to become increasingly skilled at navigating the ever-more fragmented and inadequate patchwork of public, private not-for-profit, and private for-profit providers of services to clients with mental illness and/or various additional disabilities.

According to a 2006 report conducted by the National Association of Social Workers (NASW) in the United States, case management was identified by licensed social workers as a major component of what they do on a regular basis, with many stating that more than half of their time at work is spent engaging in case management activities (Whitaker, Weismiller, & Clark, 2006). As noted by Frankel and Gelman (2012), case management is now applied in many settings that serve a wide range of clients, including those with long-term mental illness, developmental disabilities, persons living with AIDS, ex-offenders released from prison, families involved with child welfare agencies, the elderly, and many other populations considered to be vulnerable or "at risk."

Core Functions of Case Management

Although the patchwork of available services for clients in need undergoes constant change, the basic core functions of case management remain essentially the same. Case managers begin by engaging clients in the planned change process prior to or during the completion of a comprehensive biopsychosocial-cultural assessment. The assessment is then followed by planning, linking, monitoring, and regular evaluation of service plan adequacy and effectiveness (Summers, 2001). The overall purpose of case management involves assisting persons in need by facilitating access to services that are designed to meet those needs. In many situations, case management is not a one-time activity. Clients engaged and served by case managers are often those with complex needs that create multiple challenges in daily living. As a result, clients who require case management services will quite often need ongoing support in order to maintain an optimal level of functioning.

Figure 15.1   Core Functions of Case Management

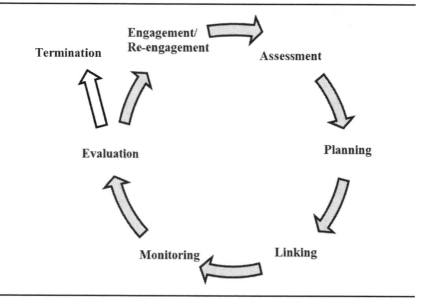

Locating and enhancing the necessary supports for clients within their home environments can be a daunting task requiring time, attention, creativity, and perseverance on the part of the social worker. In addition, case management is not always as simple as connecting clients to the services they need. In some cases, the fit between client and service provider may not be a good one, even though it may have initially seemed to be. This may be due perhaps to a problem such as service providers advertising programs that in reality they do not (for any number of reasons) adequately fund or staff. In addition, the fit between the culture of a client and the cultural milieu of a service provider may not be a good one. There can also be other issues that should be considered in relation to goodness of fit. For example, services targeted at certain age groups or clients with particular issues or diagnoses need to be considered in the development of appropriate service plans. For example, a case manager would not refer an elderly client to an agency designed to help families with young children. Likewise, a person in need of addictions treatment may not be an appropriate client for individual psychotherapy at the office of a private practice social worker. In addition, as client life situations change, reevaluation of service plans will become necessary.

Engagement

All social work service provision begins with engaging the client. The initial step in any contact with clients and the creation of any type of treatment, intervention, or service plan starts with attention to the development of a working relationship. Even after more than twenty years of intense emphasis on evidence-based approaches to practice, research in relation to client-worker relationship building demonstrates that effective work with clients will not materialize if a good working relationship with the client is not established (Luborsky, O'Reilly-Landry, & Arlow, 2011). The engagement phase is the period during which the social worker and the client will become better acquainted with each other. It is also the time during which the presenting problem is most likely to begin being addressed (Compton & Galaway, 1999).

When clients and social workers are from different cultural backgrounds, the engagement phase will also serve as a time during which issues in cross-cultural communication will arise. Because culture can have a profound impact on client-worker relationships, initial sessions with clients, especially those from distinctly different cultural backgrounds, should involve discussions of the manner in which culture influences perceptions of problems and appropriate approaches to resolving problems. Although discussions of cultural differences and similarities may take longer, it is time well spent when one considers the fact that culture influences so many facets of our lives.

Even though cultural competence and cultural awareness training are now quite common features of social work education in North America, most of that instruction, as has been discussed in previous chapters, still takes a "laundry list" approach to preparing students for work with clients who are or may be culturally different (Coggins & Hatchett, 2009). This idea of erasing individual difference by placing clients in cultural categories, with attendant expectations of uniformity in relation to culturally based beliefs and culturally prescribed behaviours, robs clients of their individual understanding of their worlds and their places within those worlds. Each client's unique understanding of her or his own sense of self as a cultural being and indeed a human being needs to be heard, explored, and validated (Ortega & Faller Coulburn, 2011).

It is important to be aware that engaging clients as a first step in any client-social worker process intended to create healing or change can be filled with challenges for the client as well as the social worker. For some, the simple idea of seeking professional help for economic difficulty, addiction, mental health issues, or any of a number of concerns can be accompanied by feelings of shame, guilt, inadequacy, or even fear. For other clients, social work services are not selected, but instead mandated. For those who are court ordered or otherwise required to submit to social work intervention, the process of engagement will quite often also include addressing all of the feelings just mentioned, as well as anger or resentment.

Because of individual and culturally based beliefs regarding the ability to care for oneself or one's family, clients may find asking for assistance to be a particularly difficult task. Often, clients may feel that asking for help is an indication of weakness or personal failure. In almost all cases, it is difficult for anyone (social workers included) to admit to personal or financial problems that exceed their capacity to manage or solve. Part of effective engagement is the ability to have empathy for clients who are in need of assistance. Although there have been volumes written about empathy, the stages of empathy, and empathic responses to clients, the concept of empathy is not particularly complicated. Empathy quite literally means stopping and taking the time to put oneself in the life situation of another person. Indeed, empathy can go a long way in helping those of us who are social workers in regard to managing our own reactions to clients who may initially appear to be hostile, defensive, uncooperative, evasive, resistant, or many of the other negative and judgmental terms that are used to describe behaviours that may confound initial efforts to engage people in the helping process.

Social workers should be cognizant of the fact that clients may face multiple barriers to accessing and receiving services that meet their needs while still respecting cultural and personal differences. At the level of the agency, social workers need to be vigilant, looking for potential barriers that may limit the likelihood of clients to seek or access services. For example, agencies that require clients to identify sex or gender in a manner that conforms with a typical Euro-Western binary (male or female) approach to self-identification becomes an immediate barrier or even affront to a person having a gender identity that is not represented or even considered. Allowing all people to self-identify as a matter of typical agency practice can go a long way in helping those from marginalized sexual minority populations feel more welcome. This of course has to be followed up with an organizational commitment to a broader and more inclusive understanding of diversity. It should also be noted that agency attempts at sensitivity to existing or potential client populations may range from minor investments in positive organizational change, such as appropriate gender diversity sensitivity training for staff, to a more robust commitment demonstrated by the employment of persons from various sexual minority populations.

The increasingly diverse nature of identity in relation to culture, ethnicity, and race means that the process of collecting of demographic information must allow those seeking services to define themselves on their own terms rather than forcing people to select placement in a predesignated group with which they may not comfortably identify. Social workers and others who regularly interact with clients in a variety of settings need to be aware of their own socially constructed biases in relation to physical appearance and identity. For example, the reaction of a social worker in Oklahoma who said to a tribally enrolled Indigenous American client, "Funny, you don't look Native. I thought you were African American" not only offended a person seeking services, but also demonstrated the power of social construction as it relates to race, ethnicity, and identity. In another instance, a Canadian social worker in Atlantic Canada was informed by a coworker that regular remarks about clients who do or do not "look Aboriginal" was creating concern because the agency served a large Indigenous Canadian population characterized by a great degree of variety in physical appearance. These examples demonstrate the importance of allowing clients to determine their own identities, meaning that a wide variety of agencies serving people in many capacities need to develop more affirming approaches to client self-determination as it relates to identity on many levels.

Another area of concern for social workers during the engagement process with clients has to do with beliefs or personal biases the practitioner may have regarding people in need of services. A social worker who views those in need of assistance or help in healing as unnecessarily dependent, or in some way having character flaws, will have difficulty seeing the inherent dignity and worth of individuals or perhaps even entire communities or populations. Moreover, personally held negative biases on the part of the social worker or other helpers will limit the ability of those individuals to foster the sort of affirming and collaborative working relationship necessary to effect positive and lasting healing or change.

The engagement phase should be used as an opportunity to convey genuine concern for clients (Kirst-Ashman & Hull, 1999). Clients and social workers are brought together for a wide variety of reasons and in a multitude of settings. For some, social work services are mandated by entities such as courts or parole boards. In other situations, social work services are actively sought by clients. However, whether those receiving services from social workers are mandated or voluntary, engaging clients will be a necessary first step in the helping, healing, or planned change process. If the engagement phase is successfully completed, the end result will be an agreement between the social worker and client to proceed with assessment and the development of a plan for change, helping, or healing (Coggins & Hatchett, 2009).

Assessment

Assessment is the next step in case management following engagement of the client. Assessment involves the development of a comprehensive understanding of the needs of clients, which includes identifying strengths as well as challenges and limitations. As noted in chapter 14 on micro-level biopsychosocial-cultural assessment, the assessment process begins with the investigation of a broad range of biological, physical, psychological, emotional, social, cultural, economic, and even political factors that have an impact on the lives of clients. In case management, the initial assessment is viewed less as a diagnosis and more as a process of gathering baseline data that informs the direction of social work intervention or assistance. As new information and circumstances necessitate a modification in the initial planned change process, treatment plan, or care plan, the social worker will engage the client in an evaluation of changes that are needed. Furthermore, these changes can range from proposing new problem resolution strategies to termination of the client-worker relationship.

Planning

Planning is the phase of case management that involves the formulation of a service plan and the identification of appropriate service providers. Planning involves the development of a detailed plan of action that clearly identifies the role of the client, the role of the social worker, and the role of other service providers in the development of a service plan (Coggins & Hatchett, 2002). The initial service plan is directly linked to the initial assessment, and changes in the service plan will result from subsequent modifications that stem from an ongoing evaluation and reassessment process. All case management planning must include the client as a participant in the process, to the greatest degree possible (Rothman & Sager, 1998).

Give a person a fish and you have fed her/him for a day, but teach that person to fish and s/he will be fed for a lifetime, is the loose (and more gender-inclusive) recounting of what many believe is an old Chinese proverb emphasizing the virtues of empowering people through fostering skill development versus simply giving them something each time a need arises. As those who have been in the field of social work practice for many years know, helping a client build skill in problem solving is of far greater value than simply providing needed resources each time a crisis develops. Clients who are genuinely involved and included as partners in developing and putting into place a service plan that engages them in all phases of the process will be more invested than those for whom plans are, for the most part, developed by others. Likewise, clients who become active participants in problem solving and planned-change processes will also be better prepared to exercise self-determination in a way that increases not only their capacity for more effective social functioning, but their self-esteem and eventual self-sufficiency as well (Moxley, 1997).

In the course of planning for the provision of services, case managers will encounter clients with varying degrees of capacity to participate in assessment and service planning processes. Nevertheless, it is of critical importance that social workers strive to include even those who have limited capacity for full participation in an assessment and service planning process as a result of severe mental illness, intellectual disability, physical illness, and so forth. The key to inclusion of clients cannot be easily reduced to a set of recommendations. Social workers must learn to become creative in their thinking when it comes to involving clients whose capacity to participate in assessment and service planning has been compromised.

A good example of including clients with limitations in the assessment and service planning process would be that of a social worker with a client who was on a respirator. In this particular case, the client could not speak, but was able to listen and understand. During the assessment and service planning process the social worker was in a hospital room with the client and the client's spouse. In most cases, those completing an assessment and developing a plan of care would be tempted to complete the process by largely ignoring the client and speaking instead with the spouse. However, in this case the social worker wanted to retain an emphasis on client involvement. Instead of proceeding with the assessment and plan as usual, she took an approach that reformulated many of the questions in a manner that required only a yes or no answer. Each time the client wanted to respond in the affirmative, he would move his left foot. In this way, the social worker included the client in the process, and demonstrated to the spouse a different way of communicating. When asked by her supervisor where she learned the technique, the social worker responded, "I didn't read it anywhere. I just asked myself what I would do if I couldn't talk but still wanted to let people know what I was thinking." Six months later, after the man regained some ability to speak, he asked his spouse to take him to see the social worker who had developed the home care plan. He thanked the social worker for not leaving him out of the planning process and said that her thoughtfulness gave him the inspiration to, as he said, "get well."

Problem Partialization—An important initial step in the process of working collaboratively with the client to develop a service plan involves partialization of the presenting problem identified in assessment, followed by prioritizing what issues or concerns will be addressed first, second, third, and so forth. Problem partialization is a useful tool for case managers. However, it is not confined to case management alone. Social workers, counsellors, and others often use problem partialization when helping clients dismantle problems that initially appear complex to the degree of feeling insurmountable. The process of problem partialization is one in which clients are assisted in breaking problems down into component parts. A client may say something such as "Everything is a mess," which is of course quite vague. However, a client making such a statement is clearly indicating the need for engagement in a process that examines the component parts of a presenting problem.

For example, a client who says that "university classes are getting to be too much" might be engaged by a social worker in a discussion of course loads, assignments, home life, workplace demands, and so forth. During the discussion, the terms *university classes* and *too much* would be more clearly defined and then broken down by course name, the demands of each course, and the degree of difficulty the student is experiencing in the completion of assignments. This would be followed by targeting the most problematic classes and devising a plan to address the identified concerns. Next, the demands of home life, work, and perhaps interpersonal relationships would all be examined in relation to the original problem of managing courses. The end product would be a list of concerns, each of which would be more limited in scope and more clearly defined, making them more manageable.

Managing courses, addressing issues at work, and feeling unsupported at home may all emerge as broader concerns for the person in this case who sees university course work as overwhelming. The broader presenting problems must be broken down into more specific areas of concern, followed by the identification of component parts of each problem for which a plan may then be devised. In this example, a social worker engaged in a planned change process with a client would work with the client to create a plan to address identified problems with attention to realistic desired outcomes. This may involve referral to other agencies, or the provision of services within the social worker's employing agency. In either case, the social worker and client need to be engaged in a collaborative process that emphasizes the importance of client priorities and the skill of the social worker in helping the client shape her or his desired outcomes in a way that is informed by existing constraints and opportunities presented by the client's total biopsychosocial-cultural environmental context.

Problem Prioritization—Problem prioritization follows the process of problem partialization and requires of the social worker the capacity to assist the client in understanding the need to address problems in a particular order. This does not mean that client priorities are to be overridden by the social worker. Instead, the purpose of prioritization is to help the client anticipate the possible outcome of certain choices to address identified problems in a particular order. This idea of informed client self-determination is not new to social work, and is in fact enshrined in ethical practice across North America. Simply agreeing to work on improving a difficult situation by deciding to support any goal a client identifies as important does not guarantee a good outcome. Problem identification and prioritization requires a collaborative professional relationship in which the client and social worker will work together to define their respective roles and responsibilities in the development of a detailed service plan as a component of a planned change process.

Figure 15.2   Problem Partialization

Presenting Problem	Component Parts	Plan(s)
Difficulty managing each course	Abnormal Psychology 1. Twenty-page paper due in three weeks 2. Final exam in six weeks 3. Thirty to forty pages of reading each week 4. New terminology that requires extra time to find definitions	1. Dedicate more time to reading, allowing for time to look up definitions of unfamiliar terms 2. Create flash cards to help with memorization of unfamiliar terms
	Introduction to Social Welfare 1. Fifteen-page paper due in three weeks 2. Thirty to forty pages of reading each week 3. Many dates and policy initiatives to memorize	1. Begin writing fifteen-page paper 2. Use flash cards to memorize dates and policies
	Statistics for the Social Sciences 1. Mathematic terms that are new 2. Symbols that are unfamiliar 3. Concepts that are difficult to understand 4. A final project (due in five weeks) that requires application of statistical concepts to a real life example	1. Access tutoring services 2. Meet with a study group 3. Create a list of unfamiliar terms with accompanying definitions 4. Begin planning for final project
Problems managing workload	Complete inventory assessment due in three weeks 1. Staff has been reduced from four to three due to illness 2. Additional hours have been requested by management to complete inventory 3. Staff member out due to illness will not return for three weeks	1. Speak with supervisor about the conflict between workload and course load 2. Ask if temporary help can be hired 3. Inform supervisor of inability to extend working hours by explaining course load demands
Difficulties related to home life	Family members (partner and two teenage children) have not been helpful with household chores, making studying difficult	1. Request family meeting to discuss the problem 2. Let family members know that support is needed 3. Work with family members to devise a solution

For example, a client who wants to complete a college degree, but is currently unemployed and living in a rented apartment, would need to be engaged in a process of devising short- and long-term objectives. The desire to increase knowledge and develop employable skills must be weighed against the reality of needing shelter, food, clothing, and a plan to secure an income. The social worker serving the client in this example would need to engage that client in a discussion of pressing immediate needs versus future plans. This does not mean that a client's aspirations should be dismissed or completely set aside. Instead, immediate needs can become part of a longer-term plan to strive for life goals beyond basic survival or employment for the sake of a basic income alone.

The task of the social worker in this, or any problem prioritization process, is to engage the client in an assessment of potential outcomes linked to choices or possible consequences resulting from actions. Again, if the client in this example were to ignore the need for maintaining a place of residence dependent on a basic income, and instead try to enroll in college courses as a full-time student, eviction from her or his residence would result in a cascade of undesirable occurrences. Without an income, the client wanting to attend college would soon be without a residence, meaning that applying for college admission, securing funding for college, having a place to sleep and study, and possessing financial resources needed to prepare for advanced education would result in making the dream of a college degree much more difficult, if not wholly unattainable.

Clearly the client in this case would need to attend to the issue of employment as a first step in planning for her or his future. The social worker in this situation might help the client by developing a plan that identifies the most pressing current needs and then working with that client to link the process of meeting current needs to a longer-term plan to attend college courses to increase employable skills and income potential. The following example of prioritizing the steps needed to address a current problem also illustrates the sequencing of actions required to achieve specific desired end states. The social worker in this case example might be working in an employment services program for unemployed or underemployed individuals. Although the following example of problem prioritization in service plan development is presented in an ideal form, few plans are completed exactly as they are initially designed, meaning that the client and social worker will likely be involved in an ongoing process of modifying, revising, and redeveloping service plans in order to address needs and achieve objectives.

Linking

Linking follows planning in the case management process. Linking is the act of connecting clients with agencies, organizations, or persons capable of providing services designed to meet specific needs. To be effective in serving clients with a vast array of needs, strengths, and capabilities, social workers must

Figure 15.3   Problem Prioritization

Needs Ranked in Order of Urgency	Planned Action(s)	Desired Outcome(s)
Very little food in the home	1. Refer client to local emergency food pantry	Secure two weeks of basic food supplies
Overdue electric bill must be paid	1. Help client contact the electric company to negotiate a late payment schedule 2. Assist client in completion of application for assistance with utilities	Continuation of electric utility service
Full-time employment	1. Assist client in review of employable skills 2. Help client develop an updated résumé 3. Inform client of job openings that match skills 4. Client will contact employers to schedule interviews 5. Provide client with transportation assistance 6. Client will complete job interviews	Secure full-time employment
Long-Term Objective(s)	**Planned Action(s)**	**Desired Outcome(s)**
Attend college for two years	1. Client will be assisted in completing an application for admission to college 2. Client will be assisted in completing an application for a grant to cover tuition and costs	Completion of culinary arts degree

become skilled not only at assessment and planning, but also at brokering services for clients. The role of services broker has a long tradition in social work. When acting in the role of a broker, a social worker identifies, locates, and links clients with needed and appropriate services (Barker, 2003). To be effective in relation to linking clients with service providers, case managers must become knowledgeable regarding many types of service providers in their communities and regions. This requires developing either written or electronic directories of various service providers covering a broad range of potential service needs. Moreover, that knowledge of providers cannot be limited to human services alone. A comprehensive approach to quality case management also requires awareness of service providers capable of addressing financial, legal, medical, employment, educational, and various additional needs that are identified in the development of client service plans.

Case managers who are involved in the act of linking clients with appropriate potential service providers might begin the process of knowledge building by amassing service directory information, much of which is published and made available at no cost by various governmental departments, as well as private nongovernmental organizations. Case managers will find that the creation of service provider logs or provider databases, while valuable, are in need of regular attention to ensure that information is up to date. Agencies and organizations are often in constant states of change that may include expansion, contraction, or even closure. In addition, public and nongovernmental service providers may be involved in the development of programs designed to meet the needs of emerging client populations or attract financial support from funding sources tied to local, provincial/state, or federal priorities.

In addition to the creation and maintenance of directory information, it is also vital to keep up-to-date information regarding key contact persons, especially in those agencies to which the case manager most often refers clients for service. Scheduling visits to various agencies, meeting important contact people for lunch, spending time with representatives of agencies and organizations at local conferences, and simply making time to meet key individuals for face-to-face conversations will facilitate the referral process. Quality positive professional relationships are valuable when it comes to serving clients. People who know you and respect you as a professional are often much more likely to make the extra effort required to secure needed services for one of your clients than would be the case for a stranger. This is not to say that any one individual would not otherwise be professional. It simply highlights the fact that all of us, as human beings, will tend to make an additional effort to help those people we know. Therefore, getting to know people who are part of your service provider network may go a long way in relation to facilitating the referral process and service provision outcome.

It is important for case managers to be aware of policies regarding eligibility for services provided by various agencies and organizations. In many cases, federal, provincial/state, and even municipal policies dictate who may receive services from human service agencies and charitable organizations. For example, undocumented immigrants in the United States are not eligible for many forms of social welfare, including assistance through the Supplemental Nutrition Assistance Program (SNAP), Medicaid, and a host of other public benefits (Fix, Zimmermann, & Passel, 2001).

In cases where clients are subject to treatment that results in a level of service provision differing from that of other clients referred to the same agency, the case manager may need to act as an advocate. Although one might think that those in the helping professions would be more open and accepting of diversity, case managers who refer clients for services elsewhere still need to be vigilant regarding potential for discriminatory practices within the service provider environment. The reality is that lingering forms of discrimination based on socioeconomic class, age, gender, disability, sexual orientation, religion, and even race still exist. Although cases of blatant discrimination may be less common than in the past, subtle forms of racism, marginalization, and exclusion still occur.

In a discussion of racism within clinical settings, Sue and fellow researchers identify the many ways in which dominant culture service providers engage in the invalidation of and aggression toward clients from different racial and ethnic backgrounds. Although clearly not overt, these subtle forms of hostility directed toward clients have a negative impact on the formation of positive working relationships that are necessary for progress toward objectives developed in the process of creating service plans, as well as the alliances that must be forged between clients and the service providers to whom they have been referred (Sue et al., 2007). Therefore, advocacy as a function of case management, although often thought of as advocating for services, may also include vigilance in relation to discrimination based on race or other factors. As a result, social workers, in their roles as case managers, need to devote time and attention to ensuring that clients referred to providers for care are receiving the same quality of services offered to other clients served by those individuals or agencies (Summers, 2001).

Another component of linking has to do with a client's ability to follow through on seeking and receiving the services for which she or he has been referred. Some clients may have a great deal of skill in relation to navigating complicated and often-confusing service delivery systems, while others may need more guidance. A component of assessing client strengths and needs should include an evaluation of her or his capacity to effectively follow through with a referral. Some clients may have a history of accessing services, making them more familiar with the process, while others may be quite unfamiliar. Clients with severe mental health or medical conditions, or those with cognitive impairments will likely have limited capacity to follow through with a referral process. Other clients may need only verbal instructions and a minimal amount of written information, such as addresses and telephone numbers, in order to be successful in locating and accessing needed services from the appropriate providers. Some clients may actually need to be accompanied on the first visit to another provider to ensure that the process of referral and initial contact is successful. Whatever the case may be, it is incumbent upon the case manager to assess the degree of guidance needed with clients as some may be particularly fragile or vulnerable.

Monitoring

Monitoring is a process that involves vigilance. Service plans, once in place, must be attended to regularly. This is done to make sure that collaboratively devised plans are meeting the needs of the clients with whom they have been developed. Monitoring requires ensuring that clients and providers are following through with an approach to addressing a variety of needs that also include those portions of plans that have been agreed to by various providers to whom clients have been referred (Summers, 2001). As stated earlier, it is of critical importance that clients are involved as much as possible in all stages of service plan development. If a client has not been included and involved in the development of a service plan, a low level of investment in the various parts of the plan may result in diminished effectiveness. Some case managers with large client caseloads and limited time may be tempted to bypass a task that can seem unnecessarily time consuming. However, with minimal client input, there is often minimal investment which then, in many cases, results in clients not following through with other service providers to whom they have been referred. Monitoring also requires checking in with clients to ensure that service providers are in compliance with agreed-upon service plans. In cases where agencies, or professionals within agencies, have not provided agreed-upon services, the case manager may need to act as an advocate on behalf of the client to ensure that services are provided, or if availability of other providers allows, refer the client to another agency.

Evaluation

Evaluation of a service plan may result in termination of the case manager-client relationship or the development of a modified or even new service plan. Evaluation involves a review of service-related objectives to determine the degree to which each has been met. In the current social and economic climate, simply referring clients to service providers will not be sufficient to determine whether or not objectives have been met (Frankel & Gelman, 2012). Evaluation means developing measurable objectives that can be used to determine not only the effectiveness of a case management service plan, but also to guide any changes in service delivery that emerge in the evaluative process.

Termination

Ideally, a client-worker relationship is terminated because collaboratively developed service objectives included in a service plan have been achieved. Depending on the plan developed, this may mean that a client has had her or his needs appropriately met, has successfully developed skill related to managing her or his life without the need of service providers, is now capable of maintaining her- or himself within the community using a combination of semiformal and informal supports, or has transitioned to another service provider and no longer needs help from the agency within which the original case management service plan had been initiated. However, a decision to terminate a professional case manager relationship with a client may be the result of many external factors beyond the control of the case manager or the client being served. For example, some services are time limited, meaning that a relationship must come to an end when a maximum number of service hours have been reached. Also, some clients may have a change in economic status that disqualifies them for services requiring an income below a particular threshold. Moreover, changes in residence such as relocation to another city or region may make a continuation of a client-worker relationship untenable. In other cases, a client may simply end contact with the case manager, even though attempts have been made to reestablish a connection. Finally, there are even situations that include the death of a client. This is always a possibility, especially when case management agencies or programs serve medically fragile or terminally ill clients, or when clients are from high-risk groups such as sex trade workers, intravenous drug users, homeless populations, and so forth.

Supportive Counselling

A very important aspect of case management is supportive counselling. Although counselling and psychotherapy may include similar initial engagement techniques such as asking open-ended questions, seeking clarification, paraphrasing, and summarizing, supportive counselling tends to be short term and focused on immediate concerns. Psychotherapy may address imme-diate concerns as well, but also includes work on underlying issues and well-established problematic behaviours on which the client wishes to focus attention. Additionally, psychotherapy often includes the development of insight that holds the potential for helping clients in a more global sense.

An example of supportive counselling might be helping a client reduce stress by serving as a person to whom she or he can vent frustrations or express concerns. Supportive counselling may also include helpful recommendations such as deep-breathing exercises or increased physical activity designed to facilitate stress management. However, psychotherapy would go well beyond listening and recommending stress-reduction techniques to explore environ-mental causes and triggers for stress coupled with an exploration and evalua-tion of the client's capacity to effectively cope with stressful life events or circumstances. Moreover, psychotherapy in the case of stress reduction will likely be directed toward the development of insight that holds promise for modifying established problematic behaviours and emotional responses to stress that impede the achievement of optimal functioning for clients. In case management, supportive counselling will be one component of a broader inter-vention and service plan that is generally focused on meeting a variety of client needs. However, in psychotherapeutic work with clients, identifying and work-ing on emotional and behavioural issues will be central to the helping process.

Professional Documentation

Finally, skill in relation to professional documentation is critical in the field of social work and in other affiliated helping professions such as psychology and counselling. Learning how to produce professional documentation provides a record of contact between social workers and clients who can inform the direc-tion of case management service planning. In an era of increasing litigiousness, professional record keeping can also protect the social worker and her or his employing agency from unfounded allegations of misconduct related to ser-vices sought by clients and rendered by providers. Professional documentation that details client-worker contact can be subject to subpoena in court cases involving client and social worker interactions. Inappropriate, unprofessional, or incomplete documentation can leave social workers vulnerable. Therefore, the development of skill in relation to professional documentation is crucial to pro-fessional practice. This topic will be addressed at greater length in chapter 16.

CONCLUSION

Possessing the ability to engage client systems in planned change processes represents an important set of skills required for the provision of high-quality professional direct practice in social work. Although what is commonly known as clinical social work involves the development of an advanced skill set related to work with individuals and families, the ability to competently perform case management tasks remains indispensable. This is especially true for social workers engaged in direct practice with clients having multiple needs that require matching them with a variety of service providers. Therefore, understanding assessment, service planning, and the functions of linking clients to services, combined with monitoring progress toward service goals, will enhance the effectiveness of treatment, helping, or healing plans. Indeed, as the lives of clients served by social workers become increasingly complex, the ability to focus on intrapsychic or behavioural issues to the exclusion of other concerns in the external environment is a condition that will rarely exist for people who either seek or are referred to social workers. Therefore, developing knowledge, skills, and abilities in relation to case management service provision will remain as an essential and central element of direct practice in social work.

Chapter Sixteen

Comprehensive Clinical Practice

INTRODUCTION

Clinical social workers and other clinical practitioners should clearly possess the ability to engage clients in comprehensive biopsychosocial-cultural assessment processes. The comprehensive assessment provides baseline data that will shape the nature of the relationship engaged in by client and clinician, who together will develop a treatment/healing/care plan. Likewise, clinical practitioners should also be adept at working collaboratively with clients to develop treatment objectives that address presenting problems or issues in a manner that can be tracked and measured. This can be done, for example, by monitoring specific behaviours, recording changes in emotional states, progress in symptom management, or measuring increases in the ability of clients to effectively problem solve.

As stated in chapter 14, the process of assessment in social work should begin with an exploration of the client's lived experience. This is done by utilizing an ecological systems theoretical foundation that is informed by various perspectives and viewed through various lenses. As was highlighted in the *Individualized Worldview*, social and economic justice, Indigenous perspectives, racism, feminism, cultural diversity, sexual minority experiences, and many other personal and macrosocietal factors influencing the lives of clients need to be considered in selecting the most appropriate course of action in the provision of a wide array of social work services. In this chapter, assessment, diagnosis, and treatment planning will be presented in a manner that considers the client in context. In other words, mental illness, emotional distress, and behavioural problems will be understood as being influenced by multiple and interconnected social, cultural, economic, biological, and political systems. Material related to diagnosis, treatment planning/care planning, service provision, and documentation is presented in a way that recognizes current realities, but also strives to advance comprehensive, holistic, and culturally relevant practice.

CLINICAL PRACTICE AND CASE MANAGEMENT FUNCTIONS

In clinical practice and case management (the two most common arenas of work with clients at the micro level), there are some important areas of commonality

Figure 16.1   Micro-Level Clinical Practice and Case Management

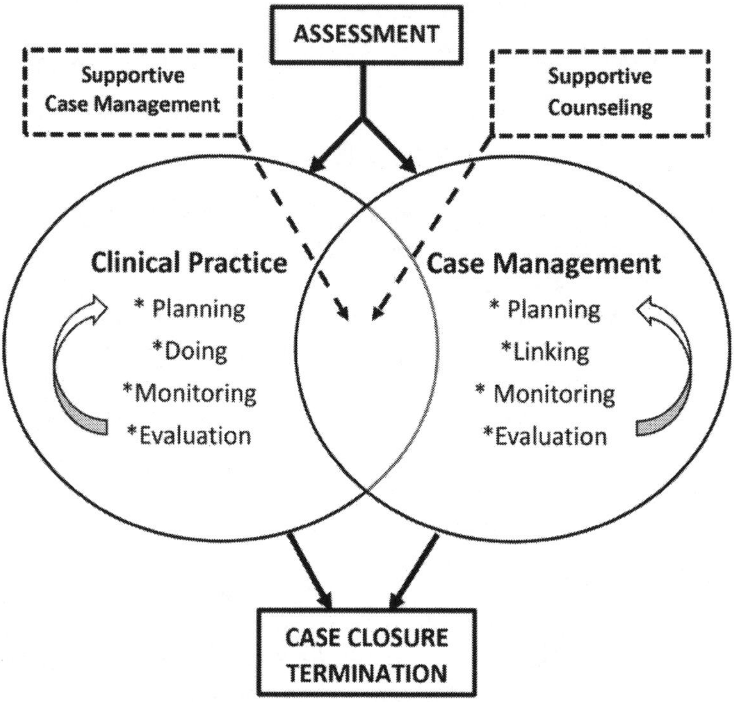

as well as recognized difference. In addition, overlap between the two also occurs. For example, clinical social workers will at times be required to engage in supportive case management activities related to unexpected events in the lives of clients that are external to clinical treatment. This may involve tasks such as advocating for clients or linking them with service providers to address identified needs. As mentioned in chapter 15, case managers, while focused on connecting clients with providers capable of addressing unmet needs, will also be called upon to provide supportive counselling to those they serve.

DIAGNOSIS IN CLINICAL WORK WITH CLIENTS

Assessment and planning for the provision of clinical services by social workers and other behavioural/mental health professionals generally include some form of diagnosis or the formulation of a diagnostic impression. The development of diagnoses ranging from identifying what needs to be targeted in treatment, healing, or helping to the use of actual formalized diagnostic categories and codes has a long history in the helping professions. As was stated in chapter 8 on Indigenous North American theory and practice, the Nahuatl peoples of central Mexico were treating recognized and categorized forms of mental illness long before the arrival of Europeans (Morales, Sheafor, & Scott, 2012, p. 406).

The more familiar Euro-Western tradition related to the identification and classification of mental illness and behavioural health conditions, although not nearly as old as that of the Nahuatl peoples of Mexico, has a history dating back to before the turn of the twentieth century, and continues into the present era with the application of the *Diagnostic and Statistical Manual of Mental Disorders*, 5th edition (DSM-5) which has replaced the DSM-IV-TR. The DSM-5 uses an approach that also includes information guiding clinicians in the application of World Health Organization diagnostic codes found in the tenth revision of the *International Classification of Diseases and Related Health Problems*, known as the ICD-10.

While the intention of developing and using a system of classification has its merits, the move from earlier versions of the DSM to the current system has not been easy, smooth, or free of criticism. The DSM was first published in 1952. The second edition (DSM-II) was released in 1968. The third edition (DSM-III) was published in 1980, and represented the first break from a psychodynamic theoretical foundation. The DSM-III emphasized normal versus abnormal behaviour from a biomedical perspective, and also introduced the multiaxial system which would remain an important component of the DSM until the introduction of the DSM-5 in 2013 (American Psychiatric Association, 2013). With each new addition of the DSM, the number of identified disorders has increased. In addition, the social milieu of the times has had an impact on the formation of the manual. For example, prior to the 1974 printing of the DSM-II, homosexuality had been listed as a disorder (Spitzer, 1981). Moreover, the shift in treatment for mental health conditions from an almost-exclusively psychodynamic orientation to a biomedical approach in the DSM-III followed two decades of profound social change which ushered in a multitude of theories that challenged psychodynamic dominance in psychotherapy.

In spite of having a long history, the formulation of a diagnosis in relation to clients with mental or behavioural health conditions remains controversial. As Corrigan (2007) argues, the process of diagnosis and labeling may indeed increase the stigma experienced by those with mental health conditions. With the most recent changes found in DSM-5, many are concerned about the pathologizing of behaviours that were previously within the normal range, creating potential for even greater stigma in relation to mental illness (Ben-Zeev, Young, & Corrigan, 2010). Although some practitioners would prefer to treat clients without attaching diagnostic labels, the fact remains that many funding sources, including the federal government in Canada and the United States have for years often required the use of standardized diagnoses found in the DSM as a prerequisite for funding of mental health treatment (Davis, 2006). This means that in both countries the DSM (now the DSM-5 or ICD-10 equivalent) continues to be an important factor in the field of mental health practice for social workers and other professionals involved in the delivery of direct clinical services to those seeking treatment for mental health conditions.

There are many ways in which mental health conditions and symptoms can and have been categorized. Some systems emphasize etiological approaches based on identifying and understanding underlying causes (Frey, 2003). Although such approaches recognize the importance of treating symptoms, addressing the original cause of the problem is seen as critical to producing lasting improvement. Therefore, if social or environmental issues are identified as causative factors in mental illness, symptom identification in the establishment of a diagnosis will be viewed as wholly inadequate and misdirected. For example, recent changes in the understanding of how oppression impacts mental health has led social workers, psychologists, and even physicians to consider poverty as an underlying condition that may cause and exacerbate mental health conditions such as anxiety and depression (Funk, Drew, Freeman, Faydi, & World Health Organization, 2010).

Holistic approaches, such as those featured in programs serving Indigenous populations or used by Indigenous helping professionals/healers, often include an emphasis on biological, psychological, spiritual, social, and emotional factors that may either cause or influence mental health conditions, or facilitate healing (Nebelkopf & King, 2003). Indigenous healing not only emphasizes a multifaceted approach to understanding the causes of mental distress or mental illness, but also an integrative approach to healing or treatment that includes attending to emotional, physical, social, and spiritual aspects of one's existence. This is why Indigenous healing practices focus on health and healing of the person and community, which may also include healing ceremonies, meaningful participation in culturally specific activities, and even the involvement of family members in the healing process (Cohen, 2006).

There are also syndromal approaches that group observed behaviours, and emotional states reported by clients into syndromes, which are clusters of "behaviour patterns, personality traits, or physical symptoms that occur together to form a specific disorder or condition" (Barker, 2003, p. 427). The DSM has utilized a system of organizing different mental disorders that places symptoms into categories, and groups patterns of symptoms together. As a result, a syndromal approach was combined with a categorically oriented classification system that relied on observed and reported symptoms in persons with mental illness. In addition, from 1980 until the implementation of the DSM-5 in 2013–2014, the DSM also included what was known as a multiaxial system that grouped mental disorders and other conditions into broad categories. Under the multiaxial system, there were five axes utilized for assessing various aspects of mental and emotional health in clients. The multiaxial system was intended to produce a diagnosis that provided a more complex and comprehensive understanding of mental disorders within the context of medical, social, and environmental factors that impacted the lives of clients. According to the DSM-IV-TR, the multiaxial system was designed to encourage the use of a biopsychosocial model in relation to clinical practice in mental health that did not reflect dominance of any one school of thought in the field of practice with clients who have been diagnosed with mental disorders (APA, 2000). The DSM-IV TR included the following axes:

Figure 16.2   DSM-IV-TR Axes

AXIS I
Clinical Disorders
Anxiety Disorders
Mood Disorders
Schizophrenia
Other Psychotic Disorders
Axis II
Personality Disorders
Mental Retardation
AXIS III
General Medical Conditions
AXIS IV
Psychosocial and Environmental Problems:
These include conditions or situations that influence the diagnosis, treatment, or prognosis of a client's mental disorder such as: family problems, social environment problems, educational problems, occupational problems, housing problems, economic problems, problems with access to health care, problems with the legal system, and other problems (war, disasters, etc.).
AXIS V
The Global Assessment of Functioning (GAF) Scale:
The primary scale for Axis V, the GAF Scale measures level of functioning on a scale of 1 to 100.

Another approach to diagnosis is one in which the mental health practitioner utilizes any of a number of dimensional models. Dimensional models emphasize the importance of evaluating behaviours and emotional states that are, for example, placed along a continuum from minimal or mild, to severe.

With certain disorders, such as autism and attention deficit hyperactivity disorder (ADHD), the current DSM-5 combines a categorical approach with a dimensional approach in the development of diagnoses. For the final draft of the DSM-5, the idea was one of improving the categorical approach to diagnosis through the incorporation of dimensional concepts (Swanson, Wigal, & Lakes, 2009). With dimensional models for use in diagnosis, the grouping of symptoms along a continuum might allow for more flexibility and accuracy.

Indeed, dimensional approaches do allow for a higher degree of precision in development of diagnoses or diagnostic impressions. However, the grouping of previously less-severe diagnoses along a continuum with more-severe conditions may increase stigma that results from association with the more-severe level of a diagnostic category (Ben-Zeev, Young, & Corrigan, 2010). In addition, the use of dimensional approaches in the development of diagnoses will require training in making accurate distinctions between levels of severity. If this is not done, the dimensional approach runs the risk of being inaccurately applied, much in the same manner as has long been the case with the Global Assessment of Functioning Scale, Axis V of the DSM-IV. As students and practitioners are well aware, the Global Assessment of Functioning Scale often ends up being of little use in either diagnosis or treatment because of the wide range of variability in terms of evaluating client functioning.

Figure 16.3   Dimensional Model

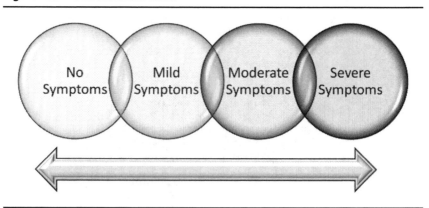

Yet another approach to diagnosing clients with mental health problems involves the concept of different "perspectives" originating with the work of Adolf Meyer and Karl Jaspers at the Johns Hopkins University School of Medicine in Baltimore, Maryland (Peters, Taylor, Lyketsos, & Chisolm, 2012). The perspectives approach includes four perspectives in relation to persons with mental health problems or diagnoses. These include (1) the disease perspective which focuses on physical illness attributed to functional problems within the client's physical self, including the brain; (2) the dimensional perspective which emphasizes understanding symptoms that occur along a continuum as being related to the variable natural attributes of persons with mental health conditions or diagnoses; (3) the behavioural perspective focuses on identifying maladaptive behaviours that occur in persons with psychiatric disorders, but also emphasizes working with those individuals to modify or change behaviour; and (4) the life story perspective which looks at the lives of clients in terms of experiences and events, with attention to how those aspects of clients' lives have had an impact on current mental health status (Peters et al., 2012).

The intention of the perspectives approach in the assessment of clients is to develop a more comprehensive understanding of each individual that acknowledges the intersection of multiple aspects of physical/biological, psychological, social, and emotional components of mental health conditions in

Figure 16.4   Perspectives Model

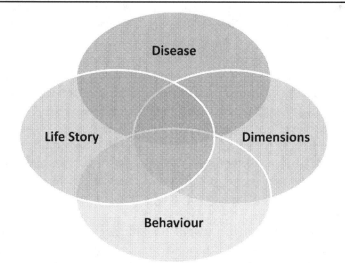

the creation of a more well-rounded diagnosis or diagnostic impression of clients with problems related to mental health. Although not as fully integrative as some Indigenous models, the perspectives model does recognize the importance of the interaction between physical, psychological, and social aspects of clients' lives in regard to mental illness and the multiple variables requiring attention in the process of treatment.

TREATMENT PLANNING

Treatment planning in social work goes by many names, such as healing and care planning, which quite often depends on the mission of an agency, the preference of the clinical practitioner, or even the popularity of a particular term at any given point in the history of various helping professions, including social work. In agencies where social workers are employed, treatment plans may be called plans of care, intervention plans, care plans, healing plans, problem-solving plans, planned change processes, or service plans. Although this list is far from exhaustive, it does demonstrate the variety of terms used to designate that aspect of the client-social worker interaction related to addressing the problems, issues, or concerns for which the client has sought or been referred for clinical mental health services.

The entire purpose for assessment and diagnosis, or the development of some sort of diagnostic impression, is to identify what concerns or problems will be worked on in the action or *doing* phases of clinical work with clients. Some mental health practitioners use psychological testing in the identification and clarification of presenting problems that will become the focus of treatment (Maruish, 2002, pp. 64–65). However, most mental health practitioners, social workers in particular, do not rely on purely intrapsychic factors in the formulation of diagnostic impressions or the development of treatment plans. As has been noted throughout this book, multiple factors play a contributing role in the issues clients face. Therefore, clinical treatment, healing, or care plans will often include some objectives that address difficulties encountered by clients at the interface between themselves and other persons or systems in their environments. Moreover, the macrosocietal and intersecting influences of racism, homophobia, sexism, ageism, gender discrimination, economic deprivation, colonization, and other oppressive social, legal, and political forces must be recognized as having the potential for profoundly impacting physical and/or mental well-being. Therefore, clinical practitioners cannot hold the external physical, social, economic, or political environment faultless in the formulation of diagnoses or diagnostic impressions that will lead to the development of appropriate treatment, healing, or care plans.

Therapies and therapists that largely ignore the complex and often oppressive lived realities of clients do them an injustice by taking a neutral stance on the influence of physical, social, economic, and political environments, while focusing almost exclusively on the need to change how clients view or respond to problems. Finally, developing treatment objectives that recognize the importance of social location, marginalization, social or economic injustice, and oppression must not end at the point of identifying negative influences on client well-being. A well-crafted treatment or healing plan should also seek to identify client strengths, capacities for effective problem solving, mastery of difficult tasks or problem situations, and innate personality factors that may contribute to positive treatment or healing outcomes.

Another important consideration in work with clients has to do with the influence of forces external to the client and the clinical practitioner. While many social workers and other mental health practitioners would like to think that engaging a client in treatment planning, planned change, or other processes is free of outside influences, the truth is that purely client-and-clinician-driven plans for addressing problem resolution or change are virtually nonexistent, with the possible exception of those rare cases in which clients have sufficient resources to pay privately for indeterminate periods of psychotherapeutic treatment. However, for the vast majority of those clients with whom social workers come into contact, a combination of client preferences, agency or program objectives, funding sources, socially influenced behavioural expectations, and even legal obligations impact the formulation of service/treatment plan development. Long-term outpatient treatment is largely a thing of the past for conditions such as depression, anxiety, posttraumatic stress, and a myriad of other diagnosed mental disorders that do not qualify clients for continuing service as persons with major mental illness.

In the current North American political and economic climate, clients are generally limited to a certain number of sessions provided by qualified mental health practitioners. A mix of public, nongovernmental (private nonprofit), and private for-profit mental health agencies and practitioners constitute the service environment. Some individuals have mental health benefits as part of their employer-based benefit packages, while others do not. In some cases, those seeking help for nonemergency mental health concerns will be required to pay for services. Those who are able to receive help from nongovernmental/ nonprofit providers or community mental health centres will likely pay for services on a sliding scale, meaning of course that those with the lowest incomes pay the lowest fees and those with higher incomes pay larger amounts. Persons seeking help from private practitioners may either be funded through various sorts of public or private insurance, or pay the full amount out of pocket. As a result, only the wealthy few in society will be able to afford treatment that is not constrained by government funding, insurance coverage, or ability to pay. Therefore, many mental health practitioners now emphasize developing measurable treatment objectives, often in the initial session.

Doing

The act of engaging in the process of treatment, healing, or working through the steps of a care plan as part of direct practice involves the client and the professional practitioner. Each plays a part in this reciprocal relationship and journey toward improved well-being for the client. Although this process of *doing* may be focused on behavioural or emotional concerns, biological, social, psychological, cultural, and even spiritual factors may at times play more prominent roles during the process of collaborative work between the client and clinical practitioner. Moreover, one or more elements of a client's internal or external world may become the primary focus of attention at different points during treatment or healing—shifting and phasing as internal states and external environments undergo change.

EXPANDED ECOLOGICAL SYSTEMS APPROACH TO ASSESSMENT FOR TREATMENT PLANNING

Because most ecological systems approaches to assessment are concerned with understanding difficulty experienced at the interface between the client and other systems, it is important to spend time prior to and at the beginning of the planning process for treatment or healing to engage clients in an assessment and diagnostic or problem identification process that considers the contexts within which they live their lives. If this important step is ignored or minimized in search of purely intrapsychic causes for distress, clinical service planning and the actual work engaged in by the client and her or his mental health practitioner will likely fail to achieve maximum positive outcomes, or could simply result in clients terminating treatment they feel is not meeting their needs.

Carefully examining the complexity of clients' lives from an ecological systems theoretical perspective encourages the mental health practitioner and the client to identify and explore multiple stressors and supports that may impact problem identification and the formation of treatment objectives. However, an ecological approach to assessment that will inform the *planning* and *doing* phases of clinical work must go beyond the older and more limited person in social environment approach. To fully understand clients' lives, current emotional states and overall mental health must be understood in relation to the natural environment, human-made environments, physical well-being, cultural systems, political/societal contexts, and spiritual/religious practices or communities of identity.

A comprehensive picture of the complexity of multiple factors impacting the lives of clients will reduce the temptation of clinicians to divorce the person from important biological, social, and cultural realities that need to be addressed in collaboratively developed treatment or healing plans intended to improve mental health or behavioural outcomes. Understanding that clients' lives have a complex set of interconnections that may function in ways that are supportive and harmonious, tense and difficult to manage, or shifting and changing will help the practitioner and the client in planning for treatment, change, or healing. As client and social worker develop a clearer understanding of the web of connections within which the life of the client is experienced, the direction of treatment, change, healing, or service planning becomes clearer.

In the case of any particular client, the approach to mental health treatment or healing selected is generally linked to diagnosis. However, diagnosis or the process of identifying specific disorders, conditions, issues, or behaviours that will become the target of intervention, treatment, or healing need to be understood within the context of multiple influences on what is most often referred to as the presenting problem. Feelings of depression, internal emptiness, anxiety, low self-esteem, loneliness, excessive shyness, anger, or any of a multitude of emotional concerns can have vastly different origins for people who seek or are referred for help. Social workers and other mental health practitioners make the best choices for effective treatment, healing, or intervention when they have worked together with clients to blend the subjective experience of a problem or concern from the perspective of a client with the more objective understanding gained by the social worker during the assessment process.

As already stated in this and previous chapters, an assessment should be done from an ecological systems theoretical perspective that includes biological, psychological, social, cultural, and spiritual aspects of a client's life. In

Figure 16.5   Expanded Ecological Systems Assessment for Treatment Planning

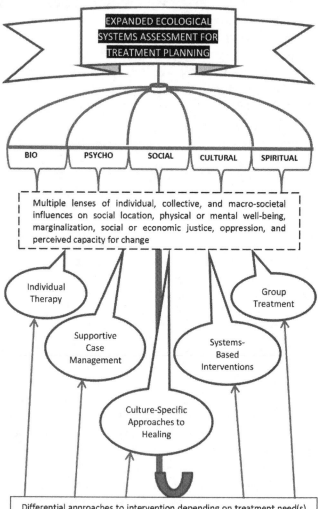

addition, social workers must filter information gathered in the assessment process through the multiple lenses of individual, collective, and macrosocietal influences on social location, physical or mental well-being, marginalization, social justice, economic justice, oppression, and perceived capacity for change. A person who is referred to a clinical social worker may report feelings of depression. However, understanding the causes of depression within the context of the life of a client may result in very different approaches to intervention, treatment, healing, and problem solving or planned change.

Developing a diagnosis or diagnostic impression that provides a more complete picture of presenting emotional and/or behavioural issues within the context of multiple dimensions (physical/biological/environmental, psychological, social, cultural, and spiritual) will heighten awareness of the impact and intersection of various aspects of clients' lives. Moreover, a holistic and inclusive approach to assessment will provide crucial information about what events and circumstances precipitate, exacerbate, or serve to maintain problematic mental health conditions that may also include behaviours sufficiently troubling to the client so as to warrant attention in the treatment or healing process.

Figure 16.6   Selecting an Approach to Psychotherapeutic Work

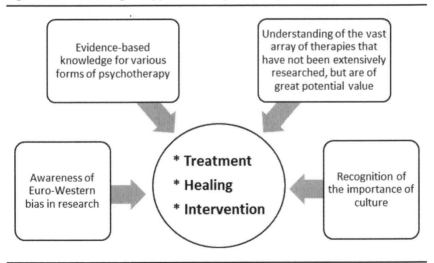

Clinical social workers and other mental health practitioners are also responsible for making decisions about potentially effective psychotherapeutic and environmental interventions. The initial task that informs and guides the direction of treatment, healing, or other forms of work with clients is the completion of a biopsychosocial-cultural assessment of clients' lives. Because the clinical social worker or other mental health professional is most likely to have a greater knowledge of theory and practice related to mental and behavioural health, it is she or he who will be most responsible for presenting or suggesting treatment options to clients. Again, it is crucial that providers of psychotherapeutic services do not fall into the trap of ignoring the external world of clients by overemphasizing an examination and analysis of the internal intrapsychic aspects of clients' lived experiences. As Saleebey (2002) makes clear, social workers and other mental health practitioners have had a history of looking for pathology in clients (Rankin, 2007). Seeking purely or even primarily intrapsychic causes for emotional or behavioural issues can lead mental health practitioners to overlook important environmental factors impacting the lives of clients they serve.

In addition to examining issues, concerns, problems, or difficulties experienced by clients as they interface with other elements of their physical and social environments, mental health practitioners should have a good understanding of what evidence-based/evidence-informed approaches to treatment or healing are likely to be effective with various presenting problems and/or client populations. This means being sufficiently skilled at understanding research in order to be a good consumer of research findings, as well as seeking continuing education opportunities that will enhance skill in the use of evidence-based/evidence-informed psychotherapeutic techniques. Nevertheless, as was stated in chapter 7, there are many potentially effective approaches to treatment that have not yet been subjected to extensive study, or which current Euro-Western-oriented research methods may not be able to adequately evaluate.

Culture is another consideration in treatment. It has long been known that many forms of psychotherapy grounded in Euro-Western cultural beliefs and values have been less effective with non-Western populations. Although all clients will have differences in beliefs, values, attitudes, and behaviours, some can be quite pronounced, as may be the case for clients from culturally distinct populations. Therefore, clinicians working with clients who may have worldviews that vary, sometimes substantially, from the North American Euro-Western majority will need to be particularly careful in selecting approaches to treatment that resonate with the client's cultural, social, and even spiritual sense of self. The following example of a client referred to a clinical social worker has been provided to demonstrate the phases of assessment and treatment planning consistent with the principles and approaches discussed in this chapter.

Case Example: Mr. Stanley

Mr. Stanley is an Anglo-American male living in a rural community in the Midwest of the United States. Mr. Stanley is fifty-nine years of age and has been referred to a clinical social worker. Mr. Stanley has been diagnosed with depression, and the psychiatrist at the rural mental health centre has asked the social worker if he could help him (Mr. Stanley) cope with his depression. An ecologically oriented assessment completed by the social worker and Mr. Stanley reveals no prior history of mental illness, including depression. In addition, Mr. Stanley has no history of substance use or abuse problems. Being an English-speaking Anglo-American heterosexual male, living in a predominantly Anglo-American rural community, Mr. Stanley has no history or perceived sense of having been marginalized or discriminated against due to race, gender, income, ethnicity, or sexual orientation. Having been raised in a middle-class family as a Roman Catholic in a predominantly Catholic community, Mr. Stanley states that he is "pretty much like everyone else" with the exception of the illness that has impacted his health, finances, and his ability to care for his wife and youngest child, age sixteen.

Since becoming ill three years ago, Mr. Stanley has sold his home to pay for living expenses and medical care. The family now lives in a rental property that is insufficiently insulated, making winter a particularly difficult time for Mr. Stanley, who due to his asbestosis is prone to respiratory infections. In addition, his wife and son have taken on part-time jobs to supplement the family income. This has caused additional emotional distress for Mr. Stanley because he feels he has failed in his role as a provider. Because the provider role for Anglo-American males in the Midwest is culturally significant, Mr. Stanley now expresses feelings of worthlessness. This, coupled with remarks about being "better off dead," led to psychiatric intervention and referral to a clinical social worker.

During the completion of a comprehensive biopsychosocial-cultural assessment, several issues emerged:

1. Mr. Stanley has a health condition known as asbestosis. Asbestosis is a progressive, chronic, debilitating lung disease. Mr. Stanley had been exposed to asbestos while working in the hulls of large ships on the lower Great Lakes. The scarring that has occurred in his lungs makes it difficult for him to breathe. As a result, Mr. Stanley cannot walk more than two city blocks without experiencing respiratory distress.

2. Mr. Stanley is currently unemployed and is unable to work due to asbestosis-related symptoms.

3. Mr. Stanley has not yet reached retirement age. Therefore, he has been fighting with the Social Security Administration to secure a determination of disability. A disability determination would make Mr. Stanley eligible for Medicare and provide him with a monthly income.

4. Mr. Stanley is currently receiving income assistance and Medicaid. However, Mr. Stanley expresses feeling shame for having to depend on what he calls "welfare," stating that the Social Security Administration should approve his "disability" which is a benefit derived from a system Mr. Stanley feels he has contributed to and therefore earned.

The social worker in the case of Mr. Stanley did address the issue of depression and potential suicidality, but was equally engaged in case management activities designed to target various systems that had negatively impacted Mr. Stanley and his immediate family. The social worker advocated for Mr. Stanley in relation to housing and was able to secure a townhouse that was better insulated and very near the medical facility where Mr. Stanley received his care. The social worker also assisted Mr. Stanley by linking him with providers of legal assistance who could help him in his dispute with the Social Security Administration. This referral resulted in a disability determination that included retroactive payment of benefits. The additional funds allowed the family to purchase a more reliable vehicle, relieving concerns about winter driving. As Mr. Stanley's life circumstances improved, so did his emotional state. After six months, Mr. Stanley was no longer taking antidepressant medication. Mr. Stanley and the social worker terminated their relationship with a reminder that he (Mr. Stanley) could contact the social worker if the need arose in the future.

In this particular case, depression was a reaction to life circumstances and difficult experiences at the interface between Mr. Stanley and other systems, with the Social Security Administration being primary. By engaging Mr. Stanley in an ecological systems-oriented comprehensive biopsychosocial-cultural approach to assessment, the social worker was able to work in collaboration with him to identify and direct change efforts toward specific targets. By working together to partialize problems and prioritize mutually established actions, the social worker and client attended to the underlying factors that contributed to and maintained depression in Mr. Stanley. Instead of pathologizing Mr. Stanley's depressive state, the social worker was able to help him understand and address his situation in the following manner:

1. Mr. Stanley was engaged in a process of looking at all the factors that have contributed to his current living situation and emotional state.
2. Mr. Stanley was given reading material related to the link between physical health and depression.
3. Mr. Stanley assumed certain tasks such as following up with his attorney and scheduling additional physical examinations related to a determination of physical disability.
4. Finally, Mr. Stanley agreed to meet regularly with the clinical social worker to discuss feelings of depression and low self-esteem. For the individual sessions focused on depression, the social worker used cognitive-behavioural therapy. Mr. Stanley appreciated what he called a "scientific" approach to addressing his symptoms.

The treatment/service plan combined charting of emotional and behavioural objectives with weekly discussions focused on progress made toward increasing responsiveness of external systems. The overall effectiveness of the combined ecological systems and cognitive-behavioural approach to intervention and treatment was supported by the fact that depression lifted and had not returned at the point of a six- and twelve-month follow-up.

MONITORING AND EVALUATION

Social workers or other mental health service providers should be involved in evaluating progress toward agreed-upon treatment/healing/service plan objectives. For many practitioners, this is done using standardized scales that measure anxiety, depression, and so forth. Other practitioners combine client self-report with the single-subject design method (described in chapter 7). In some settings clinical social workers, psychologists, and even psychiatrists are required to utilize agency or even government-approved tools to measure client progress. Often, this is also coupled with a requirement to use certain approved evidence-based psychotherapies, as outlined within the US Department of Veterans Affairs' (2012) *Veterans Health Administration Handbook*.

In most Euro-Western-oriented approaches to treatment, baseline data are gathered for the purposes of tracking change in behaviour or emotional states. However, some transpersonal approaches to treatment do not use Euro-Western methods of tracking progress, relying instead on a regular and compassionate exchange between the therapist and the client to assess growth and change. Likewise, Indigenous approaches to treatment often rely less on charting and measuring, and more on client self-report combined with observations of the healer(s) involved in the process. Whatever the case, all healing plans, clinical treatment plans, or mental health care plans have the same goal, which is improvement in emotional states or facilitating positive behavioural changes in clients referred for or seeking services. Moreover, not all interventions require extensive psychotherapy, as was demonstrated in the case of Mr. Stanley. Often, supportive case management activities combined with a brief period of psychotherapy, and perhaps pharmacotherapy, may yield even better results than a more intrapsychic and potentially pathologizing approach.

Pharmacotherapy is another important aspect of monitoring and evaluation. Those who provide psychotherapeutic or complementary supportive services need to have a good understanding of the various classes of pharmaceuticals used by psychiatrists and other medical professionals who prescribe medications for the management of mental health conditions. Many professionals utilize the annually updated *Physicians' Desk Reference* (PDR) for information on medications prescribed to manage mental health and other health conditions. Those who practice in rural and remote regions with limited access to reliable Internet connections may find references, such as the PDR, invaluable. When it comes to Internet sources of information, there are numerous reliable websites such as PDR.net, athealth.com, and WebMD.com, which serve as valuable online resources for those who seek immediate information about various medications. These sites include information on a wide range of medications commonly used to manage symptoms of mental health conditions. In the United States, the Department of Health and Human Services (DHHS), with the cooperation of the National Institute of Mental Health (NIMH), provides a very useful online guide entitled "Mental Health Medications." This guide describes the types of medications used to treat mental disorders, information on the side effects of medications, and warnings about medications as they relate to specific populations such as children and adolescents, the elderly, and pregnant women (U.S. DHHS/NIMH, 2015).

DOCUMENTATION

Without a doubt, the capacity to produce high-quality, accurate, and professional documentation is one of the most critical skills a social worker needs to develop. Well-developed assessments and progress notes serve several purposes. A more limited understanding of documentation is in relation to tracking client progress and evaluating the effectiveness of a particular intervention. However, documentation serves purposes beyond the client-worker dyad. Public, private nonprofit, and private for-profit agencies often have many employees who serve clients in different capacities. Moreover, staff turnover, movement of employees from one unit or program to another, and even retirement regularly result in the need to assign clients to other service providers within the agency. For case managers and clinical social workers, clear professional and thorough documentation not only provides a client service record for the social worker currently assigned to a particular case, but also assists future social workers and other providers for whom well-documented assessments, treatment/healing plans, or service-related activities will be instrumental to ensure continuity of high-quality service, assistance, or care.

Typical information in client files includes comprehensive assessments, plans for treatment/healing/care, progress notes, treatment/healing/care summaries, reports, confidential communication from other sources, and signed copies of releases of information. Depending on the client and source of referral, information in client files may also include court orders, probation plans, parole plans, or other federally, provincially, or state-mandated treatment orders that will often include requirements for reporting treatment compliance. Therefore, reading and understanding the limits of confidentiality and requirements to maintain privacy of client information must be part of professional activity engaged in by those providing services to clients in all settings. In addition, formal educational programming in bachelor of social work (BSW) and master of social work (MSW) programs, as well as training within agency environments, must place a clear and unambiguous emphasis on the critical nature of producing quality professional documentation. For students in social work programs, documentation is an important component of practice courses and contact with clients in field practicum placement settings. For professionals in agency settings, documentation should not be considered an afterthought, but should instead be viewed as an equally important part of the overall treatment/healing/care provision process.

Documentation is often a time-consuming but necessary aspect of work between clients and helping professionals. In line with truly collaborative approaches to work with clients, social workers or other helping professionals can also involve clients in a process of reviewing what has been and what will be included in documentation. This provides an opportunity to summarize what has been covered in sessions and does not leave the client wondering what the clinical social worker has recorded about her or him.

SOAP/SOAPIER Charting

A well-known and enduring form of documentation used in nursing is that of SOAP charting (Dziegielewski, 2003). SOAP is an acronym for Subjective, Objective, Assessment, and Plan. SOAP charting is used to record contact with clients that organizes material provided by clients and others into a predictable format that also serves to remind the attending professional of the need to include clients in the process of tracking progress toward treatment/healing/care plan objectives. The three categories of IER, an acronym for Intervention, Evaluation, and Revisions, can be added to SOAP charting documentation activities. Although SOAP/SOAPIER charting originated in the medical field, it still provides a good example of a manner in which documenting work with clients can be structured. Still, it must be acknowledged that such an approach to documentation is but one of many ways of recording interactions with clients.

S (*Subjective*)—involves the inclusion of the client's own very personal experience of a condition, concern, challenge, or problem. The subjective portion of a case note should also include direct quotes from clients. In cases where clients may be too young or unable to speak, quotes and summaries of information from other family members or caregivers can be included.

O (*Objective*)—is what has been observed by the professional. This is perhaps the most difficult part of developing client case notes because it involves taking special care to record what is observed versus what is assumed, believed, or intuited. The observed portion of case notes emphasizes the use of nonjudgemental statements that are descriptive in nature. For example, a social worker recording a session with a client might say, "Antonio entered the room looking down toward the floor, walking slowly, and speaking without looking up" versus saying that "Antonio looked depressed when he entered the office."

A (*Assessment*)—is an important function of regular monitoring of subjective and objective aspects of clients' life situations and/or emotional states. A social worker might, for example, combine client statements with observed behaviours and conclude that an adjustment or change in medication may be called for. Assessment is that portion of the client-worker relationship that calls upon the clinical social worker or other helping professional to share her or his professional judgement with the client (where possible) to identify emotional states, behavioural changes, developing strengths or challenges, and most importantly, what direction to take in treatment, healing, or care planning.

P (*Plan*)—refers to the actions taken during a session as well as what will or may be done by the clinical social worker or helping professional. The plan portion of case notes may include information about making a referral to a psychiatrist for medication adjustment or referral to a physician to address possible medical problems. In addition, a mental health professional might also work with the client to make changes in the treatment/healing/care plan by developing new objectives or including other healers.

I (*Intervention*)—will include the forms or elements of psychotherapy engaged in with clients as well as any supportive case management or other service provision activities. Intervention may also involve periodic review and comparison (with clients) of baseline data gathered at the onset of treatment with progress toward treatment/healing/care objectives. For some professionals, a portion of this information is included under the plan in case note documentation.

E (*Evaluation*)—involves an assessment of progress toward established treatment/healing/care objectives, and will include charting of change in client behaviour or reported emotional well-being. Evaluation may also lead to changes in treatment/healing/care plans.

R (*Revisions*)—are those adjustments in diagnoses/diagnostic impressions that are accompanied by the formulation of new treatment/healing/care plans that may also involve the introduction of new forms of psychotherapy, or include supportive case management activities targeted at specific systems in the client's environment.

Although SOAP/SOAPIER charting can be useful (especially for students and beginning mental health practitioners), it can be cumbersome and at times difficult to use, especially if there is little change, thereby causing the information in case notes to overlap or be repetitious (Iyer, 2001, p. 88). However, many clinical social work practitioners are not comfortable with certain elements of what is commonly referred to as the *medical model* approach to work with clients. As a result, they are often less inclined to adopt documentation methods common in nursing without major modification. Many believe that documentation practices borrowed from the medical field do not capture the richness of client-worker interactions. Therefore, a large number of social workers, psychologists, and other providers of mental health services to clients prefer a narrative approach. Use of the narrative approach in creating case or progress notes can result in a high degree of variability from one practitioner to the next. For this reason, those who use narrative approaches in documentation must take special care to ensure that crucial information is accurate, easy to locate, and does not present an impression of clients that reflects only the observations, interpretations, and evaluations of the practitioner.

Along with traditional concerns for professional assessment and record keeping that accurately reflect client care, recent decades have seen the development of documentation practices that also emphasize the importance of risk management, or in other words, the protection of service providers and their employing agencies from vulnerability in the event of an ethical complaint or lawsuit (Reamer, 2005). The rise in computerization and the concomitant increase in electronically stored, retrieved, and transmitted information have created a practice context for many social workers within which extra care, even to the point of updating or developing agency policies, has become necessary to protect client privacy and reduce legal liability through limiting access to records in paper and electronic form. This may mean that agencies will need to invest in technology, and perhaps even contract with computer specialists, to encrypt information that in earlier times would have been locked in file cabinets with keyed access available to only certain employees. In addition, agencies of all sizes need to provide comprehensive and well-designed training to new and current employees. This is necessary to ensure compliance with agency policies and procedures as well as local, provincial, state, and federal regulations or legislation related to the protection of private information. Failure to attend to employee training by adopting a *learn-as-you-go* approach will leave agencies open to potential lawsuits or other actions by clients, governing or accrediting entities, or even improperly trained or wrongfully terminated employees (Reamer, 2005). Likewise, individuals in private practice need to be up to date on all legislation related to creating, storing, and transmitting information.

Approaches to documentation are numerous and varied. Each organization should have in place some approach to recording services to clients. Therefore, social work students in field practicum placements and other helping professionals who are new to any agency that serves clients should familiarize themselves with appropriate documentation before engaging in work with individuals seeking help or who have been referred for service. However, once a social worker is familiar with agency policies and procedures, she or he also needs to be willing to question or challenge documentation protocols that are insensitive to client needs or have the potential for compromising client confidentiality. Such vigilance is an ethical requirement of social work and many other professions. Ignoring risks presented by policies related to documentation puts clients and the agency at risk.

CONCLUSION

This chapter has covered a broad range of activities engaged in by clinical social workers. Social workers and others involved in the provision of clinical services to individuals must not forget the biopsychosocial-cultural aspects of that role. By this, it is meant that external factors in the lives of clients will need to be addressed as part of any clinical treatment, healing, or care plan. Clinicians may at times be called upon to help with the management of issues outside of therapy that constitute the lived experiences of clients in their care. Clinical practitioners most definitely need skills related to engagement, assessment, planning, providing psychotherapeutic services, evaluation, and case closure or termination. However, the ability to link clients with other service providers, monitor their progress outside of the clinical relationship, and advocate for clients with particular service needs constitutes an important set of skills as well.

By keeping in mind the fact that the client-social worker relationship represents only one facet of a client's life, the clinical practitioner can better maintain a broader, balanced, and more realistic focus. Without a doubt, skilled clinical social workers can have a profound and even life-changing impact on clients with whom they work. However, those providing clinical services cannot expect that clinical intervention alone will resolve all the issues clients face in their lives. Clinical practitioners with an expanded ecological systems and anti-oppressive/social justice orientation are aware that clients' lives are intimately connected to and influenced by other biological, social, cultural, economic, spiritual, and even political realities that shape their experiences and ultimately influence the outcome of clinical intervention.

Chapter Seventeen

Social Work with Groups

INTRODUCTION

In social work practice, as is the case for closely related professions, groups are an important part of the professional work experience. While the word *group* generally conjures up ideas of treatment or therapy groups, there are many types of groups with widely varying purposes. This chapter focuses on group work, group theory, and the various types of groups encountered by social workers and other helping professionals in a wide variety of settings. This chapter includes a discussion of how groups are developed and conducted. Information on group processes for culturally different populations has been included as well, with particular attention to Indigenous populations in Canada and the United States. In addition, the importance of group work for clients with substance use disorders is accompanied by an outline of theory development in the treatment of chemical dependency/addiction. Finally, harm-reduction approaches in group work and the importance of delivering group treatment to persons with co-occurring disorders are addressed.

GROUP WORK

Group social work can take many forms. There are social workers in a variety of settings who provide information to clients, service providers, program administrators, and others in the form of educational and psychoeducational groups. Social workers often facilitate support groups, develop and deliver social skills groups, and of course, refer clients to self-help groups for a wide range of behavioural concerns. Social workers also deliver mental and behavioural health services in group settings. Service to clients in the form of group treatment can be found in outpatient mental health programs, schools, psychiatric treatment settings, juvenile detention facilities, and even in adult prisons. Social workers in host settings such as schools, hospitals, universities, and prisons will also have regular contact with other professionals as part of interprofessional/ interdisciplinary groups. Finally, virtually all those who work in agencies of any size will at some point become part of a task group. Task groups are even a common element of professional education in social work, with students regularly becoming involved in groups that are course based, developed as learning objectives in field practicum placement settings, or perhaps related to various research projects.

Types of Groups

Figure 17.1 Types of Groups in Social Work Practice

Educational

- Focused on information and skill development in a variety of settings

Psycho-Educational

- Specific to issues of health and mental health such as information about schizophrenia

Skills/Social Skills

- Designed to help participants develop skills related to managing life stresses, effectively solving problems, or interacting with others

Support

- Provision of mutual support without emphasizing behavioural change

Self-Help

- Participant-led and focused on overcoming problems such as addictions

Therapy/Treatment/Healing

- Therapeutic services provided in a group setting intended to address emotiona problems or create behavioural change

Interprofessional/Interdisciplinary

- Meeting with representatives of various professions to address client cases or agency functioning

Task

- Focus on specific work functions such as program development or project completion

Educational groups are provided in many settings by professional and paraprofessional staff. Educational groups differ from psychoeducational groups in that the focus is not on medical or mental health conditions. Educational groups are common in settings where clients are capable of performing regular activities of daily living but may need help with preparing résumés, completing job applications, filling out education or technical training grant applications, or becoming computer literate. Agencies that work with youth, ex-offenders, and other populations in need of upgrading skills and knowledge often include educational groups as part of the services they offer.

Psychoeducational groups are designed to provide mental health and health-related information to practitioners, clients, and even the family members of clients. These groups are intended to convey knowledge regarding symptoms of mental illness, pharmacological management of psychiatric disorders, the treatment of conditions, such as Alzheimer's disease, schizophrenia, depression, anxiety, and even what to expect in regard to major health concerns such as cancer treatment.

Social skills groups were very common in the 1960s through the 1980s when large numbers of persons with schizophrenia and other serious mental health conditions were deinstitutionalized. People leaving what were called mental hospitals, psychiatric hospitals, and state hospitals were generally ill prepared to live in society beyond the walls of the institution. Social skills groups, often led by social workers, were intended to help deinstitutionalized individuals develop basic skills regarding how to manage a household, go grocery shopping, complete a transaction at a bank, pay bills, and attend to various other activities of daily living. Former psychiatric patients who were now in the community would more often than not need extensive time receiving supportive services once released from the institution. While the deinstitutionalization process is essentially completed, social skills training groups are now needed for ex-offenders with serious mental health conditions leaving correctional facilities. This is because the dismantling of community supports for persons with long-term mental illness has been compounded by an increase in rates of incarceration. As a result, correctional facilities are now the de facto mental health system for many seriously mentally ill individuals who in earlier times would have been sent to state or provincial psychiatric treatment facilities (Mackrael, 2011; Torrey et al., 2014).

Social skills groups, now often simply referred to as skills groups, are still common in work with a variety of populations. There are individuals who are required to attend a variety of groups that combine behaviour change with social skill development. For example, there are groups for individuals who commit acts of domestic violence, persons who need to develop skills in relation to managing anger, and parenting groups (also called classes) for those who have become involved with the child welfare system. A new twist in the provision of social skills group work involves youths who have become so accustomed to communicating electronically that they now need help learning how to interact in face-to-face conversations with friends, family members, and others (Engelberg & Sjöberg, 2004).

Many social workers are employed in host settings where they often work alongside other professionals in organizations that may have very different purposes and missions. Social workers are employed in correctional settings, schools, hospitals, within university systems, psychiatric facilities, hospice agencies, youth justice departments, and countless other organizations or institutions. In these settings, social workers are regularly involved in interprofessional groups that are variously called interdisciplinary groups or multidisciplinary groups. Most often, interprofessional collaboration is associated with client/patient care that uses a comprehensive approach to services delivery involving multiple health and mental health providers (Ontario, 2007). However, interprofessional groups or teams may address many issues related to service delivery or organizational functioning. For example, participants in interprofessional groups might collectively review the progress of clients, patients, criminal offenders, nursing home residents, or students, depending on the setting. At the organizational level, interprofessional groups may even take on the tasks of program development or changes in agency policy. With interprofessional groups, the intention is to improve the delivery of services or agency functioning by bringing together people of varied perspectives. As a result, social workers involved in interprofessional group work will be expected to bring social work values, ethics, knowledge, skills, and perspectives to broad-range planning and implementation efforts that impact clients at many levels.

Another type of group work that is nearly ubiquitous is the *task group* (Furman, Bender, & Rowan, 2014). Task group work occurs in virtually all agency settings and may be time limited as would occur in planning for an event to honour volunteers, or more protracted as might be the case in program development and implementation. Task groups are intended to have specific outcomes. In other words, the task is either completed or left unfinished, in which case another task group will likely be formed to complete the necessary work. Many of the seemingly routine aspects of agency or institutional functioning are indeed carried out in task groups. Staff meetings, faculty meetings, and daily shift-change meetings at correctional facilities all represent task functions required for the smooth operation of work environments.

GROUP THEORY

Classic Stage Theory

Since the late 1960s, nearly every discussion of group theory has started with the stage model of Bruce W. Tuckman, an educational psychologist. In 1965, Tuckman developed a four-stage model of group development. Tuckman's stages included the four phases of *Forming, Storming, Norming*, and *Performing*. Tuckman later refined his model to include a fifth stage which resulted from his work with Mary Ann Jensen. The fifth stage, *Adjourning*, involved the completion of tasks, a reduction of dependency between group members, and termination of the group (Forsyth, 1990, p. 77). In his work, Tuckman studied the behaviour of small groups in different settings. Through this process, he identified phases that groups go through in the process of completing a task. Tuckman's stages continue to be taught to students in social work, psychology, education, counselling, and business. While the stage theory was intended for application to all types of groups, the stages presented appear better suited to task groups. However, it should be noted that Tuckman developed his stage theory because he felt that the literature on groups at that time was overrepresented by publications related to therapy groups (Tuckman & Jensen, 1977).

Critics of Tuckman's stage theory regarding group development have noted that not all groups go through all stages. While Tuckman's model does help social workers and other professionals think about the development and evolution of groups, the stages outlined perhaps suggest change more broadly, versus specific and predictable change that occurs in all groups. Finally, the model presented by Tuckman also shows clear evidence of a Euro-Western male conceptualization of process in groups. Women may, for example, engage in less conflict because of the importance of relationship building, which is more typical of feminist approaches to collective work. In addition, value placed on avoidance of confrontation combined with a strong desire to reach consensus when making decisions may occur more often in groups of individuals from societies with collectivist cultural orientations.

Figure 17.2   Tuckman's Four-Stage Model, including Jensen's Fifth Stage

Forming	Group organization
	Avoidance of controversy
	Deciding on the roles and rules
	Understanding the task(s)
Storming	Increasing tension
	Challenge of rules and roles
	Conflict
	Working through disagreements
Norming	Resolving disagreements
	Developing a sense of cohesion
	Trust increases
	Group rules and norms develop
Performing	Actual work of the group begins
	Trust is present
	Rules and norms are accepted
	Cohesion exists among members
Adjourning	Completion of task
	Reduction of dependence between group members
	Celebration or mourning of completion (not in all cases)
	Disbanding of group

GROUP TREATMENT

The Eleven Therapeutic Factors of Irvin Yalom (2005) do not represent a stage theory approach, as is the case with the work of Tuckman, but instead identify those conditions that group therapists should work to create in order to maximize the healing process of clients in therapy/treatment groups.

In the process of *instilling hope*, the first therapeutic factor, a group leader strives to create an atmosphere in which clients feel that therapy in a group setting has the potential to result in some sort of positive change. This sense of hope is believed to then create an opening for other therapeutic factors to be effective. It is also believed that clients who experience a therapist with a firm belief in the efficacy of the treatment process will be more likely to be hopeful. As treatment progresses, positive change in group members can have a compounding effect in relation to instilling hope.

Figure 17.3   Yalom's Eleven Therapeutic Factors

| *Instilling Hope* |
| *Universality* |
| *Imparting Information* |
| *Altruism* |
| *Corrective Recapitulation* |
| *Development of Socializing Techniques* |
| *Imitative Behaviour* |
| *Interpersonal Learning* |
| *Group Cohesiveness* |
| *Catharsis* |
| *Existential Factors* |

(Furman, Bender, & Rowan, 2014, pp. 15-18)

The second therapeutic factor, *universality*, develops when clients realize they are not alone in their emotional pain or distress. When clients see that others also suffer, and often in quite similar ways, a sense of sister- and brotherhood develops that can facilitate healing. As group members share their pain and struggles, others become more willing to share without shame.

The third therapeutic factor involves therapists *imparting information*. When therapists impart information within the treatment group setting, it may be done in the form of psychoeducation, such as telling clients about the emotional and physical symptoms of anxiety, depression, anorexia, complicated bereavement, cognitive distortions, and so forth. However, information provided may also include observations regarding negative communication, defensiveness, or verbal attacking behaviour that has developed in the treatment session. When this is done, the therapist will also ask group members to comment on why potentially destructive or defensive communication has developed. The intention is to uncover possible fear, shame, anger, sadness, or upsetting thoughts that are holding group members back from being truly present and honest in the session.

Altruism is the fourth therapeutic factor in Yalom's approach to group work. Being altruistic means giving of oneself for the sake of another without an expectation of something in return. When altruism is present in group treatment, clients seem to transcend their own issues and develop a desire to be part of a larger social unit committed to collective healing. This allows participants in the treatment process to come to the aid of those group members who are for the moment vulnerable and in need of support. Many years earlier, Adler also saw the capacity to develop true and unselfish concern for others as an extremely important aspect of personal development. According to Adler, the act of being altruistic served to inhibit egocentric thinking and preoccupation with oneself (Mosak & Maniacci, 2011).

The fifth therapeutic factor is *corrective recapitulation* of clients' experiences in their families of origin. Because so many clients in treatment have had problematic family lives that included negative messages about self-worth, as well as more damaging experiences such as emotional and physical abuse, the need to develop healthier ways of viewing oneself is crucial. The treatment group becomes a place for corrective processes through which clients are able to heal and develop greater self-esteem.

The sixth therapeutic factor entails the *development of socializing techniques*. As clients develop insight about themselves and their relationships, they can use the group setting to practice new relational skills. The group can become a place of role-playing, rehearsal, and the development of comfort with new ways of interacting with others. The development of socializing techniques in group settings has long been a component of chemical dependency treatment.

The seventh therapeutic factor, *imitative behaviour*, is a concept found in social cognitive theory. Clients in group treatment may in time develop patterns of effective communication and ways of relating to others that have been modeled by therapists and group members. When clients can reproduce modeled behaviours, the new skills learned can be of great use outside of treatment.

The eighth therapeutic factor is *interpersonal learning*. Because the group setting is about learning, healing, changing, and growing, the support that groups can provide clients in their progress toward emotional healing and/or development is quite valuable. In treatment groups, people can learn important lessons about how to relate to others while also receiving feedback, encouragement, and if needed, important constructive criticism. Group treatment environments serve as a safe place to make mistakes, an environment in which to be vulnerable, and a setting where the difficulties of others can provide insight into one's own problems in life.

Group cohesiveness, the ninth therapeutic factor, is one in which people feel a sense of togetherness and belonging. In cohesive treatment groups, clients value other members and value being part of the group. Cohesive treatment groups can also provide a sense of unconditional positive regard between members. This sense of feeling that one is valued and cared for allows for sharing of feelings and thoughts that might otherwise be concealed for fear of being shamed or rejected.

The tenth therapeutic factor is *catharsis*, which is an old psychoanalytic term that refers to the release of repressed emotions. Intense emotional releases can occur in groups with a high degree of cohesion and altruistic support for one another. Catharsis generally involves the release of deeply held and often painful emotions that clients have carried within themselves for a very long time, often years.

The eleventh and final therapeutic factor in treatment is a group of factors that Yalom referred to as *existential factors* or the inescapable realities of life. It means being cognizant of the fact that life and living includes happiness and sadness, pleasure and pain, and that while life can seem cruel and unfair at times, it can also include times of great joy, emotional release, and connection with others. Existentialism means that clients are able to develop a feeling of acceptance in life that is made easier by understanding that others have times of happiness as well as experiencing their own inescapable pain, suffering, and sorrow.

Yalom's therapeutic factors have applications beyond therapy groups. While not all therapeutic factors are or even need to be present in other groups, certain factors are necessary for effective functioning in all groups. For example, imparting information, cohesiveness, and interpersonal learning are as useful in task groups and support groups as they are in treatment groups. Likewise, self-help groups involve interpersonal learning, the development of socializing techniques, and even make space for catharsis. So, while Yalom's Eleven Therapeutic Factors may not represent an organized sequential theoretical approach to understanding group processes, they do provide valuable information and even direction for social workers and others involved in developing, leading, and creating the opportunity for many groups to take place.

Group Size, Structure, and Membership

The size and structure of a group depends on the purpose of the group. Information-sharing groups of the type one might conduct at a school, community centre, or as part of in-service training within an organization are often educational or psychoeducational in nature. Because these groups are not designed to foster sharing of highly personal information or emotions, they can be larger than therapy/treatment or healing groups. Some educational and psycho-educational groups can be presented in much the same manner as conference workshops.

Support and self-help groups are usually smaller, as this helps to ensure intensive discussion and dialogue (Furman et al., 2014, p. 18). Typically, adult groups may have between six and ten members, while children and youth groups should have between four and six members. Support and self-help groups are also generally open to accepting new members at any time. In support groups, social workers or other group leaders tend to take a less directive role and are often peripheral to what happens in the sessions. While social workers, psychologists, or other professionals may welcome new participants and provide opening and closing remarks at each session, the bulk of the work and the direction of the groups will be determined by the members (Furman et al., 2014, p. 70).

Self-help groups differ from support groups. While social workers or other professionals may be instrumental in connecting clients to a self-help group, the groups themselves are led by the members participating. Social workers and chemical dependency counsellors quite often refer clients to Alcoholics Anonymous (AA) and other twelve-step groups, but they do not lead the groups in their roles as helping professionals. This does not mean that a social worker or counsellor in recovery will never lead a twelve-step group; however, it will not be done as a professional treatment group leader. Instead, when professional social workers or counsellors lead self-help groups, the professional role is set aside and their participation is that of a group member. One final note: social workers and other helping professionals who do attend self-help groups as participants do not attend the same groups as their clients. Taking this important step helps maintain critical client-worker boundaries for those working as professionals in chemical dependency/addictions treatment settings.

Therapy/Treatment Groups

Therapy/treatment groups are designed to help clients with emotional and behavioural problems. Therapy/treatment groups are a safe place where emotional issues, past traumas, behavioural concerns, and any number of problems can be addressed in the company of others who are dealing with the same or similar troubles in life. In therapy/treatment groups, the group leader is nearly always a trained professional who guides the group treatment process and keeps group members on track. Therapy/treatment groups are generally limited in size, and most of the literature on groups indicates that keeping group size smaller is related to lower dropout rates and better outcomes (Burlingame, 2010).

Social workers or other professional group treatment providers begin the process of offering a group by selecting the population (e.g., persons coping with depression, anxiety, or anger issues) and then interviewing potential participants to see if they are open to a group treatment process. In some settings, the person providing group treatment may not be able to prescreen participants. However, if the option to meet with potential group members is possible, prescreening is a good first step. In the prescreening process a professional practitioner is looking for potential therapy/treatment group participants who will fit with the intended purpose of the group, have the potential of working well with others, and of course are interested in group treatment. Still, there will be times when people receiving individual treatment may need to be referred to a group as an alternative to having no ongoing treatment at all. This is a common occurrence for those who have exceeded the number of individual sessions covered by insurance. In such cases, group treatment may not be the ideal choice, but it does represent a better alternative than abrupt termination of treatment.

Once a therapy/treatment group has been formed, the initial session should include a detailed discussion of confidentiality, the limits of confidentiality, and the importance of not discussing group issues outside of group—even with other group members. The initial session should also include rules regarding no shaming, verbal attacking, or racist, sexist, or otherwise-demeaning language. In some groups (anger management, for example), additional rules such as not touching another group member, not getting out of one's seat, and not threatening group members are also often part of a group agreement. In some cases, group members actually sign a contract. In others, the group rules might remain posted in the room. Whatever the case may be, group rules need to be understood and agreed to by all in order for therapy/treatment groups to proceed beyond the initial session.

There are many different types of treatment groups in terms of theoretical foundation. The orientation to treatment is often a reflection of the professional practitioner leading the group. However, in the age of managed health care, as is the case in the United States along with limited access to mental health services, for Canadian and American populations, time-limited therapy/treatment groups and brief therapies have become the most popular. Well-researched and more easily manualized approaches to group treatment such as solution-focused brief therapies, cognitive-behavioural therapies, problem-focused therapies, and emotion-focused therapies rank among the most common. However, not all clients are best served by dominant Euro-Western approaches to treatment. For some clients, the conditions of group cohesion or the ability to trust others enough to open up in treatment take additional time. For example, clients in correctional settings take much longer to develop the level of trust necessary for self-disclosure in group treatment settings (Coggins & Fresquez, 2001). Likewise, practitioners in rural reserve or reservation-based Indigenous communities often find that clients need a substantially longer time to trust the therapist or counsellor leading a group and fellow group members participating in treatment or healing that takes place in group settings.

INDIGENOUS GROUP WORK FOR HEALING

For Indigenous North American clients, or clients from cultural groups that are distinctly different from the Euro-Western majorities of Canada or the United States, approaches to group treatment may be more effective if cultural safety and familiarity are part of the process. The idea of cultural safety was first identified by Maori nurses in Aotearoa (New Zealand). The concept of cultural safety is one in which people from specific populations are able to receive services from persons who are culturally similar to themselves, with the understanding that those who can best provide services in a manner that feels safe and supportive are those who come from the same cultural background (Milliken, 2008). For Indigenous North Americans, this means using culturally specific and relevant group treatment techniques that connect clients to an important sense of cultural identity. While each Indigenous community will have healing ceremonies and other treatment protocols that are unique to their specific population groups, some broad concepts can provide a general framework from

which social workers and other practitioners can craft treatment group structures that fit with the clients they serve, thus creating a climate of increased
cultural safety.

Medicine Wheels

There are many versions of the Medicine Wheel that are used in different
groups. A *Medicine Wheel*, when used in the context of Indigenous North American healing, refers to a circle that encompasses the totality of human existence
in relation to all other aspects of creation, meaning that physical, psychological, spiritual, and emotional aspects of life are to be understood in terms of balance, harmony, and connection (Vukic, Gregory, Martin-Misener, & Etowa, 2011).
As Kemppainen, Kopera-Frye, and Woodard (2008, p. 81) state when referenc-
ing an Indigenous healer, the Medicine Wheel is a "healing and connection tool
to be used for the uplifting and betterment of mankind." For some clients, the
Medicine Wheel provides a culturally familiar way of thinking about human
existence, while others may find the Medicine Wheel to be a valuable tool that
helps them reconnect with a cultural sense of self.

Talking Circles

In North America, a *Talking Circle* describes a technique used in treatment, self-
help, or healing groups, which are most often associated with group work
among Indigenous populations. The talking circle approach is generally
employed in groups that use a Medicine Wheel concept as a structure for group
work. A talking circle approach in groups is one in which treatment/healing/
helping begins with each person being given a chance to speak without inter-
ruption. Often an object such as a feather, a braid of sweet grass, or a purposely
selected "talking stick" is passed from one person to the next in a sunwise (clock-
wise) direction. When an individual receives the object, she or he can choose to
speak or pass the object along to the next person. The belief in a talking circle
is that all are encouraged to speak, but no one is forced to do so. While an individual is holding the object, she or he can speak without being interrupted,
questioned, countered, or confronted. If someone wants to come back to a
point made, she or he will have a chance when the feather or talking stick makes
it around the circle.

Some groups may use a talking stick or other object to open or close a
group; other groups may adopt a rule of making a full circle and then switch-

ing to an open discussion format. In other groups, the feather, stick, or other object will make many rounds until everyone has had a chance to speak, and everything that group participants may wish to say has been said. There are variations on the talking circle approach, but the idea of a deliberate and respectful approach to allowing each person the chance to speak is quite different from Euro-Western group treatment that may need regular intervention by the group leader to create space for members who do not readily or quickly participate.

Working with Indigenous North American populations requires an understanding of the legacy of historic trauma and colonization that researchers and practitioners identify as being the root cause of many behavioural and emotional problems (Gone, 2013). In some groups, it may take time for participants to process what they are hearing and become comfortable sharing. The more deliberate and empowering approach to treatment/healing that is part of a talking circle process demonstrates a foundation in Indigenous North American theory for practice which emphasizes the development of personal willingness to engage in deep reflection.

Recovery Medicine Wheel: A North American Indigenous-Centered Approach

The *Recovery Medicine Wheel* (RMW) was originally designed for use by Indigenous North American persons recovering from addiction or those who had been raised in homes where parents or caregivers had been addicted to drugs or alcohol. After the mid-1990s, the RMW also became popular as a wellness model. The RMW has been used much in the same way as the twelve-step model of AA in that the model provides structure for self-help groups seeking personal reflection and healing in recovery. However, the RMW also provides a structure for discussion in group therapy/treatment/healing, even beyond issues of chemical dependency or other forms of addiction.

There are four areas, also known as directions, within the wheel that correspond to the four realms of human existence: (1) North—The Physical Realm, (2) East—The Realm of Knowledge and Enlightenment, (3) South—The Spiritual Realm, and (4) West—The Realm of Introspective Thought (Coggins, 1990). Each of these realms features four steps, for a total of sixteen steps altogether. Each step starts in the same manner—with the individual stating aloud or silently to her- or himself, "Beginning today I will," which is followed by the step he or she intends to focus on. In groups, the group leader or group members

Figure 17.4   Recovery Medicine Wheel

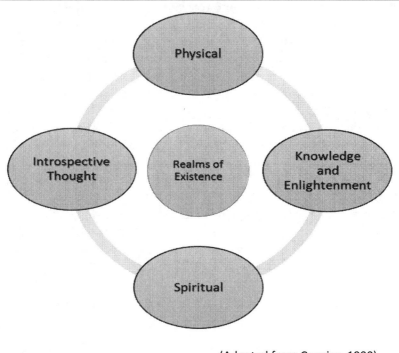

(Adapted from Coggins, 1990)

might read a step and then invite discussion, or use a talking circle approach, allowing each member to say what the step has brought to mind.

North—The Physical Realm

Beginning today I will:

1. Take good physical care of myself.
2. Regain balance in my life by developing an understanding of the important connection between the physical, psychological, spiritual, and emotional parts of my existence.
3. Stop inflicting pain (either physically or emotionally) on others or myself.
4. Come to an understanding that change is a process. (I can't expect miracles overnight).

East—The Realm of Knowledge and Enlightenment

Beginning today I will:

1. Reawaken to all of creation and to all of the beauty that exists in the world around me.
2. Make a commitment to release myself from a narrow view of life and begin to grow, learn, and gain new knowledge.
3. Remember that I have a sacred right to live my life as I wish and the need to bring harmony and balance to my existence by respecting the life rights of others.
4. Work on understanding the changes I must make in order to achieve personal harmony, balance, and freedom.

South—The Spiritual Realm

Beginning today I will:

1. Come to an understanding of my special relation to Mother Earth. (Release my pain to Mother Earth).
2. Come to an understanding of my special relation to Father Sky.
3. Seek a greater understanding of my sacred connection to all of the universe.
4. Reconnect with and nurture my own spirit.

West—The Realm of Introspective Thought

Beginning today I will:

1. Speak honestly with myself.
2. Look at my problems and my accomplishments with a willingness to commit myself to positive growth and change.
3. Examine the ways in which I have tried to manipulate, control or manage the lives of others and make a commitment to stop this behavior.
4. Acknowledge that change in my life must begin with me.

(Coggins, 1990, p. 14)

Unlike the twelve steps of AA, the RMW does not ask for an admission of powerlessness or a requirement of surrender. This is particularly important for populations that have experienced a great deal of personal and collective loss, as is the case for many Indigenous North Americans. Instead, the RMW invites people to make a commitment to change. RMW treatment goals emphasize the achievement or restoration of harmony, centeredness, balance, and freedom from emotional pain combined with a desire to achieve holistic wellness that addresses all four realms of human existence (Coggins, 1990).

Ho'oponopono

Ho'oponopono is a traditional Hawaiian approach to resolving conflict that predates contact with Europeans. In earlier times, it was used in family intervention. However, it is now used in family settings and in treatment groups. This Hawaiian approach to treatment or healing differs markedly from Euro-Western and Indigenous North American Medicine Wheel methods of involving clients in group treatment. In *ho'oponopono* an elder or a professional, such as a specially trained social worker, assumes the role once filled by a *kahuna* (Hurdle, 2002). A *kahuna* would be somewhat analogous to a *curandera/curandero*, or a traditional Indigenous North American healer such as a Diné medicine man or Anishinabe spiritual and counselling healer.

The *ho'oponopono* is usually opened with a prayer and is followed by discussion of the presenting problem in which those present have the opportunity to give specific details about their concerns (Shook, 1985). *Ho'oponopono* can last hours or even be spread over more than one day (Hurdle, 2002). In the healing process, participants do not speak directly to one another. Instead, they share their feelings, frustrations, and wishes by directing their comments to the elder, social worker, or counselling professional leading the *ho'oponopono*. When all has been said, and the issues brought up in the process have been worked out, the family or group bond is reaffirmed, and the *ho'oponopono* is declared complete and closed with a prayer. As is common at the end of the process, the family or group often shares a meal and sometimes engages in a positive activity together. After a *ho'oponopono* has been closed, the issue addressed in the process is never to be spoken of again. Those who use *ho'oponopono* must first be trained in the process. According to Mokuau (1990) and Hurdle (2002, p. 189), once the process is understood by the practitioner, it can be used in a number of settings outside of work with families. For example, *ho'oponopono* has also become an approach to treatment in schools and residential treatment centres.

CHEMICAL DEPENDENCY/ADDICTIONS TREATMENT

Substance use disorders are among the most common mental health/behavioural issues in North America affecting every level of society (O'Brien & McKay, 2007, p. 145). Perhaps the most common setting for group work is in the area of substance use disorders, also referred to as chemical dependency and/or addictions. Although addictions can also include gambling, Internet use, and other addictive behaviours, here the term *addictions* is being used in relation to substance use and abuse. While not directly addressed in this chapter, it should still be noted that gambling and other addictions are serious public health issues, and many of the same treatment modalities used to address substance use disorders are also common in the treatment of non-substance-related addictions.

Groups and Recovery

Nearly all programs designed to treat chemical dependency/addictions use treatment groups and self-help groups as key components of program design. The language of chemical dependency/addiction treatment in relation to defense mechanisms used by clients is derived from Neo-Freudian ego-psychology. Terms such as *denial, rationalization, projection, intellectualization,* and others are still common in many treatment settings. However, actual treatment in much of North America is based on a combination of behavioural and cognitive approaches, motivational interviewing, and solution-focused therapy with additional support and structure being provided by self-help (usually twelve-step) groups, and relapse prevention groups (Roth & Fonagy, 2005, pp. 323–324). There are also other approaches to treatment that involve family therapy, pharmacotherapy, and combination treatment for persons who are dual diagnosed with substance use disorders and major mental illness such as bipolar disorder or schizophrenia.

Traditionally, treatment groups for persons with chemical dependency/ addictions problems have depended on the development of a positive peer environment in which group members have a commitment to abstaining from drugs and alcohol. In addition, chemical dependency/addictions treatment has also been a specialized field that in many places requires specialized training and certification. Total abstinence as a treatment outcome has been common in North America since the very beginning of treatment programming for persons with substance use disorders. Early North American theories or beliefs about persons with addictions issues were based in religious teachings about moral character or just seen as a general lack of will. In the twentieth century, Freudian theoretical concepts about early maternal deprivation were replaced by genetic and disease theories of addiction. However, toward the end of the century, a biopsychosocial understanding of substance use, abuse, and addiction came to predominate. Nevertheless, much research continues

Figure 17.5   Theories of Addiction and Chemical Dependency

The Genetic Theory

- Addiction is viewed as an inherited condition in much the same manner as one would inherit a predisposition to breast or prostate cancer

The Disease Concept/Theory

- Addiction is the result of an inherited predisposition to addictive substances, or a physiological change that occurs in response to years of drug or alcohol consumption

The Psychodynamic Theory

- Needs related to nurturing are not met early in development, leading to addiction as a way of compensating for emotional harm and deprivation

The Behavioural Theory

- Addiction is formed and sustained through a combination of both positive and negative reinforcement

The Behavioural/Social Learning Theory

- Based on social cognitive theory and sees addiction as a voluntary learned behaviour

The Bio-Psychosocial Theory

- Physiological, behavioral, environmental, and sociocultural factors interact with and contribute to the development of addiction

(Adapted from Coggins & Hatchett, 2009)

---

to be focused on looking for a genetic link to addiction, often ignoring the impact of factors such as poverty, racism, colonization, generational trauma, forced assimilation, and multiple forms of marginalization or exclusion.

Harm-Reduction Groups

Although harm reduction is not generally accepted as an approach to the treatment of substance use disorders in North America, harm reduction has been common in Europe for several decades (Denning & Little, 2012). While harm reduction has not been a major component of chemical dependency/

addiction treatment in the United States or Canada, it has been used in other settings to help mitigate the harm to individuals and society. Needle exchange programs and free condom distribution to fight the spread of HIV and hepatitis-B are good examples of harm reduction. Even designated driver campaigns and free taxi rides for intoxicated people on New Year's Eve are examples of harm reduction. However, when it comes to a recognized and diagnosed addiction, abstinence is still the overwhelming goal of treatment.

As outlined by Denning and Little (2012, p. 16), harm reduction as a treatment goal has three primary principles: first, work with clients should be collaborative and not assume that total abstinence is the goal for treatment; second, access to treatment should not include barriers such as an agreement to total abstinence under threat of dismissal from treatment; and third, success in treatment should include reduction in substance use or substance use patterns that have negative and potentially life threatening consequences. Counselling with clients in need of developing harm-reduction treatment goals often relies on the techniques of motivational interviewing (MI). As discussed in chapter 12, MI is specifically designed to help clients in need of motivation for positive change. MI emphasizes working with clients in a manner that helps them identify risks, dangers, and the need for change. While many treatment programs are still advocating total abstinence for all clients involved in treatment, harm reduction is gaining ground and may represent a viable alternative for certain resistant or hard-to-reach populations.

Mental Illness and Addiction

Chemical dependency/addictions treatment takes place in a variety of settings. Most clients who enter treatment for problems related to substance use and abuse have had some sort of life issue that has created a sense of urgency about receiving treatment. There may be a threat of job loss, divorce, or even an impending health crisis. However, the traditional manner of viewing addictions (generally one in which a middle-class white male has an alcohol problem) obscures the very important issue of co-occurring disorders and the involvement in criminal activity for persons with major mental illness and substance use disorders. As stated by Easton (2005, p. 197), it is critical that we as a society be aware of the central role substance use and abuse play in criminal behaviour for persons with mental health problems. Often, persons with chemical dependency/addictions and mental health issues become involved with the criminal justice system as a result of criminal violations-related drug posses-sion, drug use, domestic violence involving alcohol or drugs, and driving under the influence of drugs or alcohol.

However, difficulty accessing mental health and substance abuse treat-ment outside the criminal justice system has resulted in an increased popula-tion of persons with co-occurring disorders in correctional facilities that often are not equipped to provide adequate treatment (Torrey et al., 2014). The Multi-State Treatment Advocacy Center Report (2014) on treatment of persons with mental illness in prisons and jails in the United States identifies the "root cause" of the problem as being related to the ongoing closure of state psychiatric hospitals coupled with the failure of politicians and other officials to provide adequate treatment for persons with mental illness once they have been dein-stitutionalized (Torrey et al., 2014, p. 6).

Providing services to clients with co-occurring disorders requires an under-standing of mental illness and addictive processes in the context of family and community. A systematic review of varying approaches to treatment for per-sons with co-occurring severe mental illness and substance use disorders, pub-lished in 2008 indicates that group therapy is an important and effective component of overall treatment when combined with incentives for compli-ance, better known as contingency management (Drake, O'Neal, & Wallach, 2008). In the same report, case management and interventions designed to reduce involvement with the criminal justice systems were also seen as having a positive impact on treatment outcomes.

For social workers and others providing group and individual services, the issue of the co-occurring disorders of substance abuse and mental illness speaks to the need for increasing service availability and removing barriers to comprehensive approaches for persons who need a combination of psychiatric, psychosocial, and chemical dependency/addiction treatment services. Like-wise, facilitating combined individual, family, and group treatment services could go a long way in working to improve treatment outcomes for multi-problem clients with mental illness and substance use disorders. While many treatment programs make referral to twelve-step self-help groups a general practice, it is important to remember that persons with substance abuse and mental illness may not be readily accepted in groups that maintain a singular focus on addiction. Furthermore, twelve-step groups are generally ill-equipped to address symptoms of mental illness that may arise during self-help meet-ings. Therefore, training of social workers and other professionals for group work that addresses substance abuse and mental illness in combination is crucial for populations at risk for self-harm or for becoming criminal offenders or reoffenders as a result of behaviours related to co-occurring mental illness and chemical dependency/addiction.

CONCLUSION

Group work will continue to be an important component of service provision within social work and other helping professions. In addition, social workers and other group workers will undoubtedly be involved in task and interprofessional (multidisciplinary) groups during the course of their professional careers. While it is important to develop professional skill related to the delivery of insight-oriented, solution-focused, cognitive-behavioural, and addictions treatment group sessions, social workers and other group workers must also be prepared to shift from therapy/treatment modes to skills training and psycho-educational approaches as the need arises in the course of work with groups. Students in social work field practicum placements should fashion learning agreements that include opportunities to develop and deliver various forms of groups. Finally, the importance of honouring differences in relation to the structure and delivery of group work services to culturally and socially diverse client populations will continue to be of critical importance as diversity within North American society increases.

Chapter Eighteen

Organizational Theory and Practice

INTRODUCTION

Organizations represent an arena for social work practice that is not often considered when preparing students for direct work with clients. In other professional educational programs, such as counselling or psychology, attention to working with organizations as the client system may be minimal to absent. Because many graduate social work programs have concentrations or specializations that divide students into direct micro practice or administration and program evaluation tracks, those who select the direct-practice route generally receive very little information about organizational theory and practice. However, the number of advanced generalist master of social work (MSW) programs continues to grow, especially in the United States. Therefore, it is likely that many students entering field practicum placements at the MSW level will have organizational or even community-level field practicum experiences. While the inclusion of this chapter in this particular text and the community practice chapter that follows do not pretend to provide all the information needed for practice with and within larger systems, together they represent a recognition of the importance of organizational and community theory, particularly in social work.

Change in any organization, including human service organizations, can come in many forms. Professional practitioners working in the arena of organizational change will sometimes do so as an employee of the organization advocating from within. In other situations, those who are administrators may need to initiate an organizational assessment and change process. In some organizations, professional practitioners may be brought in from outside as consultants who assess organizational functioning and recommend change. Working with an organization as the client requires shifting focus from smaller client systems such as individuals, families, or groups, to larger entities that may also include several smaller collections of individuals in separate units, each with their own subcultures. In this chapter, the organization will be thought of and discussed as the client system, with the intention of understanding what it takes to assess and intervene in organizational settings.

ORGANIZATIONAL THEORY

Before beginning with a discussion of assessment and intervention, it is important to look at the history of organizational theory development. Human service organizations and other organizational settings that serve people do not produce tangible items such as cars, radios, televisions, or other durable goods, but they are still impacted by a history of organizational theory as it relates to the structure of supervisor-worker relations, and the manner in which the efficient use of resources influences organizational viability. In essays, and later in his book *Economy and Society: An Outline of Interpretive Sociology*, published posthumously in Germany, Max Weber (1922/1978) outlined what he observed as being the characteristics of capitalist bureaucratic organizations that had developed during a period of rapid industrial expansion in the latter part of the nineteenth century.

Figure 18.1   Weber's Characteristics of Bureaucratic Organizations

1. *Positions are grouped into a clearly defined hierarchy*

2. *Workers selected on the basis of technical skill*

3. *Positions have a defined sphere of competence*

4. *Positions reflect specialization based on training*

5. *Positions typically demand full-time employment*

6. *Positions are career-oriented*

7. *Rules and procedures are outlined to coordinate activities*

8. *A central system of records is maintained*

9. *Impersonality governs employee relationships*

10. *A clear distinction exists between public and private lives*

(Weber, 2009, pp. 196-197)

While Weber may have lived, worked, and theorized well over a hundred years ago, his observations and ideas about organizations are still in many ways with us today in the twenty-first century. Anyone who has worked in a large organization will most likely recognize Weber's ten characteristics of bureaucratic organizations. Although organizations have changed in many ways, the hierarchical structure of more traditionally organized workplaces still retain many of the characteristics outlined by Weber.

Scientific Management Theory

The scientific management theory of Frederick Winslow Taylor was focused on developing management techniques that would reduce the friction between workers and supervisors that existed in a majority of North American organizations in the early part of the twentieth century. Taylor believed that adopting his scientific principles would not only create harmonious relations between workers and management, but that they would also lead to higher productivity. Taylor is perhaps best known for his desire to identify the "one best way" to accomplish any particular work-related task, thereby maximizing worker efficiency.

Taylor sought to match worker skills with tasks. He is also credited with developing the "piece-rate" approach to work which means that workers were to be paid on the basis of their productivity. Taylor believed this created an incentive to be more productive. As Taylor (1911/1998) stated, the basic principles related to maximizing productivity and profitability are as follows:

1. Maintenance of high wages and low unit production costs to achieve maximum productivity.

2. Use of research and experimentation to identify the one best way to complete manufacturing tasks.

3. Use of scientific principles to match workers with the tasks for which they are best suited.

4. Scientific training and development of employees as a means of maximizing work efficiency.

5. Close and friendly cooperation between management and labour to ensure that work tasks are completed in accordance with scientific principles.

Taylor's concepts of scientific management may seem more suited to factory work than human service agency activities, and large-scale assembly-line production operations like that of the Ford Motor Company did indeed build their operations on Taylor's theoretical concepts (Lægaard, 2006). While a rigid adherence to Taylor's scientific concepts has been tempered by other theories and shifts in workplace culture, his ideas continue to influence the structure of organizations in relation to the completion of certain work-related tasks. In addition, his ideas of training a specialized workforce, like those of Weber, remain with us today. Furthermore, Taylor's obsession with finding the "one best way" to perform a task might also seem strangely antiquated and simplistic in its positivist faith in scientific absolutes. Yet the profession of social work, along with others such as counselling, psychology, and psychiatry, need to ask if our own current obsession with manualized approaches to treatment that strive to identify the single most effective therapy for each specific psychiatric diagnosis is perhaps similarly positivist and simplistic.

Universalistic Management

The approach of French theorist Henri Fayol developed around the time of Weber and Taylor, but did not become widely read in English-speaking countries until 1949, following the translation of his work from French (Lægaard, 2006, p. 16). Whereas the work of Taylor had emphasized the roles and tasks of workers, Fayol focused his attention on the role of managers in the workplace. Fayol developed six *scalar* principles, or chains of authority, that were intended to improve overall organizational functioning.

Fayol also had other concepts, such as fairness in terms of pay for employees, as well as just treatment of line workers as management tools for increasing worker loyalty and boosting productivity (Wren & Bedeian, 2009).

Human Relations Theory

Most social workers and others in the helping professions tend to like the sound of human relations when it comes to managing workers in an organizational environment. However, George Elton Mayo was more concerned with manipulating the workplace environment to increase productivity than he was with the emotional well-being of employees in the workplace. Mayo, born in Australia, achieved prominence in the fields of industrial sociology and

Figure 18.2   Fayol's Scalar Principles—Chains of Authority

Scalar Principle

•A pyramid-shaped structure within the hierarchy of the organization.

Unity of Command Principle

•Each employee is to have only one immediate supervisor to whom she or he reports.

Span of Control Principle

•Supervisors should have no more than eight employees for whom they are responsible.

Exception Principle

•Line employees should be responsible for carrying out regular work related tasks outlined by standard procedural rules, whereas supervisors are to be responsible for situations that are not covered by standard procedural rules.

Departmentalization Principle

•Division of labour should focus on grouping together those employees who engage in similar functions.

Line-Staff Principle

•Line-staff functions are viewed as central to organizational task completion, whereas supervisor functions are seen as playing a supportive or advisory role.

(Netting, Kettner, & McMurty, 2004, p. 219)

---

industrial psychology as a result of research designed to determine the impact of workplace environmental changes on the level of worker productivity (Kistaiah, 1991). Among his most famous work was the research conducted at the Western Electric plant near Chicago, Illinois, now known as the Hawthorne experiments.

The Hawthorne experiments, conducted between 1924 and 1927, represent seminal foundational work in the areas of organizational design and human behaviour in the workplace (Franke & Kaul, 1978). The study focused on the effect of manipulating lighting to see if differences in light levels had an impact on worker productivity. It was hypothesized that manipulating the work environment would be the more important factor affecting the productivity of workers. However, the results of the Hawthorne experiments produced no clear measurable connection between productivity and varying levels of workplace illumination (DuBrin, 2011). Instead, Mayo and his team of researchers found that social factors, such as group identity and a sense of solidarity, had an impact on production levels. The core concepts of the Human Relations Theory regarding human behaviour in the workplace environment are as follows:

1. Levels of production are set by social norms, not physiological capacities or the physical environment (a concept that stands in direct opposition to scientific theories).

2. The need of workers to belong to a group is of more importance than monetary incentives or working conditions in terms of influencing productivity.

3. The informal social networks and groups that develop in the workplace environment have a strong influence on worker behaviour.

4. It is important for supervisors to pay particular attention to the social forces influencing organizations.

5. The cooperation of workers develops more fully as a result of democratic leadership. (DuBrin, 2011, pp. 23–24)

Theory X and Theory Y

Douglas McGregor is credited with developing the organizational theories of X and Y, in relation to the way in which managers view employees. Theory X is seen as an authoritarian style of management, while Theory Y is characterized as a participative style (Borkowski, 2011). In accordance with his theoretical constructs, those supervisors of employees who take a Theory X approach to management see people as generally lazy and requiring threats of job loss or loss of pay as incentives to be more productive. Also, those who ascribe to a Theory X model believe that workers cannot be trusted to accept responsibility, meaning that they must be controlled and closely managed. Conversely, those who manage in accordance with Theory Y believe that people want to view their work as important and will therefore seek responsibility. Also, followers of Theory Y believe that for human beings, work is just as important as rest or recreation. Figure 18.3, adapted from Borkowski (2011), compares basic assumptions of Theory X to Theory Y.

Figure 18.3   McGregor's Theory X versus Theory Y

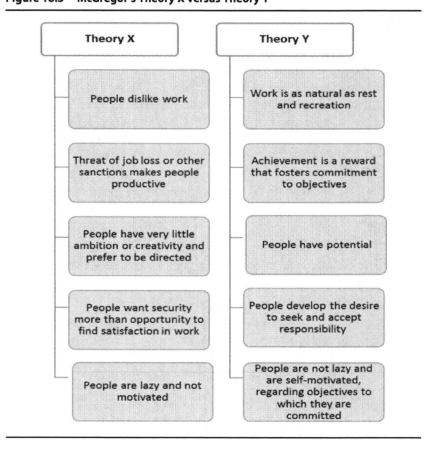

Theory Z

William G. Ouchi, born in Hawaii, developed a theory of organizational management based on the Japanese system for supervising employees. From the 1960s to the 1980s, Japan had a very successful economic system and changed from being a low-wage economy to a high-wage economy, with higher employee job satisfaction and lower turnover rates. Ouchi believed Japanese management methods could be adapted to US corporations, making them more productive as well. In his book *Theory Z*, Ouchi (1981) gives a detailed description of this approach. A synopsis of the basic principles is shown in figure 18.4:

Figure 18.4   Ouchi's Principles of Theory Z

Theory Z Principles	
	Job security through long-term employment
	Informal control with implied rules
	Explicit, formalized measures of performance
	Evaluation and promotion are a slow process
	Careers have a moderate level of specialization
	Managers demonstrate interest in and concern for the whole person, including her or his family

Management by Objectives (MBO) Approach

More than fifty years ago, Peter Ferdinand Drucker devised a way of looking at organizational efficiency and employee supervision known as Management by Objectives (MBO). While not an actual theory, MBO is more of an approach to management, and serves as an organizing tool for planning which is found in numerous organizational settings (Drucker, 1954). Many who work or have worked in human service agencies will recognize the MBO approach in which agency goals and objectives are accompanied by the development of personal goals and objectives among employees. Most annual and semiannual evaluations of employees include the development of strategies to achieve personalized work-related objectives that fit within larger organizational objectives and goals. MBO strives to improve organizational functioning by aligning goals and attendant objectives throughout the various units of the organization. The development of objectives in the MBO approach will include time lines and measures by which achievement can be gauged. When objectives are properly executed, MBO can become a successful approach to managing a business or agency and thus a very common approach to evaluating the productivity of employees in large and small organizational environments (Rodgers & Hunter, 1991).

SMART Approach

In 1981, George T. Doran introduced SMART objectives as an approach to maximizing organizational efficiency. SMART is the acronym for the development of Specific, Measurable, Achievable, Realistic, and Time-based objectives in organizational settings (Doran, 1981). Doran built on the MBO concepts developed by Drucker and created an approach to setting objectives that clearly spelled out how to make progress toward the completion of specific tasks, projects, skills development, or service outcomes easier to evaluate. When using the SMART approach, objectives are developed to be clearly measurable and time limited while also taking into consideration the potential for being realizable and achievable. The objective setting process can be difficult for many individuals. This is particularly true for those who have not previously been involved in developing objectives.

The SMART approach is now quite common in many organizational settings. This approach is even used in education, where it has been applied to the development of Individualized Education Plans (IEPs) for students receiving special education services.

Figure 18.5   Doran's SMART Objectives

Specific	Objectives should be specific in terms of what one intends to achieve
Measurable	Objectives must be clearly measurable
Achievable	Objectives should be designed with achievability in mind
Realistic	Objectives need to be achievable given time and existing available resources
Time-based	Objectives need to have clear and specific dates for achievement

(Adapted from Doran, 1981)

Decision Making

Herbert A. Simon emphasized the importance of decision making in the context of available knowledge. Simon focused on theorizing in relation to administration and developed a behavioural model, which looks at the actions of the "administrative man" versus the "economic man" (Lægaard, 2006, p. 31). For an analysis of decision making in accordance with Simon's thinking, it is important to understand the context within which decisions are made, combined with the reference point (knowledge, ideology, beliefs) of the decision maker. While the *economic man* is understood as having all information and knowledge available to guide rational decisions, the *administrative man* is constrained by

1. information that is often incomplete, imperfect or even misleading;
2. the complex in nature of most problems;
3. the limitations of skills and abilities in relation to human information processing;
4. the reality that decision making is quite often done in an environment of limited time; and
5. conflicting preferences in relation to organizational goals. (Lægaard, 2006, p. 31)

In other words, Simon's approach to understanding decision making in organizations takes into account the reality of environments within which decisions are made—meaning that most people who make administrative decisions do not match the situational ideal of the *economic man*, but are instead forced to decide upon a course of action in any given situation with limited knowledge, limited skills and abilities, or both.

Organizations as Open Systems

Following the theorists and theorizing of the late nineteenth century until the middle of the twentieth century were those individuals who questioned the idea of organizations as closed systems. Challenges to older theories were based on questions about those aspects of organizational functioning in relation to the external environment that could not be entirely accounted for from within the organization itself. By the 1960s, systems theory had become quite popular in terms of explaining many social phenomena that occur in contexts ranging from families to entire communities. Katz and Kahn (1978) developed an approach to analyzing organizations as systems, which was based on general systems theory.

Thinking about organizations in this manner fostered an analysis of organizations in the context of the larger task environment within which the organization operated. In addition, the general systems theory orientation led administrators to think of

1. the boundaries between the organization and other systems;
2. the physical location of the organization within a building or buildings in communities that were embedded in larger geographically defined systems;
3. the types of employees within the organization; and
4. the internal-external cultural context that shaped values, beliefs, and assumptions upon which the organization bases its operations. (Katz & Kahn, 1978, pp. 3–4)

Organizational Goals and Natural Systems

Political Parties, by Robert Michels (1962), is often described as representing the beginning of modern political science. The manner in which he speaks of orga-

Figure 18.6　Human Services Organizations as an Open System

Input	Throughput	Output
•Funding	•Treatment	•Treatment Success
•Clients	•Staff Training	•Staff Development
•Staff		

Feedback Loop

nizations (political parties in particular) and the tendency of those organizations to fall subject to the control of oligarchs, is regularly referred to in discussions of how long-term career officials shape organizations to retain power and to perpetuate the organization (Bonnell, 2011). This *iron rule of oligarchy* posits that as soon as organizations have been formed, power within them will naturally gravitate up the hierarchy toward permanent officials. This is followed by a second law which suggests that regardless of the original purpose of the organization, survival of the organization will come to take precedence (Parry, 2005).

Organizations may have noble and well-intentioned original missions. However, once the shift to preservation is made, original organizational goals are replaced by survival goals. This phenomenon, known as *goal displacement*, occurs when organizations modify, neglect, or even abandon original goals in order to maintain or build the organization (Warner & Havens, 1968). For example, an agency may have been established with the singular intention of serving the homeless. However, when funding for homeless services becomes scarce, the agency decides to develop programs to serve veterans of war who are returning home or ex-convicts who have recently been released from prison, both of which represent more income-generating opportunities. The original mission of helping the homeless becomes secondary to survival and growth. When viewed from a natural systems perspective, organizations are understood as doing what they need to in order to survive, just as biological organisms do. This may, however, result in substantial differences between the *real* goals and the official *stated* goals of the agency.

Feminist Critiques of Organizational Theory

Feminist critiques of traditional organizational theory emphasize the importance of giving voice to marginalized or excluded groups, such as women and underrepresented minorities. The traditional Euro-Western binary construction of thinking has structured theorizing about organizations into categories, such as rational/irrational, culture/nature, and mind/body with the first term often seen as male and preferable to (as well as privileged over) the second, which is identified with female (Mumby, 2000, p. 12). This approach of dichotomizing the world is indeed arbitrary and favours dominant Euro-Western male ways of theorizing about organizations. In social work or other human service settings, feminist values and approaches to organizing that emphasize positive and affirming relationship building as a means of facilitating organizational outcomes are not as easily divided into discrete opposing binary categories.

Organizations have long been developed, studied, and defined by males. Therefore, male models of theory in relation to organizations have not paid enough attention to alternative (specifically feminist) approaches to organizing that value relationship building and consensus over Euro-Western patriarchal and hierarchical structuring of organizational environments. Feminist practice in organizations has yielded a form of decision making, labelled *modified consensus*, which differs from dominant hierarchical assumptions about the way in which people in organizations make decisions (Iannello, 1992). It is true that organizations operating on a modified consensus basis will have people in specialized positions for some functions, and the organization will also have a director. However, the directorship is designed to attend to perfunctory aspects of agency/organizational operations, while the larger and more critical decisions about organizational purpose and direction are decided upon by a collective that seeks consensus from all involved.

Managing Diversity

R. Roosevelt Thomas Jr., an African American, was one of the pioneers of diversity issues in organizational settings. In 1991, Thomas emerged on the scene as a leader in diversity thinking because he advocated for things, such as racial and cultural differences, in the workforce to be viewed as strengths. Thomas was clear that the world and the United States itself were changing. He stressed that American corporations would need to embrace diversity in order to survive at home and in a global business climate that was highly competitive and culturally diverse (Thomas, 1992). Until his untimely death in 2013, Thomas worked tirelessly to move North American corporations beyond the "melting pot" concept, which was actually an expectation to conform to the Euro-Western white majority, regardless of one's race or culture. Instead, he encouraged cultural diversity in the organizational setting by stressing the importance of pluralism and having pride not only in one's own cultural differences, but in the diversity of one's workplace as well.

While the workplace of North America has become more diverse, the racism Thomas had fought against has not vanished. Rasmussen and Salhani (2010) discuss racism and the ways in which racial aggression toward the racially and culturally different have become less overt, but still present. This more-covert racism is in the form of microaggressions that create cumulative stress for those exposed to it on a regular basis. Solórzano, Ceja, and Yosso (2000, p. 60) describe microaggressions as "subtle insults (verbal, nonverbal, and/or visual) directed toward people of colour, often automatically or unconsciously."

An example of a microaggression that demonstrates lingering but unspoken racism is found in the remarks of a Euro-American social work educator who expressed surprise that her Indigenous (Native American) colleague had ideas about urban planning and mental health policy outside of strictly Native American issues. Her comment, "I didn't think you would be interested in things like that," made the Indigenous educator feel as though his ideas were only considered valid when confined to Indigenous issues. Over time, and after experiencing a number of such microaggressions, he began to joke to close friends that he had stepped out of his "Indian box" again. While able to see some degree of humour in the situation, he also admitted to feeling excluded from general discussions of social policy. His remarks were "they have to tolerate me, but they don't yet see me as fully human and equal," serving to demonstrate, as Miller and Garran (2008, p. 97) propose, that microaggressions accumulate like thousands of paper cuts versus one deep wound. In North America (Canada and the United States), many organizations and institutions champion diversity, but hidden within this is the reality of racial tokenism and multicultural compartmentalizing combined with an unspoken expectation of assimilation. While diversity may be outwardly celebrated, many organizations remain reluctant to fully embrace difference. Therefore, the challenge to managing diversity addressed by Thomas more than twenty years ago continues today.

Organizational Culture

When thinking about organizations, the concept of culture may seem somewhat strange. Generally when one thinks of culture, it is in relation to ethnic groups, societies, or even nations. However, all organizationally based workplaces develop cultures that shape the behaviours of people who work there. According to Hill and Jones (2008), *organizational culture* is comprised of

[t]he specific collection of values and norms that are shared by people and groups in an organization and that control the way they interact with each other and with stakeholders outside the organization. (p. 403)

Since the 1980s, organizational culture, as a concept, has been written about by Edgar Schein, and his research in the area of organizational culture focuses on the ways in which the attitudes, beliefs, values, and basic assumptions of organizations develop and how they are maintained. Schein (2010) defines *organizational culture* as

> [a] pattern of basic assumptions invented, discovered, or developed by a given group as it learns to cope with its problems of external adaptation and internal integration that has worked well enough to be considered valid and therefore, to be taught to new members as the correct way to perceive, think, and feel in relation to those problems. (p. 18)

Central to Schein's understanding of organizational culture is the concept of three levels of culture, which range from the most visible and easily detected to the deepest and least visible to casual observers. These levels are identified as *Artifacts*, *Espoused beliefs and values*, and *Basic underlying assumptions* (Schein, 2010, p. 24). The following is a brief description of each of these levels that includes examples based on Schein's work.

Figure 18.7   Schein's Levels of Culture

Artifacts	*Examples:*

- Artwork, posted mission statements, plaques, and portraits
- Type and level of technology used
- Dress codes
- How employees greet and interact with one another
- Rules regarding telecommuting
- Open or closed office doors
- Layout of the work space

Espoused Beliefs and Values	*Examples:*

- Organizational ideology
- Mission and vision statements
- Aspirations of the organization as a whole
- Ideal organizational values (real values may differ)
- Ideal expected behaviour (actual behaviour may differ)

Basic Assumptions	*Examples:*

- Beliefs that are accepted as unquestioned truths
- Assumptions regarding the nature of the environment within which the organization must function or compete
- Assumptions about clients served by the organization

Culture in organizations does, of course, reflect what is found in the society outside of the workplace environment. Organizations exist as entities embedded in what Schein (2010) refers to as macro cultures. These macro cultures are comprised of the values, beliefs, attitudes, social norms, and behavioural expectations that exist at the national, regional, and ethnic group level (Schein, 2010). Workers who form organizational cultures and subcultures do so with ideas about human behaviour that have been shaped by social contexts outside of the organization. Therefore, while organizations do develop their own cultures, those cultures include assumptions about leadership, fairness, appropriate levels of productivity, gender relations, tolerance, pluralism, and a multitude of underlying beliefs and values that exist in macro-cultural contexts found throughout North America and beyond.

ASSESSING ORGANIZATIONS

The starting point for intervention with organizations is assessment. As is the case with individual clients, the role of the social worker, administrator, or consultant is to assess strengths and challenges faced by the organization. Organizations and organizational units can range from those who are very committed to change to others that are being required to change following decisions by upper-level administration or even as the result of court orders. In the assessment of organizations, several factors need to be considered. Often, those individuals who assume the task of assessing and intervening in organizations are administrators. Administrators are generally tasked with managing organizational culture to maximize worker morale and productivity. Administrators assessing organizations will need to consult with line staff, division, or program managers, and in some cases, boards of directors. When problems are found throughout the organization, independent consultants may be brought in from outside to conduct an assessment and make recommendations regarding needed change. Outside consultants who are contracted to assess organizations start where the client is, meaning developing a better sense of organizational culture through observation during the engagement process with staff and administration.

There are organizations that have all employees engaged in similar work, making for a more collegial and less hierarchical structure, meaning that employees are not in environments with well-defined superiors and subordinates. This sort of structure is common in small and start-up organizations (Netting, Kettner, & McMurtry, 2004). Other organizations have more traditional bureaucratic structures with well-established chains of command, employees in specialized positions, and clear hierarchies (Schriver, 1995). In some organizations that utilize feminist and non-Euro-Western approaches to task completion and program development, decision making will likely involve a high degree of consensus building, as is typical in settings where a modified consensus model of organizational administration predominates. In other, often larger and more institutional environments such as universities, child welfare agencies, psychiatric hospitals, or correctional settings, administrative structures are more clearly hierarchical in nature with administrators making decisions that are then communicated downward to departments or units.

Managerial Styles

Assessments of organizations require an understanding of the manner in which administrators manage their employees. In large organizations, there are several layers of administration. Conversely, small organizations with less hierarchical organizational structures may have only one supervisor or director. Managerial style does indeed have an impact on organizations. Kouzes and Posner (1987) discuss organizational administration in terms of leadership qualities and managerial qualities. In accordance with their description of leadership and management, *leadership qualities* are understood as the ability to influence others, while *management style* is the "creation of results together, with, and through people" (Lægaard, 2006, p. 85).

Figure 18.8   Leadership and Management Qualities

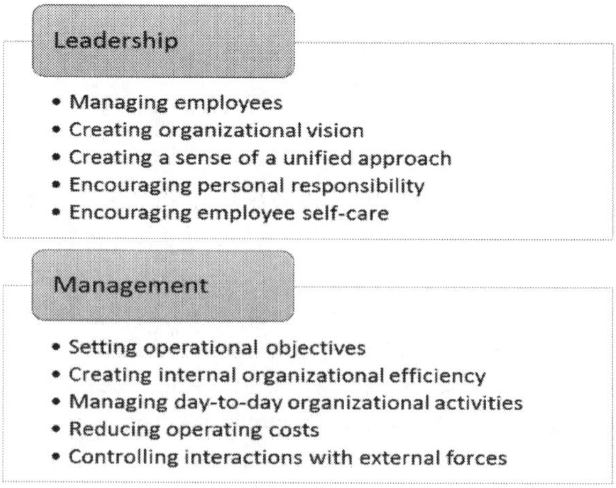

Leadership

- Managing employees
- Creating organizational vision
- Creating a sense of a unified approach
- Encouraging personal responsibility
- Encouraging employee self-care

Management

- Setting operational objectives
- Creating internal organizational efficiency
- Managing day-to-day organizational activities
- Reducing operating costs
- Controlling interactions with external forces

(Adapted from Kouzes & Posner, 1987)

For Lægaard (2006), the work of Kouzes and Posner is presented in terms of managers versus leaders, with managers being those administrators who exhibit management qualities, while leaders are those who demonstrate leadership and management characteristics (Lægaard, 2006, p. 85).

Another useful tool for understanding leadership in organizations, especially for the purposes of assessing leadership style, is the classic continuum of leadership behaviour concept first developed in 1958 by Tannenbaum and Schmidt (1982). This continuum, which was later updated, reflects thinking related to McGregor's Theory X and Theory Y in relation to the manner in which administrators view employees and the role they, as managers, play in the organization. The continuum ranges from a democratic and relation-oriented management style at one end of the continuum to an authoritarian task-oriented management style on the other (Tannenbaum & Schmidt, 1982).

Employee behaviour is impacted by organizational structure and the approach that each organization or work unit takes in relation to decision making regarding task completion or the development of organizational objectives. In addition, the culture of an organization in terms of established norms, beliefs, behaviours, and values contributes greatly to the workplace climate (Schein, 2010). A well-developed and positive organizational culture can contribute greatly to employee morale (Brody & Nair, 1995). Conversely, when an organization is characterized by a broad-based sense of dissatisfaction, commitment to organizational objectives will be weak, leading to the development of a

Figure 18.9   Management Continuum

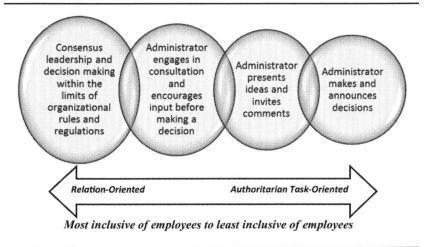

culture in which employees feel that their contributions to the organization are not valued by the administration (Coggins & Fresquez, 2001).

In organizational settings, one of the major tasks of administrators is the management of organizational culture (Schein, 2010). Therefore, social workers and other consultants generally begin the cultural assessment process by meeting with administration to identify those components of the organizational culture that may be in need of modification (Brody & Nair, 1995). This is somewhat like a problem identification process in the assessment phase of work with individual clients. Those who engage in assessment and intervention with organizations often need to work with administrators to identify inconsistencies or ambiguities in current organizational rules and regulations; approaches taken in relation to problem solving; fair treatment of employees; practices related to hiring, evaluating, or terminating employees; and a vast range of day-to-day organizational functions. This initial process is necessary so that the next phase of assessment can proceed with an understanding of beliefs and values that are espoused by those at the administrative level.

During an organizational assessment process, questions about agency/organizational culture, such as possible gender bias, subtle acts of exclusion based on culture, race, sexual orientation, and other forms of marginalization, need to be discussed with administrators as concerns that will be explored. In addition, it is important to also highlight organizational strengths that can be included in a solution-focused approach to bringing about organizational change. Once organizational culture has been studied closely and carefully, the specific values, norms, beliefs, attitudes, and behaviours identified can be looked at in terms of how they either impede or support achievement of organizational goals and objectives (Schein, 2010).

However, assessing the values, beliefs, and attitudes of employees is not easy. While it is true that a consultant can begin by simply observing behaviour, the degree to which employees will act as they normally do may be influenced by a concern about being targeted for some sort of reprimand. In larger organizations, anonymous surveys can be used, but care must be taken to avoid questions that might identify specific employees by unit, job, title, and so forth. A good example of this is found in the climate survey of an organization that asked for the race, gender, and title of all respondents to the survey questionnaire. In one department, the supervisor was an African American female. In her response to the climate survey, she wrote a comment that said, "I am the only African American female supervisor in the entire organization, so I think you will know who I am." Clearly, knowing about the organization and even including focus groups of employees in a process of reviewing survey items before actual distribution is a good idea.

In smaller organizational environments, employees may be even more reluctant to voice their concerns. In such cases, the completion of a final assessment and organizational change plan must be very carefully constructed so that no information can be traced back to a particular employee. For example, in a social work case management department of a large organization where there were problems with the intake process, the final report, which was shared with the agency director, was followed by an employee disciplinary proceeding. This was done because the director believed the intake worker was attempting to undermine her authority. The actions of the director were based on information included in the agency assessment that had been produced by the consultant. In this case, it might have been more appropriate for the consultant to bring up her observations of the intake process and ask the director to generate possible solutions which could then be shared in a meeting with all agency employees. A more careful assessment of management style might have identified the potential for bullying behaviour in the case management unit director, or confidential discussions with that director might have revealed fears of reprimand from administrators above her who had requested consultant services. Whatever the case, failure to be very careful about revealing sensitive information in a final assessment and organizational change recommendation can have negative consequences within the workplace environment.

Workplace Bullying

The concept of workplace bullying is relatively new to North America. Thinking of bullying in the work environment originated in Scandinavia in the 1980s (Einarsen, Hoel, Zapf, & Cooper, 2011). The concepts of sexual harassment and racial discrimination are well understood and the enforcement of laws related to these issues has been in place for quite some time in the United States and Canada. However, workplace bullying is different. In fact, it was not until the late 1990s and the early 2000s that workplace bullying was even a consideration for employers and researchers in North America (Einarsen et al., 2011). Workplace bullying is generally not discussed in textbooks. Organizational culture is a common theme, but bullying, which is all too often a component of the working experience, is glaringly absent from many organizational assessment strategies.

Assessing for workplace bullying includes identifying risk factors and developing strategies for controlling those risk factors. Workplace bullying is not a one-time event. Instead, *workplace bullying* is a consistent process of "harassing, offending, socially excluding someone or negatively affecting someone's work tasks," which occurs "repeatedly and regularly (for example, weekly) and over a period of time (for example, about six months)" (Einarsen et al., 2003, p. 15). According to the Public Services Health and Safety Association (PSHSA) of Ontario (2010), workplace bullying should not be confused with rigid management styles, and can take many forms. Rowell (2005), states that 81 percent of bullies are managers, 14 percent are peers, and 5 percent are lower-ranking staff. Workplace bullying can involve open hostile exchanges and public shaming, or it can assume more subtle and often much more common forms such as the following:

1. Excluding someone from social events in the workplace,

2. Playing potentially harmful practical jokes,

3. Purposely withholding important information, and

4. Sabotaging the work of a coworker. (Rowell, 2005, p. 378)

Bully bosses are particularly difficult to deal with because they are often protected by upper-level management. According to the Canadian Centre for Occupational Health and Safety (CCOHS, 2014), bully bosses will often choose staff who are hardworking, dedicated to their work, and liked by others. This is done because the bully boss sees these individuals as threats. While some bully bosses may openly threaten employees, most will use less obvious but still very upsetting and demoralizing forms of bullying. As outlined by PSHSA (2010), bully bosses are more likely to

1. sabotage a person's work, including setting unrealistic goals or deadlines, assigning an employee too much work, withholding information and job responsibilities;

2. replacing proper work with demeaning jobs, giving an employee an unreasonable amount of unpleasant jobs or tasks, or taking away projects or work assignments the employee enjoys;

3. over-monitoring of work, by engaging in constant checking of an employee's work and/or constantly tracking an employee's whereabouts, when no such need for tracking is warranted;

4. excessive or unjustified criticism or verbal aggression, trivial fault finding including, regularly threatening an employee with disciplinary action;

5. demeaning and constant criticism including, personal attacks of a person's private life and/or personal attributes in front of other employees; and

6. social isolation (silent treatment) or exclusion from social events in the workplace. (pp. 2–3)

Unfortunately, when employees try to resolve problems and issues, bully bosses will retaliate. As CCOHS (2014) reported, bully bosses will utilize performance evaluations, which they negatively slant to withhold pay raises, bonus payments, and other income incentives including specialized trainings, promotions, and transfers to other departments. Often, a bully boss fosters a toxic work environment, which can have negative effects, including increased absenteeism and turnover, decreased productivity, reduced motivation and morale, and poor customer service (CCOHS, 2014).

Many organizations have policies and procedures related to filing grievances against coworkers, supervisors, and directors. However, bullying continues, even in organizations that have antibullying policies. This may indicate that drafting and adopting antibullying regulations with occasional or inconsistent enforcement is not sufficient. Instead, organizations may need to adopt a broader approach to workplace environmental health that includes staff well-being as an important organizational outcome (Woodrow & Guest, 2014).

The Environmental Context of Human Service Organizations

Human service agencies/organizations can vary widely in regard to mission, vision, and the type(s) of clients to whom they provide services. Just as culture is important to understanding the human behavioural elements of workplace environments, identification of the organizational task environment is also critical to assessment, analysis, and intervention. Assessment of the organizational *task environment* involves identification of funding sources, skill level of employees, relationship to other service providers (including competitors), capacity to meet organizational objectives, and of course, the clients served by the agency (Netting et al., 2004, pp. 261–263).

Figure 18.10   Task Environment

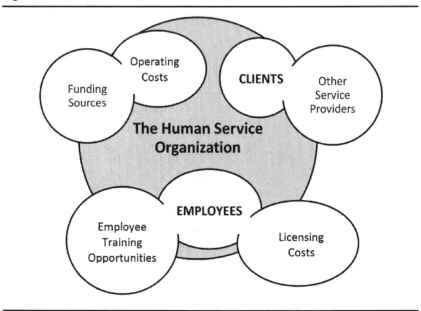

An assessment of the task environment exposes internal and external factors that can influence organizational functioning. Clearly, agencies that are facing funding reductions or cuts will be focused on locating new sources of revenue. At other times, competition from service providers in the task environment will perhaps require placing an emphasis on developing new programs or making changes to existing programs in order to keep existing clients and perhaps identify and attract new service populations.

Funding in particular is a constant concern for organizational administrators. Some human service organizations are *public*, meaning they are funded by municipalities, counties, provinces/states, or federal governments. Adult protection services, like protective services for children, are good examples of provincial/state-operated and publicly funded human service organizations. Another example of a public human service agency would be provincial or state-run human services departments that provide social services and income assistance to eligible people and families in need.

Human service can also be found in the private sector in the form of *private nonprofit* agencies, which are also referred to as *voluntary* agencies. In the United States, these agencies are also commonly called 501(c)(3) agencies, a reference to the federal tax code that allows for tax-exempt status if the agency is engaged in charitable work. In Canada, this same type of organization is referred to as a nonprofit organization (NPO), with similar tax-exempt status for charitable work. Organizations that are private and nonprofit tend to focus on specific client groups, such as at-risk youth, survivors of domestic violence, and homeless families. Private nonprofit organizations are funded through various sources, such as municipal budget allocations, provincial/state and federal grants, churches or charitable organizations such as United Way, and endowments or trusts.

Proprietary or *for-profit* organizations, which help people with a variety of needs, are much more common in the United States. For-profit service providers depend on clients who have private insurance coverage that will pay for services rendered or who have the ability to cover costs on their own (commonly referred to as out-of-pocket or private pay). As is the case for NPOs and 501(c)(3)s, for-profit organizations tend to focus on specific client populations. Persons with addiction problems have become very important populations in the for-profit sector. In the United States, services to the elderly are also a very large and growing sector of the for-profit human service industry. Private for-profit organizations will tend to market to people from higher-income brackets. However, they also secure government contracts. In the United States, private nursing home facilities, private practice social workers, and private for-profit chemical-dependency treatment programs regularly contract with or bill state governments for services provided to clients who qualify for publicly funded medical care, mental health care, and chemical-dependency treatment services.

Those who engage in assessment and intervention designed to improve organizational functioning must be keenly aware of the funding concerns as they relate to organizational survival. A shift in federal or provincial/state funding priorities can have a serious impact at the public or private nonprofit organizational level, especially if funding upon which the agency depends shifts away from populations traditionally served. Social workers or other professionals intervening in settings that are experiencing changes related to agency/organizational growth, shifting service delivery priorities, or rapid downsizing may need to be available to help employees process their feelings and concerns. Frustration, anger, or even fear can be present as they reassess their roles as service providers in a climate of change that will impact organizational priorities or perhaps lead to their own termination due to lack of sufficient monetary support for agency functions.

Assessments of organizations can produce a wide range of findings, just as is the case in work with individuals. For example, some organizations may have a large number of employees who are very committed to high-quality service delivery, but have not been properly trained to complete certain tasks. Therefore, engaging employees in skill-development workshops and other training opportunities would be important actions to recommend in relation to organizational change (Garvin & Tropman, 1992). In-service training, which involves the upgrading of employee skills, or the provision of information that will enhance job performance is a recommendation often made by consultants. In other organizations, employees may feel that they are not appreciated for the contributions they make, or that administrators point out only mistakes while ignoring important accomplishments. In such cases, agency/organization administrators may need to receive their own training regarding managing employees.

Issues such as racism, gender discrimination, or conflicts between employees and management are common areas where social workers might become involved in organizational change efforts (Garvin & Tropman, 1998, p. 150). Social workers and other professionals who intervene in organizational environments may be called upon to play a number of roles. In some cases, consultation regarding development of funding opportunities may be necessary. This could mean engaging certain employees (generally administrators) in grant-writing workshops. In other cases, the organization may be in need of educational or psychoeducational services. For example, a social worker or other professional might be asked to provide in-service training regarding appropriate workplace behaviour in relation to workplace bullying, cultural sensitivity, or the prevention of sexual harassment. Professional practitioners intervening in organizations might also end up advocating on behalf of employees who have grievances against their employers. In such instances, social workers may intervene by serving on behalf of unions as mediators in labour negotiations or even as strike organizers when negotiations break down.

CONCLUSION

This chapter began with a review of organizational theory that was designed to help social workers and other practitioners understand the forces that have shaped organizational environments. From the late 1800s until the present, organizations have increasingly become the setting within which most people, including social workers, are employed. Therefore, understanding organizational structure, culture, and purpose is an indispensable component of under-graduate and graduate social work education—even for those who view them-selves as preparing to be purely direct micro-level practitioners. Moreover, while assessing and intervening in organizations may not be part of a social worker's current practice aspirations, it is true that many MSW-level practitioners end up working in administrative positions at some point in their careers. Therefore, it is important to understand the basic elements of assessment and intervention at the organizational level.

Chapter Nineteen

Community Theory and Practice

INTRODUCTION

The concept of community has undergone many changes over time. Communities are often conceived of as being place based, meaning they have an identifiable geographic location. However, communities can also be composed of those having common ethnic origins, religious traditions, or political affiliations. Communities can exist at one's workplace, through membership in a labour union, within a specific educational setting, or any other location where people gather and work together to advance collective interests, provide mutual support, or address common concerns. Communities are formed for many purposes. Communities can develop as a result of commitment to social justice; however, they can also be formed for the purposes of advancing racist agendas, limiting the rights of women, or exerting social and economic control over the lives of others. Moreover, since the advent of the Internet, communities can now exist partially or entirely online.

INDIGENOUS COMMUNITIES

In North America, countless Indigenous communities had existed for tens of thousands of years prior to the arrival of Europeans. Indigenous populations defined their communities and themselves in relation to the lands they occupied. Generally, land and identity as a people were viewed as having a sacred element often found in creation stories and spiritual beliefs that placed different groups in specific locations with instructions to care for the lands they had been given by the Creator (Sando, 2008). For Indigenous Peoples, of what are now the modern-day nations of Mexico, the United States, and Canada, community included connections with not only human beings, but also animals, land, water, and indeed all aspects of the natural environment. The often-heard Indigenous North American term "all my relations" refers to this very connection in which people are bound together with other human beings, all other living creatures, land, water, and air, much like the strands of a spider web that link together in an interconnected and interdependent manner (Brown, 2007).

This multifaceted conceptualization of community was quite different from Euro-Western approaches which even today most often define community as existing within the limited realm of human-to-human interactions and relations. Because Indigenous populations recognized a very real and physical connection to the land, their varied and geographically specific understandings of the relationship between humans, plants, animals, birds, fish, reptiles, insects, and all other aspects of the natural environment predated the Euro-Western scientific study of the relationship between the elements of various ecosystems, now known as ecology. Added to this was a powerful spiritual component that included an individual and collective responsibility to care for the natural environment in a way that sustained the earth's ability to bring forth life. It was through this recognition of the importance of overall environmental health that Indigenous Peoples were able to survive for generations within their territories (Brown, 2007).

Figure 19.1   Precontact Indigenous Conceptualization of Communities

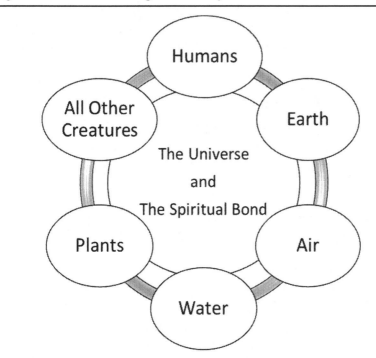

Within broader geographic Indigenous communities, there were also communities of leaders, helpers, healers, farmers, educators, hunters, gatherers, elders, clans, and friends, to name but a few. So, within Indigenous populations of North America, communities were defined by a spiritual and life-sustaining connection to the land, one's role(s) within the larger collective, and one's family and friendship networks. Although Indigenous communities have been radically altered by disease, genocide, colonization, capitalism, and the more recent forces of corporate colonization (known more benignly as globalization), elements of precontact community formation, social structure, and collective action remain strong. In some locations, such as the pueblos of New Mexico or the villages of arctic and subarctic Canada, traditional approaches to community formation and the importance of subsistence activities continue to exist. In other areas, such as urban settings, Indigenous populations have developed communities that have geographic and nongeographic elements. Whereas some Indigenous people are exclusively urban dwellers, many others have ties to reserve communities (Andersen, 2013). As a result, contemporary urban life for Indigenous North American people is often only one part of an existence that also includes ongoing membership and participation in life that takes place in reserve, reservation, pueblo, village, or ranchería communities that may be distant from the urban environments in which they currently reside.

THEORY IN RELATION TO COMMUNITY

Two of the most common theoretical foundations for assessment and analysis of communities are human ecology theory and community systems theory. Although both theoretical orientations share a concern for the manner in which community subparts interact with one another, human ecologists place more emphasis on community structure and function, while community systems theorists focus on subsystem boundaries and the analysis of tension, conflict, or complementarity that occurs at the interface between subsystems. In social work, community systems theory has often predominated. However, human ecological theory has reemerged as an important theoretical orientation due to the growing concern for understanding structural barriers combined with increased awareness of the role played by the physical environment.

Human Ecology Theory

Ecological theorists emphasize the importance of interaction between the human inhabitants of geographical communities and the physical space within which they reside. Human ecology theory began in Chicago in the 1930s and was modeled after concepts of ecology in the natural environment (Netting, Kettner, & McMurtry, 2004). Ecological theory, when applied to communities, is concerned with analyzing the way in which land is utilized by different populations within defined geographic regions. Any view of a geographic (place-based) community from the air will reveal the different uses for land in different areas. Some land may be devoted to park space, other areas may have high-density housing, certain sections of land may be set aside for industrial development, and so forth. Land use is a particularly important element of community analysis because competition over land also reveals who has political and economic power.

Core Concepts of Human Ecology

Important concepts found in human ecological theory are the ideas of competition, population density, segregation, integration, centralization, decentralization, and succession. Population density refers to the concentration of individuals within a given area. Segregation and integration, described in greater detail later in this chapter, has to do with the way in which racial, ethnic, religious, and socioeconomic groups are concentrated within a geographic area.

Figure 19.2   Core Concepts of Human Ecology

Competition

- Competition among groups for land combined with competing ideas regarding land use

Centralization versus Decentralization

- Differences in density and distribution of population, housing, and services

Succession

- The manner in which certain racial groups, ethnic population groups, or income groups replace one another within communities

Segregation versus Integration

- The way in which racial, ethnic, religious, and socioeconomic groups are dispersed within a geographic area

Competition—Competition in a community "is primarily about the acquisition or possession of land among competing groups" (Netting et al., 2004, p. 138). Land use and competition for land represents an important level of analysis. However, competition for land should not be understood as an entirely urban phenomenon. There are many examples of disputes over land use in rural and remote regions of North America. Indigenous North American populations across Canada and the United States still have many land claims that are not settled, and each new discovery of resources in the Arctic, or the need for oil pipeline right of ways renews the conflict between Indigenous North American populations and federal governments of the United States and Canada.

Centralization and Decentralization—Centralization and decentralization involves the analysis of not only the patterns of population density, but also the way in which populations or even services are dispersed or concentrated throughout a city or region. For example, some city neighbourhoods are located in food deserts. According to the American Nutrition Association (ANA, 2015) *Nutrition Digest* newsletter, *food deserts* are areas "often short on whole food providers, especially fresh fruits, vegetables, and other healthful foods" and are generally found in impoverished areas. As a result, residents often rely on local convenience stores and fast-food restaurants, which offer a wealth of processed, sugary, and fat-laden foods, known to contribute to obesity and the development of chronic health conditions such as diabetes (ANA, 2015). Food deserts are not exclusive to urban areas. Rural food deserts exist as well. In remote communities in Canada and the United States, high prices, lack of competition, and limited availability of fresh fruits, vegetables, and other nutritious foods in local rural stores restrict healthy options, especially for those who have limited budgets.

While it may seem logical to think of economically disadvantaged communities as having high population density and low service density overall, an analysis of centralization and decentralization in a low-income community may reveal unexpected findings, such as a concentration of predatory business establishments. Payday lenders are an example of just such predatory business behaviour. Typical services offered by payday lenders include pay advances or cheque cashing, with very high service fees, and the issuance of small loans with extremely high interest rates. Moreover, payday establishments regularly locate in or near economically disadvantaged communities in which residents are less likely to gain or have access to traditional banking facilities (Gallmeyer & Roberts, 2009). For example, in economically disadvantaged communities, such as the North End of Winnipeg in Manitoba, payday lenders have increased their presence where traditional banks have pulled out (Brennan, 2012). Another example is found in the work of a graduate social work student in a macro-level field placement at New Mexico State University, who in 2009 studied the location of payday lenders in the city of Albuquerque. While mapping their location, she found that payday lenders were more heavily concentrated in or near lower-income neighbourhoods and along the public transportation routes used by low-income and immigrant workers. Payday lenders are of course not the only predatory enterprises or the only problem faced by disadvantaged populations. Any assessment of disadvantaged communities across North America will reveal businesses, such as dollar stores and small independent grocery stores, that will often sell lower-quality merchandise at higher prices than one would encounter for the same- or better-quality items in more affluent communities.

Cities and rural municipalities have often grown and developed in ways that marginalize certain populations. Urban infrastructure may proceed in a manner that cuts off racial or ethnic minority communities, especially if those communities are also economically disadvantaged. In some locations, major highways are built around or through neighbourhoods with little consideration for either access or integrity. Moreover, municipalities may devote a great deal of resources to development in higher-income areas in ways that relegate certain neighbourhoods to the periphery. When this occurs, the flight of businesses and higher-income residents intensifies.

Succession—Succession is another concept found in human ecological theory. Succession is a term used to describe the manner in which certain racial groups, ethnic population groups, or income groups replace one another within communities. Succession can occur multiple times in a particular community, causing that community to take on new and often very different characteristics (Fellin, 1995). Assessments of communities often reveal waves of immigrants, internal migrants, or economic groups that have followed one another as residents of neighbourhoods. Understanding when, how, and why communities have changed may provide valuable insight regarding prevailing images of the community held by residents and outsiders.

Succession is of particular interest because many communities in North America, particularly urban communities, experience changes over time with different waves of immigration. A good example of ethnic succession would be Hamtramck, Michigan. In the early 1900s, Hamtramck started out as a German settlement. Shortly thereafter, Polish immigration resulted in a population shift that, by 1970, saw Hamtramck become an almost exclusively Polish community. After the decline of the auto industry, the ethnic character of the city changed again. By the 2010 US Census, Hamtramck was much smaller, but also much more diverse with just slightly over half of the population identifying as white and non-Hispanic. In addition, only 2,495 Hamtramck residents out of 22,493 in the 2010 census declared Polish ancestry.

When succession is ethnic, neighbourhoods experience a change in populations that includes different religious institutions, businesses, and cultural celebrations. In the late nineteenth and early twentieth centuries, ethnic populations, primarily from Europe, would immigrate to those North American urban enclaves that offered a combination of housing they could afford and a sense of cultural familiarity. As their children assimilated into the new nation and majority culture, they would often disperse, leaving their ethnic communities to live elsewhere. New groups would then occupy the developing void, and in so doing, change the ethnic character of the area, but not necessarily increase the economic wealth of the community.

This process occurred many times over in cities across the continent. In some of the literature on communities, the ethnic enclaves of presumably upwardly mobile immigrant groups are also referred to as "stepping stone" communities. This speaks to the expectation of temporary poverty and a belief that immigrants will assimilate to majority culture capitalist expectations regarding work and wealth accumulation. When communities are seen as temporary, assistance to those living in poverty will tend to be targeted and directed at helping individuals escape their communities versus helping those communities flourish.

Segregation and Integration—Over the course of North American history, social and legal segregation has resulted in communities that have a distinct racial and cultural character. In Chicago, African Americans who left the legally sanctioned racism of the South found themselves in socially segregated communities in the North. In the early 1900s, Chicago was only 2 percent African American. However, by 1970, the African American population of the city was close to 34 percent (Grossman, 1995). To this day, the neighbourhoods on the south side of Chicago remain largely African American. The growth of the African American population was followed by other population groups, such as Latinos from the Caribbean, Mexico, and Central America.

In the United States, racial fears often prompted older established white ethnic populations to flee urban areas for the suburbs once the racial composition of urban communities began to change. This phenomenon dubbed "white flight" created clear racial lines between older city neighbourhoods and those in the new suburbs beyond city limits (Boustan, 2010). As a result, communities that were once Irish, Polish, Italian, and German had now become home to African Americans and a wide variety of Latino population groups. When racialized populations succeed Euro-American/Euro-Canadian or white ethnic immigrant populations, the lingering racism of North American majority culture societies presents barriers to economic mobility and movement from core city communities to suburban or even rural communities.

In the United States, racism is most often thought of as relations between Euro-Americans and African Americans or Latinos. In Canada, the public social myth has long been one of multiculturalism. However, much like the American concept of the "melting pot," those most welcome in the mix will generally have ethnic roots in Europe. While it may be true that Canada has been somewhat more inclusive of immigrant people of colour, racism against visibly Indigenous (Aboriginal) Canadians remains quite strong. As a result, the movement of Indigenous Canadians to urban areas reflects the social segregationist pressures that influenced patterns of African American urban settlement in the United States during the twentieth century.

Succession in communities also has a strong economic component in many cases. As communities see changes in employment, such as the decline in manufacturing that has taken place across central Canada and the industrial regions of the United States, communities that were once home to many middle-class families have experienced net population losses, combined with a decline in household incomes. Changes such as these alter the character of communities as businesses and services withdraw, creating infrastructural instability. As a result, social networks may begin to unravel and entire generations of young working-age individuals may move great distances to find work, as has occurred in numerous parts of Atlantic Canada.

Conversely, some communities experience the opposite, with urban redevelopment that is driven by young urban professionals who are building careers but may not be able to build homes in high-priced neighbourhoods. In such situations, people with income growth potential may opt instead for purchasing and renovating houses that are on the fringes of economically depressed neighbourhoods. In time, others may do the same and eventually the entire area may be populated by middle- and upper-income families. This process is commonly known as *gentrification* (Lees, Slater, & Wyly, 2008). While this change might be good for the local tax base, the increased land values and property taxes, combined with the reduction in available and affordable rental properties, will force lower-income and often minority families and individuals out, changing the character of the community.

Environmental Racism and Environmental Health Justice

Although not actually part of the original human ecological conceptualization of communities and their characteristics, environmental racism and environmental health justice have become important factors to consider for social workers and others who intervene in and on behalf of communities. In 1981, the term *environmental racism* was coined by Benjamin Chavis, an African American civil rights leader who believed it is a form of racial discrimination when environmental laws and local regulations result in the deliberate exposure of communities of colour to toxic and hazardous waste sites and facilities. This, along with the systemic exclusion of minorities in the planning, policy making, enforcement, and remediation of environmental issues has had a direct impact on the livelihood of communities of colour (Holifield, 2001). Chavis also believed that intent was not needed to fulfill the definition of environmental racism, and in 1986 he conducted a landmark national study, *Toxic Waste and Race in the United States of America* (Chavis & Lee, 1987), which statistically provided a direct correlation between race and the location of waste throughout the United States. In 1990, the term *environmental racism* became widely popular following a conference that focused on race and environmental hazards, held at the University of Michigan's School of Natural Resources.

Simply put, *environmental racism* refers to the disproportionate burden placed on poor and minority communities of colour in relation to the contamination of the physical environment (Kaufman, 2003). As a term, environmental racism was initially used in the United States to highlight the fact that many African American communities were subject to a disproportionately high number of contaminated properties and sites of toxic waste disposal (Holifield, 2001). However, for Latino and Indigenous populations of the United States, the story has been much the same (Krieg, 1998)—destroying environments while stripping mineral wealth from Native American reservation lands as has occurred on the Navajo and Hopi reservations, and locating landfills near or even in low-income Latino communities as has occurred in places such as Sunland Park, New Mexico. This speaks directly to the power differential between corporate interests and Indigenous or Latino communities of colour.

In Canada, environmental racism has become a topic of discussion in relation to rural communities, First Nations, and urban areas where visible minority communities and economically disadvantaged communities (often one and the same) are subject to a larger share of industrial development (Smandych & Kueneman, 2010). For many years, the Alberta tar sands have been a target of Indigenous and non-Indigenous environmentalists who have become alarmed by rising numbers of chronic and terminal illnesses among First Nations populations living in close proximity (Smandych & Kueneman, 2010). In 2012, the *Idle No More* movement was initiated by Indigenous Canadian women who were concerned about environmental health nationwide. Participants in the movement have held rallies across Canada, which inspired similar events in the United States. The sentiment of the Idle No More movement, as posted on their website, is eloquently captured in the words of Eriel Deranger (n.d.) of the Athabasca Chipewyan First Nations:

> Our People and our Mother Earth can no longer afford to be economic hostages in the race to industrialize our homelands. It's time for our people to rise up and take back our role as caretakers and stewards of the land.

As defined by Nordenstam (1995), *environmental health justice* is "the provision of adequate protection from environmental toxicants for all people, regardless of age, ethnicity, gender, health status, social class, or race" (p. 52). The health of physical environments has recently become much more of a concern for social workers and other professionals engaging in community assessment and intervention activities. While physical environmental factors may have been a focus of community organizing efforts in many regions of North America, social work has been far more attentive to the social environment, with only passing mention of physical environmental issues (Zapf, 2009). Other professions and disciplines, such as community development, have been more focused on economic and infrastructural concerns than on planning for environmental sustainability. The attention to environmental health appears to be bringing society back to an appreciation for our dependence on a healthy natural physical environment. Those who advocate a different relationship with nature, such as *deep ecologists*, stress that we as humans need to understand other life forms as having value and worth equal to that of our own (Kaufman, 2003). This new approach to living in harmony with the planet is actually bringing us full circle to the Indigenous concept of "all my relatives."

Human Ecological Assessment

With the growing interest in developing sustainable communities for human habitation, the human ecological movement, which had for many years been superseded by other theories of community, offers value in terms of thinking about communities in a more holistic way. The capacity of communities to serve as healthy and intact physical environments combined with meeting the social and economic needs of residents fits well with the current emphasis being placed on sustainable development. Social workers and other practitioners who assess communities using a human ecological orientation focus on the capacity of communities to meet the needs of those who live there.

For more than thirty years, communities have been thought of in terms of basic functions, such as production, distribution and consumption of goods and services, socialization of community members, social control, the opportunity for social participation, and mechanisms for providing mutual support as key aspects of communities (Warren, 1978). However, communities have changed and no longer control many aspects of daily existence such as the production, distribution, and consumptions of goods and services, to the degree that had once been the case. Globalization, developments in transportation, and the advent of the Internet have resulted in the erosion of community boundaries in many areas. People now bank online with large multisite corporations, have long-distance electronic social networks, and purchase food shipped from distant locations for sale in pan-regional or even multinational corporate stores. Therefore, thinking in strictly local terms no longer fits with contemporary realities. While some aspects of communities found in older models still remain, many have been transformed by technology and the forces of globalization.

Marten (2001) provides a detailed outline of a community assessment that looks at social environments, as well as physical environmental, cultural, economic, and international influences of the lives and living conditions of human beings. In Marten's outline, the development and existence of communities are considered in relation to social, physical, economic, and geopolitical forces.

Figure 19.3 Marten's Community Assessment

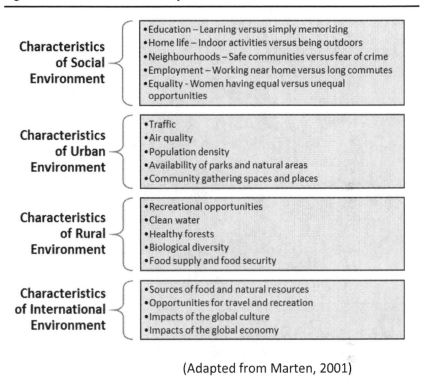

| Characteristics of Social Environment | •Education – Learning versus simply memorizing
•Home life – Indoor activities versus being outdoors
•Neighbourhoods – Safe communities versus fear of crime
•Employment – Working near home versus long commutes
•Equality - Women having equal versus unequal opportunities |

| Characteristics of Urban Environment | •Traffic
•Air quality
•Population density
•Availability of parks and natural areas
•Community gathering spaces and places |

| Characteristics of Rural Environment | •Recreational opportunities
•Clean water
•Healthy forests
•Biological diversity
•Food supply and food security |

| Characteristics of International Environment | •Sources of food and natural resources
•Opportunities for travel and recreation
•Impacts of the global culture
•Impacts of the global economy |

(Adapted from Marten, 2001)

COMMUNITY SYSTEMS THEORY

Human ecologists place an emphasis on understanding community structure, function, and the various community subparts in analyses of communities. While these aspects of community are important to community systems theorists, the focus of attention is instead on assessment, analysis, and understanding systems, subsystems, system boundaries, and interconnections between various community subparts (Coggins & Hatchett, 2009).

According to community systems theorists, communities consist of multiple systems that are interconnected, overlapping, and coexisting with one another (Warren, 1978). Community systems are marked by a diversity of subsystems. Furthermore, subsystems often have goals that differ, regularly resulting in con-

Figure 19.4   Community Subsystems

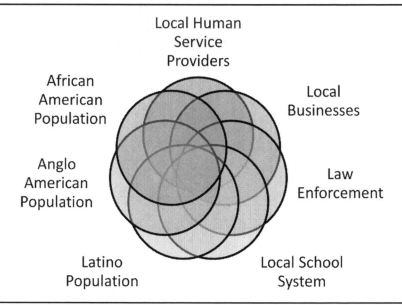

Local Human
Service
Providers

African
American
Population

Local
Businesses

Anglo
American
Population

Law
Enforcement

Latino
Population

Local School
System

flict. Because of power differentials, some community systems or subsystems can exert a greater influence on communities as a whole than is true for less powerful, marginalized, or excluded populations representing opposing systems and subparts. For example, a major employer in a community or region will likely have more power in terms of influencing land use and taxation policies than would be the case for small groups of people, such as individual landowners. Likewise, certain populations, such as wealthier residents or predominant ethnic groups, may exert the greatest share of power in communities.

Community Assessment, Utilizing Ecological and Systems Theory-Based Approaches

Communities represent a complex set of systems and subparts engaged in a constantly evolving and dynamic process. From a human ecological and systems perspective, assessment is designed to identify community characteristics and conditions typical of an ecological approach, combined with a community systems orientation that examines the nature of relationships occurring at the interface between various systems and subparts of systems. A human ecological and systems theoretical orientation to the process of data collection and analysis can be further enhanced by the addition of a modified ethnographic methodological approach that utilizes observation and participant observation in conjunction with information provided by a wide range of community residents.

It is important to remember that if a practitioner is working with or through a university or involved with a human services agency, some of the information gathered in a community assessment may need to be approved by an institutional review board or ethics review board that oversees research conducted

Figure 19.5   Community Assessment—Ethnographic Method

ETHNOGRAPHIC METHOD

•Activities Engaged in by Community-Level Practitioner

Observation

- Observation involves directly experiencing the community and recording observations without judgement. The process requires documentation of all that is seen, heard, felt, or experienced.

Participant Observation

- Participant observation requires involvement in community life as a participant. This can include attending community events, eating in local restaurants, meeting with shop owners, or even attending local church services, while also observing and recording what occurs.

Semi-structured Interviews

- Semi-structured interviews address broad areas of concern or interest. A community-level practitioner may want to ask residents, business owners, and service providers about a variety of community issues.

Structured Interviews

- Structured interviews use open-ended questions and focus on specific questions of concern in the community. The community practitioner might ask about crime, recreational activities for youth, importance of preserving language and culture, or questions about specific service needs.

Surveys

- Surveys are often quantitative. In some settings, community practitioners may use surveys as an additional source of information about a community. For example, community Elders who say Indigenous language preservation is important might be asked to answer a series of questions about language in relation to culture.

using human subjects. Regulations differ by nation, province, or state. There are also additional regulations regarding work with Indigenous First Nations populations. However, in most cases, information that is intended for research purposes, wider public dissemination, or publication must first be approved by the appropriate human subjects review entity.

Working to develop a composite view of a community will help in the assessment process. This approach will give community-level practitioners important insights into community life. Meeting with teachers in local schools, police officers, mail carriers, shop owners, local community organizers, religious leaders, community advocates, informal leaders, elected representatives, and human service providers can be quite helpful. In addition, it is also important to seek diverse opinions or observations that may be found through the inclusion of residents from different age and ethnic groups, or populations such as the homeless that are often marginalized and discounted. By meeting with a variety of people who work and/or live in the community, challenges and strengths become more clearly defined than would be the case if one relies on written information alone. No social worker, caseworker, or counsellor would use a client case file as the only source of information in the development of a

Figure 19.6   Ecological and Systems Community Assessment

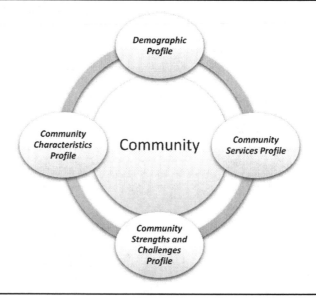

service plan. Speaking directly with the client is necessary to grasp the true level and type of need as well as identifying existing strengths and capacities possessed by the client. The same is true for a community. Written information about a community is an incomplete approach. To truly understand a community, it is necessary to meet the people who constitute the community.

Demographic Profile

A *demographic profile* of a community is a good starting point in relation to understanding important aspects of the community being assessed. Demographic data for communities can be located in city or region-wide public libraries, local libraries, and through online sources. In Canada, Statistics Canada, and in the United States, the US Census Bureau, have all of their current census data available online, as well as archived census data from previous years. Other sources of information, such as local, regional, and national crime statistics, are also available through online sources. In Canada, the Bureau of Justice Statistics and the Royal Canadian Mounted Police websites can be a good source of data, while in the United States, the Federal Bureau of Investigation (FBI) has a surprising wealth of information on diverse topics such as hate crimes and human trafficking which might be important in an assessment of a community. Other sources, such as Amnesty International and the Southern Poverty Law Center, provide an alternative perspective to information presented by federal and local governments.

A demographic profile of a community can be quite varied. However, some of the basic questions to be answered include the population of the community with information about different racial and ethnic groups, income levels, and age categories represented among community members. Important information about different housing types, such single-family dwellings, apartments, condominiums, high-rise developments, and social housing (public housing), can be combined with the condition of housing stocks. For example, some neighbourhoods may be very well maintained, while others have a great deal of housing stock in need of various degrees of repair. In rural settings, housing stock, access to potable water, adequate and safe means of waste disposal, and percentages of electrification may be important information to include.

Levels of formal education attainment and other forms of knowledge acquisition among community members can often be revealing and may present strengths in relation to planning organizing efforts during the intervention phase of work with a community. Income levels, employment levels, and the types or availability of employment opportunities are also important aspects of a comprehensive approach to community assessment. Finally, because each community is different, there may be additional important data or information that can be included in an assessment. If additional data are needed, relevant, and especially if the information is valued by community residents, they should be included in the assessment.

Community Characteristics Profile

The *community characteristics profile* builds on information included in the demographic profile. As stated above, a modified ethnographic methodological approach to data collection requires the community-level practitioner to immerse her- or himself in the community as a way of understanding community life. The community characteristics portion of the assessment includes a description of community size, defined community boundaries, the physical appearance and layout of the community, and other observed characteristics that community-level practitioners and community members consider to be important.

As the various profiles in a community assessment are completed and reviewed, salient features of community identity and life should begin to emerge. For example, what are the predominant languages used in the community? Are there specific important religious or spiritual practices that shape community life? What are common local cultural values (e.g., sharing, individualism, collective effort, fairness, competition, connection to the land) that bind residents together? Are there competing or conflicting cultural values systems in the community? To what degree is the community open to differences in sexual orientation or gender expression? The community characteristics portion of the assessment should also include information related to individuals or groups that experience oppression or marginalization. Finally, an assessment of community characteristics needs to include information about who holds financial and political power within the community, and who does not. These, and other questions, are clarified as salient community characteristics identified by the community practitioner in collaboration with others in the community.

Community Services Profile

The *community services profile* involves an assessment of available health and mental health services; educational, financial and employment services; and social and recreational services or opportunities that exist within the community. This portion of the assessment should include the range, adequacy, and accessibility of other services as well. A services profile may also include the role of institutions, such as schools, churches, mosques, synagogues, ethnic community centres, and other organizations involved in meeting the needs of community residents.

Community Strengths and Challenges Profile

Often those who assess communities are able to identify problems, but are less inclined to put the same amount of effort into identifying community strengths. For this reason, omitting the term *problems* and instead identifying challenges can be a useful way of reframing difficult circumstances faced by communities. As is the case with individual clients, in which problems are reframed as needs, the conversion of problems to challenges can be helpful in shifting one's thought process from a diagnostic problem identification mode to an action-oriented approach needed to confront a challenge. The community strengths and challenges profile should also consider the potential of the community to engage in change efforts designed to create an environment that values and supports social justice and healthy community functioning. Likewise, an assessment of strengths and challenges should not overlook the importance of natural helping networks that are composed of families, friends, and caring neighbours. Finally, the importance of cultural pride or collective identity, in combination with a commitment to social justice, can be seen as either strengths or challenges. Where they exist, cultural pride or collective identity can be drawn upon to face challenges. Where they do not exist, developing cultural pride or a sense of affirming inclusiveness that fosters a collective identity may represent a challenge that community members can rally around.

COMMUNITY INTERVENTION

Without a doubt the most enduring and widely known approaches to community intervention are Jack Rothman's (1974) Models of Community Practice, which are Locality Development, Social Planning/Policy, and Social Action. Rothman's models were originally introduced in 1968 and have since been updated, but still retain the core concepts found in the original schema (Rothman, 2001, p. 27).

Locality Development Model

The *Locality Development Model* of community practice is broad based, inclusive, and process oriented. Those using this model strive to involve a wide range of community members in the community developmental process. In accordance with this approach, community members are to be included in planning, implementing, and evaluating the process. Key elements of this approach include educational objectives directed toward bringing awareness to a problem, democratic participation, voluntary cooperative efforts, the idea of "self-help," and fostering the development of leadership at the local level. With locality development, there is a high degree of participation by members of the community.

Community members are the drivers of change and the beneficiaries of change efforts. A locality development effort is not designed to change the existing social or political order. Instead, emphasis is placed on the process of helping community members to work collectively in the identification of shared goals (Rothman, 2001). Locality development examples include a community cleanup/fix-up campaigns, a neighbourhood watch organization, the creation of community gardens, or targeting the removal of graffiti.

Social Planning Model

The *Social Planning Model*, as an approach to work with communities, is a more task-oriented, deliberate, rational, and planned technical process in relation to addressing substantive social problems (Cox, Erlich, Rothman, & Tropman, 1974). Social planning differs from locality development in that it does not define problems. Working to develop community capacity for problem solving or advocacy-related social change is not the approach used in this model of community practice. Instead, social planning addresses problems already defined by communities or advocacy groups.

In social planning efforts, the degree of community participation can vary widely. However, population groups affected by social planning efforts are not included as participants in the planning and change process to the degree found in locality development. With social planning, the degree of participation by beneficiaries will vary. Participation may take the form of responding to survey questionnaires, serving as a member of an advisory board or committees, or even being asked to participate as voting member on a planning committee (Rothman, 2001). Social planning examples include the creation of Medicare, the development of Social Security, the institution of a regional mental health delivery system, the creation of a citywide gang intervention task force, or a homelessness outreach program targeting families.

Social Action Model

Practitioners utilizing the *Social Action Model* in communities begin with the assumption that a disadvantaged population or segment of a population is in need of organizing in order to be effective, in terms of making demands on the larger community or on different levels of government for increased resources or more fair, equitable, and just treatment. The basic organizing concepts of a social action approach are social justice, democracy, the redistribution of power, provision of needed resources, and inclusion in decision-making processes regarding issues that impact the community (Rothman, 2001). Social action examples include environmental groups such as Greenpeace, First Nations and Métis protests related to land claims, union organizing related to fair treatment of workers, or movements to protect the reproductive rights of women.

Figure 19.7   Rothman's Models of Community Practice

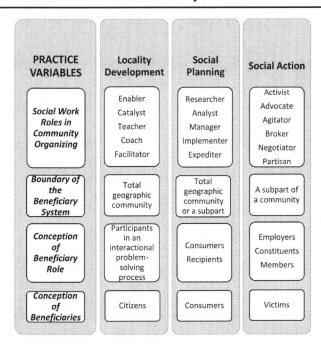

PRACTICE VARIABLES	Locality Development	Social Planning	Social Action
Social Work Roles in Community Organizing	Enabler Catalyst Teacher Coach Facilitator	Researcher Analyst Manager Implementer Expediter	Activist Advocate Agitator Broker Negotiator Partisan
Boundary of the Beneficiary System	Total geographic community	Total geographic community or a subpart	A subpart of a community
Conception of Beneficiary Role	Participants in an interactional problem-solving process	Consumers Recipients	Employers Constituents Members
Conception of Beneficiaries	Citizens	Consumers	Victims

(Portions adapted from Rothman, 1995)

In 2008, Rothman refined, updated, and in some cases changed the language of his original three models. As a result, Locality Development became *Community Capacity Development*, Social Planning/Policy was renamed *Planning and Policy*, and Social Action was recast as *Social Advocacy* (Rothman, 2008, p. 142). While it is true that the most recognizable and perhaps most enduring models for intervention in communities are those of Rothman, there are other models that have existed for quite some time. For example, Weil and Gamble (1995) present the additional practice models of Organizing Functional Communities; Community Social and Economic Development; Program Development and Community Liaison; Coalitions; and Social Movement and Social Reform.

Organizing Functional Communities

Organizing functional communities involves collaborating with people to identify and focus on particular causes. This approach to organizing and intervention can include several communities. The target for change is often some type of behaviour. A good example of this form of community intervention would be a designated driver campaign to reduce alcohol-related accidents and fatalities.

Community Social and Economic Development

Community social and economic development as a strategy for community intervention involves working with grassroots organizations, with an emphasis on economic and social development. Asset mapping is often used in this approach. Asset mapping is similar to creating a strengths-and-challenges profile designed to identify the positive components of communities and the barriers that exist in relation to moving a change effort forward. A good example of community social and economic development would be working with community members to create a plan designed to attract human service providers or businesses to the area.

Program Development and Community Liaison

The *program development and community liaison* approach to intervention is based within an organization. Community practitioners work collaboratively with concerned community members to identify existing needs that are not being met, as well as emerging needs that will need to be addressed. The development of a cultural identity program for urban Indigenous teenagers or the creation of culturally relevant programming for Asian immigrants would be examples of this approach.

Coalitions

A *coalitions* approach involves bringing different community groups or populations together to build a larger and more powerful force for community change. Examples of coalitions might include several service providers that come together to address a common problem, or bringing together groups of parents with young children and elderly community residents who have a common concern about crime and safety.

Social Movement and Social Reform

Social movement and social reform as an approach to intervention has many of the same problem definitions and tactics that would be found in Rothman's Social Action Model of community organizing. This approach to organizing is very much focused on social justice. The biggest difference with this approach is that organizing is seen as taking place outside of established structures. Good examples of a social movement and social reform approach to organizing for change would be the Occupy Wall Street movement in the United States, the Idle No More movement in Canada, and the Indigenous land rights protests in Chiapas, Mexico.

CONCLUSION—
COMMUNITY-BASED SOCIAL WORK PRACTICE

Evidence-based or at least evidence-informed practice has become very much a topic of discussion and attention in social work, psychology, psychiatry, and counselling at the micro level. Macro practice, especially at the level of community, has been less of a concern for evidence-based practice development. Perhaps this is because community practice is not nearly as common as it was in the 1960s and early 1970s. However, this does not mean that those working in communities cannot develop their own measures of effectiveness in relation to macro practice. Indeed, social workers and other community-level practitioners can and should work collaboratively with communities to formulate measurable outcomes related to community-level intervention.

Outcomes measures may be quantitative in nature, such as a reduction in drunk-driving fatalities or an increase in young people graduating high school. Evaluating the effectiveness of community intervention can also be qualitative and focused on aspects of community life that do not readily lend themselves to precise quantitative measurement. However, any measure of success needs to be sensitive to and grounded in the culture of the community engaged in a collective assessment, change, or developmental process. As would be the case with an individual client, a community intervention should include a collaboratively developed intervention/helping/healing plan that is designed to fit the unique nature of the client (in this case, the community) in context.

Chapter Twenty

The History and Purpose of Field Instruction

INTRODUCTION

This textbook has included a great deal of information ranging from the history of social work to the changing ethnic, racial, social, cultural, economic, political, environmental, and even technoenvironmental nature of North America in the twenty-first century. In addition, this book has featured a number of theoretical perspectives and approaches to practice with the intention of linking theory to practice in a manner that demonstrates the importance of competency development in relation to the knowledge, skills, and abilities that are required of professional social work practitioners. The reason the final chapter of this book focuses on field practicum is because the practicum setting is the place where social work students put what they have learned in the classroom into action as they engage and work with clients. This chapter will provide a brief history of the manner in which field practicum has become a key element of social work education. This chapter also includes information regarding the components and requirements of the field practicum experience as well as the roles played by educators, field instructors, and students. Finally, this chapter will conclude with a discussion of social work accreditation and social worker regulation in Canada and the United States.

FIELD PRACTICUM

The Canadian Association for Social Work Education-Association Canadienne pour la Formation en Travail Social (CASWE-ACFTS) in Canada, and the Council on Social Work Education (CSWE) in the United States stress the importance of the field practicum as a central component of social work education. The Educational Policy and Accreditation Standards (EPAS) in the United States (2008 and 2015) identify field education as the "Signature Pedagogy" meaning that field practicum experience is central to educating and socializing students within the profession (Wayne, Raskin, & Bogo, 2010, p. 327). The field practicum is indeed a defining component of preparation for professional practice in social work. Nearly all social work students look forward to their field placements with a great deal of anticipation and undoubtedly anxiety. After all, it is in the field placement that the knowledge one has acquired is now ready to be translated into skill demonstration and continued skill development in a real-life agency setting. The integration of material learned in the classroom and the guided acquisition of field-based skills result from the linking of classroom instruction with learning provided by qualified agency-based field instructors.

In field instruction, all involved should be focused on advocating for student needs, in relation to learning. This means that field instructors, and those serving as faculty field liaisons, need to monitor placements to ensure that they are high-quality learning environments that meet the needs of students. Likewise, students need to be honest about their learning experiences in field settings with attention to not just the completion of required hours, but also a willingness to seek out opportunities to apply what they have learned in the classroom to direct interaction with clients. Depending on the setting, the client may be narrowly conceived of as an individual or family, or more broadly defined in terms of an entire organization, a community, or a marginalized population for whom legislative advocacy is needed. This makes it very important for those serving as field practicum directors or coordinators to ensure a good fit between student learning needs and available high-quality practicum placement opportunities.

Classroom settings may provide rich and varied experiences that offer opportunities to experiment with the application of concepts, theories, and evidence-based interventions to practice. However, classroom experiences alone are not enough to produce well-rounded social work practitioners. Social work, like other allied professions that involve interaction with human beings, requires that a portion of professional education take place within the context of a supervised internship. The social work internship, most often referred to as the practicum placement, has been an important part of social work education since the early years of the twentieth century (Royse, Dhooper, & Rompf, 1996). However, the type of field practicum experience students are involved in now began developing in the 1960s when the CSWE established clear standards that required an integration of classroom and field-based learning (Royse et al., 1996). It was also during this period that the CSWE developed guidelines for the field practicum instruction, making learning that occurred in the field setting much more involved than the apprenticeship approach that was used in the early years of the profession (Austin, 1986). Field placements now involve the creation of learning agreements, also referred to as learning contracts, which help structure and guide the learning process. Students in field practicum placements are expected to complete a minimum number of contact hours during which they will meet with clients, maintain a client caseload, perform other typical social work duties related to organizational or agency functioning, and meet weekly with their field instructors to review progress toward fulfillment of objectives outlined in the learning agreement.

As can be seen in figure 20.1, many requirements for social work programs in Canada and the United States are similar. However, the two notable differences occur at the bachelor of social work (BSW) level and in the specialization or concentration year of the master of social work (MSW). The BSW degree in Canada requires seven hundred hours in the practicum placement. Those who have graduated from BSW programs with overall grade point averages necessary for acceptance in graduate social work programs (usually 3.0 or higher on a 4.0 scale) can go directly into a one-year specialization and/or advanced study MSW. In the United States, the content in an accredited BSW program is considered equivalent to the foundation year (first year) of an accredited MSW program. However, because BSW programs in Canada require three hundred more practicum hours than do American BSW programs, those entering one-year Canadian MSW programs may choose a practicum placement requiring four

Figure 20.1   Field Practicum Requirements

CANADA	UNITED STATES
•BSW programs must provide students with a minimum of 700 practice hours	•BSW programs must provide students with a minimum of 400 hours of field education
•One-year MSW programs must provide students with a minimum of 450 practicum hours or the completion of a thesis or memoir, in an area of specialization	•MSW programs must provide students with a minimum of 900 hours of field education divided into two practicum placements: a foundation placement and a concentration placement
•Pre-MSW/Foundation MSW students must complete a 450-hour practicum placement before entering the second year	•MSW advanced-standing programs must provide students with 450 hours of field education

hundred and fifty practice hours, or have the option of engaging in research or advanced study resulting in a thesis or memoire. This route is particularly popular for those who plan to pursue a doctoral degree in social work, or for those with a great deal of practice experience who wish to engage in advanced study in an area of interest. Therefore, the BSW in Canada is the true direct-practice degree, whereas the MSW can be either an advanced direct-practice degree or a degree that involves a higher level of engagement in research-related activities.

In the United States, as in Canada, the BSW degree is a generalist practice degree. The four-year BSW in Canada and the United States involves completion of a liberal arts foundation followed by two final years during which most or all of the student's courses will be in social work. The BSW in the United States also requires a minimum of four hundred hours of supervised practicum placement experience (CSWE, 2008). As was noted in figure 20.1 comparing American and Canadian MSW programs, at the MSW level, a student in the United States will be required to complete a minimum of nine hundred hours of supervised field experience. This experience is divided into two separate practicum placements, one at the foundation level and one at the concentration level. Because many MSW students enter their respective graduate programs after successful completion of undergraduate education in social work, the BSW practicum fulfills the requirement of the foundation field practicum placement. This means that those accepted as advanced-standing students will need to complete just one year of graduate education at the MSW level, and will therefore need to complete only the concentration practicum. Also, as is the case in Canada, generally only those students with a BSW and a grade point average of 3.0 or higher (on a 4.0 scale) will be accepted to one-year advanced-standing programs. Some MSW programs in the United States and Canada may set their grade point average at 3.5 or higher, while others may accept students on a provisional basis with undergraduate grade point averages that fall between 2.5 and 2.99 on a 4.0 scale.

In Canada and the United States, the BSW-level practicum experience will be more structured and closely supervised, especially in the first semester or term. The BSW practicum experience is designed to give students the opportunity to develop a broad range of generalist social work practice skills for application to intervention and service planning with individuals, families, groups, organizations, and communities. Graduating BSWs should be able to demonstrate competence in the areas of engagement, assessment, intervention, and evaluation of their own practice (DuBois & Miley, 2011). This includes the ability to effectively engage in supportive counselling, case management, resource development, community organizing, and policy advocacy, all against a backdrop of theory and evidence-based practice related to work with various client systems of various sizes and at various levels (individual, family, group, organization, community, Indigenous Nation, and the broader society).

Master-level students in foundation practicum placements are expected to demonstrate skill development commensurate with the successful completion of a BSW practicum placement experience. Master-level students in an advanced practicum placement have the opportunity to develop additional skills specific to their respective chosen areas of concentration/specialization. Some of the typical advanced placement settings can be in Indigenous (Aboriginal)-centred practice environments, bilingual practice environments, community mental health, school social work, medical social work, military social work, clinical practice, addictions, family-centered practice, corrections, administration, program evaluation, community organization, policy analysis and advocacy, and many more. Because MSW programs vary across Canada and the United States, it is important for social workers with specific preferences in relation to graduate-level professional development to locate programs that fit their educational needs.

The field practicum experience can be in the form of either a *block placement* or *concurrent placement*. Block placements are field practicum placements in which students fulfill practicum hour requirements as a capstone experience following the completion of coursework. Some programs, such as the University of Texas (UT) at Austin in the United States, have been very innovative in the use of the block placement approach in the concentration year. At UT-Austin the field practicum block placement in the master of science in social work (MSSW) program requires thirty-six hours per week in the spring semester, or eighteen hours per week in both spring and summer semester. The UT-Austin approach to field instruction allows for placements in locations far distant from where students have completed coursework. In those MSW programs that utilize the block placement approach, placements are usually accompanied by regular field seminars that may take place in the region where students are placed, or through the use of various forms of distance-education applications. *Concurrent placements* are not capstone experiences but are instead integrated into the program of study. Concurrent placements are usually offered two or three days a week, with students attending courses on the days they are not in field.

BSW programs are most often structured in a manner that includes concurrent placements. However, there are a growing number of programs that offer a summer block placement or the opportunity for students to select block or concurrent placement options. Ryerson University in Toronto is one such example, offering the typical BSW concurrent placement, as well as a summer block placement option designed to accommodate working students. With more students entering BSW and MSW programs as nontraditional students, social work programs have found it necessary to make changes that will meet their needs.

Those who favour block placements as having greater value, due to immersion in the field-based learning experience, posit that the opportunity for development of skills more closely approximates a real-world working environment of the sort students will likely encounter after graduation. Conversely, those in social work education who have traditionally favoured concurrent placements over block placements have long argued that the integration of the field practicum experience and material learned in the classroom is more readily achieved when both educational experiences are occurring simultaneously (Rogers, Collins, Barlow, & Grinnell, 2000). Undoubtedly, both forms of placement have their benefits and their drawbacks. The primary concern with concurrent placements is related to students encountering client or workplace issues they have not yet addressed in the classroom. For example, a student may be placed at an agency that becomes involved in a community social action initiative before she or he has received any macro practice course-based instruction. With the block placement format, the concern always exists that supervision and connection with the social work program may become strained for students who are no longer taking regular courses beyond the practicum placement and field seminar. However, attention to high-quality intensive supervision and field seminars that link practicum learning to programmatic objectives can serve to mitigate such potential problems to a large extent.

An additional approach to linking field and classroom learning is the *modified block placement*. This is yet another approach to completing both field experience hours and required coursework. In a modified block placement, the majority of the student's time is spent in the placement setting and a shorter (in terms of weeks, not hours) but more concentrated period of time is spent in the classroom. This is the approach used by the Smith College School of Social Work. At Smith, students attend concentrated courses in summer sessions followed by extended block placements during the regular academic school year which runs from September through late April. A modified block placement such as the one used at Smith far exceeds the required field placement hours and includes close and regular supervision.

Field Seminar

The field seminar accompanies the field practicum and is in addition to supervision the student receives through her or his field instructor in the field placement setting. The field seminar course often includes assignments such as case presentations, assessments, research article critiques, and so forth. The seminar is structured in a manner that will help students integrate learning experiences in the field with material presented in class. In general, the field seminar is a required course at the BSW level and the foundational level in the MSW. At the advanced or second year of the MSW, some programs offer regular weekly field seminar courses, while others may have students meet on a monthly or semimonthly basis. The field seminar, when properly structured, should allow for the discussion of client cases and field practicum experiences in an environment that fosters and supports student interaction directed toward the application of theory, ethics, and core social work principles to practice with client systems of various sizes.

Roles and Responsibilities

The field practicum experience should be a collaborative effort that includes the student as learner, the field instructor as both supervisor and facilitator of learning, and the faculty field liaison who is the person tasked with ensuring programmatic objectives are being met in a supportive and high-quality learning environment. Finally, added to this is the role of the seminar instructor. The seminar instructor is the person who strengthens the bond between classroom learning and field practicum experiences through the use of activities and assignments linking course-based instruction to field-based practice skill development and demonstration (CASWE-ACFTS, 2012; CSWE, 2008).

All social work programs distribute field practicum manuals to their students. These manuals serve as guiding documents in relation to the objectives of the BSW or MSW program in which the student is enrolled. In Canada, all programs accredited through the CASWE-ACFTS are mandated to provide students with information about things such as administrative structures (i.e., student, field instructor, faculty liaison, etc.), student behaviour, the behaviour of field instructors and agency staff toward students, guidelines for resolving things such as allegations of harassment, and a host of other issues. In addition, students entering field practicum placements in Canadian BSW and MSW programs are provided information regarding the protection of client confidentiality and confidential material in written or electronic form. Finally, social work programs must ensure that efforts have been made to provide a wide variety of placement options for students with disabilities (CASWE-ACFTS, 2012, p. 14). In the United States, field manuals contain material covering essentially the same topic areas and issues that are of concern to accredited programs in Canada. The CSWE EPAS (2008, 2015a) in the United States also requires programs to have a well-developed design for the field practicum component of their respective programs that clearly identifies structured approaches to student supervision, coordination of programmatic and agency-based activities, and clear criteria for measuring student achievement of requisite field-related competencies.

The Student

Students in field placement have the dual requirement of compliance with programmatic objectives and agency regulatory policies. For example, agencies that have specific dress codes will often expect students to adhere to the policy. Likewise, expectations related to professional behaviour and a whole host of agency-based policies will be required of student interns in various agency settings. However, because students are in a learning role, some differences will exist. Agency staff members are aware that students are learning, and in many settings, specific tasks and learning experiences are designed for student interns. For example, an outpatient mental health agency that receives referrals from inpatient psychiatric clinics may arrange for student interns to visit a clinic, even though this is not a regular part of the job for social workers in that particular setting. As has already been stated, students in field practicum settings are expected to complete a minimum number of supervised field practicum hours. Students are also held responsible for completing hours that may be missed due to illness or other absences from the field practicum setting. While programs may vary in relation to how hours missed are made up, all social work programs are clear that hours missed must be completed before graduation from the BSW or MSW program can occur. This means that the student, the field instructor, and the faculty field liaison must be involved in the development of concrete plans to complete missed hours in the field practicum.

Although students in field settings will share client-related information through the use of logs, journals, and other field seminar assignments, it is important to note that when clients are written about in all seminar assignments or discussed in oral presentations, client confidentiality must be protected. Therefore, students need to become accustomed to disguising key aspects of client identities in the preparation of written work that takes place outside of the agency setting. For example, a student who is presenting material on a specific client would avoid using the client's name, actual address, real telephone number, and so forth. In addition, if a student is discussing a client born on December 12, 1987, the actual date on an assessment assignment in seminar can be modified. For example, in oral class presentations, the client can be presented as someone who was born in December of 1987 with no specific day included. This would be accompanied by the use of letters versus names, as in "Ms. G." versus using the client's entire first name or last name. In addition to protecting client confidentiality in field seminar presentations, all seminar students are asked to refrain from discussing presented cases outside of class. Many programs even require students to sign confidentiality agreements before entering their field placement settings. In those cases where students do violate client confidentiality, they are required to demonstrate clear and compelling ethical and/or legal reasons for their actions (CASW, 2008, pp. 7–8; NASW, 2008, 1.07 [c]). Even in those cases where the student has what she or he believes to be compelling reasons to break confidentiality, the field instructor and field faculty liaison should be consulted prior to taking any action. Following the proper approach to resolving ethical concerns or dilemmas in relation to confidentiality requires strict adherence to professional standards. Failure to do so could result in the student's dismissal from field, and in some cases, even the social work program in which she or he is enrolled.

The Field Instructor

The field instructor plays a critical role in the field-based component of social work student learning. In the field setting, the student, the field instructor, and the school are all part of a formal professional relationship that includes curriculum-based learning objectives as well as agency or organizational-based policies and regulations. The field instructor serves as a model of proper professional behaviour, a teacher, mentor to a developing professional, supervisor, and even evaluator of student progress toward learning objectives. A good practicum instructor possesses a solid knowledge base and is also able to set aside sufficient time to supervise the student learning process, matching student learning needs with assigned cases that will challenge but not overwhelm the student intern. As a general guide, a person who wishes to serve as field instructor at the BSW level must have a bachelor's degree in social work from an accredited program and at least two years of direct-practice experience. For field placements at the MSW level, the requirements for field instructors include the possession of a master's degree in social work from an accredited program and two years of post-MSW direct-practice experience. There are cases where an additional layer of supervision may be added. This occurs in settings where a highly qualified field instructor exists, but she or he does not have a social work degree. In such cases, a qualified social worker may be brought in to provide the necessary supervision as a way of ensuring compliance with CASWE-ACFTS or CSWE accreditation standards.

In most social work programs, field instructors have a special status as sessional or adjunct faculty. This status may also include library privileges and low-cost or free continuing education credits that can be used toward fulfillment of registration or licensing requirements. Most social work programs provide some sort of regular field instructor training opportunity twice each year (fall and spring) and in some cases special summer training for field instructors may be provided. As mentioned earlier, field instructors must set aside time each week to provide supervision to students in their agencies. Field instructors are also expected to include students in orientation sessions designed to familiarize them with their organizational placement settings. Field instructors are indeed a valuable part of the field practicum education experience, playing a key and very central role in the professional development of students in social work programs (Rogers et al., 2000).

The Faculty Field Liaison

The primary task of the faculty field liaison is to ensure that students in field practicum settings are engaged in an applied educational experience that provides learning consistent with educational objectives (Royse et al., 1996). The faculty field liaison is accountable to the social work program and the social work profession in relation to the development of professional social work graduates (Royse et al., 1996). The faculty field liaison sometimes serves as a student advocate when agency settings are not complying with agreed-upon opportunities for learning or required hours of supervision. The liaison is also available to the field instructor in cases where students are not attending to required learning tasks or complying with agreed-upon agency rules and regulations such as proper attire or informing the supervisor of absences. The faculty field liaison, in conjunction with the field instructor, also serves a gatekeeping function on behalf of the social work profession. As gatekeepers, efforts should be made to ensure that social work graduates entering the profession have also demonstrated competence in the application of knowledge that occurs in the field setting.

In addition to serving as the liaison between field placement settings and social work programs, liaisons are also quite often called upon to serve as seminar instructors. In programs where liaisons do provide some of the classroom-based instruction, linkages between the field and the social work program may actually be enhanced. However, field instruction must be valued by social work programs across North America as being equal in importance to other elements of social work education. There are still many places where in spite of having been identified as key, central, and a signature pedagogy, field is not as highly valued within faculties as research, funded grant production, and of course, publication (Valentine, 2004). Moreover, faculty members serving as both field liaisons and seminar instructors run the risk of being overburdened, especially when they are also expected to attend to other programmatic responsibilities such as teaching courses, serving on committees, and providing advising or guidance for students involved in research and thesis projects.

The Learning Agreement/Contract

Although there are general objectives (Canada) or competencies (United States) for every social work program, each student has unique learning needs and every field practicum experience is different. Therefore, all students in field practicum placements are expected to develop learning agreements, also referred to as learning contracts. The learning agreement is developed by the student in consultation with the field instructor and often, her or his field seminar instructor and faculty field liaison. Learning agreements from ten years ago were quite variable, and sometimes did not adequately address learning objectives or competencies. Since then, accrediting bodies in Canada and the United States have developed updated guidelines for social work programs. These guidelines strive to ensure that programmatic curricula and field practicum experiences reflect the core values and purposes of the social work profession. With this in mind, learning agreements/contracts should be structured in a manner that addresses objectives or competencies, and also includes the activities that will demonstrate attention to student learning that is in line with accrediting standards. Learning agreements will differ for each student, depending on the agency and the type of learning experience (i.e., micro, mezzo, or macro practice). As a result, agency-specific objectives and activities related to work with specific populations and different client systems will also be part of the learning agreement beyond CASWE-ACFTS- or CSWE-mandated objectives and competencies.

CONCLUSION

The practice of social work in North America has evolved a great deal since the early days of the profession. Social workers are now found in settings such as community mental health centres, homeless shelters, schools, hospitals, prisons, universities, and even the halls of government. Social workers function as case managers, psychotherapists, administrators, educators, researchers, policy analysts, community organizers, and elected officials, just to name a few. While the commitment of the social work profession to improving society and helping the vulnerable endures, the manner in which social workers are educated, evaluated, and regulated has undergone profound change.

Accreditation in the United States

In the United States, the CSWE is the regulatory body that accredits social work programs nationwide. The 2008 EPAS demonstrated a move toward outcome-based social work education, which has continued with the adoption of the 2015 EPAS. Social work education has moved away from an almost-exclusive focus on what is taught (content) to one that emphasizes pedagogy (how one teaches) and the outcome of that instruction (CSWE, 2008, 2015a). Instructional outcome effectiveness is measured through the evaluation of the degree to which students have attained core competencies in the classroom and demonstrated concomitant practice behaviours in the practicum placement setting. CSWE (2015b, pp. 3–8) has articulated nine broad areas of competency that include the ability of each social work graduate to

1. demonstrate ethical and professional behaviour;
2. engage diversity and difference in practice;

3. advance human rights and social, economic, and environmental justice;

4. engage in practice-informed research and research-informed practice;

5. engage in policy practice;

6. engage with individuals, families, groups, organizations, and communities;

7. assess individuals, families, groups, organizations, and communities;

8. intervene with individuals, families, groups, organizations, and communities; and

9. evaluate practice with individuals, families, groups, organizations, and communities.

Along with core competencies, each social work program must shape curricula and field practicum placements in a manner that addresses designated foundational practice behaviours (CSWE, 2015b). These practice behaviours serve as evaluative measures of both instructional effectiveness and student achievement. This move toward a competency-based approach that is demonstrated in terms of practice-related behaviours shifts the primary focus from the front end of the education process (content) to the outcome of education as an entry-level professional BSW or MSW social worker. In other words, the interest is now in what a social work graduate is able to do with knowledge acquired versus emphasizing the content of what students are exposed to in their professional education. Content is still important, but it must now be linked to achieving a measurable level of professional competence.

Accreditation in Canada

Social work programs in Canada are accredited by the CASWE-ACFTS. In Canada, the CASWE-ACFTS has traditionally emphasized programmatic inputs over evaluation of outcome measures in the form of competencies (Birnbaum & Silver, 2011). As a result, this more traditional approach to social work program assessment focuses on what is being taught to students (Birnbaum & Silver, 2011). A more recent shift in accreditation of Canadian social work programs has resulted in the development of core learning objectives as outlined in the CASWE-ACFTS (2012) Accreditation Standards. The CASWE-ACFTS (2012) core learning objectives for students in accredited Canadian social work programs are as follows:

1. Identify as a professional social worker and adopt a value perspective of the social work profession.

2. Adhere to social work values and ethics in professional practice.

3. Promote human rights and social justice.

4. Support and enhance diversity by addressing structural sources of inequity.

5. Employ critical thinking in professional practice.

6. Engage in research.

7. Participate in policy analysis and development.

8. Engage in organizational and societal systems' change through professional practice.

9. Engage with individuals, families, groups, and communities through professional practice. (pp. 9–11)

Although the new standards do represent what appears to be a move toward competency development similar to CSWE core competencies, the CASWE-ACFTS core learning objectives and the attendant subsections of each learning objective are actually more oriented toward internalization of values, ethics, and guiding professional principles, with an expectation that professional practice will follow and flow naturally from identification with the profession. This differs from the American emphasis on the demonstration of skills that are observable and therefore believed to be more easily measurable.

Unlike the purported practice behaviour-based emphasis of CSWE, the CASWE-ACFTS stresses the knowledge a student should possess as a result of receiving a social work education in an accredited program. This emphasis on knowledge exposure and development of an *end-state* professional identity versus the demonstration of practice behaviours results in differences related to evaluating student success. By this it is meant that accreditation of social work programs in Canada places less emphasis on evaluation of demonstrated student skills, focusing instead on more broadly stated programmatic objectives

Figure 20.2   CSWE Competencies versus CASWE-ACFTS Core Learning Objectives

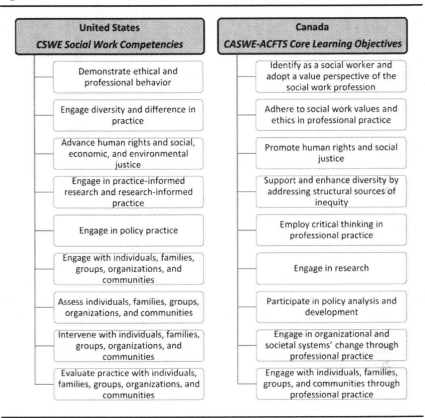

United States CSWE Social Work Competencies	Canada CASWE-ACFTS Core Learning Objectives
Demonstrate ethical and professional behavior	Identify as a social worker and adopt a value perspective of the social work profession
Engage diversity and difference in practice	Adhere to social work values and ethics in professional practice
Advance human rights and social, economic, and environmental justice	Promote human rights and social justice
Engage in practice-informed research and research-informed practice	Support and enhance diversity by addressing structural sources of inequity
Engage in policy practice	Employ critical thinking in professional practice
Engage with individuals, families, groups, organizations, and communities	Engage in research
Assess individuals, families, groups, organizations, and communities	Participate in policy analysis and development
Intervene with individuals, families, groups, organizations, and communities	Engage in organizational and societal systems' change through professional practice
Evaluate practice with individuals, families, groups, organizations, and communities	Engage with individuals, families, groups, and communities through professional practice

with the implicit understanding that students gain knowledge that will then be translated into appropriate professional practice. As a result, graduate-level courses in social work tend to measure knowledge acquisition through the completion of assignments that emphasize library research related to writing theme or term papers relevant to topics presented in their courses. In addition, midterm and final essay examinations may be used in conjunction with classroom oral presentations. While in-class skill demonstration is much more common at the BSW level, the assessment of direct-practice skill acquisition at the master's level in Canada is more often relegated to field practicum placement settings and seminar courses.

Regulation of Social Workers

A critical issue for American social work programs has been preparation for licensure following graduation. In a 2011 article published by the *Clinical Social Work Journal*, author Bruce Thyer discusses the fact that many schools of social work in the United States have ignored the importance of licensure for students who will need to pass a licensing exam in order to further their careers. The Association of Social Work Boards (ASWB), which develops the various licensing exams, has worked together with the National Association of Social Workers (NASW) to create materials addressing critical social work practice skills. Yet, many schools of social work have forged ahead with little apparent concern for postgraduation licensure passage rates. As a result, some schools fare quite poorly with less than 50 percent of graduates passing licensing exams on their first attempt (Thyer, 2011). It has been argued by some faculty members in many locations that they do not want to "teach to the exam." However, the licensing exam which utilizes knowledge, skills, and abilities (KSAs) identified by ASWB (2013b) is not that markedly different from core content in most social work programs in the United States and Canada.

In the United States, social workers at the master's level must pass a licensing exam developed by ASWB. In most states, BSW-level practitioners are also required to pass a licensing exam in order to practice as licensed social workers. At the bachelor's level, ASWB (2015, p. 15) organizes the examination into the following content areas:

- Human Development, Diversity, and Behaviour in the Environment 27%
- Assessment 28%
- Direct and Indirect Practice 26%
- Professional Relationships, Values, and Ethics 19%

At the master's level, ASWB (2015, p. 16) organizes the examination into the following content areas:

- Human Development, Diversity, and Behaviour in the Environment 28%
- Assessment and Intervention Planning 24%
- Direct and Indirect Practice 21%
- Professional Relationships, Values, and Ethics 27%

In addition to the bachelor's and master's examinations, ASWB (2013a) also provides licensing examinations for *Advanced Generalist* and *Clinical* practitioners/social workers. According to the *ASWB Examination Candidate Handbook* (ASWB, 2015, p. 17), the generalist exam, in particular, includes items related to policy analysis and advocacy, and theories and methods of social change. What many do not realize is that CSWE- and CASWE-ACFTS-accredited programs shape what become the ASWB examinations, not the other way around. In addition, those individuals who function as item writers for the various exams represent a broad and diverse range of ethnic, racial, gender, geographic, academic, and practitioner populations from across North America.

At the present time, successful passage of a licensing exam is not universally required throughout Canada. Currently, Alberta is the only province that requires social workers at all levels to pass a licensing exam, while British Columbia requires only advanced clinical practitioners to pass the ASWB clinical exam (ASWB, 2013a). In addition, many experienced clinical social work practitioners in Canada also complete the clinical social work exam developed by ASWB as a way of establishing credibility in relation to competence, but in most jurisdictions passing the exam is not required. However, this is not to say that Canadian social work educators and professionals are uniformly opposed to the development of some form of regulation beyond registration with social work organizations in the various provinces. In fact, the debate regarding licensure has been ongoing in Canada since at least the 1990s (Birnbaum & Silver, 2011), following the passage of the Agreement on Internal Trade (AIT) (Industry Canada, 2007) which was designed to streamline and harmonize regulations and standards throughout Canada, including consumer protection. The portion of the legislation impacting social work is included in Chapter 7 of the AIT (Industry Canada, 2007). The synopsis of organizations covered is found on the Industry Canada website under Chapter 7, Labour Mobility, and reads as follows:

- Government departments, ministries and agencies must comply with the provisions of this chapter.
- Governments will ensure compliance with the obligations of this chapter for: regional, local, district and other forms of municipal governments; and, occupational regulatory bodies and non-governmental organizations that exercise authority delegated by law.
- Other non-governmental organizations such as unions, education and training establishments, and professional associations have been asked to comply.

- More than 400 occupational regulatory bodies have achieved compliance or are actively working to comply with the provisions of the Labour Mobility chapter.

In the summer of 2009, the ASWB conducted a North American social work practice survey, in which twenty thousand social workers were randomly selected to participate in the survey, four thousand of whom were from Canada (Halpern, 2010). The survey found a great deal of similarity between the two nations regarding social work practice settings and social work practice-related activities. In 2010, the Canadian Council of Social Work Regulators (CCSWR) was formed and incorporated. Shortly thereafter, the CCSWR (2012) secured a Human Resources and Skills Development Canada grant to fund a project designed to identify entry-level competencies for beginning social work practitioners in Canada.

Although this move has potential merit, there is widespread and growing concern that CCSWR has developed an entry-level competency profile for social work professionals that looks more like the English Health and Care Professions competency profile which includes very little in relation to social and economic justice or intervention with larger systems to create positive social change. Unlike Canadian or American accreditation standards or even the various ASWB examinations, the CCSWR profile (as is the case for the English social work competency profile) is criticized by many for being exceedingly casework-based and individualistic in its orientation. This has led a large number of social work educators in Canada to resist professional licensure over concerns that preparation for licensure will have a negative impact on the profession. Preparing students for direct practice with individuals and families in a manner that emphasizes licensure requirements does hold the potential for marginalizing the importance and development of skills needed to engage in policy advocacy, social and economic justice activities, and the furthering of antiracist and anti-oppressive approaches to intervention with multiple systems at all levels.

Licensure of social work professionals is in the early stages in most parts of Canada. There are many who fear that practitioners in remote communities and in First Nations practice environments may be pushed out by licensed social workers who are graduates of accredited programs. In this move toward establishing a minimum level of practice-related competence, care must be taken to ensure that social workers who are credentialed must also have a culturally grounded understanding of the people they intend to serve. For this reason, the voices of Indigenous, rural, and remote populations need to be heard. There are universities such as Wilfred Laurier and the University of Manitoba that have developed Indigenous (Aboriginal)-centered MSW programs. Universities in other provinces—the universities of Calgary and Northern British Columbia, for example—have made great strides in addressing rural social work. These universities, and many others across the country, in concert with Indigenous and rural organizations, need to be at the forefront of shaping the credentialing process and preparing social workers for culturally appropriate and affirming practice. Moreover, this preparation of practitioners needs to be a process that strives to create a better fit with the diversity of the Canadian context not only in major metropolitan areas, but in practice environments beyond urban centres as well.

Final Remarks

As of February 2015, the CSWE website in the United States listed 504 accredited baccalaureate social work programs, 235 master-level accredited social work programs, and 35 additional programs in candidacy. In 2015, the website for the CASWE-ACFTS listed 39 programs in Canada that are accredited or have pre-accreditation status. Together, as of 2015, North America has 813 social work programs that are accredited or in candidacy. Certainly, the founding women (and their male allies) of the profession likely could not have even dreamed of so much growth and development in a profession that started with a handful of summer training programs in the late 1800s and early 1900s. Indeed, social work has even grown beyond both the United States and Canada with programs, departments, faculties, and schools found throughout the world.

It is unclear what the future holds for any of us. Global climate change, large-scale migration, environmental destruction, worldwide political strife, technological developments, globalization, and the concentration of wealth in the hands of the few are among the many forces that will profoundly alter the social and physical worlds we are all part of. More than ever, social work needs to be a voice of hope that will work with others to shape the future in a way that helps to heal and care for the planet we inhabit; that values the work of our human rights activists; that recognizes the contributions of our healers, thinkers, researchers, scholars, and teachers who care deeply for the well-being of others; that honours the wisdom of our Indigenous Elders; that upholds the values of dignity, equality, inclusion, fairness, and compassion for each of us; and that strives to make this world a better place. It is also hoped that this book will play at least a small part in helping to achieve those ends by preparing social workers for competent, professional, and culturally appropriate and affirming practice.

References

Ablon, J. S., & Jones, E. E. (2002). Validity of controlled clinical trials of psychotherapy: Findings from the NIMH Treatment of Depression Collaborative Research Program. *American Journal of Psychiatry, 159*(5), 775–783. doi: 10.1176/appi.ajp.159.5.775.

Abrams, L. S., & Moio, J. A. (2009). Critical race theory and the cultural competence dilemma in social work education. *Journal of Social Work Education, 45*(2), 245–261. doi: 10.5175/JSWE.2009.200700109.

Abrams, P. (2010, January 2). "Limbaugh lauds (socialist) medical care in Hawaii." *Huffington Post Canada*. Retrieved from http://www.huffington post.ca/.

Acierno, R., Hernandez, M. A., Amstadter, A. B., Resnick, H. S., Steve, K., Muzzy, W., & Kilpatrick, D. G. (2010). Prevalence and correlates of emotional, physical, sexual, and financial abuse and potential neglect in the United States: The national elder mistreatment study. *American Journal of Public Health, 100*(2), 292–297. doi: 10.2105/AJPH.2009.163089.

Adler, G., & Hull, R. (1971). *Carl Gustav Jung. Psychological types, the collected works of C. G. Jung, Volume 6*. Princeton, NJ: Princeton University Press.

Agren, D. (2010, August 10). Mexican states ordered to honor gay marriages. *The New York Times;* Reprints. Retrieved from http://www.nytreprints.com.

Ainsworth, M. D. S. (1973). The development of infant-mother attachment. In B. Cardwell & H. Ricciuti (Eds.), *Review of child development research* (Vol. 3, pp. 1–94). Chicago: University of Chicago Press.

Ainsworth, M. D. S., Blehar, M. C., Waters, E., & Wall, S. (1978). *Patterns of attachment: A psychological study of the strange situation*. Hillsdale, NJ: Erlbaum.

Akerlund, M., & Cheung, M. (2000). Teaching beyond the deficit model: Gay and lesbian issues among African Americans, Latinos, and Asian Americans. *Journal of Social Work Education, 36*(2), 279–292.

Aleman, M. (2014). Immigrant women survive domestic abuse thanks to protection from a federal law. *Borderzine: Reporting Across Fronteras*. Retrieved April 13, 2015, from http://borderzine.com/2014/02/immigrant-women -survive-domestic-abuse-thanks-to-protection-from-a-federal-law/.

Alinsky, S. D. (1971). *Rules for radicals: A practical primer for realistic radicals.* New York: Random House.

Allen-Mears, P., & Lane, B. A. (1987). Grounding social work practice in theory: Ecosystems. *Social Casework, 68*(9), 515–521.

Alloy, L. B., Acocella, J., & Bootzin, R. R. (1996). *Abnormal psychology: Current perspectives* (7th ed.). New York: McGraw-Hill.

Almeida, R. (2005). Asian Indian families. In M. McGoldrick, J. Giordano, & N. Garcia-Prieto (Eds.), *Ethnicity & family therapy* (3rd ed., pp. 377–394). New York: Guilford.

American Nutrition Association (ANA). (2015). USDA defines food deserts. *ANA Online Publications: Nutrition Digest Newsletter, 37*(3). Retrieved from http://americannutritionassociation.org/newsletter/usda-defines-food-deserts.

American Psychiatric Association (APA). (2000). *Diagnostic and statistical manual of mental disorders* (4th ed., text revision). Washington, DC: Author.

American Psychiatric Association (APA). (2013). *Diagnostic and statistical manual of mental disorders* (5th ed.). Arlington, VA: Author.

American Society of Human Genetics (ASHG). (2008, November). *The American Society of Human Genetics: Ancestry testing statement.* Retrieved from http://www.ashg.org/pdf/ASHGAncestryTestingStatement_FINAL.pdf.

Americans with Disabilities Act (ADA). (1990). *Americans with Disabilities Act of 1990—ADA—42 US code chapter 126: Equal opportunities for individuals with disabilities, Section 12101. Findings and purpose.* Washington, DC: US Department of Justice, Civil Rights Division. Retrieved from http://www.ada.gov/archive/adastat91.htm.

Andersen, C. (2013). Urban aboriginality as a distinct identity in twelve parts. In E. J. Peters & C. Andersen (Eds.), *Indigenous in the city: Contemporary identities and cultural innovation* (pp. 46–68). Vancouver: University of British Columbia Press.

Anderson, K. (2011). *Life stages and Native women: Memory, teachings, and story medicine.* Winnipeg: University of Manitoba Press.

Anderson, L., Krathwohl, D., Airasian, P., Cruikshank, K., Mayer, R., Pintrich, P., . . . Wittrock, M. (2000). *A taxonomy for learning, teaching, and assessing: A revision of Bloom's taxonomy of educational objectives.* New York: Pearson, Allyn & Bacon.

Ansbacher, H. L., & Ansbacher, R. (1956). *The individual psychology of Alfred Adler*. New York: Basic Books.

Ariel de Vidas, A. (2008). What makes a place ethnic? The formal and symbolic spatial manifestations of Teenek identity (Mexico). *Anthropological Quarterly, 81*(1), 161–205. doi: 10.1353/anq.208.0008.

Arlow, J. A. (1995). Psychoanalysis. In R. Corsini & D. Wedding (Eds.), *Current psychotherapies* (5th ed., pp. 15–50). Itasca, IL: F. E. Peacock.

Armitage, A. (2003). *Social welfare in Canada* (4th ed.). Don Mills, ON: Oxford University Press.

Arviso-Alvord, L., & Cohen-Van Pelt, E. (1999). *The scalpel and the Silver Bear: The first Navajo woman surgeon combines western medicine and traditional healing*. New York: Bantam Books.

Association of Social Work Boards (ASWB). (2013a). *About the exams.* Culpepper, VA: Author. Retrieved from https://www.aswb.org/exam-candidates/about-the-exams/.

Association of Social Work Boards (ASWB). (2013b). *Exam content outlines.* Culpepper, VA: Author. Retrieved from https://www.aswb.org/exam-candidates/about-the-exams/exam-content-outlines/.

Association of Social Work Boards (ASWB). (2015). *ASWB examination candidate handbook* (Rev. 2/2015). Culpepper, VA: Author. Retrieved from https://www.aswb.org/wp-content/uploads/2013/12/Candidate-Handbook.pdf

Atherton, J. S. (2013). *Learning and teaching: Piaget's developmental theory.* Retrieved from http://www.learningandteaching.info/learning/piaget.htm.

Austin, D. M. (1986). *A history of social work education*. Austin: School of Social Work, University of Texas at Austin.

Babad, M. (2014, April 22). Canada's middle class richest in study of big nations. *The Globe and Mail, Report on Business, Business Briefing.* Retrieved from http://www.theglobeandmail.com/report-on-business/top-business-stories/canadas-middle-class-now-worlds-richest-study-suggests/article18090490/.

Bachelor, A. (2013). Clients' and therapists' views of the therapeutic alliance: Similarities, differences and relationship to therapy outcome. *Clinical Psychology & Psychotherapy, 20*(2), 118–135. doi: 10.1002/cpp.792.

Backhouse, C., & Flaherty, D. (1992). *Challenging times: The women's movement in Canada and the United States.* Quebec City, QC: McGill-Queen's University Press.

Baffoe, M. (2009). The social reconstruction of "home" among African immigrants in Canada. *Canadian Ethnic Studies Journal, 41–42*(3–1), 157–173. doi: 10.1353/ces.2010.0026.

Baines, D. (1997). Feminist social work in the inner city: The challenges of race, class, and gender. *Affilia, Journal of Women and Social Work, 12*(3), 297–317. doi: 10.1177/088610999701200304.

Baines, D. (2011). *Doing anti-oppressive practice: Social justice social work.* Black Point, NS: Fernwood.

Bakker, P. (1997). *A language of our own: The genesis of Michif, the mixed Cree-French language of the Canadian Métis.* New York: Oxford University Press.

Bandura, A. (1977). *Social learning theory.* Englewood Cliffs, NJ: Prentice Hall.

Bandura, A. (1986). *Social foundations of thought and action: A social cognitive theory.* Englewood Cliffs, NJ: Prentice-Hall.

Bandura, A. (1989). Social cognitive theory. In R. Vasta (Ed.), *Annals of child development, Vol. 6. Six theories of child development* (pp. 1–60). Greenwich, CT: JAI.

Bandura, A. (2006). Toward a psychology of human agency. *Perspectives on Psychological Science, 1,* 164–180.

Barker, R. L. (2003). *The social work dictionary* (5th ed.). Washington, DC: National Association of Social Workers Press.

Bartlett, A. A. (1996). The exponential function, XI: The new Flat Earth Society. *The Physics Teacher, 34*(6), 342–343.

Battle, K., Torjman, S., & Mendelson, M. (2006). *More than a name change: The universal child care benefit.* Ottawa, ON: Caledon Institute of Social Policy.

Beaver, R. (2013, July 29). *Sacred Seven Grandfather Teachings: Wisdom-Respect-Love-Honesty-Courage-Humility-Truth.* Retrieved November 12, 2013, from http://ronniebeaver.myknet.org/.

Beck, A. T., Freeman, A., & Associates. (1990). *Cognitive therapy of personality disorders.* New York: Plenum.

Beck, A. T., & Weishaar, M. E. (1989). Cognitive therapy. In R. J. Corsini & D. Wedding (Eds.), *Current psychotherapies* (4th ed., pp. 285–317). Itasca, IL: F. E. Peacock.

Beister, F. P. (1957). *The casework relationship*. Chicago: Loyola University Press.

Belanger, Y. D. (2014). *Ways of knowing: An introduction to Native studies in Canada* (2nd ed.). Toronto: Thompson Nelson.

Bell, V. (2011). Maslow's humanistic psychology. In C. Jarrett (Ed.), *30-second psychology* (p. 122). Lewes, UK: Prospero Books-Ivey Press.

Ben-Zeev, D., Young, M. A., & Corrigan, P. W. (2010). DSM-V and the stigma of mental illness. *Journal of Mental Health, 19*(4), 318–327. doi: 10.3109/09638237.2010.492484.

Berg, I. K., & Dolan, Y. (2001). *Tales of solutions: A collection of hope-inspiring stories*. New York: Norton.

Bergmann, U. (2012). *Neurobiological foundations of EMDR practice*. New York: Springer.

Berman, J. (2013, July 17). $10.20 per hour needed to survive even in America's cheapest county. *HuffPost: Business Online*. Retrieved May 16, 2014, from http://www.huffingtonpost.com/2013/07/17/worker-wage_n_3610530.html?utm_hp_ref=business.

Birnbaum, R., & Silver, R. (2011). Social work competencies in Canada: The time has come. *Canadian Social Work Review/Revue Canadienne de Service Social, 28*(2), 299–303.

Bodnar, L., & Wisner, K. (2005). Nutrition and depression: Implications for improving mental health among childbearing-aged women. *Biological Psychiatry, 58*(9), 679–685.

Bonnell, A. G. (2011). Oligarchy in miniature? Robert Michels and the Marburg branch of the German Social Democratic Party. *German History, 29*(1), 23–35. doi: 10.1093/gerhis/ghq146.

Borden, W. (2009). *Contemporary psychodynamic theory and practice*. Chicago: Lyceum Books.

Borges, G., Nock, M. K., Abad, J. M. H., Hwang, I., Sampson, N. A., Alonzo, J., . . . Kessler, R. C. (2010). Twelve month prevalence of and risk factors for suicide attempts in the WHO World Mental Health Surveys. *The Journal of Clinical Psychiatry, 71*(12), 1617–1628. doi: 10.4088/JCP.08m04967blu.

Borkowski, N. (2011). Overview and history of organizational behavior. In N. Borkowski (Ed.), *Organizational behavior in health care* (2nd ed., pp. 3–14). Sudbury, MA: Jones and Bartlett.

Bouchard, D., & Martin, J. (2009). *The seven sacred teachings of White Buffalo Calf Woman*. Vancouver, BC: More Than Words (MTW) Publishers.

Boustan, L. P. (2010). Was postwar suburbanization "white flight"? Evidence from the black migration. *The Quarterly Journal of Economics, 125*(1), 417–443. doi: 10.1162/qjec.2010.125.1.417.

Bowlby, J. (1969). *Attachment and loss. Vol. 1. Attachment.* New York: Basic Books.

Bowlby, J. (1988). *A secure base: Clinical applications of attachment theory.* London: Routledge.

Bowler, D. E., Buyung-Ali, L. M., Knight, T. M., & Pullin, A. S. (2010). A systematic review of evidence for the added benefits to health of exposure to natural environments. *BMC Public Health, 10*(1), 456.

Bradley, C. B., Maschi, T., O'Brien, H., Morgen, K., & Ward, K. (2012). Faithful but different: Clinical social workers speak out about career motivation and professional values. *Journal of Social Work Education, 48*(3), 459–477. doi: 10.5175/JSWE.2012.2010.00043.

Brennan, M. (2012). *The changing landscape of financial services in Manitoba: A location analysis of payday lenders, banks and credit unions* (Unpublished doctoral dissertation). University of Manitoba, Winnipeg.

Bretherton, I. (1992). The origins of attachment theory: John Bowlby and Mary Ainsworth. *Developmental Psychology, 28,* 759–775.

Bretherton, I., & Munholland, K. A. (2008). Internal working models in attachment relationships: Elaborating a central construct in attachment theory. In J. Cassidy & P. R. Shaver (Eds.), *Handbook of attachment: Theory, research, and clinical applications* (2nd ed., pp. 102–130). New York: Guilford.

Brisbane, F. L. (2000, December). *Cultural competency: An ingredient for avoiding unintentional racism.* Paper presented at the 14th Annual Counseling People of Color Conference: An International Perspective, San Juan, PR.

Brody, R., & Nair, M. D. (1995). *Macro practice: A generalist approach.* Wheaton, IL: Gregory Publishing.

Brown, J. E. (2007). *The spirit legacy of the American Indian: A commemorative edition with letters while living with Black Elk.* Bloomington, IN: World Wisdom.

Burke, B. L., Arkowitz, H., & Menchola, M. (2003). The efficacy of motivational interviewing: A meta-analysis of controlled clinical trials. *Journal of Consulting and Clinical Psychology, 71*(5), 843–861. doi: 10.1037/0022-006X.71.5.843.

Burke, M., Marlow, C., & Lento, T. (2010, April). *Social network activity and social well-being.* Paper presented at the Carnegie Mellon Human-Computer Interaction Institute (CHI) 2010, Pittsburgh, PA.

Burlingame, G. M. (2010). Small group treatments: Introduction to special section. *Psychotherapy Research, 20*(1), 1–7. doi: 10.1080/10503301003596551.

Burns, C., & Krehely, J. (2011, June 2). *Gay and transgender people face high rates of workplace discrimination and harassment.* Washington, DC: Center for American Progress. Retrieved from http://www.americanprogress.org/ issues/lgbt/news/2011/06/02/9872/gay-and-transgender-people-face -high-rates-of-workplace-discrimination-and-harassment/.

Burtch, B., & Haskell, R. (2010). *Get that freak: Homophobia and transphobia in high schools.* Black Point, NS: Fernwood.

Buvat, J. (2012). Sexual dysfunction in men. In K. Schenck-Gustafsson, P. R. DeCola, D. W. Pfaff, & D. S. Pisetsky (Eds.), *Handbook of clinical gender medicine* (pp. 446–456). Basel, Switzerland: Karger.

Canada. Parliament. House of Commons. Centre for Research on Work Disability Policy. (2010). *Federal poverty reduction plan: Working in partnership towards reducing poverty in Canada: Report of the Standing Committee on Human Resources, Skills and Social Development and the Status of Persons with Disabilities, Candice Hoeppner, MP, Chair: Parliament of Canada, Fortieth Parliament, third session, November 2010.* Ottawa: Author.

Canadian Association for Social Work Education (CASWE-ACFTS). (2012). *CASWE Standards for Accreditation—May 2012.* Ottawa, ON: Author. Retrieved from http://caswe-acfts.ca/wp-content/uploads/2013/03/ CASWE-ACFTS-Standards-11-2014.pdf.

Canadian Association of Social Workers (CASW-ACTS). (2000). *In critical demand: Social work in Canada volume 1—Final report (2000).* Retrieved September 2014, from http://www.casw-acts.ca/en/critical-demand -social-work-canada-volume-1-final-report-2000.

Canadian Association of Social Workers (CASW-ACTS). (2005a). *Code of ethics.* Toronto: Author. Retrieved from http://www.casw-acts.ca/sites/default/ files/attachements/CASW_Code%20of%20Ethics.pdf.

Canadian Association of Social Workers (CASW-ACTS). (2005b). *Guidelines for ethical practice.* Toronto: Author. Retrieved from http://www.casw -acts.ca/sites/default/files/attachements/CASW_Guidelines%20for%20 Ethical%20Practice.pdf.

Canadian Association of Social Workers (CASW-ACTS). (2012). *Canada social transfer project: Accountability matters.* Ottawa, ON: Author. Retrieved from http://casw-acts.ca/sites/default/files/policy_statements/Canada%20 Social%20Transfer%20Project%20Accountability%20Matters_Final%20 Report_E_.pdf.

Canadian Centre for Occupational Health and Safety (CCOHS). (2014, May 28). *Bullying in the workplace.* Retrieved June 4, 2014, from http://www.ccohs .ca/oshanswers/psychosocial/bullying.html.

Canadian Council of Social Work Regulators (CCSWR). (2012, October). *Entry- level competency profile for the social work profession in Canada.* Halifax, NS: Author.

Carniol, B. (2005). *Case critical: Social services and social justice in Canada* (5th ed.). Toronto: Between the Lines Publishing.

Carter, E. A., & McGoldrick, M. (Eds.). (1999). *The expanded family life cycle: Individual, family, and social perspectives.* Boston: Allyn & Bacon.

Castañeda, C. (1984). *The fire from within.* New York: Simon & Schuster.

Castellanos, M., Nájera, L., & Aldama, A. (2012). *Comparative indigeneities of the Americas: Toward a hemispheric approach.* Tucson: University of Arizona Press.

Centers for Disease Control and Prevention (CDC). (2009). *Chronic diseases: The power to prevent, the call to control: At a glance 2009.* Atlanta, GA: Author. Retrieved from http://www.cdc.gov/chronicdisease/resources/ publications/AAG/chronic.htm.

Centers for Disease Control and Prevention (CDC). (2012). *Suicide: Fact sheet. Fact at a glance.* Washington, DC: CDC, National Center for Injury Preven- tion and Control (NCIPC), Division of Violence Prevention. Retrieved from http://www.cdc.gov/violenceprevention/pdf/Suicide-DataSheet-a.pdf.

Chatters, L. M., Taylor, R. J., & Jayakody, R. (1994). Fictive kinship relations in black extended families. *Journal of Comparative Family Studies, 25*(3), 297–312.

Chavez, C., Ski, C., & Thompson, D. (2012). Depression and coronary heart disease: Apprehending the elusive black dog. *International Journal of Cardiology, 158*(3), 335–336.

Chavis, B. F., & Lee, C. (1987). *Toxic waste and race in the United States: A national report on the racial and socioeconomic characteristics of communi- ties with hazardous waste sites.* New York: United Church of Christ Commis- sion for Racial Justice.

Chernesky, R. H. (2003). Examining the glass ceiling: Gender influence on pro- motion decisions. *Administration in Social Work, 27*(2), 13–18.

Chou, W. Y. S., Hunt, Y., Beckjord, E., Moser, R., & Hesse, B. (2009). Social media use in the United States: Implications for health communication. *Journal of Medical Internet Research, 11*(4), e48. doi: 10.2196/jmir.1249.

Churchman, A., & Mitrani, M. (1997). The role of the physical environment in culture shock. *Environment and Behavior, 29*(1), 64–86. doi: 10.1177/001391659702900103.

Clark, K. (2004). Blood quantum and Indian identification. *The Dartmouth College Undergraduate JL, 2*, 40.

Coggins, K. (1990). *Alternative pathways to healing: The recovery medicine wheel.* Deerfield Beach, FL: Health Communications.

Coggins, K. (1996). *Life in a southwest prison: A study of the culture of the penitentiary of New Mexico* (Unpublished doctoral dissertation). University of Michigan, Ann Arbor. Retrieved September 9, 2013, from http://mirlyn.lib.umich.edu.

Coggins, K. (1998). *Families at risk: Planning for prevention/intervention in a traditional Native American community.* Report prepared for the Tribal Administration of the Pueblo of Jemez (Walatowa), New Mexico. Maintained and distributed by the Pueblo of Jemez, at the discretion of the governor.

Coggins, K., & Fresquez, J. E. (2001). *Working with clients in correctional facilities: A guide for social workers and corrections professionals.* Peosta, IA: Eddie Bowers.

Coggins, K., & Fresquez, J. E. (2007). *Working with clients in correctional settings: A guide for social workers and corrections professionals* (Rev. ed.). Peosta, IA: Eddie Bowers.

Coggins, K., & Hatchett, B. F. (2002). *Field practicum: Skill building from a multicultural perspective.* Peosta, IA: Eddie Bowers.

Coggins, K., & Hatchett, B. F. (2009). *Field practicum: Skill building from a multicultural perspective* (2nd ed.). Peosta, IA: Eddie Bowers.

Cohen, K. (2006). *Honoring the medicine: The essential guide to Native American healing.* New York: Ballantine.

Cohen Konrad, S. (2013). *Child and family practice: A relational perspective.* Chicago: Lyceum Books.

Cohen-Mansfield, J., & Werner, P. (1998). Predictors of aggressive behaviors: A longitudinal study in senior day care centers. *Journal of Gerontology, 53B*(5), P300–P310.

Colvin-Burque, A., Zugazaga, C. B., & Davis-Maye, D. (2007). Can cultural competence be taught? Evaluating the impact of the SOAP model. *Journal of Social Work Education, 43*(2), 223–242. doi: 10.5175/JSWE.207.200500528.

Compton, B. R., & Galaway, B. (1999). *Social work processes*. Pacific Grove, CA: Brooks/Cole.

Congress, E. P. (2008). Individual and family development theory. In N. Coady & P. Lehmann (Eds.), *Theoretical perspectives for direct social work practice* (2nd ed., pp. 119–144). New York: Springer.

Cooper, M., & Granucci Lesser, J. (2008). *Clinical social work practice* (3rd ed.). Boston: Pearson.

Corey, G. (2005). *Theory and practice of counseling and psychotherapy* (7th ed.). Belmont, CA: Wadsworth.

Corey, G. (2009a). *Case approach to counseling and psychotherapy* (7th ed.). Belmont, CA: Thomson–Brooks/Cole.

Corey, G. (2009b). *Theory and practice of counseling and psychotherapy* (8th ed.). Belmont, CA: Thomson–Brooks/Cole.

Cormier, S., Nurius, P. S., & Osborn, C. J. (2009). *Interviewing and change strategies for helpers: Fundamental and cognitive behavioral interventions* (6th ed.). Belmont, CA: Brooks/Cole, Cengage Learning.

Corrigan, P. W. (2007). How clinical diagnosis might exacerbate the stigma of mental illness. *Social Work, 52*(1), 31–39. doi: 10.1093/sw/52.1.31.

Cotto, L. (2008). *Exploring the experiences of clinicians treating Latino clients who utilize folk healing practices* (Unpublished master's thesis). Smith College, Northampton, MA.

Council on Social Work Education (CSWE), Commission on Accreditation. (2008). *2008 EPAS handbook*. Alexandria, VA: Author. Retrieved from http://www.cswe.org/Accreditation/2008EPASHandbook.aspx.

Council on Social Work Education (CSWE), Commission on Accreditation. (2015a). *EPAS revision*. Alexandria, VA: Author. Retrieved from http://www.cswe.org/Accreditation/EPASRevision.aspx.

Council on Social Work Education (CSWE), Commission on Accreditation. (2015b). *Final 2015 educational policy (EP)*. Alexandria, VA: Author. Retrieved from http://www.cswe.org/File.aspx?id=79793x.

Cox, F. M., Erlich, J. L., Rothman, J., & Tropman, J. E. (1974). *Strategies of community organization* (2nd ed.). Itasca, IL: F. E. Peacock.

Crain, W. C. (1985). *Theories of development* (2nd ed.). Englewood Cliffs, NJ: Prentice-Hall.

Crawford, J. (1996). Seven hypotheses on language loss causes and cures. *Stabilizing Indigenous Languages*, 53–69. Paper adapted from speech given at the second Symposium on Stabilizing Indigenous Languages, May 4, 1995, Northern Arizona University, Flagstaff.

Dahlberg, L. L., & Krug, E. G. (2002). Violence: A global public health problem. In E. G. Krug, L. L. Dahlberg, J. A. Mercy, A. B. Zwi, & R. Lozano (Eds.), *World report on violence and health* (pp. 1–56). Geneva, Switzerland: World Health Organization.

Dalal, F. (2002). *Race, colour and the process of racialization: New perspectives from group analysis, psychoanalysis, and sociology.* New York: Routledge, Psychology Press.

Davidson, L., & Linnoila, M. (Eds.). (2011). *Risk factors for youth suicide.* New York: Routledge.

Davidson-Hunt, I., Deutsch, N., & Miller, A. (2012). *Pimachiowin Aki cultural landscape atlas: Land that gives life.* Winnipeg, MB: Pimachiowin Aki Corporation.

Davis, S. (2006). *Community mental health in Canada: Theory, policy and practice.* Vancouver: University of British Columbia Press.

De Jong, P., & Kim Berg, I. (2008). *Interviewing for solutions* (3rd ed.). Belmont, CA: Thompson Higher Education.

Denning, P., & Little, J. (2012). *Practicing harm reduction psychotherapy: An alternative approach to addictions* (2nd ed.). New York: Guilford.

Deranger, E. (n.d.). Idle No More movement [Web comment]. Retrieved May 25, 2014, from http://www.idlenomore.ca/.

De Shazer, S. (1988). *Clues: Investigating solutions in brief therapy.* New York: Norton.

De Shazer, S., Dolan, Y. M., Korman, H., Trepper, T. S., McCollum, E. E., & Berg, I. K. (2006). *More than miracles: The state of the art of solution focused therapy.* New York: Haworth.

Dewane, C. J. (2008). 10 leadership strategies for women in social service management. *Social Work Today, 8*(2), 38.

Dewsbury, D. A. (1992). Comparative psychology and ethology: A reassessment. *American Psychologist, 47*(2), 208–215. doi: 10_1037/0003-066X .47.2.208.

Dobson, K. S., Backs-Dermott, B. J., & Dozois, D. J. A. (2000). Cognitive and cognitive-behavioral therapies. In C. R. Snyder & R. E. Ingram (Eds.), *Handbook of psychological change* (pp. 409–428). New York: Wiley.

Dolgoff, R., Harrington, D., & Lowenberg, F. (2012). *Ethical decisions for social work practice* (9th ed.). Belmont, CA: Brooks/Cole, Cengage Learning.

Doran, G. T. (1981). There's a S.M.A.R.T. way to write management's goals and objectives. *Management Review, 70*(11), 35–36.

Douglas, C. (2011). Analytical psychotherapy. In R. Corsini & D. Wedding (Eds.), *Current psychotherapies* (9th ed., pp. 113–147). Belmont, CA: Brooks/Cole.

Dove, E. R., Byrne, S. M., & Bruce, N. W. (2009). Effect of dichotomous thinking on the association of depression with BMI and weight change among obese females. *Behaviour Research and Therapy, 47*(6), 529–534. Retrieved from http://dx.doi.org/10.1016/j.brat.2009.02.013.

Drake, R. E., O'Neal, E. L., & Wallach, M. A. (2008). A systematic review of psychosocial research on psychosocial interventions for people with co-occurring severe mental and substance use disorders. *Journal of Substance Abuse Treatment, 34*(1), 123–138.

Drolet, M., & Mumford, K. (2012). The gender pay gap for private-sector employees in Canada and Britain. *British Journal of Industrial Relations, 50*(3), 529–553. doi: 10.1111/j.1467.8543.2011.00868.

Drucker, P. F. (1954). *The practice of management.* New York: Harper & Row.

D'Souza, M. S., & Markou, A. (2011). Neuronal mechanisms underlying development of nicotine dependence: Implications for novel smoking-cessation treatments. *Addiction Science & Clinical Practice, 6*(11), 4–16.

DuBois, B., & Miley, K. (2011). *Social work: An empowering profession.* Boston: Allyn & Bacon.

DuBrin, A. J. (2011). *Essentials of management* (9th ed.). Boston: Cengage Learning, South-Western College Publishing.

Dunn, C., Deroo, L., & Rivara, F. P. (2001). The use of brief interventions adapted from motivational interviewing across behavioral domains: A systematic review. *Addiction, 96,* 1725–1742.

Duran, E., & Duran, B. (1995). *Postcolonial psychology.* Albany: State University of New York Press.

Dziegielewski, S. F. (2003). *The changing face of health care social work: Professional practice in managed behavioral health care* (2nd ed.). New York: Springer.

Easton, C. (2005). Commentary: Substance abuse and criminality in the mentally disordered defendant. *Journal of the American Academy of Psychiatry and the Law, 33*(2), 196–198.

Eaton, Y., & Ertl, B. (2000). The comprehensive crisis intervention model of Community Integration, Inc. Crisis Services. In A. R. Roberts (Ed.), *Crisis intervention handbook: Assessment, treatment, and research* (2nd ed., pp. 373–387). New York: Oxford University Press.

Edwards, R. L., Shera, W., Nelson Reid, P., & York, R. (2006). Social work practice and education in the US and Canada. *Social Work Education, 25*(1), 28–38. doi: 10.1080/02615470500477821.

Efird, R. (2010). Distant kin: Japan's "war orphans" and the limits of ethnicity. *Anthropological Quarterly, 83*(4), 805–838. doi: 10.1353/anq.2010.0021.

Einarsen, S., Hoel, H., Zapf, D., & Cooper, C. L. (Eds.). (2003). *Bullying and emotional abuse in the workplace: International perspectives in research and practice.* New York: Taylor & Francis.

Einarsen, S., Hoel, H., Zapf, D., & Cooper, C. L. (Eds.). (2011). *Bullying and harassment in the workplace: Developments in theory, research, and practice* (2nd ed.). Boca Raton, FL: CRC Press.

Elder, G. (1996). Human lives in changing societies: Life course and development insights. In R. Cairns, G. Elder, & E. Costello (Eds.), *Developmental science* (pp. 31–62). New York: Cambridge University Press.

Elder, G., & Rockwell, R. (1979). The life-course and human development: An ecological perspective. *International Journal of Behavioral Development, 2*(1), 1–21.

Ellis, T. J. (2015). *A review of the literature: Therapeutic alliance and the importance of facilitating the development of relational skills in clinical psychology students* (Unpublished doctoral dissertation). Biola University, La Mirada, CA.

Engelberg, E., & Sjöberg, L. (2004). Internet use, social skills, and adjustment. *CyberPsychology & Behavior, 7*(1), 41–47. doi: 10.1089/109493104322820101.

Engle, K. (2010). *The elusive promise of Indigenous development: Rights, culture, strategy.* Durham, NC: Duke University Press.

Esbensen, A. J. (2010). Chapter four: Health conditions associated with aging and end of life of adults with Down syndrome. *International Review of Research in Mental Retardation, 39*, 107–126. doi: 10.1016/S0074-7750(10)39004-5.

Esses, V. M., & Gardner, R. C. (1996). Multiculturalism in Canada: Context and current status. *Canadian Journal of Behavioural Science/Revue canadienne des sciences du comportement, 28*(3), 145–152. doi: 10.1037/h0084934.

Etchison, M., & Kleist, D. M. (2000). Review of narrative therapy: Research and utility. *The Family Journal, 8*(1), 61–66.

Evans, D. L., Charney, D. S., Lewis, L., Golden, R. N., Gorman, J. M., Krishnan, K. R. R. K., . . . Valvo, W. J. (2005). Mood disorders in the medically ill: Scientific review and recommendations. *Biological Psychiatry, 58*(3), 175–189.

Evans, D. R., Hearn, M., Uhlemann, M., & Ivey, A. (2008). *Essential interviewing* (7th ed.). Belmont, CA: Thompson Higher Education.

Fall, K., Holden, J., & Marquis, A. (2004). *Theoretical models of counseling and psychotherapy*. New York: Brunner-Routledge.

Fässberg, M. M., Orden, K. A. V., Duberstein, P., Erlangsen, A., Lapierre, S., Bodner, E., . . . Waern, M. (2012). A systematic review of social factors and suicidal behavior in older adulthood. *International Journal of Environmental Research and Public Health, 9*(3), 722–745. doi: 10.3390/ijerph9030722.

Feder, J. L. (2015). Mexico's quiet marriage equality revolution. *BuzzFeed News World*. Retrieved April 12, 2015, from http://www.buzzfeed.com/lester feder/mexicos-quiet-marriage-equality-revolution#.wjNQpPYyK4.

Fellin, P. (1995). Understanding American communities. In J. Rothman, J. L. Erlich, & J. Tropman (Eds.), *Strategies of community intervention* (5th ed., pp. 114–127). Itasca, IL: F. E. Peacock.

Felthous, A., & Sass, H. (Eds.). (2007). *The international handbook of psychopathic disorders and law—Volume II—Laws and policies*. Chichester, UK: Wiley.

Fiore, L. (2011). *Life smart: Exploring human development*. New York: McGraw-Hill.

First, M. B., & Tasman, A. (Eds.). (2004). *DSM-IV-TR mental disorders: Diagnosis, etiology and treatment*. Hoboken, NJ: Wiley.

Fix, M., Zimmermann, W., & Passel, J. S. (2001). *The integration of immigrant families in the United States*. Washington, DC: Immigration Studies, The Urban Institute.

Flay, B. R. (1986). Efficacy and effectiveness trials (and other phases of research) in the development of health promotion programs. *Preventive Medicine, 15*(5), 451–474.

Fleming, W. C. (2003). *The complete idiot's guide to Native American history*. Indianapolis, IN: Penguin.

Flexner, A. (1915, May). *Is social work a profession?* Paper presented at the National Conference of Charities and Corrections, 42nd Annual Session, Baltimore.

Forsyth, D. R. (1990). *Group dynamics*. Pacific Grove, CA: Brooks/Cole.

Franke, R. H., & Kaul, J. D. (1978). The Hawthorne experiments: First statistical interpretation. *American Sociological Review, 43*(5), 623–643.

Frankel, A., & Gelman, S. (2012). *Case management: An introduction to concepts and skills* (3rd ed.). Chicago: Lyceum Books.

Franklin, C., & Jordan, C. (1999). *Family practice: Brief systems methods for social work*. Pacific Grove, CA: Brooks/Cole.

Freeman, A., & Reineke, M. A. (1995). Cognitive therapy. In A. S. Gurman & S. B. Messer (Eds.), *Essential psychotherapies: Theory and practice* (pp. 182–225). New York: Guilford.

Freud, S. (1905). Three essays on the theory of sexuality. In J. Strachey (Ed. and Trans.), *The standard edition of the complete psychological works of Sigmund Freud, 7* (pp. 123–245). London: Hogarth.

Frey, R. J. (2003). Diagnostic and statistical manual of mental disorders. *Gale encyclopedia of mental disorders*. Retrieved November 10, 2013, from http://www.encyclopedia.com/doc/1G2-3405700121.html.

Frey, W. H. (2012, December 13). Census projects new "majority minority" tipping points. *Brookings Research Series: State of Metropolitan America, 60*. Retrieved March 12, 2014, from http://www.brookings.edu/research/opinions/2012/12/13-census-race-projections-frey.

Frick, W. B. (Ed.). (1995). *Personality: Selected readings in theory*. Itasca, IL: F. E. Peacock.

Frideres, J., & Gadacz, R. (2012). *Aboriginal Peoples in Canada* (9th ed.). Toronto: Pearson.

Funk, M., Drew, N., Freeman, M., Faydi, E., & World Health Organization (WHO). (2010). *Mental health and development: Targeting people with mental health conditions as a vulnerable group*. Geneva, Switzerland: Mental Health and Poverty Program, WHO.

Furman, R., Ackerman, A., Loya, M., Jones S., & Negi, N. (2012). The criminalization of immigration: Value conflicts for the social work profession. *Journal of Sociology and Social Welfare, 39*(1), 169–185.

Furman, R., Bender, K., & Rowan, D. (2014). *An experiential approach to group work* (2nd ed.). Chicago: Lyceum Books.

Galan, F. J. (2001). Experiential approach with Mexican-American males with acculturation stress. In H. E. Briggs & K. Corcoran (Eds.), *Social work practice* (pp. 283–302). Chicago: Lyceum Books.

Galanti, G. A. (2000). An introduction to cultural differences. *Western Journal of Medicine, 172*(5), 335–336.

Gallmeyer, A., & Roberts, W. T. (2009). Payday lenders and economically distressed communities: A spatial analysis of financial predation. *The Social Science Journal, 46*(3), 521–538. doi: 10.1016/j.soscij.2009.02.008.

Garvin, C. D., & Tropman, J. E. (1992). *Social work in contemporary society.* Englewood Cliffs, NJ: Prentice-Hall.

Garvin, C. D., & Tropman, J. E. (1998). *Social work in contemporary society* (2nd ed.). Needham Heights, MA: Allyn & Bacon.

Gay, L. R., & Airasian, P. (2003). *Educational research: Competencies for analysis and applications.* Columbus, OH: Merrill Prentice Hall.

Geertz, C. (1973). *The interpretation of cultures.* New York: Basic Books.

Germain, C. B., & Gitterman, A. (Eds.). (1980). *The life model of social work practice: Advances in theory and practice.* New York: Columbia University Press.

Gibson, B. E., Secker, B., Rolfe, D., Wagner, F., Parke, B., & Mistry, B. (2012). Disability and dignity-enabling home environments. *Social Science & Medicine, 74*(2), 211–219.

Gill-Hopple, K., & Brage-Hudson, D. (2012). Compadrazgo: A literature review. *Journal of Transcultural Nursing, 23*(2), 117–123.

Gilligan, C. (1982). *In a different voice: Psychological theory and women's development.* Cambridge, MA: Harvard University Press.

Gingerich, W. J., Kim, J. S., Stams, G. J. J. M., & MacDonald, A. J. (2012). Solution-focused brief therapy outcome research. In C. Franklin, T. S. Trepper, W. J. Gingerich, & E. E. McCollum (Eds.), *Solution-focused brief therapy: A handbook of evidence-based practice* (pp. 95–111). New York: Oxford University Press.

Gingerich, W. J., & Peterson, L. (2013). Effectiveness of solution-focused brief therapy: A systematic qualitative review of controlled outcome studies. *Research on Social Work Practice, 23*(3), 266–283.

Ginsberg, L. H. (1998). *Careers in social work.* Boston: Allyn & Bacon.

Gitterman, A., & Germain, C. (2008). *The life model of social work practice: Advances in theory and practice.* New York: Columbia University Press.

Gladwell, M. (2008). *Outliers: The story of success.* New York: Little, Brown.

Glasgow, R. E., Lichtenstein, E., & Marcus, A. (2003). Why don't we see more translation of health promotion research to practice? Rethinking the efficacy-to-effectiveness transition. *American Journal of Public Health, 93*(8), 1261–1267. doi: 10.2105/AJPH.93.8.1261.

Gogtay, N., Vyas, N. S., Testa, R., Wood, S. J., & Pantelis, C. (2011). Age of onset of schizophrenia: Perspectives from structural neuroimaging studies. *Schizophrenia Bulletin, 37*(3), 504–513. doi: 10.1093/schbul/sbr030.

Goldberg, J., & Ernst, C. (2012). *Managing the side effects of psychotropic medications.* Arlington, VA: American Psychiatric Association-American Psychiatric Publishing.

Goldberg, M. L. (2010). And the world's most gender equal country is. . . . *UN Dispatch: United Nations News & Commentary Global News—Forum.* Retrieved October 10, 2013, from: http://www.undispatch.com/tag/human-development-report.

Goldenberg, H., & Goldenberg, I. (2013). *Family therapy: An overview* (8th ed.). Belmont, CA: Brooks/Cole, Cengage Learning.

Goldney, R., Ruffin, R., Fisher, L., & Wilson, D. (2008). Asthma symptoms associated with depression and lower quality of life: A population survey. *The Medical Journal of Australia, 178*(9), 437–441.

Gonçalves, M. M., Matos, M., & Santos, A. (2009). Narrative therapy and the nature of "innovative moments" in the construction of change. *Journal of Constructivist Psychology, 22*(1), 1–23.

Gone, J. P. (2013, August). A community-based treatment for Native American historical trauma: Prospects for evidence-based practice. *Spirituality in Clinical Practice, 1*(S), 78–94. doi: 10.1037/2326-4500.1.S.78.

Gonzales, M. (2009). *Mexicanos: A history of Mexicans in the United States.* Indianapolis: Indiana University Press.

Good, G., & Beitman, B. (2006). *Counseling and psychotherapy essentials: Integrating theories, skills, and practice.* New York: Norton.

Gould, K. H. (1995). The misconstruing of multiculturalism: The Stanford debate and social work. *Social Work, 40*(2), 198–205. doi: 10.1093/sw/40.2.198.

Graham, J., Swift, K., & Delaney, R. (2012). *Canadian social policy—An introduction* (4th ed.). Toronto: Pearson.

Green, R. G., Baskind, F. R., Mustian, B. E., Reed, L. N., & Taylor, H. R. (2007). Professional education and private practice: Is there a disconnect? *Social Work, 52*(2), 151–159. doi: 10.1093/sw/52.2.151.

Greenburg, J. R., & Mitchell, S. A. (1983). *Object relations in psychoanalytic theory*. Cambridge, MA: Harvard University Press.

Greene, R. R. (2008). *Social work with the aged and their families* (3rd ed.). New Brunswick, NJ: Transaction.

Grossman, J. R. (1995). African American migration to Chicago. In M. G. Holli & P. d'A. Jones (Eds.), *Ethnic Chicago: A multicultural portrait* (4th ed., pp. 303–340). Grand Rapids, MI: Eerdmans.

Grossmann, K. E., & Grossmann, K. (1999). Mary Ainsworth: Our guide to attachment research. *Attachment and Human Development, 1*, 224–228.

Gutiérrez Nájera, L. (2012). Challenges to Zapotec indigenous autonomy in an era of global migration. In M. Castellanos, L. Nájera, & A. Aldama (Eds.), *Comparative indigeneities of the Americas: Toward a hemispheric approach* (pp. 227–242). Tucson: University of Arizona Press.

Guy-Sheftall, B. (Ed.). (1995). *Words of fire: An anthology of African American feminist thought*. New York: Norton.

Hacker, J., & Pierson, P. (2013). The paradox of voting—for Republicans: Economic inequality, political organization, and the American voter. In J. H. Nagel & R. M. Smith (Eds.), *Representation: Elections and beyond* (pp. 139–165). Philadelphia: University of Pennsylvania Press.

Halpern, J. (2010). Social work practice analysis. *Connections, 16*(24), 3. Halifax: Nova Scotia Association of Social Workers.

Halpern, J. (2013). The sandwich generation: Conflicts between adult children and their aging parents. In D. D. Cahn (Ed.), *Conflicts in personal relationships* (pp. 143–162). New York: Routledge.

Hanson, J., & Kurtz, D. V. (2007). Ethnogenesis, imperial acculturation on the frontiers, and the production of ethnic identity: The Genizaro of New Mexico and the Red River Métis. *Social Evolution and History, 6*(1), 3–37.

Hardaway, R. (1999). African American communities on the western frontier. In S. Tchudi (Ed.), *Community in the American west* (pp. 131–145). Reno: The Nevada Humanities Committee.

Hardy, C., & Bellamy, S. (2013). *Child and youth health: Caregiver-infant attachment for Aboriginal families*. Prince George, BC: Public Health Agency of Canada, National Collaborating Centre for Aboriginal Health (NCCAH).

Harrigan, M., Baldwin, S., & Hutchinson, E. (2013). The human life course: The journey begins. In E. Hutchinson (Ed.) & Contributing Authors, *Essentials of human behavior: Integrating person, environment, and the life course* (pp. 374–418). Thousand Oaks, CA: Sage.

Harris, M., & Kottak, C. (1963). The structural significance of Brazilian racial categories. *Sociologia, 25*(3), 203–208.

Harvey, D. (2005). *A brief history of neoliberalism.* New York: Oxford University Press.

Hatchett, B., Duran, D., & Timmons, E. (2000). Family and church support for African Americans with HIV/AIDS. *Journal of Family Ministry, 14*(32–37).

Hatzenbuehler, M. L. (2011). The social environment and suicide attempts in lesbian, gay, and bi-sexual youth. *Pediatrics, 127*(5), 896–903. doi: 10.1542/peds.2010-3020.

Hatzenbuehler, M. L., & Keyes, K. M. (2013). Inclusive anti-bullying policies and reduced risk of suicide attempts in lesbian and gay youth. *Journal of Adolescent Health, 53*(1), S21–S26. doi: 10.1016/j.jadohealth.2012.08.010.

Hayes, C. C., Follette, W. C., & Follette, V. M. (1995). Behavior therapy: A contextual approach. In A. S. Gurman & S. B. Messer (Eds.), *Essential psychotherapies: Theory and practice* (pp. 128–181). New York: Guilford.

Hegar, R. L., & Scannapieco, M. (Eds.). (1999). *Kinship foster care: Policy, practice and research.* New York: Oxford University Press.

Heinonen, T., & Spearman, L. (2010). *Social work practice: Problem solving and beyond* (3rd ed.). Toronto: Nelson Education.

Henggeler, S. W. (2011). Multisystemic therapy: An overview of clinical procedures, outcomes, and policy implications. *Child Psychology and Psychiatry Review, 4*(1), 2–10.

Henggeler, S. W., Schoenwald, S. K., Borduin, C. M., Rowland, M. D., & Cunningham, P. B. (2009). *Multisystemic therapy for antisocial behavior in children and adolescents.* New York: Guilford.

Herek, G. (2012). *Facts about homosexuality and mental health.* Retrieved from http://psychology.ucdavis.edu/rainbow/html/facts_mental_health.html.

Herma, J. L., & Arlow, J. A. (2000). Psychoanalysis. *Microsoft Encarta 2000.* Redmond, WA: Microsoft Corp.

Hettema, J., Steele, J., & Miller, W. R. (2005). Motivational interviewing. *Annual Review of Clinical Psychology, 1,* 91–111. doi: 10.1146/annurev.clinpsy.1.102803.143833.

Higgins, J. (2008). Depopulation impacts. *Newfoundland and Labrador Heritage Web Site: Society and Culture, Community, Outports.* Retrieved May 20, 2014, from http://www.heritage.nf.ca/society/depop_impacts.html.

Hill, C. W., & Jones, G. R. (2008). *Strategic management: An integrated approach.* Mason, OH: South-Western Cengage Learning.

Hinde, R. A. (1989). Ethological and relationship approaches. In R. Vasta (Ed.), *Annals of child development, Vol. 6: Six theories of child development* (pp. 251–285). Greenwich, CT: JAI Press.

Hofmann, S. G., Asnaani, A., Vonk, I. J. J., Sawyer, A. T., & Fang, A. (2012). The efficacy of cognitive behavioral therapy: A review of meta-analyses. *Cognitive Therapy Research, 36*(5), 427–440. doi: 10.1007/s10608-012-9476-1.

Holifield, R. (2001). Defining environmental justice and environmental racism. *Urban Geography, 22*(1), 78–90. doi: 10.2747/0272-3638.22.1.178.

Hopkins, L., Thomas, J., Meredyth, D., & Ewing, S. (2004). Social capital and community building through an electronic network. *Australian Journal of Social Issues, 39*(4), 369–379.

Horvath, A. O. (2015). Therapeutic/working alliance. In R. L. Cautin & S. O. Lilienfeld (Eds.), *Encyclopedia of clinical psychology set.* Hoboken, NJ: Wiley-Blackwell.

Howatt, W. A. (2000). *The human services counseling toolbox: Theory, development, technique, and resources.* Scarborough, ON: Thomson–Brooks/Cole.

Hsiao, W. C., Kappel, S., & Gruber, J. (2011). Act 128—Health System Reform Design: Achieving affordable universal health care in Vermont—Updated January 21, 2011. Montpelier: Legislative Council and the Vermont Health Care Reform Commission.

Hubert, H. B., Bloch, D. A., Oehlert, J. W., & Fries, J. F. (2002). Lifestyle habits and compression of morbidity. *The Journals of Gerontology Series A: Biological Sciences and Medical Sciences, 57*(6), M347–M351. doi: 10.1093/gerona/57.6.M347.

Hurdle, D. E. (2002). Native Hawaiian traditional healing: Culturally based interventions for social work practice. *Social Work, 47*(2), 183–192. doi: 10.1093/sw/47.2.183.

Hutchinson, D. L. (2000). Out, yet unseen: A racial critique of gay and lesbian legal theory and political discourse. In R. Delgado & J. Stefancic (Eds.), *Critical race theory: The cutting edge* (2nd ed., pp. 325–333). Philadelphia: Temple University Press.

Hutchinson, E. D., & Charlesworth, L. (2013). Theoretical perspectives on human behavior. In E. Hutchinson (Ed.), *Essentials of human behavior: Integrating person, environment, and the life course* (pp. 35–108). Thousand Oaks, CA: Sage.

Hutchinson, E. D. (Ed.), & Contributors. (2011). *Dimensions of human behavior: Person and environment* (4th ed.). Thousand Oaks, CA: Sage.

Iannello, K. P. (1992). *Decisions without hierarchy: Feminist interventions in organization theory and practice.* New York: Routledge.

Industry Canada. (2007). *Agreement on international trade: Chapter seven, Labour mobility.* Ottawa, ON: Author.

Ingram, R. E. (1984). Toward an information-processing analysis of depression. *Cognitive Therapy and Research, 8*(5), 443–477.

Ivey, A., & Ivey, M. (2007). *International interviewing and counseling: Facilitating client development.* Belmont, CA: Thomson–Brooks/Cole.

Iyer, P. W. (Ed.). (2001). *Nursing malpractice* (2nd ed.). Tucson, AZ: Lawyers and Judges Publishing.

Jaimes, M. A., & Halsey, T. (1992). American Indian women at the center of Indigenous resistance in contemporary North America. In M. A. Jaimes (Ed.), *The state of Native America: Genocide, colonization, and resistance* (pp. 311–344). Boston: South End Press.

James, R. K., & Gilliland, B. E. (2013). *Crisis intervention strategies* (7th ed.). Belmont, CA: Brooks/Cole, Cengage Learning.

Johnson, Y. M., & Munch, S. (2009). Fundamental contradictions in cultural competence. *Social Work, 54*(3), 220–231. doi: 10.1093/sw/54.3.220.

Johnston, L. (2012, May 31). Native American medicine (Web article). *Perspectives in Holistic Health.* Retrieved from http://www.healingtherapies.info/Native-American%20Medicine.htm.

Jones, T., & Perry, J. (2012). *Contemporary issues in California archeology.* Walnut Creek, CA: Left Coast Press.

Jordan, C., & Franklin, C. (2011). *Clinical assessment for social workers: Qualitative and quantitative methods.* Chicago: Lyceum Books.

Jung, C. (1964). *Man and his symbols.* New York: Doubleday.

Kail, R. V., & Cavanaugh, J. C. (1996). *Human development.* Pacific Grove, CA: Brooks/Cole.

Kana'iaupuni, S. M., & Malone, N. (2006). This land is my land: The role of place in Native Hawaiian identity. *Hulili: Multidisciplinary Research on Hawaiian Well-Being, 3*(1), 281–307.

Kanel, K. (2012). *A guide to crisis intervention* (4th ed.). Belmont, CA: Brooks/ Cole, Cengage Learning.

Kaplan, H. I., & Sadock, B. J. (1998). *Synopsis of psychiatry: Behavioral sciences/ clinical psychiatry* (8th ed.). Baltimore: Williams & Wilkins.

Kaplan, M. S., Huguet, N., McFarland, B. H., & Mandle, J. A. (2012). Factors associated with suicide by firearm among US older adult men. *Psychology of Men & Masculinity, 13*(1), 65–74. doi: 10.1037/a0023173.

Kaslow, N. J., & Celano, M. P. (1995). The family therapies. In A. S. Gurman & S. B. Messer (Eds.), *Essential psychotherapies: Theory and practice* (pp. 343–402). New York: Guilford.

Katz, D., & Kahn, R. L. (1978). *The social psychology of organizations* (2nd ed.). New York: Wiley.

Kaufman, C. (2003). *Ideas for action: Relevant theory for radical change.* Cambridge, MA: South End Press.

Kemppainen, D., Kopera-Frye, K., & Woodard, J. (2008). The medicine wheel: A versatile tool for promoting positive change in diverse contexts. *Collected Essays on Learning and Teaching: The Evolving Scholarship of Teaching and Learning, 1,* 80–84.

Kenney, G. M., Dubuy, L., Zuckerman, M., & Huntress, M. (2012). Opting out of the Medicaid expansion under the ACA: How many uninsured adults would not be eligible for Medicaid? *Urban Institute, Health Policy Center Newsletter,* 1–3.

King, T. (2012). *The inconvenient Indian: A curious account of Native people in North America.* Toronto: Doubleday Canada.

Kirst-Ashman, K. K., & Hull, H. G. Jr. (1999). *Understanding generalist practice* (2nd ed.). Chicago: Nelson-Hall.

Kistaiah, M. (1991). George Elton Mayo. In D. R. Prasad, V. S. Prasad, & P. Sathyanarayana (Eds.). *Administrative thinkers* (pp. 122–135). New Delhi: Sterling.

Knegt, P. (2011). *About Canada: Queer rights.* Black Point, NS: Fernwood.

Knopf, K. (2008). *Decolonizing the lens of power: Indigenous films in North America* (Vol. 100). Amsterdam: Rodopi.

Knox, K. S., & Roberts, A. R. (2008). The crisis intervention model. In N. Coady & P. Lehmann (Eds.), *Theoretical perspectives for direct social work practice: A generalist-eclectic approach* (2nd ed., pp. 249–274). New York: Springer.

Kohlberg, L. (1963). The development of children's orientations toward a moral order. *Human Development, 6*(1–2), 11–33.

Koltko-Rivera, M. E. (2006). Rediscovering the later version of Maslow's hierarchy of needs: Self-transcendence and opportunities for theory, research, and unification. *Review of General Psychology, 10*(4), 302–317. doi: 10.1037/1089-2680.10.4.302.

Koning, H. (1992). The legacy of Columbus. *Social Justice, 19*(2), 35–38.

Kottak, C. (1991). *Cultural anthropology* (5th ed.). New York: McGraw-Hill.

Kouzes, J. M., & Posner, B. Z. (1987). *The leadership challenge: How to get extraordinary things done in organizations.* San Francisco: Wiley, Jossey-Bass.

Krasilnikov, P., & Tabor, J. (2003). Ethnopedology and folk soil taxonomies. Crop and soil sciences. In W. H. Verheye (Ed.), *Encyclopedia of life support systems (EOLSS),* developed under the auspices of the United Nations Educational, Scientific and Cultural Organization (UNESCO). Oxford, UK: EOLSS Publishers. Retrieved November 10, 2013, from: http://www.eolss.net.

Krentzman, A. R., & Townsend, A. L. (2008). Review of multidisciplinary measures of cultural competence for use in social work education. *Journal of Social Work Education, 44*(2), 7–32. doi: 10.5175/JSWE.2008.200600003.

Kreuger, L., & Neuman, W. L. (2006). *Social work research methods: Qualitative and quantitative applications.* Boston: Pearson.

Krieg, E. J. (1998). The two faces of toxic waste: Trends in the spread of environmental hazards. *Sociological Forum, 13*(1), 3–20.

Kropf, N., & Tandy, C. (1998). Narrative therapy with older clients: The use of a meaning-making approach. *Clinical Gerontologist, 18*(4), 3–16.

Krupnick, J. L., Sotsky, S. M., Elkin, I., Simmens, S., Moyer, J., Watkins, J., & Pilkonis, P. A. (2014). The role of the therapeutic alliance in psychotherapy and pharmacotherapy outcome: Findings in the National Institute of Mental Health Treatment of Depression Collaborative Research Program. *Focus, 4*(2), 269–277. Retrieved from http://dx.doi.org/10.1176/foc.4.2.269.

Krysik, J. L., & Finn, J. (2007). *Research for effective social work practice.* Boston: McGraw-Hill.

Lægaard, J. (2006). *Organizational theory.* Frederiksberg, Denmark: Ventus, Bookboon.com.

Laplanche, J., & Pontalis, J. (2006). *The language of psychoanalysis.* London: Karnac Books.

LaVeist, T., & Isaac, L. (2013). *Race, ethnicity, and health: A public health reader* (2nd ed.). San Francisco: Wiley.

Leahy, R. L. (Ed.). (2004). *Contemporary cognitive therapy: Theory, research, and practice.* New York: Guilford.

Lee, E., & Mock, M. R. (2005). Asian families. In M. McGoldrick, J. Giordano, & N. Garcia-Prieto (Eds.), *Ethnicity & family therapy* (3rd ed., pp. 269–289). New York: Guilford.

Lees, L., Slater, T., & Wyly, E. (2008). *Gentrification.* New York: Routledge.

Leigh, J. W. (1998). *Communicating for cultural competence.* Boston: Allyn & Bacon.

Leigland, S. (2007). Beyond freedom and dignity at 40: Comments on behavioural science, the future, and chance. *The Behavioral Analyst, 34*(2), 283–295.

Levinson, D. (1978). *The seasons of a man's life.* New York: Knopf.

Levinson, D., & Levinson, M. (1996). *The seasons of a woman's life.* New York: Ballantine.

Lewis, H. D. (2001). Third parties beware: The Texas Supreme Court strengthens psychotherapist-client confidentiality in *Thapar v. Zezulka. Houston Journal of Health Law and Policy, 1*(1), 263–296.

Linhard, T. (2005). *Fearless women in the Mexican Revolution and the Spanish Civil War.* Columbia: University of Missouri Press.

Luborsky, E., O'Reilly-Landry, M., & Arlow, J. (2011). Psychoanalysis. In R. Corsini & D. Wedding (Eds.), *Current psychotherapies* (9th ed., pp. 15–66). Belmont, CA: Brooks/Cole.

Lundy, C. (2011). *Social work, social justice, and human rights: A structural approach to practice* (2nd ed.). Toronto: University of Toronto Press.

Macias, A. (1980). Women and the Mexican Revolution, 1910–1920. *The Americas, 37*(1), 53–82.

Mackrael, K. (2011, December 6). Canada's prisons are becoming warehouses for the mentally ill. *The Globe and Mail, Health Section.* Retrieved from http://www.theglobeandmail.com/news/politics/canadas-prisons -becoming-warehouses-for-the-mentally-ill/article4236899/.

Madigan, S. (2013). Narrative therapy. In M. Davies (Ed.), *The Blackwell companion to social work* (4th ed., pp. 455–458). Malden, MA: Wiley.

Madson, M., Mohn, R., Zuckoff, A., Schumacher, A., Kogan, J., Hutchison, S., Magee, E., & Stein, B. (2013). Measuring client perceptions of motivational interviewing: Factor analysis of the client evaluation of Motivational Interviewing Scale. *Journal of Substance Abuse Treatment, 44*(3), 330–335.

Main, M., & Solomon, J. (1990). Procedures for identifying infants as disorganized/disoriented during the Ainsworth Strange Situation. *Attachment in the Preschool Years: Theory, Research, and Intervention, 1*, 121–160.

Manitoba Historical Society. (2013, March 6). *Historical site of Manitoba: Red River floodway (Winnipeg).* Retrieved May 6, 2014, from http://www.mhs .mb.ca/docs/sites/redriverfloodway.shtml.

Marr, G. (2014, April 22). Canada leading ranks of shrinking middle class. *National Post: Financial Post, Economy.* Retrieved from http://www.national post.com/scripts/Canada+leading+ranks+shrinking+middle+class/ 9766434/story.html.

Marten, G. G. (2001). *Human ecology: Basic concepts for sustainable development.* Sterling, VA: Earthscan, International Institute for Environment and Development.

Martin, D., & Yurkovich, E. (2014). "Close-knit" defines a healthy Native American Indian family. *Journal of Family Nursing, 20*(1), 51–72. doi: 10.1177/ 1074840713508604.

Maruish, M. E. (2002). *Essentials of treatment planning.* New York: Wiley.

Maslow, A. (1954). *Motivation and personality.* New York: Harper Collins.

Maslow, A. (1970). *Motivation and personality* (3rd ed.). New York: Harper Collins.

Matlin, M. (2004). *The psychology of women* (5th ed.). Belmont, CA: Wadsworth/ Thompson Learning.

Mayo Clinic. (2012, June 9). *Diseases and conditions: Suicide and suicidal thoughts, symptoms.* Retrieved April 23, 2014, from http://www.mayo clinic.org/diseases-conditions/suicide/basics/symptoms/CON-20033954.

McCarty, T. L., Romero-Little, M. E., Warhol, L., & Zepeda, O. (2014). Critical ethnography and Indigenous language survival. In T. L. McCarty (Ed.), *Ethnography and language policy: Some new directions in language policy research and praxis* (pp. 31–51). New York: Taylor & Francis.

McCormick, R. (2009). Aboriginal approaches to counselling. In L. Kirmayer & G. Valaskakis (Eds.), *Healing traditions: The mental health of Aboriginal Peoples in Canada* (pp. 337–354). Vancouver: University of British Columbia Press.

McDermott, J., Tseng, W., & Maretzki, T. (1980). *Peoples and cultures of Hawaii: A psychocultural profile.* Honolulu: University of Hawaii Press.

McGibbon, E. A., & Hallstrom, L. K. (2012). Oppression and the political economy of health inequalities. In E. A. McGibbon (Ed.), *Oppression: A social determinant of health* (pp. 167–185). Halifax, NS, & Winnipeg, MB: Fernwood.

McGilly, F. (1998). *An introduction to Canada's public social services: Understanding income and health programs* (2nd ed.). Toronto: Oxford University Press.

McGoldrick, M., Gerson, R., & Petry, S. (2008). *Genograms: Assessment and intervention* (3rd ed.). New York: Norton.

McGoldrick, M., Giordano, J., & Garcia-Prieto, N. (Eds.). (2005). *Ethnicity & family therapy* (3rd ed.). New York: Guilford.

McLeod, J. (2010). *Beginning postcolonialism* (2nd ed.). Manchester, UK: Manchester University Press.

McMillan, J. H. (2004). *Educational research: Fundamentals for the consumer* (4th ed.). Boston: Allyn & Bacon.

McWhirter, J. J., McWhirter, B. T., McWhirter, A. M., & McWhirter, E. H. (1998). *At-risk youth: A comprehensive response* (2nd ed.). Pacific Grove, CA: Brooks/Cole.

Meichenbaum, D. H., & Deffenbacher, J. L. (1985). Stress inoculation training. *The Counseling Psychologist, 16*(1), 69–90. doi: 10.1177/0011000088161005.

Meichenbaum, D. H., & Deffenbacher, J. L. (1996). Stress inoculation training for coping with stressors. *The Clinical Psychologist, 49*(1), 4–7.

Meyer, M., & Beezley, W. (2000). *The Oxford history of Mexico.* New York: Oxford University Press.

Michels, R. (1962). *Political parties: A sociological study of the oligarchical tendencies of modern democracy.* New York: The Free Press.

Miller, G. (2010). *Learning the language of addiction counseling* (3rd ed.). Hoboken, NJ: Wiley.

Miller, J., & Garran, A. M. (2008). *Racism in the United States: Implications for the helping professions.* Belmont, CA: Thomson–Brooks/Cole.

Miller, J. B. (1991). The development of women's sense of self. In J. V. Jordan, A. G. Kaplan, J. B. Miller, I. P. Stiver, & J. L. Surrey (Eds.), *Women's growth in connection: Writings from the Stone Center* (pp. 11–26). New York: Guilford.

Miller, W. R., & Rollnick, S. (2002). *Motivational interviewing: Preparing people for change* (2nd ed.). New York: Guilford.

Miller, W. R., Zweben, A., DiClemente, C. C., & Rychtarik, R. G. (1994). *Motivational enhancement therapy manual: A clinical research guide for therapists treating individuals with alcohol abuse and dependence* (NIH Publication No. 94-3723). Rockville, MD: National Institute on Alcohol Abuse and Alcoholism.

Milliken, E. J. (2008). *Toward cultural safety: An exploration of the concept for social work education with Canadian Aboriginal Peoples.* (Unpublished doctoral dissertation). Memorial University of Newfoundland, St. John's.

Minuchin, S. (1974). *Families and family therapy.* Cambridge, MA: Harvard University Press.

Miserandino, M. (2012). *Personality psychology: Foundations and findings.* Boston: Pearson.

Mokuau, N. (1990). The impoverishment of Native Hawaiians and the social work challenge. *Health and Social Work, 15*(3), 235–242.

Monk, G. (1997). How narrative therapy works. In G. Monk, J. Winslade, K. Crocket, & D. Epston (Eds.), *Narrative therapy in practice: The archaeology of hope. The Jossey-Bass psychology series* (pp. 3–31). San Francisco: Jossey-Bass.

Morales, A. T., & Sheafor, B. W. (1998). *Social work: A profession of many faces* (8th ed.). Needham Heights, MA: Allyn & Bacon.

Morales, A. T., Sheafor, B. W., & Scott, M. (2012). *Social work: A profession of many faces* (12th ed.). Boston: Allyn & Bacon.

Morgan, A. (2000). *What is narrative therapy? An easy-to-read introduction.* Adelaide, Australia: Dulwich Centre Publications.

Morgensen, S. L. (2012). Theorising gender, sexuality and settler colonialism: An introduction. *Settler Colonial Studies, 2*(2), 2–22. doi: 10.1080/2201473X.2012.10648839.

Mosak, H., & Maniacci, M. (2011). Adlerian psychotherapy. In R. Corsini & D. Wedding (Eds.), *Current psychotherapies* (9th ed., pp. 67–112). Belmont, CA: Brooks/Cole.

Moses, M. S. (2004). Social welfare, the neo-conservative turn and educational opportunity. *Journal of Philosophy of Education, 38*(2), 275–286. doi: 10.1111/ j.0309-8249.2004.00382.x.

Moxley, D. P. (1997). *Case management by design: Reflections on principles and practices.* Chicago: Nelson-Hall.

Muir, B., & Booth, A. (2012). An environmental justice analysis of caribou recovery planning, protection of an Indigenous culture, and coal mining development in northeast British Columbia, Canada. *Environment, Development, and Sustainability, 14*(4), 455–476. doi: 10.1007/ s10668-011-9333-5.

Mumby, D. K. (2000). Communication, organization, and the public sphere: A feminist perspective. In P. M. Buzzanell (Ed.), *Rethinking organizational and managerial communication from feminist perspectives* (pp. 3–23). Thousand Oaks, CA: Sage.

Nathan, P. E., & Gorman, J. M. (Eds.). (2007). *A guide to treatments that work* (3rd ed.). New York: Oxford University Press.

The National Alliance on Mental Illness (NAMI). (2009, October). *Depression in older persons fact sheet.* Arlington, VA: Author.

National Association of Black Social Workers (NABSW). (n.d.[a]). NABSW: Code of ethics. Washington, DC: Author. Retrieved October 3, 2013, from http://nabsw.org/?page=CodeofEthics.

National Association of Black Social Workers (NABSW). (n.d.[b]). NABSW: History. Washington, DC: Author. Retrieved October 3, 2013, from http://nabsw.org/?page=History.

National Association of Social Workers (NASW). (1996). *Code of ethics of the National Association of Social Workers.* Washington, DC: NASW Press.

National Association of Social Workers (NASW). (2008). *Code of ethics of the National Association of Social Workers.* Washington, DC: NASW Press.

National Association of Social Workers (NASW). (2013). *NASW—Standards for social work case management* [Pamphlet]. Washington, DC: Author.

Naylor, T. (2010). Neoliberalism: Neoconservatism without a smirk. *Second Vermont Republic Essays.* Retrieved October 8, 2013, from http://vermont republic.org.

Nebelkopf, E., & King, J. (2003). Holistic system of care for Native Americans in an urban environment. *Journal of Psychoactive Drugs, 1*(35), 43–52. doi: 10.1080/02791072.2003.10399992.

Nelson, G. (2006). Mental health policy in Canada. In A. Westhues (Ed.), *Canadian social policy: Issues and perspectives* (4th ed., pp. 245–266). Waterloo, ON: Wilfrid Laurier University Press.

Netting, F. E., Kettner, P. M., & McMurtry, S. L. (2004). *Social work macro practice* (3rd ed.). New York: Longman.

Niemi, R. G., Weisberg, H. F., & Kimball, D. (Eds.). (2010). *Controversies in voting behavior* (5th ed.). Washington, DC: CQ Press.

Nordenstam, B. J. (1995). Transformation of grassroots environmental justice into federal agency environmental policy. *AAAS/EPA environmental science and engineering fellowship reports* (pp. 51–66). Washington, DC: American Association for the Advancement of Science and the United States Environmental Protection Agency.

Nydegger, C. N. (2014). Asymmetrical kin and the problematic son-in-law. In N. Datan, A. L. Greene, & H. W. Reese (Eds.), *Life-span developmental psychology: Intergenerational relations* (pp. 99–124). New York: Psychology Press.

Nye, R. (1981). *Three psychologies: Perspectives from Freud, Skinner, and Rogers* (2nd ed.). Monterey, CA: Brooks/Cole.

O'Brien, C. P., & McKay, J. (2007). Psychopharmacological treatments for substance use disorders. In P. E. Nathan & J. M. Gorman (Eds.), *A guide to treatments that work* (3rd ed., pp. 145–178). New York: Oxford University Press.

Odhiambo Atieno, E. S. (1992). *Burying S. M.: The politics of knowledge and sociology of power in Africa.* Portsmouth, NH: James Currey and Heinemann.

Ontario, HealthForceOntario, Interprofessional Care Steering Committee. (2007). *Inter-professional care: A blueprint for action in Ontario—July 2007.* Toronto: Author. Retrieved from www.healthforceontario.ca/UserFiles/file/PolicymakersResearchers/ipc-blueprint-july-2007-en.pdf.

Ortega, R., & Faller Coulburn, K. (2011). Training child welfare workers from an intersectional cultural humility perspective: A paradigm shift. *Child Welfare, 90*(5), 27–49. Atlanta, GA: Child Welfare League of America.

Ortiz, A. (1969). *The Tewa world: Space, time, being, and becoming in a pueblo.* Chicago: University of Chicago Press.

Ouchi, W. G. (1981). *Theory Z: How American business can meet the Japanese challenge.* Boston: Addison-Wesley.

Palmater, P. D. (2012). Harper's manifesto: Erasing Canada's indigenous communities. *Rabble.ca*. Retrieved October 8, 2013, from http://rabble.ca.

Palmer, H. (1976). Mosaic versus melting pot? Immigration and ethnicity in Canada and the United States. *International Journal, 31*(3), 488–528.

Papadopoulos, R. (2006). *The handbook of Jungian psychology: Theory, practice, and applications*. New York: Routledge.

Parry, G. (2005). *Political elites*. Colchester, UK: ECPR Press.

Paterlini, M. (2007). There shall be order. The legacy of Linnaeus in the age of molecular biology. *EMBO Reports, 8*(9), 814–816. doi: 10.1038/sj.embor .7401061.

Patient Protection and Affordable Care Act (PPACA). (2010). *Affordable Care Act*. Washington, DC: Department of Labor. Retrieved from http://www.dol .gov/ebsa/healthreform/.

Payne, M. (2005). *Modern social work theory* (3rd ed.). Chicago: Lyceum Books.

Payne, M. (2006). *Narrative therapy*. Thousand Oaks, CA: Sage.

Payne, M. (2013). "Deemed unsuitable": Black pioneers in western Canada. *The Canadian Encyclopedia, Historica Foundation of Canada*. Retrieved October 6, 2013, from http://www.thecanadianencyclopedia.com.

Payne, M. (2014). *Modern social work theory* (4th ed.). Chicago: Lyceum Books.

Pear, J. (2010). *A historical and contemporary look at psychological systems*. New York: Psychological Press.

Peat, D. (1987). *Synchronicity: The bridge between matter and mind*. Toronto: Bantam.

Perlman, H. H. (1957). *Social casework: A problem-solving process*. Chicago: University of Chicago Press.

Perry, R. (2003). Who wants to work with the poor and the homeless? *Journal of Social Work Education, 39*(2), 321–341.

Peters, M. E., Taylor, J., Lyketsos, C. G., & Chisolm, M. S. (2012). Beyond the DSM: The perspectives of psychiatry approach to patients. *The Primary Care Companion to CNS Disorders, 14*(1). doi: 10.4088/PCC.11m01233.

Pincus, A., & Minahan, A. (1973). *Social work practice: Model and method*. Itasca, IL: F. E. Peacock.

Pittenger, D. J. (2005). Cautionary comments regarding the Myers-Briggs Type Indicator. *Consulting Psychology Journal: Practice and Research, 57*(3), 210–221. doi: 10.1037/1065-9293.57.3.210.

Popple, P. R. (2008). Social services. In T. Mizrahi & L. E. Davis (Eds.-in-Chief), *Encyclopedia of social work, 20*(4), 98–101. Washington, DC, and New York: NASW Press and Oxford University Press.

Popple, P. R., & Leighninger, L. (2011). *Social work, social welfare, and American society* (8th ed.). Boston: Allyn & Bacon.

Prendergast, N. (2011). Sankofa: Reclaiming my voice through Canadian black feminist theorizing. *Canadian Woman Studies, 29*(1–2), 121–126.

Prochaska, J. O., DiClemente, C. C., & Norcross, J. C. (1992). In search of how people change: Applications to addictive behaviors. *American Psychologist, 47*(9), 1102–1114.

Prochaska, J. O., & Prochaska, J. M. (2009). Change (stages of). In S. J. Lopez (Ed.), *The encyclopedia of positive psychology, volume I: A–M* (pp. 125–128). Malden, MA: Wiley-Blackwell.

Public Services Health & Safety Association (PSHSA). (2010). *Bullying in the workplace: A handbook for the workplace* (2nd ed.). Toronto: Author.

Pumphrey, M. W. (1959). *The teaching of values and ethics in social work education: A project report of the curriculum study* (Vol. 13). New York: Council on Social Work Education.

Purnell, L. D. (2014). *Guide to culturally competent health care* (3rd ed.). Philadelphia: F. A. Davis.

Putnam, R. D. (1995). Bowling alone: America's declining social capital. *The Journal of Democracy, 6*(1), 65–78. doi: 10.1353/jod.1995.0002.

Rambo, A., West, C., Schooley, A., & Boyd, T. V. (Eds.). (2012). *Family therapy review: Contrasting contemporary models.* New York: Routledge.

Ramey, H. L., Tarulli, D., Frijters, J. C., & Fisher, L. (2009). A sequential analysis of externalizing in narrative therapy with children. *Contemporary Family Therapy, 31*, 262–279. doi: 10.1007/s10591-009-9095-5.

Rankin, P. (2007). Exploring and describing the strength/empowerment perspective in social work. *IUC Journal of Theory and Practice, 14.4.* Retrieved October 28, 2013, from http://www.bemidjistate.edu/academics/publications/social_work_journal/issue14/articles/rankin.htm.

Rasmussen, B., & Salhani, D. (2010). A contemporary Kleinian contribution to understanding racism. *Social Service Review, 84*(3), 491–513.

Reamer, F. G. (2005). Documentation in social work: Evolving ethical and risk-management standards. *Social Work, 50*(4), 325–334. doi: 10.1093/sw/50.4.325.

Reamer, F. G. (2006). *Social work values and ethics* (3rd ed.). New York: Columbia University Press.

Reber, A. S. (1995). *The Penguin dictionary of psychology* (2nd ed.). London: Penguin.

Reed, B. (2012). The lies Republicans tell about Obama and welfare. *The Nation*. Retrieved October 28, 2013, from http://www.thenation.com/blog/.

Reid, W. J. (1988). Brief task-centered treatment. In R. A. Dorfman (Ed.), *Paradigms of clinical social work* (pp. 196–219). New York: Brunner-Routledge.

Reid, W. J., & Fortune, A. E. (2002). The task-centered model. In A. R. Roberts & G. J. Greene (Eds.), *Social workers' desk reference* (pp. 101–104). Oxford, UK: Oxford University Press.

Rieckmann, T., McCarty, D., Kovas, A., Spicer, P., Bray, J., Gilbert, S., & Mercer, J. (2012). American Indians with substance use disorders: Treatment needs and comorbid conditions. *The American Journal of Drug and Alcohol Abuse, 38*(5), 498–504. doi: 10.3109/00952990.2012.694530.

Risley-Curtiss, C. (2010). Social work practitioners and the human-companion animal bond: A national study. *Social Work, 55*(1), 38–46. doi: 10.1093/sw/55.1.38.

Roberts, A. R. (1991). Conceptualizing crisis theory and the crisis intervention model. In A. R. Roberts (Ed.), *Contemporary perspectives on crisis intervention and prevention* (pp. 3–17). Englewood Cliffs, NJ: Prentice-Hall.

Roberts, A. R. (Ed.). (2000). *Crisis intervention handbook: Assessment, treatment, and research* (2nd ed.). New York: Oxford University Press.

Roberts, A. R. (Ed.). (2005). *Crisis intervention handbook: Assessment, treatment, and research* (3rd ed.). New York: Oxford University Press.

Robinson, B. (2013, June). *Same-sex marriages (SSM) and civil union. 2013-APR: Current status: In the US, Canada, South America, Europe, etc.* Religious Tolerance.org: Ontario Consultants on Religious Tolerance. Retrieved October 7, 2013, from http://www.religioustolerance.org/hom_mar16.htm.

Rodgers, R., & Hunter, J. E. (1991). Impact of management by objectives on organizational productivity. *Journal of Applied Psychology, 76*(2), 322–336. doi: 10.1037/0021-9010.76.2.322.

Rogers, C. R. (1957). The necessary and sufficient conditions of therapeutic personality change. *Journal of Counseling Psychology, 21*(2), 95–103. doi: 10.1037/h0045357.

Rogers, C. R. (1986). Carl Rogers on the development of the person-centered approach. *Person-Centered Review, 1*(3), 257–259.

Rogers, G., Collins, D., Barlow, C. A., & Grinnell, R. M. Jr. (2000). *Guide to the social work field practicum: A team approach.* Itasca, IL: F. E. Peacock.

Roseborough, D. J. (2006). Psychodynamic psychotherapy: An effectiveness study. *Research on Social Work Practice, 16*(2), 166–175. doi: 10.1177/1049731505281373.

Roth, A., & Fonagy, P. (2005). *What works for whom* (2nd ed.). New York: Guilford.

Rothman, J. (1974). Three models of community organization practice. In F. M. Cox (Ed.), *Strategies of community organization: A book of readings* (2nd ed., pp. 22–38). Itasca, IL: F. E. Peacock.

Rothman, J. (1995). Approaches to community intervention. In J. Rothman, J. L. Erlich, & J. E. Tropman (Eds.), *Strategies of community intervention* (5th ed.). Itasca, IL: F. E. Peacock.

Rothman, J. (1998). *From the front lines: Student cases in social work ethics.* Boston: Allyn & Bacon.

Rothman, J. (2001). Approaches to community intervention. In J. Rothman, J. L. Erlich, & J. E. Tropman (Eds.), *Strategies of community intervention* (6th ed., pp. 27–64). Belmont, CA: Wadsworth/Thomson Learning.

Rothman, J. (2008). Multi modes of community intervention. In J. Rothman, J. L. Erlich, & J. E. Tropman (Eds.), *Strategies of community intervention* (7th ed., pp. 140–170). Peosta, IA: Eddie Bowers.

Rothman, J., & Sager, J. S. (1998). *Case management: Integrating individual and community practice* (2nd ed.). Boston: Allyn & Bacon.

Rowell, P. (2005). Being a target at work: Or William Tell and how the apple felt. *Journal of Nursing Administration, 35*(9), 377–379.

Royse, D., Dhooper, S. S., & Rompf, E. L. (1996). *Field instruction: A guide for social work students* (2nd ed.). White Plains, NY: Longman.

Rudd, M. D., Joiner, T. E., & Rajab M. H. (2001). *Treating suicidal behavior: An effective time-limited approach.* New York: Guilford.

Sadock, B. J., Kaplan, H. I., & Sadock, V. A. (2007). *Kaplan & Sadock's synopsis of psychiatry: Behavioral sciences/clinical psychiatry.* Baltimore: Lippincott Williams & Wilkins.

Sadock, B. J., & Sadock, V. A. (2007). *Kaplan and Sadock's synopsis of psychiatry* (10th ed.). Philadelphia: Lippincott Williams & Wilkins.

Saleebey, D. (2002). *The strengths perspective in social work practice* (3rd ed.). Boston: Allyn & Bacon.

Sando, J. S. (2008). *Nee Hemish: A history of Jemez Pueblo.* Santa Fe, NM: Clear Light.

Sarinen, S., Matzanke, D., & Smeall, D. (2011). The business case: Collaborating to help employees maintain their mental well-being. *Healthcare Papers, 11,* 78–84.

Sawchuk, P. H., & Kempf, A. (2008). *The migrant worker as racialized commodity: Exploitation and resistance in Canadian guest worker programs.* Toronto: Ontario Institute for Studies of Education, University of Toronto.

Schachar, R., & Ickowicz, A. (2014). Funding for mental health research: Looking ahead. *Journal of the Canadian Academy of Child and Adolescent Psychiatry, 23*(2), 84–85.

Schein, E. H. (2010). *Organizational culture and leadership* (4th ed.). San Francisco: Wiley, Jossey-Bass.

Schiff, J. W., & Moore, K. (2006). The impact of the sweat lodge ceremony on dimensions of well-being. *American Indian and Alaska Native Mental Health Research: The Journal of the National Center, 13*(3), 48–69.

Schmidt, C. (2011). Blind rush? Shale gas boom proceeds amid human health questions. *Environmental Health Perspectives, 119*(8), a348–a353. doi: 10.1289/ehp.119-a348.

Schott, L., & Cho, C. (2011). *General assistance programs: Safety net weakening despite increased need.* Washington, DC: Center on Budget and Policy Priorities.

Schriver, J. M. (1995). *Human behavior and the social environment: Shifting paradigms in essential knowledge for social work practice.* Needham Heights, MA: Allyn & Bacon.

Schur, L., Kruse, D., & Blanck, P. (2013). *People with disabilities: Sidelined or mainstreamed?* New York: Cambridge University Press.

Seligman, M. E. P. (1995). The effectiveness of psychotherapy: The *Consumer Reports* study. *American Psychologist, 50*(12), 965–974. doi: 10.1037/003-066x.50.12.965.

Sevel, J., Cummins, L., & Madrigal, C. (1999). *Social work skills demonstrated.* Needham Heights, MA: Allyn & Bacon.

Shaffer, D. R., Wood, E., & Willoughby, T. (2002). *Developmental psychology: Childhood and adolescence.* Scarborough, ON: Nelson/Thomson.

Sharma, T. (2012). Client centered therapy for self-growth. *International Journal of Management and Computing Sciences (IJMCS)*, *2*(3), 32–38.

Shook, E. V. (1985). *Ho'oponopono: Contemporary uses of a Hawaiian problem-solving process.* Honolulu: University of Hawaii Press.

Silko, L. M. (1993). *Sacred water.* Tucson, AZ: Flood Plain Press.

Smandych, R., & Kueneman, R. (2010). The Canadian-Alberta tar sands: A case study of state-corporate environmental crime. In R. White (Ed.), *Global environmental harm: Criminological perspectives* (pp. 87–109). Portland, OR: Willan.

Solórzano, D., Ceja, M., & Yosso, T. (2000). Critical race theory, racial micro-aggressions, and campus racial climate: The experiences of African American college students. *The Journal of Negro Education 69*(1/2), 60–73. Retrieved from http://www.jstor.org/stable/2696265.

Somers, J. (2007, March). *Cognitive behavioural therapy, core information document.* Vancouver, BC: Simon Fraser University, Summit–Institutional Repository, The Centre for Applied Research in Mental Health and Addiction (CARMHA) under the direction of the Ministry of Health, Mental Health and Addiction Branch.

Specht, H., & Courtney, M. (1994). *Unfaithful angels: How social work has abandoned its mission.* New York: The Free Press.

Spiegler, M. D., & Guevremont, D. C. (1998). *Contemporary behavior therapy* (3rd ed.). Pacific Grove, CA: Brooks/Cole.

Spitzer, R. L. (1981). The diagnostic status of homosexuality in DSM-III: A reformulation of the issues. *American Journal of Psychiatry, 138*(2), 210–215.

Stalker, C., & Hazelton, R. (2008) Attachment theory. In N. Coady & P. Lehmann (Eds.), *Theoretical perspectives for direct social work practice* (2nd ed., pp. 149–178). New York: Springer.

Stancliffe, R. J., Lakin, K. C., Larson, S. A., Engler, J., Taub, S., Fortune, J., & Bershadsky, J. (2012). Demographic characteristics, health conditions, and residential service use in adults with Down syndrome in 25 US states. *Intellectual and Developmental Disabilities, 50*(2), 92–108. doi: http://dx.doi.org/10.1352/1934-9556-50.2.92.

Stannard, D. (1992). *American holocaust: Columbus and the conquest of the New World.* New York: Oxford University Press.

Statistics Canada, Minister of Industry. (2007, October). *Family violence in Canada: A statistical profile 2007* (Catalogue no. 85-224-XIE). Ottawa, ON: Statistics Canada, Minister of Industry, Canadian Centre for Justice Statistics.

Statistics Canada, Minister of Industry. (2012, September). *Census in brief. Fifty years of families in Canada: 1961 to 2011: Families, households and marital status, 2011 Census of Population* (Catalogue no. 98-312-X2011003). Ottawa, ON: Author.

Statistics Canada, Minister of Industry. (2013). *Aboriginal Peoples in Canada: First Nations People, Métis and Inuit, National household survey, 2011* (Catalogue no. 99-011-X2011001—ISBN: 978-1-100-22203-5). Retrieved October 7, 2013 from: http://www12.statcan.gc.ca/nhs-enm/2011/as-sa/99-011-x/99-011-x2011001-eng.cfm.

Steele, M. (2010).The quality of attachment and Oedipal development. *Psychoanalytic Inquiry: A Topical Journal for Mental Health Professionals [Special Issue: Contemporary perspectives on the Oedipus complex], 30*(6), 485–495. doi: 10.1080/07351690.2010.518529.

Stockholm International Peace Research Institute (SIPRI). (2012). *SIPRI Yearbook 2012: Armaments, Disarmament and International Security.* Washington, DC: Oxford University Press. Retrieved October 3, 2013, from http://www.sipri.org/yearbook/2012.

Stuart, P. H. (2008). Social work profession: History. In T. Mizrahi & L. E. Davis (Eds.-in-Chief), *Encyclopedia of social work, 20*(4), 156–164. Washington, DC, and New York: NASW Press and Oxford University Press.

Sue, D., Sue, D. W., & Sue, S. (1994). *Understanding abnormal behavior* (4th ed.). Boston: Houghton Mifflin.

Sue, D. W. (1981). *Counseling the culturally different.* New York: Wiley.

Sue, D. W. (2006). *Multicultural social work practice.* Hoboken, NJ: Wiley.

Sue, D. W., Capodilupo, C. M., Torino, G. C., Bucceri, J. M., Holder, A. M. B., Nadal, K. L., & Esquilin, M. (2007). Racial microaggressions in everyday life: Implications for clinical practice. *American Psychologist, 62*(4), 271–286. doi: 10.1037/0003-066X.62.4.271.

Summers, N. (2001). *Fundamentals of case management practice: Exercises and readings.* Belmont, CA: Wadsworth/Thompson Learning.

Surrey, J. L. (1991). The self-in-relation: A theory of women's development. In. J. V. Jordan, A. G. Kaplan, J. B. Miller, I. P. Stiver, & J. L. Surrey (Eds.), *Women's growth in connection: Writings from the Stone Center* (pp. 51–66). New York: Guilford.

Swanson, J. M., Wigal, T. L., & Lakes, K. D. (2009). DSM-V and the future diagnosis of attention-deficit/hyperactivity disorder. *Current Psychiatry Reports, 11*(5), 399–406. doi: 10.1007/s11920-009-0060-7.

Tannenbaum, R., & Schmidt, W. H. (1982). *How to choose a leadership pattern* (No. 73311). Boston: Harvard Business Review, Reprint Service.

Tanney, B. L. (1995). Suicide prevention in Canada: A national perspective highlighting progress and problems. *Suicide and Life-Threatening Behavior (1995—The American Association for Suicidology), 25*(1), 105–122. doi: 10.1111/j.1943-278X.1995.tb00396.x.

Taylor, F. W. (1998). *The principles of scientific management.* Mineola, NY: Dover. (Original work published 1911).

Teater, B. A. (2013). Motivational interviewing. In M. Davies (Ed.), *The Blackwell companion to social work* (4th ed., pp. 451–454). Malden, MA: Wiley.

Teixeira, R. (2013, May 8). When will your state become a majority-minority? *Think Progress: Trending.* Retrieved March 12, 2014, from http://think progress.org/election/2013/05/08/1978221/when-will-your-state -become-majority-minority/.

Thomas, R. R. (1992). *Beyond race and gender: Unleashing the power of your total workforce by managing diversity.* New York: AMACOM.

Thornton, R. (1987). *American Indian holocaust and survival: A population history since 1492.* Norman: University of Oklahoma Press.

Thyer, B. A. (2011). LCSW examination pass rates: Implications for social work education. *Clinical Social Work Journal, 39*(3), 296–300. doi: 10.1007/s10615-009-253x.

Toray, T. (2004). The human-animal bond and loss: Providing support for grieving clients. *Journal of Mental Health Counseling, 26*(3), 244–259.

Toropov, B., & Buckles, L. (2004). *The complete idiot's guide to world religions* (3rd ed.). New York: Alpha, Penguin Group, Beach Brook Productions.

Torres, E. (2006). *Healing with herbs and rituals: A Mexican tradition* (T. L. Sawyer, Ed). Albuquerque: University of New Mexico Press.

Torrey, E. F., Zdanowicz, M. T., Kennard, A. D., Lamb, H. R., Eslinger, D. F., Biasotti, M. C., & Fuller, D. A. (2014, April 8). *The treatment of persons with mental illness in prisons and jails: A state survey.* Arlington, VA: Treatment Advocacy Center. Retrieved from http://tacreports.org/storage/ documents/treatment-behind-bars/treatment-behind-bars.pdf.

Towers Watson, National Business Group on Health. (2012). *North America: Pathway to health and productivity, 2011/2012 Staying@Work survey report. North America.* New York: Author.

Treasure, J. (2004). Motivational interviewing. *Advances in Psychiatric Treatment, 20*(3), 331–337. doi: 10.1192/apt.10.5.331.

Trepper, T. S., McCollum, E. E., De Jong, P., Korman, H., Gingerich, W. J., & Franklin, C. (2012). Solution-focused brief therapy treatment manual. In C. Franklin, T. S. Trepper, W. J. Gingerich, & E. E. McCollum (Eds.), *Solution-focused brief therapy: A handbook of evidence-based practice* (pp. 20–38). New York: Oxford University Press.

Tribe, L. (2004). *Lawrence v. Texas*: The "Fundamental Right" that dare not speak its name. *Harvard Law Review, 117*(6), 1893–1955.

Tryphon, A., & Vonèche, J. (Eds.). (1996). *Piaget-Vygotsky: The social genesis of thought.* New York: Psychology Press.

Tuckman, B. W., & Jensen, M. A. C. (1977). Stages of small-group development revisited. *Group & Organization Management, 2*(4), 419–427. doi: 10.1177/105960117700200404.

Tylor, E. B. (1958). *Primitive culture: The origins of culture* (vol. I). New York: Harper Torchbooks.

Underhill, R. M. (1991). *Life in the pueblos.* Santa Fe, NM: Ancient City Press.

US Bureau of Labor Statistics. (2014). *Occupational outlook handbook, 2014–15 edition*, social workers. Washington, DC: Author. Retrieved September 2014, from http://www.bls.gov/ooh/community-and-social-service/social-workers.htm.

US Census Bureau. (2011, November). *2010 census briefs. The older population: 2010* (C2010BR-09). Washington, DC: Author.

US Census Bureau. (2012, April). *2010 census briefs. Households and families: 2010* (C2010BR-14). Washington, DC: Author.

US Central Intelligence Agency (US CIA). (2013a). *The world factbook* 2013–14: North American: Canada. Washington, DC: Author. Retrieved from https://www.cia.gov/library/publications/the-world-factbook/geos/print/country/countrypdf_ca.pdf.

US Central Intelligence Agency (US CIA). (2013b). *The world factbook* 2013–14: North American: United States. Washington, DC: Author. Retrieved from https://www.cia.gov/library/publications/the-world-factbook/geos/print/country/countrypdf_us.pdf.

US Department of Health and Human Services (US-DHHS). (1999). US public health service: *The Surgeon General's call to action to prevent suicide, October 1999.* Washington, DC: Author.

US Department of Health and Human Services (US-DHHS). (2009). *Code of Federal Regulations—Title 45—Public Welfare—Department of Health and Human Services—Part 46—Protection of Human Subjects* (Revised January 15, 2009—Effective July 14, 2009). Washington, DC: Author. Retrieved November 10, 2013, from http://www.hhs.gov/ohrp/humansubjects/ guidance/45cfr46.html.

US Department of Health and Human Services, National Institutes of Health, National Institute of Mental Health (US-DHHS/NIMH). (2015). *Mental health medications. Overview: Which groups have special needs when taking psychiatric medications?* Updated April 2015. Bethesda, MD: Author. Retrieved from http://www.nimh.nih.gov/health/topics/mental-health-medications/ mental-health-medications.shtml#part_149869.

US Department of Veterans Affairs. (2012). *Veterans Health Administration handbook* (VHA 1160.05), *local implementation of evidence-based psychotherapies for mental and behavioral health conditions.* Washington, DC: Author.

US Global Change Research (GCR) Program. (2014). *2014 national climate assessment.* Washington, DC: Author. Retrieved from http://nca2014 .globalchange.gov/report.

Valentine, D. (2004). Field evaluations: Exploring the future, expanding the vision. *Journal of Social Work Education, 40,* 3–11.

Van der Kooij, J., De Ruyter, D., & Miedema, S. (2013). "Worldview": The meaning of the concept and the impact on religious education. *Religious Education: The Official Journal of the Religious Education Association, 108*(2), 210–228. doi: 10.1080/00344087.2013.76785.

Venner, K. L., Feldstein, S. W., & Tafoya, N. (2006). *Native American motivational interviewing: Weaving Native American and western practices. A manual for counselors in Native American communities.* Albuquerque: University of New Mexico, Center on Alcoholism, Substance Abuse, and Addictions.

Verhoeven, N. (2011). *Doing research: The hows and whys of applied research* (3rd ed.). Chicago: Lyceum Books.

Vromans, L. P., & Schweitzer, R. D. (2010). Narrative therapy for adults with major depressive disorder: Improved symptom and interpersonal outcomes. *Psychotherapy Research, 21*(1), 4–15. doi: 10.1080/10503301003591792.

Vukic, A., Gregory, D., Martin-Misener, R., & Etowa, J. (2011). Aboriginal and western conceptions of mental health and illness. *Pimatisiwin: A Journal of Aboriginal and Indigenous Community Health, 9*(1), 65–86.

Vygotsky, L. S. (1978). *Mind in society: The development of higher psychological processes*. Cambridge, MA: Harvard University Press.

Wallace, A. (1952a). *The modal personality structure of the Tuscarora Indians as revealed by the Rorschach test*. Washington, DC: United States Government Printing Office.

Wallace, A. F. (1952b). Individual differences and cultural uniformities. *American Sociological Review, 17*, 747–750.

Wallace, W. (1971). *The logic of science in sociology*. Chicago: Aldine-Atherton.

Walsh, J. (2013). The psychological person. In E. D. Hutchinson (Ed.) & Contributing Authors, *Essentials of human behavior: Integrating person, environment, and the life course* (pp. 109–152). Thousand Oaks, CA: Sage.

Walsh, W. M., & McGraw, J. A. (2002). *Essentials of family therapy: A structured summary of nine approaches* (2nd ed.). Denver, CO: Love.

Warner, W. K., & Havens, A. E. (1968). Goal displacement and the intangibility of organizational goals. *Administrative Science Quarterly, 12*(4), 539–555.

Warren, R. L. (1978). *The community in America* (3rd ed.). Chicago: Rand McNally.

Waters, P. L., & Cheek, J. M. (1999). Personality development. In V. J. Derlega, B. A. Winstead, & W. H. Jones (Eds.), *Personality: Contemporary thought and research* (2nd ed., pp. 126–161). Chicago: Nelson-Hall.

Watt, L. M., & Cappeliez, P. (2000). Integrative and instrumental reminiscence therapies for depression in older adults: Intervention strategies and treatment effectiveness. *Aging & Mental Health, 4*(2), 166–177. doi: 10.1080/13607860050008691.

Wayne, J., Raskin, M., & Bogo, M. (2010). Field education as the signature pedagogy of social work education. *Journal of Social Work Education, 46*(3), 327–339. doi: 10.5175/JSWE.2010.200900043.

Weber, M. (1978). *Economy and society: An outline of interpretive sociology*. Berkeley & Los Angeles: University of California Press. (Original work published 1922)

Weber, M. (2009). *The theory of social and economic organization*. New York: The Free Press.

Webster's II New Riverside University Dictionary. (1984). Boston: Houghton Mifflin.

Weil, M. O. (1995). Women, community, and organizing. In J. E. Tropman, J. L. Erlich, & J. Rothman (Eds.), *Tactics and techniques of community intervention* (3rd ed., pp. 118–133). Itasca, IL: F. E. Peacock.

Weil, M. O., & Gamble, D. N. (1995). Community practice models. In R. L. Edwards & National Association of Social Workers (NASW) (Eds.), *Encyclopedia of social work* (19th ed., pp. 577–594). Washington, DC: NASW Press.

Weisman, A. D. (1991). Bereavement and companion animals. *OMEGA—Journal of Death and Dying, 22*(4), 241–248. doi: 10.2190/C54Y-UGMH-QGR4-CWTL.

Werth, B. (2011). *Banquet at Delmonico's: The Gilded Age and the triumph of evolution in America.* Chicago: University of Chicago Press.

Whitaker, T., Weismiller, T., & Clark, E. (2006). *Assuring the sufficiency of a frontline workforce: A national study of licensed social workers—executive summary.* Washington, DC: National Association of Social Workers, Center for Workforce Studies.

White, M. (2006). Externalizing conversations revisited. In A. Morgan & M. White (Eds.), *Narrative therapy with children and their families* (pp. 2–56). Adelaide, Australia: Dulwich Centre Publications.

White, M. (2007). *Maps of narrative practice.* New York: Norton.

Whittlesey-Jerome, W. (2009). Research in social work. In K. Coggins & B. Hatchett, *Field practicum: Skill building from a multicultural perspective* (2nd ed., pp. 203–213). Peosta, IA: Eddie Bowers.

Whooley, M. A. (2012). Diagnosis and treatment of depression in adults with comorbid medical conditions: A 52-year-old man with depression. *Journal of the American Medical Association, 307*(17), 1848–1857. doi: 10.1001/jama.2012.3466.

Willi, J. (1999). *Ecological psychotherapy: Developing by shaping the personal niche.* Seattle, WA: Hogrefe & Huber.

Williams, C., & Garland, A. (2002). A cognitive-behavioural therapy assessment model for use in everyday clinical practice. *Advances in Psychiatric Treatment, 8*, 172–179. doi: 10.1192/apt.8.3.172.

Wilson, S., & Rice, S. (Eds.). (2010). Group work with older adults. In G. L. Greif & P. H. Ephross (Eds.), *Group work with populations at risk* (3rd ed., pp. 115–135). New York: Oxford University Press.

Winkelman, M. (1999). *Ethnic sensitivity in social work.* Dubuque, IA: Eddie Bowers.

Winks, R. (1997). *Blacks in Canada: A history* (2nd ed.). Montreal, QC: McGill-Queen's University Press.

Wolf, E. R. (1982). *Europe and the people without history*. Berkeley: University of California Press.

Wolitzky, D. (1995). The theory and practice of traditional psychotherapy. In A. Gurman & S. Messer, *Essential psychotherapies: Theory and practice* (pp. 12–54). New York: Guilford.

Wong, P. T. P. (2008). *Brief manual of meaning-centered counselling and narrative therapy*. Toronto: Meaning-Centered Counselling Institute.

Wood, D., Bruner, J., & Ross, G. (1976). The role of tutoring in problem solving. *Journal of Child Psychology and Child Psychiatry, 17*, 89–100.

Woodrow, C., & Guest, D. E. (2014). When good HR gets bad results: Exploring the challenge of HR implementation in the case of workplace bullying. *Human Resource Management Journal, 24*(1), 38–56. doi: 10.1111/1748-8583.12021.

Wozniak, R. H. (Ed.). (1994). *Behaviourism: The early years*. London: Routledge/Thoemmes Press.

Wren, D. A., & Bedeian, A. G. (2009). *The evolution of management thought* (6th ed.). Hoboken, NJ: Wiley.

Wu, L. F. (2011). Group integrative reminiscence therapy on self-esteem, life satisfaction and depressive symptoms in institutionalised older veterans. *Journal of Clinical Nursing, 20*(15–16), 2195–2203. doi: 10.1111/j.1365-2702.2011.03699.x.

Yalom, I. D. (2005). *The theory and practice of group psychotherapy* (5th ed.). New York: Basic Books.

Yen, H. (2013, June 13). Census: White majority in US gone by 2043. *Associated Press*. Retrieved March 12, 2014, from http://usnews.nbcnews.com/_news/2013/06/13/18934111-census-white-majority-in-us-gone-by-2043.

Zapf, M. K. (2009). *Social work and the environment: Understanding people and place*. Toronto: Canadian Scholars' Press.

Zapf, M. K. (2010). Social work and the environment: Understanding people and place. *Critical Social Work, 11*(3), 30–46. Retrieved from http://www1.uwindsor.ca/criticalsocialwork/2010-volume-11-no-3.

Zunz, S. J. (1991). Gender-related issues in the career development of social work managers. *Affilia, Journal of Women & Social Work, 6*(4), 39–52. doi: 10.1177/088610999100600403.

Index

About the Author

Kip Coggins has bachelor's and master's degrees in social work from Michigan State University and a doctoral degree in social work and anthropology from the University of Michigan. He is of Indigenous Anishinabe—Odawa and Ojibwa—heritage from his original home in Northern Lower Michigan, as well as having French Canadian roots in the provinces of Quebec and New Brunswick. His career in social work has been vast and varied, including micro, mezzo, and macro practice. In addition, he has more than twenty years in academia in the state of New Mexico, in the Texas-New Mexico-Chihuahua border region, and in Manitoba, Canada.

For his entire career in social work education, he has wanted to write a book about social work practice in North America. In 2011, an opportunity to live and work in Canada arose in the form of an academic position with the faculty of social work at the University of Manitoba. While in Manitoba, he engaged in extended and in-depth study related to social work education. The time spent meeting with practitioners and academics in Canada has been combined with his experience in the United States. The result is a textbook that takes a truly North American approach to preparing social work students for practice in a diverse North American context.